THE NEW INTERNATIONAL COMMENTARY
ON THE NEW TESTAMENT

GORDON D. FEE
General Editor

The Epistle
to the
GALATIANS

by

RONALD Y. K. FUNG

WILLIAM B. EERDMANS PUBLISHING COMPANY
GRAND RAPIDS, MICHIGAN

In Memory of

Philip S. Henman

December 21, 1899–November 8, 1986

© 1988 Wm. B. Eerdmans Publishing Company
255 Jefferson Ave. S.E., Grand Rapids, Michigan 49503
All rights reserved
Printed in the United States of America

99 98 97 96 95 94   8 7 6 5 4 3

Library of Congress Cataloging-in-Publication Data

Fung, Ronald Y. K., 1937-
The Epistle to the Galatians.
(The New international commentary on the New Testament)
Bibliography: p.xix
1. Bible. N.T. Galatians—Commentaries.
I. Title.   II. Series.
BS2685.3.F86   1988   227'.4077   88-11252
ISBN 0-8028-2509-5

CONTENTS

EDITOR'S PREFACE

In accordance with the policy of keeping the New International Commentary on the New Testament up to date by revision or replacement, a new volume on Galatians is now presented.

The original NICNT volume on Galatians was one of the earliest in the series: it was published in 1953, and was the work of Dr. Herman N. Ridderbos, who was for many years professor of New Testament Theology at the Theological Seminary of the Reformed Churches of the Netherlands in Kampen. In the decades since its appearance, study of Galatians has continued. New issues have emerged and older positions have been refined, and in this developing situation today's reader expects to find some help.

Dr. Ronald Fung has devoted many years to the study and interpretation of Galatians. He gained his doctorate in the University of Manchester with a dissertation on the relation between righteousness and faith in Paul's thought. This dissertation involved a detailed examination of the evidence of Galatians and Romans. In their report on the work, his examiners remarked that it may come to be recognized as the definitive answer to the question whether justification by faith is the central motif in Paul's understanding of the gospel or only (in Albert Schweitzer's phrase) a "subsidiary crater." Dr. Fung's research left no room for doubt that justification by faith—an experience as well as a doctrine—is the heart and core of Paul's gospel.

Since then he has published a full-length commentary on Galatians in Chinese, and he now presents another to English-speaking readers. I have read the major part of this work as it appeared month by month throughout 1983 and 1984 in the British periodical *Harvester,* and I think it important that it be made available to as wide a public as possible. Galatians is full of interpretative problems, but Dr. Fung gives careful consideration to each one of them, and offers to each a well-reasoned solution.

Both as a former mentor of Dr. Fung and as an appreciative student of his work, I have the utmost pleasure and confidence in commending this commentary to others. If nowadays we take it for granted that Christianity means freedom from spiritual bondage, we can do so because the case for

Christian freedom was defended so vigorously by Paul in Galatians at a time when it was under attack. Therefore anyone who helps us to understand this document and derive profit from it is a public benefactor.

F. F. BRUCE

AUTHOR'S PREFACE

Although I did not know it then, the foundations for a commentary on Galatians were partially laid during the time I spent as a post-graduate student at the University of Manchester. My research project involved a detailed exegetical treatment of the first eleven chapters of Romans and almost the whole of Galatians, the major exceptions being Gal. 4:12-20 and 5:13–6:10. That deficiency was made good during a six-month sabbatical leave in 1979-80 granted by the China Graduate School of Theology, when I wrote the first draft of a commentary on Galatians in Chinese, which appeared in 1982. Subsequently an opportunity was given me to attempt a serialized commentary on the same epistle in English for the British periodical *Harvester*, which published about half of my manuscript. That manuscript has been considerably revised for publication in The New International al Commentary series.

A number of distinguished commentaries on Galatians have been published in English. Those of Lightfoot, Burton, Betz, and Bruce are especially noteworthy. I believe that there is still room for a fresh treatment of a number of the problems which interpretation of Paul's letter raises and especially for an examination of the letter specifically as Paul's most direct defense and exposition of justification by faith, which is so much the heart of Paul's understanding of the gospel and of Christian experience.

I owe a special debt of gratitude to Professor Bruce. Not only did he supervise my thesis work at Manchester University; he also most graciously supplied a foreword for my Chinese commentary, and he has now bestowed on me a yet greater "second benefit" (2 Cor. 1:15, AV, RV) by giving the present volume a place in the New International Commentary.[1] How much this commentary owes to the labors of others—not least to the writings and influence of my esteemed mentor—will quickly be obvious, and the footnotes will indicate something of my indebtedness.

---

1. I should like to express my appreciation to the editorial staff of Eerdmans for the initial suggestion that my work be adapted to form the new NICNT volume on Galatians and, in particular, to Dr. John W. Simpson, Jr., who executed the task of adapting my typescript to the NIC format with impressive competence.

I take the opportunity offered here of making two other personal acknowledgements. First, I would like to record my lasting gratitude to the late Philip S. Henman, Esq., formerly Chairman and Honorary Treasurer of the Board of Governors of London Bible College,[2] who over two decades ago generously financed my three years of study at that institution and remained for many years thereafter a kind and praying friend. I also express my deep gratitude to all those whose support made it possible for me to pursue advanced theological studies in America and Great Britain.

Throughout this commentary the primary aim has been to provide a continuous exposition of the text, particular attention being given to the doctrine of justification by faith as it finds expression in this letter. The study behind this commentary is based on the Greek text of the twenty-sixth edition of the Nestle-Aland *Novum Testamentum Graece* (1979). Where it was considered necessary or desirable to refer in the text to the original, I have attempted to ensure that the reader with little or no knowledge of New Testament Greek will be able to follow the point being made. At the same time ample attention is given to details of grammar and syntax, in the hope that this might be of help especially to theological students. The English text cited, unless otherwise indicated, is that of the New English Bible.

RONALD Y. K. FUNG

2. Mr. Henman was on the Board from December 1944 to November 1970, being Honorary Treasurer from December 1945 and Chairman from May 1958. The son of a Baptist minister, he was also Honorary Superintendent of the Hook Free Evangelical Church in Surbiton, Surrey, for many years, and at various times chairman or vice-chairman of several missionary societies and the Keswick Convention.

In public life Mr. Henman was Chairman and Managing Director of the Transport Development Group, a worldwide transport company which by the time of his retirement in 1969 (forty-eight years after he joined the company out of which the group was born) had eighty subsidiaries in Britain, three in Australia, and seven in Europe. In addition he was Chairman of the London Chamber of Commerce, a member of the Grand Council of the Confederation of British Industries, and Vice President of the Institute of Transport. During his retirement he served as High Sheriff of Surrey from 1971 to 1972 and was appointed a Deputy Lieutenant of the county in 1979.

An obituary which appeared in *The Times* described Mr. Henman as "a leading figure in the world of import and export cargo" and "a noted philanthropist." A tribute in the London Bible College *Review* for Summer 1987 said: "A devoted husband and family man, he was never flamboyant in his life style or in anything he did." Mr. Henman's daughter, Mrs. Mary Clark, wrote of her father in a letter to me: "He was a man of so many 'parts' that it is difficult to be concise. . . . As a father and grandfather who introduced us to so many people and interests, he was always a pleasure to be with."

ABBREVIATIONS

Alford
H. Alford, *The Greek Testament,* with revision by E. F. Harrison (reprint in two double vols., Chicago, 1958), 3.1-67 on Galatians.

AnBib
Analecta Biblica

Arichea-Nida
D. C. Arichea, Jr., and E. A. Nida, *A Translator's Handbook on Paul's Letter to the Galatians* (Helps for Translators 18; Stuttgart, 1976)

AV
Authorized (King James) Version

BAGD
W. Bauer, *A Greek-English Lexicon of the New Testament and Early Christian Literature,* trans. and adapted by W. F. Arndt and F. W. Gingrich, second edition ed. by F. Danker (Chicago, 1979)

Barclay
William Barclay, *The Letters to the Galatians and Ephesians* (Daily Study Bible; revised edition, Philadelphia, 1976)

Barrett
C. K. Barrett, *Freedom and Obligation. A Study of the Epistle to the Galatians* (Philadelphia, 1985)

BC
The Beginnings of Christianity, ed. F. J. Foakes-Jackson and K. Lake (London, 1920-33)

BDF
F. Blass and A. Debrunner, *A Greek Grammar of the New Testament and Other Early Christian Literature,* trans. and ed. by R. W. Funk (Chicago, 1967)

Betz
H. D. Betz, *Galatians* (Hermeneia; Philadelphia, 1979)

BFBS
Ἡ Καινη Διαθηκη, ed. G. D. Kilpatrick (London, 1958)

BibTr
The Bible Translator

BJRL
Bulletin of the John Rylands (University) Library (Manchester)

Bligh
J. Bligh, *Galatians: A Discussion of St. Paul's Epistle* (London, 1969)

BNTC
Black's New Testament Commentaries

Bring
R. Bring, *Commentary on Galatians* (E.T., Philadelphia, 1961)

Brinsmead
B. H. Brinsmead, *Galatians—Dialogical Response to Opponents* (SBLD 65; Chico, Ca., 1982)

Bruce
F. F. Bruce, *The Epistle to the Galatians* (NIGTC; Grand Rapids, 1982)

BS
Bibliotheca Sacra

Burton   E. D. Burton, *The Epistle to the Galatians* (ICC; Edinburgh, 1921)
BZ   *Biblische Zeitschrift*
CBC   Cambridge Bible Commentary
CBQ   *Catholic Biblical Quarterly*
CGSTJ   *CGST Journal* (China Graduate School of Theology, Hong Kong)
CGTC   Cambridge Greek Testament Commentary
Cole   R. A. Cole, *The Epistle of Paul to the Galatians* (TNTC; Grand Rapids, 1965)
Duncan   G. S. Duncan, *The Epistle of Paul to the Galatians* (MNTC; London, 1934)
EBC   *Eerdmans Bible Commentary* (= *New Bible Commentary, Revised* [1970]), ed. D. Guthrie et al. (Grand Rapids, 1987)
EGT   *The Expositor's Greek Testament*, ed. W. R. Nicoll (5 vols.; 1897-1910; reprint, Grand Rapids, 1961)
Ellicott   C. J. Ellicott, *St. Paul's Epistle to the Galatians* (London, 1867)
EQ   *Evangelical Quarterly*
E.T.   English Translation
EvTh   *Evangelische Theologie*
Exp   *Expositor*
ExpT   *Expository Times*
FS   *Festschrift*
Fung   R. Y. K. Fung, *Gospel Truth and Christian Liberty. A Commentary on Galatians* (Hong Kong, 1982) [in Chinese]
Guthrie   D. Guthrie, *Galatians* (NCBC; revised edition, 1973; Grand Rapids, 1981)
Hays   R. B. Hays, *The Faith of Jesus Christ. An Investigation of the Narrative Substructure of Galatians 3:1–4:11* (SBLD 56; Chico, Ca., 1983)
Hendriksen   W. Hendriksen, *Galatians* (Grand Rapids, 1969)
HNTC   Harper's New Testament Commentaries
Howard   G. Howard, *Paul: Crisis in Galatia* (SNTSM 35; Cambridge, 1979)
HTR   *Harvard Theological Review*
HTS   Harvard Theological Studies
Hunter   A. M. Hunter, *Galatians, Ephesians, Philippians, Colossians* (Layman's Bible Commentary; Atlanta, 1966)
IBD   *Illustrated Bible Dictionary*, ed. J.D. Douglas, rev. ed. N. Hillyer (three volumes with single pagination; Wheaton, 1980)
IBS   *Irish Biblical Studies*
ICC   International Critical Commentary
IDB   *Interpreter's Dictionary of the Bible*, ed. G. A. Buttrick et al. (four vols.; Nashville, 1962; Supplementary Volume 1976)
JAAR   *Journal of the American Academy of Religion*

JBL	*Journal of Biblical Literature*
JETS	*Journal of the Evangelical Theological Society*
JJS	*Journal of Jewish Studies*
JSNT	*Journal for the Study of the New Testament*
JTS	*Journal of Theological Studies*
KEK	Kritisch-exegetischer Kommentar über das Neue Testament
Lightfoot	J. B. Lightfoot, *The Epistle of St. Paul to the Galatians* (1865; reprint, Grand Rapids, 1962)
LXX	Septuagint
Machen	J. G. Machen, *Notes on Galatians,* ed. J. H. Skilton (Philadelphia, 1972)
Martin	R. P. Martin, *1 Corinthians–Galatians* (Scripture Union Bible Study Books; Grand Rapids, 1968)
Metzger	B. M. Metzger, *A Textual Commentary on the Greek New Testament* (London, 1971)
MHT	J. H. Moulton, W. F. Howard, and N. Turner, *A Grammar of New Testament Greek* (four vols.; Edinburgh, 1906-76)
Mikolaski	S. J. Mikolaski, "Galatians," *EBC*, 1089-1104
MM	J. H. Moulton and G. Milligan, *The Vocabulary of the Greek Testament* (Grand Rapids, 1930)
MNTC	Moffatt New Testament Commentary
Moule	C. F. D. Moule, *An Idiom Book of New Testament Greek* (second edition, Cambridge, 1959)
MT	Masoretic Text
NASB	New American Standard Bible
NCBC	New Century Bible Commentary
NEAJT	*Northeast Asia Journal of Theology*
NEB	New English Bible
Neill	W. Neill, *The Letter of Paul to the Galatians* (CBC; Cambridge, 1967)
Nestle-Aland	*Novum Testament Graece,* ed. E. Nestle, K. Aland et al. (twenty-sixth edition; Stuttgart, 1979)
N.F.	Neue Folge (New Series)
NICNT	New International Commentary on the New Testament
NIDNTT	*New International Dictionary of New Testament Theology,* ed. C. Brown (3 vols.; Grand Rapids, 1975-78)
NIGTC	New International Greek Testament Commentary
NIV	New International Version
NovT	*Novum Testamentum*
NS	New Series
NTS	*New Testament Studies*
O'Neill	J. C. O'Neill, *The Recovery of Paul's Letter to the Galatians* (London, 1972)
Phillips	*The New Testament in Modern English,* trans. by J. B. Phillips (New York, 1958)

Pinnock   C. H. Pinnock, *Truth on Fire: The Message of Galatians* (Grand Rapids, 1972)

Rendall   F. Rendall, "The Epistle to the Galatians," *EGT* III: 121-200

RGG   *Die Religion in Geschichte und Gegenwart,* ed. K. Galling et al. (third edition; 7 vols.; Tübingen, 1956-65)

Ridderbos   H. N. Ridderbos, *The Epistle of Paul to the Churches of Galatia* (NICNT; Grand Rapids, 1953)

Robertson   A. T. Robertson, *A Grammar of the Greek New Testament in the Light of Historical Research* (1934; reprint, Nashville, n.d.)

Ropes   J. H. Ropes, *The Singular Problem of the Epistle to the Galatians* (HTS 14; Cambridge, Mass., 1929)

RSV   Revised Standard Version

RV   Revised Version

SBLD   Society of Biblical Literature Dissertation

SBT   Studies in Biblical Theology

Schlier   H. Schlier, *Der Brief an die Galater* (KEK; Göttingen, 1965)

SJT   *Scottish Journal of Theology*

SNTSM   Society for New Testament Studies Monograph

Stott   J. R. W. Stott, *The Message of Galatians* (Downers Grove, 1968)

StTh   *Studia Theologica*

StudEv   *Studia Evangelica*

TB   *Tyndale Bulletin*

TDNT   *Theological Dictionary of the New Testament,* a translation by G. W. Bromiley of *Theologisches Wörterbuch zum Neuen Testament,* vols. 1-4 ed. by G. Kittel, 5-9 ed. by G. Friedrich, index vol. (10) compiled by R. E. Pitkin (Grand Rapids, 1964-76)

Thayer   *A Greek-English Lexicon of the New Testament, Being Grimm's Wilke's Clavis Novi Testamenti,* trans., rev., and enlarged by J. H. Thayer (1886; reprint, New York, n.d.)

TNTC   Tyndale New Testament Commentaries

TOTC   Tyndale Old Testament Commentaries

Trench   R. C. Trench, *Synonyms of the New Testament* (1880; reprint, Grand Rapids, 1953)

TSFB   *Theological Students Fellowship Bulletin* (Leicester, U.K.)

UBS   United Bible Societies

VE   *Vox Evangelica*

Vine   W. E. Vine, *An Expository Dictionary of New Testament Words* (1939, 1952; contained in *An Expository Dictionary of Biblical Words* [Nashville, 1985])

WTJ   *Westminster Theological Journal*

Wuest   K. S. Wuest, *Galatians in the Greek New Testament* (Grand Rapids, 1944)

WUNT   Wissenschaftliche Untersuchungen zum Neuen Testament

Zerwick	M. Zerwick, *Biblical Greek* (E.T., Rome, 1963)
ZNW	*Zeitschrift für die neutestamentliche Wissenschaft*
ZTK	*Zeitschrift für Theologie und Kirche*

BIBLIOGRAPHY

For commentaries on Galatians and other frequently cited works see Abbreviations, pages xiii-xvii.

Abbott, T. K., *The Epistles to the Colossians and to the Ephesians* (ICC; Edinburgh, 1897).

Allen, L. C., "The Old Testament in Romans i-viii," *VE* 3 (1964) 6-41.

Allison, D. C., Jr., "The Pauline Epistles and the Synoptic Gospels: The Pattern of the Parallels," *NTS* 28 (1982) 1-32.

Annand, R., "Note on the Three 'Pillars,'" *ExpT* 67 (1955) 178.

Aune, D. E., Review of B. H. Brinsmead, *Galatians—Dialogical Response to Opponents* (SBLD 65; Chico, Ca., 1982), *CBQ* 46 (1984) 145-147.

Aus, R. D., "Three Pillars and Three Patriarchs: A Proposal concerning Gal 2:9," *ZNW* 70 (1979) 252-261.

Baeck, L., "The Faith of Paul," *JJS* 3 (1952) 93-110.

Bammel, E., "Galater 1, 23," *ZNW* 59 (1968) 108-112.

———, "Νομος Χριστου," *StudEv* 3 (1964) 120-128.

Banks, R., *Paul's Idea of Community* (Grand Rapids, 1980).

Barclay, J. M. G., "Mirror-Reading a Polemical Letter: Galatians as a Test Case," *JSNT* 31 (1987) 73-93.

———, "Paul and the Law: Observations on Some Recent Debates," *Themelios* NS 12 (1986-87) 5-15.

Barclay, W., "A Comparison of Paul's Missionary Preaching and Preaching to the Church," in *Apostolic History and the Gospel* (F. F. Bruce *FS*), ed. W. W. Gasque and R. P. Martin (Grand Rapids, 1970), 165-175.

———, *Flesh and Spirit: An Examination of Galatians 5:19-23* (Nashville, 1962; reprint, Grand Rapids, 1977).

Barrett, C. K., "The Allegory of Abraham, Sarah, and Hagar in the Argument of Galatians," in *Rechtfertigung* (E. Käsemann *FS*), ed. J. Friedrich, W. Pöhlmann, and P. Stuhlmacher (Tübingen and Göttingen, 1976), 1-16.

———, *The Epistle to the Romans* (HNTC; New York, 1957).

———, *The First Epistle to the Corinthians* (HNTC; New York, 1968).

———, *From First Adam to Last* (New York, 1962).

———, "Galatians as an 'Apologetic Letter'," *Interpretation* 34 (1980) 414-417.

————, "I am Not Ashamed of the Gospel," *AnBib* 42 (1970) 19-50.

————, "New Testament Eschatology. I. Jewish and Pauline Eschatology," *SJT* 6 (1953) 136-155.

————, *New Testament Essays* (London, 1972).

————, "Paul and the 'Pillar' Apostles," in *Studia Paulina* (J. de Zwaan *FS*), ed. J. N. Sevenster and W. C. van Unnik (Haarlem, 1953), 1-19.

————, "Shaliaḥ and Apostle," in *Donum Gentilicum* (D. Daube *FS*), ed. E. Bammel, C. K. Barrett, and W. D. Davies (Oxford, 1980), 88-102.

————, *The Signs of an Apostle* (Philadelphia, 1972).

Barth, M., "Justification. From Text to Sermon on Galatians 2:11-21," *Interpretation* 22 (1968) 147-157.

————, "Rechtfertigung. Versuch einer Auslegung paulinischer Texte im Rahmen des Alten und Neuen Testaments," *AnBib* 42 (1970) 137-209.

Bartlet, V., "Only Let us be Mindful of the Poor," *Exp* V: ix (1899) 218ff.

Bauckham, R. J., "Barnabas in Galatians," *JSNT* 2 (1979) 61-70.

Bauernfeind, O., "Die Begegnung zwischen Paulus und Kephas Gal. 1, 18-20," *ZNW* 47 (1956) 268-276.

Beasley-Murray, G. R., "Baptism in the Epistles of Paul," in *Christian Baptism,* ed. A. Gilmore (London, 1959), 128-149.

————, *Baptism in the New Testament* (1962; Grand Rapids, 1973).

Beker, J. C., *Paul the Apostle: The Triumph of God in Life and Thought* (Philadelphia, 1980).

Belleville, L. L., " 'Under Law': Structural Analysis and the Pauline Concept of Law in Galatians 3:21–4:11," *JSNT* 26 (1986) 53-78.

Berényi, G., "Gal 2, 20: a Pre-Pauline or a Pauline Text?" *Biblica* 65 (1984) 490-537.

Berger, K., "Almosen für Israel: zum historischen Kontext der paulinischen Kollekte," *NTS* 23 (1976-77) 180-204.

Black, M., *Romans* (NCBC; 1973; reprint, Grand Rapids, 1981).

Bligh, J., "The Church and Israel according to St. John and St. Paul," *AnBib* 17-18 (1963) 1: 151-156.

Blinzler, J., "Lexikalisches zu dem Terminus. τὰ στοιχεῖα τοῦ κόσμου bei Paulus," *AnBib* 17-18 (1963) 2: 429-443.

Blommerde, A. C. M., "Is There an Ellipsis between Gal. 2, 3 and 2, 4?" *Biblica* 56 (1975) 100-102.

Borgen, P., "Paul Preaches Circumcision and Pleases Men," in *Paul and Paulinism* (C. K. Barrett *FS*), ed. M. D. Hooker and S. G. Wilson (London, 1982), 37-46.

Bornkamm, G., *Early Christian Experience* (London, 1969).

————, *Paul* (E.T., New York, 1971).

————, "The Revelation of Christ to Paul on the Damascus Road and Paul's Doctrine of Justification and Reconcilation. A Study in Galatians I," in *Reconciliation and Hope* (L. Morris *FS*), ed. R. Banks (Grand Rapids, 1974), 90-103.

Bosworth, E. I., "The Influence of the Damascus Vision upon Paul's Theology," *BS* 56 (1899) 278-300.

Braun, H., *Gerichtsgedanke und Rechtfertigungslehre bei Paulus* (Leipzig, 1930).

Bring, R., "Das Gesetz und die Gerechtigkeit Gottes. Eine Studie zur Frage nach der Bedeutung des Ausdrucks τέλος νόμου in Röm. 10:4," *StTh* 20 (1966) 1-36.

Bruce, A. B., *St. Paul's Conception of Christianity* (New York, 1894).

Bruce, F. F., "'Abraham Had Two Sons.' A Study in Pauline Hermeneutics," in *New Testament Studies* (R. Summers *FS*), ed. H. L. Drumwright and C. Vaughan (Waco, 1975), 71-84.

_____, *The Acts of the Apostles: The Greek Text with Introduction and Commentary* (second edition; Grand Rapids, 1952).

_____, *The Book of Acts* (NICNT; Grand Rapids, 1954).

_____, "The Conference in Jerusalem—Galatians 2:1-10," in *God Who is Rich in Mercy* (D. B. Knox *FS*), ed. P. T. O'Brien and D. G. Peterson (Homebush West, NSW, 1986), 195-212.

_____, "The Curse of the Law," in *Paul and Paulinism* (C. K. Barrett *FS*), ed. M. D. Hooker and S. G. Wilson (London, 1982), 27-36.

_____, *The Epistle to the Ephesians* (London, 1961).

_____, *The Epistle to the Hebrews* (NICNT; Grand Rapids, 1964).

_____, *The Epistles to the Colossians, to Philemon, and to the Ephesians* (NICNT; Grand Rapids, 1984)

_____, *1 and 2 Corinthians* (NCBC; 1971; reprint, Grand Rapids, 1980).

_____, "Further Thoughts on Paul's Autobiography: Galatians 1:11–2:14," in *Jesus und Paulus* (W. G. Kümmel *FS*), ed. E. E. Ellis and E. Grässer (Göttingen, 1975), 21-29.

_____, "Galatian Problems. 1. Autobiographical Data," *BJRL* 51 (1968-69) 292-309.

_____, "Galatian Problems. 2. North or South Galatians?" *BJRL* 52 (1969-70) 243-266.

_____, "Galatian Problems. 3. The 'Other' Gospel," *BJRL* 53 (1970-1971) 253-271.

_____, "Galatian Problems. 4. The Date of the Epistle," *BJRL* 54 (1971-72) 250-267.

_____, "Galatian Problems. 5. Galatians and Christian Origins," *BJRL* 55 (1972-73) 264-284.

_____, "Is the Paul of Acts the Real Paul?" *BJRL* 58 (1975-76) 282-305.

_____, "Jesus and Paul," *TSFB* 46 (Autumn 1966) 21-26.

_____, "Jesus is Lord," in *Soli Deo Gloria* (W. C. Robinson *FS*), ed. J. M. Richards (Richmond, 1968), 23-36.

_____, "Justification by Faith in the non-Pauline Writings of the New Testament," *EQ* 24 (1952) 66-77.

_____, *The Letter of Paul to the Romans* (TNTC; second edition; Grand Rapids, 1985).

_____, *The Letters of Paul: An Expanded Paraphrase* (Grand Rapids, 1965).

_____, *New Testament History* (London, 1969; Garden City, 1971).

_____, "Paul and Jerusalem," *TB* 19 (1968) 3-25.

————, "Paul and the Historical Jesus," *BJRL* 56 (1973-74) 317-335.

————, "Paul and the Law of Moses," *BJRL* 57 (1974-75) 259-279.

————, *Paul: Apostle of the Heart Set Free* (Grand Rapids, 1977).

————, "Salvation History in the New Testament," in *Man and His Salvation. Studies in Memory of S. G. F. Brandon,* ed. E. J. Sharpe and J. R. Hinnels (Manchester, 1973), 75-90.

————, "Some Thoughts on Paul and Paulinism," *VE* 7 (1971) 5-16.

————, *The Time Is Fulfilled* (Grand Rapids, 1978).

————, *Tradition Old and New* (Grand Rapids, 1970).

————, "When is a Gospel not a Gospel?" *BJRL* 45 (1962-63) 319-339.

Buchanan, J., *The Doctrine of Justification* (Grand Rapids, 1955).

Buck, C. H., Jr., "The Date of Galatians," *JBL* 70 (1951) 113-122.

Buckingham, L. G., "The Date of the Epistle to the Galatians," *ExpT* 51 (1939-40) 157f.

Bultmann, R., "Christ the End of the Law," *Essays Philosophical and Theological* (London, 1955) 36-66.

————, *Existence and Faith. Shorter Writings of Rudolf Bultmann* (New York, 1961).

————, *Faith and Understanding,* I (E.T., New York, 1969).

————, "Das Problem der Ethik bei Paulus," *ZNW* 23 (1924) 123-140.

————, *Theology of the New Testament,* I (E.T., New York, 1951).

————, "Zur Auslegung von Gal. 2, 15-18," *Exegetica* (Tübingen, 1967) 394-399.

Burton, E. D., *Syntax of the Moods and Tenses in New Testament Greek* (third edition, 1898; reprint, Grand Rapids, 1976).

Calder, W. M., "Adoption and Inheritance in Galatia," *JTS* 31 (1930) 372-374.

Callan, T., "Pauline Midrash: The Exegetical Background of Gal. 3:19b," *JBL* 99 (1980) 549-567.

Calvin, J., *The Epistles of Paul the Apostle to the Romans and to the Thessalonians* (E.T., Grand Rapids, 1961).

Carson, D. A., *Divine Sovereignty and Human Responsibility* (Atlanta, 1981).

Catchpole, D. R., "Paul, James and the Apostolic Decree," *NTS* 23 (1976-77) 428-444.

Chadwick, H., "St. Paul and Philo of Alexandria," *BJRL* 48 (1965-66) 286-307.

Chilton, B. D. "Galatians 6:15: A Call to Freedom before God," *ExpT* 89 (1977-78) 311-313.

Clarke, W. K. L., *New Testament Problems* (London, 1929).

Cohn-Sherbok, D., "Paul and Rabbinic Exegesis," *SJT* 35 (1982) 117-132.

————, "Some Reflections on James Dunn's 'The Incident at Antioch (Gal. 2.11-18),'" *JSNT* 18 (1983) 68-74.

Collins, J. J., "Rabbinic Exegesis and Pauline Exegesis," *CBQ* 3 (1941) 15-26, 145-158.

Conzelmann, H., "Die Rechtfertigungslehre des Paulus. Theologie oder Anthropologie?" *EvTh* 28 (1968) 389-404.

Cook, R. B., "Paul . . . Preacher or Evangelist?" *BibTr* 32 (1981) 441-444.

_____, "St Paul—Preacher, Evangelist or Organizer?" *ExpT* 93 (1982) 171-173.

Cooper, K. T., "Paul and Rabbinic Soteriology: A Review Article," *WTJ* 44 (1982) 123-139.

Cosgrove, C. H., "The Law has given Sarah No Children (Gal. 4:21-30)," *NovT* 29 (1987) 219-235.

Cranfield, C. E. B., *The Epistle to the Romans* (ICC; 2 vols. with single pagination; Edinburgh, 1975, 1979).

_____, "St. Paul and the Law," in *New Testament Issues,* ed. R. Batey (London, 1970), 148-172.

_____, *The Gospel according to St. Mark* (CGTC; revised edition, Cambridge, 1977).

Creed, J. M., Review of J. H. Ropes, *The Singular Problem of the Epistle to the Galatians* (HTS 14; Cambridge, Mass., 1929), *JTS* 31 (1930) 421-424.

Crownfield, F. R., "The Singular Problem of the Dual Galatians," *JBL* 64 (1945) 491-500.

Cullmann, O., *Christ and Time* (E.T., rev. ed., Philadelphia, 1964).

_____, "Dissensions within the Early Church," in *New Testament Issues,* ed. R. Batey (New York, 1970), 119-129.

_____, *The Early Church,* ed. A. J. B. Higgins (E.T., Philadelphia, 1956).

Dahl, N. A., "Die Messianität Jesu bei Paulus," in *Studia Paulina* (J. de Zwaan *FS*), ed. J. N. Sevenster and W. C. van Unnik (Haarlem, 1953), 83-95.

_____, *Studies in Paul* (Minneapolis, 1977).

Davies, W. D., *Christian Origins and Judaism* (London, 1962).

_____, *Jewish and Pauline Studies* (Philadelphia, 1984).

_____, *Paul and Rabbinic Judaism* (fourth edition, Philadelphia, 1980).

_____, "Paul and the Law: Reflections on Pitfalls in Interpretation," in *Paul and Paulinism* (C. K. Barrett *FS*), ed. M. D. Hooker and S. G. Wilson (London, 1982), 4-16.

_____, *The Setting of the Sermon on the Mount* (Cambridge, 1964).

Deissmann, G. A., *St. Paul. A Study in Social and Religious History* (E.T., London, 1912).

de Lacey, D. R., "Jesus as Mediator," *JSNT* 29 (1987) 101-121.

Dibelius, M., "The Apostolic Council," in *Studies in the Acts of the Apostles,* ed. H. Greeven (E.T., London, 1956).

_____, and Kümmel, W. G., *Paul* (E.T., Philadelphia, 1953).

Dodd, C. H., *According to the Scriptures* (New York, 1953).

_____, *The Apostolic Preaching and Its Developments* (1937; London, 1951).

_____, "Ἔννομος Χριστοῦ," in *Studia Paulina* (J. de Zwaan *FS*), ed. J. N. Sevenster and W. C. van Unnik (Haarlem, 1953), 96-110.

_____, *The Epistle of Paul to the Romans* (MNTC; London and New York, 1932).

_____, *The Meaning of Paul for Today* (London, 1966).

_____, *New Testament Studies* (New York, 1954).

_____, *The Old Testament in the New* (Philadelphia, 1963).

Donaldson, T. L., "The 'Curse of the Law' and the Inclusion of the Gentiles: Galatians 3.13-14," *NTS* 32 (1986) 94-112.

Drane, J. W., *Paul: Libertine or Legalist?* (London, 1975).

Dunn, J. D. G., *Baptism in the Holy Spirit* (SBT 15; Naperville, Ill., 1970).

———, *Jesus and the Spirit* (Philadelphia, 1975).

———, "Paul's Understanding of the Death of Jesus," in *Reconciliation and Hope* (L. Morris *FS*), ed. R. Banks (Grand Rapids, 1974), 125-141.

———, "The Incident at Antioch (Gal. 2.11-18)," *JSNT* 18 (1983) 3-57.

———, "The New Perspective on Paul," *BJRL* 65 (1982-83) 95-122.

———, "Once More—Gal 1 18: ἱστορῆσαι Κηφᾶν. In Reply to Otfried Hofius," *ZNW* 76 (1985) 138-139.

———, "The Relationship between Paul and Jerusalem according to Galatians 1 and 2," *NTS* 28 (1981-82) 461-478.

———, "Works of the Law and the Curse of the Law," *NTS* 31 (1984-85) 523-542.

Dupont, J., "The Conversion of Paul, and its Influence on his Understanding of Salvation by Faith," in *Apostolic History and the Gospel* (F. F. Bruce *FS*), ed. R. P. Martin and W. W. Gasque (Grand Rapids, 1970), 176-194.

———, *The Sources of Acts* (E.T., London, 1964).

Easley, K. H., "The Pauline Usage of ΠΝΕΥΜΑΤΙ as a Reference to the Spirit of God," *JETS* 27 (1984) 299-313.

Edersheim, A., *The Life and Times of Jesus the Messiah* (third edition, 1886; reprint, two vols., Grand Rapids, 1962).

Ellis, E. E., "'Those of the Circumcision' and the Early Christian Mission," *StudEv* 4 (1968) 390-399.

Ellison, H. L., *The Message of the Old Testament* (Grand Rapids, 1969).

———, *The Mystery of Israel* (Grand Rapids, 1968).

Erickson, E. J., "ΟΙΔΑ and ΓΙΝΩΣΚΩ and Verbal Aspect in Pauline Usage," *WTJ* 44 (1982) 110-122.

Fannon, P., "The Influence of Tradition in St. Paul," *StudEv* 4 (1968) 292-307.

Filson, F. V., *A New Testament History* (Philadelphia, 1964).

Flanagan, N., "Messianic Fulfilment in St. Paul," *CBQ* 19 (1957) 474-484.

Flemington, W. F., *The New Testament Doctrine of Baptism* (London, 1964).

Foerster, W., "Die Δοκοῦντες in Gal. 2," *ZNW* 36 (1937) 286-292.

Fridrichsen, A., "The Apostle and His Message," *Uppsala Universitets Årsskrift* 1947: 3, 1-23.

Fung, R. Y. K., "The Forensic Character of Justification," *Themelios* NS 3 (1977-78) 16-21.

———, "Further Observations on Paul's Gospel and Apostleship," *CGSTJ* 1 (July 1986) 80-99.

———, "The Impotence of the Law: Toward a Fresh Understanding of Romans 7:14-25," in *Scripture, Tradition, and Interpretation* (E. F. Harrison *FS*), ed. W. W. Gasque and W. S. LaSor (Grand Rapids, 1978), 34-48.

———, "Justification by Faith in 1 & 2 Corinthians," in *Pauline Studies* (F. F. Bruce *FS*), ed. D. A. Hagner and M. J. Harris (Grand Rapids, 1980), 246-261.

_____, "Justification, Sonship, and the Gift of the Spirit: Their Mutual Relationships as Seen in Galatians 3–4," *CGSTJ* 3 (July, 1987) 73-104.

_____, "Ministry in the New Testament," in *The Church in the Bible and the World*, ed. D. A. Carson (Grand Rapids, 1987), 154-212.

_____, "The Nature of the Ministry according to Paul," *EQ* 54 (1982) 129-146.

_____, "A Note on Galatians 2:3-8," *JETS* 25 (1982) 49-52.

_____, "The Relationship between Righteousness and Faith in the Thought of Paul, as Expressed in the Letters to the Galatians and the Romans" (2 vols.; unpublished Ph.D. thesis, Manchester University, 1975).

_____, "Revelation and Tradition: the Origins of Paul's Gospel," *EQ* 57 (1985) 23-41.

_____, "The Status of Justification by Faith in Paul's Thought: A Brief Survey of a Modern Debate," *Themelios* NS 6 (1980-81) 4-11.

Furnish, V. P., *Theology and Ethics in Paul* (Nashville, 1968).

Gager, J. G., "Some Notes on Paul's Conversion," *NTS* 27 (1980-81) 697-704.

Garnet, P., "Qumran Light on Pauline Soteriology," in *Pauline Studies* (F. F. Bruce *FS*), ed. D. A. Hagner and M. J. Harris (Grand Rapids, 1980), 19-32.

Garvie, A. E., "Did Paul Evolve His Gospel?" *Exp* VIII: ii (1911) 180-192.

_____, *Studies of Paul and His Gospel* (London, 1911).

Gaston, L., "Israel's Enemies in Pauline Theology," *NTS* 28 (1982) 400-423.

Gaventa, B. R., "Galatians 1 and 2: Autobiography as Paradigm," *NovT* 28 (1986) 309-326.

Geyser, A. S., "Paul, the Apostolic Decree and the Liberals in Corinth," in *Studia Paulina* (J. de Zwaan *FS*), ed. J. N. Sevenster and W. C. van Unnik (Haarlem, 1953), 124-138.

Gibson, E. C. S., "Sources of St. Paul's Teaching," *Exp* II: iv (1882) 33-45, 121-132, 209-220, 278-293, 343-355, 421-429.

Godet, F., *Commentary on the First Epistle to the Corinthians* (E.T., 2 vols., 1886; reprint, Grand Rapids, 1957).

Gordon, T. D., "The Problem at Galatia," *Interpretation* 41 (1987) 32-43.

Grant, R. M., *Historical Introduction to the New Testament* (New York and Evanston, 1963).

Greig, J. C. G., "The Eschatological Ministry," in *The New Testament in Historical and Contemporary Perspective* (G. H. C. MacGregor *FS*), ed. H. Anderson and W. Barclay (Oxford, 1965), 99-131.

Grosheide, F. W., *The First Epistle to the Corinthians* (NICNT; Grand Rapids, 1953).

_____, "The Pauline Epistles as Kerygma," in *Studia Paulina* (J. de Zwaan *FS*), ed. J. N. Sevenster and W. C. van Unnik (Haarlem, 1953), 139ff.

Grundmann, W., "Gesetz, Rechtfertigung und Mystik bei Paulus," *ZNW* 32 (1933) 52-65.

Gundry, R. H., "Grace, Works, and Staying Saved in Paul," *Biblica* 66 (1985) 1-38.

Gunther, J. J., *Paul: Messenger and Exile* (Valley Forge, 1972).

———, *St. Paul's Opponents and their Background* (Leiden, 1973).

Guthrie, D., *New Testament Introduction* (Downers Grove, 1970).

———, "The New Testament Approach to Social Responsibility," *VE* 8 (1973) 40-59.

Haenchen, E., *The Acts of the Apostles* (E.T., Philadelphia, 1971).

Hall, D. R., "St. Paul and Famine Relief. A Study in Gal. 2:20," *ExpT* 82 (1970-71) 309-311.

Hanson, A. T., *Paul's Understanding of Jesus* (Hull, 1963).

———, *The Pioneer Ministry* (London, 1961).

———, *Studies in Paul's Technique and Theology* (Grand Rapids, 1974).

Hanson, R. P. C., *The Acts* (New Clarendon Bible; Oxford, 1967).

Harrison, E. F., *Acts: The Expanding Church* (Chicago, 1975).

———, *Introduction to the New Testament* (second edition, Grand Rapids, 1971).

———, *A Short Life of Christ* (Grand Rapids, 1968).

Harvey, A. E., "The Opposition to Paul," *StudEv* 4 (1968) 319-332.

Hatch, W. H. P., *The Pauline Idea of Faith in its Relation to Jewish and Hellenistic Religion* (Harvard, 1917).

Hays, R. B., "Christology and Ethics in Galatians: The Law of Christ," *CBQ* 49 (1987) 268-290.

Headlam, A. C., *St Paul and Christianity* (London, 1913).

Hemer, C. J., "Acts and Galatians Reconsidered," *Themelios* NS 2 (1976-77) 81-88.

———, "Observations on Pauline Chronology," in *Pauline Studies* (F. F. Bruce *FS*), ed. D. A. Hagner and M. J. Harris (Grand Rapids, 1980), 3-18.

Hendriksen, W., *Colossians & Philemon* (Grand Rapids, 1971).

Héring, J., *The First Epistle of Saint Paul to the Corinthians* (E.T., London, 1962).

Herron, R. W., Jr., "The Origin of the New Testament Apostolate," *WTJ* 45 (1983) 101-131.

Hester, J. D., "The Rhetorical Structure of Galatians 1:11–2:14," *JBL* 103 (1984) 223-233.

Higgins, A. J. B., "The Growth of New Testament Theology," *SJT* 6 (1953) 275-286.

Hill, D., *Greek Words and Hebrew Meanings* (Cambridge, 1967).

———, "Salvation Proclaimed: IV. Galatians 3:10-14: Freedom and Acceptance," *ExpT* 93 (1981-82) 196-200.

Hodge, C., *Commentary on the Epistle to the Romans* (rev. ed. 1864; reprint, Grand Rapids, 1950).

Hofius, O., "Gal 1:18: ἱστορῆσαι Κηφᾶν," *ZNW* 75 (1984) 73-85.

Holl, K., *Gesammelte Aufsätze zur Kirchengeschichte. II. Der Osten* (Tübingen, 1928).

Hollander, H. W., de Jonge, M., and Tuinstra, E. W., "A New Type of Help for Translators," *BibTr* 35 (1984) 341-346.

Holtz, T., "Der antiochenische Zwischenfall (Galater 2.11-14)," *NTS* 32 (1986) 334-361.

Hooker, M. D., "Paul and 'Covenantal Nomism'," in *Paul and Paulinism* (C. K. Barrett *FS*), ed. M. D. Hooker and S. G. Wilson (London, 1982), 47-56.

Hoskyns, E. and Davey, E., *The Riddle of the New Testament* (third edition, London, 1947).

Houlden, J. L., "A Response to James D. G. Dunn," *JSNT* 18 (1983) 58-67.

Hughes, J. J., "Hebrews ix 15 ff. and Galatians iii 15 ff. A Study in Covenant Practice and Procedure," *NovT* 21 (1979) 27-96.

Hughes, P. E., *Paul's Second Epistle to the Corinthians* (NICNT; Grand Rapids, 1962).

Hultgren, A. J., "Paul's Pre-Christian Persecutions of the Church: Their Purpose, Locale and Nature," *JBL* 95 (1957) 97-111.

_____, "The *Pistis Christou* Formulation in Paul," *NovT* 22 (1980) 248-263.

Hunter, A. M., *Introducing New Testament Theology* (London, 1957; reprint, 1973).

_____, *The Message of the New Testament* (Philadelphia, 1944).

_____, "St. Paul in the Twentieth Century," *ExpT* 61 (1949-50) 356-360.

Hurtado, L. W., "The Jerusalem Collection and the Book of Galatians," *JSNT* 5 (1979) 46-62.

Inglis, G. J., "The Problem of St. Paul's Conversion," *ExpT* 40 (1928-29) 227-231.

Jeremias, J., *The Central Message of the New Testament* (London, 1965).

_____, "Zur Gedankenführung in den paulinischen Briefen," in *Studia Paulina* (J. de Zwaan *FS*), ed. J. N. Sevenster and W. C. van Unnik (Haarlem, 1953), 146-154.

Jewett, P. K., *Man as Male and Female* (Grand Rapids, 1975).

Jewett, R., "The Agitators and the Galatian Congregation," *NTS* 17 (1970-71) 198-211.

_____, *Paul's Anthropological Terms* (Leiden, 1971).

Jones, M., "The Date of the Epistle to the Galatians," *Exp* VIII: vi (1913) 193-208.

_____, *The New Testament in the Twentieth Century* (London, 1914).

Käsemann, E., *Perspectives on Paul* (E.T., Philadelphia, 1971).

Kertelge, K., "Gesetz und Freiheit im Galaterbrief," *NTS* 30 (1984) 382-394.

_____, *"Rechtfertigung" bei Paulus* (second edition, Münster, 1971).

_____, "Zur Deutung des Rechtfertigungsbegriffes im Galaterbrief," *BZ* N.F. 12 (1968) 211-222.

Kidner, D., *Psalms 73-150* (TOTC; Downers Grove, 1975).

Kilpatrick, G. D., "Gal. 1:18 ἱστορῆσαι Κηφᾶν," in *New Testament Essays: Studies in Memory of T. W. Manson,* ed. A. J. B. Higgins (Manchester, 1959), 144ff.

_____, "Peter, Jerusalem and Galatians 1:13–2:14," *NovT* 25 (1983) 318-326.

Kim, S., *The Origin of Paul's Gospel* (WUNT, second series, 4; Tübingen, 1981; Grand Rapids, 1982).

King, D. H., "Paul and the Tannaim: A Study in Galatians," *WTJ* 45 (1983) 340-370.

Klein, G., "Rechtfertigung im NT," *RGG* V, cols. 825-828.

Knox, J., *Chapters in a Life of Paul* (London, 1954).

Kümmel, W. G., "'Individualgeschichte' und 'Weltgeschichte' in Gal. 2:15-21," in *Christ and Spirit in the New Testament* (C. F. D. Moule *FS*), ed. B. Lindars and S. S. Smalley (Cambridge, 1973), 157-173.

――――, *Introduction to the New Testament* (E.T., revised edition, Nashville, 1975).

――――, *Römer 7 und die Bekehrung des Paulus* (Leipzig, 1929).

Küng, H., *Justification* (E.T., London, 1964).

Ladd, G. E., *A Theology of the New Testament* (Grand Rapids, 1974).

――――, "Eschatology and the Unity of New Testament Theology," *ExpT* 68 (1956-57) 268-273.

Kuss, O., *Der Römerbrief* (two fascicles; Regensburg, 1957-1959).

Lake, K., *The Earlier Epistles of Paul* (London, 1911).

Lambrecht, J., "The Line of Thought in Gal. 2.14b-21," *NTS* 24 (1977-78) 484-495.

Lampe, G. W. H., *The Seal of the Spirit* (London, 1951).

Lang, F., "Gesetz und Bund bei Paulus," in *Rechtfertigung* (E. Käsemann *FS*), ed. J. Friedrich, W. Pöhlmann and P. Stuhlmacher (Tübingen and Göttingen, 1976), 305-320.

Lee, E. K., *A Study in Romans* (London, 1962).

Leenhardt, F. J., *The Epistle to the Romans* (E.T., London, 1961).

Liao, P. S. H., "The Meaning of Galatians 4:21-31: A New Perspective," *NEAJT* 22/23 (March/September 1979) 115-132.

Lightfoot, J. B., *Notes on Epistles of St. Paul* (London, 1895; reprint, Grand Rapids, 1980).

Linton, O., "The Third Aspect. A Neglected Point of View. A Study in Gal. 1-2 and Acts 9 and 15," *StTh* 3 (1950) 79-95.

Lohmeyer, E., "Probleme paulinischer Theologie. II. 'Gesetzeswerke,'" *ZNW* 28 (1929) 177-207.

Longenecker, R. N., *New Testament Social Ethics for Today* (Grand Rapids, 1984).

――――, *Paul, Apostle of Liberty* (New York, 1964).

――――, "The Obedience of Christ in the Theology of the Early Church," in *Reconciliation and Hope* (L. Morris, *FS*), ed. R. Banks (Grand Rapids, 1974), 142-152.

――――, "The Pedagogical Nature of the Law in Galatians 3:19–4:7," *JETS* 25 (1982) 53-361.

Longworth, A. V., "'Faith' in Galatians. A Study of Galatians 2,16–3,29," *StudEv* 2 (1964) 605-610.

Lowe, J., "An Examination of Attempts to Detect Development in St. Paul's Theology," *JTS* 42 (1941) 129-142.

Lührmann, D., "Gal 2 9 und die katholischen Briefe. Bemerkungen zum Kanon und zur regula fidei," *ZNW* 72 (1981) 65-87.

Lull, D. J., " 'The Law was Our Pedagogue': A Study in Galatians 3:19-25," *JBL* 105 (1986) 481-498.

Lyonnet, S., "Pauline Soteriology," in *Introduction to the New Testament*, ed. A. Robert and A. Feuillet (E.T., New York, 1965), 820-865.

Machen, J. G., *The Origin of Paul's Religion* (Grand Rapids, 1925).

Mackintosh, H. R., *The Christian Experience of Forgiveness* (London, 1927, reprint, 1961).

Manson, T. W., *On Paul and John*, ed. M. Black (London, 1963).

_____, *Studies in the Gospels and Epistles*, ed. M. Black (Manchester, 1962).

Marshall, I. H., *The Acts of the Apostles* (TNTC; Grand Rapids, 1980).

_____, *1 and 2 Thessalonians* (NCBC; Grand Rapids, 1983).

_____, "Preparation for Exposition: Galatians 5:16-26," *TSFB* 70 (Autumn 1974) 7-10.

_____, "The Development of the Concept of Redemption in the New Testament," in *Reconciliation and Hope* (L. Morris *FS*), ed. R. Banks (Grand Rapids, 1974), 153-169.

Martin, R. P., *New Testament Foundations* (2 vols., revised edition, Grand Rapids, 1986-1987).

Martyn, J. L., "Apocalyptic Antinomies in Paul's Letter to the Galatians," *NTS* 31 (1985) 410-424.

_____, "A Law-Observant Mission to Gentiles: The Background of Galatians," *SJT* 38 (1985) 307-324.

Marxsen, W., *Introduction to the New Testament* (E.T., Philadelphia, 1968).

Meeks, W., Review of H. D. Betz, *A Commentary on Paul's Letter to the Churches in Galatia* (Hermeneia; Philadelphia, 1979), *JBL* 100 (1981) 304-307.

Michel, O., *Der Brief an die Römer* (KEK; fourteenth edition, Göttingen, 1977).

Mickelsen, A. B., *Interpreting the Bible* (Grand Rapids, 1963).

Mitton, C. L., *Ephesians* (NCBC; London, 1976; Grand Rapids, 1981).

Moffatt, J., *Introduction to the Literature of the New Testament* (New York, 1911).

_____, "Paul and His First Critics," *Exp* VIII: xxii (1921) 69-80.

Moo, D. J., " 'Law,' 'Works of the Law,' and Legalism in Paul," *WTJ* 45 (1983) 73-100.

Moore, G. F., *Judaism* (three vols., Cambridge, Mass., 1927-1930).

Morris, L., *The Apostolic Preaching of the Cross* (third edition, Grand Rapids, 1965).

Moule, C. F. D., "A Note on Gal. 2:17, 18," *ExpT* 56 (1944-45) 223.

_____, "Obligation in the Ethic of Paul," in *Christian History and Interpretation* (J. Knox *FS*), ed. W. R. Farmer, C. F. D. Moule, and R. R. Niebuhr (Cambridge, 1967), 389-406.

_____, *The Epistles to the Colossians and to Philemon* (CGTC; Cambridge, 1957/1968).

Moulton, H. K., "Tired of Doing Good?" *BibTr* 26 (1975) 445.

Munck, J., *Paul and the Salvation of Mankind* (E.T., Richmond, 1959).

———, "Paul, the Apostles, and the Twelve," *StTh* 3 (1950) 96-110.

Mundle, W., "Zur Auslegung von Gal. 2.17, 18," *ZNW* 23 (1924) 152-153.

Murray, J., *Redemption Accomplished and Applied* (Grand Rapids, 1955).

———, *The Epistle to the Romans* (NICNT; two vols., Grand Rapids, 1959, 1965).

Newman, B. M., *"Translating 'Seed' in Galatians 3.16, 19,"* *BibTr* 35 (1984) 334-337.

Nock, A. D., *St. Paul* (London, 1938).

Nygren, A., *A Commentary on Romans* (E.T., Philadelphia, 1949).

Orchard, J. B., "The Ellipsis between Galatians 2, 3 and 2, 4," *Biblica* 54 (1973) 469-481.

———, "Once Again the Ellipsis between Gal. 2, 3 and 2, 4," *Biblica* 57 (1976) 254-255.

———, "The Problem of Acts and Galatians," *CBQ* 7 (1945) 377-397.

Parkin, V., "Συνεσθίειν in the New Testament," *StudEv* 2:3 (1964) 250-253.

Parratt, J. K., "Romans i.1 and Galatians iii.5—Pauline Evidence for the Laying on of Hands?" *ExpT* 79 (1968) 151-152.

Paulsen, H., "Einheit und Freiheit der Söhne Gottes—Gal 3:26-29," *ZNW* 71 (1980) 74-95.

Pfleiderer, O., *Paulinism* (2 vols.; E.T., London, 1891).

Plummer, A., *The Second Epistle of St Paul to the Corinthians* (ICC; Edinburgh, 1915).

Prokulski, W., "The Conversion of St. Paul," *CBQ* 19 (1957) 453-473.

Räisänen, H., "Galatians 2.16 and Paul's Break with Judaism," *NTS* 31 (1984-85) 543-553.

———, "Legalism and Salvation by the Law: Paul's Portrayal of the Jewish Religion as a Historical and Theological Problem," in *Die paulinische Literatur und Theologie,* ed. S. Pederson (Århus and Göttingen, 1980), 63-83.

———, "Paul's Conversion and the Development of His View of the Law," *NTS* 33 (1987) 404-419.

Ramsay, W. M., "Paul's Attitude towards Peter and James," *Exp* V:iv (1896) 43-56.

———, "St. Paul and the Jewish Christians in A.D. 46," *Exp* V:iii (1896) 174-190.

———, *St. Paul the Traveller and the Roman Citizen* (reprint, Grand Rapids, 1960).

Reicke, B., "Der geschichtliche Hintergrund des Apostelkonzils und der Antiocheia-Episode, Gal. 2, 1-14," in *Studia Paulina* (J. de Zwaan *FS*), ed. J. N. Sevenster and W. C. van Unnik (Haarlem, 1953), 172-187.

———, "The Law and the World according to Paul," *JBL* 70 (1951) 259-276.

Reumann, J., *"Righteousness" in the New Testament* (Philadelphia, 1982).

Richardson, A., *An Introduction to the Theology of the New Testament* (London, 1969).

Richardson, P., *Israel in the Apostolic Church* (SNTSM 10; Cambridge, 1969).

_____, "Pauline Inconsistency: I Corinthians 9:19-23 and Galatians 2:11-14," *NTS* 26 (1979-80) 347-362.

Ridderbos, H. N., *Paul: An Outline of His Theology* (E.T., Grand Rapids, 1975).

_____, *Paul and Jesus* (E.T., Philadelphia, 1958).

Rigaux, B., *The Letters of St. Paul* (E.T., Chicago, 1968).

Robertson, A., and Plummer, A., *The First Epistle of St Paul to the Corinthians* (ICC; second edition, Edinburgh, 1914).

Robertson, A. T., *Word Pictures in the New Testament* (6 vols., Nashville, 1933).

Robinson, D. W. B., "The Circumcision of Titus, and Paul's 'Liberty,'" *Australian Biblical Review* 12 (1964) 24-42.

Robinson, J. A., *St. Paul's Epistle to the Ephesians* (London, 1904).

Robinson, J. A. T., *Redating the New Testament* (Philadelphia, 1976).

Russell, E. A., "Convincing or Merely Curious? A Look at Some Recent Writing on Galatians," *IBS* 6 (1984) 156-176.

Sampley, J. P., "'Before God, I do not lie' (Gal. i.20): Paul's Self-Defence in the Light of Roman Legal Praxis," *NTS* 23 (1976-77) 477-482.

Sanday, W., "St. Paul the Traveller," *Exp* V: iii (1896) 81-94.

_____, "The Early Visits of St. Paul to Jerusalem," *Exp* V: iii (1896) 253-263.

_____, and Headlam, A. C., *The Epistle to the Romans* (ICC; fifth edition, Edinburgh, 1902).

Sanders, E. P., "On the Question of Fulfilling the Law in Paul and Rabbinic Judaism," in *Donum Gentilicum* (D. Daube FS), ed. E. Bammel, C. K. Barrett, and W. D. Davies (Oxford, 1980), 103-126.

_____, *Paul and Palestinian Judaism* (London, 1977).

_____, *Paul, the Law, and the Jewish People* (Philadelphia, 1983).

Schlatter, A., *The Church in the New Testament Period* (E.T., London, 1955).

_____, *Der Glaube im Neuen Testament* (fifth edition, Stuttgart, 1963).

Schmithals, W., *The Office of Apostle in the Early Church* (E.T., New York, 1969).

_____, *Paul and the Gnostics* (E.T., Nashville, 1972).

_____, *Paul and James* (E.T., SBT 46; London, 1965).

Schnackenburg, R., "Apostles before and during Paul's Time," in *Apostolic History and the Gospel* (F. F. Bruce FS), ed. W. W. Gasque and R. P. Martin (Grand Rapids, 1970), 287-303.

_____, *Baptism in the Thought of St. Paul* (E.T., New York, 1964).

Schoeps, H.-J., *Paul: The Theology of the Apostle in the Light of Jewish Religious History* (E.T., Philadelphia, 1961).

Schreiner, T. R., "Is Perfect Obedience to the Law Possible? A Re-examination of Galatians 3:10," *JETS* 27 (1984) 151-160.

_____, "Paul and Perfect Obedience to the Law: an Evaluation of the View of E. P. Sanders," *WTJ* 47 (1985) 245-278.

Schürer, E., *The History of the Jewish People in the Age of Jesus Christ (175*

B.C.–A.D. 135), New English Version, ed. G. Vermes, F. Millar, and M. Black (3 vols.; Edinburgh, 1973-1987).

Schwartz, D. R., "Two Pauline Allusions to the Redemptive Mechanism of the Crucifixion," *JBL* 102 (1983) 259-268.

Schweitzer, A., *The Mysticism of Paul the Apostle* (E.T., London, 1931).

_____, *Paul and His Interpreters* (E.T., London, 1912).

Scott, C. A. A., *Christianity according to St. Paul* (Cambridge, 1927).

Scroggs, R., "Paul and the Eschatological Woman," *JAAR* 40 (1972) 283-303.

Silva, M., "Betz and Bruce on Galatians," *WTJ* 45 (1983) 371-385.

_____, "The Pauline Style as Lexical Choice: ΓΙΝΩΣΚΕΙΝ and Related Verbs," in *Pauline Studies* (F. F. Bruce *FS*), ed. D. A. Hagner and M. J. Harris (Grand Rapids, 1980), 184-207.

Smith, M., "Pauline Problems. Apropos of J. Munck, 'Paulus und die Heilsgeschichte,'" *HTR* 50 (1957) 107-131.

Snaith, N. H., *The Distinctive Ideas of the Old Testament* (London, 1940).

Stanley, D. M., "Paul's Conversion in Acts: Why the Three Accounts?" *CBQ* 15 (1953) 315-338.

Stendahl, K., "The Apostle Paul and the Introspective Conscience of the West," *HTR* 56 (1963) 199-215.

_____, *Paul among Jews and Gentiles* (Philadelphia, 1976).

Strack, H. L., *Introduction to the Talmud and Midrash* (E.T., 1931; reprint, New York, 1972).

Talbert, C. H., "Again: Paul's Visits to Jerusalem," *NovT* 9 (1967) 26-40.

Tannehill, R. C., *Dying and Rising with Christ* (Berlin, 1967).

Taylor, G. M., "The Function of πίστις Χριστοῦ in Galatians," *JBL* 85 (1966) 58-76.

Taylor, V., *Forgiveness and Reconciliation* (London, 1941).

Thrall, M. E., "The Origin of Pauline Christology," in *Apostolic History and the Gospel* (F. F. Bruce *FS*), ed. W. W. Gasque and R. P. Martin (Grand Rapids, 1970), 304-316.

Torrance, T. F., "One Aspect of the Biblical Conception of Faith," *ExpT* 68 (1956-57) 111-114.

Toussaint, S. D., "The Contrast between the Spiritual Conflict in Galatians 5 and Romans 7," *BS* 123 (1966) 310-314.

Turner, N., *Grammatical Insights into the New Testament* (Edinburgh, 1965).

Vielhauer, P., "Gesetzesdienst und Stoicheiadienst im Galaterbrief," in *Rechtfertigung* (E. Käsemann *FS*), ed. J. Friedrich, W. Pöhlmann and P. Stuhlmacher (Tübingen and Göttingen, 1976), 543-555.

Vos, G., *The Pauline Eschatology* (Grand Rapids, 1930).

Wagner, G., *Pauline Baptism and the Pagan Mysteries* (E.T., Edinburgh and London, 1967).

Wainwright, A., "Where Did Silas Go? (and What Was His Connection with Galatians?)," *JSNT* 8 (1980) 66-70.

Walker, W. O., Jr., "The Timothy-Titus Problem Reconsidered," *ExpT* 92 (1981) 231-235.

Watson, N. M., "Some Observations on the use of δικαιόω in the Septuagint," *JBL* 79 (1960) 255-266.

Wedderburn, A. J. M., "Article Review: *Paul: Crisis in Galatia*," *SJT* 33 (1980) 375-385.

Weizsäcker, C., *The Apostolic Age of the Christian Church*, I (E.T., London, 1894).

Wendland, H. D., *Die Mitte der paulinischen Botschaft* (Göttingen, 1935).

Wenham, D., "The Christian Life: A Life of Tension?" in *Pauline Studies* (F. F. Bruce *FS*), ed. D. A. Hagner and M. J. Harris (Grand Rapids, 1980), 80-94.

Whiteley, D. E. H., *The Theology of St. Paul* (Oxford, 1964).

Wilckens, U., "Die Bekehrung des Paulus als Religionsgeschichtliches Problem," *ZTK* 56 (1959) 273-293.

————, "Statements on the Development of Paul's View of the Law," in *Paul and Paulinism* (C. K. Barrett *FS*), ed. M. D. Hooker and S. G. Wilson (London, 1982), 17-26.

————, "Was heisst bei Paulus: 'Aus Werken des Gesetzes wird kein Mensch gerecht'?" *Rechtfertigung im neuzeitlichen Lebenszusammenhang* (Gütersloh, 1974), 77-106.

Wilcox, M., "The Promise of the 'Seed' in the New Testament and the Targums," *JSNT* 5 (1979) 2-20.

————, "'Upon the Tree'—Deut 21:22-23 in the New Testament," *JBL* 96 (1977) 85-99.

Williams, C. S. C., *The Acts of the Apostles* (HNTC; second edition, New York, 1964).

Williams, S. K., "Justification and the Spirit in Galatians," *JSNT* 29 (1987) 91-100.

Wilson, R. M., "Gnostics—in Galatia?" *StudEv* 4 (1968) 358-367.

Windisch, H., "Das Problem des paulinischen Imperativs," *ZNW* 23 (1924) 265-281.

Winger, M. "Unreal Conditions in the Letters of Paul," *JBL* 105 (1986) 110-112.

Winter, P. "I Corinthians XV. 3b-7," *NovT* 2 (1957-58) 142-150.

Witherington, B., III, "Rite and Rights for Women—Galatians 3:28," *NTS* 27 (1980-81) 593-604.

Wood, H. G., "The Conversion of St. Paul: Its Nature, Antecedents and Consequences," *NTS* 1 (1954-55) 276-282.

Young, N. H., "*Paidagogos:* The Social Setting of a Pauline Metaphor," *NovT* 29 (1987) 150-176.

Ziesler, J. A., *The Meaning of Righteousness in Paul* (SNTSM 20; Cambridge, 1972).

INTRODUCTION

I. THE LOCATION OF THE GALATIAN CHURCHES

The Epistle to the Galatians is addressed to "the Christian congregations of Galatia" (1:2b). Where exactly these "churches" (AV, RV, RSV, NIV) were situated is a much debated question. This problem arises because by the time Paul wrote Galatians the term "Galatia" had acquired two meanings:[1] (a) in its ethnographical sense, it denoted the old Galatic region in the central plateau of Asia Minor originally inhabited by the Gauls, that is, North Galatia; (b) as a political division, it referred to the whole of the Roman province called Galatia, which also included the region to the south in some of the cities of which—Pisidian Antioch, Iconium, Lystra and Derbe—Paul had founded churches during his first missionary journey (Acts 13:13–14:28). The question is: Was Galatians written to the churches of North or South Galatia? This question is important in its own right, as a historical problem in biblical study, but also because it has a bearing on the issue of the time when the letter was written.[2]

Up till the nineteenth century, the view that Paul wrote to the churches of North Galatia held sway. This North Galatian hypothesis, given its classic expression by J. B. Lightfoot in that century and subsequently forcefully stated by James Moffatt,[3] is still championed by many scholars today, predominantly but not exclusively in Germany.[4] The South Galatian hypothesis, first laid on a firm archaeological foundation by W. M. Ramsay, who based his arguments for the case on the facts of historical geogra-

---

1. On the historical and political background of this term, see, e.g., Bruce 3-5; *Paul,* 163; Betz 2.
2. Cf. Harrison, *Introduction,* 274, who also mentions a third reason: "it has a bearing on one's conception of Paul's objectives and procedures as a missionary." This is true; at the same time, one's prior conception of those matters, gained independently of the present question, is bound to influence one's decision on this question.
3. See Lightfoot 18-35; Moffatt, *Introduction,* 90-94.
4. E.g., Kümmel, *Introduction,* 296-298; Marxsen, *Introduction,* 46; Betz 3-5; Harrison, *Introduction,* 272-274; Grant, *Introduction,* 185.

1

phy,[5] is followed by the majority of modern interpreters—at least as far as the English-speaking world is concerned.[6] We will not rehearse in detail here the arguments which have been used in the debate,[7] but only mention three considerations in support of the South Galatian hypothesis which commend themselves to us as particularly cogent: (a) what is known of the geographical situation at the time: none of the main roads in Asia Minor even passed through North Galatia, so that had Paul wanted to go to preach the gospel there he would not have set out from Lystra (cf. Acts 16:1, 6);[8] (b) Paul's evangelistic strategy: it is obvious from Acts that Paul consistently concentrated his efforts on the main roads and centers of communication in the Roman Empire, and until the end of the third century South Galatia was more important than North Galatia and correspondingly more developed;[9] (c) the silence of Acts regarding the establishment of churches in North Galatia: this silence, over against the author's explicit mention of churches in South Galatia, would be extremely difficult to explain if the controversy

5. See Bruce 8-9; "Galatian Problems. 2," 250-252.

6. One hesitates to speak of a "majority" *simpliciter*, in view of the seemingly conflicting statements by Guthrie, *Introduction*, 457 ("Most modern scholars lean to the South Galatian theory"), and Betz 4 ("today most commentators tend to favour the territory hypothesis"). (Or is the discrepancy more apparent than real, since "scholars" may be presumed to denote a wider group than "commentators"?) In the middle of this century, Hunter, "St. Paul," 357, said: "In this country, we are now almost all 'South Galatianists', and I cannot think of a recent British commentator on Galatians prepared to defend the old view." The picture does not appear to have changed significantly since. Some modern champions of the South Galatian theory are: Guthrie 15-27; *Introduction*, 450-456; Bruce 10-18; "Galatian Problems. 2"; Hemer, "Acts and Galatians," 82-85; Martin, *Foundations*, 2:145-148; Robinson, *Redating*, 55.

7. We have done so in our earlier work: Fung 7-11. Betz 5 dismisses "the pros and cons of the two theories" as "mostly speculative." But then one is at a loss to know on what basis the author reaches the conclusion that the North Galatian hypothesis is "more probable" than the South Galatian theory. This seems to add substance to the complaint of Bruce 14, where he speaks of the disquieting superficiality with which the North Galatian hypothesis is defended by many of its champions today, illustrating his statement by reference to the arguments of Willi Marxsen and W. G. Kümmel (14-17).

8. See Bruce 13; "Galatian Problems. 2," 258; Hemer, art. cit., 82 with n. 6. In the complaint referred to in the previous note, Bruce finds it "especially disquieting to see how little attention is paid to the relevant data of historical geography." He (8; "Galatian Problems. 2," 252, n.1) aptly cites J. A. Findlay, *The Acts of the Apostles* (London, 1934), 166: "It is significant that all those who know the geography of Asia Minor well are 'South Galatianists' to a man." In this connection, special attention may be drawn to the article (n. 6 above) by the late C. J. Hemer, who had "for many years specialized in the historical geography of Asia Minor, particularly in the New Testament period" (editorial introduction to article). At the time of his untimely death on June 14, 1987, he "had almost completed a study of the historicity of Acts" (editorial comment in *EQ* 59 [1987] 347).

9. See Bruce 9; "Galatian Problems. 2," 253; Hemer, art. cit., 82, 85.

reflected in Galatians had been a controversy with the churches in North Galatia.[10]

For these and other reasons, the position taken in this commentary is that the recipients of the letter were the churches of South Galatia, that is, the churches in the cities of Pisidian Antioch, Iconium, Lystra, and Derbe. That the letter is addressed to these churches collectively suggests that a certain relationship existed between them, that there were similarities as regards both their external circumstances and their internal conditions. It will become evident from the contents of the letter that they were together being threatened by heresy, and it was in response to their common need that Paul wrote this circular letter.

II. THE IDENTITY OF THE GALATIAN AGITATORS

In the only place in the letter where the addressees are called "Galatians," Paul asks the rhetorical question: "Who has bewitched you . . . ?" (3:1, RSV, NASB, NIV). This picks up the reference in 1:7 to certain preachers of "another gospel" who were distorting the gospel of Christ, thereby unsettling the minds of the Galatians. These agitators, who feature in every chapter of the letter (2:4-5; 4:17; 5:10, 12; 6:12-13), though never directly addressed by Paul, were well known enough to both him and the original recipients of the letter, but for the modern commentator the question of their identity constitutes a second introductory problem that is keenly debated. We here note, and discuss briefly, some of the more recent interpretations which differ from the traditional understanding of the agitators as Judaizers.[1]

Kirsopp Lake's suggestion that they were local Jews seeking to win the Galatians over as proselytes to Judaism[2] appears less natural, in view of the clear evidence of judaizing activity at least as far as Antioch and Syria-Cilicia (Acts 15:1, 24), than the supposition that such activity extended to

---

10. Cf. Guthrie 23. Acceptance of this "argument from silence" presupposes a high estimate of "the historical reliability of the itineraries in Acts," which Betz 4 calls "another hypothesis." In this connection, the completion and eventual publication of C. J. Hemer's unfinished work (see n. 8 above) is eagerly awaited. D. A. Carson writes in an obituary delivered at Hemer's funeral service: "Those of us who have read parts or all of this unfinished study can attest its importance. Far from being a rehash of old arguments, this manuscript provides a fresh, detailed and balanced evaluation of the primary material."

1. For a more comprehensive survey, see, e.g., Brinsmead 9-21.

2. K. Lake, *BC* V: 215.

the churches of Galatia from elsewhere.[3] It faces the further difficulty that Paul's opponents seem to have been Christians, whose "gospel" bore some resemblance to the authentic gospel (1:6-7).[4]

J. H. Ropes, elaborating an earlier thesis put forth by Wilhelm Lütgert, maintains that Paul was battling on two fronts: on the one hand, Judaizers (not intruders from outside but local Gentile Christians who had yielded to the pressure of local synagogue Jews and were now themselves judaizing) and, on the other hand, libertine radicals (also Gentile Christians) who wished to sever all association with Judaism.[5] This view is open to the fatal objection that there is really no evidence that Paul had to wage war on a double front in Galatia;[6] Ropes's major presupposition that the same gnosticizing tendency as was present in Corinth "would naturally present itself elsewhere" has also been called into question.[7]

Johannes Munck argues that the opponents were some of Paul's own Gentile converts who, considering themselves insufficiently instructed by Paul, now wished to conform to the practice of the Jerusalem church.[8] But while Paul addresses his own converts in the second person, the opponents are referred to throughout in the third person (a distinction most clearly seen, e.g., at 4:17); comparison with a similar approach in the Corinthian letters, where "offenders within the church of Corinth are rebuked in the second person, while interlopers from elsewhere are denounced in the third person," strongly suggests that in Galatians as well the agitators have come from outside.[9]

Walther Schmithals's thesis that the Galatian heretics were Jewish Christian Gnostics[10] has gained little acceptance among scholars—deservedly so, since it is based on several dubious assumptions. The objection

---

3. Cf. Duncan xxxiii; Guthrie 161; *Introduction*, 466.

4. Cf. Brinsmead 86: "The intruders are Christians, and their heresy is essentially a Christian heresy." Betz 7 puts it even more strongly: "Except for the demand of obedience to the Torah and acceptance of circumcision, their 'gospel' must have been the same as Paul's. Otherwise it would be difficult to understand why Paul is so eager to demonstrate that they are so radically different from him."

5. Ropes, especially 27, 44-45. The main arguments of Ropes's thesis are conveniently set forth in Creed, Review.

6. Cf., e.g., Creed, Review, 422; J. Knox, *IDB* II: 340 (he suggests, however, that "Paul may be facing two kinds of Judaizers"); O'Neill 67; Bruce, "Galatian Problems. 3," 260.

7. Ropes 10; Drane, *Paul*, 81-88.

8. Munck, *Paul*, 87-134. He is followed by Bring 289-290.

9. Bruce 24-25; "Galatian Problems. 3," 259. Cf. Martyn, "Mission," 313. See also the criticism of Barrett 57, who after a string of rhetorical questions concludes: "I do not think we can follow Munck here."

10. Schmithals, *Paul and the Gnostics*, 13-46. Schmithals is followed by Marxsen, *Introduction*, 53-57.

has been raised, for instance, that the interpretation of the heretics' demand for circumcision as a means of securing release symbolically from the dominion of the flesh has no basis at all in the letter; the strong insistence on the law throughout the epistle indicates that the Galatian opponents were advocates of a Jewish legalism—which ill fits a Gnostic theory; certain tendencies which may be expected of Gnosticism (such as a thoroughgoing dualism) do not appear; and, unlike 1 Corinthians, *gnōsis* ("knowledge") plays no role in the letter.[11]

A similar attempt to identify the Galatian agitators as Jewish Christian syncretists who sought enlightenment through legal observance, including circumcision,[12] fails to satisfy, if only because it involves the unjustifiable procedure of reading the Colossian situation into Galatia and the unlikely conclusion that Paul must have himself adhered to some Jewish mystery-cult before his conversion.[13]

Robert Jewett understands the Galatian agitators to be a politically-orientated group of nomistic Christians in Judea; his hypothesis is that

> Jewish Christians in Judea were stimulated by Zealot pressure into a nomistic campaign among their fellow Christians in the late forties and early fifties. Their goal was to avert the suspicion that they were in common with lawless Gentiles. It appears that the Judean Christians convinced themselves that circumcision of Gentile Christians would thwart Zealot reprisals.

It is in this light, Jewett believes, that Galatians 6:12-13 is to be interpreted.[14] According to his theory, the agitators employed the tactic not of directly opposing Paul or his theology, but of offering a completion to it (3:3) through the way of circumcision (vv. 6-18); such an offer of perfection would exert a powerful attraction on the Hellenistic Christians of Galatia,

---

11. Cf. Kümmel, *Introduction,* 300; Guthrie, *Introduction,* 467; Jewett, "Agitators," 198, 211; Schlier 21. See also Wilson, "Gnostics," especially 360ff.; Vielhauer, "Gesetzesdienst," 544-546. Betz 7 puts it down as a *fact* that "no passage in Galatians yields any data which clearly point to those [allegedly present] gnostic traits"; he does not, however, think that this "obvious" "lack of unambiguous evidence" automatically excludes the possibility that the opponents had gnostic tendencies.

Against Marxsen's argument (*Introduction,* 55, 58) that the lack of evidence is due to Paul's own failure to understand what the opponents were teaching, Bruce 25 justly remarks: "if we cannot determine the nature of their teaching from Paul's refutation of it, we have no other evidence to guide us." Cf. Barclay, "Mirror-Reading," 76: "If Galatians is our only evidence for what the opponents believed, and if, in writing Galatians, Paul laboured under a major misapprehension about them, our search for the real opponents must be abortive."

12. Crownfield, "Singular."

13. Rightly, Drane, *Paul,* 89.

14. Jewett, "Agitators," 205-206. Cf. Reicke, "Hintergrund," 187.

who would be acquainted with it as the familiar aim alike of the mystery religions and of classical philosophy, and who, moreover, themselves had "an intensely proud spiritual self-consciousness."[15]

Though favorably received by some scholars,[16] Jewett's interpretation does not seem to be free from difficulties. The main difficulty is that the evidence in support of the claim that it was specifically Zealot pressure—as distinct from non-Christian Jewish pressure in general—which occasioned the nomistic campaign among the Gentile churches is neither substantial nor unequivocal. In view of the sharply antithetical relationship between the Zealot movement and the Christian Church at the outbreak of the Jewish War,[17] it may be doubted if the Judean Christians did entertain the conviction earlier that a nomistic campaign among the Gentile Christians would thwart Zealot reprisals;[18] the Zealots as a party[19] appear to have been more concerned with trying to overthrow the occupying power than with seeking to prevent the Judean Christians from having communion with lawless Gentiles. It is not beyond dispute that the plot against Paul's life in Jerusalem (Acts 23:12-15; cf. 20:3) was engineered by members of the Zealot party, as Jewett makes out;[20] the easy access of the conspirators to the Jewish authorities and their ready collaboration with them (Acts 23:14-15) suggests otherwise.[21] The anti-Christian persecution in Judea described in 1 Thessalonians 2:14-16, which Jewett implies was connected with the activities of the Zealots,[22] can be satisfactorily explained without the supposition of such

15. Jewett, "Agitators," 206ff., 211 (whence the quotation).
16. E.g., R. P. Martin in *TSFB* 64 (Autumn 1972) 27; *Foundations* 2: 154-156; Bruce 31-32; Davies, *Studies*, 183, who writes: "Two things in Jewett's work appeal to us: its specificity in meeting what seems to us to have been an unusually pointed crisis in the Galatian churches and its sensitivity to the fiery nationalist aspects of the period with which Christian messianism had to come to terms."
17. Cf. A. Stumpff, *TDNT* II: 886; he further points out that "Christians could not stay in Jerusalem once the rule of the Zealots had been established."
18. Jewett himself admits that the belief was probably illusory, and that the Jewish Christians had overcome their illusions by the time of the outbreak of the Jewish War ("Agitators," 205-206).
19. On the Zealots as a party, cf., e.g., A. Stumpff, *TDNT* II: 884-886; H.-C. Hahn, *NIDNTT* III: 1167f.; Bruce, *NT History*, 88-95.
20. Jewett, "Agitators," 205.
21. For, "fiercely anti-Roman as they were, they were almost as hostile to the Jewish establishment—the hierarchy and the wealthy aristocrats—as to the Romans" (Bruce, *NT History*, 95). It is to be observed that the above passages in Acts on which Jewett builds his case do not speak of "Zealots" but only of "the Jews," which cannot easily be taken to mean members of the Zealot party and is so taken neither by Haenchen, *Acts*, 649, nor by Bruce, *Book of Acts*, 457. Davies, *Studies*, 183, says (in defense of Jewett): "The absence of the party name Zealots is understandable: there was no 'party' of that name before A.D. 66 probably, although there were 'zealots.'" But the passages in Acts cited by Jewett do not speak even of "zealots" (in contrast to Acts 1:13).
22. Jewett, "Agitators," 204-205.

a connection.[23] Further, it is perhaps reasonable to assume that the Galatian agitators' "program" would show some sign of affinity with the aims of the Zealots who allegedly were exerting the pressure; but the offer to bring Gentile Christians to "perfection" (Gal. 3:3) appears remote from Zealot interests.[24]

As none of the above interpretations is really convincing, the traditional understanding of the Galatian heretics as Judaizers appears to be still the most likely view.[25] In agreement with this understanding, we take the

23. E.g., Marshall, *Thessalonians*, 77-83. It is not irrelevant to observe that, whereas J. D. G. Dunn agrees with the interpretation of R. Jewett and B. Reicke in his understanding of the socio-political situation confronting Judaism in the middle of the first century ("Incident," 7-11, especially 10-11 with 45, n. 36), Rabbi D. Cohn-Sherbok in response to Dunn has emphasized the *lack* of "concrete evidence to support his general contention that the Jewish community put pressure on Jews to conform to their heritage because of the growing threat to their religious and national prerogatives" ("Reflections," 69, cf. 70). Cf. Borgen, "Paul Preaches," 42: the theory of R. Jewett and A. Suhl "about pressure from the Zealots in Judea must . . . be discussed as only one possible background, since Philo, for one, testifies in *Migr.* 86-93 to the fact that in the Jewish communities in the Diaspora also there was a general threat of persecution against non-conformists who ignored or rejected the external observances."

24. On the "Zealot pressure" theory, of course, one could suppose that the Zealots had left the agitators free to devise their own approach to bring the Gentile Christians into nomism.

25. Cf., e.g., Lightfoot 27, 52-53; Burton liv-lv; Duncan xxi, xxxii ff.; Ridderbos 15-16; Cole 23-24, 40-41; Hunter 9 10; Bligh, 17-35; Hendriksen 40; Guthrie 10-11; *Introduction*, 465-468; Betz 7; Bruce 25-27, 31-32; "Galatian Problems. 3"; Barrett 6; *Signs*, 39-40; Schlatter, *Church*, 168-172; Filson, *NT History*, 241-243; Kümmel, *Introduction*, 298-301; Gunther, *St. Paul's Opponents*, 298-299; and, especially, Barclay, "Mirror-Reading," 88-89 (though he does not use the term "Judaizers").

According to King, "Tannaim," 345-349, Paul's opponents in Galatia were either Ebionites or, as a movement, the spiritual parent of that sect. Howard regards them as "Jewish Christian Judaizers from Jerusalem" (9) "supported by the apostles at Jerusalem," who "believed that Paul, like them, taught the necessity of circumcision and the law for salvation and were totally unaware of his non-circumcision gospel" (2), with the result that while Paul was hostile to them they were not hostile to him (11). This novel view has been justly criticized as having little to commend it (see, e.g., Russell, "Convincing . . . ?" 161-162; cf. Wedderburn, "Review," 375-378).

Brinsmead gives an elaborately constructed picture of the Galatian intruders; what follows is an attempt to present the main features of that picture, in Brinsmead's own words as much as possible. The intruders are "Christians, as well as Judaizers" (194) who "probably come from circles such as the Essenes" (159). These Christian intruders of Jewish origin (86 [1]) are efficient and authoritarian "community-apostles in Galatia" who have the communities under their spell (189, 85 [1]); "they apparently stand in a stream which is critical of 'orthodox' Jerusalem traditions, Jewish and Christian" (87), that is, they uphold "the pre-Christian traditions of Jerusalem, while flouting the leadership of the Jerusalem church and the traditions of the earthly Jesus" (109, cf. 192-193). Their traditions regarding apostleship (93-106), Abraham and his seed (107-114), the law (115-137), the sacraments (139-161), and ethics (163-185) reveal a theology that consistently has one probable source—"apocalyptic and sectarian Judaism, especially circles

Galatian agitators to be Jewish Christians who adopted a rigorist attitude towards Gentile Christians and sought to impose upon them circumcision and observance of the law as conditions necessary for salvation or—what amounts to the same thing—for a full Christian status. These Judaizers may have been connected with the "circumcision party" of the Jerusalem church

---

associated with Qumran" (195); the other important source of their theology is "early Christian tradition," and they may have also drawn on "the propaganda methods of 'apologetic' Judaism" (195-196).

In their system of theology, they have "only a preliminary place" for Jesus: "Baptism into Christ makes one a novice, as was Abraham when he had faith. One must then advance to the heart of the mystery through circumcision and the observance of calendrical law" (160)—for they "present Christianity as a mystery, with degrees of perfection," and Abraham as the model of religious quest and discovery (114). For them the Mosaic covenant is "the highest form of revealed religion" (193)—although "they do not keep all the law" (87 [8]), but "evidently understand law particularly as calendar observance" (137, cf. 135, 136), and their demand for observance of the law "focuses on circumcision and calendrical feasts" (193)—and "law-obedience is the means of achieving" the goal of "attainment of the angelic state, and the final resolution of the sexes" (160). If it is also said that they "probably have a central place for Jesus," this is meant in the sense that "He is probably a Jesus who is powerful to enable the law to be kept, a Jesus who glorifies the old covenant-dispensation" (196), for "this glorious ["cross-less"] Jesus . . . has not brought in the new age, and the law-covenant remains the most glorious revelation of God" (196-197; cf. 200: the "law of Christ could only be a reauthentication of the law of Moses").

Hence, while "their glorious Jesus fixes attention on the individual in a competitive sense, which results in a hierarchical, schismatic ecclesiology which glorifies the intruding apostles," yet because Jesus "has not yet divided the ages" (197-198), justification by faith is "just a starting-point, to which must be added a justification by works of law" (190, cf. 196-197, 198, 201: "a justification by faith plus works"); this means, in sacramental terms, that circumcision "completes that which was begun by baptism," enabling the recipient to "experience proleptically . . . something of the angelic condition" (199).

In sum, Paul's opponents in Galatia are "nomistic enthusiasts" (161) and the heresy is a "'nomistic enthusiasm.' It is enthusiastic as it grows out of traditions of the glorious apostle and the glorious Jesus; but it is nomistic, because Jesus has not yet divided the ages" (198)—hence "the intruders' program of nomistic perfection and spirituality" (180), which they present "as a completion (ἐπιτελεῖν) of a mystery of which baptism is only an initiation (ἐνάρχεσθαι)" (191).

As the title of his book indicates, Brinsmead's basic thesis is that "Galatians is throughout a dialogical response to an offending theology which is now owned by the Galatians themselves" (157, cf. 192). This presupposes that Galatians belongs to the "apologetic letter" genre (cf. 37-55, 57-87). A general criticism of Brinsmead's basic thesis is, "If the theory of an apologetic genre falls to the ground his thesis has to be seriously qualified, if not abandoned" (Russell, "Convincing . . . ?" 161; on the question of genre see section IV below); in this connection it has been observed that "his analysis of Galatians as an apologetic letter is almost entirely unrelated to his extensive discussion of the traditions of the opponents" (Aune, Review, 146). But the fundamental problem with Brinsmead's reconstruction is his methodology. As Aune rightly remarks

whose activities are illustrated in Acts 15:1, 24; it would seem that the subversive activities of that party were not confined to Syrian Antioch but extended to its daughter churches in South Galatia as well. And it was precisely their insistence on including as essential ingredients in the gospel elements which do not really belong there that made Paul denounce the agitators as perverters of the gospel.

III. THE DATE OF THE EPISTLE

It was noted above (p. 1) that the destination of the Galatian epistle has a bearing on its date of composition. On the North Galatian theory, the letter could not have been written before Paul's first visit to the Galatic region in the north, which is presumably the visit recorded in Acts 16:6; thus, it must have been written after Paul's first missionary journey (chs. 13–14) and the Jerusalem Council (ch. 15). Further, if Gal. 4:13 is taken to imply that when Paul wrote he had already visited the region twice (taking *to proteron* as "on the former of two occasions"), then the *terminus a quo* is pushed forward to a time after the visit recorded in Acts 18:23; in that case, Galatians will have to be dated no earlier than the Ephesian period of Paul's ministry during his third missionary journey.

On the South Galatian hypothesis, the letter could have been written any time after the close of the first missionary journey, if the Greek expression in Galatians 4:13 means, as it could, no more than "originally, at the first." If it is construed as implying two visits, these could be identified as Paul's initial visit on the first missionary journey to the Galatian churches in an eastward direction and the subsequent visit on the same journey when he retraced his steps in the opposite direction (Acts 14:21), in which case the date of the letter could still be any time after the close of the first missionary journey. More probably, however, the second visit would have to be identified with the one recorded in Acts 16:6, and the letter would, again, date from a time after the first missionary journey and the Jerusalem Council.

---

(147), "Even if Galatians fits one rhetorical genre (which it does not), one could not assume that every assertion has the character of reflecting an opposing position." As it is, Brinsmead "leaps from one incredible assumption to another" (Barclay, "Mirror-Reading," 83, where two typical illustrations of Brinsmead's questionable exegesis are given), with "the stones of the opponents' theological building" being taken "from a variety of quarries, of circles of literature" (Brinsmead 91). The result of such "historical-cultural libertinism" is the proposal of an impossible, "bizarre and non-analogous mélange of beliefs and practices which characterize no known Jewish and/or Christian group in antiquity" (Aune, Review, 147).

It is obvious that the solution to the problem of the date of the letter hinges on finding the most probable way of correlating Paul's Jerusalem visits recorded in Galatians 1 and 2 with those chronicled in Acts.[1] This latter problem has given rise to a variety of proposed solutions. Since the visit of Galatians 1:18-20 (G1) may by common agreement be certainly identified with that of Acts 9:26-30 (A1),[2] the real question concerns the identification of the visit of Galatians 2:1-10 (G2) with one or another of the later visits in Acts: 11:30 = 12:25 (A2), 15:2-29 (A3), 18:22 (A4), and 21:15-16 (A5).[3] It may be noted at the outset that Paul says that he went up to Jerusalem with Barnabas (Gal. 2:1) and that A2 and A3 are the only visits undertaken by Paul and Barnabas together.

A. The Theories of John Knox and Kirsopp Lake

John Knox has put forth the novel theory that G2 = A3 = A4.[4] According to this view, all three passages refer to the same conference visit, which actually occurred at the A4 position, but Luke has moved the actual occasion of it to the A3 position for tendentious reasons; A3 is, in other words, unhistorical. So is A2; this "offering" visit actually took place at the A5 position but has been moved to an earlier place in Paul's career. In Knox's scheme, therefore, Paul paid only three visits to Jerusalem: the first, some three years after his conversion (the "acquaintance" visit, G1 = A1); the second, after eleven (or fourteen) years of missionary work in Asia Minor and Greece (the "conference" visit, G2 = A4 [= A3]); the last, after "an interval of not more than three years"[5] ("offering" visit, 1 Cor. 16:4; Rom. 15:25-28 = A5 [= A2]). This elaborate and ingenious scheme is open to the objection that it does not take the evidence of Acts seriously; by completely discarding the Lukan chronology in favour of an exclusive dependence on the data of the Pauline epistles, it simply avoids the difficulties of harmonizing the two

1. On the use of Acts as a secondary witness, with Paul as the primary witness, in this connection, see Robinson, *Redating*, 33; Bruce, "Galatian Problems. 1," 292-295; cf. "Is the Paul of Acts," 282-285.

2. Three exceptions to this view are mentioned between Bruce, "Galatian Problems. 1," 300-301, and Robinson, *Redating*, 38, n. 22; for criticism, see also Guthrie, *Introduction*, 383, n. 3 to 356 (against Pierson Parker); Martin, *Foundations*, 2: 150, n. 19 (against D. R. de Lacey). For the view that G1 and A1, despite the disparities between them, do refer to the same occasion, see Robinson, *Redating*, 38; Hemer, "Acts and Galatians," 86-87; and, especially, Bruce, "Galatian Problems. 1," 299-302.

3. The abbreviations A1, G1, A2, etc., are drawn from G. B. Caird, *IDB* I: 605. In the following pages, each abbreviation may denote the scripture passage, the visit to which it refers, or both at the same time, depending on context.

4. Knox, *Chapters*, 64-73.

5. Ibid., 58.

sources.[6] Moreover, Knox's entire chronology of the life of Paul seems to hinge upon Paul's statement in Galatians 2:10 and his interpretation of it to mean that Paul launched the relief fund only after the visit of Galatians 2:1-10. D. R. Hall has cogently argued, however, that the main verb in Galatians 2:10b should be taken as a pluperfect tense ("I had made it my business"), so that the request of the Jerusalem leaders was the very thing for which Paul had been striving prior to G2 (see comment ad loc.). In view of this, Knox's hypothesis appears to rest on a rather slender basis.[7]

Following Weizsäcker, McGiffert, and Schwartz, Kirsopp Lake in *The Beginnings of Christianity* advocated the view G2 = A2 = A3: A2 and A3 refer to the same visit; they are "derived from different sources and described from different points of view," but Luke has mistaken the different sources of the tradition for descriptions of different visits.[8] Donald Guthrie rightly objects that such a theory plays havoc with the historicity of Acts "without any adequate justification."[9] Lake, indeed, mentions the following as two "clear advantages of this theory":

> (1) It is based on the known fact that Luke used "sources," and that in his gospel he repeats, on occasion, the same saying from Mark and from another source which is found to have been used by Matthew also. . . . (2) It is the only theory which can do justice to the arguments set out by Lightfoot in favour of identifying Acts xv. and Galatians ii. without doing violence to the fact that Paul says that Gal. ii. was his second visit to Jerusalem.[10]

But, while it is known that Luke used sources for his Gospel, the position with Acts is far from being the same;[11] as for the arguments set out by Lightfoot in favor of identifying A3 and G2, that is the topic to which we now turn.

6. Cf., rightly, G. B. Caird, *IDB* I: 607a; Hemer, "Observations," 9.

7. Cf. P. H. Bligh, "The Pauline Chronology of John Knox," *ExpT* 83 (1971-72) 216.

8. K. Lake, *BC* V: 195-212 (quotation from 201). According to Lake (203), Acts 11:27-30; 12:25 (?); 15:1-2; and 15:36ff. (?) are derived from an Antiochian source, while 15:3-30 is from a Jerusalem source. Cf. Nock, *Paul*, 116ff. Without subscribing to the theory of two sources, Schoeps, *Paul*, 65, also takes the position G2 = A3 = A2, regarding Acts 11:27-30 as "a somewhat confused doublet."

9. Guthrie, *Introduction*, 459. Cf. Geyser, "Paul," 129: "No ingenuity short of radical excisions from the text can bring the Apostolic Conference in harmony with the famine visit."

10. Lake, *BC* V: 201-202.

11. In 1964 Dupont, *Sources*, 166, concluded his investigations into the question of the sources used in Acts with these words: "Despite the most careful and detailed research, it has not been possible to define any of the sources used by the author of Acts in a way which will meet with widespread agreement among the critics." Marshall, *Acts*, 37,

B. The View of J. B. Lightfoot (G2 = A3)

Lightfoot's arguments in favor of the view G2 = A3, a position both traditional and adopted by the majority of modern scholars, are set out in his commentary on Galatians.[12] He derives his "positive argument from the striking coincidence of circumstances," in point of the geography, the time, the persons involved, the subject of dispute, the character of the conference, and its result, and his "negative argument from the difficulty of finding any equally probable solution, or indeed any probable solution at all besides."[13] We shall now examine these claims one by one, and shall do so over against the possibility of identifying G2 with A2.

(a) The point about *geography* would apply equally well to the identification G2 = A2. The statement that "in both [accounts] the head-quarters of the false brethren are at [Jerusalem, while] their machinations are carried on in [Antioch]" presupposes that these "false brethren" made their appearance at the time of G2, but a different understanding is possible, perhaps even preferable (see point [c]).

(b) The argument as to the *time,* that it is "the same, or at least not inconsistent," again would apply to the alternative identification, unless it is proved that the latter involves a serious problem of chronology (see p. 17 below).

(c) As for the *persons* concerned, the representatives of Antioch were on both occasions (G2 and A3) Barnabas and Paul. It seems a slight advantage to Lightfoot's identification that Titus, mentioned in Gal. 2:1, 3 as accompanying them, could be identified as being among "some of the others" mentioned in Acts 15:2; but Titus may have been omitted from mention in Acts 11:30 because he was (as Gal. 2:1 shows) clearly in a subordinate position to Barnabas and Paul or because of some other reason;[14] and even in Gal. 2, it would seem, he receives mention only because of the significance he has for Paul in the context of Paul's argument in that chapter. Then, Lightfoot states that in both accounts Cephas and James

---

notes that "nothing has happened subsequently to alter this estimate in any significant way"; he insists that while some theories may be more plausible than others, "Luke has so thoroughly worked over his sources that it is impossible to distinguish them stylistically" (39). Cf. F. F. Bruce, *EBC,* 970a.

　　12. Lightfoot 123-128. Cf., e.g., Machen 86-94; Robinson, *Redating,* 39-42.

　　13. Lightfoot 123. With regard to the positive argument, cf. Sanday, "Traveller," 87-88.

　　14. Could it be the same reason as that which would account for the fact that Titus is never mentioned in Acts, even though 2 Corinthians shows that he was one of Paul's most trusted lieutenants? One suggestion is that Titus was Luke's brother (Robertson, *Word Pictures,* 3: 224, 297; Harrison, *Acts,* 21).

appear as the leaders of "the circumcision," but this is not strictly correct: in Gal. 2:9 it is "James and Cephas and John" who appear as the "pillars" of the Jerusalem community, but John does not figure in A2 at all (except inso-far as he may be assumed to be among "the apostles"); and it is not possible to suppose that John receives no mention in Acts 15 for the same sort of reason which could account for the omission of Titus's name in Acts 11:30.

A further point in this connection is that while "the agitators are similarly described in the two accounts," it does not necessarily follow that "the false brethren" of Gal. 2:4 were present on the occasion of G2. Although vv. 3-5 are usually taken as describing something which happened during the course of that meeting, with Titus as a test case, it seems possible (and in our view preferable) to take vv. 4-5 as referring to a development subsequent to G2 and introduced here because Paul is reminded of that later occasion by the mention of Titus and circumcision (see comment on 2:3). Gal. 2:3-5 then means that on the occasion of G2, no one even raised the issue of compulsory circumcision with regard to Titus, who was so ob-viously a test case; it was only later that the question of circumcision did arise, owing to the machinations of "false brethren secretly brought in" (RSV). On this reading of the situation at G2, the difference between it and A3 becomes even more apparent; and the difference relates not only to the point in question, but also to the remaining three points in Lightfoot's argument.

(d) Thus, Lightfoot's assertion, "The *subject* of dispute is the same; the circumcision of the Gentile converts," is open to question. For while that was indeed the central issue at A3, it was not even raised at G2. Even on the more usual view that Gal. 2:4-5 describes something which took place at G2, it is arguable that the chief subject of discussion was the larger topic of Paul's gospel and the division of the missionary task (vv. 2, 9).

(e) Again, the claim that "the *character of the conference* is in general the same; a prolonged and hard-fought contest" may be doubted. While the description might serve as a general statement of what happened at A3, it hardly fits the narrative of Gal. 2:1-10 (or rather 2:1-3, 6-10), which gives the impression of a friendly atmosphere and smooth proceedings.[15] Moreover, whereas Gal. 2 depicts a private conference between the Anti-ochian delegation and the Jerusalem leaders alone, Acts 15 describes a plenary session of the church. Lightfoot's attempt to forestall this difficulty must be judged unsuccessful: he maintains that "the very form of St. Paul's expression, *anethemēn autois*, . . . *kat' idian de tois doukousin* ["I laid before them—but at a private interview with the men of repute"], implies

15. Cf. Manson, *Studies*, 176.

something besides the private conference" while "on the other hand St. Luke alludes in a general way to conferences and discussions preceding the congress (xv. 4, 5, 6)."[16] But the implications thus detected in the texts are by no means obvious; on the contrary, there are good grounds for believing that Gal. 2:2 refers to only one interview, a private interview between Paul and the Jerusalem apostles (see comment on 2:2b).

(f) Finally, Lightfoot's assessment that "the *result* is the same" can be sustained only with difficulty. Whereas Gal. 2 states that no demands were made on Paul beyond the request to remember the poor (vv. 6, 10), Acts 15 records the decision of the conference to issue certain regulations regarding table-fellowship between Jewish and Gentile believers. Again, Lightfoot seeks to forestall this difficulty by stating that the apostolic decree was not intended to be permanent and universal, and therefore not applicable to the churches formed after the Council (this presupposes that the Galatian churches were in North Galatia) and lying beyond the immediate sphere of Jewish influence, and that Paul's controversy with the Judaizers led him to rely on his own authority rather than appealing to a decree of a council in Jerusalem.[17] Over against this it must be insisted that the findings of the Council were directly relevant to the Galatian controversy: indeed, by appealing to the Jerusalem decree, Paul would be able to defeat the Judaizers *on their own grounds*, since, on Lightfoot's own admission, the Judaizers

---

16. Lightfoot 126. Robertson, *Word Pictures*, 3: 222, 225 (cf. 4: 282), specifically sets the private meeting (Gal. 2:2b) between the first (Gal. 2:2a; Acts 15:4-5) and the second public session (Acts 15:6-29).

17. Lightfoot 127f. Against the first part of Lightfoot's reasoning here Ramsay, "St. Paul and the Jewish Christians," 177-178, argued that "Paul had actually delivered it to the South-Galatian Churches (Acts xvi. 4); and he therefore did consider it binding on them." Geyser, "Paul," 136-138, suggests that in Acts 15:41 παραδιδοὺς τὰς ἐντολὰς τῶν πρεσβυτέρων is to be read with the Western text and Acts 16:4 omitted as a duplicate which was inserted at the end of the first century "to obtain apostolic authority for the universal application of the prohibition" (137; cf. F. F. Bruce, *EBC*, 993b-994a; "Paul and Jerusalem," 13-14). On the other hand, Williams, *Acts*, 188, judges that "Paul may well have delivered the decrees in fact, if he thought that the Galatian churches were within the scope of the mission from Antioch, and especially if he wrote the letter to the Galatians before the Council meeting and was now able to say that the mother-church supported his own views." In any case, there is no mention in the rest of the book of Acts of Paul delivering the decree to other churches, and he certainly did not mention the decree in writing to the Corinthians (or the Romans). The latter may mean that Paul no longer agreed with the decree when he wrote 1 Corinthians, even if he agreed with it at the time it was issued (cf. Bruce, "Paul and Jerusalem," 16); this is supported by "the clear divergence" between the teaching of 1 Corinthians 8; 10 on the one hand and the apostolic decree on the other (Catchpole, "Paul," 434). Catchpole is led, however, by theological considerations to the conclusion that "the Decree must be traced to a situation not involving Paul" (429-432, quotation from 431); for a response, see Marshall, *Acts*, 246f.

were unduly exalting the Jerusalem apostles at the expense of Paul.[18] Provided, therefore, that the reliability of Acts 15 is accepted (as it is by Lightfoot), Paul's silence about the apostolic decree must remain a major obstacle to the identification of G2 with A3.[19]

Thus, far from exhibiting a "striking coincidence of circumstances," the two accounts in fact display "important differences," and there are "some unresolved problems if we regard them as referring to the same incident."[20] A couple of these problems may now be mentioned: (a) This identification requires one to suppose that in Gal. 2 Paul omits mention of A2 because (so Lightfoot argues) it was a brief and hurried visit and Paul did not see the apostles.[21] But, as Kirsopp Lake rightly objects,

18. Robinson, *Redating*, 41, argues that "Paul had no reason to quote the decrees. The decrees presupposed in what they did *not* say . . . the non-necessity of circumcision, on which Paul affirms the concurrence of the Jerusalem apostles (Gal. 2.3). What the decrees *did* say was that when Gentiles and Jews eat together the former must be prepared to make certain concessions to the conscience of the latter. But this is not at issue in Galatians." This does not answer our objection, which is precisely this: Why should Paul not appeal to what "the decrees presupposed in what they did *not* say" to refute the Judaizers' demand for Gentile Christians to be circumcised?

Wainwright maintains that Paul, writing from either Corinth or Antioch during the course of or at the end of the second missionary journey ("Where did Silas Go?" 66), "omits altogether any mention of the council, since that would have been a matter fully dealt with by Silas" (68), who had been sent by Paul from Athens to Galatia, as Timothy had been to Thessalonica (cf. Acts 17:14-16; 18:5; 1 Thess. 3:1-2; Wainwright 67). But quite apart from the failure of this really to meet our objection, the fact that in Acts 18:5 Silas is pictured as rejoining Paul at Corinth *from Macedonia* does not inspire confidence in the thesis that he had been sent *to Galatia*. A major plank in Wainwright's argument is that the church at Thessalonica "was in the middle of a grave crisis, both doctrinally and in its everyday life," so that "the only rational explanation" for Paul's sending the young and inexperienced Timothy there instead of Silas, a "leading man" in the Jerusalem church, is that "Silas was needed for a mission even more urgent, which perhaps only he could perform" (67, cf. 68 for Silas's suitability). But 1 Thessalonians itself does not give the impression that the Thessalonian church was undergoing "a grave crisis" (see, e.g., 1:2-7; 2:13; 3:6; 4:1, 10).

19. "It is this which, on the hypothesis that Acts xv. and Gal. ii. must refer to the same event, has led so many of the ablest German scholars to regard the account in Acts xv. as wholly unhistorical" (Lake, *Earlier*, 288). A case in point is Dibelius, "Council," especially 100.

20. Marshall, *Acts*, 244. Harrison, who favors the identification G2 = A3, admits that "the point of greatest difficulty with Lightfoot's analysis is his assertion that the character of the conference is in general the same"; in the same connection, he also mentions the fact that Galatians 2 says nothing about the apostolic decree (*Introduction*, 275-276), which Silva, "Betz and Bruce," 380, n. 4, concedes is a "serious" problem. It should be observed that Marshall's judgment is completely independent of the thesis that Galatians 2:4-5 belongs to a later occasion than the rest of the passage (2:1-3, 6-10).

21. Lightfoot 127; cf. Sanday, "Early Visits," 259f. Robinson, *Redating*, 40, similarly argues that "there was no occasion for him to mention this visit." This appears

this explanation overlooks the fact that in Galatians Paul is clearing himself of the accusation that he is a disobedient subordinate of the apostles by showing that on his visits to Jerusalem he never was subordinate to them. Surely it is inconceivable that he omitted a visit which can scarcely have been unknown, especially if he could have said that the apostles were then absent;[22]

for even the leaders, whom alone (on Lightfoot's view) Paul and Barnabas saw on this visit, could conceivably have "added" something to Paul, and any omission on his part would have immediately aroused suspicion and laid him open to the charge of "suppression of the truth" by his opponents.[23] (b) Lightfoot's identification of G2 and A3 also fails to account adequately for the controversy at Antioch over table-fellowship, which happened after G2, if at A3 the matter had been settled in conference and the regulations clearly pronounced in the apostolic decree.[24] The proposal of C. H. Turner that the incident of Gal. 2:11-14 actually occurred before G2[25] is surely an unnatural way of understanding the opening words of 2:11 (see comment ad loc.).

C. The Identification of G2 with A2

If none of the hypotheses so far discussed is satisfactory, it remains to examine the identification G2 = A2.[26] This identification seems to obviate

---

strange in the light of his earlier statement that "Paul is speaking on oath (Gal. 1.20) and any *slip* or dissimulation on his part would have played into the hands of his opponents. Indeed we may say that the statements of Gal. 1–2 are the most trustworthy historical statements in the entire New Testament" (36, emphasis added). This statement would seem logically to require that Paul's "again" in Gal. 2:1 be taken to indicate that he is talking about his *second* post-conversion visit to Jerusalem, not his third.

22. Lake, *BC* V: 200-201; this remark is particularly significant in that he has in this work abandoned the G2 = A2 position adopted in *Earlier Epistles* in favor of the G2 = A2 = A3 position. Knox, *Chapters*, 52f., expresses himself very strongly on the point under discussion. Cf. Catchpole, "Paul," 434: "the extreme care shown in Gal. i. 19f. to list not only whom he saw but whom he did not see makes it much more likely that he would have mentioned a visit and explained that he saw no apostle, rather than passing over the visit *in toto*."

23. Cf. Hemer, "Observations," 15. This criticism applies equally to Manson's theory (*Studies*, 177) that G2 is to be identified with a visit unrecorded in Acts, to be placed immediately after the call of Paul and Barnabas in Acts 13:2.

24. Machen, *Origin*, 101, holds that "this question had not been settled by the Apostolic Council, for even if the Gentile Christians observed the provisions of the Apostolic Decree, table companionship with them would still have seemed a transgression of the Law." But is it not reasonable to assume that the apostles in conference would have realized this difficulty and taken appropriate measures accordingly?

25. C. H. Turner, "Chronology of the New Testament," *Hastings' Dictionary of the Bible* I: 424, referred to by Guthrie, *Introduction*, 461, n. 2. Cf. Munck, *Paul*, 101-102, on which see Davies, *Christian Origins*, 194.

26. This is upheld by, among others, Ramsay, *St. Paul the Traveller*, 57-59;

all the difficulties connected with the identification of G2 with A3, and has at least three definite advantages in its favor: First, it furnishes the best explanation of Paul's silence in Gal. 2 about the apostolic decree: when Galatians was written, the Jerusalem Council had not yet been held.[27] Second, it satisfactorily accounts for the Antioch incident recorded in 2:11-14: the "play-acting" of Peter and Barnabas becomes understandable if the Council had not yet met and the clear stipulations of the apostolic decree had not yet been laid down. Third, it gives Paul's words in 2:1 their most natural sense in the context: G2 was Paul's *second* post-conversion visit to Jerusalem, which, according to Acts, must be identified with A2.[28] Some of the major objections to this identification must now be discussed.

Lightfoot, who bases his "negative argument" for the identification of G2 with A3 on the supposed difficulty of finding any other probable solution at all, has raised two objections.[29] (a) According to him, A2 "synchronizes, or nearly so, with the persecution and death of Herod" in A.D. 44; but since an interval of "at least 12 or 13, probably 15 or 16 years" elapsed between Paul's conversion and A2, this would require an improbably early date for Paul's conversion. Most modern scholars, however, would date the famine-relief visit later than Lightfoot did, between A.D. 45 and 47,[30] and the chronological difficulty is in fact much less formidable than it is in Lightfoot's view. Still, it must be admitted that the real difficulty of this view (G2 = A2) is its chronology,[31] and we must stay with this topic a little longer.

Lake, *Earlier*, 279ff.; Garvie, *Studies*, 24ff.; "Gospel," 183ff.; Bruce 43-56; Guthrie, *Introduction*, 457-465; Martin, *Foundations*, 2: 148-152; Gunther, *Paul*, 30; Hemer, "Acts and Galatians"; "Observations." Orchard's position is the same, though he describes it ("Problem," 388) as G2 − A2 + A3, i.e., Gal. 2:1-3, 6-9 − Acts 11:29-30; Gal. 2:4-5 = Acts 15:1-2.

27. Wainwright, "Where Did Silas Go?" 67, says of this suggestion: "even this fails when we consider the situation required by this hypothesis—that emissaries of the Jerusalem church were unsettling the Galatians, and that Paul was on the point of setting out for Jerusalem to get the matter settled. In these circumstances, Paul could hardly but say, in effect, 'Hold hard: I'm going to get this matter sorted out with the leaders at Jerusalem.'" But to reason thus is to forget that the polemical purpose of Gal. 1–2 is precisely to prove Paul's *independence* of the Jerusalem leaders.

28. Cf. Marshall, *Acts*, 245. On Gal. 2:1 Lake, *Earlier*, 280, has written: "*A priori* this raises a presumption in favour of the view that St. Luke and St. Paul refer to the same visit, and the *onus probandi* is really on those who deny it." Cf. Bruce, "Galatian Problems. 1," 306.

29. Cf. Lightfoot 124f.

30. Thus Filson, *NT History*, 398 (about 45); G. Ogg, *IBD* 1: 282 (toward the end of 45 or 46, with a preference for the earlier date); Bruce, *NT History*, 254 (46); G. B. Caird, *IDB* I: 606a ("not later than the autumn of 46"); Lake, *Earlier*, 289 (46-47).

31. This is readily admitted by Hemer, "Acts and Galatians," 87; cf. "Observations," 12.

C. J. Hemer has pointed out that there are at least four uncertain factors in the case.[32] (1) It may be argued whether or not the "three years" and the "fourteen years" of Gal. 1:18 and 2:1, respectively, are to be reckoned inclusively, whereby each part of a year counts as a full year. The former option is more likely, since it is in accord with regular ancient practice, so that the two periods denote what in our reckoning would be two and thirteen years respectively.[33] (2) More debatable is whether the two periods are to be reckoned concurrently from Paul's conversion, or consecutively. J. A. T. Robinson admits that "there is no way of being certain, but," he adds, "the natural presumption is that Paul is detailing a sequence . . . and that the two intervals . . . are intended to follow on each other."[34] On the other hand, Hemer is of the opinion that "the former [way of reckoning] is natural to Paul's working," and the suggestion is worth considering that "a mention of fourteen years with this meaning is rhetorically more emphatic than would be a reference to 'eleven' years (after the first visit)."[35] It would appear that there is no way of disproving either view. (3) The date of the crucifixion has been variously estimated, but it is probably safe to say, with J. A. T. Robinson, that "the most likely date . . . is 30—the only serious alternative astronomically and calendrically being 33."[36] (4) The date of Paul's conversion is never specified. On this point, Hemer's position is eminently balanced and worthy of acceptance.

> The complex development of events in Acts 1–8 gives the impression of requiring considerable time. But this may be no more than an impression: the dynamic vigour of the infant Christian movement was such that the whole story *may* conceivably have been contained within the first few months. It *may* have extended into years: while guarding against assumptions which might seem to close the question prematurely, I am open to conviction either way.[37]

Now, given these data, many permutations are possible, thus ruling out any dogmatic chronology. While any combination of the extreme options is unlikely,[38] Hemer has suggested that

32. Cf. Hemer, "Observations," 13. Our order here is different from his.
33. Robinson, *Redating,* 37. Cf. Hemer, "Acts and Galatians," 88.
34. *Redating,* 37. Cf. Lightfoot 102; Burton 68; Duncan 35; Bring 58; Ridderbos 76; Schlier 64-65; Hendriksen 70; Betz 83; G. B. Caird, *IDB* I: 606a.
35. Hemer, "Observations," 13, and Gunther, *Paul,* 26, respectively. Cf. Ellicott 23; Rendall 157; Neill 32; Bruce, *NT History,* 254.
36. Robinson, *Redating,* 37. Similarly Bruce, *NT History,* 178-180; G. B. Caird, *IDB* I: 603b. The date 33 is favored by G. Ogg, *IBD* I: 279, 281, and Manson, *Studies,* 172.
37. Hemer, "Observations," 13.
38. E.g., (a) combining "the shortest likely options throughout" and thereby compressing "the whole period from the crucifixion to the second Jerusalem visit into

various intermediate positions are at least possible. Even 33 for the crucifixion with a lapse of fourteen years all told would give a very possible 47 for the famine visit. Or consecutive reckoning from an early dating of the conversion following 30 for the crucifixion[39] could produce a similar result. Or if the period before Paul's conversion were more extended, or if the fourteen years were near to full calendar years and the reckoning virtually non-inclusive, there is still ample time if these possibilities are combined with other shorter options. In fact each of the longer or later options . . . might be included in a conceivable reconstruction.

Hemer concludes by saying:

It seems likely that the actual truth lies in one of [the possible options] or in an adjustment between two or more of them. My guess would be somewhere in the range: crucifixion in 30; conversion *c*. 32-34; visit *c*. 46-47.[40]

In our view, Hemer has successfully shown that the identification G2 = A2 is at least not impossible from a chronological point of view.[41]

(b) Lightfoot's other objection is that according to Acts Paul's apostolic mission commenced *after* the second visit, but the Galatians account "clearly implies that his Apostolic office and labours were well known and recognized before this conference." Both parts of this statement may be disputed: Acts is one with Galatians (1:15-17) in indicating that Paul received his call to apostleship at the time of his conversion, so that his apostolic mission commenced, not after the second visit, but with his activities in Damascus;[42] and while Gal. 1:23-24 shows that Paul's labors were already known before G2, it was only *at* G2 that his apostolic office was fully recognized, not before it.

Three other factors regarded as difficulties in identifying G2 with A2 may be mentioned. (c) There is the question which caused Kirsopp Lake to abandon the G2 = A2 position in favor of the G2 = A2 = A3 position:

The obvious difficulty is that, if the whole question had really been settled beforehand by the apostles at the second visit to Jerusalem, why did they pretend to argue it all *de novo* at the meeting described

---

about fourteen calendar years," or (b) taking a start in 33 "with the later and longer reckoning of other points" (Hemer, "Observations," 13f.).

39. E.g., Gunther, *Paul*, 26 with 168-169, n. 3, dates the crucifixion at 30 and Paul's conversion (not far from September) 31.

40. Hemer, "Observations," 14.

41. On the chronological difficulties raised by Robert Jewett in his *A Chronology of Paul's Life* (Philadelphia, 1979; British title: *Dating Paul's Life*), see the responses by Hemer, "Observations," 15-16, and by Marshall, *Acts*, 205, n. 2.

42. We have argued this in "Further Observations," 83-92.

in Acts xv., as though they had never discussed, much less settled, the problem?[43]

If by "the whole question" is meant the question of circumcision for Gentile Christians, then the obvious answer is: the question was not discussed, much less settled, at G2 (as we understand Gal. 2:3-5). Even on the more usual view of these verses as a reference to events which took place at G2, the objection may be countered by saying, with I. H. Marshall, that there is "nothing improbable in the fact that a difficult subject had to be discussed more than once before agreement was finally reached, as anybody who has ever worked on a committee will realize."[44] Perhaps the question is really this: if G2 (= A2) preceded A3, why did Paul not make reference at A3 to the fact that at G2 the Jerusalem apostles had clearly recognized his apostolic office and law-free gospel, and argue that therefore they should now logically recognize also that Gentile believers ought to be free from the law? A possible answer is that Paul may indeed have argued thus at A3, but Luke has not recorded it; or, more probably, no such reference was made because more powerful arguments were close at hand in the manifest working of God among the Gentiles (Acts 15:12-18) than would be furnished by reference to an agreement (Gal. 2:9-10) which may have concealed some ambiguities which had come to light in the interval between G2 and A3 and caused tension between the two contracting parties.[45]

(d) Another objection is contained in Lightfoot's attempt to explain Paul's silence about A2 in G2. Lightfoot assumes that "the Church was suffering from Herod's persecution when St. Paul arrived"; on that assumption he maintains that circumstances then were such that it would have been impossible for Paul to hold conference with the Jerusalem apostles.[46] If this assertion is correct, it will rule out the identification G2 = A2. Lightfoot's understanding of the situation in Jerusalem at the time of A2 is based on his view of the order of events in Acts 11-12 as follows: (i) the persecution of Herod, the death of James, the imprisonment and escape of Peter (12:1-19), (ii) Paul's departure from Antioch for Jerusalem (11:30), (iii) Paul's business at Jerusalem and departure therefrom (12:25), (iv) death of Herod (12:20-24).[47] But the more probable sequence of events is (i), (iv), (ii), (iii),

43. Lake, *BC* V: 201. Similarly, Catchpole, "Paul," 435: "how can the identical issue of circumcision have arisen in an identical way only to be solved by exactly the same means (a visit by Paul and Barnabas) and with exactly the same result?"

44. Marshall, *Acts,* 205. Such an answer presupposes (it would seem) that "exactly the same result" (see previous note) is a bit of an exaggeration.

45. Cf. Bruce 124f.; "Galatian Problems. 1," 303-305; *Paul,* 154-157.

46. Lightfoot 127.

47. Lightfoot 124, n. 3. For a similar understanding of the order of events, cf. Sanday, "Traveller," 93, and, more recently, Geyser, "Paul," 127.

since it is a more natural understanding of the passage to take the whole of ch. 12 (except v. 25) as placed parenthetically between the notices of Paul's journey to (11:30) and return from (12:25) Jerusalem.[48] It seems a reasonable inference that with the return of more favorable conditions Peter returned from his secret hiding place to Jerusalem, or, if he had not left Jerusalem to start with, he came out into the open again (cf. Acts 12:17, where "elsewhere" is literally "to another place," RSV, NASB). But if Peter and the other apostles were there, then it is unlikely that Paul and Barnabas would have departed without seeing them, since (i) Barnabas, who had been dispatched by the Jerusalem church to investigate developments in Antioch (Acts 11:22), would have much to report to and discuss with the leaders, and (ii) Paul, who had now been engaged in work among the Gentiles for a good number of years, would have eagerly grasped the opportunity to secure the understanding and support of the Jerusalem apostles as he sought to win the Gentile world for Christ (cf. Gal. 2:2b).

(e) The objection based on Acts 11:30 that, since the relief fund was handed over to the elders and not the apostles, the latter were probably absent at that time may be met by the consideration that in Acts 6 almoners had been appointed to take over the relief work from the apostles and that when they were dispersed in the persecution following upon Stephen's death (Acts 8:1) such financial matters as had been in their charge may have been taken over by the elders.[49] It is therefore not unreasonable to understand that at the famine-relief visit (A2) Barnabas and Paul gave the relief fund into the hands of the elders (Acts 11:30) and at the same time took the opportunity to discuss the gospel in a private interview with Peter, James, and John (G2).[50] Luke's non-mention of the private interview need not represent a serious suppression of the truth (as Paul's omission of A2 in G2 would have appeared to his opponents to be); he may have known little or nothing of that interview; or he may have considered it unnecessary to include in his brief account of Paul's early career what was but a private discussion whose importance, at least from his (i.e., Luke's) point of view, was far outweighed by that of the subsequent Jerusalem Council.[51]

48. Cf. W. L. Knox as cited in Bruce, *Book of Acts*, 257, over against Talbert, "Paul's Visits," 39f.

49. Cf. Orchard, "Problem," 392f.; Talbert, "Paul's Visits," 39: "The question of relief . . . is not within apostolic jurisdiction, as Luke sees it."

50. Cf. Lake, *Earlier*, 285f.; Bruce, *Book of Acts*, 244 with n. 35.

51. One of the arguments used by Catchpole, "Paul," 435, in support of taking seriously "some kind of Acts xv/Gal. ii equivalence" is as follows: "if Gal. ii antedates Acts xv there is produced an irreparably dislocated sequence, in that Gal. ii. 11-14 seems to issue in a break between Paul on the one side and Barnabas and Antioch on the other, whereas in Acts xv Paul goes to Jerusalem in the closest possible connection with both." This does not sufficiently take into account the fact that Barnabas and the

21

On the basis of the above discussion, we may conclude that the balance of probability strongly favors the identification of G2 with A2. Though some uncertainty remains, there are nonetheless weighty reasons against the identification G2 = A3—we mention again, in particular, Paul's silence about the apostolic decree and his alleged omission of a second Jerusalem visit. Therefore, we shall assume the identification G2 = A2 in this commentary.

D. Two Corollaries of the Identification G2 = A2

This identification has at least two corollaries. First, if Galatians was written before the Jerusalem Council, it follows that the churches addressed must be those of South Galatia which Paul founded during his first missionary journey (Acts 13:13–14:28): Pisidian Antioch, Iconium, Lystra, and Derbe. This corollary chimes in with our earlier conclusion, which was reached on independent grounds, regarding the location of the Galatian churches (see pp. 1–9, esp. 2f. and 8f. above).

The second corollary is that Galatians is the earliest of Paul's extant letters. The logic of this position is recognized when, for instance, John Knox writes: "If we could trust entirely the accuracy of the Acts account of Paul's visit to Jerusalem, the case for the early dating would be unassailable."[52] G. B. Caird, though seemingly inclined to accept the identification of G2 = A2, would, however, assign the letter to the same period of Paul's life as 2 Corinthians and Romans; he thus suggests "a very simple alternative to this early dating of Galatians. Paul may have omitted mention of the conference of A3 in writing to the Galatians because it had no bearing on his argument."[53] This is, however, hard to accept, for Paul would then have immediately invited the charge of a serious suppression of the truth from his opponents, particularly as at A3 he had agreed to the apostolic decree and had subsequently carried it both to the church at Antioch (Acts 15:30) and also to the churches of Galatia (16:4). In the light of the polemical context of

---

other Jewish Christians in Antioch had, in withdrawing from table-fellowship with the Gentile Christians there, acted against their own convictions (συνυπεκρίθησαν, Gal. 2:13), nor does it sufficiently allow for the possibility that by the time Paul and Barnabas left for the Jerusalem conference friendly relations between Barnabas and Antioch on the one hand and Paul on the other had been restored at least to a considerable extent. The process may have been facilitated by the departure from Antioch of Peter, who had been the primary object of the message brought by the men who came from James (see comment on 2:13).

52. *IDB* II: 342b.
53. *IDB* I: 606; cf. Buckingham, "Date."

Galatians 2[54]—and Paul even calls God to be his witness that he is not lying (Gal. 1:20)—the only tenable position seems to be that Paul has enumerated all the visits he had paid to Jerusalem from his conversion up to the time of writing.[55] It cannot be over-emphasized (and therefore bears repeating) that "Paul's argument in Galatians hinges upon his frankness in confessing the total extent of his visits to the Jerusalem apostles. The omission of a visit, even if it were unimportant, would arouse suspicion."[56] This vital consideration is, in our judgment, also a fatal objection to the view that combines a South Galatian destination with a late dating of the letter, say, during Paul's Ephesian ministry.[57]

Several objections, however, against this early dating of Galatians must be discussed. (a) Compared with the Thessalonian epistles, with which Galatians, if dated early, would belong, Galatians shows little eschatological emphasis, but seems to represent a later stage of doctrinal development. But two things should be remembered: First, the degree of eschatological emphasis in each letter is determined not so much by Paul's own thinking at the time of writing as by the particular needs of the readers to whom the letter is addressed; the Thessalonians were exercised by matters such as the fate of departed believers and the date of the parousia, but the Galatians were in a different set of circumstances altogether, hence the difference in eschatological emphasis between the two letters. Second, the eschatological emphasis in some of Paul's other letters is no less distinct than in 1 and 2 Thessa-

---

54. One of T. W. Manson's three "canons" for correlating Galatians 1–2 and Acts reads: "Never to forget Paul's purpose in writing the whole letter, and the first two chapters in particular. Galatians is Paul's *apologia pro vita sua*" (*Studies*, 171; another is cited below, p. 106).

55. This point also weighs against the view that Galatians, though the *earliest* letter, was written after the Council of Acts 15 (so Rendall 146-147; Talbert, "Paul's Visits"). Cf. Garvie, "Gospel," 183: "Total silence regarding a visit of such primary importance would have been disingenuous in the extreme."

56. Hemer, "Observations," 15. The point has been most effectively argued by Catchpole, "Paul," 433f., *(d);* he writes (434):

> . . . Paul, therefore, gives a complete list of his visits to Jerusalem and indeed does more than that, for in Gal. i. 17, 21 he includes what must be regarded as gratuitous information if his purpose is only to detail his visits to Jerusalem as such. This information is not, however, gratuitous if he is aiming to give a total and complete report of his movements, a report which A. Oepke has quite rightly described as "ein förmlicher Alibibeweis [a formal proof of alibi]." In other words the record of movements from his conversion in Damascus . . . to Arabia, from there to Damascus again, from there to Jerusalem, after that to the general area of Syria and Cilicia before a further visit to Jerusalem, leaves no room for movements anywhere else. Hence, as accounts of the second visit to Jerusalem in each narrative, Gal. ii. 1-10 and Acts xi. 27-30 do indeed correspond.

57. So, e.g., Robinson, *Redating,* 55-57; Silva, "Betz and Bruce," 380.

lonians; 1 Cor. 15:51-52 and Phil. 3:21 may be cited as examples, and yet 1 Corinthians and Philippians are clearly later writings than the Thessalonian correspondence.[58]

(b) J. B. Lightfoot has argued from the style and doctrinal content of Galatians that it forms a connecting link between 2 Corinthians and Romans;[59] if this order is correct, Galatians could not be the earliest of Paul's letters. However, even if we accept that "the Epistle to the Galatians stands in relation to the Roman letter, as the rough model to the finished statue; . . . it is the first study of a single figure, which is worked into a group in the latter writing,"[60] this fact in itself does not require that Galatians be placed immediately prior to Romans, unless a particular theory of doctrinal development be assumed which requires (i) that similar ideas be regarded as originating from the same time and (ii) that the time of expression of the ideas be regarded as the time of their conception. Both parts of the assumption are unwarranted. "The more important consideration," as Donald Guthrie rightly points out, "is whether the doctrine in the Epistle to the Galatians is too mature to be placed at the earliest stage of Paul's epistles."[61] In this connection, it should be remembered that a greater number of years lay between his conversion and his earliest epistle than the period spanned by his extant letters; Paul would have had ample time (if such was needed) to achieve considerable clarity and maturity on the major themes of his faith, and his acute and active mind would have insured that this time was put to good use.[62] Thus the similarity between Galatians and Romans does not require that they be placed in immediate juxtaposition chronologically; in the words of F. F. Bruce, "Paul may equally well have reproduced in Romans some of the distinctive positions of Galatians whether Galatians was written one year or ten years before."[63] Moreover, one may reasonably maintain, with A. E. Garvie, that

> the contrast of tone and thought even between Galatians and Romans is an argument against bringing them closely together. It is not likely that Paul would deal with the topic as vehemently as he does in the one letter, and soon after discuss it as calmly as he does in the other. The one was written in the very heat of the conflict, the other when the worst of the danger was past.[64]

58. Cf. Machen, *Origin*, 82; Bruce 53-55.
59. Lightfoot 42-55.
60. Ibid., 49.
61. Guthrie 37.
62. Cf. Hemer, "Acts and Galatians," 83: "Paul's grasp of a matter so central to his message as justification was surely matured even before the earliest feasible dating of Galatians."
63. Bruce 46; "Galatian Problems. 4," 256.
64. Garvie, "Gospel," 184.

As for the order 2 Corinthians-Galatians, Lightfoot employs a cumulative argument based on three lines of support: (i) a general resemblance of the two letters consisting "not so much in words and arguments as in tone and feeling," and special coincidences involving common ideas and expressions; (ii) the accordance which the proposed order affords "with the history of St. Paul's personal sufferings at this period . . . as well as with the progress of his controversy with the Judaizers"; and (iii) the light which this order sheds on one or two incidental allusions in Galatians "which otherwise it is difficult to account for."[65] But, (i) the similarity in tone and feeling is largely that between Galatians and the last four chapters of 2 Corinthians, which are in the majority opinion of today not integral to the letter;[66] but even on the assumption of the integrity of 2 Corinthians, the similarity in question may be due to the fact that Paul's emotions were similarly stirred on both occasions rather than to the letters' being written about the same time.[67] Lightfoot himself does not "lay any great stress" on the special coincidences noted.[68] (ii) The reference in Gal. 6:17 to Paul's bearing the "marks of Jesus" on his body could, on the early dating of the epistle, refer to the result of his being stoned at Lystra (see comment ad loc.); this would make Paul's allusion more intelligible to at least some of his Galatian readers than on Lightfoot's view that Paul's language here reflects the experiences he describes in 1 Cor. 15:30-32 and 2 Cor. 1:8-10. In this case a picture of "the history of St. Paul's personal sufferings" different from Lightfoot's reconstruction would emerge. "The progress of his controversy with the Judaizers," again, is capable of a different interpretation from that of Lightfoot. He argues that since in 1-2 Corinthians Paul scarcely meets his opponents on doctrinal grounds but is concerned to defend his personal authority, but in Galatians "the doctrinal opposition has assumed a distinct and threatening form" and correspondingly the doctrine of justification is more fully stated, therefore Galatians reflects a later stage in the development of the controversy;[69] but it is equally possible to argue that 1-2 Corinthians represent a later stage than Galatians because whereas in Galatians the opponents could rely on both the doctrinal argument (insisting on the necessity of circumcision and observance of the law) and the personal argument (casting doubt on Paul's legitimacy as an apostle), in 1-2 Corinthians they had to abandon the former approach and concentrate on the latter alone because the former would have been ineffective after the apostolic decree had been promulgated

65. Lightfoot 44-45, 50, 54, respectively.
66. Hence Buck, "Date," 113, can regard Lightfoot's assumption of the integrity of 2 Corinthians as the "specific weakness of this argument for the modern scholar."
67. Bruce 47; "Galatian Problems. 4," 257.
68. Lightfoot 45.
69. Lightfoot 52-53.

at the Jerusalem Council (Acts 15).[70] (iii) The suggestion that the exhortation of Gal. 6:1 might reflect the background of the restoration of the Corinthian offender (2 Cor. 2:5-11) is possible, but that verse seems intelligible enough as a general admonition; so does Gal. 6:7-10, without having to be understood as an implied rebuke at the Galatians' slowness in contributing to the collection for the Jerusalem church.

Lightfoot admits that the reasons he gives for favoring a late date for Galatians "certainly do not amount to a demonstration," but thinks that "the arguments . . . will hold their ground against those which are alleged in favour of the earlier date."[71] We make bold to say that against his arguments, the ones we have adduced in favor of the early dating of Galatians can likewise hold their ground.[72]

(c) A final objection to regarding Galatians as the earliest of Paul's extant letters might be derived from his statement in 2 Cor. 11:32-33 that he escaped from Damascus where the ethnarch under King Aretas guarded the city in order to seize him—an incident of which a a parallel account appears in Acts 9:24-25 and which should probably be dated some three years after Paul's conversion, on the eve of his first post-conversion visit to Jerusalem. It has been suggested that "ethnarch" indicates a viceroy, thus implying that Damascus was then under the control of Aretas, and that this is supported by the absence of Roman coins in Damascus during the period A.D. 34-62.[73] It is further pointed out that "when in 37 Vitellius the governor of Syria marched against Aretas, he proceeded not to Damascus but southwards towards Petra," which shows that Damascus was still in Roman hands; Aretas, then, must have obtained possession of Damascus between 37 and 40, the year of his death. Thus the incident of Paul's escape from Damascus may be dated between 37 and 40, and his conversion some three years

---

70. Cf. Hemer, "Acts and Galatians," 83: "The circumcision question has to be argued in Galatians because the Epistle antedates the Council, but that particular issue was dead and buried before the Corinthian correspondence."

71. Lightfoot 55. The "earlier date" in context refers to that which places Galatians immediately before 1 and 2 Corinthians. In the Pauline chronology of John Knox, *IDB* II: 343a, Galatians is placed after Romans and made one of Paul's latest letters from prison.

72. The argument used by Buck, "Date," 120-121, in confirmation of Lightfoot's thesis that Galatians should be placed between 2 Corinthians and Romans has been met by Bruce's masterful rejoinder (Bruce 49; "Galatian Problems. 4," 260-261). Jones, "Date," 198-205; *New Testament*, 247-252, has raised several difficulties which to him seem to render the early date for Galatians quite impossible. For a rejoinder, see Fung 145-148; "Righteousness," 1: 600-602 (with corresponding notes on 2: 595-596).

73. So Schürer, *History*, II: 129; G. Ogg, *IBD* 1: 279; cf. P. E. Hughes, *2 Corinthians*, 424-428.

earlier, between 34 and 37.[74] In this case, Paul's first post-conversion visit to Jerusalem would be dated between 37 and 40 and his second post-conversion visit some fourteen years later, if reckoned from the first visit, between 50 and 54, a date later than that of the Jerusalem Council (*ca.* 48); Paul must then have written Galatians at a time later than the Jerusalem Council, since in the letter he refers to his Jerusalem visits as past already. Only if the fourteen years are reckoned from Paul's conversion would it be possible to date Galatians before the Council, for the date of Paul's second visit would then be between 47 and 51.

The two main supports for the view that Damascus was under Aretas's control are, however, open to dispute. To take them in reverse order, (i) there seems to be some uncertainty surrounding the numismatic evidence. According to the view already referred to, the absence of Roman coins in Damascus marked the years A.D. 34-62;[75] another view gives the date as 37-54;[76] yet another, 37-61.[77] (ii) The view that the *ethnarchēs* of Damascus means the viceroy of the Nabataean king is favored by the fact that this official had the power to guard the city; on the other hand it seems a little strange, if the ethnarch was the viceroy, that he should not have arrested Paul openly. Kirsopp Lake regards "the whole basis" of the view under discussion as "extremely frail":

> It consists entirely of the assumption that if Aretas had an ethnarch in Damascus, Damascus was in his kingdom. What are the facts concerning the word "ethnarch?" . . . The really important point is that in the first century it was used as the name of the governor of the Jews in Alexandria. No one concludes that therefore Alexandria belonged to the Jews. It is more probable, then, that the ethnarch of Aretas was a representative of the Nabataean king who looked after the Arab element in Damascus, just as the ethnarch of the Jews in Alexandria looked after Jewish interests.[78]

In this case, the passage cannot be used as the basis for dating the conversion of Paul, and the possible objection it might pose to the early dating of Galatians is also removed.[79]

74. Ogg, loc. cit.; cf. Hughes, op. cit., 427, who dates Paul's conversion between A.D. 34 and 38.

75. Similarly, Hemer, "Observations," 4.

76. Hughes, *2 Corinthians*, 425; cf. S. Cohen, *IDB* III: 492a.

77. Bruce 96.

78. Lake, *Earlier*, 322f. Cf. Gunther, *Paul*, 168f., n. 3; Bruce, *Corinthians*, 245.

79. Cf. Hemer, "Observations," 13f.: "the political background of the ethnarch's presence remains unknown, and the question cannot be decided upon the unproved assumption of Nabataean control at a date we could only guess."

"Ultimately," writes J. A. T. Robinson, "dating is almost always a matter of assessing the balance of probabilities,"[80] and the dating of Galatians is certainly a case in point. Here some remarks by C. J. Hemer are wholly apposite:

> But how does one argue for or against the correctness of any partial or hypothetical reconstruction? Only by exercising judgment, by considering whether this is the simplest and most natural and most convincing explanation of the available data. The strength of any such hypothesis consists in the amount of light it throws on the ramifications of the subject without doing violence to the evidence. If one solution tends to permit the answers to interlocking problems to explain each other, that is a strong point in its favour. But if it has to depend largely on fundamental gaps in the evidence, this should render it suspect. We may not be able to say it is wrong. It may indeed be very hard to disprove. But it does not explain so much so naturally.[81]

Judged by these criteria, the identification G2 = A2, with its corollaries of a South Galatian destination and an early date for Galatians as the earliest among the extant letters of Paul—a position to which F. F. Bruce has given definitive expression[82]—commends itself to us as preferable to any other solution to these complex and interlocking problems. On this showing, Galatians may well have been written on the eve of the Jerusalem Council (*ca.* A.D. 48)—as soon as or not long after news had reached Paul that the judaizing propagandists, whose activities in Antioch and its daughter-churches in Syria and Cilicia had given rise to the necessity for a conference between Paul and Barnabas and the Jerusalem leaders (Acts 15:1-2, 23), had extended their subversive activity into the churches of South Galatia, which, as a result, were being won over to the Judaizers' counterfeit gospel.

IV. THE GENRE OF GALATIANS

Several recent studies[1] have proposed that Galatians is to be viewed as belonging to the "apologetic letter" genre and conforming to the principles and rules of contemporary rhetoric. The "apologetic letter" has been defined as one which

---

80. Robinson, *Redating,* 33.
81. Hemer, "Acts and Galatians," 81f.
82. Bruce 3-56, especially 3-18, 43-56; cf. his series of Rylands Lectures entitled "Galatian Problems" (see Bibliography).
1. Most notably Betz, especially 14-25; Brinsmead 37-55, 57-87, 188f.; cf. Howard 48f.

presupposes the real or fictitious situation of the court of law, with jury, accuser, and defendant. In the case of Galatians, the addressees are identical with the jury, with Paul being the defendant, and his opponents the accusers. This situation makes Paul's Galatian letter a self-apology, delivered not in person but in a written form.[2]

On this understanding, the structure of the epistle has been analyzed as follows: 1:1-5 epistolary prescript; 1:6-11 *exordium* or *prooemium;*[3] 1:12–2:14 *narratio;*[4] 2:15-21 *propositio* or *partitio;*[5] 3:1–4:31 *probatio* or *confirmatio;*[6] 5:1–6:10 *exhortatio, refutatio,* or *reprehensio;*[7] 6:11-18 epistolary postscript or *conclusio.* In particular, the presentation of this analysis in H. D. Betz's commentary[8] deals with minute details in verses and half verses and "invokes numerous parallels from the rhetorical handbooks, ancient and modern, for particular elements of Paul's argument."[9] C. K. Barrett has "found the whole fresh, fascinating, and illuminating";[10] his enthusiasm is shared, at least in part, by other reviewers of Betz's magisterial work,[11] and there can be no doubt that subsequent to its appearance all serious discussion will have to take (and has taken) account of Betz's pioneering approach to the structure of Galatians.[12]

2. Betz 24.

3. Betz and Howard; Brinsmead. Brinsmead and Howard regard this section as ending with v. 10, not v. 11.

4. J. D. Hester, who has offered a modification of Betz's explanation of the rhetorical structure of 1:11 2:14 ("Rhetorical Structure"), makes the section begin with 1:11, as does Howard.

5. Betz and Brinsmead; Howard.

6. Betz and Brinsmead; Howard.

7. Betz; Brinsmead; Howard. Cf. p. 221, n. 1 below. Aune, Review, 147 points out that Brinsmead "does not really defend this label, and the passage is conspicuously absent from the detailed discussion of 'Internal Indications of Structure' (pp. 57-87)."

8. It has been acclaimed as "an outstanding achievement in biblical scholarship" (Barrett, "Galatians," 414) and "perhaps the most original commentary on Galatians that we have in any language" (Meeks, Review, 304).

9. Meeks, Review, 305.

10. Barrett, "Galatians," 416.

11. Thus, Meeks speaks of its "fresh approach to the text" and of the fact that many of the parallels which the author cites from Plutarch "illuminate the Pauline text in new ways." Meeks also says that "Betz's observations of the forms and topoi used by the Hellenistic moralists and rhetors bring life and clarity to difficult passages" (Review, 304f.). Silva admits to having moved from his "initial reaction . . . of considerable skepticism" to the place where he finds "the approach illuminating and worthy of further attention" ("Betz and Bruce," 377f.). Davies, *Studies,* 172 writes: "whether he be followed at every point or not, Betz has clarified the literary structure of Galatians in a new and very enriching manner which often carries conviction and certainly must challenge reexamination."

12. This may be said in spite of the entirely negative assessment of Betz's thesis by Russell, "Convincing . . . ?" 156-160. Not only does he "not find the attempt to

On the other hand, various points of criticism have been raised about Betz's basic thesis that "Paul's letter to the Galatians is an example of the 'apologetic letter' genre."[13] (a) Not the least difficulty of this view is that, although Betz speaks with greater confidence of the "apologetic genre" as an established literary genre in Greco-Roman antiquity than does the authority whom he cites in support of this opinion (A. Momigliano),[14] he is forced to refer "almost exclusively to rhetorical and epistolary *theory* rather than to specific examples of real apologies and real letters from antiquity," without being able to offer us "a single instance of the apologetic letter with which we can compare Galatians. We are therefore asked to interpret Galatians as an example of a genre for which no other example can apparently be cited."[15] This does not inspire confidence in his thesis.[16]

(b) It has been suggested that

> Betz appears to be aware of this [absence of even a single instance of an actual apologetic letter] as evidenced by the special pleading and urgent reasoning in connection with the divisions of the genre, e.g., exordium (44-46) or narratio (58-62) or probatio (128-131).[17]

The charge of special pleading is clearly deserved in Betz's treatment of the last section just mentioned: he remarks that the section (3:1–4:31) is characterized by "apparent confusion" and freely admits that "an anlaysis of these chapters in terms of rhetoric is extremely difficult," but he attributes this difficulty to the great success which Paul as a skilled rhetorician had "in disguising his argumentative strategy."[18] (c) Related to and lying at the back of such special pleading is, in the words of W. A. Meeks, "Betz's determination to discover a tight, sequential outline in the letter," which, particularly in discussions of the last four chapters of the letter, "leads in places to a

---

blend the argument for an apologetic genre with commentary very successful," but he also considers such a "complicated argument [as] that which seeks to justify the use of *exordium* (44-46) . . . quite offputting and obstructive for one trying to get at the text and being held up by a process producing a result which hardly justifies the complex means" (158). Cf. n. 17 below with text. Perhaps it should be borne in mind that Russell apparently has in view the needs of "the minister whose task it is to make use of commentaries especially for expository or devotional purposes" (157).

13. Betz 14.

14. Hays 243, n. 92.

15. Meeks, Review, 306; cf. Russell, "Convincing . . . ?" 159.

16. Cf. Russell, "Convincing . . . ?" 160, with reference to Meeks, Review, 306.

17. Russell, "Convincing . . . ?" 159f., adding that "the slender evidence produced from M. Hengel eg by Brinsmead [231, nn. 129, 133] hardly helps the case." Cf. n. 12 above.

18. Betz 129. Cf. Silva, "Betz and Bruce," 378; Hays 222, who says that Betz's analysis here "is of little help in grasping the construction of the argument *within* this section."

fragmentation of the text and a strangely atomistic interpretation." Meeks continues:

> One of the most unfortunate examples is the discussion of Paul's argument from Scripture in 3:6-14, which Betz insists on breaking up into five separate "proofs," with the result that he discusses each verse in isolation from its context and . . . leaves us with no clear sense of the logic of the passage.[19]

(d) An obvious question, of course, is whether the Galatians would have been likely to read Paul's letter as an apologetic letter in the technical sense.[20] But even if we confine our attention to *Paul's* intention and the actual writing before us, there are still other difficulties to be mentioned. Thus, (e) doubt has rightly been expressed whether "in the excitement and urgency of the crisis with which he was suddenly confronted Paul would have been consciously careful to construct his letter according to the canons of the rhetorical schools,"[21] particularly in view of Betz's acknowledgment that Paul is one with other Christian writers in regarding "the art of persuasion" as "something rather negative and unfitting" because of its identification with "deception, slander, and even sorcery" (cf., e.g., 1 Cor. 2:1-5).[22] (f) Then, too, the letter bears all the marks of an urgent, passionate appeal to return from apostasy or the brink of apostasy (e.g., 1:6-10; 3:1-5; 4:12-20; 5:7-12); the fact that Paul leaves out his usual epistolary thanksgiving does not go too well with the supposition that we have here a carefully constructed piece of defense rhetoric. As E. A. Russell observes, "would it not be an excellent *captatio benevolentiae* to make such a gesture [sc. thanksgiving] along with his defence?"[23]

(g) Finally, Meeks makes the important point that Betz "does not really show that [the last four] chapters [of Galatians] must be conceived primarily as *defensive*." Says Meeks:

19. Meeks, Review, 305.
20. Cf. Dunn, "Relationship," 461, who raises the question in connection with 1:12-2:14 (the *narratio*).
21. Bruce 58. Cf. Silva, "Betz and Bruce," 377; Russell, "Convincing . . . ?" 158f. To the question, "How does an angry, urgent, upset Paul manage to compose such an intricately structured epistle?" Davies, *Studies,* 361f. replies: "The question ignores two things—the physical process of writing involved, which was not as easy and casual as in our world, and also the fact that channeled, controlled, deliberate, cold anger is more effective than uncontrolled. Paul's anger was more felt *through* the disciplined structure of the epistle than it would have been had it been allowed to vent itself without form." The adequacy of this answer will likely be variously estimated by different readers.
22. Betz 54-55. Silva, art. cit., 378, notes that Betz never attempts to reconcile this fact with Paul's "apparent use of the method," and that he "never really addresses the question whether Paul actually *knew* the rhetorical textbooks."
23. Russell, "Convincing . . . ?" 159.

The monitory element in the letter is curiously neglected: only 5:1–6:10 are hortatory in Betz's scheme. Yet, if he were not so determined to make "apology" the basic type to which the letter must conform, would it not appear that the whole argument from 3:1 on is primarily designed not to defend Paul's position but to exhort the Galatians to abandon their new mentors?[24] The first part of chap. 5 makes more sense as the conclusion of the argument that goes before than as the introduction to a different style. Paraenesis in the narrow sense begins only with 5:13, which at the same time introduces a digression to avoid a misunderstanding of our objection to the course of action demanded in the main argument.[25]

Having considered above the pros and cons of Betz's hypothesis about the structure and genre of Galatians, we are bound to concur with C. K. Barrett's dictum that Betz has made too much of the "apologetic letter" genre,[26] and with Meeks's implied judgment that *apologia* is *not* the most appropriate category to apply to the letter as a whole.[27] Hence the course chosen in this commentary is to adopt a more traditional way of analysis[28] while taking note of the new approach.

24. In our view, Paul's concern in 3:1–5:12 is to argue the superiority of the gospel doctrine of grace and faith to the opponents' law-oriented version of Christianity, but his ultimate purpose is, of course, to win back his errant Galatian converts (cf. the approach of the author of Hebrews). Hence, our view of the section is not in conflict with Meeks's remarks here.

25. Meeks, Review, 305f.

26. Barrett, "Galatians," 417. Using the treatment of Abraham, Sarah, and Hagar in 4:21-31 as an illustration, Barrett concludes that "other factors in addition to Graeco-Roman models entered into its [chs. 3–4] composition and must be allowed significant weight in its interpretation." Similarly, Davies, *Studies,* 176-181 points out Betz's "neglect of the Jewish connection of the Galatians" (178, cf. 180; 182 refers to Betz's "underestimation of the Jewishness of the Galatian churches"); Davies observes, among other things, that "the exegesis and activity of the synagogue were the matrices within which much of the kind of material we find in Galatians 3 and 4 especially . . . becomes intelligible" (177).

27. Meeks, Review, 306. Cf. Aune, Review, 146f.: "apologetic letter" is "a designation which can only be applied to Galatians 1–2"; Galatians does not fit "one rhetorical genre." Perhaps both sides of the evidence will be satisfied if we accept the suggestion put forward by Howard 47 that "Paul understood the accepted procedures of epistolography and rhetoric and adapted their principles [here we would add: especially in the first two chapters but also here and there in the last four], perhaps unconsciously, to fit his own needs and style."

28. Cf. A. M. Buscemi, "Struttura della Lettera ai Galati," *Euntes Docete* 34 (1981) 409-426.

The Epistle
to the
GALATIANS

Text, Exposition, and Notes

I. AUTOBIOGRAPHICAL DEFENSE 1: BACKGROUND (1:1-10)

A. SALUTATION (1:1-5)

While adopting the basic structure of the form of greeting current at his time,[1] Paul injects new meaning into this form of greeting by (a) always replacing the general "greetings" *(chairein)* with "grace to you" *(charis hymin)*, (b) frequently adding some description of the sender and of the recipients, and (c) occasionally anticipating the contents of the letter in summary fashion by what he says in the salutation (as in v. 4 here).

1. THE SENDER (1:1-2a)

1 *From Paul, an apostle, not by human appointment or human commission, but by commission from Jesus Christ and from God the Father who raised him from the dead.* 2 *I and the group of friends now with me send greetings. . . .*

1 The writer identifies himself by his Roman cognomen "Paul" (Lat. *Paullus*) instead of his Hebrew birth-name "Saul" (Acts 13:9)—aptly so, since he is addressing predominantly Gentile readers. He refers to his status as an "apostle," a word which in the NT regularly denotes a person who is sent and invested with the authority of the commissioning party.[2] The plural "apostles" (cf. 1:17) probably has primary reference to the original twelve, who were constituted such by Jesus' call and commission of them, not only during his earthly ministry (Lk. 6:13; cf. Mt. 10:2), but also, and above all, after his resurrection (Mt. 28:19f.; Lk. 24:48f.; Acts 1:8).[3] In time, however, the term was extended to include others as the Church

---

1. "X to Y, greetings." For NT examples see Acts 15:23; 23:26; Jas. 1:1.
2. K. H. Rengstorf, *TDNT* I: 421.
3. Cf. ibid., 430. See also D. Müller, *NIDNTT* I: 131-135, with corrective note by C. Brown on 135f.

reached out to the Gentiles. Paul never identifies the apostles with the twelve and in fact designates (either expressly or by implication) others clearly outside the circle of the twelve original apostles by that title: Barnabas (1 Cor. 9:5f.), James, the Lord's brother, and other unnamed persons (1 Cor. 15:7; cf. Gal. 1:19).[4] While the term seems at times to be used in the broader, less technical sense of commissioned representatives of churches (e.g., 2 Cor. 8:23; Phil. 2:25), Paul clearly regards himself as completely equal in apostolic status to the first apostles (Gal. 2:6-9; 1 Cor. 9:1, 5). He justifies his claim to full apostolic rank on account of (a) his having seen the risen Lord (1 Cor. 9:1; 15:8; cf. Acts 22:14) and hence being qualified to bear witness to his resurrection, (b) his having received by direct revelation a call to apostleship (Gal. 1:1; 2:7; Rom. 1:1; 1 Cor. 1:1, etc.), and (c) visible, concrete evidences of his apostleship (1 Cor. 9:2; 2 Cor. 12:12; cf. Gal. 2:8f.). He seems to represent something of a new departure in denying the absolute necessity of personal acquaintance with the earthly Jesus as a prerequisite of apostleship (cf. Acts 1:21f.; Gal. 2:6) and regarding personal encounter with and commission by the risen Christ as alone sufficient.[5]

The emphatic contrast with which Paul describes his apostleship is intended to underline its divine origin: he asserts that his apostolic commission, with regard to both its source and its mediation, was from God and Christ, just as a little later on he will categorically declare that his gospel, with regard to both its source and the manner in which it was communicated to him, was a direct revelation from God (1:12, 16). Appearing at the very outset of the epistle, and read in the light of the great stress which Paul subsequently places on his independence of the Jerusalem church (1:18–2:10), his assertion reflects a polemical situation in which the dignity, indeed the validity, of his apostolic status is being challenged.[6] Possibly—if the difference in the Greek between "not from men" and "nor through man" (1:1, RSV) can be pressed—Paul's authorization was being traced back to the church of Antioch, whence he had come (Acts 13:1ff.), or to Barnabas, to whom Paul owed his introduction into the original community (Acts 9:27).[7] More probably Paul's opponents (for their identity see pp. 3–9) claimed to be standing in the true line of continuity with the Jerusalem apostles and their full and authentic gospel, and charged him with (a) falsify-

4. On James see Additional Comment 5, pp. 77f.
5. Cf. K. H. Rengstorf, *TDNT* I: 431, 422. See also Schnackenburg, "Apostles," 301. Cf. also Herron, "Origin," where the view that the apostolate originated with appointment by the historical Jesus is preferred to two other views: that it was a post-Easter development within the early Church, and that it was a reflection of the theological creativity of Paul.
6. Cf. Rengstorf, *TDNT* I: 441. *Pace* Fridrichsen, "Apostle," 21, n. 20.
7. Cf. Rengstorf, *TDNT* I: 441f.

ing that same gospel which the Jerusalem authorities had taught him by watering it down to a truncated version so as to obtain easy access to the Gentiles (cf. 1:10), and with (b) high-handed presumption in claiming to be an apostle.[8] On this showing, the effect of Paul's emphatic contrast is to say that he does not want the apostolic credentials and the complete Jerusalem version of the gospel which his opponents in Galatia claimed to have, for his authority and his gospel are alike derived from a different and higher source.[9]

"By commission from" renders the Greek preposition *dia*, which properly has the sense of mediation when used before "man" (cf. RSV) but is here used in the more general sense of agency.[10] The juxtaposition of "Jesus Christ" and "God the Father" under one preposition reflects the exalted status which Christ holds in Paul's understanding. That Christ is mentioned before God has doubtless to do with a fact of Paul's personal experience: he became an apostle through an encounter with Christ who appeared to him, and this appearance was effected by God the Father "who raised him from the dead." The latter clause thus emphasizes that it was from the *risen* Christ that Paul received his apostolic commission.

2a As sender Paul includes with himself "all the brethren who are with me" (RSV). "Brethren" is a common NT designation of believers; they have been set in a fraternal relationship with one another by virtue of their common commitment to Christ (Gal. 4:5f.; Rom. 8:29; cf. Mk. 3:35). A similar expression, "the brothers who are now with me," occurs in Phil. 4:21[11] where it is clearly distinguished from "all God's people here" in the next verse; this suggests that the phrase "all the brethren" here denotes not all the members of the church in the place from which Paul is writing,[12] but a smaller company. This "group of friends" were most likely Paul's co-workers, but suggestions as to their closer identification vary according to the view taken of the place and date of writing. What seems certain is that their mention here does not denote actual participation in the writing of the letter, for apart from this casual and general reference[13] they receive no further mention in the letter, Paul speaking throughout in the first person singular. That Paul, contrary to his usual practice, deliberately leaves his

---

8. So, e.g., Burton 3; Bornkamm, *Paul,* 18f.; Bruce 95; King, "Tannaim," 354-357, 370. See also Creed, Review, 422f.

9. Manson, *Studies,* 170, n. 1.

10. Bruce 73; A. Oepke, *TDNT* II: 68; cf. BDF §223.2.

11. The Greek is exactly the same as in Gal. 1:2, except for omission of πάντες ("all").

12. *Pace* Hendriksen 31.

13. On the significance of πάντες ("all") in its attributive position as that of summation see B. Reicke, *TDNT* V: 887.

friends anonymous militates against the view that he attempts to enhance the force of his teaching by appealing to those who saw eye to eye with him;[14] such an appeal would also be inconsistent with "the whole spirit of the epistle, in which all human authority is set aside."[15] At the same time, it seems insufficient to explain the references as, "mainly at least, an act of courtesy";[16] perhaps the best solution is to regard it as reflecting Paul's desire to indicate to the Galatians that his gospel is no personal idiosyncrasy, but something shared by his colleagues.[17]

2. THE RECIPIENTS (1:2b)

. . . to the Christian congregations of Galatia.

2b "Christian congregations" translates Greek *ekklēsiai,* usually rendered "churches" (AV, RV, RSV, NIV). It is commonly recognized that in its technical sense the term *ekklēsia* in the NT refers primarily to the entire community of believers and only secondarily to the community of believers living in a specific area. A corollary of this truth is that the Church as the total community is not a mere aggregate of individual congregations; rather the local church is the universal Church in its local manifestation. On the location of "Galatia," see pp. 1–3.

3. THE GREETING (1:3-5)

3 *Grace and peace to you from God the Father and our Lord Jesus Christ,* 4 *who sacrificed himself for our sins, to rescue us out of this present age of wickedness, as our God and Father willed;* 5 *to whom be glory for ever and ever. Amen.*

3 "Grace" replaces the normal word of introductory salutation in a Greek letter, and "peace" reproduces the customary word of greeting in a Hebrew letter. Used in combination both here and elsewhere by Paul,[18] the terms have their full and specifically Christian content: "Grace" *(charis)*

---

14. E.g., Duncan 10, who points to the use of σύν with dative instead of μετά with genitive. The same construction, however, is used in Acts 14:28 where it is obviously of the same force as μετά with genitive.

15. Lightfoot 73.

16. Burton 9.

17. Cf. Bruce 74.

18. In the opening salutations of 1 and 2 Tim. "mercy" is added between "grace" and "peace."

38

denotes God's free and unmerited favor toward sinful mankind, supremely demonstrated in the work of redemption accomplished by Christ (2:21; cf. 1:6), while "peace" *(eirēnē)* denotes basically a state of wholeness (cf. Heb. *šālôm*), which for the Christian comprises peace with God (Rom. 5:1; Col. 1:20) and, on that foundation, peace with one another (Eph. 2:14-17; 4:3) and within oneself (Rom. 15:13; Phil. 4:6f.).[19] Grace and peace are related to each other as root and fruit, or cause and effect.

The words "grace and peace to you" express perhaps not so much a pious wish as an act of impartation which is accomplished through the apostle's declaration, in much the same way as, when the commissioned disciples of Jesus pronounced "peace to this house" on those who received the message of Jesus, peace would really come upon that household (Lk. 10:5f.; cf. Mt. 10:12f.).[20]

Paul ascribes this double blessing to the unitary source of "God our Father and the Lord Jesus Christ" (NEB mg., NIV—over against NEB text, AV, RV, RSV).[21] The fact that the one preposition "from" governs both "God our Father" and "the Lord Jesus Christ"—just as in v. 1 both "Jesus Christ" and "God the Father" are governed by the one preposition "by"— suggests that "the apostle envisaged the Father and the Son as a joint source of 'grace and peace,' rather than as distinct sources or as source and channel (respectively)," and that "they sustain a single relation (not two diverse relations) to the grace and peace that come to believers."[22] This clearly reflects the preeminent place that Jesus Christ occupies in the thinking of Paul. Christ has this preeminence because to Paul Christ is God by nature (2:20; 4:4; cf. Phil. 2:6), because it was Christ who accomplished the great work of redemption (Gal. 1:4), and because he has been highly exalted by God (cf. Phil. 2:9-11). Fully consonant with his preeminent place is the triple designation of him as "the Lord Jesus Christ" (also at 6:18), the components of which indicate, respectively, his exalted rank, his saving significance (cf. Mt. 1:21), and his divine commission (cf. Lk. 4:17-21; Acts 10:38).[23]

4 If the use of the single preposition "from" in v. 3 emphasizes the unity of the source of blessing, the further description of Christ's work in

19. Cf. H. Beck and C. Brown, *NIDNTT* II: 780; W. Foerster, *TDNT* II: 412.

20. So, e.g., Ridderbos 42f.; Bring 22.

21. Cf. Metzger 589: The sequence adopted accords with Paul's usage elsewhere (Rom. 1:7; 1 Cor. 1:3; 2 Cor. 1:2; Eph. 1:2; Phil. 1:2; Phm. 3); "the apostle's stereotyped formula was altered by copyists who, apparently in the interest of Christian piety, transferred the possessive pronoun so it would be more closely associated with 'Lord Jesus Christ.'"

22. M. J. Harris, *NIDNTT* III: 1178. On the use of the formula θεὸς πατήρ ("God the Father") in this verse see G. Schrenk, *TDNT* V: 1007.

23. Ridderbos 229.

v. 4 makes it possible to say that, from the perspective of the economy of salvation, God is the author, and Christ the ground or basis, of the twofold blessing of grace and peace.[24] "The will of our God and Father" (RSV) is the ultimate, pretemporal foundation of salvation; it is "the active divine resolve which cannot remain in the sphere of thought but demands action."[25] While the name "God" denotes his omnipotence and his transcendent glory, the designation "Father" suggests that his will is based not solely on his wisdom and omnipotence, but also equally on his disposition of love.[26] It was "as our God and Father willed" that Christ sacrificed himself "for our sins," Father and Son thus acting in perfect harmony in the death of Jesus Christ, as also in Paul's call to apostleship (v. 1) and in the continual bestowal of grace and peace upon believers (v. 3).

"Sacrificed himself" is literally "gave himself" (RSV, NIV), which, like "to give one's life/body," is a traditional expression "for the death of martyrs among the Jews and soldiers among the Greeks."[27] The sacrificial terminology of the NEB rendering is fully justified in view of the context. The force of the prepositional phrase "for our sins" (also in 1 Cor. 15:3) is, primarily at least, final/prospective (indicating purpose): "for the expiation (or purging) of sins,"[28] but in view of the fact that the construction used here (*hyper* with genitive) clearly has the sense "because of" in 3 Kdms. (MT 1 Kgs.) 16:18f., it is not impossible that the preposition may also have a causal/retrospective sense, denoting "our sins" as the cause of Christ's death.

The purpose of that death is further described as the believers' "rescue . . . out of this present age of wickedness." This aspect of the purpose of Christ's death is related to the foregoing (the forgiveness of our sins) in that our sins are expressions of our bondage to the present age of wickedness.[29] Paul accepts the basic division of time into two periods which was part of the Jewish scheme of things: the present age is an era of evil, the age to come the era of righteousness and regeneration.[30] While only the former is explicitly mentioned here, the contrast between the two ages is clearly implied (cf. Eph. 1:21, the only instance in the Pauline corpus where the contrast is explicitly stated).

To Paul, the present age is evil[31] because it is subject to the sway of a

24. Schlier 31.
25. G. Schrenk, *TDNT* III: 57.
26. Ridderbos 44, n. 16; G. Schrenk, *TDNT* V: 1009.
27. F. Büchsel, *TDNT* II: 166. See further J. Jeremias, *TDNT* V: 710.
28. E. H. Riesenfeld, *TDNT* VIII: 511; cf. M. J. Harris, *NIDNTT* III: 1197.
29. Schlier 34.
30. Cf. H. Sasse, *TDNT* I: 205-207; III: 891, n. 86.
31. Gk. πονηρός, which probably brings out the positive activity of evil more than κακός does: cf. Trench 38 (§xi).

40

wicked spiritual being (Eph. 6:16; 2 Thess. 3:3; cf. 2 Cor. 4:4; Eph. 2:2) and under the control of wicked spiritual forces (cf. Eph. 6:12), chief of which are the powers of sin and death (cf. 1 Cor. 15:55f.).[32] "This present age" is thus Paul's description for the totality of human life dominated by sin and opposed to God;[33] in this context, "age" *(aiōn)* has much the same force as "world" *(kosmos)* often has in the writings of John (e.g., 1 Jn. 2:15-17) and which both words can have in Paul's letters (e.g., 1 Cor. 1:20; 2:6; 3:19). It denotes "not only the current era of world history but the way of life that characterizes it."[34]

At the same time, Paul has modified the basic structure of Jewish eschatological thought, giving it a new interpretation. The purpose of Christ's self-sacrifice according to God's will becomes, through faith, its result: by virtue of his sacrifice, those who put their trust in him are rescued out of this present age of wickedness—and, by implication, ushered into the age to come. For them, the age to come is no longer merely yet to come; Christ's self-sacrifice (with his resurrection and exaltation) is the point at which the age to come breaks into the present age and and is also the transition from the one era to the other. When sinners repent and become united with Christ through faith in him, their transference from the present age to the age to come is effected as a redemptive fact.[35] The same truth is similarly stated in Col. 1:13 in terms of the believers' rescue (NEB, NIV) or deliverance (AV, RV, RSV),[36] but there the transference effected is not from one era to another but "from the domain of darkness" to "the kingdom of [God's] dear Son."

It can be seen, therefore, that the point of departure for Paul's thought is not the individual's need and experience, but Christ's epoch-making redemptive work, the primary significance of which is *objective:* it rescues believers out of the present evil age or aeon and brings them into a new aeon, a new order of existence, subject to a different power. Its *subjective* significance for believers consists in the fact that, having been thus objectively delivered out of the present aeon, they need no longer be dominated by the evil spiritual powers of this age, but may (and must) live in

32. According to G. Harder, *TDNT* VI: 554, the present age is evil "because it is filled with the sufferings and temptations of the last time"; but it is to be noted that these are not unrelated to the power of sin.

33. Cf. Manson, *Paul and John,* 26; J. Guhrt, *NIDNTT* III: 831. "Evil" gains emphasis from its predicate position in the Greek.

34. Bruce 77. Note that "the evil ways of this present age" (Eph. 2:2) is literally "the age [αἰών] of this world [κόσμος]."

35. Cf., e.g., H. Sasse, *TDNT* I: 207.

36. The verb in Col. 1:13 (ῥύομαι) is different from the one in Gal. 1:4 (ἐξαιρέομαι, a hapax in Paul), but is no less forceful.

newness of life in the new order of existence, in the power of the new life given by God.

In this one verse Paul has described several aspects of the redemption wrought by Christ: its cause ("for our sins," that is, because of them), its means (Christ "sacrificed himself"), its purpose and effect ("for our sins," that is, for their expiation; "to rescue us"), and its origin ("the will of our God and Father"). Thereby Paul has in fact touched on the chief argument of the letter, and succinctly announced in anticipatory fashion the main contents of its doctrinal section, inasmuch as the point of the controversy between Paul and his Galatian opponents lies precisely in the significance of Christ and his redemptive work and more specifically in the bearing of this work on the law.[37] Paul will argue that since Christ has, according to God's will, already rescued believers out of the present aeon (where the law belongs), it is plainly unnecessary for them to add anything—including circumcision and observance of the Torah—to the redemption already accomplished for them by Christ.

5 Paul concludes his salutation with spontaneous praise to God the Father who, as the "Fount of every blessing," wrought salvation according to his own will. This verse in the original has no verb. Since (a) glory is a basic attribute of God and (b) 1 Pet. 5:11 uses the same grammatical construction in speaking of God's power ("power belongs to God" seems more appropriate than "power be to God"), we should probably supply "is" rather than "be."[38] The verse is, then, a declaration that glory belongs to God.

God's "glory" *(doxa)* in general denotes his divine and heavenly radiance, his loftiness and majesty,[39] but since it appears here with the article it may refer to that unique glory which belongs to God alone; interpreted by its context "the glory" (RSV) may be more specifically taken as God's fatherly character and the union of perfect wisdom, holiness, and love manifested in the redemption of mankind through Christ according to his will.[40] The description of this glory as being "for ever and ever" implies that in the eternity which is comprised of endless successive generations[41] that union of wisdom, holiness, and love will continue to be a fundamental aspect of God's glory (cf. Eph. 2:7).

Paul adds finally the word "Amen," which enhances the force and

---

37. Bring 23; Ridderbos 43; cf. Burton 14.
38. I.e., indicative ἔστιν rather than optative εἴη. Cf. G. Kittel, *TDNT* II: 248; S. Aalen, *NIDNTT* II: 47; BDF §128.5.
39. G. Kittel, *TDNT* II: 237.
40. Cf. Ellicott 5; Guthrie 61; Rendall 151.
41. On the plural αἰῶνες (literally "ages") see H. Sasse, *TDNT* I: 199; Cullmann, *Christ and Time*, 46.

confirms the veracity of his declaration.[42] The declaration may contain at the same time a summons to acknowledge God's glory and to live in the light of it;[43] should this be so, the hearers' responsive "Amen" to Paul's "Amen" (cf. 1 Cor. 14:16)[44] as the letter was read would take on added significance as a pledge to endeavor to ascribe glory to God by their lives, as well as an endorsement of Paul's ascription of glory to God at this point in the letter.

B. CONDEMNATION OF THE COUNTERFEIT GOSPEL (1:6-10)

1. THE GALATIAN CRISIS (1:6-7)

6 *I am astonished to find you turning so quickly away from him who called you by grace, and following a different gospel.* 7 *Not that it is in fact another gospel; only there are persons who unsettle your minds by trying to distort the gospel of Christ.*

6   As he departs in v. 2 from his frequent practice of giving some description of the recipients of his letter (e.g., Rom. 1:7; 1 Cor. 1:2; 1 Thess. 1:1), addressing himself simply to "the Christian congregations of Galatia," so also in place of his customary thanksgiving after the salutation (e.g., Rom. 1:8; 1 Cor. 1:4-8; 1 Thess. 1:2-10, following a common form in Greek letter writing) we find an indignant protest against the Galatians' defection and a strong assertion that there is no other gospel than the one which Paul preached to them at the first. This reflects the seriousness of the situation into which the Galatians have fallen: because they are deserting the one true gospel Paul can find in them no cause for thanksgiving to God, but can only express astonishment instead.[1]

Paul accuses the Galatians of being religious turncoats: a similar use of the word translated "turning . . . away" or "deserting" (RSV, NIV) occurs in the description of one Dionysius of Heracleia, who deserted the

---

42. Cf. H. Bietenhard, *NIDNTT* I: 99.

43. Cf. Ridderbos 44, n. 18.

44. On "Amen" at the end of Christian prayers and doxologies in general see H. Schlier, *TDNT* I: 337.

1. On θαυμάζω ("I am astonished") here cf. G. Bertram, *TDNT* III: 40; Betz 45; Brinsmead 48.

In terms of the structure of the "apologetic letter," this section (1:6-10) forms the *exordium* or *prooemium*, stating the *causa* or case without which there would be no dispute. The one central problem against which the letter is written is the Galatians' treacherous acceptance of the false gospel. "This explains why Galatians as a whole disputes a theology that has been introduced by intruders; and yet the book is directed specifically at the Galatians themselves" (Brinsmead 49, cf. 69).

Stoics for the Epicureans, as "the Turncoat."[2] "The one who called you" (NIV), consistently with Paul's usage, denotes God (cf. v. 15);[3] the Greek construction (article with participle) emphasizes the divine initiative (cf. 1 Thess. 2:12; 1 Pet. 1:15),[4] while the particular tense used (aorist) suggests that God's call to the Galatians was mediated through the apostle's preaching of the gospel (cf. vv. 8f.).

"By grace" takes Gk. *en chariti* in its instrumental sense, as indicating the means of God's call (cf. v. 15);[5] an alternative rendering, "in grace" (RV, RSV), takes it in its local sense, as indicating the sphere in which the divine call took place. But in the present context it seems preferable to regard the phrase as being used in a pregnant sense ("into, so as to be in") and as highlighting the fact that the Galatians were called to enter into (cf. AV), and remain in, grace (cf. 5:4).[6] Whether the description of this grace as the grace "of Christ" is regarded as part of the original text (AV, RV, RSV, NIV) or not (NEB) makes no difference to Paul's basic meaning here, for certainly the grace into which God calls through the gospel is manifested in Christ.

The natural implication of the words "so quickly," used of the Galatians' act of deserting the one who called through the gospel, is that no very long time had elapsed since their conversion, though the phrase is insufficient to enable us to fix precisely the length of the interval between their reception of the apostolic gospel and Paul's reception of news of their defection. It is also possible that the word translated "quickly" here (Gk. *tacheōs*) has the sense of "easily" (as in 2 Thess. 2:2; 1 Tim. 5:22).[7]

The Galatians' desertion of God was accompanied, and indeed demonstrated, by their transference of allegiance to "a different gospel." This phrase is unlikely to have been used by the persons mentioned in the next verse as a description of their own doctrine;[8] since they in opposition to Paul insisted on the necessity of circumcision and other requirements of the Jewish law (cf. 5:3; 6:12f.), they are more likely to have regarded their own teaching as the "full" or "complete" gospel (cf. 3:3, where the word translated "to make . . . perfect" may reflect their vocabulary), measured by which Paul's preaching appeared in their eyes to be but a truncated gospel.[9] The present phrase (cf. 2 Cor. 11:4) seems to be one which Paul lets slip in his agitation and which he immediately revokes by the following words

2. Gk. ὁ μεταθέμενος: see MM s.v. μετατίθημι. Cf. C. Maurer, *TDNT* VIII: 161.

3. K. L. Schmidt, *TDNT* III: 489.

4. L. Coenen, *NIDNTT* I: 275.

5. E.g., H. Conzelmann, *TDNT* IX: 395, nn. 184, 186.

6. E.g., Burton 20f.; Schlier 37; W. Foerster, *TDNT* III: 1090.

7. E.g., Schlier 36, n. 2.

8. *Pace* Burton 22.

9. Cf. Beker, *Paul*, 43f., 45.

(v. 7).[10] It is clear from the sequel (vv. 8f.) that in Paul's judgment any "gospel" that differs fundamentally from the one which he preached to the Galatians is no gospel at all, and this verdict he immediately passes on the new doctrine which was claiming the allegiance of his Galatian converts.

7   What in the previous phrase was called "a different gospel" Paul now refuses to recognize as "another gospel." If the conventional distinction between the two Greek adjectives underlying these phrases is maintained, the former means "one of a different kind" and the latter "another of the same kind."[11] But probably here, as in 2 Cor. 11:4, no essential distinction is intended; this becomes all the more likely in the light of the consideration that the word "another" ("gospel" has been supplied in translation) seems to be used somewhat pleonastically in order to introduce the following "only" or "except that."[12] "No one would think of calling this substitute message a 'gospel,' Paul implies, except with the intention of confusing the minds of believers."[13] Such a no-gospel "gospel," Paul explains, was the product of "some" (AV, RV, RSV) who of set intent wanted to "distort" or "pervert" (RSV) the gospel of Christ;[14] the vague reference does not indicate ignorance on his part of their identity but rather his disdain for them. The effect of their activity was to raise seditions among the Galatians, causing their allegiance to the gospel which they had received from Paul to be shaken.[15]

The true gospel, on the other hand, is described as "the gospel of Christ." Here the genitive is taken by some as both objective and subjective: Christ is both the content of the gospel (v. 16; cf. v. 12; Rom. 1:1-3) and also, through the apostles' preaching, the one who proclaims himself as the obtainer of peace (cf. Eph. 2:14, 17).[16] More probably, however, the geni-

---

10. H. W. Beyer, *TDNT* II: 703.

11. Gk. ἕτερος and ἄλλος respectively. Cf. Trench 357-361 (§xcv).

12. BDF §306.4. Cf. F. Büchsel, *TDNT* I: 264f.; MHT 3: 197f. Εἰ μή here is equivalent to πλὴν ὅτι in Acts 20:23.

13. Bruce 82.

14. On μεταστρέφειν ("distort") cf. G. Bertram, *TDNT* VII: 729.

15. On ταράσσειν ("unsettle") here as "political" language cf. Betz 49: the word "describes the destructive work of political agitators who cause confusion and turmoil." This is cited by Meeks, Review, 304 as an instance of Betz's "tendency to assume rather too quickly the technical usage of many terms" (another is the "political" use of μετατίθεσθαι in v. 6). Meeks's judicious warning in this connection is worth quoting in full: "Even where evidence for technical usage is available, there may be a problem. When terms are in common use in ordinary language and are also used with particular nuances in forensic or political contexts, it is not so self-evident whether in a given *epistolary* context the ordinary or technical usage ought to be heard." Other examples of the use of "political" or "military" terms are collected, apparently with approval, by Davies, *Studies,* 362, n. 11.

16. E.g., G. Friedrich, *TDNT* II: 731; W. Grundmann, *TDNT* IX: 543; Zerwick §37.

tive is simply objective, so that "the gospel of Christ" means "the gospel which tells of Christ"; this gives the most suitable meaning to the phrase, which Paul usually uses in contexts having to do with proclamation (Rom. 15:19; 1 Cor. 9:12; 2 Cor. 10:14; Phil. 1:27; 2 Thess. 1:8; cf. 2 Cor. 2:12; 9:13; 1 Thess. 3:2).

The word "gospel" *(euangelion)* is related to the verb "preach, proclaim" *(euangelizomai)*[17]—literally "bring good tidings"—and means "good tidings." In its seven occurrences in this epistle (1:6f., 11; 2:2, 5, 7, 14), with the exception of the first where the addition of the adjective "different" gives the word a pejorative tinge, it is used consistently in its basic meaning of the "good news" of God's salvation in Jesus Christ, particularly as that which embodies all the objective facts concerning the Christ-event and the meaning of those facts.

2. ANATHEMA ON PREACHERS OF A DIFFERENT GOSPEL (1:8-9)

8 *But if anyone, if we ourselves or an angel from heaven, should preach a gospel at variance with the gospel we preached to you, he shall be held outcast. 9 I now repeat what I have said before: if anyone preaches a gospel at variance with the gospel which you received, let him be outcast!*

8-9   In these verses, Paul unequivocally implies that the true gospel is that which he and his fellow missionaries preached to the Galatians and which they received at the first; this, as what follows will make abundantly clear, was the gospel of justification by faith. A solemn imprecation is pronounced impartially upon any preacher of a message which is "at variance with"[18] the original apostolic preaching, whether such a preacher be an angel from heaven or even Paul himself or one of his coworkers who first brought the gospel to the Galatians.[19] This implies (a) that the gospel embodies a core of fixed tradition which is normative so that no preaching deviating from it can be called "gospel" in the proper sense of the word, and (b) that the authority of the gospel resides primarily in the message itself and only secondarily in the messenger.[20] The different constructions used in the

17. Cf. Isa. 40:9; 52:7 (cited in Rom. 10:15); 61:1f. (applied by Jesus to himself in Lk. 4:17-19).
18. Cf. AV, RV, NIV: "other than"; BDF §236.3; Moule 51; M. J. Harris, *NIDNTT* III: 1201; Burton 28—over against RSV, NASB "contrary to"; E. H. Riesenfeld, *TDNT* V: 736; Betz 52.
19. This is the implication of the emphatic καὶ ἡμεῖς ("we ourselves").
20. Cf. Ladd, *Theology,* 382, 388, 392; G. Bornkamm, *TDNT* VI: 682.

two conditional clauses indicate that, whereas the former has in view a mere supposition made for the sake of emphasizing the uniqueness and inviolability of the gospel, the latter refers to something that is more than a possibility, something which is assumed as fact.[21] Perhaps the reference to an angelic preacher suggests that Paul has in mind specifically the Judaistic nature of the false message, since the Galatian agitators might have stressed the connection between the law and the angels through whom it was mediated (cf. 3:19), though this remains uncertain.[22]

"What I have said before" is literally "what *we* have said before" (cf. RSV), the plural denoting Paul and his coworkers in contradistinction to the singular "I now repeat."[23] In the light of this contrast, "what we have said before" is less likely to refer to the words of v. 8 than to some earlier occasion, either Paul's original visit to Galatia or, less probably, a subsequent visit.[24]

The twice-repeated "let him be accursed" (AV, RSV), coupled with the indication that this was not the first time such an anathema had been invoked, shows that it cannot be explained as "a careless utterance, expressing more accurately his immediate feelings than his general theory,"[25] but must be taken with all seriousness as indicating Paul's attitude toward any teaching that is at variance wtih the gospel. The fearful verdict, "let him be anathema" (RV), can hardly mean being "held outcast," that is, excommunicated,[26] since it envisages an angel as a possible object. It thus more likely means being delivered up and devoted to the judicial wrath of God:[27] "the kind of zeal which Israel directed against apostates to preserve her own salvation, and which Paul himself had formerly exercised against Christians, he now directs against the Judaizers to protect the church."[28] The Galatian heretics, in particular, fall under the anathema (which is an "effective invocation")[29] because, by reimposing the requirements of the law as necessary for salvation, their "full gospel" (a) undermined the message of justification by faith and presented as the road to salvation a way that

---

21. V. 8, ἐάν with subjunctive; v. 9, εἰ with indicative; cf. Burton, *Syntax*, §§242, 250; MHT 3: 115. On the variant readings in v. 8 see Metzger 590.

22. For the suggestion cf. Schweitzer, e.g., *Mysticism*, 73; but see Betz 53, n. 84.

23. Cf. Hanson, *Pioneer*, 66; Bauckham, "Barnabas," 65.

24. Cf. Cole 42 (the reference is to v. 8); Ridderbos 50, n. 21; Betz 45, 50 (the reference is to an earlier occasion); Arichea-Nida 14 (the reference is to Paul's original visit); Duncan 19 (the reference is to a later visit).

25. Smith, "Problems," 124.

26. E.g., Betz 54 and, apparently, J. Jeremias, *TDNT* III: 752.

27. Cf. NIV; J. Behm, *TDNT* I: 354f.; H. Aust and D. Müller, *NIDNTT* I: 415.

28. Garnet, "Qumran," 26.

29. Hendriksen 41.

actually leads to death (cf. 5:4) and (b) "disallowed the claim that Jesus by His death and resurrection had inaugurated the messianic age which superseded the age of law and thus in effect disallowed his title to be the Messiah."[30] The severity of the anathema is thus the measure of the significance which Paul attaches to the principle of righteousness by faith: for if any teaching at variance with the original apostolic preaching involves the messenger in the divine wrath, then only the message of justification by faith is the divinely sanctioned message, the one gospel worthy of its name.[31]

3. PAUL'S ONLY CONCERN (1:10)

10 *Does my language now sound as if I were canvassing for men's support? Whose support do I want but God's alone? Do you think I am currying favour with men? If I still sought men's favour, I should be no servant of Christ.*

10 In the more literal translation of the RV, v. 10 reads thus: "For am I now persuading men, or God? Or am I seeking to please men? If I were still pleasing men, I should not be a servant of Christ." The double reference to "pleasing men"[32] reflects the allegation of Paul's detractors, which probably was that he was "currying favour with men" by relaxing the terms of the gospel—more specifically by jettisoning the demand for circumcision and other legal requirements—in order to make conversion easy for Gentiles;[33] to this was added the charge that when it suited him Paul could also preach circumcision (5:11). He was being accused, in other words, of "being a time-server, running with the (Gentile) hares and hunting with the (Jewish) hounds in order to win converts at any price."[34]

As for "persuading men," it has been suggested that the implied answer to the first question is "Men," since elsewhere the expression appears as a description of the apostle's evangelistic activity (2 Cor. 5:11; Acts 18:4; 19:8; 28:23). On this understanding Paul's rhetorical question is directed against the charge that he was trying to persuade God to accept Gentile converts on less stringent terms than those laid down by the law,

30. Bruce, "When is a Gospel," 331.
31. The translation of vv. 8f. offered by Cook, "Paul," 442 (= "St Paul," 171b) shifts the emphasis, without sufficient reason, from the content of the gospel (which is Paul's paramount concern in these verses) to the "manner" of its presentation, "the way we presented it to you."
32. On ἀρέσκειν ("to please") cf. W. Foerster, *TDNT* I: 455.
33. E.g., Schlier 41f.
34. Neill 24.

"persuading God" being thus materially identical with "pleasing men."[35] The usual interpretation takes the two rhetorical questions as parallel with each other, so that "persuading" becomes virtually synonymous with "pleasing,"[36] and the implied answers to the two questions are "God" and "No, not men but God" respectively. The latter of these two interpretations appears to be more likely since (a) it makes for a natural connection in thought with the preceding verses, which seems required by the presence of the word "for" in the original (cf. NASB)[37] but is not provided (or at least not mentioned) by the first interpretation; (b) the word "now" would seem, particularly in view of the preceding consideration, to be used here in its Attic sense of "just now";[38] and (c) the order "men, or God" in Paul's question ("Is it men that I am persuading, or God?") naturally leads one to expect the answer "God."

According to a recent interpretation, "persuading men" is a definition of rhetoric, and "persuading God" is a "polemical definition of magic and religious quackery," while "persuading men by pleasing them is . . . one of the notorious strategies of political rhetoric and demagoguery," the "man-pleaser" (ho areskos) being "a familiar figure already in antiquity, especially his most appalling variety, 'the flatterer' "; the effect of Paul's two rhetorical questions is thus to deny that he is "a rhetorical 'flatterer,' 'persuading' or 'pleasing' men, or a magician, trying to 'persuade God.' "[39] This interpretation has the merit of explaining the phrase "persuading God" against its contemporary background, and obviating the necessity (attached to the previous view) of taking "persuading God," rather unnaturally, as virtually synonymous with "pleasing God." On either of the last two interpretations, the main sense of Paul's rhetorical questions is clear: his uncompromising attitude as reflected in the severity of his language in condemning the counterfeit gospel (vv. 8f.) is proof positive that he is no men-pleaser.

"Pleasing men" and being a "servant of Christ" are regarded as mutually exclusive (cf. Eph. 6:6; Col. 3:22). That these two are not always and necessarily so is clear from such a passage as Rom. 15:1-3, where pleasing one's neighbor "for his good, to build him up" (NIV) is enjoined as a form of imitation of Christ (cf. 1 Cor. 10:33); but often the two are

---

35. E.g., R. Bultmann, *TDNT* VI: 2.

36. Cf. NEB, RSV, NASB, NIV; BAGD s.v. πείθω 1 c; Thayer s.v. 1 b.

37. On γάρ ("for") here see Burton 31; Duncan 21.

38. Cf. MM s.v. ἄρτι; Thayer s.v. 2; G. Stählin, *TDNT* IV: 1107, n. 8.

39. Betz 46, 54f. This pejorative sense of the phrase is rejected by Meeks, Review, 304 as unsuitable to the context, where, it is maintained, "*theǭ peithein* has to be equivalent to *theǭ areskein*, always positive in Paul . . . , the positive opposite to the negative 'pleasing men.' "

incompatible with each other, particularly where it is a matter of loyalty to God or to the cause of the gospel (cf. Acts 4:19; 5:29).

In the final part of the verse, which is cast in the form of a contrary-to-fact conditional sentence,[40] the word "still" hints at a contrast with Paul's pre-conversion life: the fanatical zeal which he displayed as a devotee of Judaism was inspired not only by his desire to please God, but also by a desire to seek the favor of men (cf. 1:13f.; Phil. 3:4-6);[41] but the call of Christ had set him free from that unworthy desire, and his sole concern now was to be an obedient "servant of Christ." This self-designation as used by Paul expands the parallel "apostle of Jesus Christ" (cf. 1:1; Rom. 1:1), describing his apostolic office according to "its final basis, which consists in the fact that Christ has won Paul from the world and made him His possession."[42]

40. Cf. Burton, *Syntax*, §248.
41. So, e.g., Betz 56.
42. K. H. Rengstorf, *TDNT* II: 277.

II. AUTOBIOGRAPHICAL DEFENSE 2: PAUL'S INDEPENDENT GOSPEL AND APOSTLESHIP (1:11–2:14)

A. THE DIVINE ORIGIN OF PAUL'S GOSPEL (1:11-12)

1. NOT FROM HUMANKIND (1:11-12a)

11 *I must make it clear to you, my friends, that the gospel you heard me preach is no human invention.* 12 *I did not take it over from any man; no man taught it [to] me; . . .*

11-12a Despite their culpable defection from the gospel, Paul still addresses his readers as "my friends," literally "brethren"—a form of address familiar from the OT where it is used of fellow-Israelites, but enriched in the NT with fresh content in that all believers in Jesus are God's children and *ipso facto* brothers and sisters to one another.[1] The formulaic introductory clause, literally "I make known to you" (cf. 1 Cor. 15:1), is intended to remind the readers of something which they had forgotten, namely, the nature and origin of the gospel which Paul had preached to them.[2] Paul first asserts in general the non-human character of his gospel by stating that it is not "according to man" (NASB),[3] then supports this asser-

1. Cf. H. F. von Soden, *TDNT* I: 145; W. Günther, *NIDNTT* I: 256. See also on 1:2a above.
2. The verb "to make known" (γνωρίζειν) "is used both in LXX and NT language of immediate proclamations of the divine will" (W. Mundle, *NIDNTT* III: 314). On the textual variant δέ ("but," AV) for γάρ ("for": RV, RSV, NASB) cf., e.g., (in favor) Ellicott 11f.; Lightfoot 79f.; and (against) Burton 35f.; Zerwick §473. In the original construction, "the gospel" precedes the conjunction "that"; but the RV rendering "as touching the gospel" (treating τὸ εὐαγγέλιον as an accusative of respect; also Ridderbos 56, n. 7) is unnecessary, since the apparent irregularity may be taken as a common species of attraction whereby τὸ εὐαγγέλιον, logically the subject of the verb ἔστιν ("is"), is introduced as the object of γνωρίζω (Burton 37; cf. AV, RSV, NEB, NASB, NIV).
3. Gk. κατὰ ἄνθρωπον. On this phrase cf. J. Jeremias, *TDNT* I: 364.

tion by referring to both the source of his gospel and the manner of its communication to him.

In his negative statement, the word translated "take . . . over" (more commonly rendered "receive") is, as a correlative concept to "deliver," a technical term for the reception of tradition (cf. 1 Cor. 11:23; 15:3),[4] which implies that teaching is the means of communication. The clause "nor was I taught it" is added to enforce and explain "I did not receive it" (RSV), while the emphatic "from . . . man" (placed before both verbs in the original)[5] is probably to be understood as predicated of both verbs, so that the two negative clauses in the NEB rendering convey the single thought that it was not from any human persons that Paul received or learned the gospel.[6] Since "to teach" (cf. Col. 1:28; 1 Tim. 4:11; 2 Tim. 2:2) and "to be taught" or "to learn" (cf. Eph. 4:21; Col. 2:7; 2 Thess. 2:15), no less than "to receive" and "to deliver," are used in connection with Christian tradition,[7] Paul's emphatic denial here of his gospel having any connection with mankind appears to assume the more specific form of the claim that he is "not one of the tradition-receiving members of the church."[8]

Distrust of the accuracy of Paul's negative statement has been expressed on the grounds that if the revelation of Christ in or near Damascus had been Paul's first contact with Christ, "the revelation could not have been self-authenticating and therefore could not have been revelation at all"; Paul must therefore have had some previous knowledge of Christ, which is explained by "the presence in the community of believers of a *living memory*

---

4. Gk. παραλαμβάνω (cf. Heb. *qibbēl*), correlative to παραδίδωμι (cf. Heb. *māsar*). Cf. the cognate noun παράδοσις ("tradition") in 1 Cor. 11:2; 2 Thess. 2:15; 3:6.

5. On παρὰ ἀνθρώπου as denoting the agent, as in Mt. 18:19, cf. MM s.v. παρά.

6. Cf. BFBS; Phillips; Bruce 87.

7. On Paul's references to Christian tradition cf. Bruce, *Tradition*, 29-38; Cullmann, *Early Church*, 64; Fannon, "Influence," especially 297.

8. Schlier 46f. (my translation). Cf. K. Wegenast, *NIDNTT* III: 764; King, "Tannaim," 352-357, who thinks that Paul is denying the charge of tanna-oriented dependence, his opponents having cheapened his apostolate by making it synonymous with the concept of "teacher," "rabbi," or "tanna." Ellicott 13 thinks that ἐδιδάχθην ("I was taught") points more to subjective appropriation, while παρέλαβον ("I received") marks only objective reception; this distinction appears dubious in the light of the correct observation of G. Delling (*TDNT* IV: 14) that, as in 2 Thess. 3:6 and Phil. 4:9, παραλαμβάνειν can denote "the reception of an inner understanding of the nature and spirit of the moral life of the Christian which grows out of the contagious power of example." Arichea-Nida 17 take "received" to refer to the initial reception of the gospel and "taught" to Paul's growing understanding of its contents; but in view of the immediately following contrast with "revelation," it is more likely that both refer to the initial reception of the gospel.

of Jesus."[9] But it is difficult to see how the presupposition of a previous knowledge of Christ on Paul's part justifies distrust of his statement. For that statement "does *not* mean that the content of Christian preaching was previously unknown to him": Paul is "*not* saying that all that he has to say concerning Jesus was imparted to him by direct, ecstatic revelation"; only, the conviction, through revelation, of the resurrection of the crucified "altered at a stroke his whole attitude to what he already knew of Jesus." What he earlier regarded as a "lying message became the message of salvation, and Paul's task was now to pass it on."[10]

2. BY REVELATION (1:12b)

. . . I received it through a revelation of Jesus Christ.

12b Paul's positive statement in the original is elliptical in that an expressed verb is lacking: it simply reads "but through revelation of Jesus Christ." It might seem natural to supply in thought one of the verbs in v. 12a. In this case "I was taught [it]" is ruled out (in view of the manifest contrast between instruction and revelation) and "I received [it]" is the obvious choice (so NEB, NASB, NIV). But, as already noted, "to receive" and "to be taught" are two sides of the same coin, and the one as much as the other is set over against the idea of obtaining by revelation. Therefore, the omission of the verb may well be intentional,[11] and we are probably to understand not "received" but "it came" or "it was."[12]

The revelation here spoken of obviously refers to Christ's appearing to Paul on the Damascus road. It should not be taken[13] as referring to

9. Knox, *Chapters*, 123f.
10. A. Oepke, *TDNT* III: 583f. (emphasis added).
11. So Schlier 47, n. 1.
12. Cf. RV, RSV, Phillips; Bruce 87, respectively. According to G. Delling, *TDNT* IV: 13f., Paul's use of the verb "received" in this verse shows "closer approximation to the original Greek παραλαμβάνω" than his use of it in 1 Cor. 11:23; 15:1, 3; 1 Thess. 4:1 (which reflects Heb. *qibbēl*, more) and means "'to receive the intellectual and ethical content of religious life,' 'to inherit it in acceptance of its claim by attachment' . . . to the author of this life." It would appear that Delling assumes, with NEB, NASB, NIV, that "I received" is to be understood before "through revelation": his exposition of the meaning of the Greek verb is that of the verb thus assumed in the clause. But if "received" is not to be assumed in v. 12b, there is all the more reason to think that the verb in v. 12a (where it is actually present) is used "with closer correspondence to *qibbēl*," meaning "'to receive in fixed form, in the train of Christian tradition'" (ibid., 13).
13. As by Bosworth, "Influence," 291.

"various revelations" of the kind mentioned in 2 Cor. 12:1, thus making the revelation of the gospel not immediately a part of Paul's initial experience of encounter with Christ, but subsequent to it. The entire context suggests that the revelation here is to be closely connected with the revelation of v. 16: the revelation of the gospel to Paul is spoken of in the context of his previous opposition to Christianity (vv. 13f.), the revelation of God's Son to him (vv. 15f.), and his evangelistic activity immediately afterwards (v. 17). It is thus most natural to understand the revelation of v. 12 as identical with, or at least coincident with, the revelation spoken of in v. 16.[14]

While the genitive construction "of Jesus Christ" may be subjective (or *gen. auctoris*) and denote Jesus Christ as the revealer,[15] yet in the light of v. 16a it is more probably objective, indicating Jesus Christ as the one revealed, the content of the revelation.[16] Paul's meaning, then, is that the gospel came to him as a result of Jesus Christ being revealed to him. In this connection, the use in v. 11 of the present tense "is" after the aorist "was preached" (RSV) is significant. The aorist might be an instance of the historical "comprehensive aorist"[17] which sums up Paul's preaching activity up to the time of writing, but in view of the preceding context (vv. 8f., where both "we preached" and "you received" are in the aorist tense) the reference is more likely to Paul's original preaching to the Galatians.[18]

The different tenses in v. 11 show that, according to Paul, the gospel which came to him as a result of God's revelation of Christ, which he had preached to the Galatians in the beginning, is the same as that which he still preaches at the time of writing and to which he is now in his letter calling the readers to return (cf. 1:6; 3:1). This, as the content of the entire letter will attest (cf. especially 2:15–4:11; 5:2-12; 6:12-16), is none other than the gospel of justification by faith. Thus, according to these verses (1:11f.), it was the gospel of justification by faith which came to Paul as the result of a direct revelation of Jesus Christ.

14. It is noteworthy that Paul seems to make a sharp distinction between his Damascus experience of seeing Jesus and all his subsequent revelations (cf., e.g., W. Michaelis, *TDNT* V: 357; Kümmel, *Römer 7*, 148; Wilckens, "Bekehrung," 274) and that he firmly renounces any ecstatic basis for the apostolate (so K. H. Rengstorf, *TDNT* I: 440; K. L. Schmidt, *TDNT* III: 508). It is thus rightly said (Ladd, *Theology*, 368) that "Paul's conversion cannot be interpreted as the first true mystical experience of a great mystic" (as is done by Prokulski, "Conversion").

15. E.g., A. Oepke, *TDNT* III: 583; W. Michaelis, *TDNT* V: 357.

16. E.g., Burton 41f.; Betz 63; Bruce 89. Others take it as both subjective and objective, e.g., W. Grundmann, *TDNT* IX: 551; B. Siede, *NIDNTT* III: 751.

17. Burton, *Syntax*, §§39b, 40.

18. Burton 37.

B. PAUL'S FORMER LIFE (1:13-14)

1. PERSECUTION OF THE CHURCH (1:13)

13 *You have heard what my manner of life was when I was still a practising Jew: how savagely I persecuted the church of God, and tried to destroy it; . . .*

13 In adducing evidence for the divine origin of his gospel and thereby also for his claim to be an apostle by direct revelation—for gospel and apostleship are for him "quite inseparable: they form the two sides of the one coin bearing the impress of the authority of the one divine will"[1]—Paul appeals first to his non-Christian past, representing it as something that the Galatians had already heard of. It would seem that the history of the apostle's past as a persecutor formed part of his preaching (cf. 1 Cor. 15:8-10; Phil. 3:6; 1 Tim. 1:13) and that the Galatians had heard it from Paul himself.[2] He refers to his former "manner of life"[3] as that of "a practising Jew." The latter phrase is literally "in Judaism" (RSV, NASB, NIV); the term "Judaism" denotes objectively the Jewish religion (cf. AV, RV) and subjectively the Jewish way of life, which receives its character from the Jewish religion as its center.[4]

Of his former life Paul mentions two characteristics. The first is his persecution of "the church of God"—a reference to the universal Church as the messianic people of God in its entirety, which is, however, to be met with in various local "churches of God" (1 Cor. 11:16; 1 Thess. 2:14; 2 Thess. 1:4) representing the one universal Church.[5] In the present context the main representative is the church of Jerusalem (cf. Acts 8:3), although Paul's persecution did not stop with that church (cf. Acts 26:10f.).

"Savagely" (RSV "violently") is perhaps better rendered "intensely" (NIV); the Greek phrase basically means "beyond measure" (AV, RV), "to an extraordinary degree."[6] With what intensity Paul engaged in

1. Bornkamm, *Paul*, 18. Cf. Brinsmead 50.
2. Cf. Munck, *Paul*, 14, 24-29, 91.
3. Gk. ἀναστροφή is in itself a neutral term: G. Ebel, *NIDNTT* III: 934. The possessive ἐμήν seems little different from the simple genitive μου, both meaning "my"; cf. BDF §285.1.
4. Schlier 49. The term Ἰουδαϊσμός ("Judaism") appears first in the LXX (R. Mayer, *NIDNTT* II: 310). Kilpatrick, "Peter," 319-312 observes that Ἰουδαϊσμός, Ἰουδαϊκῶς ("like a Jew," 2:14), and Ἰουδαΐζειν ("to Judaize," 2:14), which occur only here in the NT, "seem to suggest not only a view of Israel from the outside but also a reluctance to identify with Israel" (321).
5. Schlier 49f. Cf. K. L. Schmidt, *TDNT* III: 506.
6. Cf. BAGD s.v. ὑπερβολή. Hultgren, "Persecutions," 109 (cf. 110) favors

55

persecuting the Church is illustrated by the record in Acts (8:3; 9:1f., 13f.; 22:4f.; 26:9-12, cf. 7:58-60). The rendering "tried to destroy" regards the verb as conative; but the imperfect tense is better understood in the same way as the imperfect tense of the preceding verb: while (and as long as) Paul was engaged in persecuting Christians he was actually devastating (cf. AV, RV) the Church of God.[7]

2. PROGRESS IN JUDAISM (1:14)

. . . 14 and how in the practice of our national religion I was out-stripping many of my Jewish contemporaries in my boundless devotion to the tradition of my ancestors.

14 The second feature mentioned by Paul is his advance in Judaism. "I was outstripping" is literally "I was advancing . . . beyond" (NASB, NIV).[8] "In the practice of" the Jewish religion[9] Paul was making more progress than many of his contemporaries among his own people, that is, the Jewish people;[10] here an allusion to "a contest between several young Jews who are faithful to the Law" has been detected,[11] but this is not certain. What is far more certain is that Paul's outstanding religious progress was inspired by,[12] and at the same time found expression in, a far greater zeal for his ancestral traditions than was displayed by many of his Jewish contemporaries.[13]

"to the utmost," believing that it "should be translated and interpreted to connote Paul's intensity of zeal . . . , not the alleged intensity of his violence."

7. E.g., Schlier 50, n. 5. The word πορθέω ("destroy") is used in the NT exclusively in connection with Paul's persecution of the Church (Gal. 1:13, 23; Acts 9:21), which lends credence to the suggestion that "the narrative had assumed a somewhat fixed form" (Linton, "Third Aspect," 81). This in turn supports the dictum that the use of the verb in both Acts and Galatians "is not enough to show that Luke knew Galatians" (Haenchen, *Acts,* 331, n. 3). See, however, C. Masson, "A propos de Act. 9.19b-25. Note sur l'utilisation de Gal. et de 2 Cor. par l'auteur des Actes," *Theologische Zeitschrift* 18 (1962) 161-166.

8. The same verb (προκόπτω) is used in Lk. 2:52 of Jesus. For a significant difference in NT usage between this verb and αὐξάνω, the verb used in Lk. 2:40 of Jesus' forerunner, see W. Günther, *NIDNTT* II: 130.

9. NEB thus brings to the fore, probably rightly, the subjective sense of Ἰουδαϊσμός (cf. W. Gutbrod, *TDNT* III: 383).

10. Cf. F. Büchsel, *TDNT* I: 685 (s.v. γένος).

11. By G. Stählin, *TDNT* VI: 714.

12. The participle ὑπάρχων ("being" in AV and RV) is probably used causally here; cf. Burton 47.

13. For the comparative force of περισσοτέρως (so "more exceedingly" here in AV and RV) cf. 2 Cor. 11:23; 1 Thess. 2:17 (F. Hauck, *TDNT* VI: 62). However, it is taken as elative here by RSV, NEB, NIV; Betz 68, n. 117.

Materially the same as "the tradition of the elders" of the Synoptic Gospels (cf. Mt. 15:2f., 6; Mk. 7:3, 5, 8f., 13), the traditions spoken of by Paul are probably not equivalent to just "Jewish tradition generally, both written and verbal,"[14] but are, rather, the special ancestral traditions of the party to which Paul belonged (cf. Phil. 3:5; Acts 22:3; 23:6; 26:5). That is, they are Pharisaic traditions[15] and more particularly those enshrined in the oral law transmitted and expounded in Pharisaic schools, which comprised the 613 prescriptions (248 positive commands and 365 prohibitions) of rabbinic exegesis.[16] To the Pharisee, this tradition was a living testimony to the Torah given at Sinai as well as its continuation; for Paul as a Pharisee the law in the narrow sense (the written law) *and* the oral tradition together represented the basis of his life and the stimulus to his zeal in life.[17]

It was zeal for this ancestral law, an intense personal concern for its fulfillment, which provided both the inspiration and the vehicle of expression for Paul's progress in the Jewish religion, and it would seem that his "advance" had to do, primarily and especially, with "the achievement of righteousness according to the standards and ideals of Pharisaism."[18] It was the same zeal, moreover, which led to his implacable hostility towards Christianity and intense persecution of the Church, for a direct relation is clearly implied between vv. 13b and 14b. The parallel construction of the two clauses is seen most clearly in the Greek but remains recognizable in a more literal rendering like the RV:

| beyond measure | I persecuted | the church of God |
| more exceedingly | being zealous for | the traditions of my fathers |

This parallelism serves to enhance the thought that Paul's hostility to the Church was the outcome of his devotion to the law (cf. Phil. 3:5f.; Acts 22:3f.). From this it would appear that even before he turned to Christ Paul had realized distinctly the essential incompatibility between Christianity and Judaism, and in particular the threat which the new faith posed to the supremacy of the law.[19] It does not follow, however, that this insight into the antithesis between law and faith, which was his from the outset, could not

14. F. Büchsel, *TDNT* II: 172.
15. E.g., H. F. Weiss, *TDNT* IX: 46; cf. G. Schrenk, *TDNT* V: 1022.
16. Cf., e.g., Schoeps, *Paul*, 283; W. Grundmann, *TDNT* IV: 535 with n. 31.
17. Schlier 51f.
18. Burton 46; cf. G. Stählin, *TDNT* VI: 714. A. Stumpff, *TDNT* II: 887 suggests that while this zeal was misconceived by the Jews it is nevertheless "to be estimated positively from the subjective angle."
19. Cf., e.g., Dibelius-Kümmel, *Paul*, 39; Inglis, "Conversion," 229; W. Gutbrod, *TDNT* IV: 1077f.; Ladd, *Theology*, 365. *Pace* Kertelge, *Rechtfertigung*, 226, n. 310. The point is well emphasized by Barclay, "Paul and the Law," 12 as part of the answer to the question why faith in Christ and full commitment to the Torah are mutually exclusive in Paul's soteriology.

have been further clarified and confirmed through his conflict with Jews and Judaizing Christians in the early Church. It is tempting to link Paul's early recognition of this antithesis to the observation that "to the best of our knowledge Paul as distinct from the twelve was the only apostle who came from learned circles and not from the ʿam ha-areṣ.[20]

ADDITIONAL COMMENT 1: WHY PAUL PERSECUTED THE CHURCH

Paul's orthodoxy was, according to Günther Bornkamm, the sole reason for his hostility to Christ and his zeal as persecutor: "We must get away," he warns, "from the common, but false, idea that for an orthodox Jew like himself belief in Jesus as the Messiah was of itself sufficient reason for persecution."[21] It may be observed, however, that the preaching of Jesus *crucified* as the Messiah would have been intolerable to Paul's orthodoxy, and it seems probable that in addition to, or at least in conjunction with, his devotion to the law the early Christians' preaching of a crucified Messiah also contributed to Paul's persecuting frenzy.[22] For when Paul says to the Corinthians, "Jews demand signs and Greeks seek wisdom, but we preach Christ crucified, a stumbling block to Jews and folly to Gentiles" (1 Cor. 1:22f., RSV; cf. 2:2), we may recognize the voice of one who "had stumbled over it himself."[23]

The correctness of appealing in this way to 1 Cor. 1:17-24 for an understanding of what constituted the offense of the cross for Paul is disputed by Jacques Dupont, who writes:[24]

> We cannot grant that the passage has any biographical character or that the portrayal of the Jew scandalized by the cross of Christ gives

20. K. H. Rengstorf, *TDNT* I: 438, n. 181. O'Neill 24-27 would omit Gal. 1:13f., together with vv. 22-24, as an interpolation by a later writer who wished to glorify the apostle, but his reasons are not convincing; cf. Fung, "Relationship between Righteousness and Faith," 2.169f., n. 69.

21. Bornkamm, *Paul*, 15. Cf. Schmithals, *Paul and James*, 37, n. 81.

22. Bultmann, *Faith and Understanding*, 236. Wilckens, "Statements," 17 regards the preaching of a crucified Messiah as one of two reasons for Paul's persecution of the Church (cf. n. 31 below).

23. Wood, "Conversion," 278. Cf., e.g., W. Grundmann, *TDNT* IX: 542. This point is not affected by the correct observation that Χριστός here as usually in Paul is probably only a name and does not refer to the office of Messiah (Barrett, *First Corinthians*, 55), since Christ was preached *as* the Messiah in the primitive kerygma. Moreover, "whereas his non-Jewish readers would take it as a proper name, Paul himself is fully acquainted with the title originally meant by the term" (W. Grundmann, *TDNT* IX: 540, cf. 542).

24. "Conversion," 189.

the impression of being patterned on the description of the Greek who regarded the message of the cross as folly. It would be difficult to look to this development of detailed teaching for the state of Paul's mind before his conversion.

But, granted that the passage has no specific biographical character, what Paul here says about Jews in general must apply to his pre-conversion self as a Jew as well; and while "strictly the reference in 1 C[or]. 1:18 ff. is merely to the divine folly of the *stauros* [the cross]," the stumbling-block for the Jews is "a parallel" to foolishness for the Greek, so that: "Fundamentally what is called *mōria* [folly] is only another form of the *skandalon* [stumbling block] and *vice versa*."[25] To Paul as to every other Jew, a crucified Messiah was not only an insult to his national-political messianic hopes, it was also "incomprehensible absurdity,"[26] since the Messiah was, almost by definition, one uniquely favored by God (cf. Isa. 11:2), whereas a hanged man was, according to the law, cursed by God (Dt. 21:23). That Paul must have seen in the cross[27] the decisive refutation of the claim that Jesus was the Messiah may be inferred from passages such as Mt. 27:42; Lk. 24:20f.; Jn. 12:34 and does not depend on whether Gal. 3:10-14 can be appealed to as providing evidence of how Paul once thought.[28]

The crucifixion at once rendered it unnecessary to give any serious consideration to the question of Jesus' messiahship: Jesus had been condemned not only by the court of Judaism, but by the high court of heaven itself, hence, his disciples' claim that he was the Messiah could only be blasphemy worthy of death (cf. Lev. 24:16), and their further claim that he was risen could not be treated as anything but criminal deception.[29] Thus the plain sentence of the law led Paul to dismiss the claims of the Nazarenes as blasphemous and culpably false, and this, coupled with his clear grasp of the fundamental incompatibility between Judaism and the Christian faith, impelled him to give himself wholeheartedly to what he considered the unmistakable and sacred duty of uprooting the pernicious sect of Jesus' followers.

In contrast to this understanding of the motives for Paul's persecu-

25. G. Stählin, *TDNT* VII: 354.

26. Godet, *First Corinthians*, 1: 105.

27. On the *manner* of Jesus' death as the chief basis of the element of σκάνδαλον in it, cf. Davies, *Paul*, 283f.

28. Dupont, "Conversion," 188 maintains that the latter verses "must be understood as the reflections of a Christian theologian" and that it "would not be wise to seek in them an evidence of how Paul thought when he was once a Pharisee and zealous for the law." But, in fact, the simple application of Dt. 21:23 to Jesus would have been obvious to Paul the Pharisee; it was only the reinterpretation of the cross which Paul contributed as a Christian theologian.

29. Bruce, "Some Thoughts," 6.

tion of the Church Dupont suggests that the motive for Paul's hostility is to be sought in the interpretation of Christ's death found in Paul's letters (Gal. 5:11; 6:12-16; Phil. 3:3, 18f.), according to which the saving significance of the cross rendered circumcision and the law unnecessary, and that this was what constituted the cross a stumbling-block for his opponents.[30] In maintaining, however, that "in the motives which Paul attributes to his persecutors, he is clearly recognizing the same motives as those which had turned him into a persecutor of the church,"[31] Dupont has apparently overlooked two points.

First, the early believers seem to have found no incompatibility between belief in Jesus and continuance in observance of the law (although this ceased to have a soteriological function);[32] this makes it unlikely that rejection of circumcision and the law would have stood out as a prominent feature, much less as the most prominent feature, of their belief. In fact, in the content of the primitive kerygma as reconstructed by C. H. Dodd, abrogation of the law certainly does not figure as one of the dominant themes of early apostolic preaching.[33]

That the Hebrew Christians of Jerusalem escaped the brunt of Paul's persecuting fury (cf. Acts 8:1 and 9:26) and were spared the fate of being scattered like their Hellenistic counterparts (6:1; 11:19) was probably due to their more conservative attitude to the law and their closer attachment to the temple (cf. 6:7). As for the Hellenists, one of their leaders, Stephen, was indeed accused—falsely, Luke says—of making "blasphemous statements against Moses and against God" in that he taught that Jesus of Nazareth would destroy the temple and change the customs delivered by Moses (6:11, 13f.). The first part of this accusation is not unlike the false witnesses' accusation of Jesus before the high priest (Mk. 14:56-58); in view of the close similarity between the trial of Jesus and that of Stephen, it is most natural to understand the falseness of the witnesses in Stephen's case in the same sense as in Jesus' case, that is, as consisting "not in wholesale fabrication but in subtle and deadly misrepresentation of words actually spoken."[34]

30. Dupont, "Conversion," 189-191. Cf. Schmithals, *Paul and James,* 28 with n. 56 on 29f.; Bultmann, *Existence,* 113; Räisänen, "Paul's Conversion," 406.

31. Dupont, "Conversion," 189. Cf. Wilckens, "Statements," 17, who gives as the second reason for Paul's persecution of the Hellenists (cf. n. 22 above) their claim that "any atonement through the cultus (and thereby the *Torah*), had become ineffective" on account of Jesus' death and resurrection.

32. Cf. W. Gutbrod, *TDNT* IV: 1069.

33. Dodd, *Apostolic Preaching,* 17, 24, 26. Cf. Hunter, *Message,* 24-38; Higgins, "Growth," 277. In the terminology used by Higgins, the cross's annulment of the law's validity as a soteriological principle belongs to the tertiary, not primary, elements of NT theology.

34. Bruce, *Book of Acts,* 135.

It is most probable that the accusation made against Stephen was based on some teaching which reflected the teachings of Jesus on the temple, cult, and religious observance of the law. Be that as it may, Stephen's address before the Sanhedrin (Acts 7:2-53) constituted a powerful statement designed to counter the charges levied against him. Stephen responds to the charge of blasphemy against the temple by demonstrating from the Scriptures that God, who does not dwell in houses made with hands, had never confined his presence to any particular land or place. Therefore, the Jews were guilty of virtual idolatry, in line with the rebellious conduct of their ancestors in sacrificing to idols (vv. 40-43), in that they attached permanence to the temple as a focal point of God's presence.

As for the charge of blasphemy against Moses, Stephen returns the accusation squarely upon the heads of the Jews themselves: they, in fact, not he, were the ones guilty of rejecting the law of Moses. During all the time that they had the law of Moses, they were rebellious against God and resisted his appointed messengers, the climax being the murder of the Righteous One. It is particularly noteworthy that Stephen refers to the law of Moses as "the living utterances of God" (Acts 6:38), which suggests that he regarded Moses' law more in its revelatory than in its regulatory aspect;[35] moreover, his contention is that the Jews ought to have obeyed the law of God but did not (v. 53). All this suggests that, like his Master before him, Stephen made a distinction between the law of Moses "as delivered by angels" (v. 53, RSV) and the "customs," that is, ritual prescriptions and religious require ments of the oral tradition.

At the same time Stephen teaches—by implication if not by explicit statement—a vital lesson in worship: the whole Jewish system of cult and tradition had only a limited place in God's plans for his people as but one mode of worship designed for temporary use, which must now be rejected in favor of the pure spiritual worship which the coming of Jesus had inaugurated. By recounting the rebelliousness of the Israelites during all the time that they were under the law of Moses, Stephen may have also wanted to suggest the limited place that even the Mosaic law itself, like the temple, occupied in the plan of God.

Thus, even in the case of the Hellenists (if they may be presumed to have shared Stephen's views), who were the main target of Paul's attack, their more depreciatory attitude toward the law had to do chiefly with its place (or its loss of significance) in the new era of spiritual worship inaugurated by Jesus, and not with any realization that the saving significance of the cross rendered circumcision and the law unnecessary.[36]

---

35. So, e.g., Hanson, *Acts*, 99.
36. Cf. Hultgren, "Persecutions," 98-100, 110. Räisänen, "Paul's Conver-

The second point to be mentioned against Dupont's suggestion is that the saving significance of Jesus' cross as logically involving the abrogation of the law (at least in the clarity with which it is presented in the Pauline letters) may have been Paul's own contribution; indeed, more than one scholar has stated that this was in fact the case.[37] This means that Paul's preaching added another dimension to the offense of the cross as it appeared to his opponents, which was absent from the stumbling-block of the cross as understood by Paul and his fellow Jews before the time of his conversion. We cannot attribute precisely the same motives to Paul the persecutor as Paul the apostle does to his Jewish opponents.

It may safely be assumed, therefore, that Paul's persecution of the Church was in fact caused by the offense of the cross as much as by his devotion to the law, although the offensiveness of the cross was undoubtedly rendered the more repugnant by his zeal for the law. That he should mention his devotion to the law rather than the offense of the cross as the reason for his hostility to Christian faith is understandable in a context where he is concerned to emphasize the fervor of his early attachment to Judaism. His purpose in Gal. 1:13f. is to justify his contention that the gospel came to him without human mediation (vv. 11f.): the fact that he was an ardent persecutor of the Church shows that both his inward orientation and his conduct were incompatible with the basic principles of Christianity, so that there can be no question of his having received, even unconsciously, the gospel from the hands of the apostles of Christ.[38]

C. PAUL'S CALL TO APOSTLESHIP (1:15-17)

1. GOD'S SOVEREIGN CALL (1:15-16a)

15 *But then in his good pleasure God, who had set me apart from birth and called me through his grace,* 16 *chose to reveal his Son to me and through me, in order that I might proclaim him among the Gentiles.*

---

sion," 415 suggests that "the Hellenists displayed a liberal attitude towards parts of the law, which they interpreted in spiritual or ehical terms."

37. E.g., Wood, "Conversion," 282; Wilckens, "Bekehrung," especially 285; Garvie, *Studies,* 93. *Pace* Wedderburn, "Review," 376f., who prefers to see Paul as "inheriting the form of the gospel of at least some of the Hellenists," who "preached a gospel which held that neither circumcision nor the keeping of the law was necessary for salvation."

38. So, correctly, Schlier 52. Cf. Machen, *Origin,* 61; Duncan 26. The theory that though Paul's conversion was sudden, he had experienced psychological preparation for it, is unconvincing and found to be baseless upon close examination: cf. Kümmel, *Römer 7,* 158; Fung 45-51; "Relationship between Righteousness and Faith," 1: 177-181 with 2: 173-179.

15-16a "But then" (literally "but when") signals that a complete break occurred in Paul's life when God called him to be an apostle.[1] Though the word for "God" seems to be a scribal gloss,[2] God is obviously the subject of the sentence. "In his good pleasure" (RSV "was pleased") refers to God's purpose, resolve, and choice, although here it is "not emphasized as an eternal basis."[3]

In "set . . . apart," here and in Rom. 1:1, some have seen an intentional allusion to Paul's Pharisaism,[4] but it is unlikely that such an allusion would have been caught by the readers.[5] "From birth," literally "from my mother's womb" (AV, RV), in the light of Jer. 1:5, probably means "before I was born" (RSV). In view of v. 16b, "called me through his grace"[6] refers to Paul's call to be an apostle, although the thought of his "conversion" is naturally included.[7]

The idea of God consecrating Paul[8] before his birth and subsequently calling him is strongly reminiscent of Isa. 49:1ff., where the Servant of Yahweh (addressed as Israel) is called to be a light to the Gentiles, and of Jer. 1:4f., where Jeremiah appears as one consecrated before his birth and appointed a prophet to the nations (i.e., the Gentiles). Paul's application of these biblical expressions to himself has the effect of aligning himself with those OT figures in the history of salvation: God's call to him was essentially the same as his call to them, a renewal of his will for the salvation of the Gentiles.[9] More specifically, whereas the analogy with Jeremiah reflects Paul's "apostolic self-consciousness,"[10] the allusion to Isaiah (together

---

1. This break is described by K. H. Rengstorf, *TDNT* I: 437 as "the first distinguishing mark of the Pauline apostolate" and as constituting "a basic difference between Paul and the other disciples [i.e., apostles] of Jesus."

2. Metzger 590.

3. H. Bietenhard, *NIDNTT* II: 818f., and G. Schrenk, *TDNT* II: 742, respectively.

4. The Greek words concerned are ἀφορίσας (here, aorist active participle) and ἀφωρισμένος (Rom. 1:1, perfect passive participle). "'Αφωρισμένος is the current transl. of the Heb. *pārûš* and Aram. *pārîš*, of which Φαρισαῖος [Pharisee] is the transcription" (K. L. Schmidt, *TDNT* V: 454): thus Paul, who "as a Pharisee had set himself apart for the law," has been set apart by God "for something entirely different, for the gospel of God" (Nygren, *Romans*, 45f.).

5. It is possible, though, that "Pharisaic Judaizers would have had no trouble following the implications of either his language or his insinuation" (King, "Tannaim," 358). But according to Betz 70, n. 134, there is no evidence that Paul knew of the linguistic relationship.

6. For διά here as instrumental cf. A. Oepke, *TDNT* II: 67.

7. K. H. Rengstorf, *TDNT* I: 438, observes that "so far as the sources go, Paul seems to be the first to trace back the apostolate to God Himself," 1 Pet. 1:2 being in his opinion "dependent on Pauline trains of thought."

8. To "set apart" here means to appoint: G. Dulon, *NIDNTT* I: 473f.

9. Munck, *Paul*, 26. Cf. K. H. Rengstorf, *TDNT* I: 437-441.

10. K. H. Rengstorf, *TDNT* I: 439; cf. Bruce, "Further Thoughts," 23-25.

with other similar references: cf. Rom. 15:21 with Isa. 52:15; Acts 13:47 with Isa. 49:6; Acts 18:9f. with Isa. 43:5) reveals Paul as "the Apostle specially selected to continue the work of the Servant of Yahweh."[11]

While grammatically "calling" is closely connected with "setting apart" (both being part of the substantive "who had set . . . apart . . . and called"), in time it is more closely associated with—and indeed coincident with—"revealing." In other words, the divine call came to Paul by way of God's revealing his Son to him. The phrase "to me and through me" represents two of the several possible renderings of Gk. *en emoi* : "to me" (RSV), and "through me"—to others.[12] In some instances the Greek phrase seems to have the sense "in my case" (Phil. 1:30; 1 Tim. 1:16; cf. 2 Cor. 13:3). Here, the simplest and most natural translation probably also gives the most apposite meaning: "in me" (AV, RV, NIV), that is, "within me" (Phillips) or "in (the sphere of) my soul," Paul thus stressing by the phrase "the inward and intensely personal character of God's revelation to him of the risen Jesus."[13]

The phrase should not, however, be taken to suggest a merely inward revelation without a corresponding external object, for there is little doubt that the preceding phrase ("to reveal his Son") refers to Paul's vision of the risen Christ (also attested in 1 Cor. 9:1; 15:8) on the road to Damascus (cf. v. 17). "In me" underscores the idea of inwardness already implied by the verb "reveal," which connotes a disclosure involving perception and understanding on the part of the recipient.[14] It is likely that Paul's inward, spiritual apprehension of the Christ who was revealed to him came about during the three sightless days following his encounter with the risen Christ (cf. Acts 9:9, 18f.);[15] the inward illumination and the physical vision were alike part of God's revelation to him. That vision and revelation are thus closely linked together is also indicated in 1 Cor. 15:8, where the word used of Christ's appearance to the apostle carries beyond the idea of vision the force of revelation,[16] while in 1 Cor. 9:1 the objectivity of the vision is adduced as guaranteeing the authenticity and hence the validity of Paul's vocation.

The expression "his Son" (i.e., the Son of God) is most likely not

11. Stanley, "Paul's Conversion," 336.

12. Lightfoot 82f.; Hays, "Christology," 281.

13. M. J. Harris, *NIDNTT* III: 1191; cf. Dunn, *Jesus*, 105. For further details see Fung, "Revelation and Tradition," 25f.

14. Cf. Trench 354 (§xciv); Holl, *Gesammelte Aufsätze*, 23. Bornkamm, *Paul*, 21; "Revelation," 94-97, deprecates the view that the word here is to be connected with the vision of the risen Christ, but his arguments are not convincing: cf. Fung 54, n. 142; "Relationship between Righteousness and Faith," 2: 181f., n. 140.

15. E.g., Rendall 154; Wuest 50.

16. W. Michaelis, *TDNT* V: 358 (s.v. ὁράω). Cf. Betz 64 on the common linkage of visionary experience and verbal revelation in ancient religious literature.

used simply as a recognized title for the Messiah: Paul's consistent use of it elsewhere to refer to Christ's divine sonship in the unique, ontological sense (Rom. 1:3f.; 1 Cor. 1:9; 15:20-28; Gal. 4:4; 1 Thess. 1:10)[17] suggests that the term should be similarly understood here.[18] Paul is claiming, then, that he received insight into the unique nature of Jesus' sonship (cf. Acts 9:20).

But his encounter with the risen Christ must also have meant that he recognized that Jesus was indeed the Messiah (cf. 1 Cor. 15:3, 8);[19] and since the early Christians believed that God had made Jesus Lord as well as Messiah (cf. Acts 2:36), it may reasonably be assumed that with the recognition of Jesus' messiahship there was also the recognition of his being the Lord (cf. 1 Cor. 9:1).[20]

In summary, then, the revelation vouchsafed to Paul in his Damascus

17. Cf. Sanday-Headlam, *Romans*, 8f. *Pace* Schoeps, *Paul*, 150, on which see Williams, *Acts*, 125.

18. Cf. Lyonnet, "Pauline Soteriology," 821. Bornkamm, "Revelation," 98, in accord with his view that the "revelation" of Gal. 1:12, 16 is to be understood as an objective "aeon-changing" event (cf. n. 14 above), maintains that here "'Son of God' denotes not, as usually interpreted, the Risen and Exalted One, but the Son of God 'sent' as *man*. . . ."

But Bornkamm's claim that Paul's use of the title "refers to the Incarnation" (ibid., 98) is not borne out by the evidence: (a) Bornkamm says (97) that the title occurs in Romans and Galatians "above all in the context of the Pauline doctrine of law and grace, works and faith" and refers in this connection to Gal. 1:15f.; 2:20; 4:4, 6; Rom. 5:10; 8:3, 29, 32. Of these, however, Gal. 1:15f. is the very passage in which the meaning of the christological title is being determined; Gal. 4:6 refers to the Son whose Spirit God has sent into the hearts of believers, and since the sending of the Spirit is clearly subsequent to the sending of the Son for the work of redemption (vv. 4f.), the title in v. 6 must refer to the Son as resurrected; in Rom. 8:29, with its thought of the believers' conformity to the image of God's Son, the title again plainly refers to the resurrected and glorified Christ (cf. v. 30: "he also glorified," RSV).

(b) Even if, as Bornkamm maintains (100), Rom. 1:3f.; 1 Thess 1:10; and 1 Cor. 15:20-28 are not "specifically Pauline in language or ideas" but "simply reproduce the expectation of the End common to primitive Christianity," the use of the title "Son of God" in these passages nevertheless shows that Paul's thinking about "the Son" is not confined to the incarnation, for we have no reason to believe that Paul was simply making use of "the characteristic idiom and expectation of primitive Christian missionary preaching in general" without being in agreement with it.

(c) In 1 Cor. 1:9, again, "his Son Jesus Christ," with whom believers are called into fellowship, surely refers to Christ as "the exalted, eschatological Lord" (Barrett, *First Corinthians*, 40). We may therefore regard the usual interpretation of Gal. 1:16 as preferable.

19. The content of Paul's conception of Jesus' messiahship was derived not so much from the apostles' pre-Christian messianic conception as from the pre-Pauline Christology of the Church: cf. Dahl, "Messianität," 89f.

20. This understanding agrees with the fact that "for St. Paul Christ attained to the exercise of Lordship at His resurrection" (Whiteley, *Theology*, 108 [who does qualify this statement]); indeed, "the evidence of all the New Testament strata leads to the conclusion that the title Κύριος belongs to Jesus as the one whom God has raised from the dead and enthroned alongside himself" (Bruce, "Jesus is Lord," 27).

experience of the christophany meant his realization that the crucified and risen Jesus was indeed the Messiah, Lord, and, in the unique sense of the term, Son of God.[21] The last term is of particular importance: for Paul it not only implies the uniqueness of Jesus but in Gal. 1:16 it "can connote all that was revealed to Paul at his call to be an apostle to the nations."[22]

God's purpose in revealing his Son to Paul was that he might proclaim him "among the Gentiles," that is, to all who were in Gentile lands[23]—a thought already implied by analogy with the OT figures mentioned earlier (Jeremiah, the Servant of Yahweh). "Proclaim him" is literally "preach-(as-)the-gospel him"; this confirms the thought (cf. 1:1, 12) that the gospel was revealed to Paul at the same time as, and as an inalienable component of, his call to apostleship. By themselves vv. 15-16a might be taken to reflect only Paul's thinking at the time of writing, but read (as they must be read) in connection with vv. 16b-17 they confirm that for Paul conversion and call to the apostolate coincided in time, and that both were rooted in his experience of the christophany on the Damascus road.

ADDITIONAL COMMENT 2: FURTHER OBSERVATIONS ON 1:16a

Combining our understanding of the meaning of the revelation of Jesus to Paul in v. 16 with his plain statement in v. 12 that his gospel (of justification by faith) came to him as a result of Jesus Christ being revealed to him, we may fairly infer that the principles of grace and faith, which represent the positive aspect of the doctrine of justification, were inherently involved in the recognition of Jesus in his threefold capacity as Messiah, Lord, and Son of God; that is, the recognition of this logical connection was due to revelation no less than was the recognition of Jesus in his true capacity. But since the positive aspect of the doctrine of justification implies its opposite, the negative aspect (that justification is not attainable by legal works) must also have been part of the gospel revealed to Paul.

Neither here nor elsewhere does Paul describe exactly how the revelation was communicated and apprehended, though 2 Cor. 4:6 points to a sudden flash of illumination which brought about a permanent transformation (cf. 2 Cor. 5:16). But if the divine revelation did not totally bypass

21. Cf. Kim, *Origin,* 100-136.
22. E. Schweizer, *TDNT* VIII: 384.
23. The apparent contradiction between *God* sending Paul (here) and the risen *Christ* sending him (Acts 26:17) is resolved by the considerations that "it is characteristic of his theology to assign identical functions or attributes to God and to Christ," and that "it would be entirely congruous with his general position that he should speak of the whole experience as due to the initiative of God" (Thrall, "Christology," 313, 314).

human intellect, we may venture the opinion that Paul may have arrived at his understanding of the gospel by way of a radical reorientation in his thinking which included two aspects: (a) the realization that the way of legal righteousness was a cul-de-sac—for at the very zenith of his success along the path of Pharisaic legalism, it was revealed to him that he was persecuting the Messiah in the person of his followers (cf. Acts 9:4f.; 22:7f.; 26:14f.) and was therefore in rebellion against God; and (b) the corresponding recognition that righteousness was now to be had through a believing dependence on Christ, the Lord and Son of God, alone—a recognition which would have come to Paul the more readily if (as is not impossible) he already held the belief that the age of the Torah would be replaced by the age of the Messiah. The fact that he can describe and interpret his conversion experience in terms of justification by faith in Gal. 2:16 and Phil. 3:7-9 lends support to the conclusion derived from Gal. 1:12, 16 that the gospel of justification by faith in both its negative and positive aspects was implicitly involved in the revelation to him of Jesus in his threefold capacity.[24]

In the light of this observation, it is not surprising that there is complete harmony between Paul and Jesus in their strong insistence on the central truth that salvation is by the grace of God and that faith is the means of its appropriation. This emphasis on grace and faith (which is reliance on God's mercy) underlies all of Jesus' teaching as a basic presupposition and comes to clear expression in some of his parables, notably those of the laborers in the vineyard (Mt. 20:1-16, peculiar to Matthew), the prodigal son, and the Pharisee and the tax collector (Lk. 15:11-32; 18:9-14, both peculiar to Luke).[25] This teaching is in essence the same as Paul's doctrine of justification by faith alone, although Jesus and Paul express it in different terms: Jesus says, "I did not come to invite virtuous people, but sinners" (Mk. 2:17), while Paul calls God "him who justifies the ungodly" (Rom. 4:5, RSV). The terminology is different, but the substance is the same.[26] The remarkable understanding which Paul thus shows of the central message of his Master—the more remarkable in that his letters give no evidence that he knew the parables of Jesus—is fully consonant with his claim in Gal. 1:12, 16 as explained above.

The contradiction between Gal. 1:12 (as explained above by v. 16a), where Paul claims direct revelation as the origin of his gospel, and 1 Cor.

---

24. For a more detailed argumentation of this thesis see Fung, "Revelation and Tradition," 27-30. The point needs to be emphasized, especially in view of the following fact, noted by Gordon, "The Problem at Galatia," 35: "Nowhere in any of the accounts of Paul's call is anything specific *said* [emphasis added] about justification. What *is* said, particularly in Galatians, is that Paul was called as an apostle to the Gentiles."

25. Cf., e.g., Hanson, *Paul's Understanding,* 13ff.; Bruce, "Justification," 66-69.

26. Cf. Holl, *Gesammelte Aufsätze,* 27.

15:3, where he seemingly refers to his gospel as something received by tradition, is only apparent, not real. As regards Paul's basic understanding of the gospel, revelation (Gal. 1:12) came first, tradition (1 Cor. 15:3) followed after.[27]

2. PAUL'S OBEDIENT RESPONSE (1:16b-17)

When that happened, without consulting any human being, 17 *without going up to Jerusalem to see those who were apostles before me, I went off at once to Arabia, and afterwards returned to Damascus.*

16b-17 Paul's statement here seems to be contradicted by the parallel account in Acts 9:19b-20, which contains no mention of his visit to Arabia, but instead pictures him remaining with the disciples in Damascus for several days after his baptism and then "immediately" (v. 20, RSV) preaching Jesus in the synagogues. It has rightly been observed that "the detail of the three years [between Paul's call to apostleship and his subsequent first visit to Jerusalem, Gal. 1:18] was vastly important for Paul's argument in Galatians, . . . but it was not at all important in a general history of the progress of the Church."[28] For this and other reasons, the most satisfactory solution to the apparent discrepancy between the two passages is to take Paul's "at once" seriously and literally, and to treat the same word in Acts 9:20 (NEB "soon") as meaning "immediately following his return to Damascus"—Luke having omitted, for some reason, mention of Paul's Arabian visit between his v. 19a and v. 19b.[29] Thus the sequence of events was not: conversion/call, preaching in Damascus, Arabian visit, but rather: conversion/call, Arabian visit, witness in Damascus.[30]

"Arabia" is generally taken as a reference to the Nabataean Kingdom, the northwestern boundaries of which extended to the walls of Damascus.[31] It is commonly thought that Paul went to Arabia for solitary com-

27. I have argued this at length elsewhere (Fung, "Revelation and Tradition," especially 34-41). Howard 34 maintains that Paul's purpose in Gal. 1:11f. can hardly be to argue his independence of all men, since in vv. 13f. he implies that he knew, at least in part, and opposed what the Church taught, and in 1 Cor. 15:1-7 admits having received information on the crucial events of the gospel. Elsewhere I have sought to clarify the relationship between Gal. 1:12 and 1 Cor. 15:3 (Fung, art. cit.); Howard's argument loses much of its force in the light of this clarification.

28. Machen, *Origin*, 73.

29. For detailed argumentation of this position see Fung 63-65; "Relationship between Righteousness and Faith," 2: 193-195, n. 197.

30. E.g., W. Schrage, *TDNT* VII: 835, and Guthrie 71-72; K. Lake and H. J. Cadbury, *BC* IV: 193; Catchpole, "Paul," 434, 438, respectively.

31. The view of Baeck ("Faith," 95, n. 1) that the term here is not a geographical

munion with God and reflection on his position in the light of the new revelation.[32] It is preferable, however, to regard this visit as undertaken mainly for the purpose of missionary activity (without, of course, necessarily precluding all reflection on Paul's part), for the following reasons: (a) The most natural reading of vv. 16f. is that Paul went to Arabia in response to the purpose for which the revelation had been vouchsafed, namely, that he might proclaim Christ among the Gentiles.[33] This understanding accords well with Paul's own description of his gospel as having come by direct revelation (v. 12), which should be taken with due seriousness. (b) Such a prompt response[34] would be thoroughly in keeping with Paul's Jewish awareness that "the revelation entailed the mission"[35] and particularly with his character as a man of utter sincerity and intense activity (witness his erstwhile persecution of the Church). (c) That he later had to flee Damascus to escape from the hands of the ethnarch under the Nabataean king Aretas (2 Cor. 11:32f.) would suggest that he had incurred the hostility of that king by preaching to his subjects in Arabia.[36]

Since Paul went up from Damascus to Jerusalem for his first post-conversion visit in the third year after his conversion (see on v. 18), it is clear that the sojourn in Arabia and the stay in Damascus together made up a period of two or three years, though what portion of this time was spent in Arabia cannot be ascertained from the passage itself. In any event, vv. 16b-17 emphasize the fact that immediately after his conversion Paul did not consult anyone, least of all the apostles in Jerusalem, and that even after his visit to Arabia he did not go to Jerusalem, but returned to Damascus.[37] The Greek verb behind "consulting" is used here more likely in the sense of "receiving instruction or advice from" than in the sense of "adding or

---

proper name but a general appellative, being an error for ἀραβα, which means "wilderness" in the LXX (e.g., Dt. 1:7; 2:8), is unconvincing.

32. E.g., Neill 28f.; Arichea Nida 23. This view is considered by Lowe, "Development," 132f. to be a "misapprehension both of what is meant by 'Arabia,' and of the character of the man."

33. So, e.g., Lake, *Earlier,* 320; *BC* V: 192; Schlier 58; Bligh 135f.; Betz 74; Bruce 96.

34. On this cf. K. H. Rengstorf, *TDNT* I: 438.

35. Baeck, "Faith," 95.

36. So, e.g., Haenchen, *Acts,* 334; Bornkamm, *Paul,* 27. For a response to the fourfold argument of Burton 55-57 against this understanding of Paul's Arabian visit, see Fung, "Revelation and Tradition," 30-32. The considerations offered both in that article and in my comments above confirm the view that Paul's call to be an apostle to the Gentiles was coincident with his conversion (cf., e.g., Schlier 54, n. 6; Stendahl, "The Apostle Paul," 204f. [= *Paul,* 84f.]; Kim, *Origin,* 55-66). For an answer to objections based on Acts to this view see Fung 69-72; "Relationship between Righteousness and Faith," 1: 584-587 with 2: 589f., nn. 43-53; "Further Observations," 83-86.

37. Πάλιν (RSV "again") is pleonastic: BDF §484.

contributing to" as in 2:6;[38] but still more probable in the present context is the sense of consulting with "someone who is recognized as a qualified interpreter about the significance of some sign," so that Paul's meaning here is that he did not consult the apostles about the significance of the revelation he had received, though they would be regarded within the circle of Jesus' followers as most qualified to give "a skilled and authoritative interpretation" of what he had seen and heard on the Damascus road.[39] "Any human being" is literally "flesh and blood," which denotes "man as such" without any nuance of that which is sinful,[40] though perhaps with the notion of creaturely frailty.[41]

"Going up" (cf. v. 18; 2:1) and "coming down" (Acts 11:27; 18:22; 25:6f.) are used in the NT of going to and leaving Jerusalem;[42] this usage is probably to be explained in terms of that city's geographical location in the highlands of Palestine and its religious position as the seat of the temple and the mother-city of the Church.[43] While "going up" should not be rendered "returning,"[44] the usage of the expression shows that it lends no support to the notion that Paul had never been to Jerusalem before. In the present context, the significance of Jerusalem for Paul lies in the fact that in that city were to be found those who were apostles before him (in time, not status), among whom "the twelve" must have occupied the preeminent place.[45] This emphasis on his lack of contact with Jerusalem is part of his defense, which is designed to show that he was never dependent on the Jerusalem authorities for his gospel or his commission to preach it.

The same general approach is continued in vv. 18-24, but before we consider those verses it will be useful to pause for a summary. Our study of vv. 11-17 has shown that Paul's conversion is to be understood as involving (a) recognition of the risen Jesus as Messiah, Lord, and Son of God, (b) the experience of being justified by faith apart from legal works, (c) the revelation of the basic principles of the gospel, and (d) the call to be an apostle to the Gentiles. This conclusion is consonant with the purpose and purport of

---

38. *Pace* J. Behm, *TDNT* I: 353; Howard 35.

39. Dunn, "Relationship," 462f.

40. E. Schweizer, *TDNT* VII: 128.

41. Cf. J. Behm, *TDNT* I: 172.

42. The Hebrew form of the name occurs here in vv. 17f. and in 2:1, the Hellenized form always elsewhere in Paul: E. Lohse, *TDNT* VII: 327f. with n. 225; Kilpatrick, "Peter," 318f.

43. Cf. J. Schneider, *TDNT* I: 519f.

44. That would require ὑπέστρεψα as in v. 17b or ἐπανῆλθον (cf. Lk. 10:35; 19:15).

45. Cf. Munck, "Paul, the Apostles, and the Twelve," 107, as against his later view in *Paul*, 213.

Paul's words in these verses: his gospel had no connection with mankind, but came to him by direct revelation (vv. 11f., 15-16a). This is supported by his life before his conversion, inasmuch as the very direction and principles of that life were diametrically opposite to those of Christianity (vv. 13f.), and by his conduct immediately after his conversion and call, since he went off to Arabia to preach the gospel and had no contact with Jerusalem even after his return (vv. 16b-17). Thus no human influence on the origin of his gospel—or human explanation of his commission to preach it—was possible either prior to or immediately after his conversion and call.

ADDITIONAL COMMENT 3: PAUL'S INTEREST IN THE GENTILES

If immediately after his call to apostleship Paul began preaching to Gentiles in Arabia, this means that he already had a gospel for the Gentiles, and it seems a fair inference that he preached to the Gentiles *immediately after* his conversion and call the same gospel of justification by faith which had come to him by revelation *at* his conversion and call. But is his prompt obedience in preaching the gospel to Gentiles in any way related to his background as a Pharisee?

Some scholars see in Gal. 5:11 ("if I am still advocating circumcision") evidence that before becoming a Christian Paul was "a Jewish missionary to the Gentiles along the lines taken by orthodoxy."[46] But since such alleged missionary activity on Paul's part is something "we know just nothing about,"[47] and is not clearly established by this text, we mention it only as, at most, an interesting possibility,[48] which, if verified, would render Paul's Christian activities among the Gentiles all the more intelligible.

Others suggest that Paul's training as a Pharisee under Gamaliel was such as to give him a prior interest in Gentiles. It is pointed out that the first century "was the century of Jewish history which fostered a universalistic hope without parallel in any century before or since" and moreover that "hopes for the future typical of the school of Hillel, which controlled in undiluted form the circle of Paul's teacher Gamaliel I, were those of Biblical prophetism," which envisaged the nations joining Israel in the worship and service of God in the messianic age.[49] We are therefore to believe that the Gentile question must have forced itself upon Paul in his personal contacts as

46. Bornkamm, *Paul*, 12. Cf., e.g., Bultmann, *Existence*, 113.
47. Schoeps, *Paul*, 64, n. 2.
48. So Whiteley, *Theology*, 74; Schoeps, *Paul*, 64, n. 2, 168, despite 219.
49. Schoeps, *Paul*, 220, 228f.

well as in his studies. If so, Paul at conversion would have recognized in the fact that the Messiah had come and the messianic age had dawned an imperious call to proclaim him "as a light to the nations, that [God's] salvation may reach to the end of the earth" (Isa. 49:6, RSV); and thus Paul's Jewish background would provide us with an important factor for understanding his immediate response to the call to preach to the Gentiles.[50]

Doubt has been cast, however, on one or two basic presuppositions of this view. It is pointed out that "in the Judaism of Paul's day there was no 'missionary' in the sense of one who is sent out by a religious community to propagate its faith," so that Paul's Jewish "missionary" activities are probably to be conceived as "private, occasional proselytizing activities rather than a regular, professional missionary enterprise."[51] Moreover, the traditional understanding of Gamaliel as a member of the school of Hillel is also open to question. While "later tradition makes Gamaliel the successor of Hillel as head of his school," "those earlier traditions which reflect some direct memory of the man and his teaching do not even associate him with the school of Hillel."[52] Paul's extreme zeal for the law as the reason for his persecution of the Church indicates that he probably belonged to the radical wing of the Pharisaic movement, perhaps the school of Shammai (certainly, Gal. 3:10 and especially 5:3 are more representative of that school than of the school of Hillel). If so, the likelihood is that "he was rather hostile to the Gentiles and had little interest in winning them for Judaism."[53]

Therefore, Paul's immediate response to the commission to preach to the Gentiles is probably not to be explained by reference to his background along the lines of either previous experience as a Jewish missionary to Gentiles or membership in the school of Hillel. His Gentile mission more likely followed with logical necessity from his experience of God's revelation to him:[54] since Jesus is the Messiah, the Son of God and the exalted Lord, and salvation is no longer dependent on observance of the law but only on faith in Christ as the appointed Savior of all, the message of salvation by grace through faith can be, and is to be, carried to the Gentiles as well as the Jews.[55] This was the conviction which took hold of Paul at his conversion and call, and sufficiently accounts for the immediacy of his preaching to the Gentiles.[56]

50. Cf. Baeck, "Faith," 108; Schoeps, *Paul*, 219f.

51. Kim, *Origin*, 39f.

52. Bruce, *Paul*, 50.

53. Cf. Kim, *Origin*, 41-44 (quotation from 44).

54. Cf. Pfleiderer, *Paulinism*, 1: 3.

55. On the particular importance of the title "Son of God" in this context see Bornkamm, *Paul*, 21f., 94; Betz 70f.

56. Cf., e.g., Dodd, *NT Studies*, 119; Ladd, *Theology*, 368. According to Gager, "Conversion," 701, "an important part of Paul's written legacy"—Galatians, most of

D. PAUL'S FIRST POST-CONVERSION VISIT TO JERUSALEM (1:18-20)

1. THE CIRCUMSTANCES OF THIS VISIT (1:18-19)

18 *Three years later I did go up to Jerusalem to get to know Cephas. I stayed with him for a fortnight,* 19 *without seeing any other of the apostles, except James the Lord's brother.*

18 The emphatic "I did go up" of NEB is probably intended to show a contrast with the negative "without going up" in v. 17a. In the original, Paul's statement begins with the word *epeita*, "then," which occurs also in v. 21 and 2:1 (cf. RSV), where it is translated "next" by NEB. The repeated use of this word suggests that Paul is giving a consecutive account of his career since his conversion. First to be mentioned is his first post-conversion visit to Jerusalem. This visit occurred "three years later"— reckoning, presumably, not from Paul's return to Damascus but from his conversion and call, which is the common point of reference and departure for his *not* visiting Jerusalem in v. 17 and his visit described in the present verse.[1] Whether the phrase "three years" denotes three full years[2] or, more probably, is by inclusive reckoning to be regarded as equivalent to "in the third year" (cf. the parallel expressions "three days afterwards" in Mk. 8:31; 10:34 and "on the third day" in Lk. 9:22; 18:33), Paul's point here is that he engaged in "three years" of preaching before visiting Jerusalem for the first time after his conversion, thus showing the independence both of his gospel and his commission to preach it.[3]

He further specifies the *purpose* and *duration* of the visit: he went up "to get to know Cephas"[4] and he "remained with him fifteen days" (RSV).[5] The verb translated "to get to know" (a NT hapax) is taken by some scholars

---

Romans, and his comments in Phil. 3, in which he undertakes "an extensive plea *to the effect* that the law was no longer the path to righteousness or justification before God"— "is directed at reducing his sense of dissonance by reducing the attractiveness of the rejected alternative." He further thinks that "the beginnings of an answer" to the question why Paul insistently presents himself as an apostle to the Gentiles might be found in the consideration that it was Gentile Christianity which provided Paul with the support he needed for his attempt to reduce post-decision dissonance. It is to be observed that this interesting psychoanalytic theory does not mention, let alone discuss, Paul's clear statement in Gal. 1:15f., which in my view casts serious doubts on its validity.

1. Gunther, *Paul*, 26. Cf. Schlier 59; Neill 29; Arichea-Nida 24.
2. A. B. Bruce, *Christianity*, 44, n. 2, on inadequate grounds.
3. Cf. Weizsäcker, *Apostolic Age*, 96f.
4. "Cephas" is the Aramaic name which Paul regularly uses in designating the apostle Peter except in 2:7f.
5. *Pace* Rendall 155, πρός with accusative here is equivalent to παρά with dative. Cf. Moule 52f. on Jn. 1:1; Bruce 98 on Mk. 6:3.

to mean "to make inquiry of," "to get information from"—a sense which the word is said to have in classical Greek.[6] But serious doubt is cast on the correctness of this thesis by a recent study which demonstrates (a) that that meaning cannot be substantiated for the particular construction in question (verb + accusative; not verb + double accusative or verb + accusative + indirect question) either in classical or post-classical Greek and (b) that the only correct and linguistically possible translation is "to get to know (personally)," "to get (personally) acquainted with."[7] We may take it, then, that the common Hellenistic sense of the verb, "to get to know" or "to get acquainted with" (NIV), is the intended meaning here.

Even so, the intrinsic probabilities of the situation suggest that Paul became acquainted, not only with Cephas (Peter), but also with the tradition of the earthly Jesus represented by him;[8] for (a) Peter must have been an invaluable source of information concerning Jesus' life and ministry, being traditionally the source behind the Gospel of Mark; (b) the theory of Paul's lack of interest in the historical Jesus lacks a substantial basis;[9] and (c) the two apostles can hardly have avoided talking about the earthly life and ministry of their common Lord.[10] This understanding gains confirmation from the noteworthy facts (a) that Peter and James, who appear here (vv. 18f.) as the only persons Paul met with during his first Jerusalem visit, are the only persons mentioned by name in 1 Cor. 15:1-7 in connection with what Paul had received and in turn transmitted to the Corinthians, and (b) that the resurrection appearances described there seem to fall into two series, linked respectively with the names of Cephas and James[11]—all of which suggests that it was during his first Jerusalem visit that Paul received this particular tradition.[12]

6. E.g., Edersheim, *Life*, 2: 625 with n. 2; Kilpatrick, "Gal. 1:18"; Davies, *Setting*, 453-455; Dunn, "Relationship," 465.

7. Hofius, "Gal 1:18." The rendering "to visit in order to get to know" (e.g., F. Büchsel, *TDNT* III: 396; Schlier 60; BAGD s.v. ἱστορέω) is, according to Hofius (80), also inaccurate, as the verb does not mean "to visit someone."

8. Cf. Cullmann, *Early Church*, 65; Bring 52. In his reply to Hofius, Dunn ("Once More—Gal 1:18"), while conceding that "the translation 'to get information from Cephas' does push the sense rather hard," and that "the better translation is 'to get to know Cephas,'" insists that "getting to know Cephas must, by the force of the word and the circumstances of the occasion, have included gaining information about (and indeed from) Peter."

9. See Additional Comment 4 below.

10. One might see a measure of cultural difference reflected in the illustrations used by Dodd, *Apostolic Preaching*, 16 and Machen, *Origin*, 76 in connection with this point. Dodd: "we may presume they did not spend all the time talking about the weather"; Machen: "it is highly improbable . . . that he [Paul] spent the time gazing silently at Peter as though Peter were one of the sights of the city."

11. Cf. Winter, "I Corinthians XV. 3b-7," especially 145f., 148.

12. So, e.g., Fridrichsen, "Apostle," 17, n. 9; Bruce 98, 100. On the other

At the same time, to obtain information concerning the historical Jesus *as a by-product* of getting acquainted with Peter is a totally different matter from receiving instruction in the gospel. The very word "to-get-to-know" seems to have been "chosen thoughtfully in order to avoid the impression that Paul received instruction from the authorities of Jerusalem."[13] Furthermore, the briefness of the visit—which was abruptly terminated by a plot against his life and a coincident vision confirming his call to the Gentiles (Acts 9:29f.; 22:17-21)[14]—and the apologetic context combine to rule out the possibility of what has been called "the fantastic idea" of "a late catechumenate and a crash course in missionary work with Peter."[15]

19 Paul also specifies that he did not see "any other of the apostles, except James the Lord's brother." Several passages in the NT mention Jesus' brothers (e.g., Mk. 3:31f.; Jn. 2:12; Acts 1:14; 1 Cor. 9:5). Mk. 6:3 mentions his sisters and refers to four brothers by name, the first of whom is in all probability the James of Gal. 1:19. These brothers have been regarded (a) by the Orthodox churches as sons of Joseph by a previous marriage (the "Epiphanian" view), (b) in Roman Catholic interpretation as Jesus' first cousins, the sons of "Mary wife of Clopas," who was the Virgin's sister (Jn. 19:25; the "Hieronymian" view), and (c) by Protestant exegetes as Jesus' uterine brothers, sons of Joseph and Mary (the "Helvidian" view). This last view accords best with the natural implication of Mk. 6:3, where the context suggests that the brothers, together with the sisters unspecified by name, were, like Jesus himself, children of Mary.[16]

Paul does not explain why he saw no other apostle during his visit; the other apostles may not have been present in Jerusalem at the time, possibly being engaged in missionary work in Judaea,[17] but it is best not to conjecture. The way in which the reference to James is attached as an afterthought, as it were, may indicate that he had only a subsidiary part to play in Paul's meeting with the two Jerusalem leaders, if not indeed that his meeting with Paul was almost accidental. In any case, Paul's intention here and in v. 18 is to assert that at this visit there could be no question of the apostles' bringing their authority or influence to bear on him or his gospel either as a body[18] or as individuals, since he saw only Peter and

---

hand, Héring, *First Corinthians,* 158 thinks that Paul "had doubtless received earlier in Damascus" the tradition in question here.

13. Schnackenburg, "Apostles," 290, n. 1.

14. Cf. Lightfoot 84.

15. Bornkamm, *Paul,* 28. Cf. A. B. Bruce, *Christianity,* 44; King, "Tannaim," 354f.

16. Cf. Bruce 99; W. Günther, *NIDNTT* I: 256; H. F. von Soden, *TDNT* I: 144f.

17. The suggestions of K. H. Rengstorf, *TDNT* I: 431 and Machen, *Origin,* 76, respectively.

18. Foerster, "Δοκοῦντες," 290 suggests that Paul is thinking here of the

James, who, moreover, acted as informants and not instructors or imparters of authority.[19]

ADDITIONAL COMMENT 4: PAUL'S INTEREST IN THE HISTORICAL JESUS

Two main factors have contributed to the theory that Paul had no interest in the historical Jesus: (a) the apparent paucity in his letters of references and allusions to the life and teaching of Jesus,[20] and (b) his apparent depreciation in 2 Cor. 5:16 of the knowledge of Christ "after the flesh" (AV, RV).[21] These will be considered in reverse order.

By 2 Cor. 5:16b ("even though we have known Christ after the flesh, yet now we know him so no more," RV), Paul probably means that he had a wrong conception of the Messiah.[22] The contrast that he wishes to make in this verse seems to be, *neither* (a) between his present knowledge of Jesus "after the Spirit" and his former acquaintance with the earthly Jesus,[23] since it is doubtful that this verse implies that Paul had ever been personally acquainted with the earthly Jesus;[24] *nor* (b) between his present mature stage and an earlier immature stage of his own Christian life;[25] *nor* (c) between his own present knowledge and that which the twelve had of Jesus before the cross (as though that had been merely "after the flesh");[26] *but rather* (d) between his present evaluation of Christ and his former estimation of him as based on human standards (cf. RSV, NEB, NIV).[27]

Grammatically the Greek phrase *kata sarka* ("after the flesh") goes with the verb "know," not the noun "Christ"; therefore, Paul is not speaking of knowing a "Christ after the flesh." It has been argued that "'a Christ regarded in the manner of the flesh' is just what a 'Christ after the flesh' is" and that this "Christ after the flesh" is the historical Jesus—as opposed to

---

twelve as a group, since in those early years neither Peter nor James alone could or would "commission" anyone: cf. Acts 6:2; 8:14; 11:1, 22.

19. For an answer to the objections raised by Bauernfeind, "Begegnung" against the above "commonly accepted interpretation" of this meeting between Paul and Cephas, cf. Fung 87-89; "Relationship between Righteousness and Faith," 1: 211-214 with 2: 218-219, nn. 332-346.

20. Cf. Bultmann, *Existence*, 124; J. Schneider, *TDNT* V: 193; Whiteley, *Theology*, 101.

21. Cf. Bultmann, *Faith and Understanding*, 241, 277.

22. So, e.g., W. Grundmann, *TDNT* IX: 546, with n. 343.

23. J. Weiss as quoted in Bruce, "Jesus and Paul," 22.

24. Correctly, Ridderbos, *Paul and Jesus*, 42, 139, n. 4; Rigaux, *Letters*, 48.

25. A view rightly rejected by Machen, *Origin*, 130.

26. Schoeps, *Paul*, 57.

27. E.g., E. Schweizer, *TDNT* VII: 131; Bruce, *1 and 2 Corinthians*, 208.

the exalted Christ.[28] But "the change from a carnal to a spiritual knowledge of Christ does not mean that the object of his [Paul's] knowledge has changed from the Jesus of history to the Spirit-Christ."[29] Furthermore, Paul's statement about not knowing Christ "after the flesh" is paralleled by the previous statement about not knowing "any man" after the flesh (v. 16a), thus requiring that the two statements be interpreted in the same way. But if the interpretation under review is applied to the knowledge of every man, the result is absurd.[30]

With regard to the more general consideration of Jesus' life and teaching in the letters of Paul, four points may be noted. (a) Paul lived and preached "in a new—a postmessianic—situation," in "an eschatologically different world," and it was therefore "unthinkable that he should simply transmit the teaching of Jesus."[31] (b) The epistles do not contain the missionary preaching of Paul, being addressed to Christians to whom the story of Jesus was probably already familiar.[32] (c) Paul's letters themselves do provide clear evidence of his knowledge of (by this is not meant personal acquaintance with) and interest in the earthly Jesus (e.g., Gal. 1:19; 3:13, 16; 4:4) and his teaching (cf., e.g., Rom. 13:7 with Mk. 12:17; 1 Cor. 9:14 with Lk. 10:7; 1 Cor. 10:27 with Lk. 10:8; Gal. 6:1f. with Mt. 18:15);[33] and if regard is had to Paul's preaching as recorded in Acts, a good case can be (and has been) made that "Paul's whole method of preaching involves a background knowledge of the life of Jesus."[34] (d) "The principal reason for the lack of allusion to the events of Jesus' ministry may quite simply be that Paul was not an eyewitness of these events, and preferred to confine himself to those matters of which he could speak at first hand."[35]

ADDITIONAL COMMENT 5: THE APOSTOLIC STATUS OF JAMES

Whether James is regarded as an apostle in Gal. 1:19 is not easy to determine, and the suggestion has been made that the lack of clarity regarding

28. Bultmann, *Theology*, 1: 238f.; cf. *Faith and Understanding*, 217.
29. Hoskyns-Davey, *Riddle*, 160.
30. Machen, *Origin*, 142.
31. Barrett, "Not Ashamed," 30 (= *NT Essays*, 130).
32. Cf. Grosheide, "Pauline Epistles," 141.
33. On this see, e.g., Holl, *Gesammelte Aufsätze*, 26f.; Hunter, *Theology*, 103f.; Bruce, "Paul and the Historical Jesus"; Allison, "Pauline Epistles," especially his conclusions on 10, 17, and 25.
34. Barclay, "Comparison," especially 168f.; quotation from 169.
35. Bruce, "Jesus and Paul," 25.

James's position was "intentional with Paul."[36] A negative answer to the question has been returned on the grounds that (a) if James had been regarded as an apostle, Paul would probably have written that he saw no other apostle "except Peter and James"; (b) there is no indication that James had been sent out as a missionary by Christ—instead he always appears as a leader in the Jerusalem church; (c) the description "the Lord's brother" is added to distinguish this James from the two apostles of the same name.[37] However, these arguments are not decisive: (a) The reference to James may have been added as an afterthought; (b) it would appear that James, though an unbeliever along with the rest of Jesus' family during Jesus' earthly ministry (Jn. 7:5; cf. Mk. 3:21, 31-35), was commissioned as an apostle when the risen Lord appeared to him (1 Cor. 15:7), the general rule about Jesus' appearing only to believers (cf. Jn. 14:19) being set aside in this particular case; and (c) the description "the Lord's brother" would be even more necessary if James was in fact regarded as an apostle.

An affirmative answer may, therefore, be preferred, for the following reasons: (a) The most natural understanding of the grammatical construction in this verse is to take the word "except" as referring to the whole preceding clause ("I saw none of the other apostles except . . . ," RSV, cf. NEB), not to the verb alone ("I did not see any other apostle, but I saw only . . . ," cf. NEB mg.; NIV retains the ambiguity), and thus as implying that James was an apostle.[38] (b) In the Acts account of Paul's first visit to Jerusalem after his conversion (Acts 9:26-30) Paul is said to have been introduced by Barnabas to "the apostles" (v. 27), which is probably to be understood as a generalizing plural.[39] (c) The apostleship of James is favored by the parallelism between Cephas (linked with the narrower group of "the Twelve") and James (linked with the wider group of "all the apostles") in the summary of the resurrection appearances in 1 Cor. 15:5-7 (cf. on 1:18 above).[40]

36. Schmithals, *Office*, 64f.

37. For these arguments cf. Rendall 156; Duncan 32; Munck, *Paul*, 92, n. 2; "Paul, the Apostles, and the Twelve," 107; Schlier 61 with n. 1.

38. Cf., e.g., Zerwick §470; K. H. Rengstorf, *TDNT* I: 422 with n. 93, 431; W. Günther, *NIDNTT* I: 256; Bruce 100f., who points to 1 Cor. 1:14 as a parallel to the present construction. For refutation of the view of L. P. Trudinger that the Greek is to be construed as meaning "other than the apostles I saw none," see Howard 89f., n. 118.

39. Cf., e.g., Ramsay, "St. Paul and the Jewish Christians," 184. Acts 9:26-30 is considered merely a "Lucan edifice" by Haenchen, *Acts*, 335; for a defense see Fung, "Relationship between Righteousness and Faith," 2: 217, n. 325.

40. Some regard the two groups as identical (e.g., Burton 370-372), but it seems more natural to understand "all the apostles" as a larger group than "the Twelve" (e.g., K. H. Rengstorf, *TDNT* I: 422; Barrett, *Signs*, 38f.; Grosheide, *First Corinthians*, 352).

2. AN OATH OF TRUTHFULNESS (1:20)

20 *What I write is plain truth; before God I am not lying.*

20 Paul affirms with an oath that all that he is writing is plain truth. The insertion of this affirmation at this particular point suggests that "what I write" refers primarily to the report about his first visit to Jerusalem, and especially to his last sentence in v. 19.[41] But while the oath is prompted by the claim in v. 19 that he saw none of the other apostles, there is no reason to say that it refers exclusively to that.[42] On the contrary, since any suspicion that he is not telling the truth (particularly with reference to his Jerusalem visits) would have weakened his case, Paul's asseveration must apply to all that he is writing in the autobiographical section of his letter.

It has been observed that in Roman legal procedure the proffering of oaths in court was generally discouraged, unless it was absolutely necessary; here Paul takes the voluntary oath *(iusiurandum voluntarium)* as "a forceful and even dramatic means to emphasize both the seriousness of the issue and his own truthfulness."[43] It is with good reason that Paul took his own statements so seriously, for the very truth of the gospel as he understood it was at stake in the veracity of his narrative. The vehemence of his language also implies, probably, that a different account, which misrepresented the nature and purpose of his visits to Jerusalem, was current among the Galatian churches, and that he was eager to counter this with his statement of the facts.[44]

E. PAUL IN SYRIA AND CILICIA (1:21-24)

1. HIS NON-ACQUAINTANCE WITH THE CHURCHES OF JUDEA (1:21-22)

21 *Next I went to the regions of Syria and Cilicia,* 22 *and remained unknown by sight to Christ's congregations in Judaea.*

---

41. So Schlier 62.
42. Thus Burton 61 thinks that the reference is to everything from v. 13 or v. 15 on; cf. Betz 79, n. 216.
43. Sampley, "Before God," 481f.
44. Cf. Bligh 142; Bruce 102. More specifically, Sampley, "Before God," 481f. thinks that "the appearance of the oath immediately following his denial that he saw a wider group of apostles strongly suggests that Paul's opponents have claimed that during the visit in question Paul not only learned his gospel but also received some special—perhaps collective, official, apostolic—authorization to preach it."

21 Paul informs his readers that after his first post-conversion visit to Jerusalem he went into the regions of Syria and Cilicia.[1] "Regions" (Gk. *klimata*) is here (as in Rom. 15:23) used in the general sense of "territories," "districts," and not in the more technical sense of the administrative sub-divisions of a Roman province, which are designated by a different Greek word (singular *chōra,* as in Acts 16:6; 18:23). Syria had become a Roman province under Pompey in 64 B.C.; Cilicia consisted of two parts, of which the western part (Cilicia Tracheia) was allotted to a succession of client kings, while the eastern part (Cilicia Pedias, which included Paul's native Tarsus) was united administratively with Syria from about 25 B.C. to A.D. 72, when Vespasian recombined the two parts of Cilicia into a single province. Paul is thus strictly correct in speaking of Syria and Cilicia in the same breath, since in his time they constituted the one imperial province of Syria-Cilicia governed by a legate with his headquarters in Syrian Antioch (cf. Acts 15:23, 41, where the Greek has a single article governing both "Syria" and "Cilicia"—and, in v. 23, "Antioch" as well).[2]

The order in which they are mentioned does not necessarily represent—and, according to Acts 9:30; 11:25f., in fact does not represent—the order of Paul's visits, "Syria and Cilicia" being "probably a phrase of which the order was fixed by custom," somewhat similar to "England and Wales" today.[3] More probably still, Paul is referring to these regions as the spheres of his missionary activity, with Antioch and Tarsus as the respective centers: Syria, also closer to Jerusalem geographically, is mentioned first as the chief region of his evangelistic endeavors; then follows Cilicia, which was both farther from Jerusalem and of less significance to Paul.[4]

22 Throughout this period of activity in Syria and Cilicia, which 2:1 indicates to be some eleven to fourteen years, Paul remained "unknown by sight" to the churches of Judea. Since he regularly speaks of "churches" (plural) in a province or more extensive area (e.g., 1:2; 1 Cor. 16:1, 19; 2 Cor. 8:1; cf. Rom. 16:4, 16; 1 Cor. 11:16; 1 Thess. 2:14) but of the "church" (singular) in a city (e.g., 1 Cor. 1:2; 1 Thess. 1:1), "Judaea" here is probably to be taken as denoting the Roman province of Judea, and "the churches of Judea that are in Christ" (NIV) as identical with "the churches of God in Christ Jesus which are in Judea" (1 Thess. 2:14, RSV) and also

1. For the significance of "next" see above on v. 18.
2. Cf. E. M. B. Green and C. J. Hemer, *IBD* I: 288; Bruce, *Paul,* 33.
3. K. Lake, *BC* IV: 107. The same order appears in Acts 15:23 (with "Antioch" and under a single article), 41.
4. Schlier 62. According to J. Weiss as cited in Knox, *Chapters,* 59, Gal. 2:21 merely indicates the point from which Paul's work at that time began, but cannot be taken to mean that for the fourteen years he worked only in Syria and Cilicia. Weiss is correct in what he asserts, but what he denies is an inference rendered probable by the polemical context.

with "the church throughout all Judea and Galilee and Samaria" (Acts 9:31, RSV, where "Judea" plainly has the narrower sense of a division within Palestine).

These churches consisted of groups of Christians dispersed from Jerusalem by the persecution which followed Stephen's martyrdom, "together with others which had been formed through the evangelistic outreach of Jerusalem disciples even before that";[5] the composition of the church at Damascus as reflected in Acts 22:5[6] is illustrative of the sort of situation which could have similarly obtained in Palestine itself. The NEB description of these churches as "Christian congregations" treats the characteristic Pauline expression "in Christ" in a general sense (cf. RSV "of Christ") and not in its more technical, "incorporative" force (as in 3:26-28). The formula is added here probably, as in 1 Thess. 2:14, to distinguish the Christian churches from Jewish congregations.[7]

The reference to Judea here has been taken as distinguished from and excluding Jerusalem,[8] but this is difficult to sustain. Not only is such a distinction unsupported by any indication in the context and against the simple geographical fact that Jerusalem is naturally included in Judea, but Paul's polemical interests require that the church of Jerusalem be reckoned among the churches of Judea: he is at pains here to emphasize his independence of the *Jerusalem* authorities throughout the formative phase of his apostleship, and he would be defeating his purpose were he to exclude Jerusalem by an act of mental reservation from his reference to the churches of Judaea.[9]

Paul's statement seems to be in conflict with the account in Acts of the apostle's education in Jerusalem at the feet of Gamaliel and his persecution of the church in Jerusalem (Acts 22:3f., 18f.; 26:10f.) and equally with its record of his activities in Jerusalem during his first post-conversion visit (9:26-29). This apparent contradiction has led to the conclusion that Paul's persecution of the Church did not take place in Jerusalem but was centered in and around Damascus, that possibly he had never been in Jerusalem before his conversion, and that the Acts story must be rejected out of hand.[10] Such radical conclusions are neither satisfactory nor necessary.

On the other hand, it would not do to take the clause in Gal. 1:22 in the sense of "I was becoming unknown," meaning that in the course of ten

5. Bruce 103.
6. "The Christians there" (τοὺς ἐκεῖσε ὄντας) may have the sense of "those who had gone thither": cf. Bruce, *Book of Acts*, 440f. with n. 13.
7. For a dissenting opinion cf. K. L. Schmidt, *TDNT* III: 507.
8. E.g., Lightfoot 86, 92; Machen 82; Hendriksen 64, n. 40.
9. Cf. Bruce 103f.; "Is the Paul of Acts," 286; Haenchen, *Acts,* 297.
10. Cf. Haenchen, *Acts,* 297f.; Bultmann, *Faith and Understanding,* 220; Knox, *Chapters,* 36.

(or more) years' absence Paul gradually became a stranger to the Christians of Judea,[11] since it is difficult to read the idea of "becoming" out of the periphrastic construction, which simply emphasizes the durative nature of the action. In this instance the construction is doubtless best rendered "remained unknown" (Phillips "was still personally unknown"). The suggestion that the persecution had been directed primarily against the Hellenists and resulted in their expulsion, so that years later the persecutor was naturally unknown by sight to the remaining native Jewish Christians,[12] is faced with the double difficulty that (as explained above) "Judaea" probably refers to the whole of Palestine and that the other Judean churches were in large measure the original Jerusalem church in dispersion.

The real solution would seem to consist in the combination of several considerations: Paul is referring to the time when he departed for Syria and Cilicia and to the immediately ensuing period, thus saying that he was unknown *in his new identity as a Christian*; "by sight" might be better rendered "personally" (NEB mg., NIV);[13] and the emphasis falls on the phrase "to the churches" (RSV, NIV). All that Paul means, then, is that he went away to Syria-Cilicia without becoming personally acquainted with the churches of Judea, that during the years between that departure and his second Jerusalem visit he never went back among them and presented himself to these churches as a preacher of the gospel—in short, that, although he was privately known to individual members of the churches, yet to those churches as a whole he remained personally unknown since he never appeared in their assemblies as a preacher of the gospel.[14]

Two other considerations are worth mentioning: (a) We cannot assume that the victims of the persecution must have known the man who was carrying it on, since the actual harrying of the believers could have been done by underlings.[15] (b) The present verse confirms the picture given by Acts that Paul's persecuting activity was restricted to "two places and two only, Jerusalem and Damascus. . . . It is probable that it amounts to a lightning campaign in Jerusalem, which was about to be followed by another in Damascus, when his conversion intervened."[16]

Paul's reference to his remaining personally unknown to the Judean churches is intended to attest his independence of the Jerusalem authorities in one or more different ways: (a) Presumably Judea is where Paul would

11. Rendall 157.

12. Longenecker, *Paul*, 64, n. 226 (begins on 63).

13. Cf. R. Bultmann, *TDNT* I: 116; E. Lohse, *TDNT* VI: 776.

14. Cf. Machen, *Origin*, 50; Duncan 33; Ridderbos 71; Schlier 63; Hultgren, "Persecutions," 105-107.

15. Dibelius-Kümmel, *Paul*, 47.

16. Manson, *Studies*, 172f.

have worked had he received his missionary commission from the Jerusalem apostles. (b) Possibly the Jerusalem leaders whom he did not see at his first visit were engaged in missionary work in Judea, and Paul is saying that he was not known by them. (c) It may be simply that in those early years the apostles maintained a close contact with the churches throughout Palestine,[17] so that Paul's lack of personal acquaintance with the latter *ipso facto* meant the absence of any contact on his part with the apostles.

2. HIS PREOCCUPATION WITH PREACHING IN SYRIA-CILICIA (1:23-24)

23 They only heard it said, "Our former persecutor is preaching the good news of the faith which once he tried to destroy"; 24 and they praised God for me.

23 This and the following verse plainly imply what is a likely assumption in itself, namely, that in the regions of Syria and Cilicia (v. 21) Paul continued his preaching activity. Here he relates how the churches of Judea kept hearing[18] news of such activity. The reference to Paul as "our former persecutor" indicates that the words reported are the direct speech, not of the new converts in Syria and Cilicia, but of the Judean churches as they received and disseminated the news.[19]

The "good news of the faith" is in the original simply "faith" *(pistis);* the word is taken by many in an objective sense *(fides quae creditur)* as synonymous with the gospel message (thus NEB) or the body of Christian beliefs or Christianity.[20] On the other hand, the subjective meaning of the word *(fides qua creditur)* as faith in Jesus Christ,[21] which is its consistent meaning elsewhere in the epistle (cf. 2:16, 20; 3:7-9, 11f., 14, 22-26; 5:5; 6:10), would serve better as the object of "tried to destroy." Perhaps it is best, then, to regard "faith" as being used primarily in its subjective meaning, but possibly with a transition toward the objective sense.[22]

---

17. The suggestions, respectively, of Burton 63; Machen, *Origin*, 76; Foerster, "Δοκοῦντες," 290.
18. Ἀκούοντες ἦσαν, periphrastic imperfect, like ἤμην ἀγνοούμενος ("I remained unknown") in v. 22. The masculine participle refers to the members of the church.
19. Bruce 105.
20. So respectively R. Bultmann, *TDNT* VI: 213; Betz 81, n. 255; BAGD s.v. 2. d. α.
21. Preferred by, e.g., Thayer s.v. 1. b. αA; Machen 85.
22. Ridderbos 73f. The suggestion that πίστις here might mean "the body of believers" (Kilpatrick, "Peter," 322) is, despite the use of the same verb ("tried to destroy") here as in v. 13, most unlikely.

There is no reason to suppose that Paul's evangelistic efforts were confined to Jews; in fact, in accordance with the most natural understanding of v. 17—that Paul began preaching to Gentiles immediately after his conversion and call—we should understand the objects of his evangelistic activity in Syria and Cilicia to be Gentiles also, although Jews need not have been excluded. Paul's narrative here probably implies that his work in these regions was more fruitful than his previous efforts in Arabia.

24 As often as the Judean churches heard news of his preaching activity, says Paul, they glorified (the imperfect tense denotes repeated action) God "because of me" (RSV, NIV), that is, because of the transforming grace of God manifested in him.[23] From the viewpoint of his argument for his independence, Paul's reference to the Judean Christians' hearing about his evangelistic activity and glorifying God on his account represents something of a digression, yet it is not without its own purpose of showing (a) that his gospel is in harmony with that of the primitive Church,[24] so that the Judean Christians are cordial in their attitude towards him, and (b) that therefore the Judaizers whom he is opposing are both of recent development and out of harmony with the original gospel and with the original attitude of the Judean Christians.[25] In other words, it was the Judaizers, not Paul, who had deviated from the right path.

In these verses (21-24), as in the preceding (vv. 16-20), Paul is arguing that the facts of his life show that he was not and never had been in a subordinate position to the Jerusalem leaders. Thus once again he underlines the claim that he did not owe either his missionary commission or apostolic authority or the truth of his gospel to them; and this indirectly supports his positive claim (vv. 1, 12, 16) that he derived all from God's direct call and revelation of Jesus Christ.

---

23. "For me" is literally "in me"; for this causal sense of ἐν cf. 2 Thess. 1:10, citing LXX Is. 49:3; see also on 3:8 below. Bammel, "Galater 1, 23," 110f. suggests that in 1:23f. we have to do with an extract from a martyr's hymn of the early Church: the preaching of the faith he once persecuted represents the climax in the "scale" of the persecutor's confession and repentance represented in martyr aretalogies; thus Paul is answering the charge of having been a persecutor of Christians with a testimony from the same sphere as that from which the agitators had come.

24. This is underlined by the very structure of the statement in v. 23, where the pivotal phrase "the faith which" links the statements which precede and follow it, "is [now] preaching" and "once tried to destroy," which are antithetical both in their time references (Gk. νῦν, "now," is not represented in NEB translation of the first of these clauses) and in the actions they describe.

25. Cf., e.g., Burton 65f.; Pinnock 26.

F. PAUL'S SECOND POST-CONVERSION VISIT TO JERUSALEM (2:1-10)

1. THE TIME AND REASON FOR THE VISIT (2:1-2a)

1 *Next, fourteen years later, I went again to Jerusalem with Barnabas, taking Titus with us.* 2 *I went up because it had been revealed by God that I should do so.*

1 As in 1:18, 21, the word "next" implies that Paul is giving a strictly chronological narrative of events and omitting nothing of significance for his present apologetic purpose. Seen in this light, "again" indicates that the visit described here was absolutely Paul's second post-conversion visit to Jerusalem.[1] The close link with 1:21 also implies that it was from Syria-Cilicia, most probably from Antioch, that Paul and Barnabas set out for Jerusalem. The time of this visit is specified as "fourteen years later"—the fourteen years being reckoned either from the first visit or, like that visit itself, from Paul's conversion (see on 1:18). Which is the correct view must be decided on grounds other than reference to the different temporal construction used in this verse as compared with 1:18, since the change of preposition may be only stylistic.[2]

"With Barnabas" simply indicates that this time Paul had Barnabas as a colleague: it does not imply that he claims priority to Barnabas on this occasion. If nevertheless an impression to that effect might be gained, that is because Paul himself was "for his own consciousness the decisive party."[3] According to Luke, it was Barnabas who first introduced Paul to "the apostles" (Acts 9:26f.; see under 1:19 above), presumably vouching for the genuineness of his conversion, and who subsequently sought him out from his native Tarsus and invited him to become his partner in the work at Antioch (Acts 11:25f.). Barnabas apparently remained Paul's senior colleague as far as the initial stage of the missionary journey which they took together (note the order of the two names in Acts 11:30; 12:25; 13:1f., 7)—until, after the encounter with Elymas the sorcerer in Cyprus, Paul emerged as the leader of the group of missionaries (13:13, 43,

---

1. Πάλιν ("again") is certainly to be read; its absence in some witnesses is "either accidental or the result of scribal uncertainty concerning its precise significance in the context" (Metzger 591).
2. Here διά with genitive, RV "after the space of fourteen years," cf. NASB; in 1:18 μετά with accusative, RV "after three years," cf. NASB. G. B. Caird, *IDB* I: 606a remarks that the latter interpretation "would not have occurred to anyone if the more natural interpretation had not created a chronological problem." See p. 18 above for the opinions of C. J. Hemer and J. J. Gunther (n. 35).
3. Schlier 65 (my translation).

46, 50; the order in 14:12 probably reflects Barnabas's greater age and more imposing appearance).

Two visits to Jerusalem undertaken by Paul and Barnabas together are mentioned in Acts (11:27-30; 15:1-4), and the question naturally arises as to which, if either, of these visits is to be identified with the visit mentioned in Gal. 2:1. The majority view today identifies the visit of Gal. 2 with the conference-visit of Acts 15; the position adopted in this commentary is that the balance of probability favors identification of the visit of Gal. 2 with the famine-relief visit of Acts 11. This conclusion logically implies that this letter was written to the churches of South Galatia and is the earliest of Paul's extant letters.[4]

As for Titus (who, incidentally, is never mentioned in Acts), Paul's letters reveal that he was one of Paul's converts (Tit. 1:4) who became his close associate and, on occasions, his personal delegate, as in his successful handling of the delicate Corinthian situation both with regard to Paul's personal relationship with that church (2 Cor. 2:12f.; 7:5-16) and in the matter of its participation in the Jerusalem relief fund (2 Cor. 8:6–9:5; 12:18). The singular participle "taking" suggests that his inclusion in the present party was due to the initiative of Paul, who wished to bring him along as a representative of Gentile Christians (cf. v. 3).

2a When Paul says that he went up "because of" (NASB, cf. NEB) or "in response to" (NIV) a revelation (literally "in accordance with revelation"), it is not immediately clear whether in this particular instance the revelation—which can hardly refer to the "initial revelation of Jesus Christ" to Paul[5]—took the form of a prophet's words (as in Acts 11:28; cf. 1 Cor. 14:26, 29f., where prophetic utterances are called "revelation[s]"), of the command of the Spirit to the Church (as in Acts 13:2), or of a communication to Paul alone.[6] The last possibility is perhaps the most likely; since on his previous visit to Jerusalem Paul had received a revelation to leave the city (Acts 22:17-21), it was natural that he should not wish to return until another revelation authorized him to do so;[7] moreover,

---

4. See the discussion above, pp. 9–28.

5. Howard 38. Cf. the critique by Russell, "Convincing . . . ?" 163.

6. For the three possibilities cf., respectively, e.g., Neill 34; Manson, *Studies*, 177; and A. Oepke, *TDNT* II: 457 (cf. 458; III: 585; V: 235, n. 52). Against equating the "revelation" here with the Agabus prophecy of Acts 11:28, Catchpole, "Paul," 433 observes: "The Agabus prophecy must be presumed to have occurred some substantial time before the famine in order that the prediction-realization scheme might be appropriate. But such an interval would make it difficult to take the Agabus prophecy as the direct cause of Paul's visit to Jerusalem and therefore as the content of the ἀποκάλυψις." Catchpole thinks that Paul probably refers to "an ecstatic experience in the context of community worship (cf. I Cor. xiv.6, 26)."

7. Duncan 38; cf. G. Delling, *TDNT* VII: 765. See, however, H. Balz, *TDNT* VIII: 553, n. 60.

the Paul of Acts was not over-responsive to other people's revelations which affected himself [cf. Acts 21:10-14], and the Paul of the epistles—not least the Paul of this epistle—is so constantly aware of his unmediated authorization by Christ that it is natural to conclude that, when he did anything by revelation, the revelation was personally received.[8]

The important thing about his going up "by revelation" (AV, RV, RSV) lies, however, in its corollary, which is that he made this second visit neither on his own initiative, nor at the demand of the Jerusalem authorities as though he had to render an account of himself, nor simply because he had been commissioned by the church in Antioch to go.[9] The implication of this is plain: the Pauline mission, at the time of the second visit as at the time of the first, was independent of Jerusalem (or Antioch for that matter), and, as it was with his mission, so it was with his authority and his gospel.

2. LAYING THE GOSPEL BEFORE THE LEADERS (2:2b)

I laid before them—but at a private interview with the men of repute—the gospel which I am accustomed to preach to the Gentiles, to make sure that the race I had run, and was running, should not be run in vain.

2b The first question that arises from Paul's statement is whether "before them" refers to the Jerusalem Christians or "the men of repute" (on this expression see on v. 6 below). Put differently, the question is whether there was only the one private interview or whether there was also a public meeting of the church before whom Paul laid his gospel. (How the question can arise is more easily appreciable when Paul's statement is read in the Greek.) In support of the latter view, which is favored by many interpreters, E. D. Burton has put forth the following argument:[10]

Although an epexegetic limitation may certainly be conjoined to what precedes by *de* ["but"], yet it is Paul's usual habit in such cases to repeat the word which the added phrase is to limit (cf. *anebēn* ["I

---

8. Bruce, *Paul*, 151f. Cf. Harrison, *Introduction*, 277: "Paul would hardly use [the word] revelation for something communicated to him through another when throughout chapter 1 he has been using revelation only of that which came to him directly from the Lord (1:12, 15)."

9. Machen 94 rightly points out that church commission and divine revelation are not necessarily mutually exclusive: Paul's response to the church's request was decided on the basis of direct revelation from God.

10. Burton 71.

went up"] in this v.; Rom. 3:22; 9:30; I Cor. 1:16; 2:6; Phil. 2:8—in I Cor. 3:15 it is otherwise). In this case, moreover, it is difficult to suppose that Paul should have used the very general *autois* ["before them"] if, indeed, he meant only three men, or to see why if he referred to but one interview he should not have written simply *kai anethemēn tois dokousin to euangelion* ["and I laid before the men of repute the gospel"], etc.

This argument is not compelling, however, for the following reasons: (a) A careful study of the six references given as evidence reveals that four of them have to do with the repetition of a *noun* and are therefore not really parallel with the present instance;[11] in the remaining two the repetition of the *verb* seems to be due to the presence of some intervening clause.[12] But the present instance is more akin to 1 Cor. 3:15 where the verb is immediately modified by the following phrase. (b) Considering that Paul was dictating, not writing, these words, it is not impossible that *autois* ("them")[13] was uttered as a vague anticipatory reference to be more exactly defined in the following words and still more specifically in v. 9—the more so in view of the difficult style in vv. 3-5, which may be due not merely to the fact of dictation but also to the emotional state of the author.[14] (c) It would seem precarious to dictate what an author should write in order to convey a certain meaning: it is better to ask whether that particular meaning is excluded by what is actually written—which does not seem to be the case here. (d) Paul's "privately" (AV, RV, RSV, NIV; *kat' idian*) lacks a corresponding "publicly" (*dēmosią* or *en koinǭ*). This shows that he did not have in mind a meeting with the church apart from and in addition to his meeting with the apostles.[15] (e) It is difficult to see why Paul should have, or indeed could have, set the gospel before the Jerusalem *Christians,* when his repeated insistence in the context is that he was independent of the Jerusalem *authorities.* For these reasons, it seems preferable to regard "but at a private interview" as epexegetical of "I laid before them," and as indicating that there was only the one

---

11. In these cases (Rom. 3:22; 9:30; 1 Cor. 2:6; Phil. 2:8) the noun simply has to be repeated in order to pick up its antecedent before being further described by the qualifying phrase. The repetition is rendered the more necessary in Rom. 3:22 by the intervening v. 21b and in Rom. 9:30 by the emphasis required, while in Phil. 2:8 it is an integral part of the poetic structure.

12. Thus Gal. 2:1b before ἀνέβην ("I went up") in 2:2; 1 Cor. 1:15 before ἐβάπτισα ("I did baptize") in 1:16.

13. A case of *constructio ad sensum:* BDF §282.1.

14. Nor is it impossible that, as Schlier 67 suggests, "them" = "the men of repute" here refers to the leading men of the church—the apostles—of whom the three in v. 9 were only the most prominent, although we think it more natural to take the δοκοῦντες in all three verses (2, 6, 9) as the same three men: so Foerster, "Δοκοῦντες," 286; cf. Barrett, "Paul and the 'Pillar' Apostles," 1.

15. Schlier 67, n. 1.

private interview at which Paul communicated his gospel to the apostles.[16] Presumably Paul thought that he might get a more sympathetic hearing for his law-free gospel at a private interview with the Jerusalem leaders than he would at a general meeting of the church.

It has been suggested that the phrase "in private" (NASB) implies that "the men of repute," on account of the persecution described in Acts 12, were in hiding and Paul had to confer with them one by one in their different hiding-places.[17] But the first part of this assertion may be doubted on the grounds that the death in A.D. 44 of Herod Agrippa I, who instituted the persecution, must have preceded the visit of Paul and Barnabas by some years and that James the Lord's brother does not seem to have been affected by the persecution (Acts 12:17).[18] Furthermore, the second part of this assertion hardly tallies with the impression conveyed by the most natural reading of Gal. 2:6-9, especially of the plural participles and verbs.

Paul laid his gospel before the apostles—not, as has been maintained, "with the request for counsel, approval or decision,"[19] but simply for their consideration.[20] Perhaps the idea of "decision" is justified to the extent that the Jerusalem authorities had to decide what they were to do with the gospel set before them—but only in the sense, it would seem, that "they could either accept it or reject it; there was no other alternative."[21] If even at the first visit at least a decade earlier there was already no question of Paul's seeking the apostles' authorization for his mission or message, this was even more out of the question at the later date of this second visit.[22]

But Paul did set his gospel before the apostles, and this was done, he says, "for fear that I was running or had run my race in vain" (NIV).[23] The

16. So, e.g., Schlier 67; Orchard, "Problem," 379f.; Ropes 31; Cole 62; Hollander, de Jonge, and Tuinstra, "New Type of Help," 344f. Bruce, "Conference," 197, 201 takes Gal. 2:2 as a reference to a private meeting between Paul and the Jerusalem leaders which took place in advance of the the conference proper in the absence of Barnabas and vv. 6-10 as a reference to the conference proper, at which Barnabas was present. But the use of the first person singular throughout vv. 1-9b (barring the parenthetical verses 4-5, on which see below) would seem to militate against the suggestion that two different meetings are in view in vv. 2-3 and vv. 6-10.

17. Geyser, "Paul," 131.

18. For the true order of the events recorded in Acts 12 see pp. 20f. above.

19. J. Behm, *TDNT* I: 353; rightly criticized by Schmithals, *Paul and James,* 40f.

20. Cf. Thayer s.v. ἀνατίθημι; BAGD s.v. 2; and especially Dunn, "Relationship," 466-468.

21. Cole 62.

22. The present tense "I am accustomed to preach"—in the original simply "I preach" (AV, RV, RSV, NASB, NIV)—shows that Paul's gospel had suffered no change from the time of this visit to the time of his writing.

23. On the expression "running . . . in vain" see A. Oepke, *TDNT* III: 660; O. Bauernfeind, *TDNT* VIII: 231.

Greek phrase rendered "for fear that" (*mē pōs,* also in 4:11) indicates "the accompanying and determining feeling of apprehension"[24] with which Paul communicated his gospel to the Jerusalem authorities; positively expressed, his concern was to assure that they would recognize his converts as genuine Christians and members of the Church.[25] He was concerned, in other words, with officially securing the freedom of the Gentiles from the requirements of the law and their equality of status with Jewish Christians.

Implicit in this concern for Gentile freedom was concern for the unity of the Church: Paul's anxiety was not lest refusal of recognition on the part of the Jerusalem authorities should thereby render his own work invalid and his Gentile Christians non-Christian, but lest such refusal should bring about a rupture of the one Church into two separate branches of Jewish and Gentile Christianity.[26] That Paul valued the unity of the Church highly is shown by the indefatigable efforts with which he was to organize the Gentile collection for the mother-church (cf. 1 Cor. 16:1-4; 2 Cor. 8–9; Rom. 15:25-28). Therefore, while he strongly asserted his independence of Jerusalem, he desired no dissociation from Jerusalem. Indeed, he believed that his Gentile apostolate could not be effectively discharged except in fellowship with Jerusalem: a cleavage between his Gentile mission and the mother-church of Jerusalem would mean a divided Christ (cf. 1 Cor. 1:13) and thus a frustrating of his purpose in all his previous and present efforts in the evangelization of the Gentiles.[27]

3. TITUS NOT CIRCUMCISED (2:3-5)

3 *Yet even my companion Titus, Greek though he is, was not compelled to be circumcised.* 4 *That course was urged only as a concession to certain sham-Christians, interlopers who had stolen in to spy upon the liberty we enjoy in the fellowship of Christ Jesus. These men wanted to bring us into bondage,* 5 *but not for one moment did I yield to their dictation; I was determined that the full truth of the Gospel should be maintained for you.*

24. BDF §370.2; cf. Schlier 67 as against Ridderbos 89, n. 9.
25. Manson, *Studies,* 174f. *Pace* Betz 88, who takes "running . . . in vain" unnaturally, as a reflection of "the present concern of the Galatians," which is "also the concern of the opposition."
26. So, e.g., Burton 73; Bring 61ff.; cf. Garnet, "Qumran," 26f.; and especially Dunn, "Relationship," 468. Beker, *Paul,* 90 speaks of "a divided apostolate, [which] was unthinkable to Paul (1 Cor. 5:11)," rather than a divided Church.
27. Cf. Bruce, *NT History,* 254; "Galatian Problems. 1," 303; "Paul and Jerusalem," 9; *Paul,* 152; Neill 35. For criticisms of the interpretations of Schlier 66-69, and Munck, *Paul,* 108f. see, respectively, Schmithals, *Paul and James,* 40; and Fung 100-102; "Relationship between Righteousness and Faith," 1: 220-222 with 2: 227.

3 The account of what actually took place at the private meeting with the Jerusalem leaders (v. 2) seems to be interrupted by a digression and is not resumed until v. 6. Here Paul notes what did *not* take place: Titus was not compelled to be circumcised, "Greek though he is." The latter clause correctly renders the Greek phrase[28] as concessive (so also RSV, NASB, NIV) rather than causal (Phillips) and implies that from the purely Jewish viewpoint the demand for circumcision would most readily apply to Titus as a person of Gentile origin,[29] who was, moreover, present as Paul's companion. The choice of the verb "compelled" *(anankazein)* has been taken to imply that the circumcision of Titus was strongly pressed on Paul and Barnabas, so that "was not compelled" denies not the attempt but only the success of the attempt;[30] furthermore, the context is said to imply clearly that the attempt was made (albeit unsuccessfully). This assumes that vv. 4f. belong with v. 3 to the same occasion; together these verses describe something which happened during the meeting, with Titus as a test case.

A difficulty with this usual supposition, however, has been noted by T. W. Manson:[31]

> The difficulty is that if Titus was a test case, Paul's account of it is utterly inept. Either Titus was circumcised or he was not. If he was not, it should have been simple to say so outright: "Certain false brethren wanted to have Titus circumcised, but I put my foot down." If he was circumcised, the fact would be well advertised in Galatia by Paul's opponents, and the involved and stumbling verbiage of these verses would be worse than useless as camouflage for that nasty fact.

It would seem preferable, therefore, to follow Manson and others[32] in referring vv. 4f. to an event which took place not at this Jerusalem meeting but on a subsequent occasion—as we gather, at Antioch (cf. Acts 15:1, 24)[33]—and of which Paul is reminded by his mention of Titus and circumcision.

---

28. Ἕλλην ὤν, which Moule 102 speaks of as "the most notorious instance" of ambiguity between concessive and causal; cf. MHT 3: 157.

29. Cf. H. Windisch, *TDNT* II: 515.

30. E.g., Ellicott 25f.; Lightfoot 105; Burton 76; Betz 88, n. 294.

31. *Studies*, 175f.

32. Orchard, "Problem"; Geyser, "Paul," 132-134; Bruce 111, 115-117. Their view is opposed by, e.g., Schmithals, *Paul and James*, 107, n. 14; Smith, "Problems," 118.

33. Bauckham, "Barnabas," 70, n. 20 rightly observes that "the first person plural includes Barnabas in 2:5, 9, 10"; from this he concludes that 2:4f. "cannot be a parenthetical reference to the later event at Antioch . . . because Barnabas did not then withstand the false brethren." This objection no longer applies if 2:4f. in fact refers to the period immediately before the Jerusalem Council, when Barnabas and Paul were united in their stand against the demands of the Judaizers (cf. Acts 15:2), and if Paul's οὐδὲ εἴξαμεν ("we did not yield," Gal. 2:5) can be regarded as a true plural which includes Barnabas.

This being the case, the verb "compelled" is better understood of the necessity of, rather than the attempt at, having Titus circumcised.[34] If it be insisted that the verb must contain the notion of pressure, then it might be suggested that the word is chosen in anticipation of the subsequent occasion at Antioch (cf. 2:14, where the verb appears again—NEB "insist") with a possible side-glance also at the situation in Galatia at the time of Paul's writing (cf. 6:12, where the verb appears in connection, again, with the issue of circumcision). On the understanding, then, that v. 3 belongs to the time of the private conference but vv. 4f. to a later occasion, the three verses together mean that the issue of compulsory circumcision did not even arise on the earlier occasion, though Titus, a Greek of Gentile origin, was present; and that it was brought up only at a later period as a result of the machinations of certain pseudo-Christians.

Even if vv. 4f. are taken closely with v. 3 as belonging to the same occasion, it is difficult to conclude from the text that Titus *was* circumcised. The reading which omits the words "not even" (with or without "to whom")[35] at the beginning of v. 5 does not have adequate textual support, and is immediately rendered suspect by the greatly simplified structure which results from its acceptance.[36] To take the expression "we did not yield submission" (RSV) to imply that Paul voluntarily accepted the suggestion of Titus's circumcision[37] involves treating the Greek phrase[38] as equivalent in sense to the adverb "submissively"[39]—a highly doubtful procedure.[40] And to suggest that Titus accepted circumcision of his own accord without prior consultation with Paul[41] raises the question why Paul does not then declare himself free from being responsible for Titus's circumcision. To all these views the caveat raised by Manson equally applies, as does the further objection that it is incomprehensible how the circumcision of a Gentile Christian (voluntarily accepted whether by Paul or Titus) could be interpreted by Paul as an act by which the truth of the gospel was to be maintained for the Gentiles.[42] We are bound to conclude, therefore, that Titus was *not* circumcised.

---

34. Cf. Schlier 69f.
35. I.e., omitting οὐδέ or οἷς οὐδέ; cf. AV, RV, RSV; Lake, *Earlier,* 277ff.; BC V: 197.
36. Cf. Metzger 591f.; Ellicott 27.
37. E.g., Duncan 43ff.; Gunther, *Paul,* 52; D. W. B. Robinson, "Circumcision."
38. Τῇ ὑποταγῇ: "by way of the subjection (demanded)" (Burton 84). Betz 91, n. 320 observes that "as a pleonasm the expression is emphatic."
39. Thus Moule 45; MHT 3: 220.
40. Rightly, Burton 84f.
41. E.g., Nock, *Paul,* 109.
42. Linton, "Third Aspect," 87. *Pace* Walker, "Timothy-Titus," 233a (cf.

Now if even in such an obvious case as Titus Paul did not yield to circumcision, or rather, if the question of compulsory circumcision was not even raised by the Jerusalem leaders, then it is clear that Gentile Christians were under no obligation to accept circumcision. "The non-circumcision of Titus, therefore, was in reality a decision of the principle."[43]

4 Verse 4a is more literally rendered in the RSV: "But because of false brethren secretly brought in" (RSV). One view would connect this phrase with the main verbs in v. 2, the resultant sense being that Paul went up to Jerusalem and laid his gospel before the leaders there, not because he needed their approval, but on account of the propaganda of the false brethren;[44] this involves taking v. 3 as a parenthetical assertion, which seems unnatural. It is preferable to assume that the main clause is missing (Paul is dictating under considerable emotion) and to supply, in accordance with our understanding that vv. 4f. refer to a later incident at Antioch, a clause such as "the question of circumcising Gentile converts was first raised."[45] The false brethren are contemptuously described both as having been "secretly brought in" (RSV; Gk. *pareisaktous*) and as having "sneaked in" (NASB; Gk. *pareisēlthon*)—two expressions which reinforce each other in emphasizing the furtiveness, or at least the intrusiveness, of their action.[46]

These "interlopers" Paul roundly condemns as "sham-Christians," that is, persons who called themselves and were probably regarded by others as Christians but whose conduct in fact falsified their claim to be Christian. Paul charges them with having infiltrated the ranks of the Gentile Christians (at Antioch) "to spy out our liberty which we have in Christ Jesus, in order to bring us into bondage" (NASB). The word translated "spy out" *(kataskopēsai)* "carries the nuance of inquiry with a claim to the right of supervision," and may contain an ironical reference to use of *episkopēsai* ("to supervise") by the false brethren (or the Galatian heretics).[47]

233b): "it is by no means clear whether Titus himself was or was not circumcised or, if he was, whether this was or was not done as an act of 'subjection' on the part of Paul."

43. Burton 75 (although, as we understand the situation, no actual decision was involved since the question was not even raised).

44. Machen 103f.

45. Bruce 116 (where this clause is in italics). For other suggestions see Orchard, "Problem," 381; Geyser, "Paul," 132. On the ellipsis in v. 4 see further the debate between J. B. Orchard ("Ellipsis"; "Once Again") and A. C. M. Blommerde ("Ellipsis"). The way the ellipsis is filled in NEB (cf. NIV) suggests that v. 4 is taken closely with v. 3. Zerwick §467 favors taking v. 4a and v. 6a as parallel clauses both dependent on the main clause in v. 3, but the great distance separating the two initial particles δέ ("but") makes this suggestion highly unlikely.

46. Cf. W. Michaelis, *TDNT* V: 825 with n. 14.

47. E. Fuchs, *TDNT* VII: 417 with n. 1.

In speaking of "our liberty" Paul identifies himself closely with the Gentile churches; the "liberty which we have in Christ Jesus" (NASB) refers concretely to the freedom from the necessity of circumcision for justification before God, a freedom which is based on the atoning work of Christ and appropriated by faith in that atoning work.[48] Correspondingly, the aim of the infiltrators—"to bring us into bondage"[49]—is to bring the Gentile Christians under bondage to the law, of which the act of circumcision is the epitome (cf. 5:3). It thus emerges that the interlopers were sham-Christians precisely because they had not really grasped the fundamental principle of the gospel—justification by faith apart from works of the law.

5 As suggested already, the bogus-Christians of v. 4 are in all probability to be linked with the Judaizers of Acts 15:1, 24, who came down to Antioch and taught the Gentile Christians that circumcision according to the law of Moses was necessary for salvation; it was the ensuing dispute over this matter at Antioch that led to the Jerusalem Council. There the same question was debated further by the leaders of the Church, including the apostles (Acts 15:2ff.). In the present verse, Paul informs his readers that he resolutely opposed the Judaizers' efforts: "We did not give in to them for a moment, so that the truth of the gospel might remain with you" (NIV).

In view of the consistent use of the first person singular in vv. 1, 2, 6, 7 the plural "we did not yield" (RSV) is not likely to be an instance of the editorial "we" (as NEB takes it); in saying "we" Paul may be once again identifying himself with the Gentile Christians (in this instance, those at Antioch), or else he is speaking of himself and his colleagues.[50] "Not for one moment" underlines the absoluteness of their unyielding attitude in face of the Judaizers' demands. The purpose of their firm stand is that the "truth of the Gospel" ("full" is an unnecessary addition) might remain securely in the possession of the Gentile Christians, specifically the Gentile Christians of Galatia.[51] It is clearly implied that for Paul and his colleagues to have yielded "an inch" (Phillips)[52] to the demand for circumcision of Gentile Christians would have meant letting the truth of the gospel—which speaks of justification by faith alone, apart from legal works—be wrested from their hands. This uncompromising identification of the principle of justification by faith with the "truth of the Gospel" makes it all the more intelligible why Paul should have pronounced such a severe verdict on the preachers of a different "gospel" (see under 1:8f. above).

48. Cf. Schlier 71f.; *TDNT* II: 497.
49. On ἵνα with future indicative in final clauses, see Burton, *Syntax,* §198.
50. Among whom Barnabas could be included; cf. n. 33 above.
51. On the meaning of "truth" here cf. A. C. Thiselton, *NIDNTT* III: 884; R. Bultmann, *TDNT* I: 242; and on the absolute use of "gospel" here and in 2:14 see G. Friedrich, *TDNT* II: 729 with n. 65.
52. Literally "for an hour"—the smallest unit of time (cf. Mk. 13:11, 32).

4. NOTHING ADDED TO PAUL (2:6)

6 *But as for the men of high reputation (not that their importance matters to me: God does not recognize these personal distinctions)— these men of repute, I say, did not prolong the consultation. . . .*

6 The truth implied in v. 3—that Gentile Christians were under no obligation to accept circumcision—is put in a slightly different way when Paul next states (after the parenthetical vv. 4f.), also negatively, that the Jerusalem leaders "added nothing" (RSV) to him. The repetition of the expression "men of high reputation" from v. 2 (where NEB has "men of repute" for the same Greek expression)[53] seems to indicate that it is a title given by the Jerusalem church to its leaders,[54] which Paul uses, possibly with a tinge of irony,[55] in depreciation of the arrogant and extravagant claims which the Judaizers were making for the Jerusalem leaders.[56]

Of these leaders Paul says parenthetically: "what they were makes no difference to me; God shows no partiality" (RSV).[57] Whether the particle *pote* is taken temporally ("once," "formerly," as apparently in RSV, NASB, NEB) or as simply having an intensive force ("whatever," as in NIV),[58] the past tense "were" probably refers, not to the time of Paul's second post-conversion visit in Jerusalem, but to the pre-resurrection period of the apostles' lives.[59] To "show partiality" is to "show regard for a person";[60] when this clause is used of God in reference to humans, it connotes deference on his part toward particular persons on account of some supposed advantage or "importance" possessed by them—the statement

53. According to D. Müller, *NIDNTT* III: 822, the expression οἱ δοκοῦντες ("men of repute") "is often found of a recognized authority in extra-biblical literature."
54. Barrett, "Paul and the 'Pillar' Apostles," 4f., 12, 17. An alternative suggestion is that the expression was a slogan coined by Paul's opponents in referring to the Jerusalem authorities (e.g., G. Kittel, *TDNT* II: 233). The participle δοκοῦντες refers to their present status in the estimation of the Judaizers, i.e., at the time of Paul's writing (Lightfoot 28, n. 1, 107; Guthrie 82), rather than their status at the time of Paul's second visit (Schmithals, *Paul and James*, 83f., n. 13).
55. So, e.g., K. L. Schmidt, *TDNT* III: 508; U. Wilckens, *TDNT* VII: 735; over against G. Kittel, *TDNT* II: 233, who sees "no reason to suspect irony."
56. The expression thus "allows Paul both to acknowledge the fact that these men possess authority and power and to remain at a distance with regard to his own subservience to such authority" (Betz 92). For criticism of the interpretation of the δοκοῦντες in this verse offered by Foerster, "Δοκοῦντες," 287f., cf. Fung 108f.; "Relationship between Righteousness and Faith," 2: 228f., n. 411.
57. On διαφέρει ("matters") as a "proverbial present" see Betz 94.
58. Cf. AV, RV; BDF §303; MHT 3: 196.
59. Schlier 75.
60. Cf. E. Lohse, *TDNT* VI: 779f. The Greek phrase is πρόσωπον λαμβάνειν, here and Lk. 20:21, literally "to lift the face [of a suppliant]"; cf. Mt. 22:16 par. Mk. 12:14, βλέπειν εἰς πρόσωπον, "to look on the face."

being, of course, that he does *not* give such deference.[61] Paul says that God does not regard the apostles with special favor because of some "personal distinctions" on their part—the distinctions in question having to do chiefly with their personal acquaintance (perhaps also their special relationship) with the earthly Jesus. To Paul, personal acquaintance with the earthly Jesus (cf. Acts 1:21f.) was not an indispensable prerequisite of apostleship: a personal encounter with the risen Christ and commission by him were accounted sufficient qualification (cf. 1 Cor. 9:1; 2 Cor. 11:5; 12:11f.; and see under 1:1 above).

The strong emotion under which Paul writes, already apparent from the parenthetical statement in v. 6, is further indicated by the change of construction from "as for the men of high reputation" to "these men of repute."[62] Those men, according to the NEB rendering, "did not prolong the consultation"; this takes the verb in question *(prosanatithesthai)* in a similar sense to that which it had in 1:16 ("consult").[63] But in view of the different context here, the more usual translation is to be preferred: the men of repute, Paul relates, "added nothing to me" (RSV; RV "imparted," NASB "contributed"). Here the verb recalls the cognate verb "I laid" *(anatithesthai)* in v. 2 and should probably be interpreted in connection with it: Paul laid his gospel before the men of repute for their consideration, and they on their part fully accepted it, having nothing to add by way of modification or amplification.[64] Therefore, v. 6 has to do primarily with Paul's gospel (cf. NIV); the fact that nothing was added to it by the Jerusalem apostles, like the fact of Titus's freedom from circumcision, means that Paul's law-free gospel was fully accepted and endorsed by the other apostles. It is possible, however, that the sense may be wide enough to mean that nothing was conferred on Paul over and above what he already possessed, so that the thought includes the ideas of both gospel truth and missionary commission.[65]

61. This is evidence against Munck's reading of the parenthetical statement as a sword-thrust from Paul to the effect that the "pillars," too, had a checkered past (*Paul*, 99).

62. "As for" (so also NIV) is literally "from" (RV, RSV, NASB). On the change see further BDF §467.

63. Cf. J. Behm, *TDNT* I: 353 (s.v. προσανατίθημι).

64. The emphatic "to me" (placed in the original at the beginning of the sentence) may be understood in the light of the observation that "it is in Galatians that the ἐγώ ["I"] expresses most clearly opposition to the authority of others and the assertion of Paul's own authority" (E. Stauffer, *TDNT* II: 356, cf. n. 115). Here the opposition is not to the authority of the other apostles as such, but to their authority as claimed and interpreted by the Judaizers (cf. Moffatt, "Critics," 76).

65. For the suggestion that the choice of the word "added" reflects the awkwardness of Paul's position, see Dunn, "Relationship," 469, cf. 472f.

5. AGREEMENT OVER DIVISION OF LABOR (2:7-9)

. . . 7 but on the contrary acknowledged that I had been entrusted with the Gospel for Gentiles as surely as Peter had been entrusted with the Gospel for Jews. 8 For God whose action made Peter an apostle to the Jews, also made me an apostle to the Gentiles.

9 Recognizing, then, the favour thus bestowed upon me, those reputed pillars of our society, James, Cephas, and John, accepted Barnabas and myself as partners, and shook hands upon it, agreeing that we should go to the Gentiles while they went to the Jews.

These verses, the main statement of which is in v. 9,[66] state the positive outcome of the meeting. The designation of James, Cephas, and John as "those reputed pillars of our society"—or, following the original more closely,[67] "those reputed to be pillars" (NIV)—presupposes the idea of the Church as God's temple.[68] Far from adding anything to Paul's gospel or conferring any authority on him, these "pillars" are said to have done three things, the first two providing the basis for the third.

66. They "gave to me and Barnabas the right hand of fellowship" (RSV).

67. Οἱ δοκοῦντες στῦλοι εἶναι, possibly a combination of the earlier expressions in vv. 2, 6 (οἱ δοκοῦντες, οἱ δοκοῦντες εἶναί τι) with the honorific title "the pillars": Betz 99, n. 404.

68. Cf. Eph. 2:21; 1 Pet. 2:4-7; Rev. 21:14; U. Wilckens, *TDNT* VII: 734f.

According to one suggestion, the title "pillars" originally had an eschatological connotation, referring to "the pillars of the eschatological temple" (Barrett, "Paul and the 'Pillar' Apostles," 13f.; dismissed by Schoeps, *Paul,* 73, n. 2 as "not probable"), and its origination was connected with the ascription to Simon of the name "Cephas," "Peter," "the Rock" (Mt. 16:18; cf. Barrett, *Signs,* 70). According to another suggestion, the three "pillars" were modelled on the three patriarchs Abraham, Isaac, and Jacob and their foundational role for Judaism (Aus, "Three Pillars").

Possibly the original "pillars" were Peter and the two sons of Zebedee, James and John (cf. Mk. 5:37; 9:2; 14:33), but after the execution of James by Herod Agrippa I (Acts 12:1f.) his place was taken by his namesake (Bruce 123). It has also been suggested (Annand, "Note") that Paul is here referring to the three *metae* (turning posts or markers around which chariots or runners raced) in the Roman arena; but this, like the further notion that στῦλοι ("pillars") is a playful pun on ἀπόστολοι ("apostles"), the link being provided by στῆλαι ("pillars"), must be considered far-fetched. It is equally unconvincing to see a connection between the "pillars" here and the three priests of the community council at Qumran (1QS 8.1; cf., e.g., Greig, "Eschatological," 123).

In the view of Bruce 121, "the identity of the sequence of names with the traditional order of the catholic epistles of James, Peter and John in the NT canon may be nothing more than a coincidence." On the other hand, Lührmann, "Gal 2 9," 70-72 maintains that not only their arrangement, but their acceptance into the NT canon, had some connection with the list of names in Gal. 2:9: "the intention of the expansion of the epistles section of the New Testament beyond the Pauline corpus" by the inclusion of those seven letters was "to document the common testimony of the [four] apostles to the teaching of the church" (72, my translation).

7-8 First, they saw that Paul had been entrusted with the gospel for the Gentiles just as Peter had been with the gospel for the Jews. Paul explains his having been entrusted with the gospel equally with Peter by reference to the fact that God was equally at work in both cases, enabling the two men to prosecute effectively their task as apostles: the word "for" *(gar)* shows that the effectiveness of their apostolic work is adduced as the positive proof of their apostolic commission.[69] Because the noun *apostolē* ("apostleship") does not appear in connection with Paul in v. 8b, which has simply "for me also to the Gentiles" (NASB), as it does in connection with Peter (v. 8a), it has been thought that "the apostles recognized his gospel as equal with theirs, but they never recognized him as 'apostle.'"[70] It is much more reasonable, however, particularly in view of the apologetic purpose of the passage, to understand the shorter phrase used of Paul as an abbreviation of a fuller expression which is parallel to what is said about Peter (cf. NIV).[71]

Verse 7 (in conjunction with vv. 8f.) has been taken to imply that there were two gospels, a Petrine gospel and a Pauline gospel, which represented a "theological antithesis"[72] or at least contained important differences in content.[73] Actually, however, the so-called Petrine gospel is merely the gospel as Peter preached it to the Jews, with the particular approach and emphasis appropriate to Jewish audiences, just as the so-called Pauline gospel is the same gospel as Paul proclaimed it among the Gentiles, with the particular approach and emphasis appropriate to Gentile audiences. Certainly our passage makes no suggestion that Paul and the Jerusalem authorities preached two different gospels;[74] the subject under discussion at the meeting was not the content of the gospel (cf. v. 6) but the respective

69. There is no preposition in the original before "Peter" or "me," so that the idea is probably not so much of God working effectively "in" them (cf. AV) as of God making their ministry effective (cf. RSV, NASB, NIV; Burton 94; Wuest 65). Correspondingly, the noun ἀποστολή ("apostleship") seems to refer to the discharge of their apostolic office (Ridderbos 89) rather than to the fact of their commissioning (as apparently in NEB; cf. K. H. Rengstorf, *TDNT* I: 446). According to Räisänen, "Legalism," 78 "the reference to divine 'energy' surely includes miracles and other charismatic phenomena"; this is a plausible but not necessary inference from the text.

70. Betz 98.

71. I.e., to regard εἰς τὰ ἔθνη ("to the Gentiles") as an abbreviation of εἰς ἀποστολὴν τῶν ἐθνῶν ("for [the discharge of his] apostleship to the Gentiles"). Cf. Hendriksen 83, n. 58.

72. R. Meyer, *TDNT* VI: 83.

73. Fridrichsen, "Apostle," 9ff.; Burton 91f. Cf. Martyn, "Mission," 308: "Peter pursues *the* mission to the Jews (Law-observant); Paul pursues *the* mission to the Gentiles (Law-free)."

74. The genitive constructions τῆς ἀκροβυστίας and τῆς περιτομῆς are simply genitives of indirect object (MHT 3: 211), meaning respectively "for the uncircumcision = Gentiles" and "for the circumcision = Jews," as in NEB (which, however, by printing

spheres of activity to be assigned to the two parties. Every indication is given in the context that the gospel preached by Paul (and Barnabas) was in all essentials the same as that which Peter, James, and John understood the gospel to be: thus, there is one and only one gospel (1:7, 8f.); Paul's preaching was identical with that of the primitive Church (1:23); the issue of circumcision was not raised even in the obvious case of Titus (2:3); and Peter and Paul had the same knowledge of the way of salvation (2:16).[75]

It is noteworthy that in vv. 7f. the name Peter appears instead of Cephas, which is the Aramaic form used elsewhere in Galatians and throughout Paul's other letters.[76] One suggestion is that the exceptional use of the name comes from an underlying official record of the meeting, but such a view has met with objections.[77] A discrepancy has also been detected between the status of Peter as described in vv. 7f. (where he alone is mentioned) and in v. 9 (where he appears second in the list of three), but no diminution in the status of Peter need be implied in the transition from vv. 7f. to v. 9, since in the parallel statements about Paul no diminution in his status in favor of Barnabas is implied.[78]

9 The second thing Paul says about the "pillars" is that they recognize "the favour thus bestowed upon me." In the light of vv. 7f. the "favour" (literally "grace"; Gk. *charis*) refers to the privilege of apostleship (cf. Rom. 1:5; Eph. 3:8).[79] The "pillars' " insight or perception spoken of in v. 7a *(idontes)* and their recognition or acknowledgment spoken of in v. 9a *(gnontes)*[80] lead to the third thing said of them, which is clearly expressed in

---

"Gospel" with a capital G, might lend itself to the idea that Paul refers to two different gospels). Cf. Barrett 105.

75. Interestingly, Betz 49 speaks of there being two gospels between which, however, the conference agreed, "there is no material difference." On this question of "two gospels" cf. further Fung, "Revelation and Tradition," 34-37.

76. Differently, Kilpatrick has recently suggested that "the original text of Galatians had Πέτρος throughout Gal 1:18–2:14 and that the variants with Κηφᾶς at Gal 1:18; 2:9, 11, 14 are secondary"; "someone assimilated the passages in Galatians to 1 Corinthians [1:12; 3:22; 9:5; 15:5]" ("Peter," 319, 326).

77. According to Kilpatrick, "Peter," 326, the reading Κηφᾶς does not occur in these verses because, "on the evidence, correctors were not always systematic" (cf. previous note); he thinks it also possible that "the reading Κηφᾶς once existed at Gal 2:7, 8 but has not survived in our manuscripts."

78. Bruce 123. For a discussion of both issues mentioned in this paragraph see Fung, "Note."

79. Schlier 78; *pace* Betz 99.

80. Burton 95 thinks: "It is an overrefinement to attempt to discover a marked difference between ἰδόντες ["seeing"] and γνόντες ["knowing"]." Erickson, "ΟΙΔΑ and ΓΙΝΩΣΚΩ," 117, 121 also takes them as synonymous; but some distinction such as that suggested here seems reasonable.

the rest of v. 9 in NEB, where the word "go" (supplied by the translators) obviously connotes missionary activity.[81]

But how was the agreement—granted that it had to do with the division of the mission field—understood by the contracting parties? Some understand this division ethnographically: Paul and Barnabas would preach to Gentiles, Peter and the others would preach to Jews, whether outside or within the regions where Paul preached to the Gentiles.[82] But this understanding is difficult to square with Paul's own testimony that his evangelistic efforts were directed towards Jews as well as Gentiles (1 Cor. 9:20), which is corroborated by the evidence of Acts, in which Paul is depicted as invariably beginning his missionary work in any city, wherever possible, with the Jewish synagogue. Others take the division to be strictly geographical, or mainly geographical rather than ethnic;[83] but in this case no less than in the other, defining the boundaries of the two mission fields must have been a difficult task—so much so that one scholar has roundly declared the geographical interpretation "untenable."[84]

A third option seems preferable: to regard the division as neither strictly geographical nor strictly ethnic, but as "simply a general recognition of the dispensation of God which had so far prevailed" and a general agreement giving the primary direction in which each side was to apply its respective missionary efforts and ensuring that there should be no rivalry and competition between the two sides. It was not intended, therefore, as an exclusive concordat preventing Paul and Barnabas from laboring among Jews and Peter and the others from laboring among Gentiles.[85]

The significance of this "gentlemen's agreement" at Jerusalem has been variously estimated. Some speak of it as "an unconditional surrender to the Antiochian position"; others are sure that "the Jerusalem church did not

---

81. On the ellipsis in the ἵνα clause see BDF §481; for ἵνα here as meaning "on the understanding that" see Bruce 124.

82. E.g., Schmithals, *Paul and James,* 45f., 54; Betz 100. Cf. Holtz, "Zwischenfall," 353; he thinks that in practice the Jerusalem agreement must have immediately proved infeasible.

83. E.g., Fridrichsen, "Apostle," 12, and Burton 97f., respectively.

84. Haenchen, *Acts,* 467. Cf. H. W. Beyer, *TDNT* III: 599.

85. Cf. Longenecker, *Paul,* 253; Machen 131; *Origin,* 99 (whence the quotation); Ridderbos 90; Bornkamm, *Paul,* 40. It is worth emphasizing that this "division of labor is necessary because of the cultural barriers between Jews and Gentiles, not because of a disunity in the understanding of God, his redemption of mankind, and the gospel of Jesus Christ" (Betz 100). At the same time, we may note with Bruce, *Paul,* 168 that "it was probably impossible for one who concentrated on Gentile evangelization to be at the same time an effective missionary to Jews; hence the division of mission-fields . . . was a wise decision." On the discrepancy between Paul's statement here and the tradition recorded in Mt. 28:16-20 see Bruce 124; "Conference," 204.

adopt Paul's gospel in its entirety and all its logical implications."[86] Both views seem to presuppose that the theology of the Jewish church stood over against Paul's theology, although whereas according to the one view it was a case of capitulation, according to the other it was more like an uneasy truce. But vv. 2 and 6 combine to show that "agreement between Paul's Gospel and that preached by the primitive community is confirmed, and not just established."[87] Paul himself speaks of the three "pillars" extending to him and Barnabas "the right hand of fellowship" (RSV, NASB, NIV), which was a handshake of partners signifying agreement[88] and confirmation over the matter (cf. 2 Kgs. 10:15; Ezr. 10:19 [AV "gave their hands"]; Ezk. 17:18).[89] Neither "surrender" nor "compromise" would therefore seem to be a true description of the Jerusalem agreement; rather, it confirmed an already existing unity between the gospel of Paul and the gospel as preached by the Jerusalem leaders and gave recognition to Paul's apostleship as equal to that of Peter.[90] If, as Paul's relations with the Corinthian church would suggest, some tension between Paul and Jerusalem was later caused by difficulties over the implementation of the agreement which were due at least in part to certain ambiguities inherent in the terms of the agreement,[91] that is a different matter. From the perspective of Paul's apologetic interests in this letter, the Jerusalem agreement meant that he owed neither his gospel nor his apostolic commission to the Jerusalem authorities, since he brought both with him to the meeting.[92]

86. K. Lake, *BC* V: 198, and Bornkamm, *Paul*, 30, respectively. Pfleiderer, *Paulinism*, 2: 10 goes even further.

87. W. Gutbrod, *TDNT* IV: 1065f.

88. Cf. W. Grundmann, *TDNT* II: 38; J. Schattenmann, *NIDNTT* I: 643.

89. In Ezr. 10:19 "they gave their hand" (RV) means "they all gave their hands in pledge" (NIV) or more simply "they pledged themselves" (RSV).

90. It is not for nothing that these verses (6-9) have been considered "one of the chief rocks on which the Tübingen construction was finally wrecked" (Ropes 19). (The "Tübingen construction" posited an *antithesis* between Paul with his Gentile Christianity and Peter with his Judaic Christianity, which was resolved in the *synthesis* of the Catholic Church in the second century.)

91. Cf. Bruce 124f.; *Paul*, 154-157. On the other hand Barrett, *"Shaliaḥ,"* 100-101 appears to think that a sharp tension existed from the first. He suggests that "the two parties understood the term ἀπόστολος (and ἀποστολή) in different senses": Paul's "pioneering interpretation differed from the administrative, organizational one, that sought to bring all churches into a proper relation with that in Jerusalem" (100).

92. This is reflected even linguistically in the careful choice of the perfect tense πεπίστευμαι (contrast the aorist ἐνεργήσας ["worked"] in v. 8), which here has the force of a pluperfect ("I had been entrusted"); cf. Ramsay, "Paul's Attitude," 52f., who emphasizes the significance of the variations in the tenses used. The view of Greig, "Eschatological," 126 that the interview recorded in Gal. 2 is perhaps "an understatement by Paul of an ordination ceremony" is surely ruled out of court by Paul's own claim in 1:1, to go no further.

6. THE SOLE REQUEST MADE OF PAUL (2:10)

10 *All they asked was that we should keep their poor in mind, which was the very thing I made it my business to do.*

10 Finally Paul mentions, not as a condition imposed by the Jerusalem apostles or a concession made on his part,[93] but simply as an amplification of the agreement, their sole request that he and Barnabas continue to remember the poor.[94] If "the poor" may have been a self-designation of the Jerusalem community,[95] yet here the phrase must refer primarily to the materially poor members of the Jerusalem church.[96] The request is hardly likely to have been an obligation laid upon Paul as an "apostle of Zion" to collect money for the Jerusalem community,[97] if only because the only apostolates in view are those of the apostle to the Jews and the apostle to the Gentiles (v. 8).

Similarly, the hypothesis that the collection for the poor saints in Jerusalem, which was organized in consequence of the agreement here, was exacted by the mother-church as a levy from the Gentile churches[98] has been justifiably rejected.[99] It may have been the case that "in Jerusalem the contributions of the Gentile Churches were regarded as tribute rather than charity,"[100] but there is no proof of this. If "the real analogy is not the temple tax," it is probably right to regard "the additional voluntary love offerings" occasionally sent by Jewish communities to Jerusalem as the correct analogy."[101]

Certainly Paul himself regularly speaks of the collection as a voluntary act of grace (1 Cor. 16:3; 2 Cor. 8:6), fellowship (Rom. 15:26), ministry (2 Cor. 8:4; 9:1), or bounty (9:5), albeit once also as the payment of a spiritual—not legal—debt (Rom. 15:27). In his eyes the collection was not merely a means of alleviating want; it was also a recognition of Jerusalem's special status as the mother-church of the new Israel,[102] an acknowledg-

---

93. Cf. Reicke, "Hintergrund," 182, and Betz 101, respectively.

94. On imperatival ἵνα ("that") see MHT 3: 94f.; Moule 144.

95. Cf. the later "Ebionites," literally "the poor"; E. Bammel, *TDNT* VI: 909.

96. This understanding is borne out by a comparison of Rom. 15:26 (where "the poor among God's people" rightly takes τῶν ἁγίων as partitive, not epexegetic) and 2 Cor. 8:13f.; 9:12.

97. Cf. Schoeps, *Paul,* 68f.; E. Schweizer, *TDNT* VI: 414.

98. Schweitzer, *Mysticism,* 156. U. Wilckens, *TDNT* VII: 735 seems to border on such a view.

99. E.g., G. Kittel, *TDNT* IV: 282f.; Berger, "Almosen," 198f.

100. Manson, *Studies,* 206.

101. G. Kittel, *TDNT* IV: 283; similarly, E. Bammel, *TDNT* VI: 909.

102. Cf. Bruce, "Paul and Jerusalem," 4; Schlier 80f.; K. L. Schmidt, *TDNT* III: 508.

ment on the part of the Gentile churches of their indebtedness to Jerusalem as the origin of spiritual blessings (Rom. 15:27), a demonstration to the Jerusalem church of the genuineness of the Gentile Christians' faith (2 Cor. 9:12f.), and a bond of fellowship and love and a sign of unity between Jews and Gentiles in Christ.[103] The collection, as it later gradually materialized (1 Cor. 16:1-4; 2 Cor. 8–9) and was eventually brought to Jerusalem (Rom. 15:25f.), may also have been "Paul's deliberate effort to heal the widening breach between the church in Jerusalem and those churches that looked to Paul as founder."[104]

We may reasonably surmise that more than one of these considerations (excepting the last mentioned) already converged in prompting Paul to accede to the Jerusalem leaders' request to "keep their poor in mind"— particularly as Paul immediately goes on to say, "and in fact I had made a special point of attending to this very matter."[105] That the verb (Gk. *espoudasa*; cf. NEB "made it my business") is to be thus rendered as pluperfect has been demonstrated by a recent study in which it is convincingly argued that: (a) the RSV rendering of the verb as "I was eager" (also NIV and NASB; cf. AV, RV, Phillips) is linguistically inadmissible (*spoudazein* in the New Testament refers not merely to a state of mind but also expresses an effort) as well as grammatically inept (to express a state of mind the imperfect tense, not the aorist, would be required); (b) the NEB rendering,[106] though grammatically possible, gives a sense which is alien to the context, since it makes v. 10b a statement of Paul's submission to the Jerusalem authorities whereas the preceding context has emphasized his independence of them; and (c) only the translation of NEB margin ("I had made it my business") is both grammatically possible and fitting to the context.[107]

The adoption of the pluperfect translation means that Paul is referring here to the famine-relief work which according to Acts 11:29f. was the very reason that Paul and Barnabas were in Jerusalem. If it is objected that

---

103. Cf. Bruce, "Paul and Jerusalem," 23f.; Bornkamm, *Paul*, 40f.; C. Brown, *NIDNTT* II: 827f. Taking the verse as a reference to the collection agreed upon at the apostolic council of Acts 15, Berger, "Almosen," 199 speaks of the collection as signifying "the legitimizing of the existence of uncircumcised communities and their association with Jerusalem with the help of traditional Jewish-theological categories" (my translation).

104. Ellison, *Mystery*, 21.

105. Bruce, *Letters of Paul*, 23. Cf. also n. 107 below.

106. Cf. G. Harder, *TDNT* VII: 565: "sought strenuously."

107. Hall, "Famine." Cf. J. B. Orchard, "Problem," 389 n. 20; Geyser, "Paul," 130; Hemer, "Acts and Galatians," 86 (with n. 21), 87. Bruce, "Conference," 207, while cautioning against any dogmatic affirmation that "one of [two] possible senses alone is permissible and that the other is to be excluded," rightly maintains that "the context must be allowed the determinant voice" (cf. 209f.).

the ardor implied in the main verb is unlikely to have been connected with the transfer of funds already collected,[108] it may be replied that what is in mind is probably Paul's part in *organizing* the relief fund.[109] Paul is pointing out, in other words, "that he had already taken some initiative along this line: he did not raise money for the Jerusalem church simply because the 'pillars' had asked him to do so, but as an important element in his own apostolic policy."[110] His mention of the request here serves the important apologetic purpose of saying in effect that "the full recognition given by the apostles to Paul was proved in nothing more clearly than in the fact that their only request was the very thing for which he had been striving immediately before that visit."[111]

Thus the events of Paul's second post-conversion visit to Jerusalem, like the events of his life both before and after his call by God, substantiate his claim that he received both his gospel and his apostleship directly from the risen Lord. If the earlier set of events supports this by showing that there was never a time when he was in a position to have derived his gospel and apostolic commission from the Jerusalem leaders, the events of the second visit support it by showing the full recognition given by those leaders to the gospel and apostolic office which already were his prior to the meeting of the two parties. A third major support will be furnished by the Antioch incident (2:11-21).

G. AN INCIDENT AT ANTIOCH (2:11-14)

Paul concludes his sustained defense, begun at 1:11, of his authentic gospel and apostolic status against the calumniations of his Galatian opponents by referring to an incident at Antioch which involved his opposing Peter to his face. Together with the two previous paragraphs describing respectively his first and second post-conversion visits to Jerusalem, this passage reveals an

---

108. Ridderbos 91, n. 35.

109. E.g., Duncan 38. According to Hurtado, Paul's "effort to raise an offering for Jerusalem was being misinterpreted as proof of inferiority or subservience to the Jerusalem leadership," and "the carefully-worded reference to the Jerusalem collection in Gal. 2:10 is designed to counter any misunderstandings of the enterprise by Paul's opponents in Galatia" ("Collection," 46, 52); this presupposes the identification of the Jerusalem visit of Gal. 2 with that of Acts 15—a position not followed in this commentary.

110. Bruce 127.

111. Hall, "Famine," 310b; cf. Neill 37. For a response to the entirely different interpretation of v. 10a presented by Bartlet, "Only," cf. Fung 121f.; "Relationship between Righteousness and Faith," 2: 239-241, n. 483.

interesting development in the relation between Paul and Peter: Paul is successively Peter's guest (1:18-20), his fellow-apostle (2:1-10), and his critic (2:11-14).[1] From the standpoint of his apologetic purpose, this passage goes beyond the earlier ones and brings his argument to a triumphant climax: in Jerusalem, not only was Paul not commissioned by Peter, but his independent status and work as an apostle were also officially acknowledged by the "pillars" of the church; now at Antioch, he even opposed Peter to his face when the latter engaged in conduct which Paul regarded as a deviation from the truth of the gospel.

After sketching the course of events which led up to his public rebuke of Peter (vv. 11-14a) Paul proceeds to record what he said to Peter. Where his statement to Peter ends is not entirely clear. It is most unlikely that it consists of v. 14b alone,[2] for the thought of that verse is incomplete without the explanation which follows. But to regard the whole of vv. 14b-21 as direct discourse or at least as a substantial (though not verbatim) report of what Paul said to Peter at Antioch[3] is to come up against the difficulty that v. 17 seems removed from the concrete situation at Antioch (the objection expressed there can hardly have come from Peter). Perhaps the truth lies somewhere between: Paul's recital of his address to Peter in Antioch is progressively colored by polemic against his Galatian detractors and, as it were, gradually shades into a theological discussion with his readers.[4]

Be that as it may, it suffices for our purpose to note that Paul, at any rate, seems to conceive of vv. 15-21 as a continuation of the speech "before the whole congregation" begun at v. 14b, since, (a) as already observed, v. 14b would have little meaning by itelf; (b) the plural subject "we" (v. 15), including as it does Peter and the other Jewish Christians with Paul, links up with the Antioch situation; and (c) a new section clearly emerges only at 3:1, where the readers are directly addressed.[5] The entire passage (vv. 11-21) could therefore be treated as a unit in the composition of the letter. In this commentary it is divided into two sections (vv. 11-14, 15-21) for convenience of treatment and because v. 15 clearly marks the beginning of the doctrinal section of the letter.

1. Cf. Bruce, "Further Thoughts," 26.
2. Cf., e.g., RSV, NEB; Bring 86.
3. Cf., e.g., NASB, NIV; Rendall 163f.
4. E.g., Schmithals, *Paul and James*, 77; U. Wilckens, *TDNT* VIII: 569; Reicke, "Hintergrund," 175. In terms of the "apologetic letter" structure, vv. 15-21 is the *propositio*, which has a double function: "it sums up the legal content of the *narratio* by this outline of the case and provides an easy transition to the *probatio*" (Betz 114). Meeks, Review, 305 cites this view of the passage as "an example of the scheme's power to solve exegetical problems."
5. Schlier 87.

1. THE COURSE OF EVENTS (2:11-13)

11 *But when Cephas came to Antioch, I opposed him to his face, because he was clearly in the wrong.* 12 *For until certain persons came from James he was taking his meals with gentile Christians; but when they came he drew back and began to hold aloof, because he was afraid of the advocates of circumcision.* 13 *The other Jewish Christians showed the same lack of principle; even Barnabas was carried away and played false like the rest.*

11-13 It is impossible to be certain why Peter came to Antioch. The incident related here may have occurred before the first missionary journey of Paul and Barnabas (Acts 13–14) or after their return from that tour;[6] the latter view may be preferred as making possible a simpler reconstruction of the sequence of events. In any case, it is unnatural to understand the opening words of v. 11 to regard the incident here as actually taking place before Paul's Jerusalem visit of 2:1-10;[7] much rather to be accepted is the dictum of T. W. Manson, one of whose three "canons" for correlating Gal. 1–2 and Acts reads as follows:

> Any reconstruction of the events which involves tampering with the order in Gal. i, ii is to be regarded with suspicion. And, on the other hand, a reconstruction which allows us to preserve the Galatian order should have that fact accounted to it for righteousness.[8]

Peter at first sat at table and ate with the Gentile Christians, as Barnabas and the rest of the Jewish Christians in Antioch had been doing. The expression "taking his meals" no doubt includes a reference to participation in the Lord's Supper—that the eucharist and the community love-feast were closely linked together is suggested by 1 Cor. 11:20-22, 33f.—but to make it refer exclusively[9] or even primarily to the eucharist is to narrow unduly the meaning of the original verb, which is quite general,[10] and ill accords with the equally general expression "live . . . like a Jew" (v. 14b).

---

6. Cf., e.g., Neill 39 and Bruce 128, respectively. Those who identify Gal. 2:1-10 as a description of the apostolic council naturally date the present incident after the Council: e.g., Holtz, "Zwischenfall," 346.

7. This has been done in an attempt to overcome one difficulty involved in the identification of that visit with the one recorded in Acts 15: see p. 16 above.

8. Manson, *Studies,* 171 (another was cited on p. 23, n. 54 above). Cf. Betz 61 with n. 64, who applies to Paul's *narratio* in 1:13–2:14 the rhetoricians' general rule of following the natural order of events.

9. So Schweitzer, *Mysticism,* 196; cf. G. Dulon, *NIDNTT* I: 473.

10. Cf. Lk. 15:2; Acts 10:41; 11:3; 1 Cor. 5:11; Parkin, "Συνεσθίειν," especially 252.

These verses (12f.) show that at the time of Peter's visit it was already an established custom in the Antioch church for Jewish and Gentile believers to enjoy free table-fellowship with one another, apparently on an equal footing which knew no conditions or restrictions.[11] The impression given by our text thus goes against the assumption which is sometimes made[12] that the fellowship between Jewish and Gentile Christians was facilitated by mutual consideration, with the Gentile believers continuing to keep a group of minimal rules such as the "precepts of Noah"[13] which they already observed before becoming Christians. The text further implies that Peter came into a situation which he found neither unusual nor uncongenial. By eating freely with the Gentiles Peter on his part was in effect declaring the Christian Jew as well as the Christian Gentile to be free from the law.[14] That Paul found Peter's behavior thoroughly agreeable (as v. 12a implies) indicates that the two apostles were one in their general attitude towards the incorporation of Gentile Christians into the Church.

This happy state of affairs was disrupted when "certain persons came from James."[15] This rendering correctly connects the phrase "from James" immediately with the verb "came" (and not with the noun "certain persons," as though the sense were "certain adherents or supporters of James"), thus denoting James as the sender.[16] These visitors were probably bearers of a message which either was designed "to remind the *Jewish* members of the Antiochian congregation of the obligations which all true Jews, including Jewish Christians, must observe in their dealings with Gentiles"[17] or, perhaps more likely, was addressed to Peter personally, to the effect that news of his free table-fellowship with Gentiles in Antioch was "being exploited by unsympathetic scribes and Pharisees to the detriment of the Christian cause in Judaea."[18] Whatever its precise terms, the message

11. Cf. Holtz, "Zwischenfall," 347f., 352, 353. According to Acts 11:26, this was so from the beginning of the Antiochene church's existence; cf., e.g., Lake, *Earlier*, 23; Haenchen, *Acts*, 609.

12. E.g., Filson, *NT History*, 207.

13. On these see Barrett, *First Adam*, 23-26; Dunn, "Incident," 20 with 49, n. 71.

14. This he had already done in principle on a previous occasion, when, according to Acts 10:9-48, he baptized the household of the Roman centurion Cornelius and remained for some days in his home; even earlier than that Peter lodged with a tanner, whose occupation was considered ceremonially unclean (9:43).

15. If the singular be read throughout v. 12, as preferred by Manson, *Studies*, 178f. and as indicated in NEB margin, the person concerned may have been the spokesman of a group; but the plural is probably the correct reading: Metzger 592f.

16. Cf. Ellicott 33, over against Ridderbos 96, n. 7. Barrett 13 thinks that "presumably Paul, rightly or wrongly, understood that they represented the mind of James," who "stood for Jesus and the law, at least for Jews" (14).

17. Duncan 57. Cf. Barrett 12f., 100.

18. Bruce, *Paul*, 177; cf. Manson, *Studies*, 181; and Barrett, *Signs*, 86, where

had the unfortunate effect of causing Peter gradually to draw back, finally separating himself completely from the company of Gentiles.[19]

Paul attributes the shift in Peter's behavior to his fear of "the advocates of circumcision" (RSV "the circumcision party"). This rendering of the original expression—which elsewhere in Paul (Rom. 4:12; Col. 4:11) means simply "the circumcised," that is, "the Jews"—seems justified by the fact that in v. 13 (in the Greek) Jewish Christians are referred to simply as "the Jews"; in the present instance, the expression may include both Jewish-Christian members of the Jerusalem community and non-Christian Jews.[20] This assumes that "the advocates of circumcision" are a larger group distinct from the persons who "came from James."[21]

Peter's "fear" may have been no more than a genuine concern lest he, who was head of the "home mission" work of the Jerusalem church (cf. 2:7), should appear to be (and be reported as) apostatizing from Judaism and thus prove a stumbling-block to those whom he was seeking to evangelize.[22] But the actual term used ("he was afraid"; *phoboumenos*) suggests a rather stronger emotional reaction and makes it plausible that there was more to the message from James than was suggested above: if that message had also appealed to Peter's concern for the physical safety of the Jewish Christian churches in Judea, which were already in considerable jeopardy from non-Christian Jews (cf. 5:11; 6:12) as a result of the increasing rumors of Jewish Christian fraternizing with uncircumcised Gentiles in Antioch and Galatia,[23] this would provide further explanation for Peter's behavior.[24]

---

the communication from James is seen as "a message of rebuke to . . . (Peter) with the result that [the Jerusalem authorities] had virtually excommunicated Paul along with his Gentile churches." According to Dunn, "Incident," 31-34, "the men from James made a higher demand on the God-fearing Gentile believers than the Jewish believers in Antioch itself," particularly with regard to ritual purity and tithing: on this thesis see the responses from Houlden, "Response"; Cohn-Sherbok, "Reflections," especially 70-72; and Holtz, "Zwischenfall," 351f. Catchpole is, by his examination of the evidence, "driven to one and only one conclusion: the demands laid down in Antioch are none other than the demands of the Decree" brought by the emissaries from James ("Paul," 442). But this proposal is based on an "Acts xi. 27-30 = Gal. ii. 1-10 = Acts xv. 1ff. equivalence" (438, cf. 435) which we are unable to accept; see also the response from Bruce 129f.

19. Both verbs, ὑπέστελλεν and ἀφώριζεν, are imperfect. On the relation between the two verbs see K. H. Rengstorf, *TDNT* VII: 598; cf. Holtz, "Zwischenfall," 348: both in time and materially the withdrawal preceded the separation.

20. So Manson, *Studies*, 180. Cf. Ellis, "Circumcision," 394, who suggests "Jewish Christians with a strict attitude towards the Jewish cultus and customs."

21. Cf. Schmithals, *Paul and James*, 67.

22. So Manson, *Studies*, 180f.

23. So G. Dix, as quoted and endorsed by Schmithals, *Paul and James*, 67f. with n. 12.

24. On the bearing of Peter's "fear" on the question of his primacy see O. Cullmann, *TDNT* VI: 110 with n. 56.

However well-intentioned Peter's altered behavior may have been and however much it might have been justified as an accommodation along the same lines as were later espoused by Paul (1 Cor. 9:19-23),[25] it was to Paul clearly a case of "playing false" (NASB, NIV "hypocrisy"; *hypokrisis,* better rendered "play-acting")—conduct which masked and belied Peter's genuine convictions.[26] The other Jewish Christians[27] "showed the same lack of principle" by joining him in his play-acting, with the result that "even Barnabas"—Paul's close associate, whose defection in this manner was therefore least expected and most disappointing[28]—was swept off balance and carried away into their play-acting.[29] The clear sense of *hypokrisis* shows that Peter was taken to task for failing to have the courage of his real convictions;[30] and it is for this reason that Paul says that Peter "stood condemned" (v. 11, RV, RSV, NASB).[31]

2. PAUL'S CONFRONTATION OF PETER (2:14)

14 *But when I saw that their conduct did not square with the truth of the Gospel, I said to Cephas, before the whole congregation, "If you, a Jew born and bred, live like a Gentile, and not like a Jew, how can you insist that Gentiles must live like Jews?"*

25. Cf. P. Richardson, "Inconsistency," especially 360f Richardson rightly observes that the inconsistency between that passage and Gal. 2:11-14 is "an inconsistency related to the differing demands of the two situations" (362).

26. E.g., Lightfoot 113; Burton 109; Machen 138.

27. Literally, "the rest of the Jews." On the use here of "Jews" to denote Jewish Christians see W. Gutbrod, *TDNT* III: 381.

28. Bauckham ("Barnabas") has suggested that Barnabas's minor role in this letter in spite of his prominent role in the evangelization of Galatia is to be put down to Paul's disappointment and embarrassment over Barnabas's recent defection.

29. Taking the dative case of τῇ ὑποκρίσει, with Ellicott 34f., in the pregnant sense of "by, and then into." The verb συναπήχθη ("was carried away") has, according to Betz 110, a strong connotation of irrationality.

30. E.g., Cullmann, "Dissensions," 123; Schlier 84; W. Günther, *NIDNTT* II: 469.

31. Κατεγνωσμένος does not mean "to be blamed" (AV), "clearly in the wrong" (NEB, NIV), or "'condemned' before God" (U. Wilckens, *TDNT* VIII: 568, n. 51). Rather it indicates that Peter was condemned by his conduct, which was at variance with his own inner convictions (e.g., R. Bultmann, *TDNT* I: 715: O. Cullmann, *TDNT* VI: 110; W. Schneider, *NIDNTT* II: 365). Is Barrett being entirely consistent when he says on the one hand that "Peter was acting contrary to his *true convictions*" (102, emphasis added) and on the other hand that his action was hypocritical "in that it is the attitude of a Mr Facing-both-ways" (113, n. 20; see 100-102) "trying to combine two irreconcilable principles," namely those stated in 2:15 and 2:16b-c respectively (Barrett 18f.), and that "Peter serves as the outstanding example of the man without a theological foundation, without a theological backbone . . ." (16, cf. 13)?

14 From Paul's point of view, Peter's personal inconsistency carried an even more sinister significance. When Paul says that he "opposed" Peter to his face (v. 11) on seeing that the conduct of Peter and the other Jewish Christians "did not square with the truth of the Gospel," the verb he uses (*anthistēmi*, v. 11) implies that *to him* Peter's conduct was tantamount to the beginning of an attack on the position he was maintaining at Antioch (though it was certainly not so intended by Peter). Measured by this position, which in Paul's estimation clearly represented "the truth of the Gospel," Peter's play-acting was, in fact, nothing short of a defection or deviation from that truth.[32] How that gospel truth was conceived by Paul (already intimated in the exposition on 1:12, 16) becomes explicit in Paul's address to Peter and indeed is given repeated expression in the rest of the letter.

Here, in his open rebuke of Peter, Paul states that Peter, although "a Jew born and bred" and hence not even a proselyte, himself followed the Gentile and not the Jewish way of life; his present withdrawal is thus regarded as constituting only a surprising aberration and not as representing the essential principle of his life.[33] The question based on this conditional clause points to the irrationality (*pōs* ["how"] here means "how is it" [so NASB, NIV]) of his withdrawal. The verb "insist" (*anankazō*, literally "compel") does not merely describe an attempt,[34] but implies that Peter's shift in conduct was a kind of indirect compulsion: his example as an apostle was bound to exert a moral influence on the Jewish Christians at Antioch.[35]

This had in fact actually happened (vv. 11-13): under Peter's influence the rest of the Jewish Christians had, like him, withdrawn from table fellowship with the Gentile Christians—probably because the latter were suspected of not having selected and prepared the food set before the mixed

---

32. In the Greek clause rendered "their conduct did not square with," the verb ὀρθοποδέω (a NT hapax) means "not to waver," "not to stumble" (H. Preisker, *TDNT* V: 451), while the preposition πρός has the force of "in agreement with" (B. Reicke, *TDNT* VI: 724); it denotes "not the goal to be attained, but the line of direction to be observed" (Lightfoot 113); contra Gaventa, "Galatians 1 and 2," 317: "they did not walk straight toward the truth of the gospel."

33. This is the force of the present tense of ζῆς ("you live"), which is apparently overlooked when Howard 43 says that "Peter had himself lived like a Gentile"; for such a pluperfect force the aorist tense would have been used. Cf. Betz 112, to whom the present tense "suggests that the table fellowship was only the external symbol of Cephas' total emancipation from Judaism."

34. Cf. Phillips; MHT 3: 63.

35. Schmithals, *Paul and James*, 69; W. Gutbrod, *TDNT* III: 383. On the other hand, Catchpole, "Paul," 441 takes the verb in the "undiluted" sense of making a demand and concludes that "demands were initiated by James, delivered by his emissaries, and endorsed in action by Peter." Similarly, Holtz, "Zwischenfall," 349 thinks that Peter articulated in words his expectation that the Gentile Christians subject themselves to definite Jewish ordinances in the interest of making possible full fellowship with the Jewish Christians, but he admits that the text says nothing about this.

company of Jewish and Gentile Christians in strict observance of the Jewish dietary laws. It follows that for Gentiles to "live like Jews"[36] they would have to observe the Jewish food-laws, and ultimately submit to circumcision, and that this was in practice being imposed on the Gentile Christians as a requirement for fellowship with the Jews.

The serious public consequences of Peter's conduct—which "would make a divided Church inevitable or a united Church impossible"[37]—called forth the public rebuke by Paul, who explains in vv. 15-21 the deeper issues involved in this apparently mundane matter of having meals together.[38]

36. Greek Ἰουδαΐζειν (a NT hapax) has the same meaning as Ἰουδαϊκῶς ζῆν ("live . . . like a Jew") of the previous clause: "to live according to Jewish customs and commandments": K. G. Kuhn, *TDNT* VI: 732.

37. Neill 41.

38. If Galatians is viewed as an apologetic letter, 2:14 is seen to follow the practice of the majority of the rhetoricians in bringing the *narratio* to a climax at the point where the issue to be determined begins: Paul's question to Peter reflects precisely the issue in Galatia, namely, that the Judaizers are trying to make Gentile Christians live like Jews (cf. Betz 62; Brinsmead 69).

III. MAIN ARGUMENT: EXPOSITION OF THE DOCTRINE OF JUSTIFICATION BY FAITH (2:15–5:12)

A. PAUL'S ADDRESS (2:15-21)

Structurally speaking, these verses are a continuation of Paul's address to Peter which began with v. 14b, but because of their content they are treated here as the first paragraph of Paul's doctrinal argument.[1] The passage is of paramount importance not only as Paul's first systematic treatment of justification by faith but also because it affords valuable insights into the significance of the doctrine for his understanding of the gospel.

1. PROPOSITION: JUSTIFICATION BY FAITH (2:15-16)

15 *We ourselves are Jews by birth, not Gentiles and sinners.* 16 *But we know that no man is ever justified by doing what the law demands, but only through faith in Christ Jesus; so we too have put our faith in Jesus Christ, in order that we might be justified through this faith, and not through deeds dictated by law; for by such deeds, Scripture says, no mortal man shall be justified.*

15 This verse and the next form a single, overloaded sentence in the Greek; they have been aptly described as "Paul's doctrine of justification in a nutshell"[2] and must be examined in considerable detail. Speaking "from the provisional standpoint of the Jews"[3] Paul describes himself, Peter, and the other Jewish Christians ("we ourselves") as "Jews by birth, not

---

1. They correspond to the *propositio* in the apologetic letter: cf. Betz 113; Brinsmead 51f. (See also, however, Dunn, "Incident," 55, n. 117.)
2. Schmithals, *Paul and James*, 73. It is worth noting that the terminology of justification by faith appears on the whole for the first time in v. 16: πιστεύω ("believe") once (apart from 2:7, where it has the different sense of "to entrust with"), πίστις ("faith") twice (apart from 1:23), and δικαιόω ("justify") three times.
3. E. Stauffer, *TDNT* II: 362.

Gentiles and sinners."[4] This characterization at once focuses attention on the sharp distinction between Jew and Gentile, for what made the Gentiles sinners in the estimation of the Jews was not only that they did not observe the law but also that they did not even possess it and consequently lacked the possibility of obtaining righteousness through it.[5] In the original expression, "sinners of the Gentiles" (AV, RV) or "Gentile sinners" (RSV, NIV; Gk. *ex ethnōn hamartōloi*), the two nouns are synonymous and form a single concept;[6] it accords with this that the "sinful men" of Lk. 24:7 who were to be responsible for crucifying Christ are referred to in Acts 2:23 as "lawless men" (RSV), where the adjective or adjectival substantive *(anomoi)* is used in a sense analogous to that of its adverb in Rom. 2:12 (*anomōs*, NEB "outside the pale of the Law of Moses"; cf. v. 14).

16a Paul claims for himself and the others the knowledge[7] "that no man is ever justified by doing what the law demands, but only through faith in Christ Jesus." Peter's assent to this principle is taken for granted by Paul[8] and is independently attested by the tradition of Peter's later speech at the Jerusalem conference (Acts 15:7-11, especially vv. 9, 11).

Negatively, Paul asserts that no human being is justified (NEB adds "ever" for emphasis) by doing what the law demands. To be justified means to be declared righteous before God, that is, to enjoy a status or standing of being in a right relationship with God, of being accepted by him.[9] "By doing what the law demands" is more literally "by the works of the law" (AV, RV, NASB);[10] these deeds done in fulfillment of the law's prescriptions are at the same time an expression of the Jews' self-consciousness as God's chosen people and (for them) the basis of a legal claim over against God.[11]

4. "By birth" is literally "by nature" (φύσει), i.e., by natural descent; cf. H. Köster, *TDNT* IX: 272.

5. E.g., Wilckens, "Was heisst," 86; Betz 115, n. 25.

6. Cf. Mt. 26:45 with Mk. 10:33f.; K. H. Rengstorf, *TDNT* 1: 328.

7. The term "we know" (εἰδότες, as here, or οἴδαμεν elsewhere) is usually used by Paul to introduce "a dogmatic position as something commonly known" (Munck, *Paul,* 126).

8. On this see W. Gutbrod, *TDNT* IV: 1066.

9. Cf. Fung, "Forensic."

10. In the Greek, ἐξ ἔργων νόμου, the preposition qualifies the first and not the second of the substantives which follow it, so that the meaning is "not 'by the principle of works'" (M. J. Harris, *NIDNTT* III: 1178). For justification of the common view that the phrase means "works which are commanded by the law," not "service of the law" or "legalism," see Moo, "'Law'," 91-96. The second of these interpretations of the phrase is preferred by (among others) Dunn, "Works," 527f., 529, 538.

11. Cf. Kertelge, "Deutung," 214f. Νόμος ("law") is used by Paul in a variety of senses (cf., e.g., H.-H. Esser, *NIDNTT* II: 444; W. Gutbrod, *TDNT* IV: 1069-1071; Moo, "'Law'," 75-90). It is often used (as here) without the article. "It is certainly not true that νόμος is 'a' law as distinct from ὁ νόμος, 'the' Law" (Gutbrod, op. cit., 1070). A more accurate formulation of the general distinction is that "ὁ νόμος is the Mosaic

By "the law" here Paul has in view not its ceremonial aspect only, but the law in its entirety;[12] but while it is true that Paul does not anywhere explicitly distinguish between the ceremonial law and the moral law,[13] an implicit distinction is clearly suggested in 1 Cor. 7:19 by the contrast between "circumcision" (which is a part of God's law) and the keeping of God's commands, thus separating "the ethical from the ceremonial—the permanent from the temporal."[14]

Be that as it may, the main purpose of Paul's present statement is simply to point out the total inadequacy of the law as a means of justification: v. 16d quotes the same OT text (Ps. 143:2) as is cited in Rom. 3:20, where the context (Rom. 1:18–3:20; cf. Gal. 3:10) shows that the reason for the inadequacy of the law is in the fact that all have sinned, the Jews, who occupy a privileged position in salvation history, as well as the Gentiles, who do not. The *implication* of Paul's statement, however, may well include the rejection of "any and all works as works-of-merit"[15]—that is, of "legalism"—as of no avail in the matter of justification; for "if even the works prescribed by the holy law of Israel do not contribute to justification, then *a fortiori* other works certainly do not."[16]

Positively, Paul states that it is "only through faith in Christ Jesus" that a person is justified. The genitive "Christ Jesus" (the variant order "Jesus Christ" [AV, RV, RSV, NIV] probably represents no significant difference in meaning) has been taken by some as subjective genitive, yielding a variety of meanings ranging from (a) "the faithfulness of Christ," through (b) "the faith which Christ creates in man by his revelation of God's love," to (c) "Christ's own faith," first shown in his life and subsequently reproduced in the life of the believer, and even (d) "Christ's tenure in *fidei*

Law, while νόμος is simply 'law' as such (though in the context the law in question may be the Mosaic one)" (Zerwick §177); when anarthrous νόμος refers to the Mosaic law, it may be a reflection of the rabbinic usage of anarthrous *tôrâ* as though it were a proper noun. But a surer guide to the meaning than the use of the article is the context (Moule 113; MHT 3: 177).

12. According to R. Bultmann, the reason Paul makes no distinction between the cultic and ritual and the ethical requirements of the law is that, thinking in a Jewish manner, he evaluates them not in regard to their content, but in their nature as demands (*Theology,* 1: 260f.; cf. "Christ the End," 43f.).

13. Emphatically, Bruce, "Paul and the Law," 266. Cf. Moo, "'Law'," 84f.

14. Ladd, *Theology,* 510. Cf. W. Gutbrod, *TDNT* IV: 1072, who states that Paul "works out his position" in regard to the law "primarily with reference to the ethical commandments, especially those of the Decalogue which apply to all men." Cf. also Wilckens, "Statements," 19. On the other hand Davies, "Paul and the Law," 9 thinks that 1 Cor. 7:19 is "not a reference to Mosaic commands."

15. Bultmann, *Theology,* 1: 283.

16. Küng, *Justification,* 300. Cf. R. Bultmann, *TDNT* VI: 220. On the completely negative sense of ἔργον ("work") in Paul's use whenever it is a matter of human achievement see G. Bertram, *TDNT* II: 651.

commissum" of Roman testamentary law.[17] All such interpretations founder on the fact that the clause "we too have put our faith in Jesus Christ," following immediately upon the present phrase "through faith in Christ Jesus," puts it beyond reasonable doubt that *Christou Iēsou* is to be construed as objective genitive, expressing the object in whom the faith is reposed (so the usual translation with "in").[18]

The preposition "through" designates faith in Christ as the means of justification.[19] This faith is nowhere defined in the NT (Heb. 11:1 included), but "the committal of one's self to Christ on the basis of the acceptance of the message concerning him" is perhaps as good a definition as any other.[20]

The antithesis which Paul poses between "by doing what the law demands" and "through faith in Christ Jesus" is expressed in the absolute terms of a simple "not . . . but" (AV, RSV, NASB, NIV). The over-literal translation of the RV ("a man is not justified by the works of the law, save through faith in Christ Jesus") is misleading in that it might be taken to imply that faith in Christ is the means by which conformity to law, inadequate in itself, is made effective for salvation,[21] whereas the expression rendered "save" *(ean mē)* probably introduces an exception only to "a man is not justified," not to the entire clause "a man is not justified by works of the law."[22] By adding the word "only" before "through faith in Christ Jesus" (so also RV mg.; cf. RSV at Rom. 11:20) the NEB rightly stresses faith as the *exclusive* means of justification and faithfully reflects Paul's emphasis on "the total incapacity of man for any kind of self-justification. In justification the sinner . . . stands there with his hands entirely empty."[23]

17. E.g., (a) Torrance, "One Aspect"; Longenecker, *Paul*, 150f.; "Obedience," 146f.; (b) Manson, *Paul and John*, 62; (c) A. T. Hanson, *Paul's Understanding*, 9f.; cf. *Studies*, 40, (d) G. M. Taylor, "Function," especially 73. Cf. Hultgren, "Πίστις," 250-252. The understanding of πίστις Χριστοῦ as "the faith(fulness) of Christ" has now been argued at length by Hays (see, e.g., 141-142, 175); for a response see Russell, "Convincing . . . ?" 171-173.

18. Cf., e.g., R. Bultmann, *TDNT* VI: 204 with n. 230; 210, n. 267; W. Grundmann, *TDNT* IX: 552; M. J. Harris, *NIDNTT* III: 1213; and especially Hultgren, "Πίστις," in particular 254f., 261. *Pace* Lohmeyer, "Probleme," 207, where it is taken as both subjective and objective genitive.

19. Cf. A. Oepke, *TDNT* II: 67; see also G. Schrenk, *TDNT* II: 216, n. 21. The interpretation of Deissmann, *St. Paul*, 146f., that justification "through" faith is in fact justification "in" faith confuses faith and justification, as Kertelge, *Rechtfertigung*, 184 rightly observes. This criticism applies also to Hultgren, "Πίστις," 263, where "faith in Christ" is spoken of as "identified with . . . God's justifying act in Christ."

20. Burton 123. For the various elements or aspects involved in the NT concept of faith see, e.g., R. Bultmann, *TDNT* VI: 205ff., especially 217ff.; O. Michel, *NIDNTT* I: 599-605.

21. So, rightly, Duncan 65.

22. Burton 121. Cf. Schlatter, *Glaube*, 333, n.

23. Küng, *Justification*, 238.

16b, c The exclusiveness, and hence the all-sufficiency, of faith as the means of justification receives further emphasis in the central proposition of the sentence, and that in three ways:

(a) Justification is said to be "not through deeds dictated by law" but "through this faith [in Christ]"—not *ex ergōn nomou* but *ek pisteōs Christou*. In v. 16a the preposition *ek* (= *ex*) is used with *ergōn nomou*, but *dia* appears with *pisteōs Christou*. Insofar as the change of preposition from *dia* to *ek* (*ex*) has any significance, it might be that *ek* points to the principle, whereas *dia* points to the means, of justification, so that the two together designate faith as "the principle and means of justification."[24] More probably, however, the change is simply stylistic (cf. *en pistei*, "by faith," v. 20). The same phrases are employed in Rom. 3:30—God will justify the circumcised *ek pisteōs* and the uncircumcised *dia tēs pisteōs*—where the contention of the passage that there is no distinction between Jew and Gentile (cf. also vv. 22-24) makes it clear that the change of preposition is only a rhetorical variation which "serves to underline the identity of method."[25] It is noteworthy that the change from *dia* to *ek* in Gal. 2:16 does make the antithesis between faith and works as the means of justification formally as well as materially complete: in the Christian way of salvation faith re-

---

According to a recent suggestion, v. 16a represents the view accepted by Jewish Christians and here "faith in Jesus is described as a *qualification* to justification by works of law, not (yet) as an antithetical alternative"; in v. 16c, "what were initially juxtaposed as complementary, are now posed as straight alternatives" (Dunn, "New Perspective," 112f.). This thesis is intimately bound up with the theory that the leading apostles, though willing to waive circumcision as an entry requirement for Gentile believers, still in effect expected them—*Gentile* Christians—"to live as those within the covenant in traditional terms, to maintain covenant status by, in particular, conforming with the food and purity regulations which governed the meal table" (114; cf. "Incident"). Our exegesis of the account of the Antioch incident compels dissent from this theory, and accordingly from the thesis which Dunn regards as "a slightly different way" of expressing it ("New Perspective," 113).

At a more fundamental level, the "knowledge" spoken of in v. 16a is predicated of *Paul* as well as the other Jewish Christians at Antioch, which makes it doubtful whether "what the law demands" can be narrowly restricted to the "badges of covenant membership" (circumcision, food laws, sabbath observance: Dunn, "New Perspective," 107-111; cf. "Works," 527-532, 538) and whether God's justification is correctly defined as "God's acknowledgment that someone is in the covenant" ("New Perspective," 106; for a concise description of "covenantal nomism" see Sanders, *Paul and Palestinian Judaism*, 75, 236). For if our exposition of Gal. 1:11-17 is not mistaken, it is not in such terms (works of law as badges of covenant membership, justification as acknowledgment that a person is in the covenant) that Paul describes his conversion and call. On Dunn's exegesis of 2:16 see also the remarks by Räisänen, "Galatians 2.16," 544-548, who rightly contends (546f.) that a shift in the meaning of justification after v. 16a (suggested by Dunn) is unlikely.

24. Kertelge, *Rechtfertigung*, 184 (my translation).
25. Murray, *Romans*, 1: 124. Cf. Bruce 139f.

places works and Christ replaces the law.[26] (It is also noteworthy that Paul never uses *dia pistin* ["on account of faith"—as though faith were a condition in the sense of an accomplishment] in connection with justification or salvation, "which would involve a doctrinal error."[27])

(b) The antithesis between faith and works is repeated from v. 16a. This might appear to be sheer tautology,[28] but the seeming redundancy serves the most important purpose of reinforcing the truth that faith in Christ ("this faith") is the sole and sufficient means of justification.[29]

(c) The emphatic "we too" (v. 16b; cf. NIV) or "even we" (AV, RV, RSV, NASB) resumes the emphatic "we ourselves" of v. 15 and stresses the fact that even Paul and the other Jewish Christians (who, as members of the elect people with all their privileges, might conceivably have adopted the Jewish, not Jewish Christian, standpoint of having faith supplement the works of the law) have believed in[30] Christ with the express purpose of being justified by faith in Christ alone and not by works of the law.[31] Thereby they confess that justification comes only through faith and not in any degree through deeds dictated by the law and, in the same act of believing in Christ, demonstrate the universal validity of the principle of justification by faith.[32]

16d Finally, Paul seeks to clinch the matter by adducing proof from Scripture that "no mortal man shall be justified" by legal works. He cites Ps. 143:2b, where the MT ("for no one living is righteous before you," NIV) is rendered by the LXX (142:2b) "for no one living shall be justified before you."[33] Paul's free quotation differs from the LXX original in three

26. Cf. Schlatter, *Glaube*, 335; Schlier 92.

27. Lightfoot 115.

28. It is in fact so taken by some scholars who argue that in the phrase ἐκ πίστεως Χριστοῦ the genitive is not objective ("in Christ") but subjective ("of Christ"), e.g., Longenecker, "Obedience," 147, n. 1; Barth, "*Rechtfertigung*," 203. Cf. n. 17 above.

29. On this see Murray, *Romans*, 1: 371f.

30. The expression πιστεύειν εἰς ("believe in"), which does not appear in classical Greek and the LXX, has been thought (e.g., by M. J. Harris, *NIDNTT* III: 1212) to be modelled on Heb. *heʾemîn bᵉ;* but since the LXX does not render the Hebrew preposition by εἰς but by the simple dative, the expression is more likely a distinctive Christian coinage (so Ladd, *Theology*, 271f.). The view of R. Bultmann, *TDNT* VI: 203f. that "believe in Jesus" is an abbreviation for "believe that Jesus died and rose . . ." is rightly dismissed by Moule 69, n. 3 as a curious one.

31. V. 16 is syntactically to be thus closely linked with v. 15 as constituting with it *one* sentence (so, e.g., Kümmel, "Individualgeschichte," 158f.; Wilckens, "Was heisst," 87, n. 24), over against the view which would see a caesura between the two verses with the first referring to the old order and the second to the new order (e.g., Bultmann, "Auslegung," 394; G. Klein as cited by Kümmel, op. cit.).

32. Cf. Barth, "Justification," 155.

33. G. Schrenk, *TDNT* II: 213 regards the LXX as sharpening the MT, in that it asserts "not merely universal sinfulness but the impossibility of justification." But the

respects: (a) it adds the decisive words "by such deeds" (the "deeds dictated by law," repeating *ex ergōn nomou* from the previous clause), thus giving the general expression of the psalmist a particular application; (b) it omits the phrase "before you," which is perhaps assumed;[34] (c) it replaces "everyone living" with "all flesh" (cf. Gen. 6:12)—the latter expression being "a significant expression for human existence which rebels against God or is too weak to render real obedience."[35] The substitution of one phrase for the other thus forges a link with the thought that the works of the law are performed by mankind (*anthrōpos*, v. 16a) who is flesh; it also possibly obliquely counters the Judaizers' claim that circumcised flesh was accepted as righteous before God.[36] By this adaptation of the Scripture, Paul shows that the negative half of his formula "[not] by doing what the law demands, but only through faith in Christ Jesus" was already taught in Scripture.[37]

The upshot of Paul's statement in vv. 15f., then, is (a) that justification is attained by faith in Christ alone and not by legal works, and (b) that this principle—which is illustrated in his own experience and that of the other Jewish Christians and, at least in what it denies, is supported by Scripture—applies universally to Jew and Gentile alike. That he should here (as also in Phil. 3:7-9) describe or interpret his conversion experience *as* an experience of justification by faith is in perfect accord with the conclusion derived from Gal. 1:12, 16 that the gospel of justification by faith in both its negative and positive aspects was implicitly involved in the revelation of Jesus to him as the Messiah, Lord, and Son of God: ultimately the knowledge to which he refers in v. 16 ("we know") is grounded in his encounter with Christ, and the conviction thus gained is then supported by his new understanding of Scripture.

2. DEFENSE: THE NEGATIVE ARGUMENT (2:17-18)

17 *If now, in seeking to be justified in Christ, we ourselves no less than the Gentiles turn out to be sinners against the law, does that*

latter notion is probably already hinted at in the MT itself: see Watson, "Observations," 264; cf. Hanson, *Studies*, 28.

34. Cf. E. Schweizer, *TDNT* VII: 129, over against Schlier 95, who thinks that the omission obscures the judgment situation.

35. Michel, *Römer*, 145 (my translation). On points (a) and (c) see also Barrett 19.

36. R. Jewett, *Anthropological*, 98.

37. A similar adaptation occurs in Rom. 3:20 (where "before you" is retained with an appropriate change in the personal pronoun), and "it may be inferred that for him at least this paraphrase of Ps. 143 (LXX 142):2 had become a habitual proof-text for the doctrine of justification by faith apart from works of law" (Bruce 140).

mean that Christ is an abettor of sin? No, never! 18 *No, if I start building up again a system which I have pulled down, then it is that I show myself up as a transgressor of the law.*

17 Paul now faces an objection which seems to have been not so much directly occasioned by the Antioch episode (it can hardly have come from Peter) as it was generally leveled at his doctrine of free grace. According to this objection, Paul's doctrine encourages sin (cf. Rom. 6:1, 15; Gal. 5:13-26). Paul concisely states the doctrine itself as justification "in Christ" *(en Christō)*—the prepositional phrase being a favorite expression which Paul uses with a variety of meanings and which has been described as utterly defying definite interpretation.[38] In the present instance, a locative sense seems clearly appropriate: Christ is "the scope within which" justification takes place;[39] at the same time our phrase seems to be a "counterformula" to the antithetical expression "justified by the law" *(en nomō)* in 3:11; 5:4; this suggests that *en* here has instrumental force.[40] A combination of both the locative and instrumental sense thus yields the meaning that believers are justified in virtue of the new relationship to God which is set up by incorporation into Christ;[41] in other words, justification is the result of union with Christ through faith.[42]

As Lightfoot has shown in his commentary,[43] the question "is Christ then an agent of sin?" (RSV; NASB "minister of sin")[44] may be taken either (a) as a logical conclusion from false premises, or (b) as an illogical conclusion from correct premises. In the first case, the reasoning would proceed like this: to seek to be justified in Christ is to abandon the law (premise 1); to abandon the law is to become a sinner (premise 2); then Christ abets sin (conclusion). But this is a monstrous conclusion; either premise 1 must be abandoned (as the objector would maintain) or premise 2 must be rejected (as Paul would argue). In the second case, Paul is arguing that although it is true that in order to be justified in Christ it is necessary to abandon faith in the law as a means of salvation (premise 1) and hence to become sinners in the sense of being reduced to the level of the "Gentiles and sinners" of v. 15

38. BDF §219.4. For various suggested meanings of the phrase cf., e.g., Bultmann, *Theology*, 1: 311; Bornkamm, *Paul*, 154f.; A. Oepke, *TDNT* II: 541f.; M. J. Harris, *NIDNTT* III: 1192f.; W. Grundmann, *TDNT* IX: 550f.

39. BAGD s.v. ἐν I.5.d.

40. A. Oepke, *TDNT* II: 542.

41. A. Richardson, *Theology*, 260.

42. For this sequence (faith, union, justification) cf. Buchanan, *Justification*, 203f., 265, 372, 399, 413; Hill, *Greek*, 141.

43. Lightfoot 116f.; cf. Burton 127-130, in greater detail.

44. Treating ἄρα ("then," "in that case"; cf. AV "therefore") as inferential, as frequently in Paul (e.g., v. 21; 3:7, 29; 5:11; 6:10), rather than simply interrogative, as apparently in RV, NEB, NIV.

(premise 2),[45] the conclusion does not follow that Christ thereby becomes an agent of sin (in the sense of a promoter of actual wrongdoing), support for this statement being given in vv. 18-20. This second alternative is strongly favored by the immediately following expression of revulsion—"No, never!" literally "May it never be!" (NASB)—"which elsewhere in argumentative passages always negatives a false but plausible inference from premises taken as granted."[46] On this understanding, "the whole speciousness of the objection which Paul is answering turns on the seeming identity, the real diversity, of the conceptions of sin implied in *hamartōloi* ["sinners"] and *hamartias* ["sin"] respectively":[47] as Paul will go on to explain (vv. 18-20), to become "sinners" in the sense of v. 15 is by no means the same as being actual transgressors of the law.

18 As the defense continues Paul changes from the first person plural to speak "in the supra-individual first person":[48] not only is he making a tacit reference to Peter but his remark is capable of application to anyone[49] who, like Peter, builds up what he formerly destroyed.[50] Two questions arise in the interpretation of this verse: What is meant by the "system which I have pulled down"—more literally "those things which I tore down" (RSV, cf. AV, RV)? In what sense do I then "show myself up as a transgressor of the law"?[51] The answer to the first question is: the law, which set up the wall of partition (cf. Eph. 2:14, AV) between Jews and Gentiles by means of its demands, and which, by the same means, could be perverted into an instrument for supposedly attaining merit before God.[52] The second question is more difficult to answer; several suggestions will be examined.

(a) One interpretation refers the "transgression" to the *previous action* of tearing down the law which is involved in the Jewish believer's

45. For this sense of "sinners" in v. 17 cf., e.g., H. W. Beyer, *TDNT* II: 89; Räisänen, "Galatians 2.16," 552, n. 55; as a reference to guilty humanity, K. H. Rengstorf, *TDNT* I: 328; in the sense of radical sinfulness as in v. 15, Lambrecht, "Line," 490f.

46. Lightfoot 117; cf. MHT 3: 330. V. 17 is regarded both by Bultmann, "Auslegung," 395f. and by Moule, "Note," as a statement rather than a question, although they differ in the interpretation of the verse; but nowhere else in Paul does μὴ γένοιτο ("No, never!"), used thus as an independent sentence, follow a statement (Bruce 141).

47. Burton 126.

48. Ridderbos 102.

49. Cf. E. Stauffer, *TDNT* II: 357; BDF §281; MHT 3: 39f.

50. On the negative character of the "building up" here, which is contrary to Pauline usage, cf. O. Michel, *TDNT* V: 142, n. 13.

51. The verb συνιστάνω ("show") is used here in a rare meaning rather than in its primary classical sense of "to commend": W. Kasch, *TDNT* VII: 897f.; cf. BAGD s.v. (συνίστημι) I.1.c.

52. E.g., O. Michel, *TDNT* V: 142; J. Schneider, *TDNT* V: 741; cf. C. Brown, *NIDNTT* III: 189.

acceptance of faith in Christ.[53] The present tense of the verb *synistanō* suggests, however, that the "being a transgressor" which will be demonstrated by the reerection of the law refers to a state in the present, not an act in the past. If the intended idea had been "then I show myself up as one who has transgressed the law," this could have been clearly expressed by using some form of the perfect tense.[54] Moreover, it is doubtful whether "transgressor" *(parabatēs),* which denotes one who transgresses a specific command (cf. 3:19; Rom. 4:15; 5:14), can be reduced in this way to being more or less equivalent in meaning to the more general term "sinner" (cf. v. 17a).[55]

(b) Another view identifies the "transgression" as Peter's *present conduct* of separating from the Gentiles, which, as conscious and willful violation of the will of God clearly revealed in Christ, makes him a more heinous transgressor than one who in the eyes of the Judaizers commits a technical breach of a regulation (cf. v. 17, "sinners").[56] This seems, however, to confine the statement unduly to the episode at Antioch; if, as suggested earlier, Paul is writing with an eye to the Galatian situation, then a more general interpretation of v. 18 is called for.

(c) A third view would find the key to the understanding of v. 18 in its connection with v. 19: v. 18 indirectly supports the denial of v. 17 (that justification by faith makes Christ an abettor of sin) by showing that it is, instead, when a person sets up again the validity of the law that he shows himself to be a transgressor; v. 18 is in turn supported by v. 19, where Paul points out that it was the law itself ("through the law" is emphatic by reason of its position) which caused him to die to the law, the implication being that "the rehabilitation of the law actually amounts to a transgression of its true principles."[57] This suggests that in erecting again the validity of the law one shows oneself up as a transgressor in that one thereby goes *against its real intent* (as divinely conceived), which is that of leading a person to die to it so that he may live to God (v. 19).[58] In thus taking the word "for" *(gar)* at the beginning of v. 19 as explicative of v. 18, this interpretation fails to do justice to the close connection between v. 19 and v. 20, which comes to expression in the repeated references to dying and living.[59] (It should be noted that whereas most English versions include "I have been crucified

53. E.g., Bring 91; Machen 153; Räisänen, "Galatians 2.16," 552, n. 55.
54. E.g., infinitive παραβεβηκέναι or participle παραβεβηκότα, examples of which have been found in papyri (MM s.v. παραβαίνω).
55. Rightly, Lambrecht, "Line," 487.
56. E.g., Duncan 69; Ziesler, *Righteousness,* 173.
57. Ellicott 41; cf. Lightfoot 117.
58. Cf. Burton 131.
59. Thus: "I died," "I have been crucified with Christ"; "to live . . . I now live . . . Christ lives . . . my present bodily life [literally "the life I live in the body," NIV] is lived. . . ."

with Christ" in v. 20, the Greek editions generally place the verse division after this clause so that the clause is included in v. 19. Here the numbering of the English versions is followed.)

(d) It seems preferable, therefore, to regard "for" at the beginning of v. 19 as coordinate with the same word in v. 18 (cf. NASB, against RSV "but") and as introducing a second reason for the denial of the false conclusion rejected in v. 17: Paul now sets alongside "the (hypothetical) negative proof of the *mē genoito* ["May it never be!"]" (v. 18) "the (actual) positive proof of this *mē genoito*" (vv. 19f.).[60] On this understanding of the structure of vv. 17-20, v. 18 has in view the *actual transgression* which inevitably follows a reestablishment of the law as the authority in the believer's life.[61] To speak in terms of the Antioch situation, if Peter and the other Jewish Christians upheld again the observances of the law as a necessary condition for justification (as the Judaizers were urging upon Paul's Galatian converts), then they were thereby submitting themselves afresh to the dominion of the law and were bound to become transgressors of it (cf. 5:2f.; 2:16).[62] This interpretation certainly has the advantage of being in complete harmony with Paul's teaching elsewhere on the close connection between transgression and law (cf. Rom. 4:15).[63]

3. DEFENSE: THE POSITIVE ARGUMENT (2:19-20)

19 *For through the law I died to law—to live for God.* 20 *I have been crucified with Christ: the life I now live is not my life, but the life which Christ lives in me; and my present bodily life is lived by faith in the Son of God, who loved me and gave himself up for me.*

19-20a The emphatic "I" *(egō)*, with which the positive argument in vv. 19f. against the false conclusion of v. 17b begins (in the Greek text), may be explained by the "I" *(egō)* of v. 20b (20a in Greek editions) as referring to Paul in his natural self; but the genuine first person singular is here used also representatively of all true Christians.[64] Of this "I" Paul predicates a dying "through the law . . . to the law" (RSV, NIV, NASB). A person's death to the law means that that person ceases to have any relation to the law, so that the law has no further claim or control over that person.

60. Kümmel, "Individualgeschichte," 170 (my translation); cf. Ridderbos 103.
61. E.g., J. Schneider, *TDNT* V: 741.
62. Schlier 97; Kümmel, "Individualgeschichte," 168.
63. Mundle, "Auslegung," also interprets v. 18b in the sense of Rom. 4:15, although he would understand the clause to be speaking of the Jew, not the Christian.
64. BDF §281; cf. E. Stauffer, *TDNT* II: 357.

This death is accomplished "through the law"; this is more specifically expressed in the clause "I have been crucified with Christ," which refers not in an ethical sense to a subjective experience in Christian consciousness, but to the believer's objective position in Christ.[65] By virtue of his incorporation into Christ (cf. v. 17) and participation in Christ's death Paul has undergone a death whereby his relation to the law has been decisively severed and the law has ceased to have any claim on him (cf. Rom. 7:4, 6).[66] But since the vicarious death of Christ for sinners was exacted by the law (cf. Gal. 3:13) and was "first an affirmation of [the law's] verdict,"[67] Paul's death to the law through participation in Christ's death can be said to be "through the law."[68] This death "through the law . . . to the law" means not only that the law as a false way of righteousness has been set aside but also that the believer is set free from the dominion of the law (under which there is transgression, Rom. 4:15) for a life of consecration to God (cf. Rom. 7:6).[69]

Paul's point in vv. 19-20a is thus that, although in seeking to be justified in Christ believers become "sinners" in that they do not possess the law (v. 17a), this is but an outworking of the principle of dying to the law in accordance with its own demands, and the purpose and result of freedom from the yoke of the law is not to lead them to sin, but to enable them to live for God; hence, Christ is not "an abettor of sin" (v. 17b, c).

20b As a result of his participation in Christ's death on the cross, Paul now explains (note the first "and" of NASB, NIV), the life he now lives is not lived by him—by the "I" of v. 19, the self righteous Pharisee who based his hope for righteousness and salvation on strict observance of the law—but by Christ, the risen and exalted One, who dwells in him. It is sometimes said that these words show the mysticism of Paul's experience;[70] but if the mode of expression may be somewhat "mystical," the meaning is

---

65. Cf., e.g., Ladd, *Theology*, 485; Ridderbos, *Paul*, 210; over against Duncan 71; Davies, *Paul*, 197.

66. Cf. J. Schneider, *TDNT* VII: 582.

67. W. Gutbrod, *TDNT* IV: 1076; cf. Bultmann, "Auslegung," 397.

68. The preposition διά thus has its usual instrumental force: A. Oepke, *TDNT* II: 66.

69. "To live for God" may be a case of actual result described as purpose: Ridderbos 105; cf. Zerwick §§351-353 on the tendency to confuse consecutive and final clauses. In this one verse (v. 19 in Greek editions, vv. 19-20a in English versions) Paul has succinctly combined in their logical relationship the twin thoughts of the Christian's freedom and the Christian's obligation: "Christ alone is freedom: by crucifixion with him I died to law, which is bondage. Christ alone is obligation: I died with him that through him and his resurrection I might live to God" (Barrett 52). Cf. 5:14 and comment ad loc.

70. E.g., Deissmann, *Paul*, 121f.; Duncan 73; Hunter 25.

clarified by the completely rational statement which follows.[71] Now that Paul's natural self has come to an end, his earthly existence[72] is no longer an independent life of his own, but a life of believing dependence on the Son of God, who loved him and gave himself for him.[73] To have Christ living in Paul, therefore, does not mean some kind of mystical depersonalization, as though the human "I" of Paul were absorbed into the pneumatic "I" of Christ;[74] on the contrary, Paul fully retains his identity as an "I" who sustains an "I–Thou" relationship with Christ.[75]

The new life spoken of here began when Paul "died to law—to live for God" (v. 19), which was also when "we believed . . . that we might be justified" (v. 16, RV).[76] This means that the believer's new life, which is characterized by faith in Christ and by Christ's indwelling presence, is to be dated from the time of his justification. From the perspective of Paul's argument, the point is that, although justification in Christ *does* mean that one abandons dependence on the law and becomes a sinner in that sense (v. 17), it does *not* mean actually committing sin, since it *also* and *at the same time* means living a new life of union with Christ: Christ lives in the believer, and the believer lives his present, earthly life by faith in Christ.[77]

71. Note the first "and" in NEB, which rightly takes δέ as continuative, not adversative; cf. Burton 137, 138.

72. "My present bodily life" is literally "the life which I now live in the flesh" (AV, NASB)—an instance of the non-theological use of σάρξ ("flesh") in Paul; cf. E. Schweizer, *TDNT* VII: 126.

73. This application to the individual believer of the idea of Christ's atoning love is unique in the NT. In this context the title "Son" describes the close bond of love between God and Jesus and thus emphasizes the greatness of the sacrifice (cf. Rom. 5:10; 8:32; E. Schweizer, *TDNT* VIII: 384). On "the Son of God" as the correct reading cf. Metzger 593 over against O'Neill 44f. Berényi, "Gal 2, 20," has shown that, contrary to the claim of W. Kramer and K. Wengst that Gal. 2:20b ("the Son of God, who loved me and gave himself up for me") is a pre-Pauline formula (491-509), the text may legitimately be considered "a Pauline creation" (509-537). On Christ rather than God as the object of faith, cf. M. J. Harris, *NIDNTT* III: 1214. For the suggestion that τοῦ υἱοῦ here should be regarded as subjective genitive ("faith *of* the Son of God") or at least *gen. auctoris* ("faith which *comes from* the Son of God") see Hays 167-169, 250.

74. Correctly Ridderbos, *Paul*, 232.

75. Cf. E. Stauffer, *TDNT* II: 360; Furnish, *Theology*, 176.

76. On vv. 16 and 19 as descriptions of a single event see E. Stauffer, *TDNT* II: 357.

77. Some scholars have detected a baptismal reference in vv. 19f., mainly on the strength of comparison with Rom. 6:1ff. (e.g., Schlier 99ff.; Brinsmead 73f.). But since the close association of faith and baptism in Paul's thought is not expressly formulated and considered in these verses, we are rightly warned against too hastily seeing such a reference here (Kertelge, *Rechtfertigung*, 242, cf. 241, 265. Cf. further Wendland, *Mitte*, 47; Dunn, *Baptism*, 107). Contrary to the procedure of "most interpreters [who] interpret Romans 6 into Gal 2:19-20," Betz 123 thinks that "Gal 2:19 may contain the theological principle by which Paul interprets the ritual of baptism in Romans 6."

4. DEFENSE: THE DEATH OF CHRIST (2:21)

21 *I will not nullify the grace of God; if righteousness comes by law, then Christ died for nothing.*

21 A break—and climax[78]—in the argument seems to be reached with this verse (note the asyndeton), on which the following points may be noted: (a) Paul may be regarded as stating, in an attack against his opponents, that he (unlike them) refuses to annul the grace of God.[79] But this suggested contrast between him and them is rendered doubtful by the fact that Paul does not use the emphatic personal pronoun for "I" before the verb. It thus seems more likely that he is answering an objection that he makes the grace of God null and void, the more specific reference being to his setting aside the law and its righteousness, in which (according to the Jewish viewpoint) the grace of God consisted.[80]

(b) Paul denies this charge by saying, indirectly, that "righteousness" does not come through the law, just as he explicitly stated earlier (especially v. 16) that justification does not come by works of the law. That righteousness *(dikaiosynē)* is introduced in this manner in a context dealing with justification (the verb *dikaioō*)—almost as though they were synonymous[81]—suggests an intimate relation between the two, which may be

78. H.-H. Esser, *NIDNTT* II: 120.
79. E.g., Cole 83f. Strictly speaking, the "making void" concerns, "not God's grace as such, but its practical force" (C. Maurer, *TDNT* VIII: 159).
80. E.g., Burton 140; Schlier 104.
81. For "righteousness" RSV actually has "justification." According to Ziesler, *Righteousness*, 174, the righteousness in this verse "is forensic, in that it has the aspect of acceptability, and ethical, in that it is essentially something one does";

> this righteousness must surely be equated with the new life of faith of v. 20. If righteousness were not in Christ, i.e., through *dying and rising* with him, his death would be irrelevant, v. 21. As things are, both righteousness and justification are by grace, through the Lord who dies and rises. . . . In v. 21 there is a complete answer to the charge of v. 17.

Against this view I offer three observations: (i) It is not obvious that v. 21 is a complete answer to the charge of v. 17. Rather it would seem that the charge of v. 17 is answered first negatively in v. 18 and then positively in vv. 19f., and that v. 21 is a return to the theme of vv. 15f. This also means that the righteousness in v. 21 need not be, in fact is probably not to be, equated with the new life of faith in v. 20. The very fact that v. 21 is asyndetic supports the view that in v. 21 Paul returns to the position of vv. 15f., which are concerned with forensic justification rather than ethical righteousness. (ii) That Paul's main concern is with justification, not ethical righteousness, is shown by what follows in 3:1ff.; in connection with this passage Ziesler concedes (175) that "the reckoning of faith as righteousness is apparently the same as justification by faith" (vv. 6, 8). (iii) The fact that in 3:13f.; Rom. 3:24-26; 5:9 the death of Christ is connected (directly or indirectly) with justification strongly suggests that here in Gal. 2:21 as well the issue is justification, not ethical righteousness.

briefly expressed thus: righteousness is that *status* of being in the right with God bestowed in justification, which is God's *act* of putting the believing sinner right with him.

(c) It is implied that righteousness is by the grace of God and is closely connected with the death of Christ. Indeed, since Christ's death would be "to no purpose" (RSV)[82] if righteousness were by the law, it appears that it was God's purpose that the bestowal and obtaining of righteousness be closely connected with the death of Christ, just as in the preceding context justification is connected with faith in Christ. The second and third of these three points (b, c) emerge here only indirectly or by implication and will be taken up and more fully expanded by Paul in the course of his argument in chapters 3 and 4.

ADDITIONAL COMMENT 6: THE SIGNIFICANCE OF THE ANTIOCH INCIDENT

The idea of justification by faith dominates Paul's train of thought in his "address" (2:15-21): it is directly and repeatedly emphasized in his statement that the way of justification is faith in Christ rather than works of the law (vv. 15f.) and is presupposed in his refutation of the charge that his gospel encourages sin (vv. 17-20); then the closely related concept of righteousness (regarded as attainable not by means of the law but by grace) marks the end of the passage. This is the deeper issue underlying the apparently mundane matter of table-fellowship between Jewish and Gentile Christians at Antioch.

In the light of the examination of 2:15-21 above the reason for Paul's opposition to Peter clearly emerges. To Paul, the truth of the gospel was none other than justification by faith in Christ alone and not by works of the law—a principle which applied to Jew and Gentile alike and hence was the basis of the Church's unity.[83] But by denying table-fellowship to Gentile Christians Peter was in effect declaring them to be second-class citizens, with the implication that the only way they could become first-class citizens was to go the whole way of the proselyte and accept circumcision; in the final analysis circumcision could be required as a precondition for social contact only if it was first a requirement for salvation.[84] Thus Peter's conduct not only immediately threatened the Church's unity, but in the long run compro-

---

82. This is one of two derived meanings of the adverb δωρεάν, which basically means "freely, for nothing": F. Büchsel, *TDNT* II: 167. Cf. p. 194, n. 143 below.

83. Cf. Nock, *Paul*, 103.

84. Bruce, "Further Thoughts," 28f.; *NT History*, 268; cf. Bring 79; Dibelius-Kümmel, *Paul*, 133; Räisänen, "Legalism," 80, 82.

mised the very basis of that unity; it was, at least as Paul saw it, "a fundamental assault on the order of grace in which the church lived, in favour of the order of performance, whose principle of operation is the law."[85] Behind Paul's confrontation with Peter lies the opposition of two basic principles: justification through faith in Christ alone (= salvation by the grace of God), and justification by works of the law (= salvation by man's own achievements).

From the entire Antioch incident, then, it is clear how vital Paul considers justification by faith: it is to him "the truth of the Gospel"; to hold fast to this principle of salvation is to be "acting in line with the truth of the gospel" (2:14, NIV),[86] whereas to cause this principle to be compromised is to deviate from "the straight path of gospel truth."[87] Even though he presents his doctrine in a polemical context, with the result that its formulation is in part conditioned by the position he is combating,[88] it cannot fairly be maintained (as by A. Schweitzer and others) that the doctrine is of merely polemical significance,[89] for at least two reasons: (a) It is entirely unlikely that Paul would so unhesitatingly define what he calls "the truth of the Gospel" in terms of something which allegedly had only subsidiary importance for him. (b) He describes or at least interprets his conversion experience (and indeed that of Peter and other Jewish Christians) in terms of justification by faith (v. 16), which is thus seen to stand at the beginning of the believer's experience as the foundation of the new life of faith in Christ and consecration to God (v. 19). In this connection we do well to remember that "it is always important to distinguish between the situation which merely evoked a particular expression or development of some belief and a situation which actually gave rise to the belief itself";[90] in the present instance, the former refers to the situation in which Paul found himself first in Antioch and then in Galatia, and the latter to his Damascus experience itself.[91]

85. Schlier 84 (my translation).
86. Cf. R. Klöber, *NIDNTT* III: 352.
87. Bruce, *Letters of Paul*, 25.
88. E.g., the very form of the expression ἐκ πίστεως Χριστοῦ ("by faith in Christ") suggests a deliberate choice of the preposition ἐκ, though it is less accurate than διά (on this see Lightfoot 115), in order to form an exact antithesis to ἐξ ἔργων νόμου ("by the works of the law"); see on 2:16c, pp. 116f. above.
89. Cf. Fung, "Status of Justification," especially 5-7.
90. Whiteley, *Theology*, 18. This distinction is overlooked when Räisänen, "Paul's Conversion," 407 says: "Perhaps it was in Antioch around AD 50 that Paul emerged as a preacher of justification by faith, rather than on the Damascus road in the thirties." This statement is based on the observation that there is a total absence of justification terminology from the account of Paul's call (Gal. 1:11-17); but our comment on 1:12b and Additional Comment 2 (p. 54 and pp. 66–68 above) show that the *thought* of justification is far from absent from that account.
91. Cf. A. B. Bruce, *Christianity*, 12, 50; Kertelge, *Rechtfertigung*, 226.

B. AN APPEAL TO EXPERIENCE (3:1-6)

This passage begins a major portion of the epistle (3:1–5:12), in which Paul is concerned to argue, from a scriptural and theological perspective, the superiority of the gospel doctrine of faith to the Galatian agitators' law-oriented version of Christianity. In seeking to press home his central thesis with arguments from various directions which "tumble over one another,"[1] Paul appeals first to the readers' experience and then to Scripture, and in connection with both to logical reasoning.[2]

Although v. 6 also serves to introduce vv. 7ff. and is made to begin a new paragraph in RSV, NIV, and Phillips, it is preferable to regard it as concluding the present paragraph (so NEB) for two reasons. (a) Grammatically, the use of the comparative adverb *kathōs* ("even as," AV, RV; "even so," NASB) at the beginning of v. 6 is among the cases where (as in 1 Tim. 1:3) the clause which supplies the point of reference is not present but must be supplied from the context.[3] The inferential particle *ara* in v. 7 ("then," NEB, NIV; "so," AV, RSV; "therefore," RV, NASB) also points in this direction. (b) Materially also, v. 6 properly belongs with the preceding context, for its function is to show that the Galatian converts, as those who have heard and believed the gospel, stand in the same line of faith as Abraham.

1. A SERIES OF QUESTIONS (3:1-5)

1 *You stupid Galatians! You must have been bewitched—you before whose eyes Jesus Christ was openly displayed upon his cross!* 2 *Answer me one question: did you receive the Spirit by keeping the law or by believing the gospel message?* 3 *Can it be that you are so stupid? You started with the spiritual; do you now look to the material to make you perfect?* 4 *Have all your great experiences been in vain—if vain indeed they should be?* 5 *I ask then: when God gives you the Spirit and works miracles among you, why is this? Is it because you keep the law, or is it because you have faith in the gospel message?*

Paul asks his misguided readers a series of five or six questions which, for convenience of treatment, may be reduced to three: these are found in v. 1, vv. 2, 5, and vv. 3f. respectively.

1. J. Knox, *IDB* II: 341a; cf. Schlier 118.
2. In terms of the apologetic letter 3:1–4:31 constitutes the *probatio:* Brinsmead 52; Betz 128, cf. 129. But see pp. 29f. above.
3. BAGD s.v. 1; cf. Thayer s.v. 1. In this case the answer to be supplied is "By faith, of course." Cf. Williams, "Justification," 92f.

1 "You must have been bewitched" is literally "Who has bewitched you . . . ?" (RSV, NASB, NIV). This rhetorical question, "intended as a rebuke,"[4] suggests that Paul regards his Galatian converts as having unwittingly come under the spell—the hypnotic effect—of the false teachers (the group behind the singular "who"; cf. on 1:7b).[5]

With obvious emotion (indicated by the word "O": AV, RV, RSV)[6] Paul chastizes his readers as "stupid Galatians." *Anoētoi* denotes either an insufficient or mistaken use of mental powers or a deficiency in understanding itself.[7] Whichever it is, the word also suggests that behind Paul's perception of intellectual fault lies his "adverse religious and moral judgment" of the Galatians,[8] and the result is the same: they have failed to grasp the liberty inherent in their salvation.[9]

Their foolish conduct (cf. 1:6) was the more culpable in that Jesus Christ had been publicly proclaimed before their very eyes as crucified. The word rendered "openly displayed" *(prographō)* refers not to some document or letter previously written by Paul (cf. the use of the word in Rom. 15:4; Eph. 3:3; Jude 4),[10] nor to a depiction of the suffering and dying Jesus,[11] but to the public and official character of the apostolic kerygma which set forth, like a placard for all to see, "Jesus Christ . . . crucified" (RSV, NASB, NIV).[12] The perfect participle *estaurōmenos* ("crucified") in this phrase does not merely fasten attention upon the death of Christ as the culmination and therefore summary of his life as that of "one who took the form of a servant,"[13] nor does it characterize Jesus as one hanging on the cross and to be considered as such even now, rather it describes him in his character as the crucified (and risen) One. The phrase "Jesus Christ crucified" concisely summarizes the decisive event in salvation history and, as such, the fundamental content of the Pauline kerygma.[14] If only the Galatians had fixed their eyes on that placard, it would have enabled them to escape the fascination of the false teachers; for that one phrase, had it been

---

4. BDF §146.2.

5. Βασκαίνω, "bewitch," a NT hapax allied to English "fascinate," denotes casting a spell by the evil eye: J. S. Wright, *NIDNTT* II: 559. According to G. Delling, *TDNT* I: 595, "the characteristic point of the βασκανία is that it exerts its influence without extraordinary means."

6. For the Greek particle ὦ as indicative of emotion cf. Zerwick §35; MHT 3: 33.

7. E.g., Guthrie 91 and Schlier 118f., respectively.

8. J. Behm, *TDNT* IV: 962; cf. Trench 283 (§lxxv).

9. G. Harder, *NIDNTT* III: 129.

10. So Rendall 167.

11. Rightly G. Schrenk, *TDNT* I: 771; Bornkamm, *Paul*, 159; over against, e.g., Martyn, "Mission," 315.

12. E.g., E. Brandenburger, *NIDNTT* I: 397; R. Mayer, *NIDNTT* III: 482.

13. As in Hoskyns-Davey, *Riddle*, 156.

14. Schlier 120; cf. J. Schneider, *TDNT* VII: 582.

truly understood, would have removed the ground from the Judaizers' argument (cf. on 1:4).

2, 5 The two questions of vv. 2 and 5 may be considered together, as they both employ the same antithesis: "by keeping the law" or "by believing the gospel message"/"because you have faith in the gospel message." "Answer me one question" is literally "this only would I learn from you" (RV), the Greek verb being used in the simple sense of "finding something out from someone" or "being informed."[15]

Confident that an answer to the question to be asked would constitute a decisive argument, Paul in diatribe style first asks the Galatians how it was that they had begun their Christian lives (this is the significance of "receiving the Spirit," v. 2; cf. Rom. 8:9; Eph. 1:13; Acts 2:38), and how it was that their experience of God's working among them came about (v. 5).[16] The present participles rendered "gives" and "works" (v. 5) are parts of a single substantive construction ("the one who gives . . . and works"). They could refer to the miraculous demonstrations of power which accompanied the initial preaching of the gospel to the Galatians (cf. Acts 2:43; Heb. 2:3f.);[17] in this case the question in v. 5 would repeat to some extent the one in v. 2. It is more natural, however, to take the participles as referring to God's present supply[18] of his Spirit and his continuing works of power among the Galatians. On this showing the two questions have regard, respectively, to the Galatians' initial reception of the Spirit within them and their continuing experience of his presence and power among them. The obvious answer to both questions is the same: not "by keeping the law" *(ex ergōn nomou),* but "by faith in the gospel message." *(ex akoēs pisteōs).*[19]

No doubt attaches to the meaning of the first phrase in this antithesis

---

15. BAGD s.v. μανθάνω 3; Thayer s.v. b. To D. Müller, *NIDNTT* I: 486 it is debatable whether the word is used here in a secular Greek sense or in the OT sense of learning the will of God; but the former seems clearly more appropriate to the context. K. H. Rengstorf, *TDNT* IV: 408f. would take the Greek behind "learn from you," μαθεῖν ἀφ' ὑμῶν, as meaning "learn by you," thus distinguishing it from "learn from," μαθεῖν παρά, as in 2 Tim. 3:14; but ἀπό (ἀφ') is used for παρά with the genitive (cf. BDF §210.3) and Rengstorf's entire exposition seems too subtle to be convincing.

16. Since "miracles" refers to outward deeds ἐν ὑμῖν naturally takes the meaning "among you" (e.g., Betz 135) rather than "within you" (e.g., Ellicott 50).

17. E.g., G. Bertram, *TDNT* II: 653; Burton 151f.

18. For ἐπιχορηγέω ("supply") cf. 2 Cor. 9:10; Col. 2:19. The force of the prefix is probably not simply directive (Ellicott 49), but additive (Lightfoot 136). The suggestion of Parratt, "Romans i.11 and Galatians iii.5," that "he who supplies the Spirit to you" (RSV) is not God (so NEB) but a charismatic individual who conveys the Spirit by laying on of hands is rendered unlikely by the fact that in the other two occurrences of the verb the supplier is God or Christ.

19. According to Betz 130, 136 this is evident because at the time of their experience the Galatians were outside the law and therefore could not have kept it.

(cf. 2:16), but the second phrase has been interpreted in a variety of ways, depending on whether *akoēs* is taken in an active sense ("hearing") or a passive sense ("what is heard," that is, the gospel message) and on whether *pisteōs* is regarded as active ("believing," "faith," either subjective or objective genitive) or passive ("what is believed," "the message of faith," objective genitive). The following combinations have been offered: (i) the hearing (active) of faith (active, subjective), that is, hearing that comes of faith or in faith, or that is accompanied by faith;[20] (ii) hearing (active) which leads to faith (active, objective);[21] (iii) hearing (active) which leads to faith (active, objective) and is accompanied by faith (active, subjective)—thus combining (ii) and (i);[22] (iv) hearing (active) the message of faith (passive, objective);[23] (v) faith (active, subjective) in the gospel message (passive);[24] (vi) proclamation (passive) of the message of faith (passive, objective);[25] (vii) preaching (passive) which aims at faith, demands faith, or has faith as its subject or as its content and goal (active, objective);[26] (viii) hearing (active) the gospel and believing it (active, subjective), or (by metonymy) the message (passive) of faith (active, objective), that is, the gospel that is presented to be heard and believed.[27]

That *pistis* is to be taken in the active sense of *fides qua creditur* (believing) rather than in the passive sense of *fides quae creditur* (the "faith" as content) seems reasonably clear from what precedes and what follows these verses (2:16, 20; 3:6-9, 14), but it is more difficult to decide whether *akoē* here has an active or a passive sense. We may confine ourselves to a consideration of the two major alternatives: (i) "hearing with faith" (RSV, NASB), "hearing and believing" (NEB mg., second alternative); and (v) "believing the gospel message," "faith in the gospel message" (NEB, cf. Phillips), "believing what you heard" (NIV). The latter view may be supported by reference to Rom. 10:16f., another passage which speaks of missionary preaching, where *akoe* is used three times, in the first instance

20. E.g., RSV, NASB; L. Goppelt, *TDNT* VIII: 329; G. W. H. Lampe, *IDB* II: 637a.

21. E.g., Moule 175; Scott, *Christianity*, 99, 130.

22. E.g., Guthrie 92-93. Cf. Schlatter, *Glaube*, 388f., 611f.

23. Braun, *Gerichtsgedanke*, 80.

24. E.g., NEB, NIV; Sanders, *Paul and Palestinian Judaism*, 482f., 492.

25. Betz 128 with n. 3, 130, 132.

26. E.g., (a) Hatch, *Pauline Idea of Faith*, 33, n. 1; (b) R. Bultmann, *TDNT* VI: 213; (c) Ellicott 47; (d) G. Kittel, *TDNT* I: 221.

27. Bruce 149, thus considering (i) ("hearing the gospel and believing it") and (vii) ("the gospel itself, which is presented to be heard and believed") as alternatives; but cf. 147, where the translation of the text ("the message of faith") shows preference for the latter. W. Mundle, *NIDNTT* II: 175 gives both (i) ("hearing in faith") and (vii) ("the apostolic message which has faith as its content"), without indicating whether these are to be combined or regarded as alternatives, or, if the latter, where his preference lies.

(v. 16) certainly, and in the second and third (v. 17) probably, in the passive sense of the report or message—that which is heard.

It is preferable, however, to take *akoē* in Gal. 3:2, 5 in the active sense of "hearing," on the following grounds: (a) Even though the antithesis in these verses is between faith and law and not between hearing and doing,[28] *akoēs* taken as active ("hearing") does still present a better contrast with "observing" (NIV). (b) Although on the other view the preposition *ek* *(ex)* might be rendered "as the result of, in consequence of,"[29] yet in Pauline usage *ek* usually denotes a direct rather than a remote causal relationship. Therefore, it would not be entirely accurate to say that "the gospel message" (*akoēs* taken in the passive sense) is the direct cause of the Galatians' receiving the Spirit, whereas "hearing and believing" (*akoēs* taken in the active sense) is the direct cause. (c) The active sense for *akoē* is supported by the context just as the active sense of *pistis* is. The Galatians' reception of the Spirit *ex akoēs pisteōs* is set down in parallel fashion with God's dealings with Abraham, whom God justified not "by a message about faith" or "a message which produces faith" (even though this is true enough in itself; cf. Rom. 10:17a), but "by faith," in order that believers might receive the promised Spirit "through faith" (v. 14). This conclusion of the discussion in v. 14 clearly refers back to v. 5 and describes the correspondence between what God did for Abraham and what the community has received; hence the chief idea in vv. 2, 5 is faith, and the reference in *akoē* is not to an independent notion standing over against faith, but to a process—hearing—which belongs with and is carried out in faith.[30]

We may therefore take the rendering of RSV, NASB, and NEB mg. (second alternative) as giving *exegetically* the true sense (though *materially* the rendering of NEB and NIV is not incorrect). The two questions are then a reminder that it is by reason of their believing response to the proclamation of "Jesus Christ crucified" that the Galatians initially received the gift of the Spirit and even now continue to experience his power. Since the present

28. Rightly, Ellicott 47.
29. Thayer s.v. II.6; BAGD s.v. 3.f. Hays 179f. rightly calls the NEB rendering ("by believing the gospel message")

> an interpretive paraphrase which is impossible to justify as an actual translation of Paul's words. This would require us to take πίστεως as the object of the preposition ἐξ, with ἀκοῆς understood to mean "the (gospel-)message" and taken as an objective genitive dependent on πίστεως. Because of the word-order, however, such a construction is awkward and far-fetched. The point may be illustrated by comparing the parallel expression διὰ νόμου πίστεως in Rom. 3:27. Would anyone want to suggest that Paul means to say here that boasting is excluded "through believing the Law"?

Cf. the first sentence of n. 10 on p. 113 above.
30. For these reasons see Schlatter, *Glaube,* 611.

reality of the Spirit is the pledge of the eschatological salvation that is to come (e.g., 2 Cor. 1:22; 5:5; Eph. 1:14),[31] the significance of Paul's twice-repeated question lies in its implied answer that salvation is not by deeds dictated by law, but by a believing response (v. 2) to the message of Christ (v. 1). Thus the same relation stands between faith and salvation as we have seen to exist between faith and justification (2:16).

3-4 These three questions (two in the Greek) are connected and may, like those in vv. 2 and 5, be considered together. The fundamental question is that of v. 3b: "Having begun by the Spirit, are you now being perfected by the flesh?" (NASB). To "look to the material to make you perfect" (NEB) would indeed be a stupid thing to do,[32] and would cause all the previous experiences of the Galatians to be in vain.

Because of the ambiguity of the Greek verb *paschō*, which could indicate either suffering or any sort of experience, v. 4a has been variously rendered: (a) in a neutral sense (perhaps to preserve the ambiguity) as "did you experience so many things . . . ?" (RSV, cf. AV, RV); (b) as an indication that the Galatian Christians had suffered for their faith (NIV, cf. NASB, Phillips), and (c) taking the Galatians' experiences in a positive sense as in NEB: "all your great experiences."[33] Since vv. 2 and 5 speak of the reception of the Spirit and the miraculous works of God's power in their midst, the NEB rendering seems to suit the context best,[34] although the second view cannot be absolutely excluded as impossible.[35] Also disputed is the force of the clause in v. 4b, which may be taken either as a threat (all their experiences would become worse than useless) or as an encouragement (Paul does not consider the situation irretrievably hopeless).[36]

To return to the fundamental question: "Beginning with the Spirit" (NIV) no doubt refers to the inception of the Galatians' Christian life when the Spirit was imparted and received by their hearing with faith (v. 2) the message of Christ (v. 1). But the precise meaning of the second of the two clauses of the question is less easy to determine.[37] The issue is not so much whether the verb *epiteleisthe* is to be taken as middle ("bring to completion") or passive ("be brought to completion," i.e., as in NEB, "to make

---

31. E. Schweizer, *TDNT* VI: 422; cf. J. Schniewind and G. Friedrich, *TDNT* II: 584.

32. V. 3a should be thus connected with v. 3b (as in Lightfoot 135) rather than with v. 2 (as in Duncan 80).

33. Cf., e.g., (a) B. Gärtner, *NIDNTT* III: 723; (b) Bruce 150; (c) BAGD s.v. πάσχω 1.

34. Cf. W. Michaelis, *TDNT* V: 912 with 905, n. 3; Betz 134.

35. Cf. Machen 169f.

36. E.g., Ridderbos 115f. and Hendriksen 115f., respectively.

37. In σαρκὶ ἐπιτελεῖσθε the dative is probably modal rather than strictly instrumental: E. Schweizer, *TDNT* VII: 133, n. 269.

you perfect"), as whether it means here (a) simply "ending" (RSV) or "trying to attain your goal" (NIV) as opposed to "beginning" (cf. Phil. 1:6),[38] or (b) "perfecting" or "being made perfect."[39] As it turns out, the two questions are closely related in the versions, in that those that take the verb as middle give it the simple meaning of "ending" (RSV, NIV), whereas those that take it as passive give it the sense of "being perfected" (AV, RV, NASB, NEB). On the assumption that the prefix *epi* probably has "additive" or "perfective" force here,[40] we may prefer the latter rendering and regard Paul as making an ironic reference to the Judaizers' claim to "make perfect" the Pauline version of Christianity which the Galatians had received by insisting on their "keeping the law" as a necessary complement.[41]

Paul is placing works of the law under the heading of "flesh," a word which in its characteristic Pauline usage denotes human nature in its fallenness, apart from the regenerating grace and sanctifying power of God's Spirit.[42] Works of the law fall into this category because they deceive a person into thinking that he can be justified before God by his own strength (i.e., by keeping the law), which is "flesh."[43] "Having begun by the Spirit" (NASB), on the other hand, "implies that man lives, not in his own strength, but by another power."[44] Once again, as in 2:15-21, the contrast is between faith and works of the law; only this time the faith/works antithesis is brought into connection with, and indeed given expression through, the new antithesis between the Spirit and the flesh. Having received the Spirit (who is the pledge of final salvation [2 Cor. 1:22; 5:5; Eph. 1:14]) by faith, the Galatians have no need to look to fleshly works of the law to bring them to perfection. The two principles, Spirit-faith and flesh-works, are mutually exclusive.

2. AN ANSWER FROM SCRIPTURE (3:6)

6 *Look at Abraham: he put his faith in God, and that faith was counted to him as righteousness.*

---

38. Also G. Delling, *TDNT* VIII: 62.
39. E.g., Vine 8.
40. Cf. n. 18 above.
41. Cf., e.g., Ridderbos 114; Schlier 123f.; Brinsmead 79. This interpretation is viewed with suspicion by Barclay, "Mirror-Reading," 82; in his final tabulation of results, however, he considers it "conceivable" that the opponents talked of "completing" Paul's work (89).
42. Cf. E. Schweizer, *TDNT* VII: 133; A. C. Thiselton, *NIDNTT* I: 680f.
43. Bultmann, *Theology,* 1: 240; cf. Wuest 86.
44. E. Schweizer, *TDNT* VI: 428. Cf. R. Bultmann, *TDNT* II: 868.

6 Although the answer to the questions in vv. 2 and 5 is self-evident, Paul characteristically drives the point home by going to the Scriptures for the definitive answer; the word at the beginning of v. 6 rendered "even as" (AV, RV) or " even so" (NASB; Gk. *kathōs*) contains the idea of a norm or measure.[45] Paul quotes almost verbatim from the Septuagint of Gen. 15:6, using this text because of the association of belief and righteousness—Abraham's faith in God and that faith being counted to him for righteousness. Paul has in mind Abraham's believing acceptance of God's concrete promise to him concerning his descendants (LXX Gen. 15:5b, "thus shall your seed be"); this is borne out by the fact that Paul's analysis in Rom. 4:17-22 of Abraham's faith is based on the context in which Gen. 15:6 occurs.

According to Jewish interpretation at the time of Paul, Abraham's faith was a meritorious work: Abraham "put his faith in God," and therefore God counted that act of faith for what it was, as righteousness.[46] Since Paul employs the quotation of Gen. 15:6 in confirmation of the implied answer to the question in vv. 2, 5 (by "hearing with faith" and not by "works of the law"), it is clear that he does not take the "counting" as an accounting of Abraham's merit, or even in the sense that Abraham's faith was regarded or estimated by God as if it were righteousness (the one quality being taken for the other).[47] Rather, he takes it in the sense that Abraham was considered to stand in a right relationship (i.e., was given the status of being "right") with God, simply by virtue of his faith in God, and not by virtue of meritorious achievement before God.[48] In this way Paul makes a radical break with Judaism, probably also giving a corrective to an interpretation of the same verse being taught to the Galatians by the Judaizers.[49]

While faith does not intrinsically have the value of righteousness[50] and is not itself righteousness in the sense of a meritorious work, it is probably not arbitrary that faith (as distinct from some other quality) is reckoned for righteousness. As James Denney observed,[51]

> The spiritual attitude of a man, who is conscious that in himself he has no strength, and no hope of a future, and who nevertheless casts himself upon, and lives by, the word of God which assures him of a future, is the necessarily and eternally right attitude of all souls to God. He whose attitude it is, is at bottom right with God.

45. Ridderbos 118, n. 1.
46. Cf. H. W. Heidland, *TDNT* IV: 290.
47. Sanday-Headlam, *Romans,* 100; Thayer s.v. λογίζομαι 1.a.
48. Cf., e.g., G. Schrenk, *TDNT* II: 204; Cranfield, *Romans,* 1: 231f.
49. Barrett, "Allegory," 6f.; Cranfield, *Romans,* 1: 229f.
50. Rightly, H. W. Heidland, *TDNT* IV: 289; *contra* Ziesler, *Righteousness,* 182.
51. *EGT* II: 621a.

Furthermore, according to Rom. 4:22 and its preceding context, Paul himself suggests that Abraham's faith was counted to him for righteousness because it gave glory to God and constituted trust in his faithfulness and power.

Now to have righteousness "counted" to one and to be justified are synonymous expressions: this may already be gathered from a comparison of vv. 6 and 8 of Gal. 3 (cf. also v. 11a and v. 11b), but appears most clearly from Rom. 4:1-3.[52] In appealing to Gen. 15:6 Paul's intention is to show that "what the Galatians might have known on the basis of their experience (verses 1-5) is in accord with what the Scriptures have to say about Abraham":[53] that righteousness, or justification, comes about through faith, and not through works of the law. If it be asked how Abraham's one act of trusting God's promise to him can be cited in support of the Christian way of "hearing with faith" the message of Christ, the answer would seem to lie in the consideration that that one act was part of Abraham's commitment of his whole self to God, and that the faith which justifies is similarly total self-commitment to God; in other words, the kind of faith which Abraham had "is precisely that of which the gospel speaks."[54]

It is clear that in Paul's own mind the case of Abraham (receiving righteousness through faith) provides an obvious parallel to that of the Galatians (receiving the Spirit through hearing and believing the gospel and not by keeping the law). In other words, Paul takes it for granted that Abraham's being justified by faith *proves* that the Galatians must have received the Spirit by faith also; and this argument from Scripture falls to the ground *unless* the reception of the Spirit is in some sense equated with justification. For if this were not so, it could be objected that even though Abraham was indeed justified by faith, it does not necessarily follow that reception of the Spirit also has to be dependent on faith; conceivably while justification is by faith the gift of the Spirit could be conditioned on works. We may take it, then, that Paul conceives of receiving the Spirit in such close connection with justification that the two can be regarded in some sense as synonymous, so that in the Galatians' receiving the Spirit their justification was also involved.[55]

52. Cf., e.g., Calvin, *Romans*, 84; Hodge, *Romans*, 112.
53. Ridderbos 117.
54. Bruce, *Time is Fulfilled*, 65. Cf. Hill, "Salvation Proclaimed: IV," 197a. This is not to deny, of course, that faith in Gal. 3 is more christocentric, in Rom. 4 more theocentric (Beker, *Paul*, 97, 103). But self-commitment to God and self-commitment to Christ necessarily involve each other (cf. Jn. 14:1).
55. Cf. H. W. Heidland, *TDNT* IV: 292. Hays 179, n. 16 rightly remarks that "the observation that Paul appeals *to* the Galatians' experience of the Spirit as a premise *from which* he can argue deals a serious blow to Betz's theory that Galatians is an apology written 'in defense of the Spirit' (25)," and that in this respect "Betz's hypothesis about the purpose of the letter contradicts his exegetical observations about 3:1-5."

Thus, just as in the previous passage (2:15-21) Paul interpreted his own conversion experience in terms of justification by faith, so also in the present passage (3:1-6) the Galatians' initiatory experience of receiving the Spirit is regarded as at least involving justification by faith, if not being totally synonymous with it. This again shows that to Paul justification stands at the inception of the Christian life as an integral part of the Christian experience and gives the lie to the theory that justification represents but a "subsidiary crater" (A. Schweitzer) on the periphery of Paul's theology and is of polemical significance only.[56]

C. FROM CURSE TO BLESSING (3:7-14)

From the personal question, "How did you Galatians gain your acceptance with God?" (3:1-6), Paul passes on to the more general question, "Who are the people whom God accepts and on what basis are they accepted?"[1] Once again he appeals for scriptural support to the case of Abraham, which has already served as confirmation of his (implied) answer to the personal question. Here the argument revolves largely around the matter of sonship to Abraham: it appears that the judaizing opponents had argued, probably on the basis of Gen. 12 and 17 (esp. 17:9-14), that in order to share in the blessings promised in God's covenant with Abraham, it was necessary to become a child of Abraham—which meant circumcision and observance of the law.[2] Against this Jewish understanding Paul offers his own Christian interpretation; hence the frequent occurrences of Abraham's name, which give a certain coherence to the discussion in chapters 3 and 4.[3] Paul's purpose in the present passage is to show that, over against law, which

---

56. Schweitzer, *Mysticism*, 225. Cf. the final paragraph of Additional Comment 6 above (p. 127).

1. Duncan 83.

2. Herein perhaps lies a difference of emphasis between these Judaizers and more "orthodox" Judaism: "For the Rabbis the proselyte is not incorporated into sonship of Abraham. . . . The Judaisers were ready to accept full incorporation to sonship on the condition of fulfilment of the Law" (W. Foerster, *TDNT* III: 784, n. 35). This difference of emphasis would remove what Harvey, "Opposition," 325f. regards as the "fatal" difficulty in the view that ch. 3 has circumcision in view.

3. Cf. 3:6, 7, 8, 9, 14, 16, 18, 29; 4:22—all the instances in the epistle. Cf. Martyn, "Mission," 317-320, who observes that the major issue in "the exegetical catena of 3.6-29" is that of the identity of Abraham's descendants; this, Martyn suggests, is due to Paul's knowledge "that the Galatians are currently hearing a great deal about Abraham and about the identity of his descendants" (319, 318). "Paul takes up the traditions about Abraham in hope of neutralizing their [the false teachers'] Law-observant mission" (320); thus, "in the main it is not they [the false teachers] who are reacting to Paul's theology, but rather he who is reacting to theirs" (323).

involves a curse (vv. 10-12), faith is the way to blessing and as such makes one a child of Abraham (vv. 7-9), the transition from curse to blessing being provided in and by Christ (vv. 13f.).

1. FAITH: THE WAY TO BLESSING (3:7-9)

> 7 *You may take it, then, that it is the men of faith who are Abraham's sons.* 8 *And Scripture, foreseeing that God would justify the Gentiles through faith, declared the Gospel to Abraham beforehand: "In you all nations shall find blessing."* 9 *Thus it is the men of faith who share the blessing with faithful Abraham.*

7 "You may take it" rightly understands the verb *ginōskete* as imperative rather than indicative (so RSV).[4] Paul begins by asking his readers to recognize[5] that the true children of Abraham[6] are exclusively "the men of faith" (*hoi ek pisteōs;* cf. v. 9)—those who are justified by faith in Christ and whose life is guided by the principle of faith. In contrast to "the circumcision party" (2:12, RSV; *hoi ek peritomēs*) these may be called "the faith party";[7] the preposition *ek* in these contrasting expressions designates "circumcision" (that is, the law) and "faith" as the characteristic features of the two groups.[8]

Sonship to the patriarch depends on this "genealogy of faith which goes back to Abraham"; the determinative factor is no longer physical but spiritual descent.[9] This truth, which Paul regards as logically involved ("then" represents the inferential particle *ara*) in Abraham's experience of receiving righteousness through faith, he proceeds to demonstrate by explicating the meaning of God's dealings with Abraham for the Gentiles.

8 Paul's citation of God's promise to Abraham is a conflation of

4. Rendall 168 argues that the imperative would require the aorist γνῶτε (cf. γνῶθι in Heb. 8:11); but Heb. 13:23 has the present γινώσκετε, which Lightfoot 137 takes to be imperative.

5. R. Bultmann, *TDNT* I: 703, cf. 708 (s.v. γινώσκω).

6. That "sons" includes "daughters" is clear from v. 26 with its context, especially v. 28.

7. Cole 92; Pinnock 38.

8. Cf. Zerwick §135. Hays maintains that the primary meaning of the phrase in this verse is "those who are given life on the basis of (Christ's) faith" (201), of which Abraham's faith is a "a foreshadowing" (202). "This interpretation hinges upon the claim [cf. 154] that ἐκ πίστεως in verses 7 and 9 should be understood as an allusion to Hab 2:4, understood messianically" (ibid.). But Hab. 2:4 is not cited until 3:11, and it is surely much more natural to construe the phrase by its immediately preceding context (v. 6) as a reference to *Abraham's* faith; this interpretation is also supported by Rom. 4:16.

9. G. Schrenk, *TDNT* V: 1005 (whence the quotation); J. Jeremias, *TDNT* I: 9.

Gen. 12:3c (cf. 28:14c) and 22:18a (cf. 18:18b; 26:4c) in the LXX; the words "all nations" from 22:18a are substituted for "all the families" in 12:3c so as to bring in the word "nations" *(ethnē)*, because of its current use in the sense of "Gentiles."[10] In the MT the Hebrew niphal verb *nibrᵉkû*, "bless," may have reflexive force, in which case the meaning is "shall pray to be blessed as Abraham was blessed" (cf. RSV and NEB at Gen. 12:3c; 18:18a), and the rendering "shall find blessing" in our verse may be an attempt to bring out the distinctive sense of the niphal. *Nibrᵉkû* is usually taken, however, in a passive sense.[11] In any case the LXX translators understood the Hebrew verb in the passive sense and rendered it as unambiguously passive in the Greek. It is in this sense that Paul understands the original promise and sees its fulfillment in the mission to the Gentiles.

Citing God's promise to Abraham, then, Paul says that Scripture "declared the Gospel to Abraham beforehand,"[12] thereby recognizing in God's promise to Abraham an announcement of the gospel in advance.[13] Paul is able to do so because he takes the "in you" *(en soi)* of the quotation, not (as the Judaizers no doubt did) in its locative and genealogical sense of physical relationship with Abraham, but, in accordance with the precise force of Heb. *bᵉ* (translated *en* in the LXX in Gen. 12:3 and 18:18) and particularly in the light of the Christ-event, in its instrumental sense, as "by means of you" (so NIV "through you," both in Galatians and in the two OT references). By his believing response to God's promise Abraham had "given occasion to the establishment and announcement of the principle that God's approval and blessing are upon those that believe."[14] Paul further explains that Scripture's declaration to Abraham was due to its "foreseeing"

10. Sanders, *Paul, the Law*, 21 contends that Paul's quotation is based on Gen. 18:18, not 12:3, "since Paul's major intention is to include the Gentiles, and the term *ethnē* does not appear in 12:3" (cf. Beker, *Paul*, 375, n. 14). It would seem, however, that the main intention of Paul's quotation is to prove the pivotal position which Abraham occupies in salvation history as the archetype of justification by faith (cf. vv. 7, 9); hence the real emphasis is on the phrase ἐν σοί, which does not appear in Gen. 18:18 (although ἐν αὐτῷ does).

11. R. E. Clements, *Abraham and David* (London, 1967), 15, n. 3, cited by Bruce 156. Cf. Gen. 12:3c; 18:18a, AV, RV, NASB, NIV.

12. This personification of Scripture, in which he may simply be following a rabbinic mode of expression (cf. Schlier 129), shows that he identifies Scripture with God's own speaking (G. Schrenk, *TDNT* I: 753; cf. C. Brown, *NIDNTT* III: 491).

13. The Greek verb (προευαγγελίζω, a NT hapax) indicates "preaching the gospel by anticipation," not "preaching a preliminary gospel" (rightly Hanson, *Studies*, 64). This should be clearly borne in mind, even though from another point of view it can be said that when the blessing came to the nations in Christ God's promise to Abraham was fulfilled and "the προ-ευαγγέλιον became the εὐαγγέλιον" (G. Friedrich, *TDNT* II: 737).

14. Burton 161.

(the participle has causal force)[15] that God would justify the Gentiles[16] through faith.[17] The significance of God's promise to Abraham lies, therefore, not merely in its value "as documentation of the theme that the Gospel is to be preached to the Gentiles,"[18] but in its testimony that the doctrine of justification by faith was implicitly involved and anticipated in the promise to Abraham.

We may, therefore, reconstruct Paul's reasoning in v. 8 as follows: Abraham received righteousness by faith (v. 6); his believing response was the occasion of the establishment of the principle of justification by faith; God foresaw that he was to justify the Gentiles according to this principle;[19] this principle was announced as the timeless principle of the gospel (this is the force of the present tense of the verb "justify") when God (in Scripture) made the promise to Abraham that through him all the nations (that is, the Gentiles) would be blessed.

9 From all this it follows[20] that "it is the men of faith" who are blessed with believing[21] Abraham: since God has promised that the Gentiles will be blessed through Abraham and since his blessing was in the first instance that of justification by faith, then those who exercise faith in God are blessed—that is, justified—"along with Abraham, the man of faith" (NIV).[22] This conclusion may now be linked with the statement of v. 7: according to the Judaizers, only the sons of Abraham can have a part in his blessing; but Paul has shown that those who are blessed along with Abraham are men of faith (v. 9); hence it is the men of faith who are the sons of Abraham (v. 7).[23]

15. "Foreseeing" gives the accurate meaning of the Greek participle (cf. K. Dahn, *NIDNTT* III: 515), although "to know in advance" has also been suggested as a suitable rendering (W. Michaelis, *TDNT* V: 381).

16. A reference to "all nations in distinction from Israel as the *gôyim*" (K. L. Schmidt, *TDNT* II: 369).

17. NEB thus takes ἐx as equivalent to διά; cf. MHT 3: 260, and the discussion above of 2:16b, c, point (a) (pp. 116f.).

18. Dodd, *According*, 44.

19. Beker, *Paul*, 98 refers to this as "a basic salvation-historical principle." With regard to the statement of P. Jacobs and H. Krienke, *NIDNTT* I: 695 (s.v. προοράω) that the verb is "not used in the NT . . . to describe the activity of God," it is to be remembered that "Scripture foreseeing" is a personification: it is God's foreseeing that is expressed in Scripture (cf. Wuest 95).

20. "Thus" represents Gk. ὥστε, which is here simply an inferential particle (cf. Moule 144).

21. Πιστός is to be taken in this sense (cf. RSV, NASB, NIV) rather than as meaning "faithful" (cf. AV, RV), since it is on Abraham's faith rather than his faithfulness that the context lays stress (Vine 61).

22. That Paul says "share the blessing" rather than "are justified" probably reflects the vocabulary of his opponents (cf. Burton 162). On the interpretation of this verse by Howard 57 see the just criticism of Wedderburn, "Review," 381f.

23. On Paul's argument in this passage as reflecting one of two kinds of typologi-

2. LAW: INVOLVING A CURSE (3:10-12)

10 *On the other hand those who rely on obedience to the law are under a curse; for Scripture says, "A curse is on all who do not persevere in doing everything that is written in the Book of the Law."* 11 *It is evident that no one is ever justified before God in terms of law; because we read, "he shall gain life who is justified through faith."* 12 *Now law is not at all a matter of having faith: we read, "he who does this shall gain life by what he does."*

Having argued *for* justification through faith (vv. 7-9), Paul now strengthens his position ("on the other hand" is literally "for," Gk. *gar*) by arguing *against* the possibility of justification by legal works. For this purpose he employs three OT passages.

10 In a deliberate contrast with "the men of faith" (vv. 7, 9) Paul states that "all who rely on observing the law" (NIV)—that is, all who hold to legal works as the means of justification (and as the guiding principle of life)—are under a curse.[24] He then immediately grounds this statement by quoting Dt. 27:26a.

A word which occurs twice in Paul's quotation (*pas,* cf. AV, RV, RSV, NASB "everyone . . . all things"; NEB "all . . . everything") is not represented in the Hebrew of the MT of the verse quoted, but is in the next verse (Dt. 28:1); but Paul's twofold "all" is probably the result not of his fusing two quotations but more simply of his following the LXX text of Dt. 27:26a,[25] which by inserting the two instances of *pas* adds emphasis to what is expressed in the MT (cf. NEB's "any" and "all" in that verse).

By substituting "everything that is written in the Book of *the* Law"[26] for the Septuagint's "all the words of *this* law" (MT also has "this law"), Paul further generalizes the original denunciation of "the man who does not uphold the words of this law by carrying them out" (NIV in Dt. 27:26) into a curse on "every one who does not abide by all things written in the book of the law, and do them" (RSV in Gal. 3:10): whereas "this law" refers to the twelve curses pronounced from Mount Ebal (the "Shechemite dodecalogue"; Dt. 27:15-26), "the law" is in Paul's mind a reference to "the written Torah (cf. Dt. 31:26; Jos. 1:8) in all its details."[27]

---

cal exegesis occasionally employed by the rabbis, namely, that in which "the action of a Biblical personage is presented as an archetypal model," see Cohn-Sherbok, "Exegesis," 122f.

24. Anarthrous κατάραν has the effect of "curse opposed to blessing" (Hendriksen 127, n. 94).

25. Cf., e.g., Grundmann, "Gesetz," 57, over against Cole 96.

26. On the phrase "the Book" cf. G. Schrenk, *TDNT* I: 617 (s.v. βιβλίον).

27. Bruce 158. For the view that "Paul's argument does not misrepresent the original intention of the passage" see Bruce, "Curse," 28f. (with ref. to M. Noth).

Paul's meaning in v. 10 is, therefore, that all who hold to legal works are under the curse pronounced by the law itself upon all who do not observe the law completely.[28] The words presuppose that no one does observe the law completely, although Paul does not pursue this line of reasoning, but concentrates on the declaration of the authoritative scripture.[29]

Paul's claim in the present verse has occasioned much difficulty among scholars; it has, in fact, been described as "the most difficult problem" in Galatians and Romans.[30] It is maintained, for instance, that Paul has misrepresented Pharisaism in that "in Jewish belief no idea was more stressed than the infinite and unceasing willingness of God to forgive the penitent sinner," so that "the observance of the Law did not for a Jew involve the pitiless antithesis of complete success and complete failure which Paul here portrays"[31] and that "Paul's definition of righteousness as perfect conformity to the law of God would never have been conceded by a Jewish opponent."[32] On the other hand, it has been observed that the doctrine of the necessity of doing all the law is not absent in Palestinian Judaism.[33]

28. Cf. 5:3; Jas. 2:10; F. Hauck, *TDNT* IV: 577. It is importing an alien thought into the context to take Paul's meaning to be that they are cursed because, from the viewpoint of Christ, legal works do not fulfill the law in the true sense (e.g., Bring, "Gesetz," 22f.; Kertelge, *Rechtfertigung*, 209). On D. P. Fuller's interpretation see the criticism of Bruce 158 and Sanders, *Paul, the Law*, 54, n. 34 and the discussions in Moo, "'Law,'" 97f. and Schreiner, "Perfect Obedience . . . Possible?" 155f.

According to Sanders, *Paul, the Law*, 21 the thrust of this verse "is borne by the words *nomos* and 'cursed,' not by the word 'all,' which *happens* to appear" (emphasis added). But even if, for the sake of argument, one concurs with his "conclusion that the *emphasis* is not on the word 'all'" (22, emphasis added), it is doubtful if that word—which, after all, also appears in Dt. 28:1, 15, 58; 30:10 (LXX)—can be dismissed as a happenstance that has no significance for Paul. See also n. 54 below.

29. "Scripture says" is literally "it is written," on which cf. G. Schrenk, *TDNT* I: 747. It has been objected that the presupposition just mentioned is contradicted by Paul's own testimony in Phil. 3:6, where he describes himself as having been blameless with respect to legal righteousness (Bring, "Gesetz," 22). It is probably true, however, that his claim there is "an illusion of the Pharisee's heart" (Cranfield, "Law," 151) which had not realized the deepest intentions of the law (cf. Lk. 18:11f.). Rom. 1:18–3:20; 5:13, 20; and 7:5ff. show clearly enough that Paul the Christian has a very different view of the demands of the law and its fulfillability. On Paul's view of the fulfillability of the law see, e.g., Schreiner, "Paul and Perfect Obedience" (against E. P. Sanders), especially 278; "Perfect Obedience . . . Possible?" 159 (against H. Schlier, whose interpretation of Gal. 3:10 is similar to that of Sanders [cf. *Paul, the Law*, 54, n. 28]).

30. K. Lake, *BC* V: 217, n.

31. Nock, *Paul*, 30.

32. Moore, *Judaism*, 1: 495; 3: 151.

33. Cf. Longenecker, *Paul*, 41f. (where the references given include Jas. 2:10, reflecting Palestinian Judaism). See also W. Grundmann, *TDNT* IV: 536; H. Braun, *TDNT* VI: 480; p. 222, n. 8 below.

It would therefore appear that Paul's claim in v. 10b is not entirely removed from the realm of Jewish thought, and it becomes unnecessary to account for it in terms of his lack of expert knowledge,[34] his having presented his earlier convictions in a distorted way, or his argument being dictated by polemical considerations and influenced by his rabbinic training. In any case, "the limited part that repentance plays in Paul's soteriology suggests that he approached the whole question with different presuppositions from those of the rabbis";[35] his argument here is probably part of his Christian interpretation of the law in the light of the Christ-event, as will become clear in the discussion of v. 13 below.

11 Secondly, Paul states that it is clear that no person is ever justified in God's sight "in terms of law" (NEB) or "by the law" (AV, RV, RSV, NIV, NASB). He justifies this statement by quoting Hab. 2:4b, in which (as in Gen. 15:6) the two concepts "righteous" and "faith" appear together and which is doubtless chosen for that reason. The MT of Hab. 2:4b can be represented by "the righteous will live by his faith" (NASB, NIV, RSV) or "by his faithfulness" (NASB mg., NIV mg., RSV mg., NEB mg.), that is, by steadfastness in waiting for the vindication of God's justice in the face of enemy oppression. The LXX, on the other hand, has "the righteous one will live by my faithfulness" *(ho de dikaios ek pisteōs mou zēsetai)* or (if *mou* be taken as objective genitive) "by faith in me." There is a variant reading placing *mou* immediately after *ho de dikaios* and thus yielding the sense "my righteous one will live by faith," which is the form quoted in Heb. 10:38a (so NIV). Paul omits the possessive pronoun *mou* (without any significant alteration of meaning) and apparently understands the statement to mean: "he who is righteous by faith shall live" (NASB mg.).[36]

On the other hand, it has been argued in favor of the translation "the righteous shall live by faith" (RV; AV, NASB, and NIV are similar) that (a) the original Hebrew certainly does not bear the other meaning and it is contrary to both the MT and the LXX to link "by faith" with "the righteous one" rather than with "will live"; (b) the order of the words in Paul's quotation is not what would be most favorable to the other rendering; (c)

---

34. As by Nock, *Paul*, 30f.

35. Bruce 160. Gundry, "Grace," 34 accounts for Paul's infrequent use of the terms "repentance" and "forgiveness" as follows: "Paul so deeply felt the falling short of God's glory through sin that he did not think trying to keep the law, *let alone repenting to receive forgiveness for failures to keep it*, adequate. The more the law abets sin's lordship because of human weakness, the less adequate is repentance to take care of guilt; *for repentance implies a change of behavior.*"

36. That Hab. 2:3f. was a traditional *testimonium* from the earliest period is clearly shown by Dodd, *According*, 51.

Paul's argument seems best sustained by linking "by faith" with "live"; and (d) this construction forms a more exact antithesis to the words "shall live by them" in v. 12 (RSV, NASB).[37] At least one scholar has judged that the understanding reflected in the RSV and NEB renderings "is inspired more by Lutheran dogma than by a calm consideration of the evidence";[38] others, while agreeing that the text is construed by Paul as in RSV and NEB, question the "somewhat violent use of the quotation" and speak of "the Pauline distortion of Habakkuk."[39]

Against these objections may be set the following considerations: (a) The particular meaning which the quotation had for Paul and which he intended for his readers is to be gathered primarily from the context in which he employs it and the part which it plays in his argument.[40] The expression "justified . . . by the law" in v. 11a, not to speak of the wider context from 2:15 onwards (where the concern is with how a man may be justified, not how the righteous shall live), naturally suggests the association of "by faith" with "the righteous one" rather than with "shall live."[41]

(b) That the order of the words quoted (the placement of the modifying prepositional phrase after the noun rather than between the article and the noun) would be amenable to this interpretation may be deduced from Paul's writing elsewhere "the Israel according-to-flesh" (ton Israēl kata sarka, 1 Cor. 10:18) rather than "the according-to-flesh Israel" (ton kata sarka Israēl): "the righteous-one by-faith" (ho dikaios ek pisteōs) could similarly be intended to mean the same as "the by-faith righteous-one" (ho ek pisteōs dikaios).[42]

(c) While Heb. 'emûnâ strictly means "steadfastness" or "fidelity" rather than "trust" or "faith," the former is based on the latter. As it has been well said, "can there be any 'fidelity' on man's part, such as God can reward with the great gift of 'life,' which does not ultimately have its roots in man's attitude of 'faith' in God?"[43]

(d) Furthermore, "if it is 'faith' which makes the 'just' man worthy to receive life, what is it but his faith which gives him originally his title to be called 'just'?"[44] Seen in this light, Paul's application of the Habakkuk text

---

37. Cf. Ellicott 54; G. Schrenk, *TDNT* II: 191 with n. 71.

38. Hanson, *Paul's Understanding*, 7.

39. Taylor, *Forgiveness*, 48 and Schoeps, *Paul*, 202, n. 3, respectively.

40. Burton 166.

41. Cf. Sanders, *Paul, the Law*, 53, n. 23. That a double entendre is intended here is improbable (rightly M. J. Harris, *NIDNTT* III: 1177f.).

42. This answers the objection of Michel, *Römer*, 55.

43. Duncan 94f. Cf. Lightfoot 155, who thinks that in Hab. 2:4 the word has something of the "transitional or double sense": constancy springing from reliance on Yahweh.

44. Duncan, loc. cit.

as though it read "he who is righteous-by-faith" does no violence to the prophet's intention: he simply "strips faithfulness to its core of faith in God"[45] and in so doing expresses the abiding validity of the prophet's message.[46] The quotation in Rom. 1:17 is to be similarly construed.[47]

Paul's argument in v. 11 is, then, to this effect: because Scripture says that it is he who is righteous (that is, justified) *by faith* that will live, it follows that no one is justified by works of the law (irrespective of one's success or failure in keeping it).[48]

12 Thirdly, Paul demonstrates the incompatibility of faith and law by quoting Lev. 18:5b: "the man who obeys [literally "does"] them will live by them" (NIV), where "them" refers to Yahweh's "statutes and . . . ordinances" (RSV) mentioned in v. 5a—although for Paul's readers the word would most readily recall "all things written in the book of the law" (Gal. 3:10b, RSV). This being the principle of law, the contrast with the principle of faith is clear: the one says, "he who is righteous by faith shall live"; the other, "he who practices them shall live by them" (NASB). "Shall live"[49] occurs in both Hab. 2:4 and Lev. 18:5 and justifies the juxtaposition of the two passages in accordance with the rabbinic exegetical principle of *gᵉzērâ šāwâ* ("equal category").[50] But while the goal envisaged

---

45. Allen, "Romans i-viii," 8. Cf. G. Quell, *TDNT* II: 177, n. 2.

46. Cf. Collins, "Exegesis," 152. According to Hays, "the ambiguity of Paul's formulation allows him to draw multiple implications out of the Habakkuk text" (156). Hays discusses the question "by *whose* faith shall the righteous live?" (155-157), and responds with a threefold answer (156):

> (a) The Messiah will live by (his own) faith(fulness). [Cf. 151-154 for the argument that ὁ δίκαιος is Christ.]
> (b) The righteous person will live as a result of the Messiah's faith(fulness).
> (c) The righteous person will live by (his own) faith (in the Messiah).

Hays claims that "Paul's thought is rendered wholly intelligible only if all of these interpretations are held together and affirmed as correct" (ibid.). In our view, however, both (a) and (b) are doubtful, and only (c) is correct—as an answer to the question "by whose faith will 'he who is righteous by faith' live?"

47. Cf. Cranfield, *Romans*, 1: 102; C. Brown, *NIDNTT* III: 368. On the somewhat different use of Hab. 2:4 in Rom. 1:17 as compared with its use in Gal. 3:11 see Beker, *Paul*, 96.

48. Ziesler, *Righteousness*, 177 would give "righteous" here "its full and usual meaning, forensic and ethical"; but since v. 11b is intended to provide the scriptural ground for the statement of v. 11a, it is reasonable to understand "righteous" as strictly defined by "justified," which admittedly (178) is declaratory (only).

49. On the middle voice of the verb cf. Zerwick §226.

50. Barrett, *First Adam*, 40, n. For the principle see Strack, *Introduction*, 94; Jeremias, "Gedankenführung," 148. It has been argued that the use of Lev. 18:5 to "fortify" Hab. 2:4 "directly implies a contrast between living by the law and living by faith" and therefore favors the rendering "the righteous shall live by faith" for v. 11b (Hanson, *Studies*, 41f.; Hanson goes on to identify "the righteous" as "the Righteous One," that is, the Messiah). But it may equally be argued that the very parallelism of the

is the same, faith and law appear as two diametrically opposed and mutually exclusive principles. Paul's point is proved: "the law is not based on faith" (NIV).[51]

Thus, by means of these three scriptures, Paul demonstrates that while faith is the way to blessing (vv. 7-9) the law, as a principle diametrically opposed to faith and not based on faith (not *ek pisteōs*), can never bring justification (which is only through faith, *ek pisteōs*). The law can only bring its own curse (vv. 10-12). The impossibility of being justified by legal works is in v. 10 based, by implication, on the fact that no one keeps the law perfectly, while in vv. 11f. the basis is of a more dogmatic nature: "the law could not justify (= give life, Gal. 3.21) in any case, since it rests on works, and only faith gives life."[52] This can also be expressed in terms of 2:21: "it is out of the question that the way of the Law should lead to salvation, since this would render the Christ event pointless."[53] Thus, both the factual-experiential and the dogmatic approaches figure in Paul's argumentation here, as they do in Romans; "it appears that the twin pillars of human weakness and salvation-history, not just salvation-history, uphold justification by faith alone."[54]

---

words ὁ δίκαιος ἐκ πίστεως ζήσεται ("he who is righteous by faith shall live") and ὁ ποιήσας αὐτὰ ζήσεται ("he who practices them shall live") favors "he who is righteous by faith," corresponding to "he who practices them," the two scriptures furnishing opposing answers to the question—not *"How* will one live?" but *"Who* shall live?"

51. This interpretation is opposed by Bring, "Gesetz," 9f., 20ff. Elsewhere he maintains that "it is not the opposite of *faith* that is demonstrated in the quotation in vs. 12b, but the opposite of *righteousness by the law* as Paul understood its meaning"; this judgment is based on his understanding of Paul as meaning that "the promise of life belongs, not to the observance of law, but to the fulfilment which took place when Christ fulfilled the law" (Bring 130)—an understanding which is rightly judged to be "off the mark" (Hanson, *Studies*, 48; cf. Dunn, "Works," 541, n. 51).

Cohn-Sherbok, "Exegesis," 130f., sees in vv. 11f. Paul's use of Rabbi Ishmael's thirteenth rule of exegesis which states that two contradictory passages are to be resolved by a third if possible: here the contradiction between Hab. 2:4 and Lev. 18:5 is resolved by Gen. 15:6, already quoted in v. 9 and referred to again in v. 14 (similarly King, "Tannaim," 365; Schoeps, *Paul*, 177f.). This explanation seems unsatisfactory for two reasons: (a) Lev. 18:5 is cited to show, by its very antithesis to Hab. 2:4, which is mentioned *first*, that justification can never be by way of law—hence no resolution of any contradiction is necessary since none is seen by Paul. (b) Gen. 15:6 only confirms the one principle (Hab. 2:4) against the other (Lev. 18:5) and so would in any case offer no "reconciliation of conflicting passages." For a more satisfactory treatment cf. Dahl, *Studies*, 161ff. (especially 161-164, 171-174).

52. Sanders, *Paul and Palestinian Judaism*, 483, n. 37; "Question of Fulfilling," 106.

53. H. Braun, *TDNT* VI: 480.

54. Gundry, "Grace," 27. In *Paul and Palestinian Judaism*, 483, n. 37, E. P. Sanders wished to "emphasize more the dogmatic character of Paul's view"; cf. "Ques-

3. CHRIST: PROVIDING THE TRANSITION (3:13-14)

13 *Christ bought us freedom from the curse of the law by becoming for our sake an accursed thing; for Scripture says, "A curse is on everyone who is hanged on a gibbet."* 14 *And the purpose of it all was that the blessing of Abraham should in Jesus Christ be extended to the Gentiles, so that we might receive the promised Spirit through faith.*

In a forceful and abrupt introduction, Paul presents Christ as the deliverer from the curse of the law and the one who obtains the blessing of Abraham for believers. The reference to "Christ" is emphasized by the word's initial position in the sentence and by the sentence's asyndetic entry into the course of the text. Four main features of Paul's argument in these verses may be noted.

13 (a) Christ in his death is described as "having become a curse" (RSV, NASB)—a conclusion Paul arrives at by the use of the rabbinic exegetical principle of "equal category" (already mentioned in regard to v. 12), which in the present instance works in the following manner. In the LXX both Dt. 27:26 (quoted in v. 10) and Dt. 21:23 (quoted in v. 13) begin with words based on the same verbal stem ("curse"):[55] 27:26 pronounces a curse (*epikataratos*, verbal adjective) upon everyone who fails to render perfect obedience to the law, and 21:23 declares to be accursed (*kekatēramenos*, perfect participle) everyone who hangs upon a tree (or pole). By bringing these two texts together and interpreting the latter in terms of the former, Paul understands Jesus' death on the cross (to which a curse was attached according to Dt. 21:23)[56] as a bearing of the curse of God

---

tion of Fulfilling," 108; he now maintains in *Paul, the Law*, 20-27 (especially 23-27) that Gal. 3:10-12 has only the dogmatic reason in view, since Paul does not hold the view that the law cannot be fulfilled. On this last point see, however, n. 29 above.

55. (Ἐπι)καταράομαι. The common stem appears only in the LXX; in the MT two different Hebrew words are used. The reading ἐπικατάρατος in Paul's quotation of Dt. 21:23 in v. 13 "may be due to assimilation . . . of this quotation to the words of Gal 3:10" (Wilcox, "Upon the Tree," 87).

56. "Gibbet" is literally "tree" or "wood," Gk. ξύλον. Ξύλον in the sense of "cross" is a distinctive NT use of the word (J. Schneider, *TDNT* V: 39). Acts 5:30 and 10:39 suggest that Dt. 21:23 was already applied to the crucifixion of Christ before Paul, thus showing the early acceptance by Jesus' followers of the fact that their Master died the death on which the law pronounced a curse. Barrett 30 observes that in the earliest period rabbinic interpretation apparently took "of God" in Dt. 21:23 (literally "he that is hanged is the curse of God" [RV mg.; NASB mg. is similar]) as an objective genitive ("the body hanging on a tree is an affront to God"); he surmises that it was "probably . . . in the realm of anti-Christian propaganda that the genitive was taken to be subjective: 'God lays his curse upon everyone who hangs on a tree.'"

incurred (according to Dt. 27:26) by all who fail to continue in obedience to the law.

In its original OT context the "hanging" does not refer to hanging as a means of execution but to the hanging of a body on a tree or stake (cf. Dt. 21:22) after execution in some other way, in order to expose the condemned to shame.[57] But in its application to Jesus the "hanging" obviously refers to crucifixion. This, however, is consonant with the fact that already "in many OT passages the Heb. *tlh* does not refer to the supplementary Heb. punishment but to the customs of hanging, impaling and crucifixion customary elsewhere"[58] and with the application in Jewish law of the principle of Dt. 21:22f. to the hanging of both living persons and of corpses.[59]

The word "curse" in the expression "having become a curse" is evidently used by metonymy: Christ "became a curse" in the sense that he submitted to the curse pronounced by the law of God, or it could be an instance of *abstractum pro concreto:* "curse" = "bearer of the curse."[60] It is significant that Paul avoids using of Christ the expression that is used in the LXX of Dt. 21:23 ("accursed by God"): the implication of such an expression would conflict with Paul's view of Christ's death as his supreme act of obedience to God's redemptive will (cf. Rom. 5:19; 2 Cor. 5:19).[61]

(b) Christ's submission to the curse is said to be "for our sake" or "for us" (RSV). The personal pronoun "us" *(hēmōn)* is understood by some as referring to Jews only.[62] But it probably includes Gentiles as well, since

---

57. J. Schneider, *TDNT* V: 39, n. 12.

58. G. Bertram, *TDNT* III: 918.

59. Bruce 165. The exegesis (proposed by G. Klein and adopted by Schoeps, *Paul,* 179) which gives to the Hebrew participle *tālûy* of Dt. 21:23 the dual meaning of both "hanged" and "elevated" (cf. Jn. 8:28; 12:32) is open to the fatal objection that with Paul, in distinction from John, the exaltation of Jesus begins only with the resurrection; this interpretation would also "involve the absurd sense: 'An exalted one is accursed by God'" (Bruce 166).

60. H. Riesenfeld, *TDNT* VIII: 509; F. Büchsel, *TDNT* I: 450. In view of the insistence of some that the curse of the law and the curse of God are to be sharply distinguished (e.g., Burton 164f., 168, 172; he even asserts that "to miss this fact is wholly to misunderstand Paul" [168]), it is necessary to emphasize that, while "the curse is the curse of the Law, since the Law expresses it," "yet it is also the curse of God, for the Law is the revelation of God" (F. Büchsel, *TDNT* I: 450).

Dunn, "Works," 536 would understand "the curse of the law" as having to do "primarily with that attitude which confines the covenant promise to Jews as Jews," as "the curse of a wrong understanding of the law." This meaning seems ill-suited to the idea of Christ as the bearer of the curse. The remark of Räisänen, "Galatians 2.16," 548 that "it is altogether impossible to read chapter 3 as an attack on just a particular *attitude* to the law," has its bearing here.

61. Bruce 165.

62. E.g., Machen 179; Betz 148. Cf. Donaldson, "'Curse of the Law,'" 107, n. 3. Donaldson himself interprets 3:13-14a "as a radical reinterpretation, in the light of the cross event, of a Jewish pattern of thought in which the inclusion of the Gentiles is seen

both alike fail to keep the law perfectly and therefore stand under the curse which the law pronounces; if Gentiles do not possess the Mosaic law (cf. "Gentile sinners," 2:16), they nevertheless have the equivalent of the law within their hearts and consciences and are in principle subject to its curse (cf. Rom. 2:12-15). It would seem, therefore, an inadequate explanation of Paul's meaning to say that "it is by the deliverance of Israel from the curse of the Law that God made it possible for the blessing promised to Abraham to extend to the Gentiles";[63] rather, the Gentiles must themselves be redeemed from the curse before they can receive the blessing of Abraham.[64] Moreover, the "we" of v. 14b, which picks up the "us" and "our" of v. 13a, surely includes "the Gentiles" of v. 14a, thus confirming that v. 13a already has Gentiles as well as Jews in view. "For our sake" renders a Greek phrase *(hyper hēmōn)* which in itself need not mean any more than "on our behalf"; the sense "in our place," however, is conceded by many scholars as at least a derived meaning warranted here by the context.[65]

(c) By submitting to the curse of the law on behalf of his people, both Jew and Gentile, Christ redeemed them from the law's curse and condemnation.[66] He neutralized the curse for them, so that they, on whom the curse

---

as a consequence of the eschatological redemption of Israel" (100, cf. 102, 106), so that "those who are redeemed from the curse of the law are Jewish Christians exclusively" (94). An important factor in his argument is his claim that "the same 'eschatological model' [namely, "the redemption of Israel is the necessary prelude to the blessing of the Gentiles," 99] underlies both Gal 3:1–4:7 and Rom 11" (106); this claim is made possible by the supposition that the actual sequence in Rom. 11—"Jewish remnant—'fulness of the Gentiles'—salvation of 'all Israel' "—is also "a revision of this eschatological model" (100).

63. Duncan 99.

64. Cf. Schlier 136f.; F. Büchsel, *TDNT* I: 450; Howard 59f.; Sanders, *Paul, the Law,* 68f., 88, n. 20; Williams, "Justification," 91f.; Lull, " 'The Law Was Our Pedagogue,' " 481, n. 1. See also Donaldson, " 'Curse of the Law,' " 107, n. 2.

65. E.g., Zerwick §91; Moule 64; H. Riesenfeld, *TDNT* VIII: 509; W. Mundle, *NIDNTT* I: 417; M. J. Harris, *NIDNTT* III: 1197.

66. The NEB rendering "bought . . . freedom" clearly brings out the basic components of the meaning of Gk. ἐξαγοράζειν (here and in 4:5): the payment of a price issuing in release from a state of slavery or captivity. Elsewhere in Paul (1 Cor. 6:20; 7:23) the simple form of the verb (ἀγοράζειν) is explicitly connected with the idea of a price ("bought at a price"), which other NT writers specify as "the precious blood of Christ" (1 Pet. 1:19, RSV; cf. Rev. 5:9). It is doubtful, however, that such use of redemption vocabulary implies a recipient to whom the ransom or purchase price is paid; perhaps the most that can be said is that it indicates that Christ's action on behalf of his people is at tremendous cost to himself—even at the cost of his own life. (Marshall, "Development," 153f., n. 4, has suggested that in discussion of redemption terminology a distinction be made between two terms: "price" should be used "for those cases where some *payment* or exchange is *received* by the person from whom the captive is delivered," and "cost" "for whatever *expenditure* of money, life and effort is *demanded* on the part of the redeemer.")

rightfully falls because of their failure to keep the law, now become free from both its demands and its curse. Christ was able to neutralize the curse because in his death he satisfied the claim of the law by fulfilling it in his life, so that "this liberation from the curse of the Law . . . confers both an actual and also a legally established freedom."[67]

Verse 13 thus represents Christ's death as a vicarious bearing of the curse of the law which delivers his people from the same curse.[68] This is in simple terms Paul's Christian interpretation of Christ's death on the cross.[69] Like the early disciples before him, after his conversion Paul had to rethink the meaning of the cross. The confession of Jesus' messiahship involved in his conversion (cf. 2 Cor. 5:16; see p. 66 above) made it imperative for Paul to explain Jesus' accursed death on the cross in a way consistent with his

Apart from the OT (e.g., Ex. 15:13; Isa. 43:1), another possible background of the redemption metaphor in the NT is that of *redemptio ab hostibus*, the release and return to their native lands of prisoners of war on payment of a ransom by a fellow citizen (W. Elert, "Redemptio ab Hostibus," *Theologische Literaturzeitung* 72 [1947]: 265-270, cited by Marshall, op. cit., 158 with n. 5). As for the contemporary practice of sacral manumission (in which the slave provided the priests with his own purchase price, and they in the name of the god they worshipped then purchased with that price the slave's freedom from his master), there are at least two vital differences (which are really two sides of the same coin) between it and Christ's redemption: (a) In Paul "the divine Purchaser does not pay only in appearance as in sacral redemption, but in the most bitter reality, so that the parallel breaks down at the decisive point" (F. Büchsel, *TDNT* I: 126). (b) "In sacral redemption it is really the slave who finally purchases his own redemption. Hence, we are better advised to find the basis of Paul's thinking in the ordinary redemption and purchase of slaves" (K. H. Rengstorf, *TDNT* II: 275, n. 106). But if any reference to sacral manumission was indeed intended, then "a vivid contrast was implied: the gods did nothing to effect emancipation, it was the slave who had slowly amassed the necessary sum of money; God in Christ, however, had done all that was necessary to effect emancipation" (Leenhardt, *Romans*, 101f.).

67. F. Büchsel, *TDNT* I: 126. Cf. Schlier 140; Ridderbos 126; Kertelge, *Rechtfertigung*, 211.

68. For the idea that Christ's death is presented in this verse as a vicarious, substitutionary death cf., e.g., Morris, *Preaching*, 55f., 58f.; Hunter 28f.; F. Büchsel, *TDNT* I: 450f. Examples of other views are: (i) According to Burton 168-171 Christ sets people free, not from the curse of the law, but from the misconception that God deals with mankind on a legalistic basis. This has rightly been called "an unjustifiable modernization of Paul's thought" (Ridderbos 126, n. 9); (ii) Whiteley, *Theology*, 137 and Dunn, "Paul's Understanding," 139-141, respectively, describe Christ's death as "participatory" and "representative" rather than substitutionary (for criticism cf. Kim, *Origin*, 276f., n. 3).

69. Cf. W. Grundmann, *TDNT* IX: 544. Cf. also, however, Wilcox, "Upon the Tree," who holds (in support of N. A. Dahl) that "Gal 3:13a-14 [*sic*] is a fragment of Jewish-Christian midrash taken over by Paul" (99). Bruce, "Curse," 32 suggests a good reason why Paul's explanation is not repeated in his later letters: "There is, perhaps, a certain accidental quality about it, as though the redemption effected by Christ in his death depended on the external form of his death—death by crucifixion. . . . But the saving essence of the death of Christ lay in the spirit in which he accepted it."

glorious resurrection and exaltation; this Paul does by means of the exegetical device explained above.

It has rightly been said that "this use of the text of Deuteronomy [21:23] might be described as a brilliant controversial device."[70] But it would be wrong to think of Paul's initial development of it only in connection with controversy. He must have made use of this text himself to refute the early Christians' claim of a crucified Messiah; now that he was forced by the evidence of Jesus' resurrection to acknowledge that claim, he was compelled to reconcile its validity with the judgment of the law in Deuteronomy. The solution to the scandal of the cross found in our passage must therefore have occurred to him sooner rather than later in his Christian life. As H. R. Mackintosh put it, "He had no need to await the outburst of controversy; he had a Judaist in his own heart, with whom from the outset he was bound to reach an understanding."[71]

14 (d) This verse describes the purpose for which Christ redeemed his people from the curse of the law. NEB's "that . . . so that" (cf. NASB, NIV) seems to regard the second clause as subordinate to the first; but the two clauses, both introduced by *hina*, are probably to be taken as coordinate (cf. AV, RV, RSV).

The first clause makes a statement from the perspective of salvation history:[72] it was in Jesus Christ—the one who delivered his people from the curse of the law by vicariously bearing it upon himself (v. 13) and who is the offspring of Abraham in whom all the Gentiles were to be blessed (v. 16)— that the Gentiles receive Abraham's blessing, which (as vv. 8 9 have shown) is that of being justified through faith. In this way Christ's coming opened to the Gentiles the door of faith and of justification through faith apart from the works of the law.[73]

The second clause expresses the same truth in terms of individual spiritual experience: "the blessing of Abraham which has been revealed in Christ is received in the gift of the promised Spirit."[74] This gift of the Spirit

70. Headlam, *Paul*, 83.

71. Mackintosh, *Forgiveness*, 103. Cf. Bruce, *NT History*, 229; "Some Thoughts," 6.

72. By "salvation history" I mean that divine sequence of events recorded in Scripture which take place in history in accordance with God's plan, which are directed toward the salvation of his people, and which thus both reveal God's salvation and are themselves the means through which God's salvation is wrought. Cf. Cullmann, *Christ and Time; Salvation in History* (New York, 1967); "The Relevance of Redemptive History," in *Soli Deo Gloria* (W. C. Robinson *FS*), ed. J. M. Richards (Richmond, 1968), 9-22; Kuss, *Römer*, 275-291; Bruce, "Salvation History," especially 79f., 82-87.

73. Cf. E. Schweizer, *TDNT* VI: 426, n. 624: "Paul is thinking of a Pentecost of Gentile Christianity, the basic outpouring of the Spirit on the Gentiles."

74. Schlier 140 (my translation). Another way of stating the relationship of the two ἵνα clauses to each other is as follows: "Verse 14 summarizes the preceding argument

(who is the substance of the promise)[75] is to be received "through faith," literally "through the faith"—the faith spoken of in vv. 7, 9, 11f. In the original promise to Abraham there was no mention of the Spirit but only the blessing of justification by faith, and yet here Paul conceives of the fulfillment of that promise as constituted above all in the bestowal of the Spirit upon those who have faith.[76] It is thus manifest that in Paul's thinking the blessing of justification is almost synonymous (it is certainly contemporaneous) with the reception of the Spirit (cf. p. 136 above, the next to last paragraph on 3:6).[77]

Before proceeding further in the text of Paul's letter, we pause to summarize in four statements our findings from this passage (3:7-14) which bear upon the subject of justification by faith.

(a) Paul shows from God's promise to Abraham that faith is the way to the blessing of justification (vv. 8f.); works, on the other hand, can never justify (vv. 10-12). Thus, justification through faith is not only illustrated in Paul's own conversion (2:15ff.), in the experience of the Galatian converts (3:1ff.), and in the case of Abraham (3:6), but is also seen to be intended from the time of Abraham as God's abiding principle of dealing with mankind; the announcement of this principle to Abraham was a proleptic announcement of the gospel (v. 8).

(b) Justification by faith is closely linked with sonship to Abraham, since being blessed with Abraham, which is identical with being justified by faith (v. 9), is said to be equivalent to being sons of Abraham (v. 7). Justification by faith is also closely linked with reception of the Spirit, so much so that the two may be equated (v. 14). Thus we can establish an intimate relationship between these three ideas: justification by faith, sonship to Abraham by faith, and reception of the Spirit by faith. The obvious common factor is faith: the men of faith are, as regards the formal side, sons of Abraham; as regards the material side, they are justified and receive the

---

in chiastic fashion, the first *hina* clause . . . reiterating the positive point of 3:8 (the blessing of Abraham for the Gentiles), the second, the positive assertion of 3:1-5 (the Spirit is received through faith)" (Sanders, *Paul, the Law*, 22).

75. NEB "the promised Spirit" rightly takes τοῦ πνεύματος as genitive of definition; so, e.g., Moule 175f. On the variant reading εὐλογίαν ("blessing," instead of "promise") see Metzger 594.

76. Ropes 36 speaks of the two—the blessing of Abraham and the gift of the Spirit—as "identical." Cf. H. W. Beyer, *TDNT* II: 763; H.-G. Link, *NIDNTT* I: 214; J. D. G. Dunn, *NIDNTT* III: 701.

77. Cf. Williams, "Justification," 93-95. Berényi, "Gal 2, 20," cites Gal. 3:13-14 as an excellent example of Paul's use of paradox: v. 13a-b (Christ redeemed us from the curse of the law by becoming a curse on our behalf) and vv. 13b-14a (Christ's becoming a curse resulted in blessing for the Gentiles) each constitute a paradox.

gift of the promised Spirit. The near-equation of justification and reception of the Spirit repeats and confirms what we found in examining vv. 1-6, while the presentation of justification in terms of sonship to Abraham reflects and confirms what was seen in 2:14-21, that is, the polemical orientation of the doctrine of justification, the formulation of which has been shaped in part by the position being combated.

(c) Justification through faith is set in the context of salvation history: God's promise to Abraham that the Gentiles would be blessed by means of faith (v. 8) was fulfilled in Christ, whose death delivered the Gentiles from the curse of the law and opened to them the door of justification by faith (vv. 13-14a).

(d) Justification through faith, viewed from the experiential point of view, is based upon the salvation-historical event of Christ's death (vv. 13, 14b): it is Christ's bearing of the law's curse in his death that made reception of the Spirit through faith possible. This provides the key to understanding the relation between righteousness and Christ's death which was noted but not defined in our discussion of 2:16; it can now be said that righteousness or justification has its objective ground in the vicarious death of Christ, and that the purpose of that death is fulfilled in the bestowal of justification (and of the Spirit) through faith.

D. THE LAW AND THE PROMISE (3:15-22)

Still basing his arguments on the biblical story, Paul now seeks to show that God's promise to Abraham temporally preceded the covenant given at Sinai, and that this historical fact supports the doctrine he is defending, that justification is by faith apart from works of the law.

1. THE PRIORITY OF THE PROMISE (3:15-18)

15 *My brothers, let me give you an illustration. Even in ordinary life, when a man's will and testament has been duly executed, no one else can set it aside or add a codicil.* 16 *Now the promises were pronounced to Abraham and to his "issue." It does not say "issues" in the plural, but in the singular, "and to your issue"; and the "issue" intended is Christ.* 17 *What I am saying is this: a testament, or covenant, had already been validated by God; it cannot be invalidated, and its promises rendered ineffective, by a law made four hundred and thirty years later.* 18 *If the inheritance is by legal right, then it is not by promise; but it was by promise that God bestowed it as a free gift on Abraham.*

153

15 Paul begins his argument for the priority (and permanence) of the promise to Abraham with a human analogy (literally "I speak according to man," cf. AV, RV). V. 15b begins in the Greek with *homōs*, which is usually understood to carry the meaning "nevertheless" (cf. AV, RV "yet") and to be shifted forward from its natural position before "no one" by "trajection" (cf. 1 Cor. 14:7).[1] Less probably, the word could, if accented differently, be translated "also" or "likewise" (i.e., as with God's covenant; cf. NIV "Just as . . . , so it is in this case").[2]

"Will and testament" represents Gk. *diathēkē,* which is the LXX translation of Heb. *berît,* "covenant." In support of the rendering "covenant" in our verse (AV, RV, NASB, NIV) it has been said that "the whole force of the argument demands that the *diathēkē* of verse 15 be of the same type as that in verse 17."[3] But this seems to overstate the case, since "the point of comparison is simply that of inviolability, unalterability and therefore absolute validity."[4] Although some scholars prefer not to tie down the meaning here to one or the other,[5] the many legal terms in the passage clearly suggest that the word is being used in the sense of Hellenistic law and point to "will, testament" as the more correct interpretation.[6] It is possible, however, to take *diathēkē* here in its original meaning of "an arrangement, a settlement drawn up and legally in force."[7] This option seems to have an advantage over the other two, since it simplifies the divine-human comparison without affecting the point of the analogy.[8]

The NEB rendering of v. 15b ("when a man's will and testament . . . or add a codicil") seems to presuppose the practice of Roman law, in which "the testator . . . could add a codicil at any time that he chose, but after his death (or before it, for that matter) nobody else might do so"[9]—the validation of the will coming only after the testator's death (cf. Heb. 9:16f.). If (as has been maintained) the verse has Greek procedure in view, then Paul

---

1. E.g., Thayer s.v.; MHT 3: 337.
2. E.g., BDF §450.2, followed by BAGD s.v. In this case the second object of comparison would have to be regarded as following (vv. 17f.; cf. 1 Cor. 14:9) rather than preceding ὅμως.
3. Morris, *Preaching,* 91. Cf. Hughes, "Hebrews ix 15ff. and Galatians iii 15ff."
4. J. Behm, *TDNT* II: 129.
5. E.g., Clarke, *NT Problems,* 154, n. 1; Whiteley, *Theology,* 85f.
6. Cf., e.g., Behm, loc. cit.; F. Hauck, *TDNT* V: 760; G. Stählin, *TDNT* IX: 459, n. 172.
7. Ridderbos 130.
8. It would render unnecessary, e.g., the explanation that "no regard is paid to the fact that in the case of God's testament the presuppositions of this validity . . . are very different from that of a human will, i.e., the death of the testator" (J. Behm, *TDNT* II: 129; cf. III: 1099). Cf. n. 24 below.
9. Bruce 171.

might be referring to the validation of a will by duly registering it and depositing it in the public record office of a city, after which "not even the testator was permitted to alter it, unless such permission had been expressly written into it";[10] in this case it would be preferable to speak of the will being "confirmed" (AV, RV), "established" (NIV), or "ratified" (RSV, NASB) rather than "executed." It has also been suggested that the reference is to the Jewish institution of *mattenat bārî*, which had to do with the irrevocable gift of a healthy person.[11] Still, perhaps taking *diathēkē* in its original sense of a disposition or settlement will most readily permit a simple understanding of Paul's words without need of modification: "When a deed of settlement is properly signed, sealed and delivered and the property legally conveyed, not even the original owner can revoke it or alter its terms."[12] Whatever the precise background of the human analogy, Paul's point is plain: even a human legal settlement is irrevocable in nature.

16 Next, Paul draws attention to a fact of biblical history, namely, that "the promises were pronounced to Abraham and to his 'issue.'" The plural "promises" refers to God's promise to Abraham as this was repeated on several occasions and couched in different expressions;[13] but in view of the association of the "inheritance" with the promise in v. 18, Paul may have in mind particularly that clause in the promise which concerned the giving of the land to Abraham and his descendants as an everlasting possession (Gen. 13:15; 17:8; cf. 12:7; 15:7).[14] Paul doubtless understands this in a spiritual sense,[15] although he does not pause to make this explicit.

Paul interprets the "issue" as a reference to Christ. He is well aware of the collective sense of *sperma* (Greek) or *zera'* (Hebrew) in the Genesis passages;[16] his identification of the "issue" spoken of in the promise as the Christ of history is not derived from a direct exegesis of the OT texts, but rather from an interpretation of them in the light of the Christ-event. His argument seems to be this: in the promise to Abraham, "it" (the subject of "does not say" is probably Scripture, as in v. 8, or possibly God) does not use the plural "issues," referring to many, but "issue," which, being a noun

10. Bruce 170f., describing the view of W. M. Ramsay.
11. Betz 155f. (following E. Bammel).
12. Bruce 170.
13. Cf. Burton 184. Note the alternation between the plural, here and in v. 21, and the singular, vv. 17, 22.
14. See Lightfoot 142 for two considerations which would seem to limit the references to Gen. 13:15 and 17:8.
15. Cf. Rom. 4:13, where the promise to Abraham and his offspring appears in the form "that the world should be his inheritance"—a promise which is fulfilled in the penetration of the gospel of justification by faith into the world of the Gentiles.
16. Cf. Rom. 4:18, where Abraham's offspring of Gen. 15:5 is identified with the many nations of Gen. 17:5, interpreted as Gentile believers.

in the singular number, can refer to a single person—in fact, it does refer primarily to one individual, Christ.[17]

This piece of Pauline interpretation[18] is charged with being "allegorical in the sense that it no longer takes into account the original meaning of the words and has overstepped the limits set to allegory in rabbinical hermeneutics."[19] Over against this, however, it should be remembered that (a) the word "issue," both in Hebrew and in Greek, can be used to designate *one* definite descendant (e.g., Gen. 4:25; 1 Sam. 1:11);[20] (b) parallel arguments based on the singular or plural of Heb. *zera'* are not wanting in rabbinic literature;[21] and (c) Paul is speaking from the standpoint of fulfilled prophecy in the conviction that the "issue" of the original promise can, in the event, refer only to Christ.[22] According to Paul's reading of history, then, Christ "is the true Heir of the promise, of the universal inheritance, and He determines the fellow-heirs"[23]—as vv. 26-29 will show.

17 With the words "What I am saying is this" Paul proceeds to apply the human analogy to the divine dealings in history: "a covenant"

17. On Paul's argument here as an example of one mode of rabbinic direct or explicit exegesis (fastening on "the strict sense of a term"), cf. Cohn-Sherbok, "Exegesis," 120f. For the suggestion that the clue to Paul's interpretation of the "issue" as Christ lies "in the link-word ξύλον (ʿṣ), found in both Deut 21:23 (cf. Gal 3:13) and Gen 22:6a, 7b, 9," see Wilcox, "Upon the Tree," especially 97f.

18. Burton 509 reckons with the possibility that v. 16b ("It does not say . . . Christ") is an early editorial comment which became incorporated in the text; this is definitely maintained by O'Neill 50f. It is true that Paul's interpretation of "issue" here is at variance with that given in v. 29, but "Pauline dialectic leads not uncommonly to formal logical contradictions" (A. Oepke, *TDNT* IV: 619, cf. n. 82). It is also true that the omission of v. 16b would leave "a consistent connection" (Burton, loc. cit.); in this case the "issue" in v. 19c would find its antecedent in the "issue" of v. 16a. But, on the other hand, the reference to the arrival of the "issue" finds a more natural explanation in v. 16b than in v. 16a (cf. vv. 23-25, where the "coming" of faith is connected with the coming of Christ).

19. Schoeps, *Paul*, 181, n. 3 (cf. 42, n. 2). But here this reminder is apt: "The 7 rules of Hillel and the 13 of Ishmael . . . show what can be gleaned from the literal wording" (F. Büchsel, *TDNT* I: 263, n. 24).

20. Schoeps is therefore not accurate in saying that Paul's deduction from the singular of Gen. 22:18 is "both in contradiction to the meaning of the word and to Biblical linguistic usage" (*Paul*, 181). Cf. Wilcox, "Promise," who observes that the application of the promises (of the "seed" to Abraham and to David) to the Messiah "seems to have begun already with Jewish thought and exegesis" (16).

21. Cf. Bruce 172f.; Longenecker, *Paul*, 59, n. 204.

22. Cf. Newman, "Seed." The matter is well expressed by Collins, "Exegesis," 150: "The apostle bases his conclusion on two grounds: the use of the singular noun and the conviction that Christ is par excellence the seed of Abraham. In the first one can detect the scribe, but in the second the Christian is more in evidence." Ultimately, however, "the argument is not a grammatical one but a theological one" (C. Brown, *NIDNTT* III: 524).

23. J. Schniewind and G. Friedrich, *TDNT* II: 583. Cf. S. Schulz, *TDNT* VII: 545.

(RV, RSV, NASB)[24] had been validated by God[25] and therefore in force long before the giving of the law, which came only 430 years later.[26] From this minor premise, and the major premise already laid down in v. 15b, the conclusion follows that the law cannot possibly invalidate the original settlement so as to render the promise ineffective.[27] It is thus clear that Paul regards the promise to Abraham as a divinely ratified settlement or covenant and argues from its considerable priority to the law that its provisions cannot be made null and void by the later introduction of the law.[28]

18 Since the "promises" of v. 16a are spoken of as "covenant" in v. 17b, whose principal content is in turn referred to as "the promise" in v. 17c (the Gk. has *epangelia*, "promise," in the singular; cf. AV, RV, RSV, NASB, NIV), we might speak of the original "covenant of prom-

24. It is interesting to note that NEB translates the single word διαθήκη as "a testament, or covenant"—thus correcting itself, as it were, or at least providing an alternative. To speak of God ratifying a *will* (e.g., Hooker, "Paul," 50f.) in this instance is to complicate the thought unnecessarily, as may be demonstrated by the following comment: "The image and the thought are here very contradictory, for whereas a human will comes into effect only with the death of the testator, the will and testament of God (v. 15 . . .) . . . is put into effect as soon as it is drawn up, and from that point on it is exclusively and incontrovertibly valid" (J. Behm, *TDNT* III: 1100); cf. n. 8 above. If it be insisted that the same sense be given to διαθήκη in vv. 15 and 17, the best word would seem to be, not "covenant" or "will," but "legal settlement" (see above on v. 15).

25. On the variant reading with εἰς Χριστόν see Metzger 594.

26. It is with reference to this law that the covenant is said to have been "confirmed *before* of God" (AV) or "*previously* ratified by God" (RSV, NASB). The figure 430 appears also in the MT of Ex. 12.40 as the period of Israel's sojourning in Egypt, and in the LXX (and Samaritan text) of the same verse as covering the time of Israel's sojourning in Egypt "and in the land of Canaan." Gen. 15:13 (cf. Acts 7:6) gives the round figure of 400 years as the predicted period of Israel's oppression in Egypt. It is plausible that "Paul was probably following what was a common rabbinic explanation in his own time as well as later," namely, that "the covenant with Abraham was made thirty years before Isaac's birth" (King, "Tannaim," 366), from which event the lesser number, which applied to Abraham's offspring, is reckoned (Dahl, *Studies*, 169, n. 17). The precise solution of the chronological difficulties—which in any case probably would not be of any particular interest to Paul (cf. Lightfoot 144; Betz 158)—seems to have eluded the commentators, but fortunately this does not in the least affect Paul's argument here, which emphasizes only the considerable length of time separating the law from the promise.

27. "Paul's point is that what God has said is already in force by the mere fact that He has said it" (W. Foerster, *TDNT* III: 784, n. 36). This is borne out by the perfect participle προκεκυρωμένην ("validated") as well as by the emphatic ὑπὸ τοῦ θεοῦ ("by God").

28. This temporal argument appealing from the law back to the Abrahamic promise "has an exact parallel in Jesus' reference in the question of divorce to the ordinance of creation as revealing a deeper and more original form of the will of God" than the provision of the Mosaic law (Schoeps, *Paul*, 180). For other examples of this temporal argument as an accepted rabbinic method see Longenecker, *Paul*, 123, n. 63. The "law" here is identified by J. Guhrt, *NIDNTT* I: 370, with the elaborations of late Judaism; but on this see the editorial comment by C. Brown (371f.).

ise."[29] Its nature is underlined yet again when Paul points out that it was "by a promise" (v. 18b, RSV) that God bestowed the inheritance as a free gift on Abraham.[30]

As H. Schlier observes, three things are emphasized in this brief statement: (a) it is God who has made the decision, which therefore stands and is not to be broken; (b) the decision was for promise, not law; and (c) it was a gracious decision which forestalled all merit and excluded every meritorious achievement.[31] Since Abraham is a "conclusive test case"[32] and the OT event "still retains its (exemplary) meaning,"[33] the inference becomes inevitable (v. 18a): the inheritance is not "based on law" (NASB), more specifically the Mosaic law—if it were, the inheritance would belong to "those who rely on obedience to the law" (v. 10)—but is rather based on a promise and hence on faith. For just as Abraham was justified by faith in God's promise (v. 6), so "the men of faith" are the true children of Abraham (v. 7) and will inherit Abraham's blessing (v. 9).[34]

2. THE PURPOSE OF THE LAW (3:19-22)

19 *Then what of the law? It was added to make wrongdoing a legal offence. It was a temporary measure pending the arrival of the "issue" to whom the promise was made. It was promulgated through angels, and there was an intermediary;* 20 *but an intermediary is not needed for one party acting alone, and God is one.*

21 *Does the law, then, contradict the promises? No, never! If a law had been given which had power to bestow life, then indeed righteousness would have come from keeping the law.* 22 *But Scrip-*

---

29. This phrase in fact occurs in Barrett, *First Adam*, 60. Hooker ("Paul," 51), however, thinks that Paul does not speak of God's original promises to Abraham in terms of a covenant, the term διαθήκη being used (in her opinion) in the sense of "will" (cf. n. 24 above).

30. Ridderbos 136, n. 13 says that χαρίζομαι without the object (as here) is a technical term for the law of inheritance, meaning: make a grant, deed something by will. But it is more natural to supply the object from the context; cf. BAGD s.v. 1.

31. Schlier 149f.

32. Guthrie 103 (he notes the emphatic position of "to Abraham"). Cf. E. Hoffmann, *NIDNTT* III: 72.

33. BDF §342.5. Cf. Moule 14f., who calls this "the Perfect of Allegory"; p. 206 below, with n. 11.

34. "In laying the supreme emphasis on [the promise to Abraham] Paul parts company with Judaism. For Judaism the great thing was the deliverance from Egypt together with the giving of the law. . . . Paul reverses the emphasis. Judaism would read the patriarchal narratives in the light of Sinai. Paul insists on looking at Sinai from the standpoint of the promise to Abraham" (Manson, *Paul and John*, 45). Cf. Barrett, "Allegory," 15.

ture has declared the whole world to be prisoners in subjection to sin, so that faith in Jesus Christ may be the ground on which the promised blessing is given, and given to those who have such faith.

19 But if the law is something which, as Paul makes out, came later than the promise and has no power to make the promise ineffective, the question inevitably arises: "Why then the law?" (RSV).[35] This question about "the purpose of the law" (NIV) cannot be adequately answered without the place and significance of the law in salvation history being shown,[36] and the NEB rendering puts the question in a form which is general enough to accommodate this aspect as well. In any event, the question is one which Paul no doubt found it necessary to answer in responding to the Judaizers, but which also may have presented itself to Paul himself as something of an inner necessity.[37] The answer is given in vv. 19b-22, from which a number of points will be noted.

(a) The law was given "to make wrongdoing a legal offence" (v. 19a). This rendering rightly regards the Greek phrase as indicating the purpose and not the cause (cf. AV, RV, RSV, NASB, NIV: "because of transgressions") for which the law was given.[38] The more precise meaning of the phrase has, however, been variously interpreted as: (i) "to check transgressions"; (ii) "to reveal transgressions," that is, to bring them to light and to expose sin as transgression (cf. Rom. 3:20; 4:15; 5:13); (iii) "to evoke and increase transgressions," that is, to call them forth by stimulating latent sin into activity (cf. Rom. 7:7f., 13)—a meaning which logically includes (ii) and is therefore sometimes combined with it as "to reveal and provoke transgressions"; and (iv) "to awaken a conviction of sin and guilt" and thus of the need of a Savior.[39] Since in the context Paul is more concerned with

35. Cf. NASB; BDF §480.5; BAGD s.v. τίς 3.a.
36. Cf. Schlier 151; Sanders, *Paul, the Law,* 66f.
37. Cf. Dibelius-Kümmel, *Paul,* 65f.
38. Gk. τῶν παραβάσεων χάριν. On the variants παραδόσεων ("traditions") and πράξεων ("deeds") Metzger 594 makes no comment beyond what may be implied in an exclamation mark.
    Lull, "'The Law Was Our Pedagogue,'" 483 argues for the causal sense of χάριν "as introducing the *prior* condition that had caused God to 'add' the Law": "*because* of transgressions" means "in order to *deal with* the transgressions that had occurred." A later statement—"The function of the Law before (or until) the coming of the 'offspring' was merely to punish *and prevent* transgressions" (485, emphasis added; cf. 489: "to *curb* or *prevent* transgressions," emphasis original)—shows that Lull is combining the causal sense of χάριν with its final sense, more particularly with view (i) as we have listed them in the text. Cf. p. 169, n. 7 below.
39. E.g., (i) O'Neill 52, 78; (ii) Cranfield, "Law," 162; Martin 112f.; W. Günther, *NIDNTT* III: 585; (iii) A. Oepke, *TDNT* IV: 618; J. Schneider, *TDNT* V: 740; Grundmann, "Gesetz," 58; (iv) Hendriksen 140; Pinnock 45. For the interesting sugges-

the objective facts of salvation history than with the subjective development of faith in the individual (see on vv. 22ff. below), (iv) appears less appropriate. While (i) is in accord with the Jewish understanding of the law as a hedge against sin,[40] it is ruled out by Paul's explicit teaching elsewhere. Between (ii) and (iii) it is difficult to choose: we may either regard (ii) as expressing all that is intended by Paul here, attributing to the law the simple function of revealing transgressions, that is, (as NEB suggests) of imparting to them the character of legal offenses, and see Paul as taking his description of the law's function a step further in Romans, or we may regard (iii) as representing Paul's thought here, the present phrase being "a crisp formulation of what he says elsewhere."[41] In either case, the function of the law is presented as an entirely negative one.

(b) The law was "added . . . till the offspring should come to whom the promise had been made" (v. 19b-c, RSV). Two thoughts are expressed here: (i) The law was an addition, having its beginning after the promise (v. 17); it was added (cf. Rom. 5:20), not "to the promise as a kind of supplement to it," but "to the human situation for . . . a purpose totally different from that of the promise."[42] (ii) The validity of the law ceased with the coming of "the Seed to whom the promise referred" (NIV), that is, Christ (v. 16). Thus the law here, as compared with the line of promise from Abraham to Christ, is presented as "an interim dispensation"[43] which was temporally restricted and only temporarily valid.[44]

(c) The law was "ordained through angels by the hand of a mediator" (v.19d, RV). Again, two thoughts are involved here. (i) The law was ordained through the mediation of angels. The rendering "ordained by angels" (AV, RSV)[45] poses what must be regarded as a violent contrast between Paul's estimate of the law here (even when due allowance is made for the polemical context of the passage) and that in Romans (cf. in particular

---

tion that what is in mind here is "a sacred and revised edition" of the law which "took into account the transgressions of the faithless and disobedient people," see Stendahl, *Paul*, 19f.

40. Cf. Schoeps, *Paul*, 194f.; Betz 165.

41. J. Schneider, *TDNT* V: 740. Cf. Schlier 153.

42. Bruce 176.

43. Manson, *Paul and John*, 20. Note also the observation of Barrett, *First Adam*, 60f.

44. Cf., e.g., A. Oepke, *TDNT* IV: 618; C. Maurer, *TDNT* VIII: 168; Schlier 152, 155; Bammel, "Νόμος," 123f. For the suggestion that the law here is to be understood as "not the law in the fullness and wholeness of its true character, but the law as seen apart from Christ," see Cranfield, *Romans*, 2: 859.

45. Unless "by" is taken in the sense of "by means of." Cf., e.g., Schlier 155; Schoeps, *Paul*, 182f.; Clarke, *NT Problems*, 155; Reicke, "Law," 262, 268; G. Delling, *TDNT* VIII: 35.

Rom. 2:17f.; 7:12). The generally accepted view, represented by RV, NEB, NASB, and NIV,[46] is much more likely to be correct. The role of angels as God's assistants in the promulgation of the law is employed in Jewish and early Christian tradition to enhance the glory of the law (e.g., Dt. 33:2, LXX; Acts 7:38, 53; Heb. 2:2). Here in Galatians, however, in a "specific Christianizing of the tradition," it is used to show the inferiority of the law as that which was given not directly by God but only through angelic mediation.[47] (ii) The law was ordained also "through an intermediary" (RSV)— "by the hand of," as a literal translation would represent the phrase, being a pure Hebraism for "by the agency of" (NASB).[48] The reference is probably to Moses, who clearly appears in a mediatorial role in the giving of the law (cf. Ex. 20:19; Dt. 5:5, 23-27).[49] The point of these two thoughts is that since the law was, on the one hand, proclaimed through angels and, on the other hand, communicated by the agency of an intermediary, "it had reached men only at two removes from God."[50]

20 (d) Of v. 20 it has been said that there are as many interpretations as the number of years between promise and law (cf. v. 17)![51] Two of these may be singled out for special consideration. The first understands the phrase "not . . . of one" (AV, RV) as affirming that the party for whom a mediator acts must consist of a plurality of persons, so that the verse becomes a proof that the law was given not by God but by angels. The reasoning runs as follows: For God to give the law to the people of Israel there would be no need of a mediator, since a single person can deal directly with a plurality (cf. 1 Tim. 2:5); the very fact that the law was given through an intermediary implies that on both sides pluralities were involved; and the plurality on the heavenly side cannot have been God, who is one, but the angels.[52]

The second view regards the plurality implied in "not . . . of one" as a duality of parties and understands the verse as emphasizing the one-sided nature of the promise. Here the thought is that while the very idea of

46. Cf., e.g., BAGD s.v. διατάσσω; Moule 57; M. J. Harris, *NIDNTT* III: 1182; A. Oepke, *TDNT* II: 67 with n. 6 (but cf. IV: 618).

47. Cf. G. Kittel, *TDNT* I: 83 (whence the quotation); J. Jeremias, *TDNT* IV: 866, n. 210; and especially Callan, "Midrash," 550-554.

48. Moule 184.

49. Betz 170 with n. 72 points out that in the LXX ἐν χειρὶ Μωυσῆ ("by the hand of Moses") "has become almost a formula." On the phrase ἐν χειρὶ μεσίτου ("by the hand of a mediator") here cf. especially Callan, "Midrash," 555-564, who suggests that the term μεσίτης/srswr is especially associated with two incidents in Moses' career (Ex. 20:19; 32-34).

50. Scott, *Christianity*, 43.

51. Ridderbos 139. Cf. Lightfoot 146 (up to 250 or 300); Ellicott 64 (over 400).

52. E.g., Schweitzer, *Mysticism*, 70; Clarke, *NT Problems*, 155f.; A. Oepke, *TDNT* IV: 618f.

mediation involved in the giving of the law indicates that it is of the nature of a contract between two parties, both of whom have to fulfill its terms for it to be valid, the promise is a unilateral disposition dependent solely on God's sovereign grace.[53] As we have rejected that interpretation of v. 19d which makes the law stem from the angels, we follow (with NEB, cf. NASB, NIV) the second interpretation, which also appears the more natural one.[54]

Thus far, then, in his answer to the question regarding the purpose of the law Paul has pointed to its negative function, its limited validity, its mediated communication, and its conditional nature—all of which show, by implication if not by explicit statement, that the later dispensation of law is inferior to the original covenant of promise.

21 (e) The law's inferiority to the promise does not mean that the law contradicts the promise (v. 21a).[55] Paul substantiates his emphatic denial of any such contradiction by referring again to the function of the law, but this time in a positive as well as a negative aspect. The *negative* aspect is presented here (v. 21b), and the positive aspect in the next verse. Paul's statement here has been understood in at least three ways. One view takes the verb "to bestow life" to mean: to give the ability to do what the law demands; in this view Paul is arguing from cause to effect.[56] But a difficulty is posed for this by the predominant meaning of the verb in Paul, as throughout the NT, which is: to impart life in the soteriological sense.[57] Another

---

53. E.g., Lightfoot 146f.; Betz 171f.; Robertson, *Word Pictures*, 4: 296f.

54. A recent suggestion identifies the "intermediary" (vv. 19f.) with the angel of the presence who accompanied Moses in the wilderness and spoke to him at Mount Sinai (Ex. 23:20f.; 32:34; 33:14; Acts 7:38) and regards this angel as the mediator of the angels as Moses was mediator on behalf of the Israelites (A. Vanhoye, "Un médiateur des anges en Ga 3, 19-20," *Biblica* 59 [1978] 403-411). A difficulty one finds with this view is that the final clause "God is one" then seems to lose something of the climactic force in the argument which it has in the second interpretation above (which accords well with its final position in the sentence), and becomes merely a step in the logical reasoning which concludes that the mediator referred to here is not God's mediator but (by implication) a mediator of the angels. Moreover, this concept of an angelic mediator would probably be less easy for Paul's original readers to grasp, being less explicitly grounded in the OT Scriptures than the more familiar concept of Moses as the Israelites' mediator with God. Vanhoye's view, together with that of L. Gaston, who thinks Paul refers to the tradition of the seventy angels of the nations ("Angels and Gentiles in early Judaism and in Paul," *Studies in Religion/Sciences Religieuses* 11 [1982]: 65-75), is also rejected by King, "Tannaim," 366f., n. 80). For yet another, more recent attempt at solving the enigma of Paul's words here, see de Lacey, "Jesus as Mediator," 115-117.

55. On the nicely balanced question whether τοῦ θεοῦ ("of God") is part of the original text see Metzger 594f. The substitution of τοῦ Χριστοῦ ("of Christ") for τοῦ θεοῦ is clearly inappropriate in the context, since the promises are obviously to be understood in the sense of v. 16.

56. E.g., Ridderbos 141 with n. 27; E. Hoffmann, *NIDNTT* III: 72.

57. Cf. R. Bultmann, *TDNT* II: 874f. (s.v. ζωοποιέω). Williams, "Justification," 96f. takes "make alive" here as an allusion to the work of the Spirit in releasing

view regards the verb here as the causative of "gain life" (v. 12) and meaning in effect "to justify";[58] but this makes the protasis (the "if" clause) say much the same thing as the apodosis (the "then" clause), whereas the former should provide some explanation for the latter. A third view seems preferable: Paul is arguing from the effect ("to bestow life") to the cause ("righteousness"): if a law had been given that could impart life, then righteousness, which is the prior condition of life, would have come from keeping the law.[59] In any case, the point of the statement—cast in the form of a contrary-to-fact conditional sentence[60]—is that the function of the law was not to provide the way of acceptance with God ("righteousness").[61] The law's inability to impart life is here simply stated, not explained; neither does Paul raise the question whether it is theoretically possible to obtain righteousness through the law.[62]

---

from the enslaving power of sin, and derives from this understanding of Paul's statement the implication that "righteousness *is* by means of (ἐκ) that which *can* make alive, namely the Spirit"; on this showing, "Paul appears to be linking the status of righteousness with the work of the Spirit in the closest possible way." Paul does employ the verb ζωοποιεῖν ("to bestow life") in connection with the work of the Spirit (2 Cor. 3:6; cf. 1 Cor. 15:45; see also Jn. 6:63), and this could be used to support the view that the verb as used in Gal. 3:21 contains an allusion to the work of the Spirit (a law had not been given which could, as the Spirit alone can, make alive). However, Paul's statement in this verse is, in our view, purely negative in intention as well as form, and we cannot legitimately draw from it the positive inference that righteousness is by means of the Spirit.

58. Burton 195. Cf. Sanders, *Paul and Palestinian Judaism*, 503, where "righteousness" is equated with "life."

59. Ellicott 66. Cf. p. 226, n. 32 below.

60. Winger, "Unreal Conditions," has drawn attention to the difference in form between this verse and the similarly conditional sentence in 2:21: there Paul does not employ the unreal conditional form, whereas here he does. After making "a survey of Paul's use of conditional sentences," which "shows that it is indeed 3:21 rather than 2:21 that is anomalous" (110f.), Winger concludes that in 3:21 ἄν is used "as insurance against misunderstanding" (112).

61. Ziesler, *Righteousness*, 179 maintains that here "we must give 'righteousness' its full value; righteousness by the law is that which consists in law-fulfillment and therefore claims a favourable verdict." But Paul does not actually say "righteousness by the law," only that "righteousness would have come from keeping the law." The emphasis does not fall on the conduct and character which, in the event of the condition being fulfilled, would form the basis of acceptance with God. It is, rather, on the acceptance itself. Cf. Burton 195, 469.

62. It would appear that the reason the law is unable to bestow life is not simply that "man does not in fact keep the commandments" (H. Braun, *TDNT* VI: 480; cf. W. Gutbrod, *TDNT* IV: 1072; Moule, "Obligation," 394), but also that mankind, belonging to this age and standing under the dominion of sin and the flesh, inevitably perverts them into a means of meritorious achievement, of religious boasting before God, so that keeping the law becomes a sinful effort to be independent of God and his grace (cf., e.g., W. Grundmann, *TDNT* I: 308f., IV: 573; Klein, "Rechtfertigung," col. 827; Vos, *Eschatology*, 274; Bruce, "Curse," 29).

As for the second question, if due emphasis is to be given to the word "the-

22 The *positive* aspect of the law's function is stated with the help of the figure of a jail sentence,[63] with Scripture as the magistrate,[64] "all men" (NASB) as the prisoners,[65] and sin as the jailer who carries out the sentence ("in subjection to sin"—literally "under sin," AV, RV, NASB). It has been maintained that "the singular *graphē* in the N.T. always means a *particular passage* of Scripture";[66] Paul elsewhere in his epistles indeed seems to have maintained a clear distinction between the use of the singular (Rom. 4:3; 9:17; 10:11; 11:2; Gal. 4:30) and the plural (Rom. 1:2; 15:4; 16:26; 1 Cor. 15:3, 4), but the personification of Scripture here (as in v. 8) may warrant our seeing a departure from Paul's normal practice and general NT usage.[67] Neither of the particular scriptures which have been suggested as being in view in v. 22—Ps. 143:2, quoted in Gal. 2:16, and Dt. 27:26, quoted in Gal. 3:10[68]—seems to prove Paul's point that all are consigned under sin. We can, therefore, take the singular "Scripture" here as referring not to one specific passage but to the entirety of Scripture, which does, however, pronounce its verdict through individual texts, passages such as those reflected in Rom. 3:10-18, which declare the whole world to be sinners.[69]

In Paul's analogy no reason *for* which the magistrate consigns the prisoners *to* the jailer is mentioned, though in reality that reason is sin. But, expressing the facts of the case rather than speaking strictly within the terms of Paul's imagery, we may say that God, speaking through the Scriptures, locks up all men under the condemnation of sin, providing them with no

---

oretically" the answer is probably "Yes" (cf. Ridderbos, *Paul*, 134). But what is theoretically possible is not actually possible (cf. Kertelge, *Rechtfertigung*, 72, 205, n. 221); on the plane of reality the question of the possibility of obtaining righteousness through the law need not even arise: "It is not God's purpose that any individual should attain righteousness for himself by keeping the Law; God's purpose is to offer righteousness to all through faith in Jesus Christ" (Whiteley, *Theology*, 82).

63. For the following treatment of the imagery cf. Guthrie 107.

64. The same verb (συνέκλεισεν, "declared . . . to be prisoners") is used in Rom. 11:32 ("making . . . prisoners") with God as the subject, thus showing that here Scripture is identified with God's own speaking (G. Schrenk, *TDNT* I: 754).

65. NEB "the whole world" is literally "all things" (RV, RSV); the phrase is "probably a generalizing neuter referring to persons" (Bultmann, *Theology*, 249; cf. BDF §138.1; G. Delling, *TDNT* VI: 292, n. 32). Rom. 11:32 has the masculine "all men" (NIV; i.e., as in NEB, "all mankind"); Betz 175, n. 116 rightly thinks that the two "must be identical." According to Barrett 34, "the neuter expresses comprehensiveness and universality even more strongly than the masculine πάντας would do."

66. Lightfoot 147f. (emphasis in the original).

67. Guthrie 107. Cf. G. Schrenk, *TDNT* I: 753 (more emphatically).

68. E.g., Lightfoot 147 and Howard 59, respectively.

69. E.g., Schlier 164; Hunter 30.

possibility of escape;[70] and his purpose in doing so is stated in v. 22b. Here the original word order[71] is against connecting "by faith in Jesus Christ" with "the promise" to produce "the promise by faith in Jesus Christ" (RV, NASB) and in favor of connecting the phrase (regarded as put in an emphatic position) with "may be . . . given," so that "faith in Jesus Christ" is both the objective basis on which the promise is given (so NEB, cf. NIV) and the subjective means whereby the promise is received (by "those who have such faith").[72] Interpreted in the light of v. 18, the promise may refer to the inheritance promised to Abraham, understood in its spiritual application as acceptance with God and all its attendant blessings;[73] interpreted in the light of v. 14 and our discussion thereof, the promise refers to the promise of justification by faith (after the manner of Abraham's justification) and reception of the Spirit. Hence the promise has to do, at least partially if not exclusively, with justification by faith. This understanding is supported also by the connection between vv. 21 and 22: the law could not bestow righteousness (v. 21); what it did was to shut up all people under sin so that the promise might be received by faith (v. 22); thus the promise of v. 22 clearly has to do with the righteousness mentioned in v. 21.

Paul's contention in vv. 19-22 may be summed up as follows: The law is an institution inferior to the covenant of promise and it does not bestow righteousness. Its "true effect . . . is to nail man to his sin. As the prison holds the prisoner . . . so man is shut up by the Law under sin. . . . Rightly understood, then, the Law prevents any attempt on man's part to secure

70. Συνέκλεισεν (RSV "consigned"; cf. n. 64 above) is used in Lk. 5:6 of catching fish: cf. Robertson, *Word Pictures,* 4: 297.
71. Not ἡ ἐκ πίστεως Ἰησοῦ Χριστοῦ ἐπαγγελία ("the by-faith-in-Jesus-Christ promise").
72. Cf., e.g., Schlier 165, over against Ridderbos 142. This construction also obviates the difficulty that "the promise itself, when made, contained no mention of the Messiah, let alone Jesus Christ," on account of which O'Neill 53 would omit the words "Jesus Christ" as "an understandable but incorrect gloss."
Hays gives an analysis of the narrative structure of this verse (123, Fig. 21), which, in agreement with his analyses of 3:13-14 and 4:3-6 (116, Fig. 18), "places Jesus Christ in the role of Subject, with πίστις as the power or quality" by which he "has performed an act which allows believers to receive the promise" (124); Hays further maintains (162-164) that the balance of grammatical evidence is in favor of taking the genitive as subjective. *Contextually,* however, the evidence "points in the other direction" (Bruce 181), for the following τοῖς πιστεύουσιν helps to make clear that πίστις refers to the believers' faith and that therefore Ἰησοῦ Χριστοῦ is an objective genitive. I refrain from attempting a response to Hays's theological argument in support of his interpretation, which draws on Eph. 3:12 and Rom. 5:1f., 19 for support (164-167). See also Hays, "Christology," 278-280.
73. Schlier 145.

righteousness before God in any other way than . . . that promised to Abraham."[74] There is no essential contradiction of the promise by the law, because, simply, the law is intended to serve the purposes of the promise, which has to do with justification by faith.[75]

In this section (3:15-22) Paul has again demonstrated that justification is by faith and not by works of the law. He has done it in terms of the relation between the law and the promise, by showing clearly that it is the original covenant of promise which represents God's intention in his dealings with men, and that the law is an inferior institution designed to serve the purposes of the promise. Hence the Judaizers were wrong, in the terms used in v. 16, to impose new conditions for salvation ("add a codicil") upon the original covenant of promise, which cannot be rendered null and void ("set . . . aside") in this way.

The entire passage is, in fact, an elaboration of the antithesis between law and promise already introduced in vv. 13f. As in that earlier passage (cf. especially vv. 13f. and v. 22), the doctrine of justification by faith is explained historically, that is, from the perspective of salvation history.[76] This perspective is continued in the next section (3:23-4:11). Before turning to that, however, we may briefly note again the nexus of ideas in which justification belongs: promise (vv. 16, 18, 22), inheritance (v. 18), and life (v. 21). If in 3:15-22 justification is treated primarily with reference to the promise, in the next section it is the notion of sonship (implied in the concept of inheritance) that will occupy the dominant place.

E. CHRISTIAN MATURITY (3:23–4:11)

It was suggested at the beginning of section C (on 3:7-14) that Paul's argument in chapters 3 and 4 revolves largely around the matter of sonship to Abraham, since the Judaizers had made an issue of it. We have seen how Paul demonstrates in that passage that it is the men of faith who are the sons of Abraham. In section D (on 3:15-22) we have followed his argument that the relation between the law and the promise shows that the inheritance is to be received as a promise by faith and not obtained by works of the law. There the notion of sonship to Abraham does not figure prominently, although it does lie near at hand by being implied in the idea of inheritance and through

74. W. Gutbrod, *TDNT* IV: 1074.
75. Cf. Schlatter, *Glaube*, 357.
76. As O. Michel, *TDNT* VII: 746 says of v. 22b, "This Pauline thesis is to be taken historically. It is thus connected with his apocalyptic doctrine of the aeons and is teleologically orientated to his understanding of salvation. In God's plan of salvation one thing takes place in order that something else may result."

its indirect association with the promise. In the present section, however, sonship to Abraham again comes to the fore, merging with the concept of sonship to God; in two parallel movements Paul argues that believers are sons of God and the true offspring of Abraham (3:23-29) and that they are God's full-grown sons and heirs who have put their spiritual infancy behind them (4:1-7). The section closes with a warning against relapse into slavery (4:8-11).

1. THE COMING OF FAITH: SONSHIP TO GOD (3:23-29)

23 *Before this faith came, we were close prisoners in the custody of law, pending the revelation of faith.* 24 *Thus the law was a kind of tutor in charge of us until Christ should come, when we should be justified through faith;* 25 *and now that faith has come, the tutor's charge is at an end.*
26 *For through faith you are all sons of God in union with Christ Jesus.* 27 *Baptized into union with him, you have all put on Christ as a garment.* 28 *There is no such thing as Jew and Greek, slave and freeman, male and female; for you are all one person in Christ Jesus.* 29 *But if you thus belong to Christ, you are the "issue" of Abraham, and so heirs by promise.*

Continuing the perspective of salvation history introduced in vv. 13f. and developed in vv. 15-22, Paul gives further consideration to the place of the law in the divine economy by showing the relation between law and faith as two distinct dispensations.

23 First, the earlier dispensation before the coming of "this faith" is described as one in which "we were close prisoners in the custody of law." The use of "law" (anarthrous) here, in clear distinction from "*the* law" (articular) in the next verse, suggests that Paul has in view the general principle of law and that the personal pronoun "we" therefore refers to all people: Jews and Gentiles alike were closely guarded and locked up under law, even though the Gentiles did not possess law in the same form as the Jews did.[1]

---

1. See p. 160, point (b). The first person plural in vv. 23-25 is taken as referring to Jews only by, among others, Donaldson, " 'Curse of the Law,' " 98. But the statement "we are no longer under a custodian" (v. 25b, RSV) is explained by the sentence, "you are all sons of God in union with Christ Jesus" (v. 26); this suggests that "we" includes "you." Now the following context (vv. 27-29, especially v. 28) shows that "you" refers to all Christians irrespective of *race,* status, or sex; this in turn suggests that the "we" of the previous verses also refers to *both* Jews *and* Gentiles.

The imagery of imprisonment, repeated from v. 22 and reinforced here by the synonymous figure of custody,[2] emphasizes mankind's state of confinement under law: it was law which made all people prisoners, and it was in being under law that the confinement consisted. It is noteworthy that whereas in v. 22 all were prisoners of *sin,* here they are prisoners of *law.*[3] This state of confinement under law was intended to last until the appointed time of the arrival of the faith that was to be revealed—until, that is, faith should "appear on the scene . . . or become operative" as the newly opened way of salvation.[4]

The faith in question, referred to three times in vv. 23 and 25 as "*the* faith" (articular), is the faith in Christ just spoken of in v. 22; it is the principle (and means) of salvation opposed to law and at the same time stands for the new order of eschatological salvation itself.[5] The coming of faith is therefore identical with the coming of Christ, who is the object of faith; it is the coming of Christ, making possible the coming of faith, which is the decisive point in salvation history.[6]

24 In the light of this division of time into two epochs, Paul can speak of the law being accordingly *(hōste)* "our custodian until Christ came" (RSV). The custodian (*paidagōgos,* literally "boy-leader") was usu-

---

2. The verb is probably to be understood here solely in the sense of enforced restraint (e.g., BAGD s.v. φρουρέω 2; Thayer s.v. 2; H.-G. Schütz, *NIDNTT* II: 135) without any nuance of "benevolent protection" "against self-destruction and against the influence of wicked powers" (Duncan 120f.; O. Michel, *TDNT* VII: 746, respectively), which thought seems alien to the context.

3. The near-equation of sin and law thus suggested has a parallel in Rom. 6:14, where to be under law is, by implication, to be under sin. As will be seen, a similar near-equation of the law and the flesh is suggested by Gal. 5:16-18, where the Spirit-flesh antithesis of vv. 16f. becomes in v. 18 opposition between the Spirit and the law (cf. pp. 251f. below).

4. Bultmann, *Theology,* 1: 275. Moule 169 notes that for the strange word order in the prepositional phrase εἰς τὴν μέλλουσαν πίστιν ἀποκαλυφθῆναι and in the nearly identical phrase πρὸς τὴν μέλλουσαν δόξαν ἀποκαλυφθῆναι in Rom. 8:18 one would have expected εἰς (πρὸς) τὴν πίστιν (δόξαν) τὴν μέλλουσαν ἀποκαλυφθῆναι. MHT 3: 350 suggests that this particular order may be due to the use of ἡ μέλλουσα δόξα as a set phrase; but 1 Pet. 5:1 has τῆς μελλούσης ἀποκαλύπτεσθαι δόξης (which is "the more classical construction," Bruce 182). In any case, "the participle is often separated from its adjuncts" (BDF §474.5). The preposition εἰς here probably has both temporal and final significance (cf. A. Oepke, *TDNT* II: 426f.).

5. Cf. A. Oepke, *TDNT* III: 584; Wendland, *Mitte,* 42. In the opinion of Longworth, "Faith," 609, "the term faith now hovers between a subjective and an objective meaning."

6. Cf. J. Schneider, *TDNT* II: 674. That Abraham was justified by faith shows conclusively that Paul cannot mean that prior to the "coming" of faith no one had exercised saving faith (rightly, Ladd, *Theology,* 507); in speaking as he does Paul is "thinking in redemptive-historical, eschatological categories" (Ridderbos, *Paul,* 198, cf. 174).

ally the slave who conducted the freeborn youth to and from school and who superintended his conduct generally—a function clearly differentiated from that of the teacher or "pedagogue" in the modern sense.[7] In describing the law as a *paidagōgos,* therefore, Paul does not mean that the law exerts a gradual, educative influence on people, either by inclining them toward good until they receive Christ or by enabling them to realize their own sin, turn their backs on trusting in their own merits, and desire the grace of Christ.[8] As noted earlier, Paul's primary concern in these verses (22-25) is not to describe the genesis of individual faith in terms of psychological development, but to sketch the progress of salvation history.[9] His meaning is rather that the law brought mankind into, and kept mankind under, an objectively desperate situation, from which there was no escape until the revelation of faith as a new possibility.[10] This revelation is, as we have seen, coincident with the coming of Christ; it is until the coming of Christ,[11] who

---

7. Cf. Dodd, *Meaning,* 85f.; Hanson, *Studies,* 238; Hendriksen 148, n. 107 (not *Schulmeister,* but *Zuchtmeister*). According to Young, *"Paidagogos,"* 156, "the child generally came to the pedagogue immediately after the mother, wet nurse (τίτθη) and nanny (τροφός) had completed the educational process at its most basic level. This was usually at age seven, and the boy remained in the charge of the pedagogue until late adolescence." For the role of the pedagogue see especially Young, 157-165. Young rightly insists (170-173) that "Paul's emphasis in vv. 23-24 falls on the confining and restrictive rather than either the corrective or protective functions of a pedagogue" (171). On the other hand, Lull concludes from a study of the role of the παιδαγωγός ("'The Law Was Our Pedagogue,'" 489-494) that the function of the law as παιδαγωγός to the Galatians was "to bridle the passions and desires of their flesh (see 5:16-24)" (495; cf. p. 159, n. 38 above).

8. Rightly, Schlier 169; cf., e.g., Bammel, "Νόμος," 124, n. 2; Belleville, "'Under Law,'" 60. For the views rejected here cf., e.g., A. B. Bruce, *Christianity,* 308f.; W. D. Davies, *IDB* III: 100a (= *Studies,* 237); H.-H. Esser, *NIDNTT* II: 445; D. Fürst, *NIDNTT* III: 779; Gordon, "The Problem at Galatia," 41 ("Torah protected Israel from the defiling influences of the Gentiles"), 43 ("to carry God's people safely through centuries of Gentile threats"). Cf. n. 2 above.

9. So, emphatically, Bultmann, *Theology,* 1: 266; "Christ the End," 46; *TDNT* VI: 217. Cf. Dodd, *Meaning,* 40, n. 16.

10. Cf. Bultmann, *Theology,* 1: 216; *Existence,* 136; G. Bertram, *TDNT* V: 620f.; Dodd, *NT Studies,* 123, n. 2; Beker, *Paul,* 55f. According to Belleville, "'Under Law,'" 71, the law "was intended to function as a temporary, regulatory code which . . . manages our life and hems us in to its directions and judgments. This is a somewhat neutral picture of ὑπὸ νόμου. . . . These verses do not picture a no-exit situation." However, v. 24b ("that we might be justified by faith") suggests that custody under the law was a *negative,* not neutral, state of inability as regards justification.

11. In εἰς Χριστόν the preposition has a temporal sense (as in NEB, RSV). As Young, *"Paidagogos,"* 174 observes, "εἰς with the accusative can have a temporal meaning (e.g. εἰς ἐμέ, "up to my time"), and the parallel εἰς τὴν μέλλουσαν πίστιν (3:23) demonstrates that this is [the] meaning of εἰς Χριστόν (i.e. 'up to the time of Christ')." Cf., e.g., Betz 178; Bruce 183. A. Oepke, *TDNT* II: 426f. takes it as final as well as temporal.

opened the way of faith to both Jews and Gentiles, that the law was custodian.[12]

When, in elaboration of the phrase "until Christ," Paul describes the meaning and goal of the law's activity as custodian by the clause, "that we might be justified by faith" (RSV, NIV), it is to be remembered that this righteousness is in no sense effected or prepared for by the law; rather, it is the hidden purpose of the custodianship of the law, which became clear only with the coming of Christ and faith.[13]

25 With the coming of Christ, the way of justification by faith in Christ is thrown open, not as just another possibility, but as the only way of obtaining righteousness. By saying that "we are no longer under a custodian" (RSV), Paul is in fact speaking of "the historic succession of one period of revelation upon another and the displacement of the law by Christ":[14] from the vantage point of salvation history, the validity of the law ceased with the coming of faith in the coming of Christ.

Having described the earlier dispensation of law and its displacement through the coming of faith (vv. 23-25),[15] Paul turns to describe the dispensation of faith which was inaugurated by the coming of Christ (vv. 26-29). The change from the generalizing first person plural of the earlier verses to the second person plural here seems to indicate that Paul now has the more subjective aspect of the Galatians' experience in view.

26 This verse explains why it is ("For") that with the coming of faith believers are no longer under law as a custodian (v. 25). "You . . . all" refers to all Christians irrespective of race, status, or sex (cf. v. 28); without distinction they are "sons of God" (the metaphor of inheritance requiring the masculine translation). Paul's argument seems to require that "sons" be understood in the sense of adult sons, for only so can the verse properly be regarded as providing the reason for v. 25, the sense being that just as the

---

12. On παιδαγωγός as custodian rather than tutor, see further Stendahl, *Paul*, 17-22; Longenecker, "Pedagogical Nature," 53-56. To regard the law as a "schoolmaster" (AV) or "tutor" (RV, NASB; cf. NEB) to "bring" (AV, RV) or "lead" (NASB, NIV) people to Christ and to construe Paul's words in terms of subjective, psychological development, is to come under the following caveat: "In the common interpretation of Western Christianity, . . . one could even say that Paul's argument has been reversed into saying the opposite to his original intention . . ." (Stendahl, *Paul*, 86f.).

13. Schlier 170. Cf. Bultmann, *Theology*, 1: 266.

14. Burton 200. Cf. Kertelge, *Rechtfertigung*, 207f.; Longworth, "Faith," 609f.; and p. 166, n. 76 above.

15. O'Neill 53f. would omit these verses as "a profound commentary on Paul, but commentary," but his reasons for doing so are not convincing. For a response cf. Fung 233, n. 23; "Relationship between Righteousness and Faith," 2: 102, n. 431.

custodian ceased to be necessary when the young person became of age, so the law has ceased to be valid since believers (have become and) are full-grown sons.

The two prepositional phrases at the end of the verse are taken together by AV, NASB, and NIV as forming one unit: "by (or through) faith in Christ Jesus";[16] in RV, RSV, and NEB they are separated and understood as modifying "you are all sons of God" independently of each other.[17] The latter understanding is supported by the following considerations: (a) The alleged awkwardness of adding a second modal clause to the words "you are sons" has a parallel in Rom. 3:25, where "through faith" is almost certainly to be separated from "in his blood" (RV, RSV, NEB, NASB, against AV, NIV). (b) The construction "faith in the Lord (or Christ) Jesus" indeed occurs in Eph. 1:15 and Col. 1:4, but in these instances it is not certain that en ("in") indicates the object so much as the sphere of faith.[18] (c) The idea of "faith in Christ" is clearly conveyed elsewhere in Galatians by the objective genitive ("faith of . . . ," 2:16, 20; 3:22). (d) The context shows that the second of these two phrases in 3:26 ("in Christ Jesus") must be separated from the first, being "thrown to the end of the sentence so as to form in a manner a distinct proposition, on which the Apostle enlarges in the following verses."[19]

On this understanding, then, faith, that is, faith in Jesus Christ (cf. vv. 22f., 25), is the means by which the Galatians have become God's sons,[20] while the ground of their sonship is their new relationship of "union

16. Cf. Ellicott 70. It would appear that P46, which reads διὰ πίστεως Χριστοῦ ("through faith of Christ"), has altered the original construction to make the meaning more clear (Kertelge, Rechtfertigung, 237, n. 58). Howard 97, n. 219, understands the phrase as meaning: "Through this faith (which resides) in Christ," and cites 1 Tim. 1:14 and 2 Tim. 2:1 as "similar constructions." But, to mention just one consideration, there is an important difference in that in those passages an article precedes the phrase "in Christ Jesus" (cf. n. 18 below).

17. Cf., e.g., Kertelge, op. cit., 208, n. 234; A. Oepke, TDNT II: 434, n. 54.

18. Cf. Moule 81; M. J. Harris, NIDNTT III: 1212. MHT 3: 263 with n. 2 thinks that it is probably the latter. In 1 Tim. 3:13; 2 Tim. 1:13 the article with the repetition of the preposition makes the meaning unambiguous (cf. n. 16 above).

19. Lightfoot 149. Cf. Hatch, Pauline Idea of Faith, 45, n. 1; Beasley-Murray, Baptism, 150. Hays 169 helpfully points out that the parallel with 3:28d—

(v. 26)   πάντες γὰρ υἱοὶ θεοῦ   ἐστε διὰ τῆς πίστεως   ἐν Χριστῷ Ἰησοῦ
(v. 28d) πάντες γὰρ ὑμεῖς εἷς   ἐστε   ἐν Χριστῷ Ἰησοῦ

—makes clear that "we have here an instance of Paul's characteristic formula ἐν Χριστῷ."

20. Schlier 172 takes "faith" here as approaching the meaning of the message of faith (cf. Rom. 10:8) and therefore denoting the objective means of sonship; but it seems more consistent with Paul's usage in the preceding context to take it as the subjective means of appropriation.

with Christ Jesus."[21] A reasonable inference from this is that it is faith which brings the believer into union with Christ on the basis of which sonship is bestowed.

27 The ground of the assertion in v. 26 is provided by this verse (note "for," AV, RV, RSV, NASB, NIV). Baptism is here regarded as the rite of initiation into Christ, that is, into union with Christ, or, what amounts to the same thing, of incorporation into Christ as the Head of the new humanity. This sense of the expression "baptized into" as "baptized so as to become a member of" is required by the context "on each of the three occasions which are decisive for its meaning": here, 1 Cor. 12:13, and Rom. 6:3.[22]

Baptism is also[23] regarded as "putting on" Christ, who is thought of as a garment enveloping the believer and symbolizing his new spiritual existence[24] (cf. Rom. 13:14, where the ethical aspect is primarily in view). The metaphor is probably derived from Hebrew tradition where the figure of changing clothes to represent an inward and spiritual change was common (cf. Isa. 61:10; Zech. 3:3f.).[25]

21. Cf. Thayer, s.v. ἐν I.6.b. On the omissions suggested by O'Neill 54f., cf. the response in Fung 235, n. 33; "Relationship between Righteousness and Faith," 2: 103, n. 441.

22. Dunn, *Baptism,* 112. Cf., e.g., A. Oepke, *TDNT* I: 540; M. J. Harris, *NIDNTT* III: 1209. "Baptized into Christ" (AV, RV, RSV, NASB, NIV) is sometimes taken to mean being "baptized with reference to Christ" (reflecting a Jewish idiom) and as equivalent to "baptized into the name of Christ" (cf. Acts 8:16; 19:5; so, e.g., Lightfoot, *Notes,* 295f.; H. Bietenhard, *TDNT* V: 275f.), but this seems debatable. The sense "with reference to" clearly would not fit 1 Cor. 12:13, and whereas baptism "into the name of Christ" would seem to signify a transference of the baptized person "into Christ's account" so as to become his property (the expression "into the name of" is common in commercial contexts: cf. Bruce, *Acts,* 187), baptism "into Christ" denotes rather the idea of union with Christ, as Rom. 6 clearly shows. If this distinction is valid, the use of the formula "baptized into the name of Paul/my name" in 1 Cor. 1:13, 15 gains in significance: in the face of the church's divisions, each claiming to "belong to" (RSV) the leader (cf. NIV) of its choice, Paul reminds the party associating itself with his name that they were never baptized "into his name" so as to owe allegiance to him—the implication being that their baptism had been "into the name of Christ" so that they belong to *Christ* and owe *him* their loyalty and love.

23. A. Oepke, *TDNT* I: 539 considers v. 27b to be "a heightened form" of v. 27a.

24. Ridderbos 148; *Paul,* 225.

25. So, e.g., Flemington, *Baptism,* 57f.; Beasley-Murray, *Baptism,* 148; U. Wilckens, *TDNT* VII: 689f., n. 22. It is therefore superfluous to regard the conception as derived from Gnostic circles (Kertelge, *Rechtfertigung,* 238) or from the mystery religions (Schoeps, *Paul,* 112). A. Oepke, *TDNT* II: 320 roundly declares that "the usage of Paul has nothing whatever to do with the donning of the garment or mask of the god by the initiate" (cf. Cranfield, *Romans,* 689); at the same time, it is worth remembering that "while Paul was not influenced by such ideas or practices, they could certainly have influenced some of his Gentile converts in their understanding of his teaching" (Bruce 187).

The baptism in view in Gal. 3:27 is almost certainly water baptism;[26] this being the case, its juxtaposition with faith, especially the fact that union with Christ is ascribed both to faith (v. 26) and to baptism (v. 27), raises the question of the exact relationship between the two. An extreme, mechanistic view of baptism would have us believe that it was, "for Paul and his readers, universally and unquestionably accepted as a 'mystery' or sacrament which works *ex opere operato,*" that the moment the believer receives baptism, union with Christ "takes place in him without any cooperation, or exercise of will or thought, on his part."[27] Such a view simply ignores the close connection between faith and baptism in the present instance; the fact that in this chapter faith is mentioned fifteen times and baptism only once would even by itself compel agreement with the dictum that Paul "by no means unconditionally attributes magic influence to baptism, as if receiving it guaranteed salvation."[28]

According to another view, "that which baptism symbolizes also actually *happens,* and precisely through baptism": "baptism is the moment of faith in which the adoption is realized—in the dual sense of effected by God and grasped by man—which is the same as saying that in baptism faith receives the Christ in whom the adoption is effected."[29] Here the emphasis upon a close alliance of faith and baptism is no doubt well placed; but in seeking to do justice to both ideas this view seems to make faith's efficacy dependent upon baptism as though it were only in baptism (as "*the* moment of faith") that faith receives Christ; this would logically lead to the conclusion that baptism is indispensable for the reception of Christ in whom alone salvation is to be found.[30] Such a position would, however, be clearly

---

26. Dunn, *Baptism,* 109 maintains that "baptized into Christ" is "simply a metaphor drawn from the rite of baptism to describe . . . the entry of the believer into the spiritual relationship of the Christian with Christ, which takes place in conversion initiation." In spite of the arguments put forward to support this thesis (111f.), there seems little reason to doubt that the original readers would have immediately understood v. 27a in terms of the *rite* of water-baptism (cf. Bruce, *Ephesians,* 79f.; K. H. Rengstorf, *TDNT* VI: 619), and this favors the assumption that Paul meant it to be so understood. While it is true that "to be baptized into Christ is to put on Christ," it is not true that "the sense is disrupted if we take one as a metaphor and one as a literal description of a physical act" (Dunn, op. cit., 111); there is no disruption if v. 27a describes a physical act ("baptized") and its spiritual meaning ("into Christ") and v. 27b then enlarges upon that meaning ("you have . . . put on Christ").

27. Lake, *Earlier,* 385 and Schweitzer, *Paul and His Interpreters,* 225f., respectively.

28. Bultmann, *Theology,* 1: 312; cf. Kertelge, *Rechtfertigung,* 299 with n. 7; Richardson, *Theology,* 347; G. Braumann, *NIDNTT* I: 289. The most decisive refutation of the view in question is provided by Paul himself in 1 Cor. 10:1ff.

29. Nygren, *Romans,* 233 (Nygren's emphasis) and Beasley-Murray, *Baptism,* 151, respectively. Cf. Jeremias, *Central Message,* 59.

30. For this position cf., e.g., Flanagan, "Messianic Fulfilment," 481; Lee,

opposed to Paul's teaching on the all-sufficiency of faith for salvation in Galatians itself, as would immediately become obvious if we substituted baptism for circumcision and regarded it as a condition for salvation.[31]

From the standpoint of the practice of baptism in apostolic times, when faith and baptism were not necessarily two distinct experiences separated by a period of time but two inseparable,[32] almost coincident parts of the one single experience of transition from the old existence to the new,[33] the view under discussion could well be a reflection of the actual state of affairs; but as an analysis of the *logical* relationship between faith and baptism it leaves something to be desired.

A more satisfactory view of the logical relationship between faith and baptism is represented by the statement that "St. Paul saw in Baptism the normal but not necessary, the helpful but not indispensable sign and seal put upon the act of faith appropriating the gift of God in Christ."[34] On this understanding, baptism is the "outward and visible sign of [an] inward and spiritual grace" *(Book of Common Prayer)*, and the apparent equation of faith and baptism in vv. 26f. may be explained as a natural transference of terms whereby the symbol (baptism) is said to effect that which it symbolizes or as a form of metonymy whereby what is strictly true of faith is predicated of baptism.[35] Probably Paul mentions baptism here because he is about to emphasize the oneness of those who are in Christ (v. 28, where the "all" of v. 26 recurs): the *visible* sign of this oneness is not faith but baptism; the oneness *with* Christ that is symbolized in baptism is the basis for the oneness *in* Christ (cf. Eph. 4:5, "one Lord, one faith, one baptism"). Here, as in

---

Romans, 111 (the phrase "baptismal justification" occurs repeatedly: 111-113, 133, 136f.). According to Ridderbos, *Paul,* 412, "Baptism and faith are both means to the appropriation of the content of the gospel. . . . That which the believer appropriates to himself on the proclamation of the gospel God promises and bestows on him in baptism. . . . Faith responds to the call of God through the gospel, and in baptism God takes the one thus called under his gracious rule and gives him a share in all the promises of the gospel." This seems close to saying that the believer's initial response in faith must be made effective or completed by baptism—or have we failed to grasp the author's meaning here?

31. As it has been aptly remarked in reference to Gal. 5:6, "On the same principle, neither baptism nor the want of baptism can be of any avail" (Scott, *Christianity,* 129).

32. Cf. Schnackenburg, *Baptism,* 127: "Paul would not understand it if anyone refused to be baptized; to him such an attitude would no longer be genuine faith."

33. Cf. Wagner, *Pauline Baptism,* 293f. Note the sequence "hearing-believing-being baptized" found frequently in Acts (e.g., 2:37f., 41; 8:12f., cf. vv. 35f.; 16:14f.).

34. Scott, *Christianity,* 114, cf. 122. Cf. also Neill 90; Pfleiderer, *Paulinism,* 1: 199; Robertson, *Word Pictures,* 4: 298 (baptism is "a badge or uniform of service like that of the soldier").

35. Cf. Bruce, *Colossians, Philemon, and Ephesians,* 388; Hendriksen 149.

Rom. 6, "there is an appeal in the presence of those who were in danger of forgetting spiritual facts, to the external sign which no one could forget."[36]

28 On the basis of a comparison with the parallel structures in 1 Cor. 12:12f. and Col. 3:9-11, this verse has been judged, probably rightly, to be "a fragment of an early Christian baptismal liturgy."[37] Those who through baptism have entered into union with Christ "are all one in Christ Jesus" (AV, NASB, NIV), in whom the racial, social, and sexual distinctions which obtained before are covered up, as it were, by the same garment—Christ.[38]

The three antitheses, which represent the most far-reaching distinctions of ancient society, seem to have been deliberately chosen with an eye to the threefold privilege for which a pious male Jew daily thanked God: that he was not made a Gentile, a slave, or a woman—categories of people debarred from certain religious privileges.[39] It is noteworthy that in the third antithesis the words used are not the customary terms for man and woman but the more technical terms denoting male and female,[40] thus indicating that what is in view is the general relationship between the sexes and not the specific relationship between husband and wife. The statement that there is no "male and female" in Christ does not mean, as was believed in later Gnosticism, that in the new era mankind is restored to the pristine androgynous state;[41] nor does it mean that all male-female distinctions have been obliterated in Christ, any more than that there is no racial difference between the Christian Jew and the Christian Gentile.

---

36. Machen, *Origin*, 287. Longenecker, *NT Social Ethics*, 31 is probably right in seeing in vv. 27f. "a liturgical formulation of the early Church." Paulsen, "Einheit," especially 87, thinks rather of vv. 26-28 as dealing with a traditional topic which Paul integrates into the argument of his letter especially by means of v. 29. In any case, one is at a loss to know how it can be said, as by Brinsmead 141: "In the statement of 3:27-29, Paul claims a sacramental realization of eschatological deliverance without reservation. He appears to border on enthusiasm."

37. Cf. Scroggs, "Eschatological Woman," 291-293 (quotation from 291); idem, *IDB* Supp. Vol. 966b; Witherington, "Rite and Rights," 596f.

38. Cf. Kertelge, *Rechtfertigung*, 239. For an interpretation in terms of Christ's "field of force" cf. W. Grundmann, *TDNT* IX: 552, n. 377.

39. Cf., e.g., A. Oepke, *TDNT* I: 777 with n. 4.

40. Not ἀνήρ/γυνή, but ἄρσην/θῆλυς. The formulation "male *and* female" (RV), which departs from the pattern of the preceding phrases, is presumably due to the influence of Gen. 1:27 (cf. Mk. 10:6). According to Witherington, "Rite and Rights," 597-599, in alluding to Gen. 1:27 Paul's intention is to assert, in opposition to the view of rabbinic Judaism that a woman must be connected to a circumcised male (husband or son) to ensure a place in the covenant community, that "in Christ, marriage, with its linking of male *and* female, into a one flesh union, is . . . not a requirement for believers" (599).

41. Cf. Betz 197-199 for this myth in various religious traditions, and Jewett, *Man*, 24-28 for refutation of the myth.

"In Christ Jesus" emphasizes that Paul views the elimination of these antitheses from the standpoint of redemption in Christ,[42] while the context clearly shows that the primary emphasis of the verse is on *unity* in Christ rather than on equality. The masculine gender of "one" suggests that the meaning here is that all who are in Christ form a corporate unity (NEB "one person"; cf. RV "one man"); it is this sense which provides the necessary transition from the thought of Christ as the "issue" (v. 16) to that of believers as the "issue" (v. 29) of Abraham.[43] If the notion of equality in Christ is also involved, it is only secondary and has regard to incorporation into this "one person" and membership in the community.[44]

29 As those who are united to Christ and who participate in the new existence made possible by him, believers "thus belong to Christ," and since Christ is the true offspring of Abraham (v. 16b), those who thus belong to Christ are collectively also Abraham's true "issue,"[45] and as such individually heirs in fulfillment of God's promise to Abraham.

Thus the new dispensation of faith is described in these verses (26-29) as one in which believers become sons of God through faith, since they are united to Christ by baptism, being constituted thereby Abraham's true offspring and therefore heirs of the promised inheritance.

Before going further in Paul's argument we pause to note several important considerations that arise from vv. 23-29.

(1) V. 24 states, again, that justification is through faith, but a comparison of v. 22 and vv. 23f. reveals a further point. The theme of imprisonment is repeated from v. 22a and strengthened in v. 23, and the divine purpose is described both as the imparting of the promise through faith to those who believe (v. 22b) and as justification by faith (v. 24b): just

---

42. Cf., e.g., Conzelmann, "Rechtfertigungslehre," 403; Ridderbos 149.

43. Cf. Burton 407f. If a noun is to be supplied from the context for the masculine numeral "one," the only one available is υἱός, "son" (Barrett 38, 114, n. 35).

44. Cf., e.g., Banks, *Community*, 118. An impressive list of scholars have gone beyond this to draw out important implications of Paul's statement here for women's ministry (cf. e.g., Longenecker, *NT Social Ethics*, 70-93). It seems precarious to appeal to this verse in support of any view of the role of women in the Church, for two reasons: (a) Paul's statement is not concerned with the role relationships of men and women within the Body of Christ but rather with their common initiation into it through (faith and) baptism; (b) the male/female distinction, unlike the other two, has its roots in creation, so that the parallelism between the male/female pair and the other pairs may not be unduly pressed. For further discussion of the implications of Gal. 3:28 for the question of women in ministry see Fung, "Ministry in the NT," 182-184.

45. Cf. W. Grundmann, *TDNT* VII: 782: "Abraham is the carrier of the promise for Israel and the Gentiles. The promised seed integrates those who receive Him into the bearer of the promise"—although, strictly speaking, Paul does not say "into Abraham," but only "into Christ" (v. 27).

as "through faith" in v. 24b corresponds to the same phrase in v. 22b (where it is paraphrased by NEB), so also "that we might be justified" (v. 24, RSV) corresponds to "that the promise . . . might be given to those who believe" (NASB). This means that the "promise" of v. 22b is to be understood as the promised blessing of justification; this is in harmony with our conclusion reached earlier (on v. 22) that the promise there has to do with the righteousness mentioned in v. 21. Therefore, justification by faith is seen to be the fulfillment of the promise made to Abraham, a conclusion which is in line with our earlier observation (on 3:8) that the promise to Abraham implicitly involves and anticipates the doctrine of justification by faith.

(2) From vv. 26-29 it is seen that believers are individually God's sons and collectively the true offspring of Abraham. They are God's sons since by faith they have been incorporated into Christ, the Son of God, and they are collectively the true seed of Abraham since, by virtue of their faith-union with Christ, they are one person in him who is the true "issue" of Abraham (cf. v. 16). Materially, therefore, God's sons are also the true issue of Abraham and sonship to Abraham is identical with sonship to God;[46] since the promise is fulfilled in sonship to Abraham (v. 29c), it is fulfilled in sonship to God. But we have just seen that the promise is fulfilled in justification, and earlier (on vv. 7-14: see pp. 151f. above) that it is fulfilled in reception of the Spirit; hence, justification by faith, reception of the Spirit by faith, and becoming sons of God by faith are intimately linked together as different expressions for the fulfillment of the promise.[47] From this we may infer that these three are not separate and distinct experiences but closely interwoven parts or aspects of the single experience of faith-union with Christ. Experientially, they take place at the same time in fulfillment of the same promise; logically, however, they are distinguishable and their logical relationships to one another will become clear in the next section of the text (4:1-7).[48]

(3) The promise to Abraham is seen to have a double fulfillment. From the salvation-historical point of view, it is fulfilled in Christ, the promised seed (v. 16), and in all those who are comprised in him (v. 29).

46. Ridderbos, *Paul*, 198 explains how Paul can alternately and in very much the same sense speak of "children of God" and "children/seed of Abraham": sonship originally signified "the special covenant relationship between God and Israel" (cf. Rom. 9:4), and "it is this peculiar privilege of Israel as nation [sic] that, in conformity with the Old Testament promises of redemption (cf. 2 Cor. 6:16-18), passes over to the church of the New Testament and there receives a new, deepened significance."

47. See pp. 152f. above, point (b), where the close link between justification, reception of the Spirit, and sonship to Abraham was noted.

48. Meanwhile, what is stated in the present section may be graphically presented as follows:

Experientially considered, on the other hand, it is fulfilled in the individual believer's threefold experience just referred to: justification, reception of the Spirit, becoming a son of God. These two points of view are, of course, complementary: the latter takes place in the individual when he comes to be "in Christ," an incorporation effected by faith. Hence it is by faith-union with Christ that the individual aligns himself with the central event of salvation history and partakes of the benefits accruing therefrom.

(4) The principle of justification by faith is again presented within the framework of salvation history as that which comes into force in the new dispensation, which is sharply set off from the earlier dispensation at the point where the Christ-event cuts into history. The coming of Christ as the ground of salvation also ushers in the principle of faith as the means of justification, and this is set over against the function of law which held sway until the coming of Christ and the revelation of faith:[49] the coming of Christ meant the cessation of law, so that the principle of justifying faith could take over. This division of history into two parts, with Christ as the line of demarcation, is connected with Paul's interpretation of the apocalyptic doctrine of the aeons: the present evil age (cf. 1:4) is still dominated by law, but in Christ the age to come has dawned and the law has ceased to be valid for those who through union with Christ already exist in the age to come.[50]

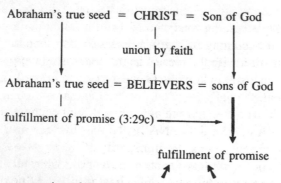

49. We might note again the parallel expressions "until faith should be revealed" (v. 23, NIV) and "until Christ should come" (v. 24). This parallelism leads Martyn, "Antinomies," 424, n. 29 to remark: "Faith is apocalypsed by coming newly on the scene"; to Martyn, this clearly indicates that "Paul's understanding of apocalypse is focused primarily not on God's *uncovering* of something hidden from the beginning of time (1 Cor. 2:10), but rather on God's new act of *invading* the human orb, thus restructuring the force field in which human beings live."

50. Cf. O. Michel, *TDNT* VII: 746; Grundmann, "Gesetz," 58. On the apocalyptic perspective of Paul's theology in Galatians see further Martyn, "Antinomies," especially 420f.

2. THE COMING OF CHRIST: SPIRITUAL MATURITY (4:1-7)

1 *This is what I mean: so long as the heir is a minor, he is no better off than a slave, even though the whole estate is his;* 2 *he is under guardians and trustees until the date fixed by his father.* 3 *And so it was with us. During our minority we were slaves to the elemental spirits of the universe,* 4 *but when the term was completed, God sent his own Son, born of a woman, born under the law,* 5 *to purchase freedom for the subjects of the law, in order that we might attain the status of sons.*

6 *To prove that you are sons, God has sent into our hearts the Spirit of his Son, crying "Abba! Father!"* 7 *You are therefore no longer a slave but a son, and if a son, then also by God's own act an heir.*

The first words (cf. RSV; 5:16; 3:17) show that these verses are intended as elaboration of what has been said in the preceding verses (3:23-29). The immediate link with the earlier paragraph is provided by the word "heir." In 3:29 the heirship is heirship in relation to Abraham, whereas here it is heirship in relation to God (cf. 4:1, 6f.), but preparation has been made for the transition by the material identity of sonship to Abraham and sonship to God already noted from 3:26-29. In the verses before us, the idea of becoming full-grown sons also mentioned in 3:26 is developed in combination with the idea of being free from slavery, as Paul explains with a human analogy how the Galatians have become full-grown sons and heirs of God.

1-2 The heir who is not yet of age is first described: he is not yet a man, but "a child" (AV, RV, RSV, NASB, NIV)—literally "an infant" *(nēpios);* the Greek term "covers the immaturity of youth as well as the incapacity of childhood" and thus denotes "a minor" in any stage of his minority.[51] As long as he is in this state of legal infancy, he is "no different from," that is, "no better off than,"[52] a slave as far as freedom of action (though not legal status) is concerned.[53] Even though *de jure* he already

---

51. Duncan 126. Cf. G. Braumann, *NIDNTT* I: 281 on the overtones of the word.

52. Both meanings of the verb διαφέρει (cf. AV, RV, NASB, NIV; and NEB, RSV, respectively) can find a place here.

53. K. H. Rengstorf, *TDNT* II: 271 remarks that "in the NT the δοῦλος ["slave"] is the classical picture of bondage and *limitation*" (emphasis added).

owns the whole estate, yet *de facto* he has no power of disposition over it; he is under the supervision of "guardians"[54] and "trustees."[55]

It has been suggested that "the tutor [NEB "guardian"] was the guardian of the child's person, the governor [NEB "trustee"] the guardian of the child's property."[56] On the other hand, it is pointed out that "there is no certain instance of the use of *oikonomos* ["trustee"] in the literature of antiquity for one who has charge of the person or estate of a minor, nor any case of the terms *epitropos* ["guardian"] and *oikonomos* appearing together"; that there are no instances in the papyri of a distinction between the two terms; and that "in the popular mind the guardian and steward was one and the same."[57] It would seem, then, that only one kind of overseer is spoken of here, "trustees" being intended to amplify and elucidate "guardians." Perhaps "Paul's association of the two terms came about because of the mention of slavery (4:3; also 4:1), since *oikonomos* ('administrator') can designate the supervisor of slaves."[58]

It is not certain whether Paul's analogy about the state of the minor lasting until the time fixed by his father is drawn from the practice of Roman law or Hellenistic law or from some other legal procedure.[59] Opinion also varies as to whether the father is represented in the analogy as still living or already deceased.[60] But these questions, like the one about the exact identity

54. Cf. RV, RSV, NASB, NIV; BAGD s.v. ἐπίτροπος 3; Thayer s.v. 2. AV has "tutors." Young, *"Paidagogos,"* 155 observes: "The ἐπίτροπος was a legal appointment whereas the παιδαγωγός was a social position made by the father. However, there are common factors in the roles which brought the words together in metaphorical usage."

55. Cf. RSV. Other renderings convey the same idea: "governors" (AV), "stewards" (RV), "managers" (NASB; BAGD s.v. οἰκονόμος 1.a; Thayer s.v.).

56. Wuest 113.

57. Longenecker, "Pedagogical Nature," 56; W. Foerster, *TDNT* III: 784 n. 37; O. Michel, *TDNT* V: 150 (translating Strack-Billerbeck III: 565), respectively. Note, however, Belleville, "'Under Law,'" 63: "While the functions of the ἐπίτροπος and the οἰκονόμος overlap, their spheres of applicability differ. Οἰκονόμος is not used in reference to Roman inheritance laws. It is an administrative term with no apparent legal connotations."

58. Betz 204; cf. Longenecker, loc. cit. On the other hand, Belleville, "'Under Law,'" 63 considers it "more likely that Paul in his use of both ἐπιτρόποι and οἰκονόμοι is merely referring to those who had effective control of the person, property, and finances of a minor (i.e. 'under the control of all types of guardians and stewards') as the plural would also suggest."

59. Cf., e.g., (Roman) Gibson, "Sources," 352f.; Betz 202; (Hellenistic) Schlier 189 with nn. 8f.; (other) W. Foerster, *TDNT* III: 784, n. 34; Ridderbos 152, n. 4; Burton 214. In the judgment of C. F. D. Moule, "it is not clear whether ἡ προθεσμία τοῦ πατρός in 4:2 ("the date set by the father") is an allusion to an actual law . . . [or] an artificial adaptation to the theological meaning of the full arrival of the time (vs. 4) when God brought his Son into the world" (*IDB* I: 49a).

60. Cf. Burton 214 and Schlier 189, respectively. Preferable is the opinion of J. I. Packer, *NIDNTT* I: 477.

of the guardians and trustees, do not affect the central point of the analogy, which is that the heir is under supervision during his minority and is freed from it at the father's appointed time.

3 The analogy is applied in vv. 3-5. To the legal minority of the heir, Paul likens the spiritual infancy of all people: the emphatic "we" here (*hēmeis*, NEB "us"), like the first person plural in 3:13f., probably embraces both Jews and Gentiles, since the transition from "we might attain the status of sons" (v. 5) to "because you are sons" (v. 6, RSV) suggests that the "we" of vv. 3-5 includes the "you," the Galatian converts of Gentile origin.[61] During this period, they were enslaved[62] under "the elemental spirits of the universe" (so also RSV). This rendering takes the Greek phrase *ta stoicheia tou kosmou* in a cosmological sense; an alternative translation renders it as "the basic principles of the world" (NIV; cf. RV "the rudiments of the world"). Which of these represents or approximates more nearly to the intended meaning is a question which will be discussed when we come to v. 9, where *ta stoicheia* occurs again. Meanwhile we may note that the servitude to the *stoicheia* in v. 3 *(hypo ta stoicheia)* is described in v. 5 as subjection to law *(hypo nomon),* so that certainly what Paul has primarily in view here is the law, and that as an instrument of spiritual bondage.

4b Now just as in the human analogy there is a time appointed by the father which marks the end of the period of minority and subjection to guardians and trustees, so in the history of salvation there came a time when "God sent his own Son." In speaking of God sending his Son Paul follows a traditional line of thought; he may even be using a pre-Pauline formula.[63] The verb "sent" "does not in itself make any christological statement,"[64] for example, about Christ's preexistence, but since Paul believed in this idea (cf. 1 Cor. 8:6; 10:4; Col. 1:15-17), it may well have been in his mind as he wrote this verse. Even if we are dealing with a pre-Pauline summary here, the idea of Christ's preexistence would probably still have been present, since "the identification of Christ with the divine wisdom through which the worlds were made was not peculiar to Paul and does not appear to have originated with him (cf. Jn. 1:2f.; Heb. 1:2; Rev. 3:14)."[65] It is to be

---

61. Cf. Burton 215; Schlier 193. On the other hand, Belleville, "'Under Law,'" 68 takes the shift from ἦμεν ("we were") to ἐστέ ("you are"), together with v. 5, as indicating that "4.1-5 refers specifically to pre-Christian, Jewish life under the law," and that Paul turns to the Gentiles only in vv. 6-11.

62. The periphrastic pluperfect (ἤμεθα δεδουλωμένοι) emphasizes the continuous state of slavery more than the simple pluperfect (ἐδεδουλώμεθα) would.

63. Cf. E. Schweizer, *TDNT* VIII: 374.

64. K. H. Rengstorf, *TDNT* I: 406. He goes on to say that it "rather derives its christological flavour from the christological context in which it is used."

65. Bruce 195.

observed that Christ was already Son when God sent him, that it was not the sending which made him the Son of God; in other words, his Sonship is to be understood not merely in a functional sense but in an ontological sense.[66]

The true humanity of the Son and his unity with mankind are underlined by a twofold statement: (a) he was "born of a woman"—the woman being not only the means of his entrance into the world but also the one from whom he took everything which is proper to mankind (though he knew no sin, 2 Cor. 5:21);[67] (b) he was "born under the law"—his very birth as man placing him immediately under subjection to the law. The participle rendered "born" probably denotes an action coincident with that indicated by the main verb "sent": God's sending of his Son coincides with the Son's being born of a woman (for another instance of the same aorist participle having coincidental force, cf. Phil. 2:7). That Paul uses here *genomenon* (from *ginomai*, "to be, to become"; cf. AV "made") and not *gennēthenta* (from *gennaō*, "to beget") cannot be construed as indicating that he does not have the virgin birth in view;[68] in the present context the former probably is simply a synonym for the latter (as *ginomai* is a "well-attested quasi-passive of *gennaō*"), so that "Paul's wording . . . throws no light on the question whether he knew of Jesus' virginal conception or not."[69] In any case, it is perhaps unlikely that Paul does have the virginal conception in view here, for the context lays emphasis on the identification of the Son of God with those he came to redeem; "hence he is stressing the likeness to us in terms of birth rather than the distinction from us in terms of conception."[70]

5   The purpose for which Christ was placed under the law is here stated. The two *hina* clauses, which are structurally parallel to each other (see RV, and cf. 3:14), have been taken as coordinate statements of the negative and positive aspects of the purpose, the latter complementing and interpreting the former,[71] but it seems more natural to regard the second clause as expressing the purpose or intended result of the first, as in NEB.[72] Christ achieved the purpose of redeeming those under law by bearing the full obligation of the law in life as well as the curse of the law in death (3:13).[73]

---

66. Cf. Ridderbos, *Paul*, 68f.

67. Cf. Ridderbos 155 with n. 10; *Paul and Jesus*, 74; *Paul*, 65.

68. *Pace* Schlier 196; Hendriksen 158f.

69. Bruce 195. Cf. G. Delling, *TDNT* V: 836: the text speaks plainly "neither for nor against" the virginal conception of Jesus. On the *assumption* that even before Paul the expression "born of a woman" had already been connected with the sending of the Son, E. Schweizer, *TDNT* VIII: 383 observes that "the formula which before Paul was explained in terms of the incarnation of the preexistent Son is referred by him to the substitutionary death on the cross, 3:13b."

70. Harrison, *Life*, 43.

71. E.g., E. Schweizer, *TDNT* VIII: 399.

72. Cf. RSV, AV, NIV; Ellicott 77; Lightfoot 168.

73. In answer to the question "How did Christ's death on the cross bring redemp-

And the purpose or intended result of this redemption was that "we," that is, both Jews and Gentiles (cf. on v. 3 above), might "attain the status of sons" or, more literally, "receive the adoption as sons" (NASB).[74] The term rendered "adoption as sons" (*huiothesia,* cf. Rom. 8:15) corresponds to Latin *adoptio* and connotes the status and "the full rights of sons" (NIV). Since the institution of adoption was not Jewish[75] but was widely known in Greek and especially Roman law, Paul most likely drew the term from the Hellenistic world; at the same time, "we should allow for the probability that in his mind it also had other associations"[76]—not least the Old Testament (cf., e.g., Ex. 4:22f.; Hos. 11:1)[77] as its theological background.

4a This freedom from law and attainment of mature sonship was accomplished by Christ in his coming "when the term was completed" or, more literally, "when the fulness of the time came" (RV, NASB).[78] The latter rendering adequately brings out the meaning of the phrase, whether the word *plērōma* ("fulness") has the active sense of "that which fills or completes" or the passive sense of "the (resulting) completeness."[79] Corresponding to the time appointed by the father in the human analogy (v. 2), the time spoken of here is fixed and appointed by God for the sending forth of his Son, the emphasis being on his sovereign determination and disposal of times and seasons. It would seem that "when the time had fully come" (RSV, NIV) does not mean that a certain divinely appointed period had elapsed (so NEB?), or that certain divinely ordained events had to transpire (cf. 2 Thess. 2:3ff.), or that God sent his Son into the world when all the

---

tion?" Schwartz, "Pauline Allusions," especially 260-263, suggests that the verb ἐξαπέστειλεν ("sent"), used by Paul only here in vv. 4 and 6, "at least in his own mind if not in that of his readers, carried the explanation: Christ's action was that of a scapegoat" (261, cf. 263). This may be correct as far as it goes; but "in the context of Gal. 3:22–4:5 the expression 'born under the law' suggests a broader reference: Christ's bearing the full obligation of the law, in life as well as in death . . ." (Longenecker, "Obedience," 146, n. 1; cf. Cooper, "Paul and Rabbinic Soteriology," 135).

74. As compared with the simple verb in 3:14 (λαμβάνειν) the compound verb used here (ἀπολαμβάνειν) may have the idea of receiving "as destined for, as promised to us" (Lightfoot 169). Cf. Thayer s.v. 1, although BAGD s.v. 1 renders it simply as "receive."

75. The term does not occur in the LXX and the practice is seldom alluded to in the OT or in rabbinical literature (cf. E. Schweizer, *TDNT* VIII: 399 with n. 12; C. F. D. Moule, *IDB* I: 48a).

76. Cranfield, *Romans,* 398. Calder, "Adoption," 374 suggests that the law of inheritance in view here is Phrygian or Anatolian.

77. Cf. Allen, "Romans i-viii," 30, who endorses the view of W. H. Rossell that the concept of adoption appears to come from the OT itself.

78. Cf. AV; BAGD s.v. πλήρωμα 5; Thayer s.v. 2.

79. These two uses cover most of the instances of the word in the OT and the NT, according to Moule, *Colossians and Philemon,* 164-169. Cf. Robinson, *Ephesians,* 255-259.

conditions were ripe for his appearance. In view of the fact that the word "came" denotes in the context (cf. 3:23, 25) the eschatological event of the coming of Christ and of the principle of justifying faith, the thought is rather that the appearance of the Son brought the "fulness of the time," marking the end of the present aeon (cf. 1:4) and ushering in the future aeon.[80] This means, for those who formerly were infants in slavery to the law, deliverance from this state and reception of the status of full-grown sons.

6 The significance of all that has been said in vv. 3-5 is now pressed home to the Galatian readers (vv. 6f.). The instatement as sons objectively accomplished by the coming of God's Son is made real in the individual believers' subjective experience through the gift of the Spirit. The rendering "to prove that you are sons" takes Gk. *hoti* as demonstrative, yielding the sense that the Spirit is sent as evidence of sonship;[81] but there is little doubt that the most natural way to understand *hoti* is to take it as causal and to translate "because you are sons" (RSV, NASB, NIV), indicating that the Spirit is sent as a result of sonship.[82] In either case sonship logically precedes the gift and operation of the Spirit, which in turn attests the reality of sonship. Sonship is not the result of the operation of the Spirit, but is attained through faith (3:26).

"Has sent" translates the same verb as is used in v. 4 of God sending his Son; here it is probably to be taken as a "collective historical aorist" referring to "the successive bestowals of the Spirit on individuals."[83] The heart stands for "the whole of the inner being of man,"[84] Gk. *kardia* bearing a similar sense to Heb. *lēḇ*, which denotes the organ of thought and will as well as the seat of the emotions. The specific activity of the Spirit, once it is sent into believers' hearts, is that of the filial cry addressing God as "Abba!

---

80. Cf., e.g., G. Delling, *TDNT* VI: 305, IX: 592; R. Schippers, *NIDNTT* I: 738; Vos, *Eschatology*, 26; Bruce, *Time Is Fulfilled*, 32. Cf. also Mk. 1:15, where Jesus' πεπλήρωται ὁ καιρός ("the time has come") bears a remarkable similarity to Paul's τὸ πλήρωμα τοῦ χρόνου ("the fulness of the time"). The latter is sometimes taken (e.g., Schlier 194; Abbott, *Ephesians and Colossians*, 18) as equivalent in substance to τὸ πλήρωμα τῶν καιρῶν (cf. NEB "when the time was ripe") in Eph. 1:10; but there the mention of "all in heaven and on earth" points to a day yet to come. Another difference is suggested by Ridderbos, *Paul*, 45, n. 2.

81. Cf., e.g., Zerwick §419; Moule 147; Hunter 33. Bruce 198 describes the NEB rendering as "a precariously free translation."

82. Cf., e.g., Burton 221; Schlier 197f.; Betz 209f.

83. Burton 223. Some have seen in it a reference to baptism: e.g., Flemington, *Baptism*, 58f.; Beasley-Murray, "Baptism in the Epistles of Paul," 139; Lampe, *Seal*, 55, n. 8. Note, however, the important concession made by Lampe (90f.) and cf. the discussion above on the relationship between faith and baptism (on 3:27).

84. J. Behm, *TDNT* III: 612. On the variant "your hearts" (AV) instead of "our hearts" see Metzger 595.

Father!"[85]—an echo of Jesus' own praying (cf. Mk. 14:36) which is also reminiscent of the beginning of the Lord's Prayer (cf. Lk. 11:2).[86] While the Spirit himself is here represented as crying within the believer's heart, the believer's own cry seems clearly implied.[87] For it is the indwelling Spirit (cf. Rom. 8:9) who teaches and enables the believer to pray using the term by which Jesus addressed God. In thus addressing God, believers show that they have "the Spirit of his Son," who is "the Spirit of sonship" (Rom. 8:15, NIV).[88] The latter phrase means probably not "the Spirit which anticipates adoption,"[89] since this ill accords with the present tenses in Rom. 8:14, 16; nor "a Spirit that makes us sons" (NEB), since "it is the Father who, by way of eminence, is the agent in adoption," not the Spirit;[90] but rather "the Spirit who imparts the assurance of sonship and enables believers to call God their Father."[91]

85. 'Abbā' is an Aramaic affectionate diminutive for "father" used in the intimacy of the family circle; it passed without change into the vocabulary of Greek-speaking Christians, although in each of its three NT occurrences (here; Rom. 8:15; Mk. 14:36) the transliteration is followed by a Greek translation. Wilcox, "Upon the Tree," 98 suggests (albeit hesitantly) that we may see in the cry of the Spirit in Gal. 4:6 a reflection of "the address of the obedient Isaac of the Akedah to his father, as given in the Palestinian targums of Gen. 22:6, 10." But nothing in the context suggests that Paul has Isaac in mind.

86. Cf., e.g., Jeremias, *Central Message*, 18; G. Kittel, *TDNT* I: 6. G. Schrenk, *TDNT* V: 1006 may well be right in saying that the cry here (cf. Rom. 8:15) "is certainly not to be restricted to the opening words of the Lord's Prayer," that "it goes beyond the use of a particular liturgical formula," and "involves a permanent attitude."

87. The view that κράζον ("crying") denotes ecstatic outcry after the manner of glossolalia is rightly rejected by W. Grundmann, *TDNT* III: 903, who takes it to denote an act of calling on God (cf. Cranfield, *Romans*, 399; Ridderbos, *Paul*, 200f., n. 64). Others think that it is an expression of confidence (Calvin, *Romans*, 170) or of the fervor of prayer (H. Greeven, *TDNT* II: 806).

88. The two are identified by, e.g., E. Schweizer, *TDNT* VIII: 392; Murray, *Romans*, 1: 296.

89. Barrett, *Romans*, 163.

90. Murray, *Romans*, 1: 296, n. 18.

91. F. Davidson and R. P. Martin, *EBC* 1031a. Cf. Murray, *Romans*, 1: 296; Ladd, *Theology*, 491.

Hays, "by applying the esoteric technology of Greimas' narrative model" (120, cf. 92-103) to the study of 4:3-6 and 3:13-14 (104-115), shows that these passages are related to each other as two formulations of the same narrative structure, as "consistent and complementary manifestations of a single story-pattern" (125), with Christ's death (even though it is not explicitly mentioned in 4:3-6) being presupposed as the central action in the gospel story (116-121). Hays does not "claim to have discovered [thereby] some unprecedented interpretation of these texts" (120), but only that Paul "was operating *(unconsciously)* on the basis of some larger principle of coherence [i.e., the gospel story] which enabled him to see these formulations as compatible or even equivalent" (92, emphasis added; cf. 86-92).

7 The upshot of this ("therefore") is impressed on the readers by the use of the second person singular "you" (v. 7):[92] each individual Galatian Christian is no longer a slave but a full-grown son, and consequently an heir.[93] "By God's own act" is more literally "through God,"[94] the idea being that the believer who is a son has also been made an heir "through the gracious act of" God (NASB marginal note), who is the source of the inheritance as well as the author of the adoption. For the Galatian Christians to put themselves under the law (or the *stoicheia* of the world) would, therefore, be to revert to spiritual infancy, whereas they are already God's full-grown sons and heirs.

We have consistently understood the references to the status of sons in vv. 5-7 in the sense of full-grown sonship, because this appears to be the sense required by Paul's argument in 3:26, and it is reasonable to suppose that this is also the sense intended in the present passage, which continues and elaborates the earlier argument.[95] While the main idea in the human analogy is that of an heir who is underage, in his application of it Paul has combined two metaphors (v. 3, "During our *minority* we were *slaves* . . .") so that, instead of saying simply "When the fulness of time arrived, God sent forth his Son . . . in order that we might come of age," he says ". . . in order that we might receive adoption as sons—and full-grown sons at that"—thus weaving together the idea of "becoming an adopted son from a slave" and that of "the heir coming of age."[96]

92. Note the successive changes in the mode of address in vv. 5-7: "we," "you" plural, "you" singular.

93. Here sonship and heirship are naturally joined together, as also in Rom. 8:17 ("children" there [Gk. τέκνα] represents the same idea as "sons" here [Gk. υἱοί]). "Heir" is understood by Cranfield, *Romans,* 406 to denote "presumably an heir of the promise made to Abraham (cf. 3:29 together with 3:26)" and not an heir of God. But "sons" in v. 5 clearly means "sons of God" and this naturally suggests that "heir" here means "heir of God"; moreover, coming immediately after "a son [of God]," "an heir" is unlikely to denote "an heir of Abraham," which would be an anticlimax (cf. Burton 224f.). Even though heirship to Abraham is materially identical with heirship to God (cf. n. 48 above), from 4:1 onwards Paul seems to have set Abraham aside temporarily, until 4:22.

94. Διὰ θεοῦ, cf. 1:1; 1 Cor. 1:9. "Through God" is the rendering of RSV, which takes the phrase, less naturally, with v. 7a.

95. Cf. A. Oepke, *TDNT* V: 653: "The status of son implies full freedom *and adulthood* as compared with legal servitude and restriction" (emphasis added).

96. It is implied that believers are full-grown sons, albeit by adoption, from the very start of their Christian experience. If the idea of being full-grown is left out of the sonship, we should have to speak of Paul having *confused,* and not just combined, the two metaphors in vv. 4f., and say that it is the idea of adoption, rather than that of coming of age, which dominates the rest of the passage until it is finally combined with the image

The human analogy itself prepares for this combination of the two metaphors by including beside the main idea of the heir also the subsidiary idea of slavery (v. 1c, "no better off than a slave"; v. 2, "under guardians and trustees"). The combination is also facilitated by the material consideration that from the spiritual point of view a person without Christ is in fact not only a minor but also a slave (v. 3).[97] Hence the coming of Christ which according to the analogy brought about mankind's coming of age as the infant heir also obtained mankind's freedom from slavery and adoption to sonship. In terms of the believer's personal experience, entry upon the full rights of the adopted son and heir who has come of age is effected by the sending of the Spirit of the Son into their hearts.

From our study of 4:1-7, two points may be emphasized in connection with Paul's exposition of the doctrine of justification by faith. (1) There is here a close-knit nexus of ideas between deliverance from enslavement to the law, adoption to sonship to God, and reception of the Spirit: the first makes the second possible, the second provides the logical basis for the third, the third furnishes the evidence for the second. But since freedom from the law implies justification by faith (cf. 3:23f.), we may say that 4:1-7 implies a close connection between justification by faith, sonship to God, and reception of the Spirit.[98] It is not surprising that this connection was already present in 3:26-29 since that section and the present section represent two parallel movements. But whereas there justification, adoption, and receiving of the Spirit appear as different aspects of a single experience, here they are presented in their logical relationship to one another.

(2) The entire discussion is, once again, carried on within the framework of salvation history. As in 3:23-29, Christ's appearance is presented as that which brings about the fullness of time, as that which puts an end to the domination of law and achieves for mankind the coming of age: the twofold (and parallel) sending of the Son (v. 4) and (the chronologically subsequent) sending of the Spirit (v. 6)[99] effected the breach between the old aeon of

---

of the heir again by the fact of inheritance (v. 7c); so, e.g., Dunn, *Baptism,* 114; E. Schweizer, *TDNT* VIII: 383, n. 360.

97. This appears to be overlooked by O'Neill 56, who says that "the images employed in verses 1-3, on the one hand, and verses 4-7, on the other hand, are strictly incompatible."

98. On justification as the basis of adoption cf. Taylor, *Forgiveness,* 78; Buchanan, *Justification,* 277; Murray, *Redemption,* 132-140.

99. Cf. E. Stauffer, *TDNT* III: 108: "The total context of salvation history" "may be seen most clearly and succinctly in G[a]l. 4:4ff.: God first sends the Son, and then, to continue the work, τὸ πνεῦμα τοῦ υἱοῦ αὐτοῦ [the Spirit of his Son]."

slavery under law and the new aeon of adoption to sonship and reception of the Spirit. Thus, salvation history and the eschatology of the two aeons are closely interwoven, and central to both is the historical event of Christ's advent, passion, and triumph.[100]

3. CULTIC OBSERVANCE: RELAPSE INTO SLAVERY (4:8-11)

8 *Formerly, when you did not acknowledge God, you were the slaves of beings which in their nature are no gods.* 9 *But now that you do acknowledge God—or rather, now that he has acknowledged you—how can you turn back to the mean and beggarly spirits of the elements? Why do you propose to enter their service all over again?* 10 *You keep special days and months and seasons and years.* 11 *You make me fear that all the pains I spent on you may prove to be labour lost.*

Since the Galatians had become full-grown sons of God (3:26; 4:1-7), their subjection to the law (or the *stoicheia*) would be not only a return as it were to infancy but a return in fact to slavery. This is the practical consideration with which Paul now directly confronts his readers.

8   Their former state, Paul reminds them, was one of ignorance of God—of "not knowing God" (RV);[101] since this may be one of those instances where "in the concept of the knowledge of God the element of knowledge emerges alongside and sometimes *prior to* that of acknowledgement,"[102] the rendering "when you did not know God" (RSV, NASB, NIV) might be preferred to NEB "when you did not acknowledge God." Their state was also one of servitude to "beings which in their nature are no gods"; *physei* (NEB "in their nature"; AV, RV, RSV, NASB, NIV "by nature"), which strengthens the denial of deity to these supposed gods, may contain an allusion to the concept of *physei theoi*, "gods that are so by their true nature," as distinct from *thesei theoi*, "those that become so by human positing."[103] In any case, Paul elsewhere makes it clear that "if there be so-called gods, . . . yet for us [Christians] there is one God, the Father" (1 Cor. 8:5f.); these so-called divinities are actually nonentities, though behind them may lurk demonic influences (cf. 1 Cor. 8:4; 10:19-21).

100. Cf., e.g., Bornkamm, *Paul*, 199; Ridderbos, *Paul and Jesus*, 64; *Paul*, 161f., 166f., 173f.; Wendland, *Mitte*, 9.
101. The Gk. phrase (οὐκ εἰδότες) is a rare instance of the classical use of οὐ with the participle (Bruce 201).
102. R. Bultmann, *TDNT* I: 705 (emphasis added).
103. H. Köster, *TDNT* IX: 255, 272. Cf. Betz 214.

9 By contrast, the Galatians' present status is described as that of those who "know" (NIV), or better (taking the aorist participle as inceptive), "have come to know" (RV, RSV, NASB) God.[104] The knowledge of God referred to here is doubtless that which was imparted to the readers by Paul's missionary preaching (cf. v. 13; 1:8) and appropriated by their personal response of faith (cf. 1:9; 3:2, 5). Being known and acknowledged by God, on the other hand, has the same sense as being called (effectually) and chosen (cf. 1:6, 15; 5:8, 13; 1 Thess. 1:4).[105] Paul's immediate correction of the active "you have come to know God" to the passive "to be known by God" (RSV)[106] has the effect of emphasizing the divine initiative.[107]

Mention of the "spirits of the elements" brings us back to the question of the meaning of "the *stoicheia* of the world" in v. 3. The Greek word can have a number of different meanings: primarily, the component parts of a series, like the letters of the alphabet; derivatively, first principles, the rudiments of learning (as in Heb. 5:12); also, the elements which make up the physical universe (cf. 2 Pet. 3:10, 12); as an astronomical term, the heavenly luminaries, especially the planets; finally, elemental or astral spirits.[108] In the NT apart from the passages just mentioned, the word occurs only in Gal. 4:3, 9 and Col. 2:8, 20.

Ta stoicheia tou kosmou (Gal. 4:3; Col. 2:8, 20) is taken by the majority of modern scholars in a cosmological sense as the elemental powers of the universe,[109] which are then more specifically identified with the angelic powers through whom the law was promulgated,[110] or with the

---

104. It is disputed whether there is any distinction of meaning between the two words for "know" in vv. 8 and 9 (οἶδα and γινώσκω respectively), with, e.g., Lightfoot 171 and Burton 230 holding the affirmative view (γινώσκω emphasizes the process or result of coming to know; cf. Erickson, "ΟΙΔΑ and ΓΙΝΩΣΚΩ," 121f.) and R. Bultmann, *TDNT* I: 703, n. 61 (on which see, however, Silva, "Pauline Style," 207, n. 44) and H. Seesemann, *TDNT* V: 116f. holding the opposite view. At least in the present instance a distinction of meaning seems warranted by the context: "By γνόντες there is . . . affirmed the acquisition of that knowledge the former possession of which is denied in οὐκ εἰδότες" (Burton, loc. cit.).

105. So, e.g., R. Bultmann, *TDNT* I: 706, 710; E. D. Schmitz, *NIDNTT* II: 400. Duncan 133 suggests the sense "acknowledged by Him as sons"; cf. Guthrie 116.

106. Technically called a case of epidiorthosis (BDF §495.3); cf. Rom. 8:34. On the use of γνωσθέντες here Silva, "Pauline Style," 202 points out that Paul has no alternative since οἶδα is not used in the passive.

107. Cf. Ridderbos, *Paul*, 247.

108. Cf., e.g., MM s.v. στοιχεῖον; Moule, *Colossians and Philemon*, 91.

109. E.g., A. S. Peake, *EGT* III: 522f.; E. Stauffer, *TDNT* III: 101; G. Braumann, *NIDNTT* I: 282; P. L. Hammer, *IDB* II: 82; Howard 66-71. Hanson, *Studies*, 8 considers this conclusion "impossible to resist." See Belleville, "'Under Law,'" 66 for seven reasons usually given in support of this identification.

110. E.g., Schmithals, *Paul and the Gnostics*, 45, n. 91; Reicke, "Law," 261-263; Bligh 337f.

spirits particularly connected with the astral bodies, the rulers of the planetary spheres believed to exercise a controlling influence over the lives and destinies of persons.[111] Others interpret *ta stoicheia* as the elementary teachings—rudimentary principles of morality and religion, more specifically the requirements of legalism by which people lived before Christ—and the *kosmos*, "the world," as mankind's habitation, which is dominated by sin.[112]

In favor of the first of these two interpretations (cf. RSV, NEB) is the strongly personal character that the *stoicheia* seem to have in the context: they appear as masters to whom service is rendered by their slaves.[113] But this, it is noted in reply, may be a case of personification, in much the same manner as the personification of the inanimate "pattern of teaching" of Rom. 6:17.[114] One objection to the first interpretation is that the sense "elemental beings" or "heavenly bodies" is not attested for *stoicheia* elsewhere until post-NT times;[115] but this has been countered by the observation that "the phrase *stoicheia tou kosmou* seems to be Paul's own contribution to religious vocabulary" and carries a particular sense which Paul has put on it.[116]

The second interpretation is said to be further supported by such considerations as the following: (a) The close connection between the *stoicheia* of the world and the time of infancy (v. 3) naturally suggests the notion of elementary teachings; in fact, the entire section 3:23–4:7 argues that believers have come of age in Christ, thus implying the opposite idea of some teaching or institution suited to the immaturity of minors.[117] (b) It is clear from vv. 3 and 5 that what Paul has primarily in view is the law as an instrument of spiritual bondage. If *stoicheia* refers to elementary, imperfect teaching, his argument is simple and direct: to accept the Jewish law or some equivalent system is to come under slavery to some imperfect doctrine. But if *stoicheia* denotes the elemental spirits, then it has to be explained how submitting to the regulations of the Jewish law is tantamount to being enslaved to these spirits.[118] As E. D. Burton remarks,

---

111. E.g., G. Bertram, *TDNT* IV: 919, VII: 726; Schlier 192; Betz 204f.

112. E.g., Lightfoot 167; Burton 510-518; Cranfield, "Law," 165; Ladd, *Theology*, 402f.; Moule 90-92; Thayer s.v. στοιχεῖον 4; Hendriksen 156f.; *Colossians*, 135-137, n. 83; Alford 39; Belleville, " 'Under Law,' " 67f.; Young, *"Paidagogos,"* 172.

113. Cf. Schlier 191; Reicke, "Law," 261.

114. Cf. Burton 517.

115. Cf., e.g., Burton 510-516; Ridderbos 153, n. 5; Moule 91f.; G. Delling, *TDNT* VII: 681-683; Blinzler, "Lexikalisches," 434-436.

116. Bruce 204.

117. Cf. Burton 517.

118. Cf., e.g., Reicke, "Law," 265-268, who answers in terms of the law's

To find the ground of the description of obedience to them [the requirements of the law] as a bondage to *ta stoicheia tou kosmou* in a remote and unsuggested connection between them and the heavenly bodies, or the physical elements of the universe, or the spirits of these elements, when the phrase is directly applicable to them in a sense appropriate to and suggested by the context and sustained by contemporary usage, is to substitute a long and circuitous course of thought for a short, direct, and obvious one.[119]

If it is a matter of choosing between these two alternatives, the relevant linguistic and contextual considerations suggest that the second is more probable. There is, however, a third option which seems to do justice to the facts of the case, including (a) the linguistic consideration that "if *stoicheion* in Galatians and Colossians is to be understood in the light of usage outside the NT, the most obvious sense is 'element,' "[120] and (b) the contextual consideration that Paul affirms a certain identification of Judaism and paganism as alike being forms of service to the *stoicheia*.[121] This view takes *stoicheia tou kosmou* as an expression contributed by Paul himself,[122] the meaning of which is to be determined from the context: using *stoicheion* "in a transferred sense for that whereon man's existence rested before Christ," Paul includes in the *stoicheia* of the world "on the one side the Torah with its statutes (4:3-5 . . .), and then on the other side the world of false gods whom the recipients [of his letter] once served, 4:8f."[123] On this understanding, the elements of the world can "cover all the things in which man places his trust apart from the living God revealed in Christ; they become his gods, and he becomes their slave."[124] This interpretation is preferred here, if only provisionally and in full recognition that the matter continues to be keenly debated.[125]

---

association with and consequent fundamental dependence on the flesh; Barrett, *First Adam*, 64f., who speaks of the recognition "that the law as Judaism knew it belonged to the age in which the elements ruled through destiny." A. J. Bandstra's attempt to identify the στοιχεῖα directly with the flesh is dismissed as "not persuasive" by Furnish, *Theology*, 117, n. 13; cf. his review of Bandstra's *The Law and the Elements of the World* (Kampen, 1964; Grand Rapids, 1965) in *JBL* 84 (1965) 192f.

119. Burton 518. See also the difficulties mentioned by Belleville, " 'Under Law,' " 66f.

120. G. Delling, *TDNT* VII: 684. Cf. Vielhauer, "Gesetzesdienst," 553.

121. Cf., e.g., Reicke, "Law," 259, 261; Schlier 193f.; Bruce 30, 202f.; Vielhauer, "Gesetzesdienst," 551.

122. That the expression was not taken over from Paul's opponents is strongly argued by Vielhauer, "Gesetzesdienst," 550-553.

123. G. Delling, *TDNT* VII: 685, 684.

124. H.-H. Esser, *NIDNTT* II: 453.

125. Thus, whereas W. Schmithals roundly declares that "nowadays it may be acknowledged as proved that in the στοιχεῖα τοῦ κόσμου we have to do with personal

The contrast between "formerly" (v. 8) and "now" (v. 9) makes any return on the part of the Galatians to the *stoicheia* absurd, that is, logically impossible.[126] For, as the repetition "back" *(palin),* "all over . . . again" *(palin anōthen)* shows, for the readers to submit to the demands of the Judaizers would represent a *"relapse to* bondage and *recommencement of* its principles. The Galatians had been slaves to the *stoicheia* in the form of heathenism; now they were desiring to enslave themselves *again* to the *stoicheia,* and to *commence* them *anew* in the form of Judaism."[127] Paul calls the *stoicheia* "weak and beggarly" (RSV):[128] "weak" because they have no power to save or justify their devotees and "beggarly" (literally "poor," as in 2:10) because they have no spiritual riches to bestow upon the Galatians—in short, they "have nothing at all to offer—but enslavement."[129]

10 Paul sees evidence of the Galatians' tendency to return to bondage to the *stoicheia* in their scrupulous observation of sacred times and seasons.[130] His statement has led to a number of interpretations.

Schmithals's view is that Paul is "employing a current familiar list which was not widespread in Jewish orthodoxy but frequently occurs above all in the apocryphal or Gnostic or gnosticizing literature," and that the tendency exhibited by the Galatians is "Gnosticism in one of its varieties."[131] This view is part and parcel of Schmithals's unconvincing theory that the Galatian heretics were Jewish Christian Gnostics; it overlooks the close similarity between Paul's wording and that of Gen. 1:14 with its

---

angelic powers" *(Paul and the Gnostics,* 45, n. 91), G. Delling equally emphatically asserts: "the reference . . . certainly cannot be to the stars. To speak of spiritual forces is a forced solution which conflicts with the linguistic findings and is hardly in accord with the context" *(TDNT* VII: 684). Blinzler, "Lexikalisches," 430-437 lists nine meanings of στοιχεῖα which have been taken into consideration in the exposition of Gal. 4 and Col. 2.

126. This seems to be the force of πῶς, rendered "how can" in RSV, NEB.

127. Ellicott 81. Cf. p. 217, n. 61 below. On θέλετε ("propose") here cf. G. Schrenk, *TDNT* III: 46 with n. 20.

128. G. Delling, *TDNT* VII: 685 sees in this description "a comprehensive judgment on all pre-Christian religion." E. Bammel, *TDNT* VI: 909 regards both στοιχεῖον and ἀσθενῆ καὶ πτωχά as terms "undoubtedly . . . used in the debate between Jew and Gentile."

129. Cf., e.g., Duncan 134; G. Stählin, *TDNT* I: 493; C. Brown, *NIDNTT* II: 828 (whence the quotation).

130. Gk. παρατηρεῖσθε ("you keep") may be used here "in the sense of watching for them, calculating their arrival (cf. the noun παρατήρησις in Lk. 17:20" (Bruce 205). The suggestion that Paul is describing only "the *typical* behaviour of religiously scrupulous people" in which the Galatians "would be engaged once they took up Torah and circumcision," and not their actual behavior at the time (Betz 217) neither does justice to the present tense of the verb nor sufficiently accounts for Paul's "fear" in v. 11.

131. Schmithals, *Paul and the Gnostics,* 44, 46.

mention of "seasons and days and years" (NIV; in the LXX the Greek words are the same as those in Gal. 4:10).[132]

Some interpreters see here a reference to (presumably pagan) "astrological superstitions," "astronomical calculations," or astronomically oriented calendar observances of certain Jewish apocalyptic circles.[133] The difficulty with this view is that it does not account for Paul's view of the observances as submission to the *Jewish* law (4:21).[134]

Others understand 4:10 as a reference to the Jewish religious calendar,[135] and this still appears to be the most natural view. On this view, "special days" are the Sabbath (cf. Col. 2:16) and other religious fast or feast days,[136] "months" are new moon observances (cf. Num. 28:11-15),[137] "seasons" are feasts or festival seasons lasting more than one day (cf. Lev. 23),[138] and "years" are Sabbatical or Jubilee years[139] or, more probably, New Year celebrations.[140] Thus "the four terms without mutual exclusiveness [cover] all kinds of celebrations of days and periods observed by the Jews."[141] In this enumeration Paul apparently intends to say that the Galatians had taken over the entire Jewish system of religious observances.[142] In his view this religious observance of sacred days and seasons according to the Jewish calendar—as an obligation imposed by the law, and not simply as a matter of custom—was a form of subservience to the *stoicheia* which could neither save nor justify its adherents but only cast them into bondage.

11 The Galatians' practice of Jewish religious observances leads Paul to fear that he might have labored over them in vain. It is possible that

---

132. Cf. Bruce 205f.

133. G. Bertram, *TDNT* VII: 726; Martin 115; Schlier 206, respectively. Against the third of these views see H. Riesenfeld, *TDNT* VIII: 148, n. 17.

134. It appears that the Jewish law is meant, despite the first, anarthrous νόμος, because of the use of the article with the second νόμος and the reference to the story of Hagar and Sarah.

135. E.g., Burton 234; H. Riesenfeld, *TDNT* VIII: 148. In the view of A. E. Harvey, "the language is so similar to that which Justin uses to refer to Jewish observances that it is difficult to believe that anything else is intended here" ("Opposition," 324).

136. Cf. G. Delling, *TDNT* II: 950; E. Lohse, *TDNT* VII: 30, n. 232.

137. Cf. BAGD s.v. μήν 2; Thayer s.v. 2; and especially G. Delling, *TDNT* IV: 641.

138. Cf. BAGD s.v. καιρός 3; Thayer, s.v. 2.d; G. Delling, *TDNT* III: 461.

139. Sabbatical Years: BAGD s.v. ἐνιαυτός 3; Hunter 34; Jubilee Years: Thayer s.v.; Schoeps, *Paul*, 77; both: Lightfoot 171; Ridderbos 162.

140. Cf. G. Delling, *TDNT* IV: 641; BAGD s.v. 3; Filson, *NT History*, 242 with n. 27.

141. Burton 234.

142. Cf. Ridderbos 162.

he would count his labors lost if the Galatians, by adhering to cultic observances as a matter of religious obligation, fail to enjoy the liberty in Christ
which is offered in the gospel; but it seems more likely that it is their
salvation, more specifically their justification, which he fears may be lost.
This understanding is supported by the following considerations. (a) The
word rendered "lost" (eikệ; "in vain," AV, RV, RSV, NASB) occurred
earlier in 3:4 in a context dealing with the matter of salvation, in particular
with the antithesis between justification by faith and justification by works.
(b) In 2:21 it is said that if righteousness were through the law, Christ would
have died to no purpose—or, "in vain" (AV).[143] The thought of Christ's
possibly having died in vain thus occurs in the context of justification. (c)
Paul will presently point out the futility of circumcision and the law, once
more in connection with the thought of righteousness (5:2, 4f.). Hence we
may assume that here also Paul is thinking of the Galatians' justification and
that he fears that they, by holding fast to their religious observances as a
means of justification, might fail to receive the justification which is available only through faith, and that consequently all the hard toil intended for
their benefit should prove to have been in vain.[144] The issue, then, is "not
the observation of religious usages as such . . . , but the basis of the justification before God":[145] the legalistic approach advocated by the Galatian
agitators and the gospel of free grace proclaimed by Paul are irreconcilably
opposed to each other.

Concluding our study of this entire section (E, 3:23–4:11), we may sum up
the major findings on the theme of justification in three propositions. (1)
Justification is clearly stated in 3:23-29 to be by faith, and this fundamental
truth is implicitly reaffirmed in what follows (4:1-7, 8-11). (2) In 3:23-29
justification by faith is presented within the framework of salvation history,
and this receives further emphasis in 4:1-7. (3) Justification by faith is seen
as the fulfillment of the promise made to Abraham (3:22, 24). As such it is
closely linked with adoption to sonship in relation to God and to reception of
the Spirit: on the one hand, it is coincident with them, all three being different aspects of the single experience of faith-union with Christ
(3:26-29); on the other hand, it provides the logical basis for adoption to
sonship, which in turn logically precedes reception of the Spirit (4:1-7).

---

143. The Greek word used is δωρεάν, not εἰκῇ. Both words, however, "take on
the sense of 'in vain,' and . . . no distinction of meaning can be seen between them in this
regard, at least in the NT" (F. Büchsel, *TDNT* II: 381). Cf. p. 126, n. 82 above.

144. That Paul has chiefly the result of his labors in mind is shown by his use of
the perfect tense κεκοπίακα ("I have labored," RSV), which refers to a past action and
its existing result.

145. Ridderbos 163.

F. A PERSONAL APPEAL (4:12-20)

This section manifestly differs from the others in the present division (III, 2:15–5:12) in that whereas the others are directly doctrinal, this section is Paul's personal appeal to his Galatian converts and has little doctrinal content. The appeal that they be not misled by the agitators but become like him in his freedom from the law (vv. 17, 12) is based on the readers' former relations with him (vv. 13-15) and on his continuing concern for them (vv. 16, 18-20).

1. PAUL'S PLEA (4:12)

12 *Put yourselves in my place, my brothers, I beg you, for I have put myself in yours. It is not that you did me any wrong.*

12 In the more literal rendering of NIV Paul's plea reads: "become like me, for I became like you" (cf. RSV, NASB). The point of reference is probably freedom from the law. In exchanging adherence to the law for faith in Christ, Paul became a "Gentile sinner," as the Galatians were (cf. 2:15, 17); he now beseeches them to become as he is, to be free from legal bondage and to know the liberty that is in Christ (cf. 5:1).[1] The last part of the verse, better rendered "You have done me no wrong" (NASB, NIV) or "You did me no wrong" (RSV), is taken by some as Paul's assurance to his converts that despite their deviation from his gospel he bore no grudge against them and by others as a statement of fact—that Paul had no reason to complain of their former treatment of him—which implies an entreaty—that they were to continue in that cordial attitude towards him and not to injure him now by ignoring his plea.[2] The latter interpretation is preferable, since it appears to make for a closer connection with the thought of the succeeding verses, in

1. Cf., e.g., Ridderbos 164f.; Schlier 208f.; Betz 222f.; E. Stauffer, *TDNT* II: 357; Hays, "Christology," 281f.
According to Gaventa, "Galatians 1 and 2," 322 the Galatians are to imitate "Paul's single-minded response to the gospel that was revealed to him. . . . To become as Paul is means to allow Christ to live in oneself (cf. 2:20) to the exclusion of the Law or of any other tradition or category (cf. 3:27-28)." On the basis of this and other observations, Gaventa maintains that in Gal. 1–2 Paul "not only defends himself and his gospel, but also offers himself as a paradigm of the work of the gospel" (326, cf. 319f.). But while it may be admitted that Paul's experiences as related in Gal. 1–2 could be considered to have the effect of "a paradigm of the reversal inaugurated by the gospel" (319), I am not convinced that it was Paul's conscious intention and design in those chapters to present "himself as an example of the working of the gospel" (313).
2. Cf., e.g., Duncan 139; Bruce 208; and Ellicott 83; Betz 223, respectively.

which Paul contrasts the Galatians' former relations with him and their present attitude toward him.

2. THEN AND NOW (4:13-16)

13 As you know, it was bodily illness that originally led to my bringing you the Gospel, 14 and you resisted any temptation to show scorn or disgust at the state of my poor body; you welcomed me as if I were an angel of God, as you might have welcomed Christ Jesus himself. 15 Have you forgotten how happy you thought yourselves in having me with you? I can say this for you: you would have torn out your very eyes, and given them to me, had that been possible! 16 And have I now made myself your enemy by being frank with you?

13 Paul's appeal is based on facts that were known to his readers. First to be mentioned are the circumstances in which he brought the gospel to them. "It was bodily illness that . . . led to . . ." is more literally "because of an infirmity of the flesh" (RV); here "flesh" is synonymous with "body" (as also in 2 Cor. 12:7).[3] The underlying Greek phrase is widely held to indicate the state *in which* Paul preached the gospel to the Galatians: he did so "in bodily weakness."[4] But the force of the original construction (*dia* with accusative) is doubtless causal: "it was because of an illness," Paul says, "that I first preached the gospel to you" (NIV).[5] The emphatic position of the phrase (well preserved in the English versions) suggests that Paul's original plan had been to go elsewhere (perhaps westward toward Ephesus) and that his missionary visit to the Galatians was due solely to his illness and his need for recuperation.[6] According to Acts 13:13f., Paul came to Pisidian Antioch from Perga in Pamphylia—a journey from the coast across the Taurus Mountains to high country some 3,600 feet above sea level.

As for the nature of his "bodily illness," scholars have diagnosed a variety of ailments, including malaria (which Paul is presumed to have contracted in the low-lying country of Pamphylia), epilepsy (suggested by the reference in v. 14 to spitting out [cf. marginal note in NASB]), ophthalmia (inferred from v. 15b and from the "big letters" with which he wrote, 6:11), and "severe neuralgia or hysteria accompanied by depres-

---

3. The very similar expression in Rom. 6:19 has a very different sense: cf. G. Stählin, *TDNT* I: 491 with n. 6.

4. Cf., e.g., Clarke, *NT Problems*, 137f.; A. Oepke, *TDNT* II: 69.

5. Cf. RSV; MHT 1: 106; BDF §223.3; E. Schweizer, *TDNT* VII: 125, n. 216.

6. Cf. Rendall 178, 137; Guthrie 119.

sion."[7] Paul's illness has further been linked with his "thorn" or "stake" in the flesh (2 Cor. 12:7f.).[8] None of these identifications, however, is certain, and we may well have to content ourselves with the bare fact that Paul was suffering from an "illness" (NIV) or "bodily ailment" (RSV) of some kind.

"Originally" represents a Greek phrase *(to proteron)* which might appear to have a bearing on the epistle's date of composition. In classical Greek the phrase would mean "on the former of two occasions" (cf. NEB mg., NASB marginal note);[9] so interpreted it would imply that when Paul wrote Galatians he had paid two visits to Galatia. These could be identified as the visits of Acts 16:6 and 18:23 respectively (on the North Galatian theory) or with the visits of Acts 13:14–14:20 and 16:6 respectively (on the South Galatian theory). On the latter theory they could also be identified as, respectively, the initial visit on the first missionary journey when Paul moved eastward from Pisidian Antioch to Derbe, and the subsequent visit on the same journey when he retraced his steps (Acts 14:21).[10] Even a strict interpretation of the phrase, therefore, does not require the conclusion that Galatians was written after the visit of Acts 16:6.

But in Hellenistic Greek *(to) proteron* lost its strict meaning (which came to be expressed by *[to] prōton*) and came to mean only "originally," "at the first." This is the sense which the phrase often bears in the NT (e.g., Jn. 6:62; 7:50; 9:8; 2 Cor. 1:15; Eph. 4:22; 1 Tim. 1:13; 1 Pet. 1:14) and probably has in the present verse as well.[11] Thus the phrase sheds no light at all on the date of the epistle: its significance "depends on the question of fact whether Paul had actually preached twice in Galatia before writing this letter; *to proteron* itself does not prove him to have done so."[12] Even if he had, there is still the question of *when* those visits took place.

14 In describing the Galatians' former attitude to him, Paul speaks first of (literally) "your trial/temptation in my flesh."[13] The Greek might mean simply that Paul's bodily condition was "a trial" (RSV, NASB, NIV) to the Galatians: apparently his illness had given his appearance a certain repulsiveness and the "temptation" (so NEB, RV) would have been for

---

7. So, e.g., Neill 69; W. Wrede and J. Klausner, as cited in Bruce 209; Wuest 125; and A. Oepke, *TDNT* III: 204, respectively.

8. So, e.g., W. Schneider and C. Brown, *NIDNTT* III: 802.

9. So, e.g., Lightfoot 175; Talbert, "Paul's Visits," 32.

10. Cf., e.g., Lake, *Earlier*, 266; Bruce 44 with n. 4, 209.

11. Cf. BDF §62; Turner, *Grammatical Insights*, 91; AV ("at the first"), RSV ("at first"), NIV ("first"), RV, NASB ("the first time").

12. Burton 241.

13. Gk. τὸν πειρασμὸν ὑμῶν ἐν τῇ σαρκί μου. The variant μου ("my") for ὑμῶν ("your") is a scribal attempt to alleviate the difficulty of the expression "your trial/ temptation"; it would yield the meaning "the trial/temptation which I caused" (cf. AV) or "the trial I was enduring" (NEB mg.). Cf. Metzger 596.

them "to show scorn or disgust" at the state of his body. But in view of what follows in the same verse it is preferable to understand the *peirasmon* of "temptation" in a fuller sense: as physical infirmity and illness were regarded by Jews and Gentiles alike as a symbol of divine displeasure or punishment (cf. Jn. 9:1f.; Acts 28:4), there would have been a natural temptation for the Galatians to despise Paul (cf. 2 Cor. 10:10) and reject his message.[14] Much to their credit, however, the temptation was successfully overcome.[15]

Far from treating Paul with contempt or disgust,[16] they welcomed him (says Paul) "as if I were an angel of God, as if I were Christ Jesus himself" (NIV). Because of the OT and Jewish view of angels as representatives of the heavenly world, to be likened to an angel is to be likened to what is divine.[17] And to be likened to Jesus Christ is an even greater honor—an honor not only appropriately bestowed on Paul here as the apostle of Christ, but promised in the Gospels to all who represent Christ (cf. the threefold enunciation of this principle in Mt. 10:40; Lk. 10:16; Jn. 13:20). The comparisons used thus show how highly Paul estimated the honor which the Galatians did him at this first missionary visit.

15 A marked contrast between the Galatians' former and present attitudes to Paul is introduced by the rhetorical question which in the original simply asks: "Where then is your *makarismos?*" This noun (its only other NT occurrences are in Rom. 4:6, 9) basically means "an act of declaring or counting as blessed or happy" (cf. the cognate verb *makarizō*, "bless"). Formerly, because they had Paul in their midst preaching the good news of salvation, the Galatians felt happy (cf. NEB, NIV) and satisfied (cf. RSV), they congratulated themselves (RV), they had "a sense of blessing"

14. Cf., e.g., Bring 212; Hendriksen 172.

15. H. Seesemann, *TDNT* VI: 32 mentions, but does not regard as necessary, the possibility that the meaning here is that "the Galatians did not fall victim to the tempter, who sought to exploit the apostle's sickness."

16. According to H. Schlier, *TDNT* II: 448, the Greek verb here (ἐξεπτύσατε) is to be taken "quite literally in the sense of the ancient gesture of spitting out as a defence against sickness and other demonic threats"; the Galatians' temptation was "to see in Paul someone demonically possessed because of his sickness"; cf. K. L. Schmidt, *TDNT* III: 820; H. Seesemann, *TDNT* VI: 32, n. 52. On the other hand, Burton 242 speaks of "the impossibility of such a sense here." The figurative sense is more likely (so Burton, Bruce 209, and AV, RV, RSV, NEB, NASB, NIV) because it represents a simpler thought and is more in keeping with the actual wording of v. 14a, which seems to imply the same object for both ἐξουθενήσατε ("you did . . . scorn," RSV) and ἐξεπτύσατε.

17. So G. Kittel, *TDNT* I: 83. There is no connection between Paul's simile here and the incident related in Acts 14:11-13, if only because the men of Lystra shortly afterwards (v. 19) turned against Paul and Barnabas (cf. Robertson, *Word Pictures*, 4: 304).

(NASB, cf. AV).[18] In that state of mind, Paul testifies, the Galatians would have plucked out their own eyes and given them to him, had that been possible.[19] It is unlikely that the language here implies eye trouble on Paul's part;[20] it may be no more than a graphic description of deep affection: to have one's own eyes torn out and given to another represents the yielding up of one's most precious possessions (cf. Dt. 32:10; Ps. 17:8; Zech. 2:8).[21]

16 All that, however, was now clean gone, and an exactly opposite state of mind had taken its place. The versions commonly render the verse as a (rhetorical) question;[22] but since the word with which the verse begins (*hōste*, RV "so then") is not used elsewhere in the NT to introduce a question, we may have here not a question but a statement.[23] Either way, Paul speaks of himself as having become the Galatians' "enemy." This probably does not mean that he had now become the object of their animosity and hate (*echthros* taken in its passive sense),[24] but rather that they now regarded Paul as someone with hostile intentions towards them (*echthros* in its active sense).[25]

Paul may have intended his words, taken as a statement, to be ironical. "By being frank with you" understands the Greek participle (*alētheuōn*, elsewhere in the NT only in Eph. 4:15) in its original meaning of "speaking the truth";[26] but more probably it refers to preaching the truth of the gospel.[27] "Here the irony has most point if 'truth' is understood to mean the actual facts of the gospel as they really are, in contrast to the deceptions of Paul's opponents":[28] he presented them with gospel truth, but they regarded him as being hostile to them! Since the verb "have . . . become" (RSV; NEB "made myself") is in the perfect tense, it is implied that the action of "telling you the truth" (RSV, NASB, NIV) took place before the writing of the present letter. The action cannot therefore be referred to the present letter; nor is it necessary to relate it to what was said in a previous letter.[29] It would seem most appropriate to understand the action as that of

---

18. If a choice had to be made, the last might be preferred as being closest to the basic meaning of the word (cf. Thayer s.v.; BAGD s.v.); but see also Betz 227.

19. On the omission of ἄν in the apodosis of this contrary-to-fact conditional sentence, cf. BDF §360.1; Zerwick §319; Burton, *Syntax*, §249.

20. For this view cf., e.g., Rendall 179; O'Neill 61.

21. Cf., e.g., Hunter 35; Cole 125; K. L. Schmidt, *TDNT* III: 820.

22. So AV, RV, RSV, NEB, NASB, NIV. Cf. BFBS, Nestle-Aland.

23. So Burton 245; Rendall 179.

24. Cf. Mikolaski 1100.

25. E.g., Lightfoot 176; Burton 244.

26. Cf. Betz 229, who takes it as the opposite of "flattering" (κολακεύω).

27. So R. Bultmann, *TDNT* I: 251; Bruce 211.

28. A. C. Thiselton, *NIDNTT* III: 887.

29. *Pace*, e.g., Duncan 140; Hendriksen 173; and Burton 245; Ridderbos 168, respectively.

Paul's initial preaching of the gospel to the Galatians, if we bear in mind that "the enmity need not be coincident with the telling."[30] The fact is that at his first visit Paul was warmly welcomed by the Galatians, but subsequently, thanks to the Galatian heretics, they became suspicious of his gospel and gave to it a critical re-evaluation. Paul marvels at what had happened: as a result of his presenting them with the truth of the gospel, he had earned their suspicion of himself as a dangerous imposter and an enemy to beware of![31]

3. FALSE ZEAL AND TRUE CONCERN (4:17-20)

17 *The persons I have referred to are envious of you, but not with an honest envy: what they really want is to bar the door to you so that you may come to envy them.* 18 *It is always a fine thing to deserve an honest envy—always, and not only when I am present with you,* 19 *dear children. For my children you are, and I am in travail with you over again until you take the shape of Christ. I wish I could be with you now; then I could modify my tone; as it is, I am at my wits' end about you.*

17 To help his Galatian converts break free from the baleful influence of the agitators, Paul exposes the latter in their true colors (cf. 6:12f.). These agitators, he acknowledges, are indeed "zealous to win you over" (NIV). But Paul notes that their intentions were dishonorable:[32] their real intent was (literally) to "exclude" (AV) or "shut you out" (RV, RSV, NASB). In view of the context, which is concerned with the interpersonal relationships, past and present, of Paul and the Galatians, the primary meaning of this "barring of the door" is probably "to alienate from the apostle and his associates";[33] but since the gospel which they preached had to do with Christ (cf. Rom. 1:3f.), the grace of God, and the believers' inheritance and privileges in Christ, alienation from Paul would mean at the same time exclusion from his gospel and the riches contained therein.

The ultimate aim of the agitators was for the Galatians to seek them (cf. NASB), not Paul, as their exclusive teachers, receiving their directions from them and obeying the law which they observed.[34] The same Greek verb

---

30. Guthrie 120 (though Guthrie favors the first view, that Paul is speaking here of his letter). We should understand "the enmity" here as referring to the Galatians' regarding Paul with suspicion (cf. on "enemy" in v. 16).

31. Cf. Bring 213.

32. Gk. οὐ καλῶς, NASB "not commendably"; cf. RSV, NIV. The adverb καλῶς is here used in a moral sense meaning "commendably, in a manner free from objection" (BAGD s.v. 2).

33. Cf., e.g., Thayer s.v. ἐκκλείω; Guthrie 121; Bruce 211; NEB, NIV.

34. Cf. Rendall 179; Burton 246.

both begins and ends the verse[35] (this is most clearly reflected in RSV), and the two instances show that the verb "may be used not only of the quest for adherents but also of the adherents' attachment to their leaders or teachers."[36] The NEB rendering of the two instances as "are envious of" and "come to envy" respectively gives the verb a sense which is more akin to its meaning in 2 Cor. 11:2 but is (to us) clearly less appropriate in the present context.

18 In accord with our understanding of v. 17, we take the first Greek infinitive in this verse not as middle (as in NIV, "to be zealous")[37] but as passive (as in NASB, "to be eagerly sought").[38] The Greek phrase behind "honest" is more fully "in a good thing" (AV; RV "in a good matter");[39] but since it clearly stands in contrast to the phrase "not commendably" in the previous verse, its meaning here is correspondingly "in a commendable manner" (both NASB), that is, with honorable intentions. Paul has already explicitly stated that the agitators' intentions were dishonorable; he now implies, by contrast, that his own intentions were honorable—for he sought nothing but that his converts be built up (edified, cf. 2 Cor. 10:8; 13:10; Rom. 15:2) in the truth of the gospel.[40] Since the dishonorable intentions spoken of in v. 17 are those of the Galatian agitators toward Paul's converts, the contrast between those and the honorable intentions mentioned in this verse suggests that these, too, have the same converts as their object of reference.

The point of v. 18 is then: "It is not good to be eagerly sought after (with honorable intentions) only when I am present with you." In other words, Paul would not mind having his converts eagerly sought after by others besides himself—as long as the motives were pure and the intentions honorable, as was the case with himself when he was with them, but was *not* the case with the agitators now.[41] His words might imply a gentle rebuke that the Galatians had allowed themselves to be thus courted by men of dishonorable intentions.

According to another interpretation v. 18a expresses the general principle that it is good for anyone—be it the Galatians, Paul, or even the

---

35. Gk. ζηλοῦσιν . . . ζηλοῦτε. The latter is probably subjunctive (so MHT 2: 75, 196; Zerwick §341; Robertson 203, 342) rather than indicative (so Robertson 325, 984; *Word Pictures*, 4: 305), although this question makes no difference to the sense.
36. Bruce 212. Cf. Thayer s.v. ζηλόω 2.a; BAGD s.v. 1.b.
37. Cf. BAGD s.v. ζηλόω 1.c.
38. Cf. AV, RV, RSV; Thayer s.v. ζηλόω 2.a; Moule 25f.; H.-C. Hahn, *NIDNTT* III: 1167. That is, the three occurrences of the verb in vv. 17f. have basically the same sense (cf. Lightfoot 176; Ellicott 89).
39. Cf. RSV, "for a good purpose"; Lightfoot 177; Burton 247.
40. Cf. A. Stumpff, *TDNT* II: 887.
41. Cf. Bring 215; Phillips.

agitators—to be eagerly sought after and made much of, while in v. 18b Paul applies this principle to himself: he would have the Galatians "always" treat him as they did when he was present with them. J. B. Lightfoot, who prefers this interpretation, acknowledges the difficulty that "it *supplies too much*"; but he thinks that "this abrupt and fragmentary mode of expression is characteristic of St Paul when he is deeply moved."[42] Furthermore, this interpretation suits the intention of the preceding context (especially vv. 12b, 14b-16) well enough: Paul wishes that the Galatians would return to their former cordial relations with him.

In favor of the interpretation we have adopted, however, is not only the contrast already noted in vv. 17 and 18, but also that in v. 19 Paul speaks of himself as being in travail again until Christ be formed in them. This is a demonstration of what it was for the Galatians to be "eagerly sought in a commendable manner" (NASB), and shows that Paul is still thinking primarily of *them* as the object of attention and care. Thus the immediate context, both preceding and following, suggests that the Galatians, not Paul, are in view in this verse. On this showing, the verse is not an echo and reinforcement of the request implied in vv. 12b, 14b-15, but a continuation of the theme of false zeal and true concern introduced in v. 17.

19 In this verse and the next, Paul is moved to speak with deep feeling by the disturbing thought of his converts being led astray by the false zeal of the agitators. The affectionate address "my children"[43] shows that Paul regards the Galatians as his children in the gospel in that he had brought them to faith in Christ (cf. 1 Cor. 4:15; 1 Tim. 1:2; 2 Tim. 1:2; Phm. 10). His love and care for them as their spiritual parent is laid bare in this verse, where he appears in the role of a mother (cf. the nursing mother of 1 Thess. 2:7). In bringing the gospel to them in the first place, he had endured "the pains of childbirth" (NIV), of which the most obvious examples were the persecutions which he (and his missionary colleagues) had to undergo (cf. Acts 13:45, 50; 14:2, 5f., 19). Faced now with the Galatians' defection from the true gospel to the counterfeit offered by the heretics, Paul experiences "over again" the pangs of labor—the sharp pains including those of perplexity (v. 20b), apprehension (v. 11), indignation (cf. 2 Cor. 11:29), and all the painful efforts required to reclaim the Galatians for the truth.[44]

42. Lightfoot 177 (his emphasis). Also in favor of this interpretation are Ridderbos 169f.; Cole 127; Hendriksen 174f.

43. So NASB (literally). The phrase is in apposition with "you" in v. 18 and hence strictly not a vocative (as it is in 1 Jn. 2:28; 3:7), although it is commonly so regarded in the English versions. The following masculine pronoun (οὕς, RSV "whom") is a case of *constructio ad sensum* (BDF §296).

44. Cf. Lightfoot 178; Ridderbos 170; G. Bertram, *TDNT* IX: 673. Ὠδίνειν

"Until you take the shape of Christ" states the time when Paul's labor pangs will cease and the purpose for which he is enduring them. In the original, the thought is more strikingly expressed as "until Christ is formed in you" (NASB, NIV). The verb used *(morphousthai)* refers to the process whereby the fetus develops into an infant; Paul's desire is to see Christ thus "formed" in his converts. If the imagery suggested by the language is unusual,[45] its intended meaning is not in doubt: to say that the image of Christ should take shape in the believers is but a more effective way of saying that "Christ should fashion them according to His own image,"[46] that in submission to him they may reflect his image and glory in their lives. It is worth noting that the noun implied by the verb denotes "essential form *[morphē]* rather than outward shape *[schēma]*"; it is here synonymous with "image" *(eikōn)*, which is the word used in Col. 3:10, a verse concerned with the same process.[47]

20 Paul confesses to being so "perplexed" (RV, RSV, NASB, NIV) about the Galatians that he does not know what to do with them. He can only express a wish[48] to be present with them at that very moment ("now")[49] and to "change [his] voice" (RV). This has been taken to mean that Paul wishes he were in possession of a heavenly language which would authenticate both his commission and his message, or that he could be right there to converse with them in person.[50] But more probably his desire is to be able to "change" (RSV, NASB, NIV) or "modify" (NEB) his "tone."[51] Apparently he believes that if only he could be present with them he would

---

("be in travail"), used figuratively here, occurs only two more times in the NT, both in a literal sense (v. 27; Rev. 12:2; cf. R. K. Harrison, *NIDNTT* III: 858).

45. As Hunter 35 observes, fetal development is to take place in them, but it is Paul who undergoes labor! On the verb cf. J. Behm, *TDNT* IV: 753f.; G. Braumann, *NIDNTT* I. 708.

46. W. Grundmann, *TDNT* IX: 545. On the other hand, Hays, "Christology," 283 translates ἐν ὑμῖν as "among you," "in your midst" and regards the text "as an expression of Paul's passionate desire that the Galatian *community* be found in the image of Christ": Paul is urging the Galatians "to participate in a paradoxical self-giving which mirrors the action of Christ who gave himself up (1:4; 2:20) and came under the law (4:6) for us."

47. Guthrie 122 (quoted); Ridderbos, *Paul*, 225, n. 41.

48. The tense of ἤθελον (literally "I was wishing") has been variously explained: as possibly an "epistolary" imperfect (Moule 9); as probably due to "the impossibility of realizing the wish" (Burton, *Syntax*, §33; cf. Betz 236, "imperfect *de conatu*"); as purely expressing a wish (G. Schrenk, *TDNT* III: 45, n. 8). Cf. p. 241, n. 129 below.

49. For this sense of Gk. ἄρτι see Thayer s.v. 2; cf. MM s.v.; Wuest 131.

50. Cf., e.g., H. Schlier, as cited in Bring 217; and Betz 236, respectively.

51. Cf., e.g., Burton 250; F. Büchsel, *TDNT* I: 251; O. Betz, *TDNT* IX: 293; M. J. Harris, *NIDNTT* III: 113.

be able to regain their trust and allegiance, so that it would no longer be necessary to use such severe language as he has found it necessary to use in reminding them of the truth and warning them against falsehood.[52] As it is, however, he is prevented from paying them a personal visit at the moment, and his heartfelt desire was perforce unfulfilled.

G. THE ANALOGY OF HAGAR AND SARAH (4:21–5:1)

The personal appeal ended, Paul makes a fresh attempt[1] to convince his readers of the correctness of his position over against that of his opponents by turning once more to the Scriptures. He refers to certain facts in the story of Hagar and Sarah (4:21-23), expounds their spiritual meaning (vv. 24-27), applies their significance to the Galatians (vv. 28-30), and concludes with a summary and appeal (4:31–5:1).

1. THE FACTS (4:21-23)

21 *Tell me now, you who are so anxious to be under law, will you not listen to what the Law says?* 22 *It is written there that Abraham had two sons, one by his slave and the other by his free-born wife.* 23 *The slave-woman's son was born in the course of nature, the free woman's through God's promise.*

21 Although Paul addresses his readers directly as "you who are so anxious to be under law," he is possibly thinking also of his detractors, for whom the argument of this section (G) would be even more telling as a counterargument to their theological point of view.[2] Here "law," as often in Paul, is anarthrous, whereas it is articular in the following clause ("the Law"). It would appear that the readers are addressed as those who wanted or desired[3] to be under law (in context, specifically the law of Moses) as a

---

52. Cf. Hendriksen 176; Guthrie 122.
1. Some think that Paul may have written this passage as an afterthought (e.g., Burton 251; Schlier 216). But this seems unlikely in view of C. K. Barrett's reconstruction of the probable background (see Additional Comment 7 below). According to Betz 240, "the allegory allows Paul to return to the *interrogatio* method used in 3:1-5 . . . by another route."
2. Cf. Cole 128f. More on this in Additional Comment 7 below.
3. Here θέλοντες ("desire," RSV) "refers to a basic resolve of the misdirected will" (G. Schrenk, *TDNT* III: 49).

religious principle, while Paul's challenge to them is to become "aware of" (NIV), and give heed to, what the Pentateuch[4] has to say by way of instruction.[5] This instruction he now draws out for his readers from a portion of the Genesis story.

22-23 First, Paul recalls three basic historical facts recorded in the law. (a) "Abraham had two sons"—Ishmael and his younger brother by fourteen years, Isaac. This common rendering takes the aorist tense of the verb as constative ("possessed") rather than ingressive (= inceptive, "acquired"),[6] but no great issue is at stake which way the aorist is interpreted. (b) The two mothers differed in status: one was a slave-woman,[7] the other was free. (c) The two sons differed in the manner of their birth: the slave-woman's son was born "in the course of nature" (literally "born according to the flesh," RSV, NASB), that is, "in the ordinary way" (NIV), by the process of natural procreation; the free woman's son was born "through promise" (RSV) or "through the promise" (NASB),[8] that is, the promise of God to Abraham recorded in Gen. 17:19; 18:10. The contrast indicated by the two prepositional phrases does not involve mutual exclusion, a "not . . . but," as if Isaac had no natural birth, particularly since v. 22 and Rom. 4:18-21 clearly imply that Abraham was his father.[9] Rather, the contrast involves a "not only . . . but also": whereas the birth of Ishmael was *simply* "according to the flesh," the birth of Isaac was *also* "through God's promise" and gained its significance from that fact.[10] This contrast and the contrast involving the status of the two women are interdependent, but it is

4. For the double sense of νόμος in this verse see W. Gutbrod, *TDNT* IV: 1071. On the distinction between anarthrous and articular νόμος in general see pp. 113f., n. 11 above.

5. This is the original meaning of *tôrâ:* cf. H.-H. Esser, *NIDNTT* II: 440; Schlier 178.

6. The latter is preferred by Ridderbos 174, n. 2; Bruce 214; cf. MHT 1: 145.

7. Gk. παιδίσκη; the word is used in the biblical literature always of the servant class (BAGD s.v.; Thayer s.v.).

8. In this phrase the preposition (διά with the genitive) "is undoubtedly to be construed instrumentally" (E. Schweizer, *TDNT* VI: 429; cf. M. J. Harris, *NIDNTT* III: 1200). On the textual question here Burton 253 thinks that "the probability that Paul would have opposed to κατὰ σάρκα a qualitative δι' ἐπαγγελίας rather than used the article in referring to a promise not previously mentioned seems to turn the scale in favor of δι' ἐπ." (cf. Rendall 181). On the other hand it is easier to account for an original longer reading giving rise to the shorter version (through accidental omission or deliberate correction) rather than vice versa.

9. Rightly, Ridderbos 175; Bruce 217.

10. Gen. 16:10 makes Ishmael also in some sense "a child of promise"; but that promise was made after his conception (cf. Lightfoot 180). Hanson, *Studies,* 91 considers this an "inconsistency," as "one of the weaknesses in his argument in Gal. 4:21f which induced Paul to leave it out of Romans."

the former which Paul regards as determinative. In the scriptural record of the birth of these two sons of Abraham[11] Paul recognizes the same opposition between reliance on self ("according to the flesh") and reliance on God ("through promise.") as exists between those who would be justifed by legal works and those who are justified by faith.

2. THEIR SPIRITUAL MEANING (4:24-27)

24 *This is an allegory. The two women stand for two covenants. The one bearing children into slavery is the covenant that comes from Mount Sinai: that is Hagar.* 25 *Sinai is a mountain in Arabia and it represents the Jerusalem of today, for she and her children are in slavery.* 26 *But the heavenly Jerusalem is the free woman; she is our mother.* 27 *For Scripture says, "Rejoice, O barren woman who never bore child; break into a shout of joy, you who never knew a mother's pangs; for the deserted wife shall have more children than she who lives with the husband."*

24 Paul calls the facts he has just enumerated "allegorical utterances"[12] and proceeds to bring out their spiritual meaning. He is not expounding the meaning of the OT passage as intended by the original writer; he is speaking of the meaning conveyed to him by the passage as it stands.[13] This so-called "allegorical" interpretation of the OT text, which he uses to buttress his argument against the Galatian heretics, is accomplished by a series of "conceptual identifications."[14] The two women stand for (literally "are," RSV, NASB) two covenants. On the one hand, Hagar stands for the covenant derived from Mount Sinai and producing children for bondage: just as the children of a slave-wife (unless acknowledged as true children by the

11. This seems to be the force of the perfect γεγέννηται ("has been born") as distinct from the aorist ἐγεννήθη ("he was born"). Cf. Rendall 181; BDF §342.5; p. 158 with n. 33 above.

12. This is the meaning which Burton 255 gives, after a full discussion, to ἀλληγορούμενα (a NT *hapax*), taking it as "a general present participle equivalent to a noun." The rendering "This is an allegory" (also RSV, cf. AV) or "This contains an allegory" (NASB, cf. RV) is, however, open to criticism: "Just as τύπος in Paul does not necessarily mean 'type,' so we are not justified in assuming that ἀλληγορούμενα means 'are an allegory.' It is a plural after all, which one would not guess from the RSV" (Hanson, *Studies*, 91). Preferable is NIV, "These things may be taken figuratively."

13. Cf. Burton 256.

14. Betz 243. O'Neill 62f. would omit vv. 24b-27. But this leaves v. 24a without the explanation which it leads one to expect, and the expectation can hardly be regarded as satisfied by v. 28. Cf. the criticisms of Barrett, "Allegory," 2.

husband and master) were destined to be slaves themselves, so the covenant of law given at Sinai committed all who embraced it to its binding power.[15]

Over against Hagar and the covenant of law which she represents (see on v. 25) stands the free woman (v. 22b), with the other covenant represented by her. The unnamed free woman is obviously Sarah while the other covenant, similarly unnamed, is obviously the covenant of faith referred to in 3:17 in contrast with the law (though the latter is not there specifically called a covenant). Paul takes it as self-evident that a straight line runs through Sarah and Isaac, the covenant of faith (because it depends on promise), the Jerusalem above (v. 26), and Christians—these being held together and interrelated by the fact that freedom can be postulated of all of them, although it is explicitly postulated of the third member only.

25 The first part of this verse presents us with a well-known *crux interpretum*. (a) The NEB rendering, "Sinai is a mountain in Arabia," presupposes the shorter text which omits *Hagar,* thus making v. 25a a simple geographical notation.[16] The thought is then that the location of Mount Sinai outside Palestine (where the central events of salvation history took place) and in a land inhabited by a subjugated people, themselves descended from Hagar, shows the connection between Sinai and Hagar. But this view faces the objection that it involves "Paul's assuming a knowledge on the part of the Galatians hardly likely to be possessed by them."[17] In all probability, therefore, "Hagar" is to be retained (with AV, RV, RSV, NASB, NIV).[18]

---

15. To the Jews "the law from Sinai was given to the descendants of Abraham through Isaac and had nothing to do with Hagar's descendants"; hence, Paul mentions Hagar specifically "to make unmistakable which of the two women represents the Sinaitic covenant" (Guthrie 124). Liao, "Meaning," 122 claims that "Paul here obviously creates a new personal understanding of διαθῆκαι as an existential term," by which "we simply mean the practical condition, or the quality, of man's life" (128, n. 23). This is necessitated by Liao's rejection of the traditional interpretation of δύο διαθῆκαι as referring to the Abrahamic and Mosaic covenants (118-121); but Paul's statement in v. 24b is too unambiguous (one of the two covenants is that derived from Mount Sinai) and its implication too plain (the other is the covenant with Abraham, cf. 3:15-17) to admit of a different interpretation.

16. Cf. Lightfoot 180f., 192f.; Rendall 181.

17. Burton 261. Cf. the criticism of Barrett, "Allegory," 11f. Metzger makes no reference to this reading.

18. Burton 259, while defending the retention of Ἁγάρ on textual grounds (he wrote prior to the discovery of P[46]), nevertheless thinks it probable that v. 25 is a scribal gloss. Cosgrove, "The Law," 228 maintains that even "when the shorter reading is followed, Hagar is still best understood as the (implied) subject of ἐστίν ["is"]." He further argues (229) that vv. 25a and 25b "must be taken as two independent justifications of the thesis of v 24"; but this presupposes the reading γάρ and results in v. 25a being taken as "perhaps an obscure proof" (see n. 23 below with the comment on it).

(b) The phrase "in Arabia" has been understood not as a topographical statement, but as a designation of the people by whom Sinai was called "Hagar"; the meaning is that the word "Hagar" represents Mount Sinai "among the Arabians."[19] But (i) Paul writes *estin* ("is") and not *kaleitai* ("is called"), and (ii) "of such a geographical expression used in this sense in such a sentence as this no example is cited."[20]

(c) Another interpretation would make Paul's statement mean "the word 'Hagar' designates in Arabic Mount Sinai."[21] But it has been objected (i) that the evidence for a linguistic connection between "Hagar" and "Sinai" here assumed is "both deficient in amount and suspicious in character," (ii) that the Arabic word *ḥagar* and the proper name Hagar are etymologically entirely distinct, and (iii) that *en tę̄ Arabią* ("in Arabia") is not at all likely to have been used by any writer for *en tę̄ Arabikę̄ glōssę̄* ("in the Arabian tongue") or for *Arabisti* ("in Arabic"), unless this was in some way indicated in the context.[22]

(d) The apparent untenability of all the above views leaves us with only two alternatives: *either*, if v. 25a is regarded as providing the reason for v. 24b,[23] we must confess ignorance of the reason why Paul links Hagar and Sinai together,[24] *or*, allowing for a less definite link between the two verses,[25] we may regard v. 25a as simply "another back-reference to Hagar the slave-wife, as though Paul were anxious to keep us reminded of the 'corresponding terms' of the analogy."[26] The latter is to us much the preferable course and v. 25a is best rendered "Now Hagar stands for Mount Sinai in Arabia" (NIV).

Representing Mount Sinai in Arabia, then, Hagar corresponds to the earthly Jerusalem of Paul's day,[27] which was in spiritual bondage[28] together

19. Ellicott 94.
20. Burton 261.
21. Schlier 220.
22. Lightfoot 195-198.
23. Note the "for" of AV, which presupposes the reading γάρ.
24. Cf. Schlier 220; Schweitzer, *Mysticism*, 211.
25. The "now" of RV, RSV, NASB, NIV seems to presuppose δέ.
26. Cole 133; E. Lohse, *TDNT* VII: 285f.; cf. P. J. Budd, *NIDNTT* I: 81; Bruce 219.
27. "Represents" is NEB's rendering of συστοιχεῖ. The cognate noun συστοιχία denotes a file of soldiers, as συζυγία denotes a rank; συστοιχεί means, then, "belongs to the same row or column with" (Lightfoot 181). Here, however, it seems to lack this concrete and strict sense, meaning simply "corresponds to" (so NIV; cf. AV, RV; Schlier 221; Burton 262; Betz 245). At the same time, the idea of "belonging to the same series" should probably be retained (cf. G. Delling, *TDNT* VII: 669 with n. 5; H.-H. Esser, *NIDNTT* II: 452; Guthrie 125).
   Gaston, "Enemies," 410 would translate v. 25b-c as follows: "It (Sinai) is in the opposite column from the present Jerusalem, for she (Hagar) serves (as a slave) with her children." This rendering puts "the present Jerusalem" in the Sarah column and makes it

with her children just as Hagar was in physical bondage with her child Ishmael. Thus the fact of bondage (albeit in two different senses) holds together Hagar and Ishmael, the Sinaitic covenant of law, the present earthly Jerusalem (which stands by metonymy for Judaism, with its trust in physical descent from Abraham and reliance on legal observance as the way of salvation),[29] and her children, that is, all who adhere to the law as the means of justification and the principle of life.

---

possible for v. 25 to support Gaston's exegesis of vv. 21-31. Gaston understands the passage "not as a digression directed against Jews but as part of Paul's proclamation of his gospel" (cf. 3:14), which "is greatly enriched by the statement that the Gentiles also inherit from Sarah and thus like her are free."

Against this thesis we would offer three observations: (a) Gaston's claim that the subject of συστοιχεῖ ("represents") "must be Sinai" (408) is highly problematic. Since in vv. 24b-25 Paul is dealing with the Hagar column, it is far more natural to take the subject of συστοιχεῖ to be Hagar (as of δουλεύει, "is in slavery," RSV) than to posit a change of subject from Sinai (v. 25b) to Hagar (v. 25c).

(b) In adopting the view that "συστοιχεῖν = to correspond to the opposite member of the pair in the other column" (404) Gaston must admit that "it is not certain whether the solution is philologically possible" (410). His definition of συστοιχεῖν goes hand in hand with his assumption that the subject of συστοιχεῖ is Sinai; they stand or fall together.

(c) Underlying and apparently determining these grammatical and philological decisions is Gaston's belief that "the present Jerusalem really cannot be detached" from the heavenly Jerusalem (410). Gaston considers it "best methodologically to try to understand Paul in continuity with the traditions of Judaism unless there are explicit grounds to the contrary" (404); this results, in the present instance, in his understanding the present Jerusalem and the heavenly Jerusalem as not opposed but related. But on the basis of what Gaston himself says, it is clear that Paul departed from Jewish tradition on this issue: for if "the entire Jewish tradition which speaks of a heavenly Jerusalem does so in the sense of a promise to the present Jerusalem" (408), the heavenly Jerusalem remains temporally distinct from the present Jerusalem; but if "Paul stands in this line but adds that Gentiles now, before the eschaton, are citizens of this heavenly Jerusalem" (421, n. 43), then to him the heavenly Jerusalem is already present—not in "the Jerusalem of today," but in the Church of believing Gentiles (and believing Jews). Hence, in Paul's analogy the present Jerusalem, whose position "in the Hagar column" is said to cause the exegetical problems (408), belongs firmly there and not to the Sarah column.

A more satisfying exegesis of v. 25 than Gaston's is given by Martyn, "Antinomies," 418-420. He thinks that Paul uses συστοιχέω here as a technical term, "thus telling the Galatians that he himself intends to speak of a *Table* of paired Opposites" (418): in saying that Hagar "is also *located in the same oppositional column* with the present Jerusalem," Paul is "correcting a similar table of opposites propounded explicitly or implicitly by the Teachers" (419).

28. Hanson, *Studies,* 96 rightly points out that the reference cannot be to the political subjection of Judea to the Romans: "most of Paul's readers were in precisely the same condition, the very people whom he describes immediately after as being free."

29. Sanders has summarized the essence of Rabbinic Judaism as "covenantal nomism"—"the view that one's place in God's plan is established on the basis of the covenant and that the covenant requires as the proper response of man his obedience to its commandments, while providing means of atonement for transgression" (*Paul and Pal-*

26 In opposing to "the Jerusalem of today" (v. 25) "the Jerusalem above" (RSV, NASB) and not, as might have been expected, "the Jerusalem to come," it might seem that Paul has confused two distinct though related forms of the concept of a new Jerusalem familiar from the OT: that which views it as coming in the eschatological future, over against the present Jerusalem (cf. Zech. 8:1-8), and that which sees it as already existing in heaven, over against the earthly Jerusalem (e.g., Isa. 62; cf. Heb. 12:22; Rev. 3:12; 21:2, 9ff.).[30] What he has actually done, however, is to mingle the two forms, the temporal and the spatial,[31] in such a way as to indicate that the Jerusalem that is to come has already arrived (note the twice-repeated "is") in the form of a heavenly, spiritual Jerusalem. He can do this the more easily because Heb. ʿôlām has both a spatial sense ("world") and a temporal sense ("age") and "the apocalyptic contrast of This Age and the Age to Come implies also the contrast of this world and the 'other' world."[32] This Jerusalem, says Paul, is "our mother"—that is, the mother of those who are Christians.[33]

27 In proof of the existence of a new Jerusalem composed of God's redeemed people, Paul quotes the Septuagint of Isa. 54:1, where a greater

---

estinian Judaism, 75; cf. 236). In this view, *"salvation is by grace but judgment is according to works; works are the condition of remaining 'in', but they do not earn salvation"*; on this decisive point of grace and works, Sanders holds, "Paul is in agreement with Palestinian Judaism" (543, emphasis original). It would appear, however, that Sanders has not sufficiently considered "the *drift* of rabbinic thought" in intertestamental Judaism, in which, "with the partial exception of the Dead Sea Scrolls, legalism is on the rise, and with it merit theology" (Carson, *Divine Sovereignty*, 94 and 120 respectively; cf. 68f., 91, 106; Gundry, "Grace," particularly 5f.). Our description of Judaism in the comments above may therefore be upheld: cf. Ridderbos 163, who even speaks of "Judaism with its *auto-soteriological* legalistic scheme of salvation" (emphasis added).

30. According to H. Schultz, "in Jewish apocalyptic tradition heavenly Jerusalem was the pre-existent place where God's glory was always present" (*NIDNTT* II: 329). To H. Strathmann, "the natural way in which the expected consummation of salvation is incidentally expressed" in this concept obviously shows that the thought "must have been a very familiar one for the apostle" (*TDNT* VI: 531).

31. Thus providing a clear example of "the New Testament's merging of the temporal sequence and the spatial gradation" (Käsemann, *Perspectives*, 98). Cf. Cosgrove, "The Law," 231: "At this point cosmic and eschatological dualism intersect, so that the present manifestation of the future, embodied in the community itself, is understood as owing its life to the world above."

32. Barrett, "NT Eschatology" 149, cf. 141.

33. The word πάντων ("all"), found in certain MSS before ἡμῶν("of us"; cf. AV, "of us all"), is to be rejected as an insertion which "gives the text a broader, pastoral application, but obscures Paul's distinction between the 'chosen ones' and the 'sons of Hagar'" (G. Zuntz, *The Text of the Epistles* [London, 1953], quoted in Metzger 596). Kidner, *Psalms,* 314-316 suggests that behind Paul's phrase stands the vision of Ps. 87 (with Isa. 54), and that Paul evidently had the LXX (Ps. 86) in mind since it is the LXX which has the additional word "mother" in v. 5.

prosperity is prophesied for restored Jerusalem as compared with the old.[34] The "barren woman," the one who was "never in labor" and the "desolate woman" (NIV)[35] in the prophecy all refer to Jerusalem before the Jews returned from the Exile; whereas the one "who has a husband" (NIV)[36] refers to Jerusalem before the Exile. The prophet says that Jerusalem as she would be after the exiles had returned would have more children than she did before the Exile robbed her of her children.

Paul finds in this prophecy a double illustration.[37] (a) Sarah, the wife who formerly "was barren" and "had no child" (Gen. 11:30), did "break into a shout of joy" when she gave birth to Isaac (cf. Gen. 21:6f.), and her children through Isaac were more numerous than those of Hagar, who "had a husband" and bore him a son, Ishmael (cf. Gen. 16). (b) It follows that the Christian Church, which corresponds to Sarah and the Jerusalem above (v. 26), was more fruitful than Judaism, which corresponds to Hagar and "the Jerusalem of today" (v. 25): whereas Judaism, in which the law held sway, limited God's people to the Jews, the Church, through the preaching of the law-free gospel, embraced Gentiles and Jews alike within the one chosen people of God. Thus in the gathering of all believers in Christ into the Church Paul sees the fulfillment of the Isaianic prophecy. His use of the prophecy in his argument is especially appropriate in that, since it can be seen as an illustration of the triumph of Sarah (and Isaac) over Hagar (and Ishmael)—besides being an illustration of the triumph of the Church over Judaism—it fits in well with Paul's treatment of the Sarah-Hagar analogy, which is tied in "with the unquestioned fact that Isaac's birth fulfilled the divine promise, belief in which had procured Abraham's justification."[38]

3. ITS APPLICATION TO THE GALATIANS (4:28-30)

> 28 *And you, my brothers, like Isaac, are children of God's promise.* 29 *But just as in those days the natural-born son persecuted the spiritual son, so it is today.* 30 *But what does Scripture say? "Drive*

34. Cosgrove, "The Law," 230 maintains that "the citation from Is. 54:1 supports not the final clause in v 26 ("which is our mother") but the main assertion: 'the Jerusalem above is free.'" But since "the quotation from Isaiah speaks of Jerusalem as a barren *woman who gives birth to many children*" (n. 41, emphasis added) but says nothing about a "free woman," it is most natural to link this with "our mother" in v. 26b.

35. Gk. ἡ ἔρημος = "the abandoned wife" (G. Kittel, *TDNT* II: 657); cf. NEB.

36. In this expression ἔχειν ("to have") is used "as a technical term for sexual intercourse" (H. Hanse, *TDNT* II: 817, n. 5).

37. Cf. Burton 264; Guthrie 125.

38. Cf. Bruce 222f. (quotation from 223). For a different, and in our view less natural, interpretation of Paul's use of the Isaianic text here see Cosgrove, "The Law," 231.

out the slave-woman and her son, for the son of the slave shall not share the inheritance with the free woman's son."

28 "And" (so also NASB) rightly understands the Greek particle *de* as continuative and explanatory (cf. AV, RV, RSV, NIV: "now") and not adversative. Since the Jerusalem above has been described as the mother of Christians (v. 26) and Isaac belongs in this series of entities, Paul can explain the significance of this description for the Galatians by pointing out that they[39] are children of promise on the pattern of Isaac (literally "according to Isaac"). Just as Isaac, son of the free woman, was born through God's promise (v. 23b), so the Galatians owe their spiritual existence as children to the promise of God. Whether they are thought of here as children of God or children of Abraham is not specified, although the context as a whole, which is concerned with the two branches of the Abrahamic family, would seem to imply the latter;[40] the emphasis is laid on the promise as characterizing the manner of their birth.[41]

If, as seems reasonable, we may interpret this promise in the light of earlier references to "promise" in the epistle,[42] then it would appear that in designating the Galatian Christians as "children of promise" Paul has in mind primarily that promise to Abraham which was in effect a promise that the Gentiles would be justified by faith (3:8). This promise found fulfillment in the context of salvation history in the coming of Christ and the opening of the door of faith to the Gentiles (3:22-25) and experientially in the Galatians when they responded with faith to Paul's preaching of Christ crucified (3:1ff.). Thus underlying, and corresponding to, the contrast between slavery (characterizing Hagar and Ishmael, the Sinaitic covenant of law, and the earthly Jerusalem of Judaism and the Judaizers) and freedom (characterizing Sarah and Isaac, the new covenant of promise, the heavenly Jerusalem, and the Christian believers) is the contrast between righteousness by law and righteousness by faith.[43]

---

39. The variant reading "we . . . are" (AV, RV, RSV) is probably a transcriber's correction influenced by v. 26 and/or v. 31: so, e.g., Burton 265; Metzger 597.

40. Cf. Burton 265. In any case, we have seen that sonship to Abraham and sonship to God are, from the spiritual standpoint, materially the same (cf. p. 178, n. 48 above).

41. The word ἐπαγγελίας ("of promise") is emphatic by reason of its position before τέκνα ("children"); its qualitative aspect is stressed through the absence of the article; and the thought is strengthened by the preceding phrase κατὰ Ἰσαάκ ("like Isaac"). This emphasis is apparent also in Rom. 9:8, which bears substantially the same sense as our verse (cf. Ridderbos, *Paul,* 343).

42. So, emphatically, Burton 265; Guthrie 126.

43. Cf. Bring 227. The contrasts which have been made up to this point may be tabulated as follows:

29 In vv. 29 and 30 Paul brings out two further points from the Genesis story. As at that time the natural-born son (literally "he who was born according to the flesh") persecuted the one "who was born according to the Spirit" (RSV, NASB), so it was in Paul's day. Ishmael's persecution of Isaac is not mentioned elsewhere in Scripture—the nearest approximation to it being his "mocking" of Isaac in Gen. 21:9 (so AV, RV, NASB, NIV). Paul's reference to this persecution may reflect a Jewish haggadah of this verse in Genesis which depicts Ishmael as bearing down, as if in fun, on Isaac with bow and arrow.[44] Alternatively, particularly in view of the post-Christian date of the tradition reflected in this haggadah, we may take the reference in the sense of Ishmael's threatening Isaac's freedom and security.[45]

As for the persecution of Christians implied in "so it is today," there is no need to confine it exclusively to the persecution by normative Judaism, such as Paul himself had taken part in (1:13, 23) and which he refers to elsewhere in the epistle (5:11; 6:12), or to the action of the Judaizers alone.[46] According to the South Galatian theory, the persecutions which the Galatians had suffered were instigated by Jews who rejected the gospel, but also involved Gentiles as the agents of persecution (cf. Acts 13:50; 14:2, 5, 19). As far as Paul himself was concerned, his persecutors were both Jews and Judaizers, and he may well have in view here persecution from both quarters, though perhaps with the Judaizers uppermost in his mind as those who were then actually troubling the Galatians.[47]

In v. 23 Isaac was described as begotten through promise, but here he is described as begotten by the Spirit. According to one view this change from "promise" to "Spirit" is "a species of trajection from the clause which

Slavery:	Freedom:
Hagar—a slave woman	Sarah—a free woman
Ishmael—born according to the flesh	Isaac—born through God's promise
the Sinaitic covenant of law	the covenant of promise (based on faith)
the present Jerusalem (= Judaism)	the Jerusalem above (= the Church)
the children of the present Jerusalem (= legalists)	the children of the Jerusalem above (= Christians)
Righteousness by Law	**Righteousness by Faith**

44. Cf., e.g., Bruce, "Abraham," 77f.; Hanson, *Studies,* 98f.; Betz 249f.
45. Cf. Ridderbos 181 with n. 12; Hendriksen 186f.
46. So Schlier 227 and Ridderbos 181, respectively.
47. Cf. Ellicott 98; Burton 266. Schlier 226f. maintains that the Galatian agitators are not in view here, because their activities are described differently in 1:7; 2:4 and 3:1. But those more specific descriptions come within the scope of the meaning of the word "persecute," which is used here in a more general sense (cf. Thayer s.v. διώκω 3: "in any way whatever to harass, trouble, molest one").

expresses the second element of the comparison,"[48] Paul's complete thought in that case being that just as earlier the one born according to the flesh persecuted the one born according to the promise, so also now the one born according to the flesh persecutes the one born according to the Spirit. In this view, "according to the Spirit" describes not Isaac, but only Christian believers.

It is, however, more satisfactory to think of "according to the Spirit" (RSV) strictly with reference to Isaac, in which case the change must mean that it was the Spirit who made the promise effectual.[49] In the case of the Christian believers of "today" it is even clearer that "Spirit," as parallel to "promise," is "the objective power of the divine promise of grace which creates [the new] life."[50] And if we are right in understanding the promise in the phrase "children of promise" (v. 28) as a reference to the promise of justification by faith, then we have an interesting and significant parallel between 3:8, 14, where the promise of justification by faith is said to find fulfillment in the reception of the Spirit, and 4:28, where the promise is seen to involve the ultimate bestowal of the Spirit.

30 The second of the two final points which Paul brings out from the story in Genesis is that Scripture commands that the slave-woman is to be cast out with her son. The quotation is from Gen. 21:10, originally the words of Sarah to Abraham, but confirmed (in v. 12) by God himself.[51] The verse seems intended to provide a consolatory thought after that of persecution in the previous verse, and one plain implication is, "The religion of promise and the religion of works cannot co-exist. God will not divide His blessing between them."[52]

---

48. Burton 266.

49. Cf. Ridderbos 182. According to Hanson the phrase τὸν κατὰ πνεῦμα [γεννηθέντα] ("the one born according to the Spirit") means "one born according to a promise uttered through the Holy Spirit." Citing 3:14 in comparison he remarks: "Here Spirit and promise are connected: a promise must be the work of the Spirit, for it implies faith" (*Studies*, 98). But τοῦ πνεύματος in 3:14 is probably a genitive of definition (yielding "the promised Spirit"); cf. p. 152, n. 75 above.

50. E. Schweizer, *TDNT* VI: 429. Cf. Ridderbos, *Paul*, 217 with n. 23.

51. V. 30 taken in conjunction with v. 27 illustrates the statement that "In proof from Scripture Paul likes to associate a verse from the Torah and a passage from the prophets" (W. Gutbrod, *TDNT* IV: 1071).

52. Pinnock 48. Cf. Bruce, "Abraham," 79: in Paul's application Sarah's demand "becomes the statement of a basic gospel truth: legal bondage and gospel freedom cannot co-exist." On the other hand, Cosgrove, "The Law," 233-235 thinks the quotation from Gen. 21:10 is applied "in warning to the Galatians" (234) and "in preparation for what is to come," namely, "the concrete exhortations to follow (see 5:1; 5:13)" (235). But 5:1 is an exhortation to stand fast in freedom, not a warning against the abuse of freedom, and while the latter note *is* sounded in v. 13, the intervening verses (2-12) are, we might say, an elaboration on the exhortation not "to be tied to the yoke of slavery

The contrast Paul sets forth by means of the Hagar-Sarah analogy has been helpfully summed up in the following basic terms: "Hagar the slave bears a son who persecutes the son of Sarah, the free woman. She and her son are cast out by divine command. The unbelieving Jews, enslaved to the Torah, persecute believing Christians, who are free in Christ. The unbelieving Jews are rejected by God."[53]

4. SUMMARY AND APPEAL (4:31–5:1)

31 *You see, then, my brothers, we are no slave-woman's children; our mother is the free woman.* 1 *Christ set us free, to be free men. Stand firm, then, and refuse to be tied to the yoke of slavery again.*

31 In Paul's treatment of the Hagar-Sarah story, the main point remains the contrast between the two branches of the Abrahamic family, and it is to this that Paul returns in his final summation of the argument. The NEB rendering brings out well the distinction (also preserved in RV, NASB) between the anarthrous *paidiskēs* ("slave-woman") and *tēs eleutheras* ("the free woman"); the article is used with the latter probably because in Paul's interpretation Sarah has been identified (by implication, not by name) as the one standing for the Jerusalem above, the Christian community of which believers are members (v. 26).

The phrase "You see, then" shows that the conclusion stated here is logically derived from what has gone before—more specifically from the fact of persecution mentioned in v. 29: It was Jews and Judaizers who were persecuting Christians (both Jewish, like Paul, and Gentile, like the Galatians) and not vice versa. "Therefore" *(dio)*, in line with the statement in v. 29, the persecuted Christians (and here Paul is thinking chiefly of Gentile Christians) correspond to Isaac, over against the persecuting Jews and Judaizers who correspond to Ishmael.[54] In substance, then, Paul argues:

---

again" (v. 1b). In other words, the flow of thought in the immediate context is against Cosgrove's understanding of the point of 4:30.

53. Hanson, *Studies*, 95.

54. Cosgrove, "The Law," 232 objects to this interpretation of διό ("then") on the grounds of (a) "the intervening position of the citation from Gen. 21:10" and (b) "the fact that the statement on persecution is introduced after v 28 (which forms the doublet of v 31) not with γάρ (or even δέ or καί) but with ἀλλά." But (a) presents no insuperable difficulty, since vv. 29f. contain the two final points which Paul brings out from the Genesis story and διό can very well refer back to the first of these points rather than the second. Furthermore, (b) may be countered by the consideration that the function of ἀλλά in v. 29 is to present a concomitant of being "children of God's promise" (v. 28),

Would you be, as the judaisers have been exhorting you to be, sons of Abraham? Be so, but observe that of the Abrahamic family there are two branches, the slave and the free. We, brethren, whose relation to Abraham is spiritual, not physical, we are the sons not of the slave, but of the free.[55]

1 This syntactically independent verse (a single sentence in the original)—with no connective particle to mark its relation to what precedes or follows—is in the nature of a "bridge verse" or "transition paragraph"[56] (cf. AV, RSV, NEB, NIV). It is on the one hand a summary of 4:21-31, if not also of chapters 3–4 as a whole, or even of 2:14–4:31 or 1:6–4:31,[57] and on the other an introduction to the exhortations of chapter 5.

Here the note of freedom is struck again before the exhortation is sounded: by offering up his life in substitutionary death for us (3:13; 4:4) Christ has set us free *tē eleutherią*. The Greek phrase is probably to be taken, not as dative of purpose or destination (as in NEB),[58] but as dative of instrument or description (RV "with freedom"), because (a) the article used with the noun marks the "liberty" as something specific (cf. AV, "the liberty wherewith . . ."), that is, the freedom Paul has been speaking of, and (b) for the idea of purpose or destination Paul employs a different expression in 5:13 *(ep' eleutherią;* cf. Rom. 8:21, *eis tēn eleutherian).*[59]

The freedom referred to is freedom from subservience to the law, "the freedom belonging to the heir, the natural son, the child of the free woman."[60] Hence the Galatians must stand firm in this freedom and refuse to submit again to "a yoke of slavery" (RSV, NASB, NIV). The "yoke" was used in current Jewish parlance in an honorable sense for the obligation

namely, being persecuted by those who are born according to the flesh; this is the major premise which, together with the minor premise ("so it is today"), leads logically to the conclusion of v. 31. Understood thus, v. 31 cannot be said to make "little sense as a logical conclusion," as Cosgrove alleges; his proposal that διό is best understood as an exhortation to the brethren comes up against the difficulty that Paul uses neither a verb of exhorting (as in Rom. 12:1, cited by Cosgrove), nor an imperative (as in Gal. 5:1), nor a hortatory subjunctive (as in 6:9, 10), but a plain first person plural indicative ("we are [not]").

55. Burton 251. Cf. Hanson, *Studies*, 99f.
56. Cole 130, n. 1, and Burton 270, respectively. On the textual question cf. Metzger 597; Burton 271f.; Schlier 229.
57. So Burton 270; Bruce 226; and Betz 256, respectively.
58. Cf. RSV, NASB, NIV ("for freedom"); BAGD s.v. ἐλευθερία; Schlier 229; Betz 255f.
59. So Bruce 226. Cf. Burton 271; Cole 136. J. Blunck, *NIDNTT* I: 719 observes that "there is in the NT no summons to contend for freedom. It is already given in what Christ has done for us." We may not forget, however, that Jude 3 does summon believers to "contend for the faith which was once for all delivered to the saints" (RSV) in which the freedom accomplished for us by Christ is offered.
60. Bring 234.

to keep the law of Moses, and the Judaizers may well have urged the Galatians to "take the yoke of the law" upon themselves.[61] But Paul bluntly points out that the ordinances of the law as demanded by the Judaizers constitute a slave's yoke, so that he uses the word in the bad sense of an imposed burden, like slavery (cf. Acts 15:10; 1 Tim. 6:1). Here the principle of justification by faith is clearly involved, for freedom from the law means for the Christian first and foremost freedom from the law as a means of justification (and secondarily as a principle of life).

In this verse we are introduced to an essential aspect of Paul's understanding of Christian salvation: the relation between the *theological indicative* and the *ethical imperative*. The two are concisely juxtaposed here: the indicative states that Christ has set believers free with the gift of freedom that is proffered in the gospel; the imperative imposes upon them the task of preserving that freedom or rather of continuing in that freedom.[62] We shall have occasion to comment again on this question of the indicative and the imperative in Paul in connection with 5:6 and, more fully, 5:26.

ADDITIONAL COMMENT 7: PAUL'S TREATMENT OF THE HAGAR-SARAH STORY

In view of Paul's statement in 4:24a, it is understandable that the present passage is commonly designated the *allegory* of Hagar and Sarah.[63] This designation implies that Paul treats the OT texts by an allegorical method, which, as a method of exegesis, "is the search for secondary and hidden meaning underlying the primary and obvious meanings of a narrative."[64] But since Paul treats the Genesis story as historically true and his use of allegory is thus to be clearly distinguished from that, say, of Philo and Josephus,[65] some scholars prefer to regard Paul's treatment as *typological*,[66]

61. Cf. Cole 136; Pinnock 49. "Again" (Gk. πάλιν, cf. 4:9) suggests that Paul "in Galatians . . . virtually equates Judaism with heathenism. To go forward into Judaism is to go backward into heathenism" (Barrett 61). Cf. p. 192 above.

62. Cf. Betz 256f., 32.

63. E.g., G. Kittel, *TDNT* I: 55; F. Büchsel, *TDNT* I: 263; E. Lohse, *TDNT* VII: 285 (repeatedly); Burton 251; Dodd, *OT in the New*, 5f. Schoeps, *Paul*, 234 regards the passage as "the clearest allegory . . . in the whole of the New Testament."

64. K. J. Woolcombe, *Essays on Typology* (1957), 40, quoted in Mickelsen, *Interpreting*, 238. Cf. Hanson, *Studies*, 94.

65. Cf., e.g., Lightfoot 198-200 (especially 199); G. Schrenk, *TDNT* I: 758; Hanson, *Studies*, 205; Chadwick, "Paul and Philo," 299; Bruce 215. Cohn-Sherbok, "Exegesis," 123f. regards Gal. 4:21-31 as an example of allegorical exegesis and cites *Gen. Rabbah* lxviii.12 in comparison. But the latter passage ignores the literal sense altogether.

66. E.g., J. Behm, *TDNT* II: 130; Bruce 217; Hanson, *Studies*, 95 (he speaks, however, of Paul's typology "beginning to verge into allegory," 161, cf. 101).

217

while others consider it to be a mixture of allegory and typology,[67] and still others speak of it as both allegorical and typological as if the terms were interchangeable.[68] Now

> in typology the interpreter finds a correspondence in one or more respects between a person, event, or thing in the Old Testament and a person, event, or thing closer to or contemporaneous with a New Testament writer. It is this *correspondence* that determines the meaning in the Old Testament narrative that is stressed by a later speaker or writer.[69]

At the basis of this typological approach stands the NT conviction that such correspondence is designed by God, who controls and overrules in history, so that the OT entities are intended to point to the greater realities of their NT antitypes. It is thus "essential to a type in the scriptural acceptation of the term that there should be competent evidence of the divine intention in the correspondence between it and the Antitype."[70] H. L. Ellison rightly warns, therefore, against "finding types where they do not exist," suggesting that we do well "to confine ourselves to those sections which the New Testament claims may be used as types, else there is the very real danger that the literal meaning is ignored." He further thinks that in the present instance "we are really dealing with an extreme case of analogy." The basic idea behind this and other NT uses of analogy is that "since all has been created by God there will be similarities in creation on all its levels."[71]

Allegory, typology, analogy—of these three terms the first would seem to be the least suitable as a description of our passage, for the reason already stated. And since "the divine intention in the correspondence" mentioned above as essential to scriptural typology seems lacking in the present instance, *analogy* may be the most appropriate term for Gal. 4:21– 5:1. But more important than the question of nomenclature is the way in which Paul makes use of the Genesis story. In this connection the following observations may be made.

(a) Paul's starting point is the historical truth of the Genesis narrative.[72] (b) Paul does, however, definitely go beyond the historical to the hidden and underlying meaning. But at the same time he seems to be merely

67. E.g., Betz 239; Lang, "Gesetz," 314; Cosgrove, "The Law," 221 with n. 12.
68. E.g., G. Delling, *TDNT* VII: 669: in "the typological interpretation in vv. 24-31," "Hagar, the handmaid, is allegorically the order of Sinai. . . ."
69. Mickelsen, *Interpreting*, 237. Cf. Ellison, *Message*, 90.
70. Van Mildert, Bampton lectures of 1814, as cited by Whiteley, *Theology*, 14.
71. Ellison, *Message*, 90. The term "analogy" is used of the passage by Bruce ("Abraham," 77, 84) alongside the term "typology" (83).
72. The charge that "Gal. 4:21-31 is an utter violation of the basic rule of

drawing out the spiritual principles underlying the actual events, so that the deeper, spiritual meaning is "in full harmony with, although additional to, the historical meaning."[73] (c) In interpreting the Genesis story, Paul has a definite central point of reference which precludes all fanciful and capricious exegesis, and this point of reference is faith in Christ.

> He expounds Scripture as one who lives in the time of its fulfilment (1 C[or]. 10:11), as one for whom the veil is thus removed which had previously lain over its reading (2 C[or]. 3:14), so that the true sense of the OT may now be seen. Allegorising is thus a means to carry through his understanding of Scripture in terms of the centrality of Christ or the Cross.[74]

It is in the light of the Christ-event and the liberty from law which it brought that Paul can understand the two women and their respective sons as representing, on the one hand, the Mosaic law and its adherents and, on the other hand, the covenant of promise and those who have faith in Christ. (d) The argument which Paul employs here does not determine his view, but only confirms an understanding already reached in some other way. The contrast between slavery and freedom corresponds to and illustrates the contrast between righteousness by law and righteousness by faith; that those who are under legal bondage correspond to Hagar the slave-woman simply illustrates the truth that righteousness and blessing do not come by way of the law; that Christians are the children of promise, as was Isaac, confirms the fact that it is people of faith (those who believe in Christ and find their righteousness in him) who are the true offspring of Abraham.

> Since the kind of OT exegesis found in this passage is by no means generally characteristic of Paul,[75] the natural inference is that there was a special reason for its use here. The reason is not far to seek: if the Judaizers in Galatia were using a similar kind of argument to persuade the Christians that sonship to Abraham entailed circumcision and observance of the law, it would be especially appropriate for Paul to turn his opponents' own weapons against them.
>
> A convincing reconstruction of the probable historical setting has been provided by C. K. Barrett. According to his analysis,[76] beginning with

---

rabbinical hermeneutics: 'No word of scripture must ever lose its original sense' (Sabb. 63a)" (Schoeps, *Paul*, 238, n. 3) is therefore entirely groundless. Cf. Hanson, *Studies*, 102.

73. Guthrie 123. Cf., e.g., Collins, "Exegesis," 156; Hendriksen 180, 182.

74. F. Büchsel, *TDNT* I: 263. Cf. G. Schrenk, *TDNT* I: 760, who says of early Christianity in general that "the fact of Christ is normative and regulative for the whole use of Scripture. . . ."

75. Cf. Hanson, *Studies*, 103; G. Schrenk, *TDNT* I: 758.

76. For the following account cf. Barrett 22-27; "Allegory," especially 6,

chapter 3 Paul is "taking up passages that had been used by his opponents, correcting their exegesis, and showing that their Old Testament prooftexts were on his side rather than on theirs" (cf. 3:6, 10, 16). In chapter 4, Paul handles the argument of the agitators based upon the two women in a similar way. The center of their theology was the concept of the people of God: the people of God had its beginnings with Abraham and the divine promise, and God's covenant with Abraham had been redefined by the Sinaitic covenant (this is the point which 3:17 is concerned to refute). God's promise was given to Abraham and his offspring, and the obligations of the offspring were clearly revealed in the law; hence, to receive the promised blessing, it was necessary to fulfill the demands of the law. The scriptural proof upon which this argument was based reached its climax in the exposition of the story of Abraham and the two women: the Sarah-Isaac-Moses-law-Jeru-salem line alone represented the true offspring of Abraham, and if the Gentiles were to have a part in it, they had to be incorporated through circumcision into Abraham's family and acknowledge the sovereignty of Jerusalem.

Against this reasoning, Paul brings out the spiritual meaning of the text apart from its literal, historical sense: he gives the name Hagar a fresh interpretation, pointing out that she represents the law and slavery. (This is why Hagar is specifically mentioned in v. 24. Paul has to make it unmistakably clear which of the two women represents the Sinaitic covenant.) Here the physical descendants of Sarah become the spiritual descendants of Hagar, while the physical descendants of Hagar, interpreted of Gentiles in general, become the spiritual descendants of Sarah. Paul then quotes Isa. 54:1 (in 4:27) to show that the future belongs with the Christian Church and not with Judaism, finally confirming this by returning to the record in Genesis (Gen. 21:9f.).

We may conclude our study of this passage by saying (a) that Paul's use of the analogy of Hagar and Sarah confirms that a polemical background existed for the epistle in general and for the doctrine of justification by faith in particular, and (b) that it also confirms, by implication, that the principle of justification by faith over against justification by legal works is a contrast that underlies the entire discussion.

11-13, 15f. Cf. also Wilckens, "Statements," 21; and Martyn, "Mission," 321-323, who has reconstructed "a sermon fragment similar to one we may imagine the [false] Teachers to have preached."

H. CONTRASTS OF THE GOSPEL (5:2-12)

In this final passage of the middle, doctrinal section (III) of the epistle, which bears the character not so much of a formal argument continued from what has preceded as of a summarizing appeal,[1] Paul again lays bare the absoluteness of the opposition between faith and works, taking issue with the latter principle as it found representative expression in the Judaizers' demand for circumcision. We may distinguish two paragraphs, dealing respectively with the contrast between faith and works (vv. 2-6) and the antithesis between the cross and circumcision (vv. 7-12).

1. FAITH VERSUS WORKS (5:2-6)

2 Mark my words: I, Paul, say to you that if you receive circumcision Christ will do you no good at all. 3 Once again, you can take it from me that every man who receives circumcision is under obligation to keep the entire law. 4 When you seek to be justified by way of law, your relation with Christ is completely severed: you have fallen out of the domain of God's grace. 5 For to us, our hope of attaining that righteousness which we eagerly await is the work of the Spirit through faith. 6 If we are in union with Christ Jesus circumcision makes no difference at all, nor does the want of it; the only thing that counts is faith active in love.

2 "Mark my words" is NEB's way of expressing the effect of *ide* ("Behold," AV, RV, NASB). The emphatic "I, Paul" is perhaps an implicit assertion of his apostolic authority, possibly an implied appeal to the fact that he could not possibly be biased toward the "liberal" law-free theology in view of his background, but more probably an indirect refutation of false reports that he had given some sanction to the Judaizers' doctrine.[2] Affirming the truth of his words with the strong asseveration "you can take it from me" (v. 3)[3] Paul makes his point in three connected statements (vv. 2-4).

The first statement is v. 2b. In form the verb *peritemnēsthe* may be passive (as understood by AV, "be circumcised") or middle (as taken by

---

1. Cf. Schlier 229. We note in passing that while Betz 253 gives *"Exhortatio"* as the heading for Gal. 5:1–6:10, this is rejected by Brinsmead (237, n. 208) in favor of *"Refutatio"* (53). Cf. p. 29, n. 7 above.

2. Cf., e.g., Betz 258; Schlier 231; and Bruce 229, respectively.

3. Literally "I testify" (AV, RV, RSV, NASB); μαρτύρομαι is used in this sense also in Acts 20:26; 26:22. Cf. H. Strathmann, *TDNT* IV: 511.

NEB, RV, RSV, NASB); here it seems best to give it the sense "submit to circumcision, let oneself be circumcised" (cf. NIV), which is aimed toward the common ground of the two voices.[4] Although this is the first mention of circumcision in direct relation to the Galatians (cf. 2:3), insistence on circumcision was certainly a central feature of the false gospel being preached by the Galatian heretics.[5] This is the issue which has been behind the entire controversy regarding sonship to Abraham (3:7ff., 29; 4:21ff.), which now emerges to the surface (5:2, 3, 6, 11f.), and which will be referred to again toward the close of the epistle (6:12-16). The verse here expresses an irreconcilable antithesis between circumcision and (faith in) Christ as two entirely different modes of receiving "profit" (AV, RV) or "benefit" (NASB) which are mutually exclusive and cannot be superimposed on each other.

3   The solemn assurance of v. 3 constitutes Paul's second statement. The present tense of "receives circumcision" (the present participle *peritemnomenǭ* as distinct from the perfect participle *peritetmēmenǭ*) shows that Paul has in view not the Jewish Christian who was circumcised, but any and every Gentile Christian who would receive circumcision as a legal obligation necessary for salvation.[6] Some infer from this statement that the agitators had contented themselves with the limited goal of circumcision together with observance of the Jewish religious calendar (4:10),[7] but this is a precarious conclusion.

In pointing out that to let oneself be circumcised is to commit oneself to observing the entire law,[8] Paul may be hammering home the logical implications of circumcision of which they had been fully informed by the agitators but had not taken sufficient account.[9] His statement also seems intended as a repetition and explanation of the first statement in v. 2 (this is probably the point of "once again").[10] The resultant meaning of the two statements is, as J. B. Lightfoot has put it:

4. So MHT 1: 162; cf. BDF §314.

5. Cf., e.g., Ridderbos 82; Harvey, "Opposition," 323; Brinsmead 64.

6. Cf. Schlier 232; Cole 139.

7. Cf. Gunther, *St. Paul's Opponents,* 83. Sanders, *Paul, the Law,* 29 (also 56, n. 58) thinks they may have adopted "a policy of gradualism."

8. H. F. Weiss, *TDNT* IX: 46, n. 211 observes that this argument is "in keeping with the Pharisaic view." Cf. Betz 259; K. G. Kuhn, *TDNT* VI: 739; and see p. 142 with n. 33.

9. Cf. Barclay, "Mirror-Reading," 75: "in other words, the Galatians may be not so much *ignorant* as *naive*." Howard 16 notes the emphasis that rests on the word "debtor" (ὀφειλέτης) "both in that it is the first word in its clause . . . and that it forms a wordplay with 'profit' (ὠφελήσει) in the previous verse." But "the entire law" also receives emphasis because of its position before the infinitive "to do," in contrast to 3:10, where "to do" precedes its object (Gundry, "Grace," 27).

10. Cf., e.g., Ellicott 102; Lightfoot 203. This seems a more natural understanding than referring it to "a statement previously made to the Galatians," probably on the

Circumcision is the seal of the law. He who willingly and deliberately undergoes circumcision, enters upon a compact to fulfil the
law. To fulfil it therefore he is bound, and he cannot plead the grace
of Christ; for he has entered on another mode of justification.[11]

4 That the "good" of v. 2 is correctly understood as justification is
substantiated by Paul's third statement. "When you seek to be justified"
plausibly gives the Greek relative clause a conditional sense and rightly
takes the verb as conative (so also, on both points, NASB, NIV).[12] If you
address the question of your justification "by way of law," that is, "by
doing what the law demands" (2:16), says Paul, then a twofold result
follows: (a) "you have been severed from Christ" (NASB, cf. NIV "alien-
ated")—the clause denotes being removed from Christ's sphere of operation[13] and hence completely cut off from relations with him; and (b) "you
have fallen away from grace" (RSV, NIV)—this presupposes the thought of
grace as a sphere or "domain" in which one stands, an idea which is also
present in 1:6; Rom. 5:2; and 1 Pet. 5:12.[14] The second clause seems clearly
explicative of the first, so that to be severed from Christ is to lose one's
standing in grace.

From this it may reasonably be inferred that justification is not
attained through the law, but by grace through Christ. But as grace on God's
part points to faith as the appropriate response on the part of mankind, and in
view of what Paul has already said about the place of faith and of Christ in
justification (especially in 2:15-21; 3:13f., 21-26), we may interpret "by
grace through Christ" to mean, "by faith, through incorporation into Christ
and on the basis of his atoning work." Once again, therefore, justification by
faith is by implication clearly contrasted with justification through the law,
the contrast being rendered all the sharper in that the Greek verbs[15] present
the consequences of any attempt at justification by law as certain and instan-

---

occasion referred to in 4:16 and 1:9 (so Burton 274f.; cf. Duncan 155; Neill 74). Burton
objects to Lightfoot's view on the grounds that vv. 2 and 3, though related, are not
identical in thought; but inasmuch as v. 3b may properly be regarded as clarifying v. 2b to
some extent, v. 3 is a repetition of v. 2.

11. Lightfoot 203. Barclay 43 provides a helpful illustration drawn from the legal
act of naturalization which shows the logic of Paul's argument in v. 3.

12. On the first point cf. Zerwick §257; Phillips; on the second cf., e.g., BDF
§319; MHT 3: 63.

13. The verb καταργέω is used with an identical meaning in relation to the law in
Rom. 7:6; cf. G. Delling, *TDNT* I: 453f.

14. Cf. W. Grundmann, *TDNT* VII: 652; W. Bauder, *NIDNTT* I: 611; Schlier
232. *Pace* W. Michaelis, *TDNT* VI: 168, n. 9, who states that "'to stand in grace' has no
basis in Paul or the NT."

15. Gk. κατηργήθητε, ἐξεπέσατε, variously called "timeless" (MHT 1: 134
with 247; 3: 73f.) or proleptic (Zerwick §257; Bruce 231) aorists.

taneous.[16] The situation is excellently described by E. D. Burton: "Logically viewed, the one conception excludes the other; experientially the one experience destroys the other."[17] In Paul's mind, justification is either *all* of grace, by faith, through Christ, or it is *nothing* at all.

5 Paul now buttresses his point by two further statements (vv. 5f.). In the first (v. 5), which is intended as an argument *e contrario* against the validity of reliance on works of the law for justification,[18] he declares that he and all true Christians on their part,[19] "through the Spirit, by faith, . . . wait for the hope of righteousness" (RSV). The word rendered "eagerly await" (NEB) is used by Paul to denote "expectation of the end" (cf. Phil. 3:20) and thus carries a distinctly eschatological sense.[20]

What is awaited is "the hope of righteousness" (AV, RV, RSV, NASB; *elpida dikaiosynēs*). This deceptively simple phrase has lent itself to a wide variety of interpretations. If "hope" is regarded as standing by metonymy for "what is hoped for" and the genitive "of righteousness" is taken as objective or appositional, then the phrase will mean "hoped-for righteousness" or "what is hoped for, that is, righteousness."[21] Of the more exact meaning of the phrase, however, there are at least four views.

(a) It is thought that the use of "hope" and "eagerly await" on the one hand and "justified" in v. 4 on the other hand requires that "righteousness" here be referred to that future justification which is spoken of in Rom. 2:13, 16. It is further held that this in turn determines the character of the righteousness which is hoped for as "ethical-forensic, with the forensic element distinctly but not exclusively in mind."[22] (b) Very similar, but without reference to the ethical aspect, is the view which takes the phrase to denote the hope of final acquittal in the last judgment, when God's verdict will be publicly pronounced.[23]

---

16. Cf. the perfects of NASB, NIV; Lightfoot 204.

17. Burton 277. Manson, *Paul and John*, 79 shows that Paul considers circumcision after baptism (= "a return . . . to the works of the law") one of three "forms of apostasy from the Gospel" which cut a person off from the body of Christ, the other two being fornication (= "a return to the works of the flesh," 1 Cor. 6:12-20) and "participation in the sacrificial meals of the heathen cults" (= "a return . . . to the service of idols," 1 Cor. 10:14-22).

18. So, e.g., Burton 278; Ridderbos 189, n. 13. Hence NIV translates γάρ ("for" in AV, RV, RSV, NEB, NASB) as "but."

19. "For to us" is NEB's attempt to reflect emphatic ἡμεῖς ("we") over against the Judaizers.

20. Gk. ἀπεκδέχομαι, as distinct from ἐκδέχομαι, "to wait." Cf. W. Grundmann, *TDNT* II: 56 (whence the quotation); Schlier 233, n. 1.

21. Cf., e.g., NEB, NIV; BAGD s.v. ἐλπίς 2.b; s.v. δικαιοσύνη 3; Thayer s.v. ἐλπίς 2.b; Zerwick §46; MHT 3: 214f.; E. Hoffman, *NIDNTT* III: 241f.

22. Burton 471. Cf. Duncan 156; Hill, *Greek*, 151.

23. Cf., e.g., G. Schrenk, *TDNT* II: 207; H. Seebass, *NIDNTT* III: 365;

Against both these views, however, is the consideration that elsewhere in Galatians (with the exception of 2:16, in a quotation from the Psalms) justification is not mentioned with reference to the future, but appears rather as something already accomplished in the present through faith in Christ.[24] It may further be doubted that the verse has justification at the last judgment in view, since elsewhere in his letters as well Paul consistently speaks of the believer's justification as something that has taken place already in the here and now (e.g., Rom. 3:24; 5:1, 9; 1 Cor. 6:11), without anywhere implying that this justification is to be publicly disclosed at the last judgment.[25] Indeed, Paul's conviction that righteousness is imparted now is "the new point in comparison with Judaism."[26]

(c) A third view takes the hoped-for righteousness in the subjective sense of "an inward personal righteousness" which is "synonymous with Christian holiness, conformity to the moral ideal."[27] But to understand "righteousness" here in this ethical sense does not accord well with v. 4, where justification appears to be a matter not of quality of life but of standing in grace, of relation to Christ. Since v. 5 is clearly intended to support v. 4 it is reasonable to expect "righteousness" in v. 5 to bear a similar sense to that which is involved in "being justified" in v. 4. And that sense is distinctly forensic, not ethical.

(d) Another suggestion regards "righteousness" here as a synonym for "the awaited eschatological blessing of salvation."[28] But while it is true that righteousness and salvation are closely associated in Paul's thought (e.g., Rom. 5:9f.; 10:9f.), they are nevertheless differentiated from each other. Rom. 5:9 clearly shows that for the Christian, justification belongs to the past ("we have now been justified," *dikaiōthentes*, aorist participle), but salvation is to occur in the future ("we shall . . . be saved," *sōthēsometha*,

---

Jeremias, *Central Message*, 65; Morris, *Preaching*, 258; Ladd, "Eschatology," 271; *Theology*, 442, 566; Ridderbos, *Paul*, 165f., 178. See especially Barrett 63-65, who expressly speaks of there being "two justifications," one in the present and the other in the future: "Justification, then, is a beginning, and a process; and it leads to a consummation, at the future judgement, when God's *initial* gracious verdict on the sinner is—or, it may be, is not—*confirmed*" (65, emphasis added).

24. Cf. Kertelge, *Rechtfertigung*, 147.
25. For substantiation of this statement see Additional Comment 8 below.
26. G. Schrenk, *TDNT* II: 205. Cf. Wendland, *Mitte*, 26; Bultmann, *Existence*, 137f.
27. A. B. Bruce, *Christianity*, 225, 226f. Similarly Schlier 233f., where the meaning given to the phrase is consistent with Schlier's understanding of justification as both forensic and ethical (89-91). Barrett 65 also says that our verse "shows a movement" in the direction of Rom. 6:19, where "righteousness means moral righteousness": "We look for the expression of our new relation to God in observable behaviour."
28. W. Foerster, *TDNT* VII: 993. Cf. Kertelge, *Rechtfertigung*, 148f.

future indicative).[29] Again, in Rom. 10:10, although "righteousness" and "salvation" stand in formal parallelism to each other, they are not identical with regard to content: whereas "righteousness" is a reference to present justification, "salvation," which resumes the thought of "you will find salvation" in v. 9, refers to salvation at the last day. Thus "the linking of *dikaiosynē* ["righteousness"] and *sōtēria* ["salvation"] unifies present and future—which are distinct."[30] This distinction answers exactly to that found in Rom. 5:9f. and is in accord with the general usage of the NT, where "the emphasis in both *sōzō* ["save"] and *sōtēria* is on the future,"[31] though the present aspect is not lost sight of (cf. Rom. 8:24; 2 Cor. 6:2). This clear distinction between "righteousness" as present and "salvation" as primarily future renders it unlikely that in our passage "righteousness" is intended as a synonym for "salvation."[32]

In view of the difficulties confronting the four interpretations discussed above, which take "of righteousness" as objective genitive or appositional genitive, the alternative understanding of the term as a *subjective* genitive appears especially worthy of consideration. In this case, we may (e) regard the term as an instance of the abstract standing for the concrete, so that the sense of v. 5b is: "we look for that which *dikaiosynē* (= *hoi dikaioi,* "the righteous") hopes for."[33] Alternatively, we may (f) give "the hope of righteousness" the sense: "the realization of the hoped for things pertaining to the state of righteousness conferred in justification" or, more simply, "the hope to which the justification of believers points them forward."[34]

The latter, (f), seems decidedly preferable to the former, since, instead of making "righteousness" stand for "the righteous," it allows the term to be understood in a sense which is both consistent with its usage elsewhere in the epistle (cf. 2:21; 3:6, 21) and consonant with the presence

29. Cf. Lyonnet, "Pauline Soteriology," 840. Foerster himself rightly observes: "In R[om]. 5:9f. δικαιωθῆναι ["being justified"] and καταλλαγῆναι ["being reconciled"] are notably distinguished from the future σωθήσεσθαι ["being saved"] by the νῦν ["now"] and the aorist participle" (*TDNT* VII: 992).

30. G. Schrenk, *TDNT* II: 207. Cf. Barrett, *Romans,* 201f.; Sanday-Headlam, *Romans,* 290. *Pace* Bultmann, who considers the terms to be "used in synonymous parallelism" (*Theology,* 1: 271).

31. W. Foerster, *TDNT* VII: 1003. Cf. G. Stählin, *TDNT* V: 430.

32. Strictly speaking, righteousness is the condition for receiving salvation or life. Cf. on 3:21b above (p. 163); Bultmann, *Theology,* 1: 270f.; *pace* Snaith, *Distinctive Ideas,* 164f.

33. Zerwick §46. Cf. MHT 3: 215.

34. So Vos, *Eschatology,* 30, and Bruce 41 (cf. 54, 232, 252), respectively. Ziesler, *Righteousness,* 179f. also takes the genitive as subjective, the phrase meaning "the hope prompted by righteousness already known." But he understands righteousness in terms of "faith working through love" and hope as "final acceptance," concluding that "righteousness in Christ is present, but the verdict on it, as on law-righteousness, comes at the Judgment."

of "you seek to be justified" in v. 4. If (f) is accepted, then the "hope" or "hoped-for things" in question probably refer to what is summed up in the terms "life," "salvation," and "glory"—each of which, at least in its characteristic Pauline usage, is related to justification as something to which it points forward.[35]

That an apparently simple expression such as "the hope of righteousness" should have occasioned such a variety of interpretations becomes more intelligible when it is remembered that the Greek genitive denotes "a relationship which is amplified by the context."[36] Having reached a decision about the meaning of that phrase, we may now consider the remainder of the verse.

The whole weight of the verse is on the two phrases "through the Spirit, by faith" (RSV), which are brought forward for emphasis since they stand for the two aspects that distinguish the Christian hope from the Jewish.[37] There is in "through the Spirit" an implied contrast with "the flesh" which is the active principle of legal righteousness (cf. 3:3),[38] while "by faith" stands in explicit and decisive contrast with "by way of law" (v. 4). The two phrases are not, strictly speaking, predicated of "righteousness": it is not explicitly stated here that it is "through the Spirit" and "by faith" that believers are justified, but only that it is "through the Spirit, by faith" that "we wait for the hope of righteousness." But since the expectation of this "hope" to which believers are pointed forward by their justification is grounded in their present experience of the Spirit and in faith, it is plainly not, and cannot be, based on works of the law, because justification, which gives rise to the hope in question, cannot itself be achieved by works of the law, but is attained only "by faith." The clear contrast beween faith and law in the immediate context (as well as in the epistle as a whole) shows beyond doubt that in Paul's thinking there can be no such thing as a hope which is being awaited on the basis of faith while the ground of that hope (namely, justification) is itself based on works of the law.

We may therefore conclude that v. 5 unmistakably implies that justification is "by faith" and not "by way of law," even though the full expression "justified by faith," which might have been expected, is lacking.[39] This lack is perhaps to be explained by the fact that the thought of vv. 5f.

35. The relation between justification and salvation has just been touched on; the relation of justification to life is clearly indicated in Rom. 5:18b, and to glory in Rom. 5:1f.; 8:30. Cf. Stott 134, where "the expectation for the future which our justification brings" is explained as "spending eternity with Christ in heaven."

36. MHT 3: 212.

37. Cf. Cole 142.

38. Cf., e.g., Ellicott 103; Burton 278. Here the Spirit is the power by which the hope of righteousness is fostered and kept alive (cf. NEB; Ellicott 104; Bruce 232).

39. On the other hand, no clear inference can be drawn from this verse regarding

relates not only to the initial act of justification but extends to the believer's subsequent life as well.

6 Paul's second statement here (the first being v. 5) explains why it is "through the Spirit, by faith" that believers await the hope of righteousness (note "for": AV, RV, RSV, NASB, NIV). That circumcision is unprofitable is repeated from v. 2, but the thought is now expanded to include *un*circumcision as well. Union with Christ Jesus (literally being "in Christ Jesus"), says Paul, makes circumcision and the want of it matters of no religious importance; they are, indeed, totally irrelevant in the realm of the Christian life.[40] Included in this, and lying at the basis of it, is the thought that circumcision has no power to effect the righteousness spoken of in v. 5, which (as maintained above) refers to much the same thing as "being justified" in v. 4. Neither does lack of circumcision, as though this lack were an advantage in seeking to be justified.[41] The only thing that counts is faith. In this assertion of the all-sufficiency of faith over against the total inefficacy of circumcision (and uncircumcision) the contrast between faith and circumcision corresponds to the contrast between faith and law spoken of in the preceding verses (vv. 4f.). This contrast dominates the thought of the present paragraph (vv. 2-6), as it does the thought of so much of the epistle as a whole.

"Active in love" represents Gk. *di' agapēs energoumenē*, on which four questions will be considered. (a) With regard to the meaning of the expression, the main issue is whether the Greek participle *(energoumenē)* should be taken as middle or passive.[42] J. B. Lightfoot thought that middle/passive *energeisthai* "is never passive in St Paul," but always middle.[43] In response to this dictum J. A. Robinson observed that *energeisthai* "is never used by St. Paul of persons, while [the active form] *energein* is always so used"—a "perfectly natural" distinction if *energeisthai* is passive—and that so far as he is aware, "there is no trace of a middle in any other writer." He therefore decides that "in St. Paul as elsewhere *energeisthai* is passive," and gives the phrase in Gal. 5:6 the sense, "faith is made operative through love."[44] In further support of the passive sense G. S. Duncan also adduces "the clear light of Gal. ii. 20," which to him shows that Paul was "brought

---

the place of the Spirit in justification. We have seen from 4:1-7 (p. 187 above, point [1]) that justification by faith issues in reception of the Spirit.

40. Cf. R. Meyer, *TDNT* VI: 83.

41. So, rightly, W. Grundmann, *TDNT* III: 398.

42. Middle: NEB; RV, RSV, NASB ("faith working through love," cf. AV); NIV ("faith expressing itself through love"). Passive: RV mg. ("faith wrought through love"); NEB mg. ("faith inspired by love").

43. Lightfoot 204.

44. Robinson, *Ephesians*, 246.

. . . to rest exclusively on *faith* by the revelation of a Saviour who *loved* him"; in accord with this understanding he takes "love" in 5:6 as well "primarily of God's love to man, rather than of the Christian's love for his neighbour."[45]

Robinson's view would offer a satisfactory explanation of the distinction in usage observed between the middle/passive form *energeisthai* and the active *energein*. But several factors favor the view that the participle in 5:6 is middle. (i) This view is simpler, since it obviates the question of who the agent is—a question to which a clear answer is not in every case readily available.[46] (ii) "It is more usual in the New Testament to say that Christ's love evokes a corresponding love in us (I Jn. iv. 19) than to say that our faith actually stems from love."[47] In keeping with this, faith (as the root) usually precedes love (as the fruit) in Paul's letters (Eph. 1:15; Col. 1:4; 1 Cor. 13:13; cf. 1 Thess. 1:3).[48] (iii) In the light of Gal. 5:13f., where explicit reference is made to love towards one another, it is difficult to define the "love" in v. 6 in terms of God's or Christ's love for the believer. But if this love must at least include the Christian's love for his neighbor, then it makes much better sense to speak of "faith working (i.e., expressing itself) through love" than of "faith made operative through love." It is not surprising therefore that the majority of Protestant interpreters and most of the major English versions concur in giving the phrase an active sense.[49]

(b) The faith which operates through love is clearly the same as the faith which justifies.[50] Does this suggest that love plays a contributory role

45. Duncan 157.

46. In the majority of instances (2 Cor. 1:6; 4:12b; Eph. 3:20; Col. 1:29; 1 Thess. 2:13) the answer would probably be "God" or "the Spirit." But the answer is not so readily forthcoming in Rom. 7:5; 2 Cor. 4:12a; Gal. 5:6; 2 Thess. 2:7. In fact, in the case of Rom. 7:5, if not also 2 Cor. 4:12a, it is difficult to give a definite answer to the question without risking unwarranted theological inferences.

47. Cole 144. Two things may be said with regard to Duncan's appeal to Gal. 2:20: (a) It is Christ's self-surrender in death, rather than Paul's faith, which is brought into immediate connection with Christ's love. (b) While "who loved me . . . ." might suggest the ground of Paul's faith (cf. Burton 139), it may legitimately be asked whether it is specifically Paul's initial conversion faith or his faith as a Christian that is here envisaged as called forth by Christ's love; the context points to the latter. Not that there is any radical qualitative difference between the two, of course: the distinction is rather the temporal distinction between faith as an initial act and faith as a continuing attitude (see n. 50 below).

48. The order in Phm. 5 is perhaps to be understood in the light of the chiastic structure of the verse.

49. Cf. (besides n. 42 above), e.g., BAGD s.v. ἐνεργέω 1.b; Thayer s.v. 3; MHT 3: 56; E. Stauffer, *TDNT* I: 50; G. Bertram, *TDNT* II: 654; M. J. Harris, *NIDNTT* III: 1182; Schlatter, *Glaube*, 372; Reumann, *Righteousness*, §105.

50. Ziesler, *Righteousness*, 165 says: "As faith is indivisible, there is no distinction of that faith which is a response to God's action in Christ (i.e., justifying faith) from that which is the Christian's continuing life."

in justification? On this question G. Bornkamm has provided an excellent answer:[51]

> We must guard against the misunderstanding current especially in Catholic theology (though Protestantism is far from exempt) that only faith made perfect in love[52] leads to justification. This represents a serious distortion of the relationship between faith, love, and justification. In speaking of justification Paul never talks of faith *and* love, but *only* of faith as receiving. Love is not therefore an additional prerequisite for receiving salvation, nor is it properly an essential trait of faith; on the contrary, faith animates the love in which it works.

Paul's words, then, are "not to be understood in a synergistic sense, as though faith through its expression of love cooperates in producing salvation";[53] he is saying simply that the faith which justifies is of such a nature that it will express itself through love.

(c) If that is the case, why does Paul describe faith as he does? It has been suggested that he explains faith along this particular line not so much because he is casting a side-glance at the loveless seducers or because he is already thinking of the warnings to follow, as because he instinctively wants to give a decisive and comprehensive delineation of the authentic life in Christ over against the falsification which his concept of faith was receiving in Galatia.[54] This understanding seems supported by the fact that the opponents are very much in view, as is evidenced particularly clearly in the following verses (vv. 7-12), and that already Paul has had to defend his doctrine of justification by faith against the charge that it encourages sin (2:17-21). Paul is once more clearing his doctrine of this allegation by pointing to the nature of faith as operating through love; his thought seems to have glided from the believer's justification to his subsequent Christian existence, which is characterized by this "expressing-itself-through-love" faith. Just as earlier Paul replied to the charge by bringing justification in Christ into relation with the new life of union with Christ (2:17, 20), so here his rejoinder presents justification by faith in inseparable connection with a life of love.[55]

(d) It remains to ask how this faith which justifies actually works through love, for certainly Paul does not mean to say that faith (even though

51. Bornkamm, *Paul,* 153 (his emphasis).
52. This takes ἐνεργουμένη as passive, but that question apart, the thought of "perfection" is plainly lacking in Paul's phrase.
53. Ridderbos 190f., n. 18. *Pace* Ziesler, *Righteousness,* 180: "It is . . . faith working through love, which wins God's favourable verdict."
54. Schlier 235.
55. On the inseparability of faith and love (i.e., good works) see Machen 220f.; Ridderbos, *Paul,* 179f.

it is faith in Christ), considered by itself, will automatically express itself in love. Here three lines of evidence converge to provide a clear answer.

First, our discussion of 2:19f. has shown that the faith which justifies also marks the beginning of a new life whose principle and power is Christ. Now in the believer's experience Christ is not distinguishable from the Holy Spirit. This appears from the fact that "there is . . . scarcely one spiritual blessing or activity which is not at one time ascribed to Christ and, at another, to the Spirit,"[56] and is seen most clearly from a passage such as Rom. 8:9f., where the phrase "within you" is predicated of both "God's Spirit" and "Christ" and both appear to be synonymous with "the Spirit of Christ." Here the relation between the Spirit, Christ, and God is perhaps most adequately explained by the thought that *"Christ dwells in us through the Spirit,* which is the Spirit equally of the Father and of the Son."[57]

In view of this "functional or practical identification" of the Spirit and Christ[58] the new life might have been described by reference to the Spirit instead of to Christ; that Paul does not actually do so in 2:19f. is probably because at this point he wishes to emphasize not the spiritual character of the new life (cf. Rom. 8:1ff.) but its existence as "a new life which acknowledges a new mastery."[59] Since Christ and the Spirit are thus identified in the believer's conscious experience, we are led to conclude that the faith which justifies marks the beginning of the new life whose principle and power is the Spirit.

This correlation between justifying faith and the Spirit, deduced from 2:20, is in complete harmony with the *second* line of evidence: In our examination of 3:1-6 it was seen that Paul regards justification by faith and reception of the Spirit as in some sense synonymous; this near equation emerged again in 3:7-14, and our study of 4:1-7 further enabled us to see that justification by faith provides the logical basis for reception of the Spirit, although the two are inseparable if distinct aspects of a single experience.[60]

From these two lines of evidence we may infer that justification marks the new life in the Spirit because the faith which is the means of justification is also and at the same time that which receives the Spirit who is bestowed on the basis of justification. This conclusion is in turn corroborated by the *third* line of evidence, which consists in (i) the explicit mention of "love" as a part of "the harvest of the Spirit" (5:22) in the believer's life, as well as (ii) the broader consideration that, throughout the section of the

56. Lee, *Romans,* 119.
57. Headlam, *Paul,* 100 (emphasis added). Cf. Richardson, *Theology,* 121.
58. Lee, *Romans,* 120.
59. Duncan 72.
60. For a review of these relationships see Fung, "Justification, Sonship," 74-79, 86-91, and especially 94f.

epistle dealing with the life of love (5:13-26), faith is not presented as "operating through love"; rather, the life of love is ascribed to the activity of the Spirit (vv. 16, 18, 25a, b).

Thus all three lines of evidence point to the Spirit as the answer to our inquiry. Faith operates through love, because the faith which is the means of justification also, at the same time, receives the Spirit (through whom Christ dwells within the believer), who is the principle and producer of the new life of love.[61]

Thus a proper understanding of the phrase "faith active in love" throws light on the relation between justification and the new life in the Spirit, permitting the conclusions (a) that justification by faith is *experientially coincident* with the beginning of new life in the Spirit and (b) that, in view of the logical sequence "justification, adoption, receiving of the Spirit" we saw earlier,[62] justification is *logically prior* to the new life in the Spirit. Our discussion also sheds light on the relation between indicative and imperative in Paul. Precisely because justification by faith means at the same time a new life in the Spirit, believers can be exhorted to conduct the manifold relationships of their lives in the Spirit's power and in accord with the Spirit's will. The ethical imperatives are therefore the natural outcome of the theological indicatives of the gospel of Christ; the gift *(Gabe)* of justification and life in the Spirit entails at the same time the task *(Aufgabe)* of a sanctified life.

ADDITIONAL COMMENT 8: JUSTIFICATION AT THE LAST JUDGMENT?

Several passages apparently contradict our earlier statement[63] that elsewhere in his writings Paul nowhere implies that the believer's justification will be publicly disclosed at the last judgment. But close examination of the relevant texts (Rom. 2:13; 3:20, 30; 5:19; 8:33f.; 1 Cor. 4:4) reveals that the contradiction is not real.

---

61. Cf. A. Oepke, *TDNT* II: 540: "The Spirit is the constantly active principle of ethical life." We need not doubt that Paul was in fact also inspired to love by the revelation of God's love in Christ (cf. Gal. 2:20c; 2 Cor. 5:14); *faith* in a loving Savior thus entails a response of *love*. Even so, the Spirit remains the dynamic of the believer's response of love, for it is the outpoured Spirit who on the basis of the historical event of Christ's death for sinners gives them the constant assurance of God's love (Rom. 5:5, 8). For a different answer from that which we have presented above, cf. A. B. Bruce, who lays emphasis on "the moral energy of faith" (as chapter 12 of his *Christianity* is entitled), especially 228f., 235.

62. See above, pp. 152f., point (b); 177, point (2); and 194, point (3). Cf. Fung, art. cit. (n. 60 above), especially 94f.

63. See p. 225 above, at n. 25.

Thus, in Rom. 2:13, while the future tense "will be justified" doubtless refers to the last judgment (cf. vv. 5, 12), Paul seems to be simply speaking from the Jewish viewpoint of a future judgment and not from a specifically Christian perspective on the matter of justification; the verse merely states "a presupposition which must be laid down to convince opponents *irrespective of the redemption in Christ*."[64] Similarly, the future tense "will be justified" (RSV) in Rom. 3:20 (as in Gal. 2:16) appears in a quotation from Ps. 143:2 and may simply reflect the Jewish viewpoint,[65] or, more probably, may be intended as a gnomic/logical future referring not to the future judgment but "rather to the certainty and universality" of what is said, that justification cannot come by works of the law.[66]

G. Schrenk regards all the remaining four passages as referring to a future justification of believers. Taking "will be made righteous" in Rom. 5:19b (as he does "will justify" in 3:30) to be "a temporal as well as a logical future,"[67] he thinks that the passage "looks to the last judgment, when they will be presented righteous, or made righteous, by God's sentence. The antithetical structure of the section leads Paul to the juxtaposition of *hamartōloi* ["sinners"] and *dikaioi* ["righteous"], and he does not say that we are now *dikaioi*."[68] But it is more likely that the future tense is being used from the standpoint of the Christ-event, so that the reference is not to the last judgment but to the justification of all who in the generations to come would reap the benefit of the cross.[69] As for Rom. 3:30 we probably have here a gnomic/logical rather than temporal future,[70] for the context shows that Paul is concerned with the *present* manifestation of God's righteousness and with the *principle* of justification (cf. esp. vv. 21, 24).

Again, Schrenk writes:[71]

> The fundamentally important and solemn declaration of R[om]. 8:33 *theos ho dikaiōn* ["It is God who pronounces acquittal"] (preceded by the future *tis enkalesei* ["Who will be the accuser?"]) obviously refers to the last judgment. Here again it is thus evident that *dikaioun*

---

64. G. Schrenk, *TDNT* II: 217 (emphasis added). Cf. Leenhardt, *Romans*, 78; Kertelge, *Rechtfertigung*, 143f.

65. G. Schrenk, loc. cit., thinks that "as a quotation it hardly provides a definitive answer to the question."

66. Murray, *Romans*, 1: 107.

67. G. Schrenk, *TDNT* II: 218.

68. G. Schrenk, *TDNT* II: 191. Cf. Dodd, *Romans*, 104; Braun, *Gerichtsgedanke*, 78.

69. Cf., e.g., Sanday-Headlam, *Romans*, 142; J. Denney, *EGT* II: 630f.; Barrett, *Romans*, 117.

70. So, e.g., Cranfield, *Romans*, 222; Murray, *Romans*, 1: 123f.; Bultmann, *Theology*, 1: 274.

71. *TDNT* II: 218.

["to justify"] is an eschatological term and that the divine justification which was accomplished at the cross, which is now believed and which is a continuing gift in the present, is to be expected as a consummated and definitive acquittal in the Last Day.

Over against this it has been maintained that the verbs "be the accuser" and "condemn" should be taken as logical futures and that the "litigation" with the powers should be regarded as in process in the present.[72] But even if we accept the view that the scene is the last judgment,[73] still nothing is said or even implied about God's pronouncing a definitive verdict of acquittal on that day. Rather, Paul's picture merely suggests that "many accusers are envisaged, but their accusations are of no account since God has pronounced his justifying sentence. There is no appeal from his tribunal."[74]

Finally, with regard to 1 Cor. 4:4 Schrenk states emphatically:

> Paul speaks most clearly of *dikaiousthai* ["being justified"] at the last judgment when he treats of retributive judgment by works, as in 1 C[or]. 4:4. . . . In the full sense a man is judicially acquitted and declared righteous only when the retributive sentence of the last judgment has been pronounced in his favour as regards the whole of his life's work.[75]

The tense of the verb, however, is decidedly against this view, since Paul says "I stand acquitted" and not "I shall be acquitted."[76] It would be better to regard the verb as used in its usual Pauline sense, the perfect tense defining "an act of God complete in the past and determining the writer's present state," so that the meaning is: Paul "*has been and continues justified* —not on the sentence of his conscience as a man self-acquitted . . . , but as an ill-deserving sinner counted righteous for Christ's sake."[77] But since (as the preceding verses make clear) Paul is here speaking not of his person but of his apostolic work,[78] it is still more probable that the verb is to be taken, not in its technical theological sense, but in its general legal meaning. Paul is saying that in spite of the fact that he "has no . . . guilty secret to share with himself" regarding his ministry—a fact which merely "speaks of human

---

72. Kertelge, *Rechtfertigung*, 150, n. 69.
73. So, e.g., Barrett, *Romans*, 173; Black, *Romans*, 126.
74. Murray, *Romans*, 1: 327.
75. *TDNT* II: 217. Cf. V. Taylor, *Forgiveness*, 43.
76. Gk. δεδικαιῶμαι (perfect), not δικαιωθήσομαι (future). Cf. Grosheide, *First Corinthians*, 101; G. G. Findlay, *EGT* II: 798.
77. G. G. Findlay, loc. cit. (his emphasis).
78. V. 4b thus means: I know nothing against myself "in my conduct as Christ's minister to you" (G. G. Findlay, op. cit., 797f.). This seems preferable to Lightfoot's view that "it is simply a hypothetical case" (*Notes*, 198). To say that Paul "is no longer conscious of sin in his state of union with Christ" (K. H. Rengstorf, *TDNT* I: 333) is surely unwarranted by this text.

ignorance rather than human innocence"[79]—he is not thereby acquitted;[80] rather he must submit himself to the decision of the Lord who alone can assess[81] the quality of his apostolic service and whose verdict alone matters. Thus understood the verse says nothing about a future justification at the last judgment.[82]

In conclusion, we are inclined to question the view which sees in these texts references to a future justification of believers. We may also doubt the view which speaks of "a strict parallelism between redemption and justification, which is also . . . both future and present."[83] Whereas redemption is by its very nature progressively realized, this does not appear to be the case with justification. Rather, it would seem that according to Paul, while an eschatological judgment still awaits believers, there is no such thing as an eschatological justification for them, in the sense of one pronounced at the final day.

2. THE CROSS VERSUS CIRCUMCISION (5:7-12)

7 *You were running well; who was it hindered you from following the truth?* 8 *Whatever persuasion he used, it did not come from God who is calling you;* 9 *"a little leaven," remember, "leavens all the dough."* 10 *United with you in the Lord, I am confident that you will not take the wrong view, but the man who is unsettling your minds, whoever he may be, must bear God's judgement.* 11 *And I, my friends, if I am still advocating circumcision, why is it I am still persecuted? In that case, my preaching of the cross is a stumbling-block no more.* 12 *As for these agitators, they had better go the whole way and make eunuchs of themselves!*

7 Paul has shown up the utter futility, indeed the positive hurtfulness, of seeking to be justified through circumcision and the law (vv. 2-6). His argument now assumes, as in 3:1-6, the form of an appeal—this time to the readers' original attitude to the gospel. Paul reminds them that they were "running well," at least when he was with them.[84] But since he bade them

79. Barrett, *First Corinthians*, 102; cf. NIV.

80. Cf. RSV, NEB, NASB; Robertson-Plummer, *First Corinthians*, 77.

81. On ἀνακρίνων here cf. F. Büchsel, *TDNT* III: 944f.; C. Maurer, *TDNT* VII: 916.

82. Cf. Kertelge, *Rechtfertigung*, 148, n. 175.

83. F. Büchsel, *TDNT* IV: 353, n. 9.

84. The metaphor of running is used by Paul to express "how the Christian life as a whole, like his apostolic service, is directed towards a goal" (G. Ebel, *NIDNTT* III: 947); cf. 2:2; 1 Cor. 9:26; 2 Tim. 4:7; Acts 20:24.

farewell someone had hindered them[85] from "following the truth." "Obeying the truth" (RSV, NASB, NIV) is identical in meaning with "obeying the gospel" in Rom. 10:16 (cf. RSV),[86] "the truth" here being that which found expression in the gospel of justification by faith apart from circumcision and the law (2:5, 14).[87] The person or persons behind the "who" of Paul's rhetorical question evidently were the same as those envisaged in 3:1 (RSV "Who has bewitched you . . . ?"), whom we have identified as Judaizers.[88]

8 Paul roundly declares their "persuasion" to be not divine in origin. The word so translated is taken by some in the passive sense (i.e., being persuaded) as referring to the Galatians' obedience or acquiescence.[89] But the active sense, referring to the Judaizers' efforts at persuading, besides being lexically defensible is more in harmony with the active "the one who calls you" (NIV).[90] This one who calls, as frequently in Paul, is God, or Christ, or God in Christ;[91] the present tense "calls" focuses on the character of God as the one who calls rather than on the time at which he called the Galatians, which is the emphasis in 1:6.[92]

9 In what appears to be a proverbial saying (cf. 1 Cor. 5:6b) Paul further illustrates the definitely evil character of the Judaizers' teaching: "a little yeast ferments the whole lump of dough."[93] "Proverbial in form, but not found outside Paul as a proverb, these words might have been associated

85. On the basic meaning of ἐγκόπτειν as "to block the way" see G. Stählin, *TDNT* III: 855 (cf. the cognate noun ἐγκοπή, "obstacle"). The verb is thus the opposite of προκόπτειν, "to clear a way," "to act as pioneer" (Lightfoot 205).

86. Cf. R. Bultmann, *TDNT* VI: 4; I: 244; A. C. Thiselton, *NIDNTT* III: 884. Following BDF §488.1b, R. Bultmann, *TDNT* VI: 4, n. 11 favors the reading τίς ὑμᾶς ἐνέκοψεν; ἀληθείᾳ μὴ πείθεσθαι μηδενὶ πείθεσθε ("Who has hindered you? Obey no one in not obeying the truth"); cf. G. Stählin, *TDNT* III: 856, n. 6. Schlier 236, n. 3 considers it improbable that Paul would have written in such an over-subtle way. Bruce 234 thinks that the addition of the last two words "may have been due to a desire to make πεισμονή ["persuasion"] (v. 8) more immediately relevant to the preceding construction."

87. Cf. Schlier 236. This seems preferable to taking "truth" here to mean "true teaching or faith," "authoritative teaching" (Bultmann, *TDNT* I: 244).

88. Behind these, of course, ultimately stands Satan himself, who is the antithesis of "God who is calling you" (v. 8): G. Stählin, *TDNT* III: 856f. Betz 264 with n. 107 identifies "who" directly with Satan.

89. So, e.g., BDF §488.1b; R. Bultmann, *TDNT* VI: 9.

90. Cf., e.g., BAGD s.v. πεισμονή; Robertson, *Word Pictures*, 4: 310; Schlier 236. There may also be a wordplay with "obey" (πείθεσθαι) in v. 7: "The result of this persuasion [πεισμονή] which did not come from God would thus be that the Galatians would no longer allow themselves to be persuaded [πείθεσθαι] by the truth" (O. Becker, *NIDNTT* I: 592f.).

91. Cf. K. L. Schmidt, *TDNT* III: 488f., 492.

92. Gk. καλοῦντος (present participle) here, over against καλέσαντος (aorist participle) in 1:6.

93. BAGD s.v. ζύμη 1; cf. NIV.

in the Christian church with the parable of the leaven [Mt. 13:33; Lk. 13:21],"[94] but a direct relation is not apparent. In any event, the saying "goes rather beyond the thought and usage of the Jewish festival [of Unleavened Bread]. It is a generally valid saying, an illustration of the truth of experience that little causes can have great effects."[95]

It is difficult to say whether "leaven" refers to the false teachers or to their teaching;[96] possibly in favor of the latter is the use of "leaven" for the hypocrisy of the Pharisees (Lk. 12:1) and the teaching of the Pharisees and Sadducees (Mt. 16:6, 11f.).[97] Moreover, the emphasis in v. 8 is clearly not so much on the individual as on his "persuasion."[98] However, the unity of teaching and person can be recognized and the situation adequately explained if we say: "The *doctrine* of the necessity of circumcision, insidiously presented by *a few*, is permeating and threatening to pervert the whole religious life of the Galatian churches."[99]

10 In spite of the Judaizers' efforts, however, Paul expresses his personal confidence concerning his converts[100] that they would "adopt no other view" (NASB). The Greek verb underlying this phrase denotes a person's " 'attitude' in which thinking and willing [leading to corresponding action] are one."[101] The standard of comparison is presumably the opinion just expressed by Paul (cf. RSV, "no other view than mine") that the Judaizers' teaching was an evil influence originating not from God and threatening the safety of the Galatian churches.[102] The implication is that the readers were as a result to obey no other gospel than that of Paul (cf. 1:6f.) and to continue in their original attitude toward that gospel (5:7).[103] This expression of confidence has been regarded as originating from "a generous and politic charity which 'believeth all things.' "[104] Paul himself refers to "the Lord," that is, Christ, as the basis or ground of his confidence,[105] and,

94. G. T. D. Angel, *NIDNTT* II: 462.

95. H. Windisch, *TDNT* II: 905. Cf. O. Michel, *TDNT* IV: 655.

96. Cf., e.g., Ellicott 107; Lightfoot 206; and Schlier 237; G. T. D. Angel, *NIDNTT* II: 463, respectively.

97. In Mk. 8:15 the warning against the leaven of the Pharisees and of Herod (or Herodians) is issued without explanation, but there also the leaven in question is probably their teaching and attitude. Cf. BAGD s.v. ζύμη 1; Cranfield, *Mark*, 261.

98. Cf. H. Windisch, *TDNT* II: 903f.

99. Burton 283 (emphasis added).

100. Gk. εἰς ὑμᾶς, RV "to you-ward."

101. Cf. Bultmann, *Theology*, 1: 214. The verb is φρονέω.

102. So Burton 284; cf. Duncan 158.

103. In this way the various answers suggested for the question "Other than what?" may be combined: Paul's gospel in general (Schlier 237), the Galatians' original attitude (Lightfoot 206), what Paul has just said. These three are directly combined by Cole 148.

104. Lightfoot 31.

105. Cf., e.g., Schlier 238; R. Bultmann, *TDNT* VI: 6. NEB "united with you"

although 4:10f. suggests that "the Galatians may already have taken another view,"[106] Paul's hope is that what he says in this letter may cause them to change their minds again (cf. 4:20 and comment ad loc.).

Paul further warns that the one[107] responsible for throwing the churches into confusion concerning the way of salvation would have to bear God's judgment.[108] The additional phrase, "whoever he may be," is perhaps not so much a reflection of Paul's ignorance of the person's identity as an allusion to this person's possible high standing in the church.[109]

11 The mention of the disturber of the churches (v. 10, cf. NASB) leads Paul to allude to a charge which had been levelled against him, namely, that he himself still preached circumcision.[110] He speaks with an upsurge of emotion which is reflected in the very structure of the sentence.[111] The following points may be noted in connection with this verse.

(a) One view of the first "still" *(eti)* holds that it conveys an implied contrast with the period before the coming of Christ, meaning, "even now, after the coming of Christ."[112] But such a reference here has been judged to be pointless,[113] and it does seem more natural to understand any and all contrasted periods of time implied by *eti* as applying to Paul himself. *Eti* has also been taken to imply that Paul had preached circumcision even as a Christian, presumably in the earlier days of his apostolic ministry.[114] This view is rightly rejected because of the lack of evidence that Paul ever advocated circumcision after he became a Christian.[115] Moreover, "an admission that he had ever preached circumcision to Gentiles would entirely

---

is a paraphrastic addition. The wordplay between πέποιθα ("I am confident"), πεισμονή ("persuasion," v. 8) and πείθεσθαι ("following," v. 7) can hardly be reproduced satisfactorily in English; for an attempt see Pinnock 70.

106. Betz 267.

107. The singular here is generic; cf. the plural "agitators" in v. 12 below and "persons" in 1:7.

108. On κρίμα as "penal judgment" cf. F. Büchsel, *TDNT* III: 942 with n. 5.

109. So Cole 148; cf. Ridderbos 193. Barrett 68 thinks that the reference is either to the ringleader of the group of invaders or to a more remote figure behind them—"James, from whom had come those who caused such disturbance in the church of Antioch" (cf. Barrett 98-102 on the latter possibility).

110. Cf. J. Knox, *IDB* II: 339b.

111. "The condition is expressed not as 'unreal' but as 'suppose I still preach circumcision,' and for the apodosis a rhetorical question is substituted" (Zerwick §311). Borgen, "Paul Preaches," 37 stresses "the grammatical form of a real case" as reflecting the opponents' accusation (cf. 44, n. 3).

112. Ridderbos 193f.

113. Ellicott 108.

114. E. Meyer, as cited in Schlier 238, n. 4. Bosworth, "Influence," 293ff. takes a similar view, but without reference to Gal. 5:11.

115. So, rightly, e.g., Ellicott 108; Cole 150; Bring 241.

destroy the case he presented in the earlier chapters of the epistle."[116] A third suggestion is that *eti* should probably be taken "in a weak sense as 'at the present moment,' with no sense of contrast with a past period."[117] But the simplest and most natural explanation is that *eti* contrasts Paul's present practice as an apostle with his former activity as a Jew.[118]

(b) The question of the life-setting of Paul's statement here is inseparably bound up with that of the agitators' identity (see section II of the Introduction, above) and has similarly given rise to various answers.[119] In

116. O'Neill 64. From this correct observation, however, O'Neill argues that "the text with ἔτι can hardly be right"; as Whiteley observes, "It is obvious why it should be left out if original, but there is no good reason why it should be included if it was not" (*Theology*, 74).

117. Cole 150.

118. So, e.g., Lightfoot 207; Burton 286; Ropes 13. Whether ἔτι in this sense provides evidence of Paul's pre-conversion activity as a Jewish missionary to the Gentiles is a question which has already been discussed: see Additional Comment 3 above (pp. 71f.).

119. For example: (i) Ropes 39f. takes Paul to be replying to a group of Gentile libertines in whose eyes Paul had not sufficiently unshackled himself from his Jewish past. But "we know nothing about such a radical antinomianism in Galatia, and it would certainly not be brought into the discussion in such an unexpected and indirect a [sic] way" (Ridderbos 193, n. 23).

(ii) J. Knox, *IDB* II: 340 takes Paul to be addressing a second group of Judaizers who—unlike those who understood Paul's position correctly at the vital point of freedom from law and circumcision and thus recognized him as an enemy—denied that he took such a radical position (in this they misunderstood him) and claimed him as their ally. But, like (i) this theory must *suppose* the presence of a second group; v. 12 evidently refers to the first group (in Knox's distinction) and there is nothing in the text to indicate that in v. 11 Paul has a different group in view.

(iii) As Munck sees it, Paul's defense is directed against those (Judaizing Gentile Christians) who were accusing him of removing circumcision from the message originally entrusted to him in Jerusalem to make it easier for Gentile converts; in doing so, the agitators were in effect claiming Paul's authority in support of circumcision (*Paul*, 90f.). But, as indicated earlier, there is no evidence that the Pauline gospel ever included circumcision.

(iv) According to P. Borgen, Paul is replying to Judaizers who claimed that he continued to preach and practice circumcision after he received his call in order to please people (1:10), that is, in order to be accepted by the Jewish community ("Paul Preaches," 41f.). At the decisive point of the meaning of "advocating circumcision," however, Borgen's reasoning appears to be problematic. On the one hand, he clearly states: "When Paul preached that the heathen Galatians should depart from the desires of the flesh . . . , then his opponents claimed that this was *the ethical meaning of circumcision*. Paul still preached circumcision, and *their* task was to persuade the Galatians to make bodily circumcision follow upon their ethical circumcision" (41, emphasis added; cf. 38f.). On the other hand, Borgen paraphrases the verse as follows: "If in his preaching against the pagan vices of desire and the passions he had preached *bodily circumcision*, then the stumbling-block of the cross ceases to exist" (40, emphasis added). Thus in the phrase "advocating circumcision" the noun is taken one moment (from the Judaizers' point of

our view the situation is best construed in terms of a charge of inconsistency on the part of Paul with regard to circumcision.[120] This charge was occasioned presumably by his policy of being a Jew to the Jews (1 Cor. 9:20) and of not discountenancing the practice of circumcision among Jewish Christians, by any earlier precedent there may have been for the circumcision of Timothy (Acts 16:3),[121] and by his opponents' failure to grasp the fundamental distinction between the voluntary undertaking of an act and the performance of the same act as a matter of religious obligation.[122]

(c) In the event of his preaching circumcision, says Paul, the "offense" (AV, NIV) or "stumbling-block" (also RV, RSV, NASB) of the cross has been removed or abolished.[123] The genitive "of the cross" may be taken as subjective genitive or genitive of origin,[124] but in view of 1 Cor. 1:23, where Christ crucified is called the stumbling-block of the Jews, it may be preferable to regard it as a genitive of definition, so that the whole phrase stands for a single concept and refers to the cross (or the preaching of the cross) as itself the stumbling-block (as in NEB).[125] In either case Paul's meaning is clear: the preaching of the cross provokes offense, or the cross itself is a stumbling-block, not merely because (as in 1 Cor. 1:23) a crucified Messiah was an object of aversion and a contradiction in terms, but rather because it stands for the way of salvation by grace through faith in the

---

view) as ethical circumcision and the next moment (from Paul's perspective) as bodily circumcision. Such a double entendre seems hardly likely in view of the unambiguously physical connotation of "circumcision" in the rest of the epistle (2:3; 5:2f.; 6:12f.).

120. Cf., e.g., Lake, *Earlier,* 306; Bruce 236f., 27.

121. If the composition of Galatians is placed after the Jerusalem Council, Gal. 5:11 can be explained by reference to Acts 16:3 (so, e.g., Filson, *NT History,* 228f.; Schlier 239). But in view of our preference for the pre-Council dating, we prefer to say, with Martin 100, that "Acts 16:3 may have had an earlier precedent."

122. Two objections have been raised against such a view: (i) there is nothing to suggest that Paul is at the moment referring to the charge of inconsistency, and (ii) such an alleged inconsistency can hardly be called a "preaching of circumcision" (Ridderbos 193, n. 23). But (i) is applicable, mutatis mutandis, to any proposed interpretation, and (ii) does not sufficiently allow for the possibility that the phrase may reflect the actual language used by the opponents themselves; moreover, as Ellicott 108 observes, the emphasis does not rest on the verb "I am . . . advocating" (literally "I am . . . preaching," NIV) but on the noun "circumcision," which in the Greek text is prominently placed between "if" and "I am still preaching" (εἰ περιτομὴν ἔτι κηρύσσω).

123. G. Delling, *TDNT* I: 454 gives κατήργηται here the sense "robbed of its effect" (cf. J. I. Packer, *NIDNTT* I: 73, "cancelled"); but the meaning he attributes to the word in 5:4 ("to take from the sphere of operation," cf. n. 13 above) seems applicable here as well (cf. BAGD s.v. καταργέω 2; Thayer s.v. 2: "cease, pass away") and indeed fits better with the understanding of τοῦ σταυροῦ ("the cross") as genitive of definition (see our comments on those words).

124. Cf. Phillips: "the hostility which the preaching of the cross provokes."

125. Cf. Schlier 239.

atoning death of the crucified One, apart from circumcision and the law, over against the way of salvation by legal works.[126]

Since the cross proclaims the way of righteousness through the death of Christ (cf. 2:21; 3:21), it inevitably constitutes a stumbling-block to those who would be justified through the law. This is because justification through legal works would enable one to speak of a "righteousness of my own," whereas the preaching of the cross offers only "the righteousness which comes from faith in Christ, given by God in response to faith" (Phil. 3:9)— thus robbing one of the possibility of making even so small a contribution as the acceptance of circumcision.[127] Paul implies that if he would preach circumcision, the offense of the cross would be removed and he would not be suffering persecution; the correctness of this assumption is borne out by the fact that the agitators' own zeal in advocating circumcision was motivated in part by a desire to avoid persecution (6:12).

12 With a touch of sarcasm the apostle expresses the wish that the "agitators"[128] would turn the knife upon themselves in self-emasculation.[129] This wished-for action has, however, been understood of the agitators' "cutting themselves off" from communion with Paul's converts,[130] but the more widely accepted meaning of the word, reflected by NEB and NIV,[131] is probably correct, since (a) "the overwhelming force of his [Paul's] argument is lost if we weaken the sense of this dramatic term to *segregari*";[132] (b) *kai*,[133] pointing as it does to a climax, compared with what precedes, implies a contrast between "receiving circumcision" (cf. vv. 2-6, 11) and the action envisaged here;[134] and (c) in Phil. 3:2 literal circumcision is similarly demoted to the status of mere mutilation.[135]

---

126. So, e.g., Burton 287; G. Delling, *TDNT* I: 454; G. Stählin, *TDNT* VII: 354.

127. Cf. Ridderbos, *Paul*, 142; Bruce 238.

128. So also NIV. Bruce 238 observes that the participle here, ἀναστατοῦντες, used of subversive activities in Acts 17:6; 21:38, is a stronger word than that used in 1:7, ταράσσοντες ("trouble," RSV).

129. Cf. NIV "emasculate themselves." The renderings of NEB and NIV correctly bring out "the causative and permissive sense" of the middle voice of the Greek verb ἀποκόψονται (Zerwick §232). Zerwick §355 also notes that the optative expressing a wish is here replaced by "a future for a desire possible of attainment but not seriously entertained"; cf. Ridderbos 195, n. 27; Betz 270. Cf. also p. 203, n. 48 above.

130. Ellicott 110; Barrett 70 says that he is "not quite sure that AV's rendering, 'cut themselves off,' [sic] is wrong." Cf. RV, Phillips, AV, the latter which understands the verb as passive.

131. Cf. RV, NASB "mutilate themselves"; Schlier 240; Betz 270.

132. G. Stählin, *TDNT* III: 854.

133. Rendered "even" in AV, RV, NASB and paraphrased as "go the whole way" in NEB, NIV.

134. G. Stählin, loc. cit.

135. Gk. κατατομή; cf. H. Köster, *TDNT* VIII: 110f.

More than one commentator has seen a tacit reference here to the sacral castration practiced by the priests of Cybele.[136] Inasmuch as the center of this cult was Pessinus in North Galatia, such an allusion would fit in better with the North Galatian theory than the South Galatian theory (which is preferred in this commentary); but the assumption itself of such an allusion is probably gratuitous.[137]

It has also been suggested that Paul is influenced here by the recollection of a saying of Jesus to the effect that mutilation is better than causing offense (cf. Mt. 5:30; 18:8). In this case Paul is implying that "the mutilation itself would be preferable to circumcision which made faith and true righteousness void by substituting righteousness by the law."[138]

It is more likely, however, that the thought here is that of self-excommunication which the verb carries in the light of Dt. 23:1 (LXX 23:2), which forbids any emasculated person to enter the assembly of the Lord: by desiring self-emasculation for the agitators Paul is wishing that they would shut themselves out of, and cease to trouble, the company of God's people.[139] In this case, "The whole expression is most significant as showing that to Paul circumcision had become not only a purely physical act without religious significance [cf. v. 6], but a positive mutilation, like that which carried with it exclusion from the congregation of the Lord"[140]—even though, we might add, Paul still recognized circumcision as a valid expression of piety in the case of Jews and Jewish Christians.

In these verses (5:7-12), then, Paul holds up the way of the cross (and therefore of faith) as the divinely-appointed means of righteousness, while he condemns in no uncertain language the way of circumcision (and therefore of works) and its advocates as being of evil origin and harmful effect.

136. E.g., Lightfoot 207; Rendall 185; Schlier 240; Ridderbos 195.
137. Cf. Bruce 238.
138. Bring 243. Cf. Duncan 161, who refers to Mk. 9:42ff.
139. Cf. G. Stählin, *TDNT* III: 855. It should be obvious that in accepting this view we are not reverting to the first meaning of the verb ἀποκόψονται mentioned above. If there is any inclination to doubt, in view of Rom. 9:3, that Paul would ever entertain such a severe wish, the following points should be kept in mind: (a) The language already employed in Gal. 1:8f. is, if anything, even stronger than what appears here. (b) "The apostle was not fastidious in his choice of linguistic media, and . . . at a time like this·the strongest expression in current speech seemed to be the best adapted to his purpose." (c) "Paul's cry is one of biting scorn and is obviously not meant to be taken literally [cf. n. 129 above]. What he is saying is simply that they ought to carry their error to its logical extreme and thereby make evident something which is indubitably clear to him, namely, that they do not belong to the community of God" (G. Stählin, *TDNT* III: 854f.).
140. Burton 289.

IV. GUIDANCE ON PRACTICAL CHRISTIAN LIVING (5:13–6:10)

Beginning with 5:13 Paul gives direct teaching and exhortations regarding the practical Christian life. That he should do this after the doctrinal exposition of the previous section (III) is in keeping with his procedure in some of his other letters (cf., e.g., Rom. 12:1ff.; Eph. 4:1ff.; Phil. 4:1ff.) and points to an important truth: doctrine is the foundation on which the Christian life is to be lived and life is the sphere in which doctrinal truths are to be applied.

A general description of life in the Spirit (5:13-26) is followed by several more specific principles (6:1-10).[1] It has been conjectured that Paul is combating here a party of libertines who considered him to be insufficiently emancipated, but the evidence is insufficient to establish the existence of such a party in Galatia.[2] More likely he is taking issue with the false position that freedom from the law issues in moral license—a conclusion either mistakenly drawn by his own converts or, more probably (cf. on 2:17, 21; 5:6), wrongly considered by his opponents to be the consequence of his preaching.[3] In any event Paul corrects the erroneous conclusion by holding up the Christian life as a life lived under the guidance of the Holy Spirit.

A. LIFE IN THE SPIRIT (5:13-26)

1. LIBERTY, NOT LICENSE (5:13-15)

13 *You, my friends, were called to be free men; only do not turn your freedom into licence for your lower nature, but be servants to one another in love.* 14 *For the whole law can be summed up in a single commandment: "Love your neighbor as yourself."* 15 *But if you go on fighting one another, tooth and nail, all you can expect is mutual destruction.*

1. O'Neill 65-71 (cf. 86) would omit 5:13–6:10 as an editorial addition—on wholly inadequate grounds in our opinion.
2. Cf. above, Introduction, section II; p. 239, n. 119 (point [i] on J. H. Ropes); Cole 152f.
3. Cf. J. Knox, *IDB* II: 340a; Kümmel, *Introduction*, 301.

13 Addressing them by the emphatic personal pronoun "you,"[1] Paul forcefully distinguishes his Galatian converts from the agitators (v. 12): those were advocates of circumcision and hence representatives of legal bondage, whereas "you were called to freedom" (RSV, NASB).[2] This verse shows that the believer's freedom is based on God's call, which is mediated through the gospel (cf. 1:6); according to 5:1 it is based on the redemptive work of Christ. It is thus seen that "in the call of the Gospel men are called to the act of Jesus Christ as the basis of a new life of freedom."[3]

But freedom from the law, far from being lawlessness, brings its own obligation with it: the proper use of freedom. (a) Negatively expressed, this means that believers are not to turn their freedom "into an opportunity for the flesh" (NASB).[4] "Flesh" denotes not merely the bodily passions and lusts, nor even strictly speaking a "lower nature" contrasted with a "higher nature" in a person, but rather the human individual in his or her sin and depravity apart from the redeeming grace of God and the sanctifying work of the Spirit.[5] Thus this "sinful nature" (NIV) embraces "the desires of body and mind" (Eph. 2:3, RSV) and produces the "works of the flesh" which Paul is to list in vv. 19-21. The word rendered "opportunity" or "occasion" (NASB; AV, RV) is used in the military sense of a base of operations (cf. its use in Rom. 7:8, 11); here the imagery suggested is of the "flesh" occupying the position of the malicious opponent and using "freedom" as a springboard for its activities.[6] In other words, the warning is against using "freedom" as a pretext for indulging the sinful nature.

(b) Positively stated, the proper use of freedom is for believers to be servants of one another through love. Paul does not speak here of love primarily as the motivation or manner of their mutual service (as with NEB and NIV "in love"), but of love as the means by which they are to serve one

---

1. Gk. ὑμεῖς. NEB, like NIV, rightly passes over in its translation the word γάρ ("for," cf. AV, etc.), which here seems to have simply continuative force equivalent to that of δέ (Zerwick §473). Cf. Betz 272, who takes γάρ to "indicate another step in the argument."

2. Literally "for freedom." Ἐπί with dative (cf. Eph. 2:10; 1 Thess. 4:7) indicates that freedom is the purpose for which believers have been called (cf. Zerwick §129; Moule 50; BDF §235.4; Robertson, *Word Pictures*, 4: 311).

3. H. Schlier, *TDNT* II: 499.

4. There is no verb in the Greek and the ellipsis is filled in different ways: "offer to" (Bultmann, *Theology*, 1: 244), τρέπετε or στρέφετε ("turn": Robertson, *Word Pictures*, 4: 311), ἔχετε ("hold": BDF §481), λαμβάνετε ("take") or ἔχετε (Bruce 240).

5. Cf. H. Seebass, *NIDNTT* I: 675f.; Ridderbos, *Paul*, 94; Ladd, *Theology*, 472f. Barrett 71f. rightly criticizes NEB's "our lower nature" as "a most unfortunate rendering, not least because it implies that we have a higher nature which if left to itself would be intrinsically good; Paul knows no such higher nature."

6. Cf. Cole 153; G. Bertram, *TDNT* V: 473 (s.v. ἀφορμή).

another (AV "by love"; RV, RSV, NASB "through love"), just as v. 6 says that faith expresses itself through love.[7] "Love" here is undoubtedly love between Christians; if believers' love for God is meant at all, it is so only as the foundation and source of their love for one another.[8]

Since the context emphasizes freedom, the strong statement "be servants" (literally "serve as slaves") raises the question why Paul intentionally describes the believers' mutual love as a form of slavery. It has been suggested that "it is the necessity of commitment and the difficulties of maintaining human relationships that cause Paul to describe the free exercise of love as a form of mutual enslavement."[9] On the other hand, Paul was perhaps influenced by the example of Jesus' love, in which, on the eve of his passion, the Master demonstrated his love for his disciples by the lowly service of washing their feet (Jn. 13:2, 5, 12).

In any event, by this striking connection between freedom and slavery Paul effectively underlines the fact that however free believers may be, they are not their own; the goal of their freedom is mutual service through love.[10] By this paradoxical mode of expression, the nature of true Christian freedom is presented not "in the Greek sense of man being the master of all his decisions,"[11] but in terms of the human capacity for serving others through love. The parallelism with v. 1 is worth observing. "In each case it is the summing up of a position already established, which becomes in turn the text for a practical appeal": as those whom Christ has set free with the freedom of the gospel, the readers must not lapse back into the slavery of legal bondage (v. 1); neither should they abuse this freedom, but "should realize the true nature and implications of Christian freedom."[12]

14 Paul goes on to give the reason (note "for," omitted by NIV) that mutual service through love is important enough to be set forth (in v. 13) as the goal of the believers' freedom. "The whole law" translates a construction which contrasts the whole or the totality with the part and thus means: "the law considered as a unit," "the law taken as a whole," or "the spirit and intention of the law."[13] NEB, like NIV, understands the verb

---

7. The article with "love" (διὰ τῆς ἀγάπης) may be anaphoric, referring back to the love mentioned in v. 6, where it is anarthrous (δι᾽ ἀγάπης). For an interesting alternation of the use and non-use of the article with the word "love" cf. 1 Cor. 13:1-3, 13a (anarthrous) and vv. 4, 8, 13b (articular).

8. Cf. Ridderbos, *Paul*, 294, 299.

9. Betz 274.

10. Cf. Duncan 163; E. Stauffer, *TDNT* I: 50; K. H. Rengstorf, *TDNT* II: 278.

11. So, correctly, J. Blunck, *NIDNTT* I: 719f.

12. Duncan 162.

13. Cf. MHT 3: 201; BDF §275.7; Zerwick §188; B. Reicke, *TDNT* V: 887; Ridderbos 201, n. 3; Bruce 141. The Greek construction is ὁ πᾶς νόμος, with the adjective in the attributive position. Had it been πᾶς ὁ νόμος, with the adjective in the

plēroō in the sense of to "sum up."[14] But the rendering "is fulfilled" (AV, RV, RSV, NASB) is to be preferred, since it is favored by (a) the context, which emphasizes practice of the law of love (v. 13; 6:1f.); (b) the evidence of Rom. 13:8 (cf. 8:4), where the verb undoubtedly means "to fulfil"; and (c) the distinction which Paul makes in Rom. 13:8f. in his use of both *plēroō* in the sense of "fulfill" and another verb in the sense of "sum up."[15]

The "single commandment"[16] quoted here is Lev. 19:18b; the primary meaning is not that we must properly love ourselves before we can love others (although this is true in itself), but that we are to love our neighbor with the same spontaneity and alacrity with which we love ourselves.[17] As for the question "And who is my neighbour" (Lk. 10:29) a definitive answer has been given by Jesus in the parable of the good Samaritan and in the Sermon on the Mount: "my neighbour" refers not merely to my compatriot or personal friend, but to anyone who may cross the path of my life (Lk. 10:30-36), including my enemy (Mt. 5:43f.). The good Samaritan would suggest to us that we are not to determine our attitude toward a person by first deciding whether he qualifies as a "neighbor" according to our definition of the term, but to endeavor to become (and be) to everyone whom we encounter (particularly if the person is in need) a neighbor—one who shows him kindness (Lk. 10:37).[18] In the context, however, Paul probably has the fellow-Christian in view.

Just as Jesus (in Mt. 22:40) holds up the two commandments of love for God and love for neighbor as that on which the law and the prophets depend,[19] so Paul here condenses the requirements of the law as a whole, particularly its moral requirements, and more specifically the ten commandments,[20] into the single commandment of love—"'One word,' not 'Ten

---

predicative position (cf. AV "all the law") the meaning would have been "the entire law (without exception of any precept)" (Zerwick §188); cf. v. 3 ὅλον τὸν νόμον, "the entire law," that is, the sum total of its precepts.

14. BAGD s.v. 3 also considers that this clause "because of its past tense is probably to be translated *the whole law has found its full expression in a single word*"; but the perfect passive πεπλήρωται here, like the perfect active πεπλήρωκεν ("has satisfied") of Rom. 13:8, is probably to be taken as a gnomic perfect expressing a general maxim (cf. Burton 295).

15. The second verb (Rom. 13:9) is Gk. ἀνακεφαλαιόω. Cf. Burton 294-296; G. Delling, *TDNT* VI: 293 with n. 40; R. Schippers, *NIDNTT* I: 738. In view of the above reasons the suggestion that Paul is "punning upon two of the meanings" of the Greek word (Cole 156) appears unlikely.

16. Literally "one word," λόγος being used in the sense of "commandment"; on this see Bruce 241.

17. Cf. Ridderbos 201f.; Cranfield, *Romans,* 677.

18. Cf. H. Greeven, *TDNT* VI: 316f.; U. Falkenroth, *NIDNTT* I: 258f.

19. On this as the meaning of κρεμάννυμι cf. G. Bertram, *TDNT* III: 920.

20. Cf. Ridderbos, *Paul,* 106.

words'; a *monologos* rather than a *dekalogos*."[21] Between Jesus' "two commandments" and Paul's "single commandment" there is no real discrepancy: for as far as moral conduct in human relationships is concerned, God's law is summed up in the one rule, "Love your neighbour as yourself" (Rom. 13:9),[22] and is satisfied by the observance of that rule. Moreover, love for one's neighbor can only spring from a prior relationship of love between the believer and God in Jesus Christ and is the concrete expression of love for God; hence, "there is here a double commandment, but no double love."[23]

Paul has repeatedly stated that believers are free from the law (cf. 4:31; 5:13) and has repeatedly appealed to the Galatians to preserve and enjoy this liberty and not to allow themselves to relapse into legal servitude (4:9-11; 5:1). Now, however, they are exhorted to serve one another through love, for by doing so they will satisfy the requirements of the law. This paradox may be explained by the following considerations: (a) Through the redemption of Christ believers have been set free from bondage to the law and are no longer under obligation to obey its statutes; (b) God's law remains a valid expression of his will, which requires that we love our neighbor as ourselves; (c) hence, what the law as a whole requires is satisfied when believers serve one another through love.[24] In other words, the believer who is free from the law is at the same time one who fulfills the law; only the way he fulfills the law is not by punctiliously observing the rules and regulations of an external code, but by the new way of love,[25] which is generated within the believer by the power of the Holy Spirit (see above on 5:6b).[26]

15 It is impossible to be certain of the exact situation to which these words were addressed, though a common view is that the agitators' teaching had somehow occasioned disputes and controversy in the Galatian church or had at least added fuel to the fire.[27] Quarrelsomeness and the like seem to

---

21. Manson, *Studies*, 189.

22. Cf. Dodd, "Ἔννομος Χριστοῦ," 101, n. 1; Ridderbos, *Paul*, 136f., 273.

23. Ridderbos, *Paul*, 299.

24. Cf. Burton 294; Wuest 151f.

25. Cf., e.g., Machen 211f.; G. Bertram, *TDNT* III: 921; R. Bultmann, *TDNT* VI: 220; *Theology*, 1: 262; Küng, *Justification*, 300; Betz 275; Bruce 243. Kertelge, "Gesetz," 390 (my translation) suggests that "only in the fulfillment of the love-commandment does the Christian preserve the freedom gained in Christ."

26. Barclay's emphasis on the role of the Spirit in enabling the believer to "fulfil the just requirement of the law" (cf. Rom. 8:4) *without* reference to the commands or law of God is well placed ("Paul and the Law," 12f., points [i] and [iii]).

27. So, e.g., Burton 297; Duncan 164; Neill 78; Hays, "Christology," 289; cf. Wedderburn, "Review," 384; Garnet, "Qumran," 24. A possible objection to this view is that it is difficult to conceive of Paul condemning disputes and controversy *related to the Galatian heresy* as "fighting one another" since in this very letter (especially chs. 3 and 4; cf. 1:8f.) he is himself engaging in theological debate with the Judaizers.

have been the particular "works of the flesh" to which the Galatians were especially prone (cf. vv. 20f., 26).[28] Whatever its cause, such conduct—as of a pack of wild animals "biting and devouring" one another (NIV)—is the opposite of "serving one another through love" and can only lead to the disastrous end of mutual annihilatio

2. THE SPIRIT THE OVERCOMER (5:16-18)

16 *I mean this: if you are guided by the Spirit you will not fulfil the desires of your lower nature.* 17 *That nature sets its desires against the Spirit, while the Spirit fights against it. They are in conflict with one another so that what you will to do you cannot do.* 18 *But if you are led by the Spirit, you are not under law.*

16 The gist of vv. 13-15—that believers have been called for freedom, not in order that they may indulge their sinful nature, but that they should serve one another through love—is further explained ("I mean this") as Paul reveals the secret of successful Christian living. The course to be followed is indicated by the imperative, "walk by the Spirit" (RV, RSV, NASB),[29] where "by the Spirit" is (in Greek) given emphasis by its position before the verb. "Walking" is a common Hebraism for "conducting one's life"[30] and thus is synonymous with "living." If the verb is taken as imperative here, the promise in the latter half of the verse (where "the desires of the flesh" is also emphatic by virtue of its position before the verb) will then be regarded as the inevitable result of life lived by the Spirit.[31]

That the guidance of the Spirit can be experienced as a reality in the life of the believer is a sign that Jeremiah's prophetic word about the new covenant has been fulfilled. In OT times the Israelites knew God's law as an external code, but in the NT dispensation the law of God is set in his people's understanding and written on their hearts (Jer. 31:31-34; Heb. 8:8-12);

28. So Bruce 250, 257; cf. 25, 240, 242.

29. NEB "if" substitutes hypotaxis for parataxis. Barrett 74 is correct in saying "The Spirit is referred to here [vv. 16ff.] because it is the second necessary counterpart to flesh. Love [vv. 13f.] is its ethical counterpart, Spirit is its theological counterpart." In Barrett's view, however, πνεῦμα ("Spirit") in Paul is not yet explicitly the third person of the Trinity, but means "the non-human centre of human life," i.e., "the divine centre available to reconstruct human life as the basis and for the practice of love" (74f.), or " the power of Christ operative and central in the life of man" (76).

30. Cf., e.g., Rom. 8:4; 1 Cor. 7:17; 2 Cor. 5:7; Eph. 4:1; Phil. 3:17; Col. 4:5; 1 Thess. 4:1; 2 Thess. 3:11.

31. RSV "do not gratify the desires of the flesh" mistakenly turns a promise into a second imperative: the construction (οὐ μή with aorist subjunctive) expresses a strong assurance (Burton 299).

God's will is now an inward principle, the result of the leading of the Spirit within the believer. To "walk by the Spirit" means to be under the constant, moment-by-moment direction, control, and guidance of the Spirit.[32] By living in this way believers can be sure that they will not "carry out" (NASB)[33] the desires of their sinful nature.

17 What was implied in the previous verse is now made explicit: the flesh and the Spirit are diametrically opposed to each other. It is this opposition which explains why walking by the Spirit will inevitably result in the desires of the flesh not being carried out. It has been suggested that "'spirit' and 'flesh' in this context are probably the constituent parts of every man," so that *pneuma* refers to the human spirit, not the Spirit of God.[34] But this is highly unlikely in view of the Spirit-flesh contrast Paul develops elsewhere (cf. Rom. 8:4-6, 9, 13), particularly in Gal. 3:3, and in view of the clear reference to the divine Spirit in both the preceding and the following verses (5:16, 18, 22, 25).

The verb "sets its desires" (NASB; more simply "desires," NIV; cf. AV, RV "lusteth") is not repeated in the elliptical second clause, which has only "and the Spirit against the flesh" (AV, RV, NASB). NEB's use of a different verb ("fights") in that clause follows J. B. Lightfoot, who wrote, "as *epithymein* cannot apply to the Spirit, some other verb must be supplied in the second clause," and suggested "strives, fights."[35] However, "the very fact that Spirit as well as Flesh can have 'desires' . . . by itself indicates that the original meaning of 'desire' is simply the direction in which one yearns"; the verb is used in a good sense in Phil. 1:23; 1 Thess. 2:17.[36] By presenting the flesh as lusting against the Spirit as much as the Spirit desires against the flesh, Paul gives the flesh an autonomy which properly belongs to it as that which stands for mankind in sin apart from the grace of God and the power of the Spirit (cf. above on v. 13).

That the flesh and the Spirit are "in conflict with one another" is clear—"the antithesis is as complete in literary form as it is in actual fact."[37]

---

32. Ladd, *Theology*, 475. Present tense περιπατεῖτε denotes continuous action (MHT 3: 75).

33. Cf. G. Delling, *TDNT* VIII: 59 (s.v. τελέω); Betz 278.

34. O'Neill 68; similarly Windisch, "Problem," 279.

35. Lightfoot 210.

36. Bultmann, *Theology*, 1: 224f. To speak of longing and desire in a good sense Paul also uses ἐπιποθέω (Rom. 1:11; 2 Cor. 5:2; 9:14), ἐπιπόθησις (2 Cor. 7:7, 11), and ἐπιποθία (Rom. 15:23): H. Schönweiss, *NIDNTT* I: 458.

37. Guthrie 135. Martyn, "Antinomies," 416 takes Paul's use of ἀντίκειται ("are in conflict") as a "technical term . . . , by which he defines the Spirit and the Flesh as a pair of opposites"—"what Aristotle might have called an instance of τἀναντία" (413): "the Spirit and the Flesh constitute an apocalyptic antinomy in the sense that they are two opposed orbs of power, actively at war with one another *since* the apocalyptic

But what is the meaning of the enigmatic last clause? If "so that" *(hina)* is taken in the final sense, then the purpose of both the flesh and the Spirit is in view: "Does the man choose evil, the Spirit opposes him; does he choose good, the flesh hinders him."[38] It is difficult, however, to regard these two opposing principles as both together realizing this purpose, or to regard as a purpose a state of continuous opposition.[39] It is preferable, therefore, to take *hina* as consecutive:[40] the result of this continuous opposition between the flesh and the Spirit is that "you do not do what you want" (NIV).

This clause has been interpreted in at least three different ways. (a) One view regards it "not as applying to both [of the preceding] clauses equally, but with definite reference to the restraint which the Spirit exercises on the flesh."[41] Such an interpretation is in harmony with the explicit promise of v. 16 as well as the general consideration that "the [Spirit-flesh] antithesis, as presented in the Pauline literature, signifies that the Holy Spirit is the antagonist and conqueror of the flesh as the seat of sin."[42] But it is open to the objection that it is logically inconsistent with the clause "they are in conflict with one another," which "seems rather to point to the *opposition* incurred than the victory gained by the Spirit."[43] Nor does it accord well with the adversative *de* ("but") at the beginning of v. 18, which suggests that decisive victory is achieved only when the Christian is actually led by the Spirit.

(b) A second interpretation takes "what you will to do" as "the promptings of the conscience," "moral strivings and yearnings," or "the purpose fixed by spiritual impulse, namely, the achievement of love (cf. v. 14f.)."[44] The picture, then, is of the believer's good desires being overcome by the desires of the flesh—a picture, in that case, which irresistibly recalls that of Rom. 7 (especially vv. 15, 19).[45] It is difficult, however, to avoid the conclusion that Gal. 5:17, taken in its context, refers to a different situation from that envisaged in Rom. 7:14-25: there Paul describes an unequal conflict between the subject's willing and doing, here it is a battle between flesh and Spirit which stands under the promise of victory; there the

---

advent of Christ and of his Spirit. The space in which human beings now live is a newly invaded space, and that means that its structures cannot remain unchanged."

38. Burton 302; cf. *Syntax*, §222. Cf. also E. Schweizer, *TDNT* VI: 429. Wenham ("Christian Life," 83 with 90f., n. 7), also, takes ἵνα as final, but "in a rather weak sense to refer to the tendency of the Spirit-flesh conflict."

39. So, rightly, Ridderbos 203, n. 9 and Guthrie 135f. respectively.

40. Cf., e.g., §BDF 391.5; Zerwick §352; Moule 142f.

41. Duncan 168; cf. Rendall 187; Mikolaski 1102.

42. A. B. Bruce, *Christianity*, 242.

43. Ellicott 115 (emphasis original).

44. Lightfoot 210, Cole 158, and G. Schrenk, *TDNT* III: 50 respectively.

45. Cf. Marshall, "Preparation," 9; Ridderbos 203f.; Hodge, *Romans*, 243.

subject is taken captive by the law of sin, here the believer, though threatened by the flesh, may prevail over it by walking according to the Spirit.[46] Thus our passage undoubtedly places the emphasis on the positive aspect of victory through obedience to the Spirit, and with this the second interpretation does not tally.

(c) A third view refers "you will" not specifically to the carnal will or the moral will, but to "the free-will in its ordinary acceptation."[47] The verse then means that in the Spirit-flesh conflict it is impossible for the believer to remain neutral: he either serves the flesh or follows the Spirit.[48] This interpretation seems best, since it is free from the difficulties involved in the other two and is consistent with the picture of opposition described in the preceding part of the verse.

18 This conditional sentence clearly shows that Paul does not regard the believer simply as a helpless spectator or an unwilling pawn in the fierce battle between the flesh and the Spirit; the assumption is rather that the Christian can overcome the flesh by siding with the Spirit.[49] Being "led by the Spirit" is in form passive; in its actual meaning, however, it is not entirely passive. The active leading of the Holy Spirit does not signify the believer's being, so to speak, led by the nose willy-nilly;[50] on the contrary, he must let himself be led by the Spirit—that is, actively choose to stand on the side of the Spirit over against the flesh.[51] Like "walking by the Spirit" (v. 16, cf. v. 25b), being led by the Spirit is a kind of "passive-active" action— actively obeying the prior leading of the Spirit (cf. Phil. 2:12f.). We can see from this that the work of the Spirit in the believer's life does not set the believer free from the warfare between flesh and Spirit.[52] "The Holy Spirit is not a perpetual motion machine which operates automatically in the life of the believer," but a Person whose working the Christian can respond

46. Cf. Bornkamm, *Experience,* 100f.; Ridderbos, *Paul,* 127, 270; Wenham, "Christian Life," 83; Toussaint, "Contrast," 310-313 (especially 312).

47. Ellicott 115; cf. Betz 279f., 280f.

48. Kümmel, *Römer 7,* 106.

49. Cf., e.g., Kümmel, *Römer 7.* The sentence is in the form of a simple or "real" condition: while the grammatical form itself does not indicate whether the condition is in fact fulfilled, yet "the fulfilment of the condition . . . is in a certain sense 'supposed' i.e. taken as a basis of argument" (Zerwick §305, cf. §§303f., 312).

50. Betz 281 seems to border on such a view when he says: "This experience of the Spirit is 'enthusiastic' in nature, and it is an experience of 'being carried away' (ἄγεσθαι). In the battle between the forces of flesh and Spirit . . . the Spirit takes the lead, overwhelms, and thus defeats evil." But it must be noted that Paul speaks of "being led" (ἄγεσθαι) and not of being "swept off" (ἀπάγεσθαι, 1 Cor. 12:2; AV "carried away," RV "led away").

51. Cf., e.g., Bultmann, *Theology,* 1: 326; "Christ the End," 62; H. Braun, *TDNT* VI: 481.

52. So, correctly, J. D. G. Dunn, *NIDNTT* III: 702.

to, depend on, and cooperate with. Therefore, the Christian faces the decision whether to follow the Spirit in this way or to give in to the flesh.[53]

Since in vv. 15-17 the conflict has been consistently spoken of in terms of the Spirit and the flesh, we might have expected Paul to say: "But if you are led by the Spirit, you are not under the flesh." Instead, he says "you are not under law." This transition from the Spirit-flesh conflict to the Spirit-law antithesis suggests two important and related truths.

(a) The law and the flesh are closely linked. According to Paul's exposition in Romans, the law, far from restraining the flesh, actually produces the opposite effect. On the one hand, the law provokes and increases sin (Rom. 7:5, 8), because the human sinful nature ("flesh") causes a person to be at cross-purposes with God's law; on the other hand, owing to the weakness of the flesh, which does not, and cannot, submit to God's law (8:3, 7), the more earnestly a person strives to keep God's law by his own efforts (= flesh), the more inextricably does he find himself in the grip of indwelling sin (7:14-25).[54] Thus the law and the flesh lead to identical results.[55] A comparison of Gal. 5:18 (where to be "under law" is contrasted with being led by the Spirit) with v. 16 (where walking by the Spirit is said to be the way to avoid carrying out the desires of the flesh) shows the implication to be plainly this: the desires of the flesh cannot be overcome by the Christian remaining under law.

(b) The renewed reference to the law (cf. v. 14) shows that Paul still has the old issue in mind: if the Judaizers upheld the law as the only safeguard against becoming slaves to the flesh, Paul asserts as an adequate safeguard the guidance of the Spirit, which to him constitutes "a third way of life," a highway distinct from, and superior to, both legalism and antinomianism.[56] These two truths may be combined by saying that to be under law is no way to overcome the desires of the flesh, and the real solution lies in being led by the Spirit.[57]

53. Wuest 154. Cf. Ladd, *Theology*, 518f.
54. For our understanding of this passage cf. Fung, "Impotence."
55. Cf. Lightfoot 209; Robertson, *Word Pictures*, 4: 312. Cf. also the opposing series of terms listed by E. Schweizer (*TDNT* VI: 431, n. 652) in which the flesh and the law stand on the same side as interpreting each other.
56. Burton 302. Cf. Guthrie 136; Betz 275f.; Wuest 139.
57. Cf. Bruce 240, 245f. Dodd observes: "The moral demand of letting Christ's Spirit rule you in everything is far more searching than the demand of any code, and at the same time it carries with it the promise of indefinite growth and development" (*Meaning*, 147). Cf. also n. 162 below.

If our exegesis of Gal. 5:16-18 is sound, this passage casts serious doubt on the correctness of Sanders's solution to the problem of Paul's apparently ambiguous attitude to the law. Sanders says that the question being addressed determines what Paul says about the law: his negative statements occur in contexts discussing how one gets "in," his positive statements in contexts discussing how one who is "in" behaves (e.g., *Paul, the*

3. THE WORKS OF THE FLESH (5:19-21)

19 *Anyone can see the kind of behaviour that belongs to the lower nature: fornication, impurity, and indecency;* 20 *idolatry and sorcery; quarrels, a contentious temper, envy, fits of rage, selfish ambitions, dissensions, party intrigues, and* 21 *jealousies; drinking bouts, orgies, and the like. I warn you, as I warned you before, that those who behave in such ways will never inherit the kingdom of God.*

To illustrate the state of opposition between the flesh and the Spirit, Paul provides representative lists of their respective activities. "The works of the flesh" (AV, RV, RSV; in Rom. 8:13 Paul refers such deeds to "the body") are concrete expressions of the flesh, that is, of fallen mankind itself, in actual living.[58] Paul's catalog of vices may not be based on any clear principles of organization. Indeed, in the opinion of H. D. Betz, "the seemingly chaotic arrangement of these terms is reflective of the chaotic nature of evil; this chaos is to be contrasted with the oneness of the 'fruit of the Spirit' and its orderly arrangement (v 22-23)."[59] Nevertheless, the fifteen items as they stand may be broadly classified into four groups, as suggested by the punctuation of NEB and NIV.[60] The table on the following page lists the various items as they are translated in six English versions and will make for easy reference as we go through the fifteen items seriatim.[61]

19 (i) In Paul's letters *porneia* is a general term for a variety of sexual irregularities (cf. NIV), including incest (1 Cor. 5:1) and sacral prostitution (1 Cor. 6:15-18).[62] In Paul's eyes, "Every other sin that a man can commit is outside the body; but the fornicator sins against his own body" (1 Cor. 6:18), meaning probably that such sins as gluttony and drunkenness (v. 10) affect only the temporary state of the body as a physical organism,

---

Law, 10, 114). Cf. Barclay, "Paul and the Law," 12: "surely the whole thrust of Paul's argument in Galatians is that Gentiles do not need to take on the yoke of the law *either* as a means of entry into God's people *or* as a pattern for their subsequent behaviour."

58. Cf. Wuest 157: ἔργα "is probably to be understood as active rather than passive, as referring to the deeds rather than to the products of the evil nature."

59. Betz 283.

60. Cf., e.g., Lightfoot 210; Burton 304.

61. The two items peculiar to the AV are not part of the original text and will be omitted from the following discussion. Φόνοι after item xiii appears to be a scribal addition prompted by recollection of Rom. 1:29 (Metzger 597f.). Chadwick, "Paul and Philo," 293 tells us that "Philo likes amassing lists of virtues and vices, and in one prodigious passage manages to piece together a catena of 144 Greek words describing vices." We may well feel relieved—and none more so than the commentator—that Paul saw fit to limit the number to fifteen in the present list.

62. There the term retains its primary sense of traffic with πόρναι, "harlots"; cf. Burton 305.

	Greek	AV	RV	RSV	NEB	NASB	NIV
(a) Sexual sins (i)	[moicheia] porneia	[adultery] fornication	= AV	= AV	= AV	immorality	sexual immorality
(ii)	akatharsia	uncleanness	= AV	impurity	= RSV	= RSV	= AV
(iii)	aselgeia	lasciviousness	= AV	licentiousness	indecency	sensuality	debauchery
(b) Religious deviations (iv)	eidōlolatria	idolatry	= AV	= AV	= AV	= AV	= AV
(v)	pharmakeia	witchcraft	sorcery	= RV	= RV	= RV	= AV
(c) Disorders in personal relationships (vi)	echthrai	hatred	enmities	enmity	quarrels	= RV	= AV
(vii)	eris	variance	strife	= RV	a contentious temper	= RV	discord
(viii)	zēlos	emulations	jealousies	jealousy	envy	= RSV	= RSV
(ix)	thymoi	wrath	wraths	anger	fits of rage	outbursts of anger	= NEB
(x)	eritheiai	strife	factions	selfishness	selfish ambitions	disputes	selfish ambition
(xi)	dichostasiai	seditions	divisions	dissension	dissensions	= NEB	= NEB
(xii)	haireseis	heresies	= AV	party spirit	party intrigues	factions	= NASB
(xiii)	phthonoi [phonoi]	envyings [murders]	= AV	envy	jealousies	= AV	= RSV
(d) Sins of intemperance (xiv)	methai	drunkenness	= AV	= AV	drinking bouts	= AV	= AV
(xv)	kōmoi	revellings	= AV	carousing	orgies	carousings	= NEB

but fornication (in this instance, union with a prostitute) establishes a relation that cannot be undone (v. 16) and is an offense against the whole person.[63] Hence the stern injunctions to "shun" or "abstain from" fornication (1 Cor. 6:18; 1 Thess. 4:3; cf. Eph. 5:3). At the same time, for all the severity with which he condemns this sin, Paul believes that it, like all other sins (except the sin against the Holy Spirit, Mt. 12:31; Mk. 3:28f.; Lk. 12:10), can be forgiven through the redemptive work of Christ (cf. 1 Cor. 6:9-11; 2 Cor. 12:21).[64]

(ii) *Akatharsia,* meaning basically "uncleanness" (AV), is used in the NT of ritual uncleanness (Mt. 23:27, a figurative use; cf. the adjective *akathartos* in Acts 10:14; 11:8) as well as of moral impurity (cf. RSV in the verse under discussion), which is the opposite of holiness (cf. 1 Thess. 4:7) and prevents fellowship with God. In the latter sense, the word appears here and elsewhere in conjunction with "fornication" (*porneia;* cf. 2 Cor. 12:21; Eph. 5:3, 5; Col. 3:5) and hence may refer specifically to impure conduct in sexual relations.[65]

(iii) *Aselgeia* appears to have a broad sense in Eph. 4:19, where the Gentiles are said to have "abandoned themselves to vice" (NEB), "greedy to practice every kind of uncleanness" (RSV). In Rom. 13:13 the word is paired with "debauchery" and thus takes on the special nuance of sexual excess. This may be the sense of the word here in Galatians as well (cf. the English versions), as well as in 2 Cor. 12:21 where the first three items in this list in Galatians also occur.[66] The sin of "indecency" (NEB) may represent an advance on "fornication" and "impurity," for it is "vice paraded with blatant impudence and insolence, without regard for self-respect, for the rights and feelings of others, or for public decency."[67] Here precisely is why *aselgeia* is such a terrible thing: "it is the act of a character which has lost that which ought to be its greatest defense—its self-respect, and its sense of shame."[68]

Paul also begins his catalogs of vices with sexual sins in Rom. 1:24; 1 Cor. 6:9; Eph. 5:3, 5; and Col. 3:5. Their prominence in these lists is due to their prevalence in current society: There is ample evidence to show that the sexual life of the Greco-Roman world at the time of the NT was sheer chaos. Such evidence has come not from Christian writers but from pagans

---

63. Cf., e.g., Whiteley, *Theology,* 214; Godet, *First Corinthians,* 1.312; Bruce, *Corinthians,* 65. For "body" in the sense of the whole person cf. H. Reisser, *NIDNTT* I: 500f.

64. Cf. F. Hauck and S. Schulz, *TDNT* VI: 594.

65. Cf. F. Hauck, *TDNT* III: 428f.; Burton 305. Cf. also Barclay, *Flesh,* 29f.

66. Cf. O. Bauernfeind, *TDNT* I: 490; Barclay, *Flesh,* 31; Burton 305f.

67. Bruce 247.

68. Barclay, *Flesh,* 33.

who were disgusted with the unspeakable sexual immorality.[69] Not surprisingly has it been said, "In nothing did early Christianity so thoroughly revolutionize the ethical standards of the pagan world as in regard to sexual relationships."[70]

20 After three words for sexual sins come two words for sins which are deviations from true religion (cf. Rev. 21:8). (iv) *Eidōlolatria* and the cognate noun *eidōlolatrēs* ("idolater") occur only in the NT and Christian writings dependent on the NT. In terms of derivation *eidōlolatria* may not be a compound of *eidōlon* ("idol") and *latreia* ("worship"), but its meaning is indeed a combination of these two ideas.[71] As the typical sin of the Gentiles, idolatry is opposed to service of "the living and true God" (1 Thess. 1:9); its fundamental error consists in the offering of "reverence and worship to created things instead of to the Creator" (Rom. 1:25, cf. vv. 19-23). As "idols" may refer to the images of supposed gods (Acts 7:41; Rev. 9:20) or the gods thus represented (1 Cor. 8:4, 7; 10:19), so "idolatry" partakes of this ambivalence of meaning.[72] Paul clearly regards idols as mere nonentities, yet he recognizes that demonic forces lurk behind them, so that to take part in a pagan sacrificial feast is to "become partners with demons" (1 Cor. 10:19-21).[73] Hence the admonition to "shun idolatry" (1 Cor. 10:14; cf. v. 7; 5:11; Eph. 5:5; Col. 3:5).

As sexual immorality was more often than not entailed in idol-worship—witness the hundreds of "sacred" prostitutes in the temple of Aphrodite in Corinth, with whom the devotees of the love-goddess entered into sexual union as an act of worship (cf. 1 Cor. 6)[74]—the idol-worshipper could be committing a double, if not triple, offense (against God and his own person, if not also against the person with whom he had sexual intercourse). In the broadest sense, of course, idolatry is the worship of anything which usurps the rightful place of God; so Paul can speak of "the ruthless greed which is nothing less than idolatry" (Col. 3:5), for the object of greed becomes an object of worship.[75]

(v) *Pharmakeia* originally meant the medical use of drugs; but it came to mean the abuse of drugs for poisoning instead of healing, finally taking on the sense of "witchcraft" (AV) or "sorcery" (RV).[76] When the erstwhile practitioners of magic arts in Ephesus committed their books to the

---

69. Cf. Barclay, *Flesh*, 24-27.
70. Duncan 171f.
71. F. Büchsel, *TDNT* II: 379f.
72. Burton 306.
73. Cf. W. Mundle, *NIDNTT* II: 286.
74. Cf. Barclay, *Flesh*, 28, 35f.
75. Cf. Barclay, *Flesh*, 35; Bruce 247.
76. Cf. Barclay, *Flesh*, 36; J. S. Wright, *NIDNTT* II: 558.

fire, the considerable value of those volumes bore eloquent witness to the prevalence of such practices in those times (Acts 19:19; cf. 8:9-11; 13:8-10) in spite of the fact that sorcery was a serious offense in Roman law.[77]

Next to be mentioned are eight items all indicative of dis-ease in personal relationships. (vi) The plural *echthrai* here (cf. RV) may be an instance of the use of "the Pluralis Poeticus for abstract subjects in a classical way," or it may refer to various concrete manifestations of the abstract sin (cf. items ix-xv, which are all plural in form).[78] The singular is used in Rom. 8:7 of unregenerate mankind's enmity towards God, but here the reference is undoubtedly to enmity among people.[79] Such enmity can exist on three levels:[80] between different classes (e.g., slaves and freemen), between different races,[81] and between individuals (e.g., Herod and Pilate, Lk. 23:12). It is important to observe, with F. F. Bruce, that "the *echthros* [enemy] is the one who cherishes the hostile thought and performs the hostile act; the object of his activity is not necessarily *echthros* towards him (the term is not inevitably correlative)." This is the obvious assumption of Jesus' teaching that his disciples love their enemies (Mt. 5:44; Lk. 6:27, 35; cf. Rom. 12:20, quoting Prov. 25:21).[82]

(vii) For the textually superior singular *eris* some manuscripts have plural *ereis* (the normal plural form is *erides,* as in 1 Cor. 1:11).[83] *Eris* is the "contentious temper" (NEB) which leads to "strife" (RV) and "discord" (NIV). Paul mentions it as a characteristic of pagan society (Rom. 1:29; cf. 13:13), but unfortunately it often gains entry into the Church as well, causing quarrels and disrupting Christian fellowship (1 Cor. 1:11; 3:3; 2 Cor. 12:20). Paul knew of some who proclaimed Christ "in a jealous and quarrelsome spirit" (Phil. 1:15, NEB), that is, "from envy and rivalry" (RSV). That even such a praiseworthy activity as the preaching of Christ (there is no doubt that the doctrine was sound, v. 18) should have been motivated by "envy and strife" (AV, RV, NASB) is surely a sobering—and searching—thought.

---

77. Bruce 248. According to W. Foerster, "For Paul witchcraft is meddling with demons" (*TDNT* II: 17); it seems more correct to say, in the light of Acts 13:4ff., that sorcery counterfeits the works of the Spirit (Guthrie 137).

78. MHT 3: 27 and Ellicott 117; Burton 309 respectively.

79. Cf. W. Foerster, *TDNT* II: 815.

80. Cf. Barclay, *Flesh,* 40-42.

81. E.g., the Greeks regarded anyone who did not speak their language as a "barbarian" or "foreigner" (βάρβαρος, Col. 3:11; 1 Cor. 14:11; NEB, one who speaks "gibberish"), while to the Jews all Gentiles were unclean and sinners (cf. Gal. 2:15).

82. Bruce 248.

83. Cf. Metzger 597. MHT 2: 131 says concerning the plural form ἔρεις: "when ει and ι were identical in pronunciation it is unlikely that such a new form would oust the regular ἔριδες . . . and produce a needless ambiguity."

(viii) *Zēlos* in itself can have a good sense and is used of "zeal" for God (Rom. 10:2) and the law of God (Phil. 3:6), for persons (2 Cor. 7:7, 11; 11:2), and for a worthwhile project (2 Cor. 9:2). But here (as also in Rom. 13:13; 1 Cor. 3:3; 2 Cor. 12:20, in all of which *zēlos* is associated with *eris*) it represents "jealousy" (RSV), a self-centered zeal which resents the good which another enjoys but is denied to oneself (cf. Jas. 3:14, "bitter jealousy") and may actively seek to harm the other person.[84]

(ix) *Thymoi* is the plural of *thymos,* which in Paul's letters (except for Rom. 2:8, where it refers to divine retribution), as in Luke and Hebrews, is consistently used of human anger—in antithesis to its usage in Revelation.[85] It is probably to be distinguished from *orgē,* particularly where the two words appear together (e.g., Eph. 4:31; Col. 3:8). Whereas *orgē* denotes a more settled state of mind (cf. Eph. 4:26: "If you are angry *[orgizesthe],* . . . do not let sunset find you still nursing it"), *thymos* is more passionate, and at the same time more temporary.[86] Hence in the verse under discussion *thymoi* is appropriately rendered "fits of rage" (NEB) or "outbursts of anger" (NASB). It is in keeping with this difference that "*thymos* tends to be used of the reprehensible anger of men, *orgē* of the righteous wrath of God," though "the distinction is not steadfastly maintained."[87]

(x) *Eritheiai* is the plural of *eritheia,* which denotes "base self-seeking."[88] The word is derived from *erithos,* "a hireling," and originally meant "working for pay"; it came to acquire the sense of "canvassing for office." Elsewhere in Paul's letters it occurs in contexts having to do with competing parties within the Church (cf. 2 Cor. 12:20; Phil. 1:17; 2:3); therefore it probably refers more specifically to that "selfish ambition" (NIV) which gives rise to rival "factions" (RV) and party "strife" (AV, cf. NASB).[89]

(xi) *Dichostasia* is used in classical Greek to mean "dispute, disunity, strife, in general, and also political opposition, revolt, [and] rebellion."[90] In its only other NT occurrence (Rom. 16:17, plural *dichostasiai,* as here), Paul warns the Roman Christians to be on their guard against those who cause "dissensions" (RSV, NASB) or "divisions" (AV, RV, NIV) and set up "hindrances" (NASB) or "obstacles" (NIV) to true

---

84. Cf. Trench 89 (§xxvi); A. Stumpff, *TDNT* II: 881f.; Barclay, *Flesh,* 46.

85. Cf. F. Büchsel, *TDNT* III: 167f.; H. Schönweiss, *NIDNTT* I: 106.

86. Cf., e.g., Morris, *Preaching,* 162; Trench 130-133 (§xxxvii); Barclay, *Flesh,* 49-53.

87. Burton 307f.

88. F. Büchsel, *TDNT* II: 661.

89. Barclay, *Flesh,* 55f.; Ellicott 117f. In 2 Cor. 12:20 the same sequence as items vii-x in our list is found.

90. G. Nordholt, *NIDNTT* I: 535.

teaching. In the present instance *dichostasiai* is associated with *eritheiai* (x) and *haireseis* (xii), which suggests the sense "divisions" (RV) or "dissensions" (NEB), that is, parties within the Church. Thus in the NT the word signifies "objective disunity" in the community, probably with a limited "political" sense.[91]

(xii) The fundamental idea in *haireseis* (plural) is "choice," the act or result of the action denoted by *haireisthai* ("to choose"); a *hairesis* (singular) is simply a body of people who have chosen the same faith and way of life (cf. Acts 5:17, the Sadducean party; 15:5; 26:5, the Pharisaic party).[92] When used in a bad sense the word denotes a "faction" (cf. 1 Cor. 11:19, RSV, NASB), with the suggestion that the private, unauthorized character of the party in question makes it distinct from, and alien to, the Church, which is the lawful assembly of the people of God.[93] If a pejorative sense already attaches to the word in Acts 24:5, 14; 28:22 (referring to the "heretical sect" of the Nazarenes), then we have there a tendency which is culminated in 2 Pet. 2:1, where the word means "heresy" in the modern sense.[94] Here in the Galatian passage, the reference is to "factions" (NASB), each exhibiting a "party spirit" (RSV) and possibly engaged in "party intrigues" (NEB).

21a (xiii) *Phthonos* (singular of *phthonoi*) is similar in meaning to *zēlos* (viii). But whereas *zēlos* can have the positive sense of "zeal," as well as the negative sense of "jealousy," *phthonos* has only the ignoble sense of "envy" (RSV) which regards another person with ill-will because of what he has or is.[95] This is not very different from *zēlos* as it is used here (cf. NEB "jealousies").[96]

Finally, Paul names two examples of the sin of intemperance. (xiv) While the use of wine is in itself no sin (cf. Jn. 2:10; 1 Tim. 5:23), excessive consumption in the form of "drunkenness" (AV) and "drinking bouts" (NEB; Gk. *methai* is a plural form) shows up repeatedly in catalogs of vices (Rom. 13:13, 1 Cor. 5:11; 6:10; in the last two passages the word used is *methysos,* "a drunkard"). Drunkenness is a nocturnal activity, ill-becoming those who belong to daylight (1 Thess. 5:6f.). Getting drunk before partaking in the Lord's Supper was an especially culpable act; it made a farce of what ought to be a sacred and solemn occasion (1 Cor. 11:20f.). A man

91. H. Schlier, *TDNT* I: 514.
92. Cf. Barclay, *Flesh*, 58f.
93. Cf. G. Nordholt, *NIDNTT* I: 535; H. Schlier, *TDNT* I: 182f.; Burton 309f.
94. Cf., e.g., Hendriksen 220, n. 166.
95. Barclay, *Flesh*, 46-49; Hendriksen 221. Cf. Trench 86-90 (§xxvi).
96. So also Burton 310. According to Trench 89 (§xxvi) φθόνος is "essentially passive," as ζῆλος is "active and energetic." But in Phil. 1:17 φθόνος is by no means passive.

given to drink is ipso facto disqualified from being a bishop or deacon of the Church (1 Tim. 3:3, 8; Tit. 1:7). Drunkenness leads to "dissipation" (NASB, NEB) or "debauchery" (RSV, NIV), but the Christian life should rather be characterized by being filled with the Spirit (Eph. 5:18) and should as such be clearly distinguishable from the experience of such Hellenistic cults as the worship of Dionysus, god of wine, with its stress on religious intoxication.[97] Between gluttony and drunkenness, the latter "is the more perilous because it weakens people's rational and moral control over their words and actions"; thus it is suggestive that in 1 Cor. 5:11; 6:10 the drunkard is neighbor to the slanderer and the swindler.[98]

(xv) *Kōmoi* is variously rendered as "carousings" (NASB), "revellings" (AV), and "orgies" (NEB). *Kōmos* (singular) is a natural companion of "drunkenness" (cf. Rom. 13:13), a characteristic feature of the pagan way of life (1 Pet. 4:3), and a concrete example of putting "pleasure in the place of God" (so NEB, 2 Tim. 3:4, Gk. *philēdonos*).

This catalog of vices is prefaced by *hatina* ("the kind of") and followed by *kai ta homoia* ("and the like") both of which show that the enumeration is representative and not exhaustive.[99] Many sins mentioned elsewhere in Paul's letters[100] are missing from this list. Of the fifteen items mentioned, the first three and the last two (groups [a] and [d]) are sins committed in the sphere of the body, but the rest (groups [b] and [c]) "might well be committed by disembodied spirits," thus showing that "the deeds of the flesh" are not necessarily physical or sensual, but embrace spiritual vices as well.[101]

Chief among the sensual sins are those having to do with sexual relations: they make up the first group, and some form of sexual offense may also be involved in the last item (xv). This suggests that lustful or sexual passions have a prominent place in the concept of the "flesh," and the suggestion is corroborated by the observation that in Paul's lists of vices (the list under discussion together with those mentioned in n. 100) "fornication" (i) occurs 8 times and "impurity" (ii) 4 times, and in five instances the list begins with "fornication" or some other sexual sin.[102]

It is obvious that sins which disrupt Christian fellowship (group [c]) also occupy a prominent place: as an apostle and a leader of the churches,

97. Cf. P. J. Budd, *NIDNTT* I: 513f.
98. Bruce 249f.
99. Cf. J. Schneider, *TDNT* V: 188: The words "and such like" are "a kind of comprehensive phrase" and "enable the reader to continue the catalogue in thought."
100. Cf. Rom. 1:24-32; 13:13; 1 Cor. 5:10f.; 6:9f.; 2 Cor. 12:20f.; Eph. 4:25-31; 5:3f.; Col. 3:5, 8f.; 1 Tim. 1:9f.; 2 Tim. 3:2-5.
101. Whiteley, *Theology*, 32 (whence the quotation); Ridderbos, *Paul*, 101.
102. F. Hauck and S. Schulz, *TDNT* VI: 593, n. 80; cf. on v. 19b above.

Paul was naturally concerned about the life of the communities, and this is reflected in his catalogs of vices (as also in his catalogs of virtues; cf., e.g., Eph. 4:2f.; Phil. 2:1ff.).[103] The length of this third group of sins (eight items, as against two or three in the others), and the fact that they do not belong to "the stock-in-trade of Jewish polemic against paganism," may indicate that it is in these forms that the "flesh" manifested itself most readily in the Galatian Christians.[104] However they might be classified, all the deeds of the flesh are manifestations of a life dictated by "self" instead of being led by the Spirit, in pursuit of one's own ends rather than in fulfillment of God's will.[105]

21b Not only are the acts of the sinful nature obvious (v. 19a, cf. NIV), they can also become a way of life. "Those who do such things" (RSV) is more accurately rendered "those who practice such things" (NASB); the participle *prassontes* denotes not an occasional lapse but habitual behavior.[106] Paul warns that "those who live like this" (NIV) will not inherit the kingdom of God. According to the general viewpoint of the Gospels, the kingdom of God was in process of inauguration during Jesus' earthly ministry and fully inaugurated with his death and resurrection. This "kingdom of God" is essentially the same as "the kingdom of his dear Son" (Col. 1:13); it is therefore sometimes designated "the kingdom of Christ and of God" (Eph. 5:5) or "the kingdom of our Lord and of his Christ" (Rev. 11:15, RSV, NIV). Insofar as the kingdom of God and the kingdom of Christ may be distinguished in Paul's usage, the kingdom of Christ seems to denote the present phase of the divine kingdom (as in Col. 1:13), which is mediatorially administered by Christ, while the kingdom of God refers to its future consummation in glory when Christ "delivers up the kingdom to God the Father" (1 Cor. 15:24).[107]

This kingdom may be inherited by the children of the King; and such are all believers in Christ, for through union with him and by virtue of his redeeming act they have become Abraham's true offspring and God's sons and heirs according to promise (3:26-29; 4:4-7). But God's reign or rule is moral in nature; those who consistently behave in ways that are opposed to God's nature (cf. 1 Cor. 6:9f.) show thereby that they have not accepted

---

103. Furnish, *Theology*, 84. Cf. E. Schweizer, "Traditional Ethical Patterns in the Pauline and Post-Pauline Letters and their Development," in *Text and Interpretation* (M. Black *FS;* Cambridge: 1979), 195-209 (cited in Bruce 247).

104. Bruce 250. Cf. above on 5:15.

105. Cf. A. C. Thiselton, *NIDNTT* I: 681.

106. Cf. Burton 312; Robertson, *Word Pictures*, 4: 313.

107. Cf. Bruce 251; *Colossians, Philemon, and Ephesians*, 372; *NT History*, 161, n. 8; B. Klappert, *NIDNTT* II: 388.

God's rule through Christ in their lives. They are no part therefore of the present phase of the divine kingdom, nor will they have a part in its future phase and its blessings, since the two phases are clearly conjoined (cf. the wording of Eph. 5:5). Paul had proclaimed this solemn truth to the Galatians when he first brought them the gospel—just as he and Barnabas had warned them that "to enter the kingdom of God we must pass through many hardships" (Acts 14:22)—and now he states it again by way of further warning. For the truth bears and needs repeating: the gospel which offers justification and freedom from the law through faith in Christ never gives the believer any liberty to turn that freedom into license, to practice "the acts of the sinful nature" (v. 19, NIV; cf. v. 13).

4. THE FRUIT OF THE SPIRIT (5:22-23)

22 *But the harvest of the Spirit is love, joy, peace, patience, kindness, goodness, fidelity, gentleness, and self-control.* 23 *There is no law dealing with such things as these.*

22 "The fruit of the Spirit" (AV, etc.) is obviously intended as a contrast to "the works of the flesh"; if the latter expression denotes deeds done by the flesh, the former refers to the concrete manifestations of the Spirit's work in the believer. The phrase directly ascribes the power of fructification not to the believer himself but to the Spirit, and effectively hints that the qualities enumerated are not the result of strenuous observance of an external legal code, but the natural product ("harvest") of a life controlled and guided by the Spirit.[108] Thus the two different expressions point to a contrast between the natural acts of the self-centered life and the ethical characteristics produced by the Spirit as the believer's life-transforming power.[109]

Elsewhere Paul speaks of the Spirit distributing a diversity of gifts separately to each individual as he wills (1 Cor. 12:11), but here the singular "harvest" shows that the nine graces mentioned are not, so to say, different jewels; rather, they are different facets of the same jewel which cohere and show forth their luster simultaneously[110]—when the Spirit is truly at work in the believer's life. H. D. Betz suggests that "the nine concepts should be taken as 'benefits' which were given as or together with the Spirit. In other

---

108. Cf., e.g., Longenecker, *Paul,* 178f.; R. Hensel, *NIDNTT* I: 723.
109. Cf. Ladd, *Theology,* 518; F. Hauck, *TDNT* III: 615.
110. Cf. Marshall, "Preparation," 8; Guthrie 139.

words, when the Galatians received the Spirit, they were also given the foundation out of which the 'fruit' was supposed to grow."[111]

It is eminently fitting that "love" *(agapē)* should stand at the head of this list of virtues. For love is "the measure and goal of freedom":[112] believers have been set free for the purpose of mutual service through love (v. 13), and the measure of their freedom is (at least in part) their ability to place themselves in loving service of their neighbors. Love is the "bond of perfectness" (Col. 3:14, AV, RV) which "binds . . . together in perfect harmony" (RSV) or "unity" (NIV, NASB)[113] all the virtues listed in Col. 3:12f.—compassion, kindness *(chrēstotēs),* humility, gentleness *(praÿtēs),* patience *(makrothymia),* mutual forbearance, and forgiveness.[114] Love is a grace superior to all the spiritual gifts, and among the graces it is greater than faith and hope (1 Cor. 12:31; 13:13). It is nothing less than a reflection of the nature of God and of Christ (Gal. 2:20; Eph. 5:1f.; cf. 1 Jn. 4:16).

God's great love (cf. Eph. 2:4-7) is completely undeserved by mankind (Rom. 5:8). Believers experience this love in their hearts through the mediation of the Spirit as part of the guarantee that their hope of future glory is no mockery (the other part being their experience of suffering-endurance-approvedness, Rom. 5:3-5). Nothing—no being, event, or object—can separate them from the love of God, which is also the love of Christ (Rom. 8:35-39). This incomprehensible love should be the controlling force of the Christian life (2 Cor. 5:14f.).

Paul's estimate of the importance of love in the Christian life may be gauged by the following considerations. (a) It is to be the atmosphere in which believers are to conduct their lives (Eph. 5:2), the garment they are to put on (Col. 3:14), the consistent motive of all their actions (1 Cor. 16:14). (b) Love is the secret of unity (Col. 2:2); it begins with love for fellow Christians (Eph. 1:15), including Church leaders (1 Thess. 5:12f.), and extends to all people (1 Thess. 3:12). (c) It is also the way to Christian maturity (Eph. 4:15),[115] the ground of Christian appeal (Phm. 9), and the proper restraint on the exercise of Christian liberty (Gal. 5:13; Rom. 14:15; 1 Cor. 8:1, 13). (d) Love is accompanied by practical action; it leads, for example, to magnanimous giving (2 Cor. 8:7f., 24) and genuine forgiveness

---

111. Betz 286.
112. H. Schlier, *TDNT* I: 50.
113. NEB includes in the term the idea of "completing the whole."
114. The three terms with the Greek appended also occur in Gal. 5:22f.
115. Taking "in love" with the words that follow. If the phrase is taken with the words that precede, then love is the manner in which the truth is to be maintained, ἀληθεύοντες meaning "maintaining the truth." Cf. Fung, "Nature of the Ministry," 142 with nn. 44f.

(2 Cor. 2:7f.). (e) Christian love is not flabby or sentimental, but keenly perceptive: it is capable of true discrimination (Phil. 1:9f.) and does not refrain from censure and warning, when such is demanded by the situation (2 Cor. 2:4; cf. 1 Cor. 16:24). Such love is not self-generated: it is the product of the Holy Spirit.[116] At the same time, Christians are exhorted to "pursue" love (1 Cor. 14:1, NASB), which, interpreted by the context of the Galatian passage under discussion, is tantamount to seeking to be led and guided by the Spirit (Gal. 5:16, 18).[117]

"Joy" *(chara)* does not mean earthly, human happiness: Paul repeatedly exhorts Christians to rejoice "in the Lord" (Phil. 3:1; 4:4; cf. 2 Cor. 13:11, NASB). This joy is "joy in the faith" (Phil. 1:25, RV, etc.) given by the God of hope along with peace in the continuous process of believing (Rom. 15:13);[118] its chief ground is the hope which derives from faith (Rom. 12:12, NEB "Let hope keep you joyful").[119] As an aspect of "the fruit of the Spirit," joy is also said to have its origin "in the Holy Spirit" (Rom. 14:17, RSV, NASB, NIV), that is to say, it is "inspired by the Holy Spirit" (NEB; cf. 1 Thess. 1:6, RSV, NIV; Lk. 10:21). Thus Paul traces the origin of joy indiscriminately to the Lord (i.e., Christ), God, and the Holy Spirit.[120] Because its origin is not human but divine, Christian joy is unperturbed by sorrow and tribulation, and indeed gives proof of its power precisely in the midst of them (2 Cor. 6:10; 8:2; 1 Thess. 1:6; cf. Rom. 5:3). This joy is maintained when we make our "requests known to God in prayer and petition with thanksgiving" (Phil. 4:6, cf. v. 4; 1 Thess. 5:16f.) and recognize that if we share in Christ's sufferings now we shall "share his splendour hereafter" (Rom. 8:17).

Paul himself was the embodiment of a joyful life. Although he later on found himself in a distressful situation in Rome, still he rejoiced because

116. Cf. Dunn, *Jesus*, 295: "love is not so much an act of man's will (cf. I Cor. 13.3) as the power of the Spirit which engages and moulds both man's emotions and his will."

117. Bruce 251f. notes that the noun ἀγάπη is found in the Septuagint (though not before), being used, e.g., of Amnon's passion for Tamar in 2 Sam. (LXX 2 Kdms.) 13:15 "and repeatedly of the mutual ardour of the lover and his beloved in Canticles." Thus, at least in the Septuagint, the contrast sometimes suggested (e.g., Trench 43f. [§xii]; Barclay, *Flesh*, 63f.) between ἀγάπη and ἔρως (which denotes specifically sexual love) does not obtain.

118. Gk. ἐν τῷ πιστεύειν; cf. NIV "as you trust in him."

119. Cf. Rom. 5:2, RSV: "we rejoice in our hope of sharing the glory of God." These three passages from Romans (5:2; 12:12; 15:13) show how closely hope is associated with joy, even though it is not listed separately here as an element in the harvest of the Spirit.

120. In a similar way Paul ascribes the distribution of the charismata to the work of the triune God: to the Father (1 Cor. 12:6) and the Son (Eph. 4:7) as their source, and to the Holy Spirit (1 Cor. 12:11) as the channel through which they proceed from the Father and the Son.

Christ was being proclaimed (Phil. 1:15-18) and decided to continue rejoicing because of his conviction that in defending the gospel he would know the Spirit's support (vv. 19f.). He rejoiced in his sufferings for the Church (Col. 1:24)—even if he was "being poured out like a drink offering on the sacrifice and service" of his converts' faith (Phil. 2:17, NIV). He considered two Macedonian churches his "joy" (Phil. 4:1; 1 Thess. 2:19f.). He rejoiced over the Roman church because the report that they obeyed the gospel had spread everywhere (Rom. 16:19), over the Colossians because they were orderly and stable in their faith in Christ (Col. 2:5), over the Thessalonians because they were standing firm in the midst of persecution (1 Thess. 3:8f.), and over the Corinthians because of their genuine repentance and the comfort and encouragement which he experienced as a result (2 Cor. 7:7-9, 16). He rejoiced when the Church was strong, even if he was weak (2 Cor. 13:9). And he rejoiced at his converts' concern and practical help for him (1 Cor. 16:17f.; 2 Cor. 7:7; Phil. 4:10; cf. 1 Thess. 3:6-8). Such was the apostle of joy who bids his readers not only "be always joyful" (1 Thess. 5:16) but also "rejoice with those who rejoice" (Rom. 12:15, RSV, NASB, NIV).[121]

Greek *eirēnē*, "peace," like Heb. *šālôm*, means more than the merely negative notion of absence of war and trouble; it denotes rather a positive state of "wholeness"—"soundness" and "prosperity." In the LXX the word "describes health of body, welfare and security, perfect serenity and tranquillity, a life and a state in which a man is perfectly related to his fellowmen and to his God."[122] In Paul, *eirēnē* appears most commonly in greetings and benedictions,[123] where God (with Jesus) is identified as the source of peace. Paul also speaks of "the God of peace" (Rom. 15:33; 16:20; 2 Cor. 13:11; Phil. 4:9; 1 Thess. 5:23) and refers to Jesus as "the Lord of peace" (2 Thess. 3:16). As opposed to "disorder" or "confusion" (AV, RV, RSV, NASB), peace is a state of normality consistent with God's will (1 Cor. 14:33). The evangel is called "the gospel of peace" (Eph. 6:15), because in it is proclaimed the eschatological salvation of the whole person (1 Thess. 5:23; cf. Rom. 8:6). Peace in this sense is based upon Christ's finished work of reconciliation: through the shedding of his blood on the cross (Col. 1:20) he has "annulled the law with its rules and regulations" (Eph. 2:15; cf. Col. 2:14), thus making it possible on the one hand for mankind to have "peace with God" (Rom. 5:1) and, on the other hand, for

---

121. On χαρά in Paul cf. E. Beyreuther, G. Finkenrath, *NIDNTT* II: 359f.; H. Conzelmann, *TDNT* IX: 369f.; R. Y. K. Fung, *A Commentary on the Epistle to the Philippians* (Hong Kong, 1987 [in Chinese]), 83f.

122. Barclay, *Flesh*, 86. Cf. Burton 425.

123. Greetings: Rom. 1:7; 1 Cor. 1:3; 2 Cor. 1:2; Gal. 1:3; Eph. 1:2; Phil. 1:2; Col. 1:2; 1 Thess. 1:1; 2 Thess. 1:2; 1 Tim. 1:2; 2 Tim. 1:2; Tit. 1:4; Phm. 3. Benedictions: Rom. 15:33; Gal. 6:16; Eph. 6:23; 1 Thess. 5:23; 2 Thess. 3:16.

Jew and Gentile to be reconciled to each other—indeed, to be created into "a single new humanity in himself" (Eph. 2:14-17).

In the Church, therefore, believers should "make every effort to keep the unity of the Spirit through the bond of peace" (Eph. 4:3, NIV), for it is to the peace of Christ that they have been called as members of a single body, and this peace should rule in their hearts and so act as arbiter in the community (Col. 3:15). Such harmony and concord is a characteristic of the kingdom of God (Rom. 14:17) and the norm for the marriage relationship (1 Cor. 7:15). "Peace" may also refer to the Christian's peace of mind, which comes from faith in God (Rom. 15:13; Phil. 4:6f.). Paul exhorts the Roman Christians to "make every effort to do what leads to peace and to mutual edification" (Rom. 14:19, NIV); peace is also among the objects of pursuit in his advice to Timothy (2 Tim. 2:22). Here in Gal. 5:22 "peace" may refer specifically to harmony in human relationships,[124] but it would be arbitrary to exclude from its meaning the inner peace which results from a right relationship with God and is reflected in concord with other people.[125]

Joy and peace are also conjoined in Rom. 14:17 and 15:13. In the first of these verses this collocation of peace and joy appears in its more logical order: for as justification through faith provides the logical basis for reconciliation with God (Rom. 5:1; 2 Cor. 5:19), so the peace of reconciliation with God is in turn the logical basis for the Christian's joy in God (Rom. 5:11). It has been suggested that, like faith, hope, and love (cf. 5:5f.), love, joy, and peace may well have formed a triad common in early Christian language: "In the upper-room discourse of the Fourth Gospel Jesus gives his disciples 'my peace' (Jn. 14:17), bids them abide in 'my love' (Jn. 15:9f.) and desires that they know 'my joy' (Jn. 15:11)."[126]

Makrothymia—"patience" or "long-suffering" (AV, RV)—is first a quality of God (cf. Ex. 34:6). Paul considers himself the object of Christ's "perfect patience" so that he could thereby be "an example to those who were to believe in him for eternal life" (1 Tim. 1:16, RSV). In Rom. 2:4 he speaks of God's "wealth of kindness, of tolerance, and of patience." Comparison with the reoccurrence of "God's kindness" later in the verse makes it likely that kindness is to be interpreted in terms of the other two members of the triad: God's kindness consists in his forbearance and patience, that is, in his graciously restraining the infliction of punishment and the execution of his wrath. This kindness (of which patience is part) is intended to lead people to repentance (Rom. 2:4b; cf. 2 Pet. 3:9), but the critic addressed in Rom.

---

124. So, e.g., Ridderbos 207; W. Foerster, *TDNT* II: 411; H. Beck, C. Brown, *NIDNTT* II: 781f.

125. Cf. Burton 314f.; Guthrie 139.

126. Bruce 253.

2:1 is warned: "by your hard and impenitent heart you are storing up wrath for yourself on the day of wrath when God's righteous judgment will be revealed" (v. 5, RSV).[127] If God "bore with great patience the objects of his wrath—prepared for destruction," that was because he chose "to show his wrath and make his power known" (Rom. 9:22, NIV); the parallelism with v. 17 suggests the meaning that God's long-suffering towards the vessels of wrath was designed to serve the more effective display of his wrath and power when these are revealed at last.

God's long-suffering toward mankind constitutes the basis and reason for the believer's patience towards others. To live up to their calling Christians must, among other things, "be patient, bearing with one another in love" (Eph. 4:1, NIV). They are to put on patience as part of the garments that suit God's own beloved and chosen people (Col. 3:12) and are to show patience not only in their relationships with other Christians, but "with all men" (1 Thess. 5:14, NASB). Patience was one of the qualities by which Paul and his associates commended themselves as servants of God (2 Cor. 6:6). In this (and other respects) Timothy followed his example (2 Tim. 3:10); nevertheless, Paul urged Timothy (and thus all who would be faithful ministers of the gospel) to "be unfailing in patience and in teaching" (2 Tim. 4:2, RSV).

In Paul's prayer for the Colossians (Col. 1:11), a closely related term, *hypomonē* (RSV "endurance," NEB "fortitude," NASB "steadfastness"), appears in conjunction with "patience." Insofar as a distinction can be drawn between the two terms, *hypomonē* denotes the ability to persist in pressing forward in spite of difficult circumstances, whereas "patience" refers to a long-suffering attitude towards other people, deferring one's anger under provocation, and refusing to retaliate for wrong done to oneself. Such a broad distinction may be present also in 2 Cor. 6:4, 6 (*hypomonē*, *makrothymia*, respectively), although it is not absolutely maintained.[128]

Chrēstotēs ("kindness"; AV "gentleness") is found in the NT only in Paul's letters, although the cognate adjective, *chrēstos*, is not so confined (e.g., Lk. 6:35; 1 Pet. 2:3, quoting Ps. 136 [LXX 135]:1). As applied to God, the word denotes his gracious attitude and action towards sinners: God's kindness, which (as suggested earlier) consists in his forbearance and patience, is aimed at the sinner's repentance (Rom. 2:4); salvation is the

127. The common linking of "hardness" with "heart" in the Greek Bible suggests that the κατά-phrase is probably a hendiadys, as suggested by NEB "in the rigid obstinacy of your heart"; cf. J. Behm, *TDNT* IV: 1009, n. 3.

128. In Heb. 6:15, e.g., μακροθυμία refers to Abraham's patient waiting for the fulfillment of God's promise and thus has to do more with circumstances than with people. On μακροθυμία in Paul see J. Horst, *TDNT* IV: 382-385. Cf. also Trench 195-200 (§liii); Barclay, *Flesh*, 91-97.

manifestation of God's kindness and his "love for mankind" (Tit. 3:4, NASB); in Jesus Christ the supreme act of God's kindness towards us was revealed (Eph. 2:7). God's kindness and severity (NIV "sternness") are contrasted with each other, and yet they are conjoined (Rom. 11:22); this suggests that his kindness is not unprincipled or sentimental.

As those who have experienced the kindness of God's salvation in Christ, believers are to clothe themselves with kindness (and other like qualities, Col. 3:12) and "be kind to one another" (Eph. 4:32, RSV).[129] Kindness is also among the qualities displayed by Paul as a servant of God (2 Cor. 6:6). It is an essential ingredient of love (1 Cor. 13:4)[130] and, like love, expresses itself in action; those who are kind treat others in the same way as God has treated them (Eph. 4:32; cf. Lk. 6:35).[131]

Agathōsynē, "goodness," occurs only in the Septuagint, the NT, and literature directly dependent on them. It has been interpreted as "the quality which a man has who is *agathos* ["good"] and therefore [as] moral excellence as well as goodness."[132] But perhaps the best way of getting at the meaning of the term is to set it alongside (or against) two other terms: (a) "Goodness" appears together with "righteousness" (*dikaiosynē*, NEB "justice") in Eph. 5:9, and the "righteous" (NEB "just") man and the "good" man are set against each other in Rom. 5:7. From these passages we can see that "goodness is an attitude of generous kindliness to others, which is happy to do far more than is required by mere justice."[133] (b) The contrast between the "good" landowner and the "evil" eyes of the complaining workers in the parable of the laborers in the vineyard (Mt. 20:15) shows that the "evil eye" (cf. Dt. 15:9; 28:54: AV, RV) denotes a grudging or hostile spirit (cf. the Deuteronomy passages in RSV, NASB, NIV), while being "good" means being generous.[134] Hence we may conclude that "goodness" in Gal. 5:22 represents a magnanimous kindliness which issues in practical generosity; it may thus be considered the antithesis to "envy" (item xiii in the list of the works of the flesh, v. 21).[135]

---

129. Here the adjective χρηστός is used; in Lk. 5:39 it refers to the mellowness of old wine, and in Mt. 11:30 the quality of Christ's yoke which is made to fit and therefore not harsh or discomfortable.

130. The verb χρηστεύεσθαι ("is kind") occurs in the NT only in this verse.

131. On χρηστότης in Paul see K. Weiss, *TDNT* IX: 490f.; E. Beyreuther, *NIDNTT* II: 106.

132. W. Grundmann, *TDNT* I: 18.

133. Mitton, *Ephesians*, 183. Cf. Robinson, *Ephesians*, 200.

134. So RSV "do you begrudge my generosity?" and NIV "are you envious because I am generous?"; cf. NASB.

135. Cf. Barclay, *Flesh*, 105-107; Sanday-Headlam, *Romans*, 404; Bruce 253f. In the two remaining instances of the term in the NT (Rom. 15:14; 2 Thess. 1:11) its meaning seems clearly different from the sense given here.

Pistis has already occurred many times in this letter in the sense of faith in God and/or Jesus Christ (2:16, 20; 3:2, 5, 7-9, 11f., 22-26; 5:5f.). Here, where ethical qualities are in view, the word does not denote that basic principle of the human relationship with God, justifying faith,[136] nor does it refer to that special faith which is one of the spiritual gifts (1 Cor. 12:9). The suggestion that the word here means trustfulness, that is, "faith in God's promises and mercies and loving trust towards men" (cf. 1 Cor. 13:7)[137] is not substantiated by the usage of the term. Rather, *pistis* here apparently means "faithfulness" (RV, etc.), "fidelity" (NEB), that is, loyalty and trustworthiness in one's dealings with others (as in Mt. 23:23; Rom. 3:3; Tit. 2:10).[138]

Paul occasionally uses the corresponding adjective *pistos* to mean "believing" (Gal. 3:9; 2 Cor. 6:15), but his normal use of it is for the person who is "faithful." (a) Faithfulness is a necessary qualification of the steward, the teacher, and the female deacon (1 Cor. 4:2; 2 Tim. 2:2; 1 Tim. 3:11). (b) Paul himself is someone "who by the Lord's mercy is trustworthy" (1 Cor. 7:25, RSV, NIV; cf. NEB "fit to be trusted"); he is thankful that the Lord has judged him worthy of his trust and appointed him to the gospel ministry (1 Tim. 1:12, cf. v. 11). (c) Several people are commended by Paul as *pistos:* Timothy (1 Cor. 4:17), Tychicus (Eph. 6:21; Col. 4:7), Epaphras (Col. 1:7), and Onesimus (Col. 4:9). (d) Paul presents Jesus Christ himself as the noblest example of fidelity and trustworthiness (2 Thess. 3:3, cf. Heb. 2:17; 3:2, 6; Rev. 1:5; 19:11). (e) God is faithful (1 Cor. 1:9; 10:13; 2 Cor. 1:18; 1 Thess. 5:24; 2 Tim. 2:13), and the sayings and teachings of the gospel are trustworthy (1 Tim. 1:15; 3:1; 4:9; 2 Tim. 2:11; Tit. 1:9; 3:8). Jesus repeatedly charged his disciples to faithfulness, as in some of the parables (Mt. 25:14-30; Lk. 12:35-48; 16:10; 19:11-27). *Pistis,* then, is the quality of being *pistos,* which "describes the man on whose faithful service we can rely, on whose loyalty we may depend, whose word we can unreservedly accept. It describes the man in whom there is the unswerving and inflexible fidelity of Jesus Christ, and the utter dependability of God."[139]

23a *Praÿtēs* does not have the negative sense of a lack of spirit, courage, vigor, and energy that its translation as "meekness" (AV, RV) or even as "gentleness" (RSV, NASB, NIV, NEB) might convey in modern English. In classical Greek *praÿtēs/praotēs* and the cognate adjective *praÿs/praos* were typically used to describe a person in whom strength and gentle-

---

136. So it is taken by Buchanan, *Justification,* 387.
137. So Ellicott 120.
138. Cf., e.g., Lightfoot 213; Burton 316; Bruce 254; R. Bultmann, *TDNT* VI: 204, n. 227.
139. Barclay, *Flesh,* 111.

ness go together.[140] In the Septuagint "gentleness" usually signifies a humble disposition which submits to the divine will.[141] In the NT "gentleness" is associated with love (1 Cor. 4:21), forbearance (2 Cor. 10:1; Tit. 3:2),[142] patience and humility (Eph. 4:2; Col. 3:12),[143] and peaceableness, that is, the capacity for "avoiding quarrels" (RSV, Tit. 3:2). In 1 Cor. 4:21 "gentleness" is contrasted with "a rod," which symbolizes chastisement.

"Gentleness" is the spirit in which the Word of God is to be received (Jas. 1:21), the erring brother restored (Gal. 6:1), and the opponents of the Lord's servant corrected with sound doctrine (2 Tim. 2:25). It should, indeed, pervade the whole of Christian living (cf. Jas. 3:13; 1 Pet. 3:4). It was an outstanding feature in the life of Jesus (Mt. 11:29; 21:5; 2 Cor. 10:1), who taught that "those of a gentle spirit . . . shall have the earth for their possession" (Mt. 5:5). That "gentleness" does not render one incapable of indignation is demonstrated by Jesus (cf. Mt. 11:29 with Mk. 3:5) and by Paul (cf. 2 Cor. 10:1 with Gal. 1:8f.; 5:12). As an ethical grace in the believer's life, "gentleness" may be described as a humble and pliable submission to God's will which reflects itself in humility, patience, and forbearance towards others, regarding even insult or injury as God's means of chastisement (cf. 2 Sam. 16:11) or training (cf. Num. 12:3).[144] It thus implies, but is not identical with, self-control.

Enkrateia—"temperance" (AV, RV) or "self-control" (NEB, etc.)—figures among the objects of pursuit in the list of virtues in 1 Pet. 1:5-7 and formed an important topic, together with righteousness and the coming judgment, in Paul's discussion with Felix (Acts 24:25). It is part of the strict discipline which every athlete, not least the spiritual athlete, goes into (1 Cor. 9:25) and is an indispensable qualification of the elder (Tit. 1:8, where the adjective, *enkratēs,* is used). The opposite of self-control is self-indulgence (Mt. 23:25, *akrasia*), the quality of being "without self-control" (2 Tim. 3:3, NASB, NIV; *akratēs*), the inability to keep one's passions under control or to resist temptation.[145] Paul teaches that unmarried persons and widows who lack self-control should marry (1 Cor. 7:9). A married couple should not deprive each other except by mutual consent and tem-

---

140. Barclay, *Flesh,* 114 (cf. 120).
141. Burton 317.
142. Ἐπιείκεια embraces the ideas of equity, fairness, and the moderation which makes allowances and does not insist on one's own; cf. Trench 153-157 (§xliii).
143. Ταπεινοφροσύνη means neither self-humiliation nor affected humility, nor yet merely the absence of pretentiousness, but the lowliness of mind which is based on recognizing one's true condition as sinful before God and absolutely dependent on him; cf. Trench 149-151 (§xlii).
144. Cf. Trench 152f. (§xlii); Ellicott 120; Lightfoot 213; Guthrie 140.
145. Cf. Bruce 255.

porarily for the purpose of undistracted prayer, lest they be tempted by Satan because of their lack of self-control (1 Cor. 7:5).

There is, however, no ascetic flavor to the self-control enjoined by Paul: he himself did not exercise self-control for its own sake; rather, in order that he might carry out his commission it was necessary for him to cast aside everything which might hinder him from reaching his goal (cf. 1 Cor. 9:25-27). Nor is self-control in the NT identical with the concept of self-control in Greek philosophical ethics, which "achieves its ethical significance from the humanistic understanding of life which has freedom as its goal"; behind that concept stands the ideal of the free and autonomous person who in self-mastery controls all things and in self-restraint maintains his freedom in face of evil passions and pleasures.[146] The NT, on the other hand, refers to "self-control" as the mastery of the self and the fashioning of one's life in the way which God desires.

It has been observed that "the word-group is more often used with a sexual connotation than otherwise; hence 'chastity' can usually be a suitable rendering."[147] It may be that in our passage too Paul has the sexual aspect primarily if not exclusively in view. Just as "goodness" may be regarded as an antithesis to "envy," "self-control" may be taken as being in contrast with the sins of "fornication, impurity, and indecency" and "drinking bouts" and "orgies"—all of which either are sexual offenses or might involve uncontrolled sensual passions.[148]

A few observations may be made on this list of ethical graces as a whole. (a) The nine items are more difficult to classify than the fifteen in the preceding list of vices. One may divide them into three groups of three, referring respectively to Christian habits of mind in their more general aspect, special qualities affecting a man's relations with his neighbor, and general principles of Christian conduct.[149] But love in the first group and fidelity and gentleness in the third have much to do with interpersonal relationships, so this division is a trifle too neat, although it certainly makes for easy memorization. Perhaps the best we can do by way of classification is to recognize that the first three items are directly associated with the Holy Spirit in Romans (5:5; 14:17), while the remaining six have to do chiefly with person-

---

146. W. Grundmann, *TDNT* II: 340f.

147. Bruce 25. Ἁγνεία ("chastity") in fact appears after ἐγκράτεια in several witnesses, as does ὑπομονή ("fortitude") in several others; but "these are obviously scribal interpolations, for if either had been present originally, no copyist would have ventured to delete it" (Metzger 598).

148. Cf. H. Baltensweiler, *NIDNTT* I: 496; Burton 318; Hendriksen 225.

149. Lightfoot 212. Cf. Nestle-Aland in loc.

al relationships.[150] Patience, kindness, and gentleness appear in 1 Cor. 13:4-7 as characteristics of love; perhaps Paul regarded love as the origin and motivating principle of the other virtues affecting personal relationships,[151] even though we hesitate to go so far as to concur that "it includes all the other gifts within itself."[152] It is surely a significant indication of Paul's experience of the Spirit's work in his own life that four aspects of the fruit of the Spirit are mentioned in his description of his apostolic ministry in 2 Cor. 6:4-10: patience, kindness, love, and joy (vv. 6, 10).

(b) H. Ridderbos[153] points out regarding these nine graces and other virtues mentioned in, for example, Phil. 4:5, 8; Col. 3:12-15, that

> even though they occur in the same terms in the non-Christian Greek ethic, in Paul's epistles [they] are always brought under the viewpoint of brotherly communion and the upbuilding of the church, and not, as in the Greek ethic, under that of character formation; they are always understood therefore as the fulfillment of the requirement of love and thus approached from the liberty and obedience in Christ.

(c) The fruit of the Spirit is not the same as the gifts of the Spirit. Only the term *pistis* is common to the list of graces here and that of spiritual gifts in 1 Cor. 12:8-11, and its meaning is not the same in both cases ("fidelity" and "faith," respectively). While both the graces of character and the gifts for ministry are alike products of the Holy Spirit, it is ethical graces more than spiritual gifts which represent Paul's distinctive understanding of the Spirit: the Spirit's most important work in the believer is to enable him to become holy.[154] We cannot say that Paul ethicized the Spirit, as if the early Church had regarded the Spirit as a non-ethical, mysterious, miracle-working power, which Paul then reinterpreted as the Christian's moral dynamic; already the primitive Church's conception of the Spirit clearly had an ethical aspect to it (e.g., Acts 5:1-5). Nevertheless a comparison with his treatment of spiritual gifts in 1 Cor. 12–14 suggests that Paul did distinguish the ethical aspect of the Spirit's activity from what may have been a less unambiguous understanding of the Spirit, and did shift the emphasis from the more outward spiritual gifts to the inner qualities which control conduct.[155]

(d) While these virtues are presented as the product of the Spirit, it is worth emphasizing again (cf. on v. 18) that the believer is not without

---

150. Cf. Guthrie 139; Bruce 255.
151. Cf., e.g., Burton 314; Ellicott 119; Ladd, *Theology*, 522.
152. E. Schweizer, *TDNT* VI: 431.
153. *Paul*, 297.
154. A. B. Bruce, *Christianity*, 248.
155. Cf. Davies, *Paul*, 217-221; Burton 313f.; Bultmann, *Theology*, 1: 337.

responsibility, "by attentive openness to God," to allow the Spirit to produce these graces in him.[156]

23b "Such things as these" *(tōn toioutōn)* shows that the list just given is, again (cf. "and the like" in v. 21), not exhaustive but representative. In Paul's statement, literally "against such there is no law" (AV, RV, RSV), "such" means "such things," if it is taken as neuter as in NASB and NIV, or, less probably, "such people," if it is taken as masculine.[157] The primary thought suggested by the statement is that while law exists for the purpose of restraint (cf. 1 Tim. 1:9) there is nothing in the manifestations of the Spirit to restrain.[158] This easily leads to the thought represented by the NEB rendering, that the manifestations of the Spirit belong to a sphere with which law has nothing to do.[159] It is possible, however, to go further and, with E. D. Burton, to regard this as "an understatement of the apostle's thought for rhetorical effect": the mild assertion as it stands "has the effect of an emphatic assertion that these things fully meet the requirements of the law (cf. v. 14)."[160] But as "these things" are "the fruit of the Spirit," Paul's words ultimately mean that "the law is not against those who walk by the Spirit because in principle they are fulfilling the law."[161] This interpretation of v. 23b, which is in full accord with Paul's teaching in Rom. 8:4, understands that although the word *nomos* is without the article and could be a general reference to any law, Paul is probably still thinking of the Mosaic law and his words are directed against the Jewish claim that the law is the divinely-given means of helping man's inclination for good to overcome his inclination for evil. He is saying that submission to the Spirit's leading is a superior way (cf. on v. 18).[162]

156. J. D. G. Dunn, *NIDNTT* III: 702. Cf. Ridderbos 207; Betz 287; and (more generally) H. Schlier, *TDNT* I: 50.
157. E.g., Bultmann, *Theology,* 1: 340f.; Ridderbos 208, n. 20.
158. Cf. Lightfoot 213.
159. Cf. Bruce 255.
160. Burton 318. Cf. H. Schlier, *TDNT* II: 501f.: "works which the Law is not against, because it is fulfilled in them."
161. Ridderbos 208.
162. Cf. Betz 289: "In view of the situation which the Galatians have to face, Paul suggests that it is more important to be enabled to act with ethical responsibility than to introduce a code of law which remains a mere demand. In other words, the introduction of the Torah into the Galatian churches would not lead to ethical responsibility, so long as the people were not motivated and enabled ethically. If they were motivated and enabled, however, the Torah is superfluous." Cf. also n. 57 above.

5. APPLICATION AND APPEAL (5:24-26)

24 *And those who belong to Christ Jesus have crucified the lower nature with its passions and desires.* 25 *If the Spirit is the source of our life, let the Spirit also direct our course.*

26 *We must not be conceited, challenging one another to rivalry, jealous of one another.*

24 In vv. 24-26 Paul applies the truth of the Spirit-flesh conflict and issues an appeal based upon it. The initial particle in v. 24 ("and"; NASB "now") introduces what seems to be the minor premise of a syllogism, the logical sequence of thought being somewhat as follows: (a) The flesh and the Spirit are opposed to each other; victory of the flesh means living in sin, but victory of the Spirit means yielding the fruit of character and conduct (major premise, vv. 17-23). (b) Now, it is a distinguishing feature of all Christians ("those who belong to Christ Jesus") that they have crucified the flesh (minor premise, v. 24). (c) Hence, they must (as a fact) be living by the Spirit and they must (as an obligation) be led by the Spirit (conclusion, v. 25).[163]

The words rendered "passions" and "desires" are in themselves neutral; here their use with the article and in conjunction with the "flesh" clearly shows that the reference is to the "works of the flesh." If a distinction is to be made between them, the "passions" (*pathēmata;* cf. Rom. 7:5) will denote the outward expressions of which the "desires" (*epithymiai;* cf. v. 16) are the inner directive force.[164]

The aorist tense of the verb rendered "have crucified" indicates that this crucifixion is decidedly in the past; this, together with the very term "crucified," suggests that the thought here is of believers' participation in the crucifixion of Christ. It is likely that the temporal reference is to their conversion or more specifically their baptism, which symbolizes their incorporation into Christ.[165] At the same time, the active voice of the verb, as contrasted with the passive "I have been crucified" in 2:20, seems to put the emphasis on believers' actions: in turning to Christ and becoming members of his body, they radically renounce fellowship with sin, whose seat is the flesh.[166]

---

163. Ellicott 121.

164. Cf. Lightfoot 213; Bruce 256; Hendriksen 226.

165. E.g., Pinnock 80; Guthrie 141; and Brinsmead 166; W. Michaelis, *TDNT* V: 931 respectively.

166. Cf. J. Schneider, *TDNT* VIII: 583; E. Brandenburger, *NIDNTT* I: 401. Both, however, understand the verb of a post-baptismal, ethical act on the part of Christians.

In another sense, Christians need continuously to crucify the flesh: they need unceasingly to seek to live in obedience to the Spirit's leading (vv. 16, 18, 25) and by the Spirit "put to death all the base pursuits of the body" (Rom. 8:13; cf. Col. 3:5). This continuous action is the practical outworking of the initiatory crucifixion of the flesh in the active sense (just explained) and is dependent upon the once-for-all passive crucifixion mentioned in 2:20. It is only on the basis of their spiritual participation in the historical crucifixion of Christ and by the Spirit's power that believers can hope to fulfill the ethical obligation to crucify the flesh with its passions and desires.[167]

25 This verse makes explicit the conclusion implicit in the Spirit-flesh conflict (vv. 17-23) and in the crucifixion of the flesh by Christians (v. 24). The statement of this conclusion is rendered very forceful by two factors: (a) there is no particle linking it with what precedes (asyndeton); (b) its chiastic (a-b-b-a) structure, preserved by RV "If we live by the Spirit, by the Spirit let us also walk," lets the stress fall on the two verbs "live . . . walk," while the phrase "by the Spirit" is emphasized by repetition. Although the statement is cast in the form of a conditional sentence, what is expressed in the protasis (the "if" clause) is assumed to be true (hence NIV "Since we live by the Spirit"). On that basis, the apodosis (the second clause) then makes an appeal, in which Paul with characteristic tactfulness includes himself ("let us").

We may make four further observations about this important verse. (a) "Living" by the Spirit is different from "walking" by the Spirit. The two expressions deal, respectively, with the Spirit as the source and sustaining power of believers' spiritual life and the Spirit as the regulative principle of believers' conduct.[168]

(b) Whereas in v. 16 the general term for "walking" was used, here the word used (*stoichein*, cf. 6:16; Phil. 3:16) implies the idea of a row or series[169] and suggests the picture of believers following a course with the Spirit as leader (cf. NEB) or marching in line (cf. NIV "let us keep in step") with the Spirit. This is, however, materially identical with "walk[ing] by the Spirit" (v. 16, RSV) and also with being "led by the Spirit" (v. 18).[170] Since *stoichein* expresses the thought of "walking in a row," and in view of

---

167. For a more elaborate treatment of what is materially the same theme cf. Rom. 6:1-11 (note especially vv. 6, 11).

168. Cf. NEB; E. Schweizer, *TDNT* VI: 428. In our view, Barrett 78 goes beyond the evidence when he takes the verse to indicate the presence in Galatia of some "who turn Christianity into emotional, ecstatic, 'charismatic,' inspiration, and have no regard to Christian ethics." Cf. n. 183 below.

169. Cf. G. Delling, *TDNT* VII: 667f.; H.-H. Esser, *NIDNTT* II: 452.

170. Cf. H. Seesemann, *TDNT* V: 944.

the following verses, it has been suggested that it refers here to the relations of Christians with one another more than to their individual conduct.[171] But even without pressing the meaning of the verb in this way we may still clearly see from the context that "keeping in step" with the Spirit does bear on the mutual relations of believers. It necessarily does so by virtue of the nature of the spiritual life.

(c) This is the third time in the same context (cf. vv. 16, 18) that Paul has pointed out the responsibility of believers to let the Spirit shape their conduct; the entire passage from v. 16 on shows plainly what place is to be held by the Spirit in the life and conduct of believers. An important truth is suggested by the very manner of Paul's general treatment of the Spirit and the flesh: E. Schweizer has noted that the use of the instrumental dative of "Spirit" *(pneuma)*[172] is not balanced by the use of the same construction with "flesh" *(sarx)*. "The *sarx,* then, is not a power which works in the same way as the *pneuma.* The *sarx* never occurs as the subject of an action where it is not in the shadow of a statement about the work of the *pneuma,* while the *pneuma* on the other hand is often presented as an acting agent with or without *sarx* in the context."[173] This observation strengthens the conclusion derived from vv. 16-18 above, namely, that believers can overcome the flesh if they submit to the leading of the Spirit, with whom victory belongs. This, basically, is Paul's answer to the question as to how believers can lead a sanctified life.[174]

(d) The juxtaposition of the indicative and the imperative in this verse indicates once again (cf. on vv. 1, 6) the close relationship between the two: the imperative is based on the indicative, and is intended to bring about in the lives of believers the practical outworking of the reality expressed by the indicative.[175] Its relation to the indicative is therefore basically that of consequence. Precisely because the Spirit is the source of their life, they are to keep in step continuously with the Spirit in their conduct. This relationship between the indicative and the imperative is defined in greater detail and precision in the Excursus below.

26 Returning to the theme of v. 15, which described behavior opposite to that of mutual service through love, Paul here puts in a negative

171. Duncan 178: "If our individual lives are lived 'by the Spirit,' let us also allow the Spirit to marshall us in our corporate relationships."

172. Dative πνεύματι in vv. 16, 18, 25; cf. instrumental διά in Rom. 8:13; 1 Cor. 12:8. Easley, "ΠΝΕΥΜΑΤΙ," 308-310 surveys the twelve instances of anarthrous πνεύματι in Paul (of which six are found in Galatians: cf. 3:3; 5:5) and concludes: "Πνεύματι for Paul regularly means 'motivated by the power (= Spirit) of God,'" the Spirit being "preeminently God's power at work in the life of the believer" (308f.).

173. E. Schweizer, *TDNT* VII: 131f.

174. Cf. Ridderbos, *Paul,* 272.

175. Ridderbos, *Paul,* 255.

form the corollary, for the Galatians, of walking by the Spirit. To "be conceited" is to boast of things that are insignificant and lacking in true worth, whether the boaster actually has them or only imagines that he has them or desires to have them.[176] The word naturally includes the ideas of "talking big"[177] and being "desirous of vainglory" (AV). The renderings "become conceited" (NIV) and "become boastful" (NASB) reflect the Gk. verb *ginōmetha* and suggest that Paul may have deliberately chosen to speak in a moderate tone, hinting that the sin of "self-conceit" (RSV) had not yet taken root in the readers, even though the very injunction is sufficient indication that they needed to be vigilant.[178]

Two participial clauses represent the twofold result or expression of idle boastfulness. It is tempting to regard the action of "provoking" (AV, etc.) or "challenging" (NEB, NASB)[179] as referring to the special temptation of the "strong," and the action of "envying" (AV, etc.; NEB "jealous") as the special temptation of the "weak" (cf. Rom. 15:1). The "strong," that is, those whose personal conscience does not present as many restrictions to their behavior, risk turning their freedom into license (cf. Gal. 5:13) and are tempted to challenge the more scrupulous to follow their conduct; the "weak," on the other hand, are hindered from following the "strong" because of their conscience, and might be tempted to respond with envy. According to this reading of the verse, Paul is implying that the way to avoid such challenge-envy behavior is for both parties to follow the leading of the Spirit —since the fruit of the Spirit is love—and to serve one another through love.[180] In Romans as well Paul presents love as the solution to a similar situation in the Roman church (Rom. 14:15): both the strong and the weak in faith (14:1; 15:1) have alike been accepted by Christ (15:7); hence the strong must not hold the weak in contempt and the weak must not pass judgment on the strong (14:3, 10). Nor must they pass judgment on each other (14:13), but are to accept one another (15:5, 7) as Christ has accepted them.

It is not clear, however, from Galatians, unlike Rom. 14–15, that Paul has two such factions in view; neither side has a monopoly on the sin of envy,[181] and both "challenging" and "envying" are said to be mutual and

---

176. Burton 324.

177. Cf. A. Oepke, *TDNT* III: 662; Ridderbos 211.

178. Ellicott 122f.

179. The verb προκαλέομαι, literally "call forth" (K. L. Schmidt, *TDNT* III: 496), occurs only here in the NT. Heb. 10:24 employs a different word, the noun παροξυσμός.

180. Cf. Burton 323; Ellicott 123.

181. The participle used here (φθονοῦντες) is cognate with the noun which appears as item xiii in the list of vices (see above on 5:19-21).

reciprocal.[182] It may be preferable, therefore, to regard both phrases as equally applicable to all the members of the community, without assuming any tacit distinction of parties on Paul's part. "While the first describes the hostile turning against each other, the latter implies the turning away from one another."[183]

Like v. 1 this verse is transitional in character: on the one hand it brings to an end the teaching on the Spirit-flesh conflict and the way to overcome the flesh, offering a final warning against the sins mentioned in vv. 13-15 (cf. v. 21); on the other hand it introduces the more directly hortatory section which follows (6:1-10). The change, however, to the second person ("you") and the direct address ("my brothers") in 6:1 show that 5:26 more properly belongs to the present chapter than to the next.[184]

EXCURSUS: INDICATIVE AND IMPERATIVE

It has been said that "No interpretation of the Pauline ethic can be judged successful which does not grapple with the problem of indicative and imperative in Paul's thought."[1] This problem arises because the (soteriological) indicative and the (ethical) imperative are not found only in separate sections of the epistles but are closely linked with each other and form a real "antinomy"; that is to say, we are confronted with "contradictory but nevertheless correlated statements, which grow out of a homogeneous state of affairs, [and] which therefore factually belong together."[2]

What is more, the same content may appear as both indicative and imperative.[3] Thus, believers have been set free by Christ and are to continue in that freedom (Gal. 5:1). They have died to sin and are also exhorted to reckon or count themselves dead to sin (Rom. 6:2, 11). They have been emancipated from sin and enslaved to righteousness, and they are to present

182. In the last phrase, dative ἀλλήλοις ("one another") is classical; the variant accusative ἀλλήλους (favored by Lightfoot 214 but rejected by Burton 324) is unclassical (Bruce 257).

183. Betz 294f. Barrett 78f. thinks that the previous verse and the following verse suggest "a context of spiritual gifts," and imply that "those who had these gifts provoke[d] others to imitate them" while "those who did not have them env[ied] those who had." But we fail to see any reference to spiritual gifts in 5:25 or 6:1 (contrast, e.g., 1 Thess. 5:19f.). Cf. n. 168 above.

184. Cf. Lightfoot 122f.; Burton 324; over against Ridderbos 211; Neill 83; NEB, where the verse is made to begin a new paragraph.

1. Furnish, *Theology*, 279.

2. Bultmann, "Ethik," 123 (my translation, here and in the quotations to follow). Cf. Michel, *Römer*, 216f.; Kertelge, *Rechtfertigung*, 255.

3. Cf., e.g., Kertelge, *Rechtfertigung*, 252; Windisch, "Imperativs," 271.

their bodily members as slaves to righteousness (Rom. 6:18, 19c). They are unleavened, and they must purge out the old leaven (1 Cor. 5:7).

The explanation of this antinomy offered by R. Bultmann, at least as this was expressed in the article already quoted, has not been found satisfactory. H. Windisch, in particular, has subjected Bultmann's construction of the matter to a detailed critique: (a) Bultmann begins with the observation that for Paul justification or release from sin is "the salvific blessing of the hereafter" which involves no change in the moral quality of a person; "it is neither something perceptible in the person nor something capable of being experienced by him in the sense of mysticism; it can only be believed."[4] But according to Windisch, "[While] this description can be correct for the actual statement of justification (Rom. 3; Gal. 2–3), for Rom. 6 it is scarcely sufficient."[5]

(b) From the point of departure just mentioned Bultmann goes on to state that the continuity between the old and the new person is "not ruptured": the one who has been justified "is the concrete person who carries the burden of his past, present and future, who therefore also stands under the moral imperative."[6] With this contention Windisch rightly expresses dissatisfaction because of the lack of supporting evidence, noting, for example, that there is no evidence for the assertion that Paul links the vindication of the imperative with the individual's burden of the past ("therefore also").[7] Positively, Windisch insists that the continuity between old and new is broken, and that the Christian is liberated from the burden of his past (cf. 2 Cor. 5:17); "and if he is placed under the imperative, that is in order to cast off the burden once and for all or again and again, and because he too must play his part, and because God has called him into his service."[8]

This emerges clearly, Windisch observes, from Rom. 6, which represents the most important statement of the Pauline derivation of the imperative from the indicative. According to this chapter the Pauline antinomy may be sharply expressed thus: "According to the teaching on the sacrament, sin (the old person, the body of sin) *is* destroyed in the baptized person; according to the following parenesis the separation from sin is an act of obedience which the Christian has yet to perform." Bultmann has not taken into consideration the antinomy *in this form*.[9]

4. Bultmann, "Ethik," 136, 135.
5. Windisch, "Imperativs," 272 (my translation, here and in the quotations to follow).
6. Art. cit. 137.
7. Art. cit. 267. Cf. Jeremias, *Central Message*, 62, who considers Bultmann "misled" in maintaining the continuity of the old and the new person, and notes (63) that Bultmann does not hold this position in his *Theology of the New Testament*.
8. Art. cit. 273 (cf. 267).
9. Ibid. 268.

(c) As Bultmann sees it, the moral claim of the imperative has acquired *"no new content"* for the believer; his moral conduct differentiates itself from that of the unbeliever only because it bears the character of obedience, and whether any moral conduct bears such a character depends on the judgment of God.[10] Against this, Windisch points out that "inasmuch as Paul recognizes active morality even in the case of the non-Christian, obedience is present also in [such a person's] case: he obeys, for instance, the law of nature."[11]

(d) The believer, according to Bultmann, never ceases to be an *asebēs* (ungodly person) and is a justified person *"always* as *asebēs"*; thus it is part of the existence of the justified person, an existence determined by God's grace, that he should also stand under the imperative:

> As therefore the moral demand expressing itself in the imperative is for [the believer] God's commandment, so at the same time the conduct of obedience corresponding to the demand is God's gift, produced by means of the *pneuma* [Spirit], without the demand losing its imperative character.[12]

Against Bultmann's assertion that the believer never ceases to be an *asebēs,* Windisch rightly remarks that Paul does not and probably could not draw this conclusion, "since he presupposes a moral renewal at the beginning, and assumes and demands as something normal full moral perfection at the end of the Christian's course of life."[13] While expressing substantial agreement with what Bultmann says about justification and faith, Windisch thus raises the fundamental question whether Bultmann's description of the relation between justification on the one hand and "the concrete essence of the Christian" and "his moral responsibility" on the other reproduces the meaning of Paul's statements;[14] by exposing the weaknesses in Bultmann's position he has shown it to be untenable.

Windisch's own solution to the antinomy is embodied in the following statement:[15]

> Unquestionably [the imperative] also sets the fulfillment of a *dikaiosynē* [righteousness] in some sense as the goal (cf. Rom. 6:19b). Now inasmuch as the doctrine of justification is the presup-

---

10. Art. cit. 138f.

11. Art. cit. 275.

12. Art. cit. 140.

13. Art. cit. 277. Cf. Kertelge, *Rechtfertigung,* 260: "The essential thing about his [Paul's] statement about the justified person is not what he was, but rather what he has become" (my translation).

14. Art. cit. 266.

15. Ibid. 271.

position of the imperative, the antinomy is easily resolved. It means: that which has become reality in the *imperceptible* sphere of the divine act is intended to be realized *visibly* now also in the earthly sphere. To the release from the dominion of sin, a person must respond with unreserved submission to the will of his redeemer. The standard and objective of this exertion is called, as with justification, *dikaiosynē*, Rom. 6:19 (2 Cor. 5:21).

Windisch's basic description of the relation between the indicative and the imperative is thus along the line of the principle "Become what you are." But since the repeated reference to *dikaiosynē* as the goal of the imperative seems to suggest that moral endeavor is to be made with the goal of attaining righteousness, it would appear that Windisch has to that degree mis-construed the motive in the Pauline imperative.[16]

Bultmann states that "Paul bases the imperative directly on the *fact* of justification, [and] *derives* the imperative from the indicative."[17] Similarly K. Kertelge writes, "The relation of the imperative to the indicative is that of *consequence*. The indicative of justification gives the reason for the imperative which belongs thereto, not vice versa."[18] In this way, Bultmann and Kertelge derive the ethical imperative specifically from the fact of justification. This is justified to the extent that Paul regards justification as the necessary foundation for the new life of the believer (see above on Gal. 2:20b; 5:6; cf. Rom. 6:14)[19] and clearly presupposes that the baptized to whom the ethical imperatives are addressed in Rom. 6:11-13 are those who are justified.

H. Küng has observed, however, that

Paul nowhere derives a moral demand from the juridical doctrine itself of justification. Even where it would seem to suggest itself

16. Cf. Longenecker, *Paul*, 178, who takes Windisch (in the passage quoted) to be interpreting Paul as saying that "while God makes us righteous by grace alone in the heavenly sphere (the indicative) we must make that righteousness truly applicable in the earthly sphere (the imperative), *and* that only as these two types of righteousness work together, the heavenly righteousness coupled with the earthly righteousness, is there bestowed the divine eschatological salvation," and notes that while Windisch bases his view of the relationship of indicative and imperative mainly on the Sermon on the Mount, he takes Paul to be saying the same thing in Rom. 6:19b (177).

17. Bultmann, art. cit. 127. Against this formulation Windisch found "in itself nothing to object to" (art. cit. 266).

18. Kertelge, *Rechtfertigung*, 258 (my translation).

19. To be "no longer under law, but under the grace of God" (Rom. 6:14b) presupposes that one has been justified by grace (cf. 5:1), which exercises its reign through the gift of righteousness (cf. 5:21b), so that the freedom from sin spoken of in 6:14a appears by implication to be the logical consequence of justification by faith. This means that the imperatives of Rom. 6:11-13 are rooted (note "for" in v. 14a) in the

naturally, namely, in the midst of his explanation of the doctrine of justification where he has to answer the libertarian objection, his ethical argument is not based directly on the justifying judgment of God, but on Baptism and burial in Christ (Rom. 6:1ff.).[20]

This noteworthy fact suggests that it is preferable to formulate the relation between the ethical imperative and the soteriological indicative not primarily by reference to justification, but by reference to the believer's union with Christ; for in union with Christ the believer has passed from the old existence to the new, and hence may and must live as one who is alive to God in Christ Jesus.[21] But it remains true that the relation of the imperative to the indicative is that of consequence. On this basis we can proceed to define in detail the basic relationship between indicative and imperative in Paul.

H. Ridderbos points out that the imperative not only has the function of bringing to manifestation and to full development the new life denoted by the indicative, but is also a constant touchstone for the reality of that life. This emerges especially clearly where the imperative answers to a conditional clause. Thus, the conditional "if" in Gal. 5:25 (cf. Col. 3:1) performs a dual function: it states "a supposition from which the imperative goes out as an accepted fact. But at the same time it emphasizes that if what is demanded in the imperative does not take place, that which is supposed in the first clause would no longer be admissible." Making the reality of the indicative conditional upon the execution of the imperative in this way is not putting the imperative cart before the indicative horse; it simply emphasizes that the

---

indicative of v. 14b, which points back to the change of status which took place at justification. Cf. n. 21 below.

20. Küng, *Justification*, 305. This statement should be seen in the light of our observation in the previous note, but may be accepted as it stands if we assume an emphasis on "deriving *directly* from *the doctrine itself.*"

21. With reference to n. 19 above, it is to be noted that the imperatives of Rom. 6:11-13 are first of all inferences (note οὕτως ["in the same way"] in v. 11 and οὖν ["so"] in v. 12) drawn from the meaning of Christian baptism as expounded in vv. 1-10, the keynote of which is the believer's union with Christ in his death and resurrection (vv. 8, 11). Thus in Rom. 6:1-14 Paul has given us a twofold foundation for the imperatives of vv. 11-13: according to the one train of thought, the new life of the baptized is an aspect of having died and risen with Christ and flows from union with him; according to the other, the new life of the baptized is grounded in and follows from justification. This double foundation is in fact one: since justification itself takes place "in Christ," by virtue of the believer's incorporation into him (Rom. 3:24b; Gal. 2:17), the ultimate basis for the new life of the baptized is union with Christ. If Paul at the same time implies that the new life is based on justification, this is in harmony with the indications given earlier in Romans that justification entails life (cf. Rom. 1:17; 5:17f.).

new life (with the Spirit as its source) must become evident in the new conduct (under the Spirit's direction) and cannot exist without it.

> The explanation of this relationship lies in the fact that the reality described by the indicative, however much to be appreciated as the gift of God and the new creation, yet exists in the way of faith . . . ; while, conversely, the execution of the imperative is not in the power of man himself, but is no less a matter of faith. Indicative and imperative are both the object of faith, on the one hand in its receptivity, on the other in its activity. . . . They represent two "sides" of the same matter, which cannot exist separated from each other.[22]

At a more fundamental level, this indissoluble connection is determined by the present salvation-historical situation and consequently by the nature of the salvation which is available for the enjoyment of believers. For while the new aeon (i.e., the age to come) has been inaugurated by the ministry, death, and resurrection of Jesus Christ, it has not yet revealed itself openly, directly, and completely; and although the old aeon (i.e., the present age, cf. Gal. 1:4) has passed away in Christ and all its evil powers have been dealt a mortal blow at the cross (cf. Col. 2:15), yet (cf. 1 Cor. 15:24) "the powers which God dethroned *still* want to repossess believers and force them to be their servants."[23] In other words, "the Christian stands in the tension of a double reality. Basically free from sin, redeemed, reconciled and sinless, he is actually at war with sin, threatened, attacked and placed in jeopardy by it. He must be called to *hagiasmos* [sanctification]."[24] Christian existence is thus set in the "in-between" time, between the "already" of salvation as a past event and present experience, and the "not yet" of salvation as future glory and complete consummation (cf., e.g., Rom. 8:18ff.). "The indicative represents the 'already' as well as the 'not yet.' The imperative is likewise focused on the one as well as the other. . . . There is in the 'not yet' the necessity for increasing, pushing ahead on the way that has been unlocked by the 'already.'"[25] In this way, the ethical imperative is seen to flow naturally and necessarily from the soteriological indicative.

---

22. Ridderbos, *Paul*, 255f.
23. Bornkamm, *Experience*, 80f.; *Paul*, 153 (whence the quotation; Bornkamm's emphasis). Cf. Kertelge, *Rechtfertigung*, 275.
24. W. Grundmann, *TDNT* I: 313. We should prefer to understand the word "sinless" in the quotation in the sense of "sanctified" (cf. 1 Cor. 1:30; 6:11; 1 Jn. 1:8).
25. Ridderbos, *Paul*, 257f. (cf. 487).

B. SPECIFIC EXHORTATIONS (6:1-10)

Following the general description of life in the Spirit (5:13-26), the present section consists of specific exhortations which may be summarized under two headings: (a) helping one another in the spirit of gentleness and humility (vv. 1-5) and (b) doing good in recognition of the rule of sowing and reaping in life (vv. 6-10).

1. HELPING ONE ANOTHER (6:1-5)

1 *If a man should do something wrong, my brothers, on a sudden impulse, you who are endowed with the Spirit must set him right again very gently. Look to yourself, each one of you: you may be tempted too.* 2 *Help one another to carry these heavy loads, and in this way you will fulfil the law of Christ.*

3 *For if a man imagines himself to be somebody, when he is nothing, he is deluding himself.* 4 *Each man should examine his own conduct for himself; then he can measure his achievement by comparing himself with himself and not with anyone else.* 5 *For everyone has his own proper burden to bear.*

1 Walking by the Spirit will mean not only avoidance of mutual provocation and envy (5:26) but also, positively, the rehabilitation of those who have lapsed into sin. The vocative "Brothers" (NIV; cf. 3:15; 4:12), which comes first in Greek, may be intended as a reminder to the readers that their membership in the same spiritual family involves mutual obligations. "A man" here obviously refers to a member of the Christian community. NEB "do something wrong . . . on a sudden impulse" captures the probable meaning of the Greek verb, which speaks not of intentional sin but of inadvertent wrongdoing.[1] The temporal significance of the verb's prepositional prefix *(pro-)* may be that "the sinner has been forcibly laid hold of by sin before he was able to reflect."[2] Whether the rendering "overtaken" (AV, RV, RSV) or "caught" (NASB, NIV, NEB mg.) be preferred, it is probably to be understood in the sense of being surprised by sin rather than being detected in it; the latter sense appears to be not well attested and is not required by the context.[3]

---

1. Cf. G. Delling, *TDNT* IV: 14f. (s.v. προλαμβάνω).

2. S. Biede, *NIDNTT* III: 750. Cf., e.g., Lightfoot 215; Hendriksen 231 with n. 170.

3. The latter sense is favored by, e.g., Ridderbos 212; W. Michaelis, *TDNT* VI: 172. For the former sense cf., e.g., Burton 327; Guthrie 142.

It is in harmony with this understanding of the verb to take the noun rendered "wrong" in the sense which it has in the papyri, where the connotation is of a "slip" or "lapse" rather than a willful "sin."[4] Since, however, in Rom. 5:20 the word is synonymous with "sin," it is unlikely to have been intended here to have the milder sense of "fault" (AV) as distinct from "sin," especially as "sin" does not occur in the hortatory section of Galatians.[5] Paul may have chosen the word translated "wrong" so that he could maintain the metaphor of letting the Spirit "direct our course" (5:25) and so draw a contrast with such a Spirit-directed life: to "do something wrong" is to fall beside the given course or fail to conform to the given standard.[6] While, therefore, the noun denotes "not a settled course of action but an isolated action,"[7] no exculpation is implied by it. In the phrase "any trespass" (RV, RSV, NASB) the word "any" is probably not to be taken absolutely: elsewhere in his letters Paul advises the withholding of fellowship from certain kinds of offenders (cf. Rom. 16:17; 1 Cor. 5:11; 2 Thess. 3:14), reserving a particularly severe treatment for the man who committed an act of "immorality such as even pagans do not tolerate" (1 Cor. 5:1, cf. v. 5).

"Even if" (RV, NASB) brings out the intensive force of the original phrase:[8] if, in spite of the injunction to walk by the Spirit in 5:25 and its reinforcement in 5:26, "someone" (NIV) should nevertheless commit an offense, the offender is to be restored. This responsibility is placed on the shoulders of "you who are spiritual" (RSV, NASB, NIV), a designation which has been interpreted as an ironical reference to some self-styled "spiritual ones" in the churches of Galatia.[9] Against this suggestion it is to be noted that (a) the existence of such a group is nowhere clearly indicated in the epistle; (b) "spiritual men" occurs in contradistinction to "men of the flesh" (apparently equated with "babes in Christ") in 1 Cor. 3:1 (RSV), both expressions representing believers in general; and (c) the exhortations of Gal. 6:1-10 are generally applicable and cannot be confined to any self-styled "spiritual ones."[10] The expression is, then, unlikely to contain any element of irony, contempt, or flattery, but describes, in terminology con-

---

4. MM s.v. παράπτωμα; Wuest 165.

5. So, rightly, W. Michaelis, *TDNT* VI: 172; cf. NIV "sin." The word translated "sin" is Gk. ἁμαρτία.

6. Burton 327. Betz 296 suggests that the offense "would fall into the kinds of things listed in 5:19-21."

7. Bruce 260.

8. On ἐὰν καί here see Burton 326.

9. E.g., Bornkamm, *Paul*, 82; Schmithals, *Paul and the Gnostics*, 46; Jewett, "Agitators," 211; Barrett 79.

10. Lightfoot 215; Ellicott 124.

sistent with that used in 5:16, 18, 25, believers whose lives are lived in conformity with the teaching of 5:16-26.[11]

Such ones are to "restore" (AV, etc.) the offender, or "set him right again." The Greek verb means "to make perfect" or "to equip" (Heb. 13:21, cf. AV, RV, NEB with RSV, NASB, NIV); it can refer to restoration of something to its original condition, for instance, fishing nets (Mt. 4:21; Mk. 1:19) or especially a fractured or dislocated bone.[12] "The life of the saints is to correspond to the grace given, and this itself is the standard to which they are to aspire. It is on this ground that in Gal. 6:1 and 2 Cor. 13:11 *katartizō* can mean to restore."[13] C. H. Dodd may be right to suggest that Paul applies here Jesus' teaching in Mt. 18:15-17 without going into the details of procedure.[14]

In carrying out the task of restoring an offender, the spiritual ones are to note two things: (a) They are to set him right again "very gently"—more literally, "in a spirit of meekness" or "gentleness" (RV, RSV, NASB). Since gentleness is an aspect of the fruit of the Spirit, those who walk by the Spirit will naturally show this quality. Here the emphasis is clearly on a spirit of considerateness towards the sinner, over against a censorious spirit. (b) They are to be watchful against falling into temptation themselves. The change from plural "you" to singular "yourself" applies the injunction to the individual (cf. 4:6f.): while the responsibility of restoring offenders belongs to the community ("you who are endowed with the Spirit") as a whole, "each one of you" has the responsibility to exercise the strictest vigilance over himself, lest the would-be restorer become an offender himself. Such vigilance is necessary because "anything can become a temptation"[15] and because no one is above the possibility of succumbing to temptation (cf. 1 Cor. 10:12). Awareness of this is conducive to the cultivation and manifestation of the spirit of gentleness enjoined here.

2 If the readiness to restore a brother who has sinned, doing so in an understanding and uncensorious spirit, is the first test of true spirituality, a second is the readiness to "bear one another's burdens" (RSV, NASB). The original word order puts the emphasis on "one another's burdens," probably in order to contrast these, not with the burdens of the law (cf. Lk. 11:46; Acts

11. So, e.g., Guthrie 142; Bruce 260; Dunn, *Jesus*, 287f. E. Schweizer, *TDNT* VI: 424, n. 605 is also of the opinion that the "spiritual ones" here are not a narrower group. The meaning of ὑμεῖς οἱ πνευματικοί is thus both broader and more specific than what is suggested by NEB. Cf. Barclay, "Mirror-Reading," 82 with n. 28 on 92: "The adjective could be a perfectly innocent description of those who walk in the Spirit."

12. Lightfoot 215.

13. R. Schippers, *NIDNTT* III: 350. Cf. G. Delling, *TDNT* I: 476.

14. "Ἔννομος Χριστοῦ," 108.

15. W. Schneider, C. Brown, *NIDNTT* III: 802; cf. H. Seesemann, *TDNT* VI: 29.

15:10, 28), but with the idea of each one bearing his own load (v. 5; cf. Phil. 2:4).[16] With "these" NEB is understanding the "heavy loads" as the difficulties of temptation and sin spoken of in v. 1, but since "the law of Christ" (v. 2b) entails much more than the mutual bearing of the burdens of temptation and sin, the "heavy loads" are better understood, more comprehensively, of all kinds of weakness (cf. Rom. 15:1), suffering, and pain—in short, any and every load that is hard to bear.[17] The maxim "bear one another's burdens," as Paul uses it here, "means that 'failure' by Christians should be regarded as part of the 'burden of life' and should be shared and borne by the Christian community."[18] When the burdens of life become simply unbearable for any member of the community, the others, if they are truly spiritual, will lighten his load by sharing his burdens and thus enabling him to stand. They will do so sympathetically and gladly, not (as in 5:10) by compulsion.

To "carry each other's burdens" (NIV) is to manifest a God-like quality (cf. 1 Pet. 5:7, quoting Ps. 55:22 [LXX 54:23]), and is certainly consistent with the fruit of the Spirit. But Paul's ground of appeal here is "the law of Christ": reciprocal burden-bearing on the part of Christians, Paul believes, completely satisfies the demands of that law.[19] The phrase "the law of Christ" *(ho nomos tou Christou)* occurs only here in the entire NT, although a similar expression "under the law of Christ" *(ennomos Christou)* is used in 1 Cor. 9:21. The occurrence of this phrase in Galatians is especially striking, since here Christ and the law are consistently opposed to each other, so much so that it is claimed that the phrase could not have been employed by Paul and must have been interpolated.[20] It is probable, however, that just as in 1 Cor. 9:21 Paul sets "being under the law of Christ" in opposition to being "outside God's law," so here he speaks of "the law of Christ" polemically, if not almost playfully, as an antithesis to "the law of Moses." It is as though he said to his converts: if you must

16. Cf., e.g., Ellicott 125, over against Lightfoot 216.
17. E.g., Burton 329; G. Schrenk, *TDNT* I: 555; W. Mundle, *NIDNTT* I: 261. The view that the reference here is to the bearing of a common financial burden (J. G. Strelan, "Burden-Bearing and the Law of Christ: A Re-examination of Galatians 6:2," *JBL* 94 [1975]: 266-276) is judged unconvincing by Bruce 261.
18. Betz 299.
19. On ἀναπληρώσετε (future indicative) as meaning "completely fulfil" cf., e.g., G. Delling, *TDNT* VI: 306. The alternative reading ἀναπληρώσατε (aorist imperative) could have the sense "fulfil then and there," the aorist tense marking the completeness of the act and thus intensifying the idea of completeness already contained in the prepositional prefix (Lightfoot 216), but it is likely to have been a scribal attempt to conform the original indicative to the preceding imperatives "restore" and "bear" (Metzger 598).
20. O'Neill 70.

observe the law (as the agitators say), do so—only make sure that the law you observe is not Moses' law, but the law of Christ.[21]

It is doubtful that Paul's unique expression here can be simply identified with the equally unique "Torah of the Messiah" of rabbinic belief;[22] even if for argument's sake we suppose that Paul's term was indeed taken over from the rabbis, he is more likely to be using it in his own intended sense than otherwise.[23] The view that "the law of Christ" refers to the body of ethical teaching which Jesus gave to his disciples and which was handed down in the Church[24] has met with the objection that there is no sufficient evidence to show that Paul knew such a tradition of ethical teaching, and that this interpretation imposes on the text an idea (that of a body of Jesus' teaching) which is not mentioned anywhere in the context.[25] And even though a case has been made out that Paul's ethical teaching shows a remarkable degree of consistency with Jesus' own teaching, thus reflecting familiarity with it,[26] this still falls short of proving that by "the law of Christ" Paul means the ethical teaching of Jesus.

The most common interpretation may well be the correct one: "the law of Christ" is the commandment of love, first promulgated by Moses (Lev. 19:18) and considered by Jesus to be the greatest of the commandments which speak of human relationships (Mt. 22:36-40), given by him to his disciples as "a new commandment" (Jn. 13:34; 15:12; 1 Jn. 3:23), and exemplified in his own life.[27] In conformity with Jesus' teaching, Paul also

---

21. Betz 300f. ("polemical"); Bammel, "Νόμος," 127f. ("almost playful"); Lightfoot 216; Guthrie 143; Bruce 241; Hays, "Christology," 275f. ("an ironic rhetorical formulation"). Hays helpfully notes that "the argumentative strategy is formally parallel to [Paul's] move in Gal 5:6, where he resolves the opposition between 'faith' and 'works' with the startling expression 'faith *working* through love.'"

22. So, e.g., Schoeps, *Paul*, 172f.; Davies, *Studies*, 179, who considers this "a technical messianic phrase" and "part of [Paul's] messianic stock in trade." Cf. Whiteley, *Theology*, 86. Without explicitly making such an identification, Martyn takes "the Law of Christ" (6:2) as an expression coined by the false teachers in Galatia for "God's Law as it has now been affirmed and perhaps also interpreted by God's Messiah" or, more simply, "the Law of God's Messiah" ("Mission," 314f., 323).

23. Furnish, *Theology*, 63f. Cf. Hays, "Christology," 274, on the view that the phrase is a slogan of Paul's opponents (so, besides Martyn, as cited in the previous note, Brinsmead 175): "no one has produced convincing evidence that the phrase ought to be attributed to Paul's opponents; and, even if the phrase *does* come from the opponents, Paul adopts it in a thoroughly positive and nonpolemical way."

24. E.g., Dodd, "Ἔννομος Χριστοῦ," 100, 108f.

25. Furnish, *Theology*, 61f.; Ladd, *Theology*, 514. Hays, "Christology," 273 pronounces the view in question "untenable."

26. Bruce, "Paul and the Historical Jesus," 325-335; *Paul*, 101-112.

27. Cf., e.g., W. Gutbrod, *TDNT* VI: 1076; G. Delling, *TDNT* VI: 306; R. Schippers, *NIDNTT* I: 738; H.-H. Esser, *NIDNTT* II: 446; Bring 274; Pinnock 82; Bruce, *Paul*, 187; "Paul and the Law," 277; Bultmann, *Theology*, 1: 344; Furnish,

regards love as both the summary and the fulfillment of the law (Rom. 13:8-10). The merit of this interpretation of "the law of Christ" is that it reasonably links the "law" with the "commandment" of Jesus and agrees with the emphasis on love in the preceding section of the letter (5:13f., 22; cf. 6:1).[28]

Materially, however, this interpretation may be linked with the two mentioned earlier. For if the law of Christ is his commandment of love, and if Jesus reinterpreted the law in terms of love both in his teaching and by his example, then obeying the law of Christ is to imitate the example of Jesus' loving character and conduct, by which his ethical teaching was confirmed (cf. Rom. 13:14; 2 Cor. 10:1).

3 In support (note "For")[29] of the injunction just given in v. 2, this verse describes that which is the opposite of gentleness and humility: spiritual pride. The Greek underlying the expression "thinks he is something" (RSV, etc.) has been used in 2:6; but whereas there its meaning is "esteemed by others as being special," here it means "to esteem oneself as someone special."[30] "Deceives" (RSV, etc.; NEB "is deluding") renders a word which means literally "to lead the mind astray" *(phrenapataō).*[31] It is stronger than simple *apataō* ("deceive, lead astray"), the difference being that with *apataō* there may be some objective basis to the opinion held,

---

Theology, 64; Barrett 83; *First Adam,* 80; Bornkamm, *Experience,* 83; Beker, *Paul,* 105 ("no doubt")

28. Ridderbos 213 (cf. *Paul,* 293) also considers love the content of "the law of Christ" without, however, linking it to Jesus' love-commandment. Guthrie 143 interprets it generally as submission to the person of Christ. Hays, "Christology," 274f. claims to have given greater specificity" to the position we have adopted by referring "the law of Christ" to the "paradigmatic self-giving of Jesus Christ": νόμος here means "a regulative principle or structure of existence, in this case the structure of existence [or "the pattern of action," 286] embodied paradigmatically in Jesus Christ" (276). But since Paul is "introducing a wordplay to contrast the shape and quality of the new obedience in Christ to the old obedience under the Mosaic law," ironically, according to the Galatians' desire (4:21), by exhorting them to live by the "law" of Christ (Hays 276), a reference to the love commandment as summarizing and superseding the Mosaic law is in our view more likely.

29. O'Neill 70 takes it to be "probably simply a strengthening word like our 'Yes'"; but more probably it gives the reason for the injunction of v. 2. Cf. Burton 330; Ellicott 126; Bruce 261f.

30. Gk. δοκεῖ εἶναί τι, "gives the appearance of being something" (BDF §131, cf. §301.1). The juxtaposition of τι ("somebody") and μηδέν ("nothing") enhances the contrast. Barrett 80f. detects in the expression in 6:3 a subtle return to the irony of 2:6, 9, where Paul describes James, Cephas, and John as those "who thought themselves to be something, who thought themselves to be pillars" (Barrett's translation).

31. Robertson, *Word Pictures,* 4: 315. The word is a NT hapax. The noun φρεναπάτης appears in Tit. 1:10, where it denotes not someone who is self-deceived (BDF §119.2), but someone who deceives others (Burton 331).

whereas *phrenapataō* implies a totally subjective delusion (cf. "when he is nothing"); this forceful verb thus intensifies the sense of "imagines himself" and accounts for the immediately following emphasis on observable facts as the measure of achievement (v. 4).[32] Paul implies that those who imagine themselves to be somebody are unable to bear the burdens of others: fancying themselves to be without sin or weakness they are unable to sympathize with others or to concern themselves with their burdens; conversely, they are more likely to treat others with gentleness and humility if they feel their own weakness.[33]

4 The injunction here is designed to prevent the self-deception described in the previous verse. The verb rendered "examine" means to "prove" (AV, RV) or "test" (RSV, NIV), as the purity of gold is tested by fire. It is used of the testing of the caliber of Christian faith by trials and of the quality of each individual's work by the fire of divine judgment (1 Pet. 1:7; 1 Cor. 3:13). "Each man" emphasizes individual responsibility in the work of self-scrutiny (cf. 1 Cor. 11:28), but the strongest emphasis is on the words "his own work" (AV, etc.), which in the Greek are emphasized by their position at the beginning of the sentence. "Work" here is collective singular, and can include both a person's "conduct" (so NEB) or his "actions" (so NIV)[34] and "the task which he is set" by God.[35] It is on his own conduct and performance that each person should concentrate, not the conduct and performance of others; he is to engage in self-assessment, not in critical evaluation of another.[36]

Paul apparently assumes that when a believer examines himself in this way that "then" he will discover some "reason to boast . . . in himself" (RSV).[37] But his real intention is not to issue a warrant for boasting, but to emphasize individual responsibility, that each person must take responsibility for himself, and indeed can take responsibility only for himself;[38] hence, if a person is to take pride in anything at all, he should find his "reason for boasting in regard to himself alone, and not in regard to another" (NASB).

32. Lightfoot 216f.; Ellicott 126.

33. Burton 330; Ellicott 126; Bruce 261f.

34. Cf. H.-C. Hahn, *NIDNTT* I: 229; Betz 302.

35. R. Bultmann, *TDNT* III: 651; cf. K. Weiss, *TDNT* IX: 86. H. Preisker's assertion that "for Paul judgment is by ἔργον [work] (1 C[or]. 3:13ff.; G[a]l. 6:4; Phil. 1:6; Col. 1:10; 1 Th[ess]. 1:3), not ἔργα [works]" (*TDNT* IV: 721, n. 107) overlooks the clear statement of Rom. 2:6; in Gal. 6:4 "work" is (as just mentioned) a collective singular, and the relevance of Phil. 1:6; Col. 1:10; and 1 Thess. 1:3 is doubtful.

36. Cf. W. Grundmann, *TDNT* II: 260: "Christians are summoned to a test of their own accreditation."

37. The noun used here is καύχημα, the ground of boasting, while καύχησις (e.g., Rom. 3:27) denotes the act of boasting.

38. Guthrie 144.

Whoever "imagines himself to be somebody, when he is nothing" will be likely to compare himself with the brother who has been caught in some trespass and thus find his ground of boasting "in regard to another"— particularly in regard to another's weakness (cf. the Pharisee's "thanks-giving" in Lk. 18:11). Paul encourages each person, however, to find his ground of boasting "in regard to himself alone," that is, in his own conduct and performance;[39] "then he can take pride in himself, without comparing himself to somebody else" (NIV).

In his own life Paul found reason for boasting in the successful prosecution of his apostolic task, a success which he attributed to God's blessing (2 Cor. 10:13-18; cf. Rom. 15:17-20, where *kauchēsis* is used), and in the clear manifestation of God's mercy and might when he found himself experiencing infirmity and tribulation (2 Cor. 11:30; 12:5, 9f.). There is no contradiction between the commendation in this verse and Paul's condemnation elsewhere of those whom he unceremoniously calls "fools" because they "measure themselves by themselves" (2 Cor. 10:12, cf. v. 15). For the two passages have different situations in view: Paul's oppo-nents were wrong to set themselves up as their own standard of comparison, when the true standard was one's commission from God and one's proper sphere as it was assigned by God; on the other hand, the Christian should measure his achievement not by reference to somebody else, but to himself alone.

5 A reason is now given to support the injunction in v. 4: "For each man will have to bear his own load" (RSV). The word translated "load" or "burden" here is different from the one used in v. 2;[40] while that verse speaks of "heavy loads" that one finds unbearable and requires assis-tance in carrying, this verse speaks of a person's "own proper burden," like the traveler's own pack.[41] The reference is probably to the ineluctable duties of life that fall to each person, including answerability to God for one's own conduct and performance.[42] The future tense of the verb "will have to bear" probably indicates certainty (cf. AV, RV, NASB) and may include a refer-

39. The phrase εἰς ἑαυτὸν μόνον ("in regard to himself alone") stands em-phatically at the beginning of the clause, forming a strong contrast with εἰς τὸν ἕτερον ("in regard to another") which comes at the end.
40. Φορτίον here, βάρος in v. 2. The difference is reflected in the renderings of NEB and RSV (= NASB, NIV), and obscured in AV and RV. The two words are regarded as having essentially the same sense by, e.g., Burton 334; Bring 275; Betz 304.
41. Cf., e.g., Rendall 189; Ridderbos 215.
42. Others interpret φορτίον here of "the particular *load* of sin and infirmities" (Ellicott 127), of "conscious guilt and shame" (Rendall 189), of "weakness and sin" (Burton 334) which each has to carry; or of "personal responsibility, i.e. of the decisions which have to be taken in the fight against temptations" (G. Schrenk, *TDNT* I: 555, n. 6). These interpretations, in our view, unduly restrict the meaning of the word.

ence to the day of judgment when each person will have to render an account to God (cf. Rom. 14:12; 2 Cor. 5:10).[43]

2. DOING GOOD (6:6-10)

6 *When anyone is under instruction in the faith, he should give his teacher a share of all good things he has.*

7 *Make no mistake about this: God is not to be fooled; a man reaps what he sows.* 8 *If he sows seed in the field of his lower nature, he will reap from it a harvest of corruption, but if he sows in the field of the Spirit, the Spirit will bring him a harvest of eternal life.* 9 *So let us never tire of doing good, for if we do not slacken our efforts we shall in due time reap our harvest.* 10 *Therefore, as opportunity offers, let us work for the good of all, especially members of the household of the faith.*

6 This verse is sometimes treated as an independent piece of advice having no clear link with either the preceding or the succeeding context.[44] The connective *de* (NASB "and") has been taken to imply a contrast (cf. RV "but") between the obligation mentioned here and the responsibility spoken of in the previous verse, the sense being that although everyone has his own proper burden to bear this does not exempt the believer from the obligation to contribute toward the teacher's support.[45] But in order for such a change in the logical sequence of thought to be clearly indicated, a much stronger form of expression than *de* would have to be used. It is preferable therefore to take this verse as providing a specific example of mutual burden bearing (v. 2), or at least as being suggested by that thought.[46]

"The one who is taught the word" is to "share all good things with him who teaches" (NASB). It is generally agreed that the verb used ("taught . . . teaches") refers at least chiefly to oral instruction;[47] it might even be regarded as a technical term for "to instruct in the faith."[48] "The instructor" here is the same as the "teacher" elsewhere in Paul (1 Cor. 12:28; Eph. 4:11), but the term is "hardly known at all in the religious vocabulary of Judaism," and may have been deliberately chosen "to emphasise the partic-

---

43. Cf. Ridderbos 215. Others (e.g., Pinnock 83; K. Weiss, *TDNT* IX: 86) think that only the latter is meant.

44. So Ridderbos 216f. Cf. NEB and NIV, where it forms a separate paragraph.

45. Ellicott 128; cf. Guthrie 145.

46. So Lightfoot 217f.; Bruce 263, and Burton 335 respectively.

47. So, e.g., Guthrie 145; Burton 337. The word is κατηχέω.

48. K. Wegenast, *NIDNTT* III: 771.

ular nature of instruction on the basis of the Gospel."[49] Or it may even have been introduced by Paul. The content of the instruction is "the word," which, as a general term like "the way of the Lord" (Acts 18:25), would include predominantly the apostolic "traditions" which had been delivered to the churches (cf. 1 Cor. 11:2; 2 Thess. 2:15; 3:6).

"All good things" does not have the article "because no totality is really involved."[50] "Share" may mean sharing what one has (cf. AV, RV "communicate") with another (i.e., active giving; cf., e.g., Rom. 12:13), sharing in what belongs to another (i.e., passive receiving; cf., e.g., Rom. 15:27), or both (cf., e.g., Phil. 4:15). Of the variety of interpretations of Paul's words here the most common is also the most likely: this takes "share" in the sense of active giving and "all good things" in the sense of physical goods (cf. Lk. 1:53; 12:18f.; 16:25); the meaning is then as NEB has it.[51] This is in accord with Paul's insistence on the right of the preacher to live by the gospel (1 Cor. 9:11, 14; 1 Tim. 5:17f.), even though he himself did not consistently exercise that right (1 Cor. 9:12b, 15-18). In fact he consistently waived that right, partly in order to provide a personal example to his converts not to live as parasites on others (2 Thess. 3:6-13; cf. Acts 20:33-35), at times in order to forestall any false attribution of mercenary motives to him (2 Cor. 11:7-12; cf. 1 Thess. 2:5-9), and partly because he was naturally sensitive about money matters (cf. Phil. 4:10-20). If in waiving this right Paul seems to have felt free to disregard a command of Jesus, this is probably because he "interpreted the Lord's command not as a duty to be performed but as a right to be claimed—or not claimed, as might be most expedient."[52]

Paul's exhortation indicates that the "teacher" had a fixed status; even if the teacher was not a full-time instructor in the faith, his work of teaching and preparation for teaching must have taken enough of his time that the community had to be responsible for his material support.[53] Here, then, we have probably the earliest extant evidence for a form of full-time or nearly full-time ministry supported by the congregation in the early Church.[54]

49. H. W. Beyer, *TDNT* III: 639.
50. MHT 3: 200. Gk. πᾶσιν ἀγαθοῖς.
51. Cf., e.g., Lightfoot 218; Ridderbos 216; Betz 306; F. Hauck, *TDNT* III: 808. For four other, different interpretations see Rendall 189; Burton 336, 339; Duncan 183; Guthrie 145.
52. Bruce 263.
53. Cf. Neill 84f.; Ridderbos 216f.; Burton 335. A. B. Bruce, *Christianity*, 372f. definitely thinks they were "full-time" workers.
54. H. W. Beyer, *TDNT* III: 639; K. Wegenast, *NIDNTT* III: 771. Cf. Barrett

7 The rule of sowing and reaping, of which Paul reminds his readers in this verse and the next, confronts them with a fundamental principle of the Christian life, as of life in general, thereby bringing them back from the narrower horizon of the more specific exhortations in vv. 1-6 to the broader view of the Spirit-flesh conflict in 5:13-26.[55] The prefatory formula—"Do not be deceived" (RSV, etc.; cf. 1 Cor. 6:9; 15:33; Jas. 1:16)[56]—warns the readers to "make no mistake"[57] about the truth of the ensuing statements. In the main statement, "God cannot be mocked" (NIV), the Greek represented by "mock" or "fool" means to turn up the nose in mockery or contempt; here "the reference is not to verbal scoffing but to the despising of God by a man's being, by his whole manner of life."[58] God is not to be fooled because he is God, not a human being; this seems to be the force of the anarthrous *theos,* which focuses not on the identity of God's person but on the nature of his being. A person cannot claim to accept the gospel and the obligations that come with it and at the same time live in obedience to the flesh instead of the Spirit. God will not be "outwitted" or "evaded"[59] in that way. *If* Paul still has his words in the previous verse in mind, he may be implying that failure on the part of those who receive instruction in the faith to carry out their financial responsibility toward the teacher is tantamount to failing to honor God, since making provision for the subsistence of the teacher of the gospel is part of the obligations entailed in the Christian way of life.[60]

An explicit reason that God is not to be mocked is provided by the latter half of the verse (note "for": AV, etc.). In the more literal rendering of the NASB—"whatever a man sows, this he will also reap"—"this" intensifies the force of "also," both together emphasizing the inexorable cause-effect relationship and exact correspondence between what is sown and what is reaped.[61] This common maxim occurs elsewhere in the Scriptures (e.g., Job 4:8; cf. Prov. 22:8; Hos. 8:7; 10:12f.), and in 2 Cor. 9:6 Paul makes use of a kindred truth to encourage liberality in giving toward "the provision of aid for God's people" (v. 1): that their reaping will be in direct proportion to

---

82: "They were rewarded for their work, though not, it seems, with a regular salary but by spontaneous sharing on the part of the person being instructed."

55. Burton 339f.; cf. Ellicott 129.

56. This has its formal roots in the Stoic diatribe according to H. Braun, *TDNT* VI: 244.

57. This rendering of the Greek is given by W. Günther, *NIDNTT* II: 459.

58. H. Preisker, *TDNT* IV: 796 (s.v. μυκτηρίζω—a NT hapax). Cf. Lightfoot 218f.; Rendall 189.

59. Cf. Burton 340.

60. So Burton 339 (definitely).

61. Cf. F. Hauck, *TDNT* III: 132f.

their sowing—a truth not without a degree of applicability to the matter of providing for the needs of the teacher (or preacher) of the gospel.

8 Paul's view has by now broadened from the specific matter spoken of in v. 6, and his application of the general maxim of sowing and reaping to the Christian life (note the initial "for," AV, etc., as in v. 7) brings him back to the theme of the Spirit-flesh conflict. NEB's "in the field of his lower nature . . . in the field of the Spirit" reflects the view of some scholars[62] who hold that the construction should be taken in the same sense as in the parable of the sower, where it denotes reception of seed by a particular kind of soil (Mk. 4:18, RSV, NIV "sown among thorns").[63] According to this understanding, v. 7 has in view different kinds of seed and v. 8 different kinds of soil; and the corresponding terminology of reaping "from the flesh" and "from the Spirit" (RSV, NASB) follows naturally.

Since, however, Paul is evidently "not constructing a condensed parable consistent throughout (like that of Mk. 4:26ff.), but employing individual terms 'sow' and 'reap' in a figurative sense, . . . *eis* is not . . . to be taken spatially but tropically."[64] We may therefore prefer the more common rendering "to his own flesh . . . to the Spirit" (RSV, NASB), which means in practical terms "to please his sinful nature . . . to please the Spirit" (NIV), in the one case by living to satisfy the desires of the flesh, in the other by following the leading of the Spirit.

The two life-styles are, like the principles determining them, entirely opposed to each other and yield completely different results. "Corruption" has been taken as bodily decay following upon sins of the flesh, as inward moral and spiritual corruption and death, or as physical and moral deterioration together.[65] In view, however, of the contrast with "eternal life" in the next clause, it would seem that Paul has chiefly the eschatological harvest in mind: "corruption" refers to physical death and disintegration, from which, for those who sow to the flesh, there is no rising to eternal life;[66] "eternal life," on the other hand, denotes that immortal life which in its future aspect is to be enjoyed by believers after their resurrection and glorification.[67] Paul here seems to regard the whole of a man's earthly life as a period of sowing, with harvest awaiting him on the last day: the eschatological yield is determined by present sowing.[68] That Paul is chiefly concerned with the end-time

---

62. E.g., Lightfoot 219; Guthrie 146; Ridderbos 218.
63. Gk. εἰς τὰς ἀκάνθας. Cf. Gal. 6:8: εἰς τὴν σάρκα, εἰς τὸ πνεῦμα.
64. Burton 342. Cf. Neill 85: "Paul's metaphor . . . is clearly not meant to be analysed for its horticultural accuracy."
65. E.g., Robertson, *Word Pictures*, 4: 316; B. A. Demarest, *NIDNTT* III: 525; Ellicott 130, respectively.
66. Cf. Burton 342; Ridderbos, *Paul*, 112.
67. Ridderbos 219.
68. Cf., e.g., S. Schulz, *TDNT* VII: 546; Betz 307, 309.

harvest is supported not only by the tense of "will reap,"[69] but also by the next verse.

"From the flesh" and "from the Spirit" (as in RSV) echo respectively "to his own flesh" and "to the Spirit," thereby strongly reinforcing the idea of reaping the fruit of one's sowing; "corruption" is a product which comes from the flesh just as eternal life is a gift which comes from the Spirit (cf. Rom. 6:21, 23). This correspondence is made doubly clear by two factors in the original sentence structure: (a) the two halves of the verse are almost exactly parallel to each other; (b) within each half, the chiastic pattern (a-b-b-a; cf. on 5:25) juxtaposes "to his own flesh" and "from the flesh," and "to the Spirit" and "from the Spirit," respectively.[70] It may also be observed that the possessive adjective "his" is predicated of the flesh[71] but not of the Spirit. Two thoughts are suggested by this deviation from exact parallelism: (a) The word "his" adds to the notion of selfishness already inherent in the term "flesh" (which represents the desires of the self).[72] (b) More importantly, the contrast between "his own flesh" and "the Spirit" shows that the two are not on the same plane: whereas "flesh" is what a human being is by nature, the Spirit is a gift from God, and to walk by the Spirit "signifies man's acceptance of the power of God which is not under his own control and which is now to shape his life instead of his own power."[73]

9 From the thought of "reaping what one sows" Paul proceeds to the general exhortation contained in this verse. "Doing good"[74] may be what is called "sowing to the Spirit" in the previous verse and may include all that is implied by that expression.[75] More probably, however, this verse is connected to the previous verse only by the thought of reaping, so that the "good" here refers generally to all that is morally good.[76] If the verb "tire" (enkakeō) implies any sense of yielding to evil (kakon), then it may contain

---

69. Gk. θερίσει, here taken as temporal as well as logical future; cf. Guthrie 147.

70. These points can be easily seen by reference to RSV or NASB.

71. As Burton 342 points out, "from the flesh," in view of the preceding "to his own flesh," is really equivalent to "from his own flesh."

72. Lightfoot 219; Ellicott 130.

73. E. Schweizer, TDNT VI: 430; cf. above on 5:25, point (c); Ridderbos 218f.; Guthrie 146. See A. C. Thiselton, NIDNTT I: 681f., for elaboration of the statement that "at this point, if not at others, the existential interpretation of the NT becomes relevant and convincing."

74. Gk. τὸ καλὸν ποιοῦντες; cf. 2 Thess. 3:13, καλοποιοῦντες. The use of the article here is probably generic, rather than introducing a proverbial phrase or representing simply Paul's personal idiosyncrasy; cf. MHT 3: 182; Moule 110f.

75. E.g., Ridderbos 219; Betz 309.

76. Burton 344.

an intentional antithesis with "good" *(kalon),*[77] which can scarcely be re-produced in English translation. Here, as in 2 Thess. 3:13, it means to "grow weary" (RSV),[78] which may easily shade off into the sense of "losing heart" (cf. NASB; Lk. 18:1; 2 Cor. 4:1; Eph. 3:13). This weariness may be caused by the delay of the long-awaited harvest (in this case the verse would still be closely linked with the previous one) or, more probably, by the sheer weakness of human nature which easily loses sight (at least for a time) of a proper sense of values.[79]

Having issued an exhortation to perseverance in well-doing, in which he once again includes himself ("let us": cf. 5:25f.), Paul points out the motivation for such perseverance (note "for") in the latter half of the verse. The Pauline expression "in due time"[80] means "the time which God has ordained and filled with content"[81] and here refers to the time of the eschatological harvest when those who persevere in well-doing will be rewarded (cf. Rom. 2:7). This condition for reward is restated at the end of the verse as "not growing faint" (NEB "if we do not slacken our efforts");[82] to grow faint is to become loose as a bow in an unstrung state, to become weak with fatigue.[83] It may be regarded as a consequence of "losing heart" (v. 9a): slackening of the mind (giving up) leads to weakening of bodily functions (growing faint). On this understanding, the conditional sentence in effect says: "If we persevere in doing good, we shall at the appointed time reap the fruit of our labors."

10 "So then" (RV, etc.) represents a phrase, found in the NT only in the Pauline writings, which is used to introduce the logical conclusion of a preceding statement. Here the connection with v. 9 may be understood as follows: just as there is a time for reaping, so there is a time for sowing; this

77. So Lightfoot 219.
78. Cf. E. Achilles, *NIDNTT* I: 563. But the rendering "tire *of* doing good" (cf. 2 Thess. 3:13: "tire *of* doing right" [similarly NIV], "grow weary *of* doing good" [NASB]; emphases added) is justly criticized by Moulton, "Tired of Doing Good?" as an impossible translation: the participle denotes action that is simultaneous with that denoted by the main verb, so that its meaning is "as long as you are doing good."
79. Ridderbos 219 and Guthrie 147 respectively.
80. Gk. καιρῷ ἰδίῳ, lit. "at its own time"; cf. 1 Tim. 2:6; 6:15; Tit. 1:3, where the plural is used.
81. G. Delling, *TDNT* III: 461.
82. Gk. μὴ ἐκλυόμενοι; cf. Mt. 15:32/Mk. 8:3; Heb. 12:3, 5, quoting Prov. 3:11. According to MHT 3: 285 the expression in classical Greek must mean "if we do not faint," but by Paul it is intended as a fact; Zerwick §441 agrees that the sense may simply be "tirelessly." It is taken as conditional by, e.g., Burton 345; *Syntax,* §436; Guthrie 147. Ellicott 131 has a point when he rejects the non-conditional sense "as adding no particular force to the general exhortation; whereas the conditional meaning serves fully to bring out the mingled warning and encouragement . . . which seems to pervade the verse."
83. Cf., e.g., Robertson, *Word Pictures,* 4: 317; C. Brown, *NIDNTT* III: 189.

being the case, we should make good use of the sowing time.[84] "As opportunity offers," which suggests the idea "when the opportunity presents itself," is perhaps more accurately rendered "while we have opportunity" (NASB);[85] the expression implies that believers do have this opportunity.[86] Corresponding to the "time" of the eschatological harvest mentioned in the last verse, the "opportunity" of this verse refers to the believer's life-time:[87] the believer has "the ethical responsibility to make sensible use of the time" at his disposal (cf. Eph. 5:16).[88]

Particular mention is made of the responsibility to "work for the good of all" or to "do good to all people" (NIV). The word for "good" here is *to agathon,* whereas *to kalon* is used in v. 9. It has been suggested that while *ta agatha* are things good in their results, such as beneficent actions, *ta kala* are things absolutely good, beautiful in themselves.[89] But Mt. 12:12 (where *kalon* is implied in the phrase "to do good") suggests that *kalon* can denote a beneficent act and can as a result be synonymous with *agathon* in that sense.[90] Be that as it may, the phrase "to all people" makes it plain that the reference here is to beneficent deeds, whether the benefit be spiritual or material. This principle of "doing good to all" is applied especially to "members of the household of faith," that is, members of the family of those whose characteristic is faith—the last word being taken in the active and subjective sense of trust,[91] not in the objective sense as equivalent to the gospel or Christianity (as in NEB "the faith").[92]

The concept of believers forming a household or family[93] finds expression elsewhere in Paul's letters (cf. Eph. 2:19; 1 Tim. 3:15). Here the distinction between the family of faith and "all people" (cf. 1 Thess. 5:15) shows that for Paul the time-honored division of mankind into Jew and Gentile was less significant than the believer-unbeliever distinction;[94] in-

---

84. So, e.g., Rendall 190; Guthrie 147.

85. Reading ὡς καιρὸν ἔχομεν. Here ὡς is probably equivalent to ἕως so that used with the indicative it means "while" (as in Jn. 12:35); cf. BDF §445.2; Ridderbos 220, n. 7; Bruce 266. Burton 345f. adopts the reading ἔχωμεν and takes the construction (ὡς + subjunctive without ἄν, cf. *Syntax,* §307) to mean "whenever we have opportunity." MHT 1: 248f. also accepts the subjunctive reading, but takes the construction as meaning "as long as we have opportunity" (i.e., in the same sense as ἕως + indicative).

86. G. Delling, *TDNT* III: 460.

87. Ridderbos 220, n. 7; *Paul,* 494. The Greek in both cases is καιρός.

88. H.-C. Hahn, *NIDNTT* II: 838.

89. Lightfoot 219.

90. Ellicott 132. In favor of this position are also Betz 309; Bruce 266.

91. E.g., Hatch, *Pauline Idea of Faith,* 50, n. 1.

92. E.g., O. Michel, *TDNT* V: 134; Lightfoot 220; R. Bultmann, *TDNT* VI: 213.

93. Cf., e.g., J. Goetzmann, *NIDNTT* II: 251.

94. So M. J. Harris, *NIDNTT* III: 1199.

deed, the racial and religious distinction of Jew and Gentile lost all significance for him (Gal. 3:28; 5:6). He reckons that the Christian has a greater responsibility toward his fellow-believers than toward other people in general;[95] this may have had to do with the actual historical situation: Christians in financial difficulties could hardly expect assistance from their pagan friends, because they had departed from the religious traditions of their neighbors, but their pagan friends would, however, expect Christians to help one another.[96] In this connection, D. Guthrie reminds us that the precedence given to the Christian community does not exclude the wider responsibility for "all"; the latter is, rather, urged on us and linked "with an even greater responsibility towards fellow believers." As for "the proportioning of responsibility between the larger and the narrower group," this "must remain a matter for individual conscience."[97]

95. Guthrie 148. Ridderbos observes that "This distinction does not point to a first and second 'rank' of love . . . but to a differentiation in fellowship and therefore in the character of showing love" (*Paul*, 300).

96. Burton 346f. Hurtado, "Collection," 53-57 regards Gal. 6:6-10 as forming *"an exhortation to participate in the Jerusalem collection"* (53, emphasis original). If that were the case, it is difficult to see why Paul did not use more explicit language (as he does in 1 Cor. 16:1-4 and 2 Cor. 9:1-5), particularly if (as Hurtado suggests) the Galatians' "backwardness" in this connection was due to "incorrect interpretation of the offering" (55).

97. Guthrie, "Social," 44.

V. SUMMARY AND CONCLUSION (6:11-18)

A. TRUE VERSUS FALSE BOASTING (6:11-16)

Before concluding his letter Paul returns once more to the antithesis of cross and circumcision, setting them forth this time as representing respectively the true and the false ground of boasting, and thus carrying a stage further his polemic against the Judaizers and their way of legal observance (cf. 5:2-12).

1. BIG LETTERS IN PAUL'S OWN HAND (6:11)

11 *You see these big letters? I am now writing to you in my own hand.*

11 With the word "see"[1] Paul draws the readers' attention to the fact that he is writing in large letters with his own hand. AV "how large a letter" takes the plural *grammata* in the singular sense of "a letter" (cf. Acts 28:21) and not letters of the alphabet, but this understanding suffers from three weaknesses: the word is not in the accusative (direct object) case but in the dative;[2] Paul consistently uses a different word for "letter" *(epistolē)*; and Galatians is not a long letter compared with some of Paul's other letters.[3] It was customary with Paul to dictate his letters orally to an amanuensis and write the concluding greeting in his own hand (cf. Rom. 16:22; 1 Cor. 16:21; Col. 4:18; 2 Thess. 3:17); here, however, he took the pen well before the concluding greeting.

---

1. Gk. ἴδετε, here to be understood as imperative (so RV, RSV, NASB, NIV) rather than indicative.
2. Πηλίκοις γράμμασιν is dative of manner; cf. RSV, NASB: "with what large letters."
3. For these reasons cf., e.g., Burton 348; Ridderbos 221, n. 1.

"I am now writing" (cf. RSV, NASB) is literally "I wrote"; the Greek is probably to be taken as an epistolary aorist (cf. AV, RV: "I have written").[4] The suggestion has been made that not only vv. 11-18 but the entire letter was written in Paul's own hand, since elsewhere in Paul's letters the epistolary aorist never refers merely to what follows (cf. Rom. 15:15; 1 Cor. 5:11; 9:15; Phm. 19, 21); it is argued that if Paul were referring to these verses only, he would have used the present tense (as he does in 2 Thess. 3:17).[5] But if, contrary to his custom, he had written in his own hand with such big letters from the beginning of the letter, it is difficult to understand why he should have waited till the end before drawing attention to this remarkable fact. Further, his usage of the epistolary aorist in the passages cited above does not suffice to prove that he cannot have used it here to refer merely to what follows. We take it, therefore, that only this section (vv. 11-18) was written in large letters with Paul's own hand.[6]

In the opinion of G. A. Deissmann, Paul's big letters "are best explained as the clumsy, awkward writing of a workman's hand deformed by toil."[7] But actually "how large" (AV, RV) denotes size only and does not imply shapelessness or irregularity.[8] It is not impossible that Paul wrote vv. 11-18 in uncial or inch-high letters, whereas the rest of the epistle was written in small cursive letters;[9] in any event the "big letters" were larger than those ordinarily used in his letters. Paul assumes that all the Galatian churches would see the big letters he was using, and this implies that "originally the one MS was taken from church to church, rather than that one was sent to each church."[10] The fact that these verses are written in Paul's own hand and are written in unusually large letters is an indication of their special importance. In conformity with the epistolary convention of the time, this autographic postscript serves to authenticate the letter and sum up its main points; it thus "contains the interpretive clues to the understanding of Paul's major concerns in the letter as a whole and should be employed as the hermeneutical key to the intentions of the Apostle."[11]

---

4. So, e.g., Moule 12, n. 1; Bruce 268. BDF §334 and MHT 3: 73 note that this view does not command universal assent.

5. Ellicott 133f.; Duncan 189; Wuest 175f.

6. Cf. also RSV, NASB, NIV; and, among the commentators, e.g., Lightfoot 221; Burton 347f.; Bring 282; Neill 87; Ridderbos 221f.; Bruce 268.

7. *Paul,* 51.

8. So, correctly, e.g., Ellicott 133; Betz 314. MHT 2: 8, n. 2 observes that even if Deissmann's interpretation of the phrase be conceded, we have no evidence that writing with large "clumsy" letters implied illiteracy in Paul's day (or that it does today).

9. Frederic Kenyon, as cited in Wuest 175.

10. Bruce 74, 268; *Romans,* 21, n. 1 (whence the quotation).

11. Betz 312f. On vv. 11-18 as epistolary postscript cf. also Brinsmead 48.

2. MOTIVES OF THE CIRCUMCISION PARTY (6:12-13)

12 *It is all those who want to make a fair outward and bodily show who are trying to force circumcision upon you; their sole object is to escape persecution for the cross of Christ.* 13 *For even those who do receive circumcision are not thoroughgoing observers of the law; they only want you to be circumcised in order to boast of your having submitted to that outward rite.*

12-13 In these verses the Judaizers are described and their motives exposed. These are people, Paul reminds his readers, who "want you to be circumcised," who indeed "are trying to compel you to be circumcised" (vv. 13b, 12a, NIV).[12] But, he adds, "even those who receive circumcision do not themselves keep the law" (v. 13a, RSV).[13] This statement has led a number of interpreters to view the agitators as something other than Judaizers of Jewish origin (again we are back to the question of who the Galatian heretics were). W. Schmithals, for example, appeals to this verse in support of his theory that the heretics were Jewish Christian Gnostics: since Judaizers are "representatives of the Pharisaic-legalist Christianity," and since v. 13a "obviously means a renunciation of the law in principle," the heretics cannot have been followers of the Jewish law.[14] But Schmithals has surely over-capitalized on this text. The expression "do not keep" is in fact ill-fitted to indicate "a renunciation of the law in principle"; the sense of categorical denial would have been much better conveyed by some other word.[15] It is not necessary to interpret Paul's statement to mean that "the *neophytes* . . . are not really won over to the way of life under the law; . . . as non-Jews they are not yet masters of the technique of fulfilling the law";[16] Paul's words need mean no more than that those who received circumcision were "not thoroughgoing observers of the law," with a tacit allusion to their

---

12. Unlike ἀναγκάζεις in 2:14, ἀναγκάζουσιν here is to be taken as conative: "try to compel." So, e.g., MHT 1: 247, 3: 63; BDF §319.

13. The editors of the UBS text consider present tense περιτεμνόμενοι adequately supported and the variant περιτετμημένοι as reflecting scribal or editorial modification (Metzger 598). The latter, the perfect participle, would include anyone who had been circumcised, even as a child—a meaning manifestly unsuited to the context (rightly Jewett, "Agitators," 202).

14. *Gnostics,* 17, 33. Others take the expression to indicate that the agitators were Gentile Judaizers under Jewish pressure, e.g., Munck, *Paul,* 88f.; Harvey, "Opposition," 324; Gaston, "Enemies," 401.

15. E.g., "to nullify" (ἀθετεῖν, 2:21), "to sever relations with" (καταργεῖν, 5:4). Cf. Jewett, "Agitators," 202 with n. 1; Barclay, "Mirror-Reading," 76, who is "pretty sure that Schmithals has been far too gullible in taking at face value Paul's accusation in 6.13."

16. Schoeps, *Paul,* 65, 77 (emphasis added).

"hypocrisy and to such practical expediences" as they might have recourse to.[17] That some Pharisees did not match profession with practice is at least suggested by the charge of hypocrisy so often brought against them in the Gospels, and it is not impossible that Paul is here applying his former standards as a strict Pharisee (cf. 1:13f.; Phil. 3:5f.) to his opponents.[18]

Even the fourfold argument put forward by E. D. Burton which he considers "decisive" against taking "those who do receive circumcision" (hoi peritemnomenoi) as the Judaizers,[19] is not unanswerable: (a) Paul's unqualified allegation that "the Jewish Christians did not keep the law" may be explained in the way just suggested. (b) Although the subject of "do not keep" (v. 13a) is the same as that of "may not be persecuted" (v. 12b, RV, RSV, NASB), the words hoi peritemnomenoi need not be superfluous; they may be regarded as a further characterization of "they" (v. 12a, AV, RV: houtoi) which throws into sharper relief the inconsistency of their motives: they both receive circumcision themselves and try to force it upon the Galatians, yet their object is not to keep the law (cf. 5:3) but to escape persecution.

(c) It is true that the present participle peritemnomenoi is indeed not to be taken as synonymous with the perfect peritetmēmenoi, as "circumcised persons," but in the same sense as the singular is used in 5:3, "persons who receive circumcision" (cf. above on 5:2).[20] But it may still be taken as a general present, albeit (in the light of Burton's strictures) in a rather loose and imprecise way, denoting the people in question as "the circumcision party, the advocates of circumcision."[21] Our point is not affected even if the word is taken as middle, rather than passive, voice and in a causative sense ("causing to be circumcised").[22]

(d) Burton's appeal to 5:3 ("which shows that the judaisers had not as yet endeavoured to bring the Galatians under obedience to the whole

---

17. Ridderbos 223. Cf. Wilson, "Gnostics," 364. Barrett 87 prefers "to take this accusing clause closely with the adversative clause that follows: 'in demanding your circumcision they are not keeping the law but indulging a desire to glory in your flesh. It is not the law but their own sense of self-importance that impels them to act as they do.'" But on this view it is difficult to account for the emphasis on οὐδὲ . . . αὐτοί, and the proposed meaning would be more naturally conveyed by a different Greek construction (e.g., with ἀλλά omitted and with the participle θέλοντες used in place of indicative θέλουσιν).

18. Wilson, loc. cit.

19. Burton 353f. He takes v. 13a to mean that those who have been converted to the Judaizers' position "do not undertake to keep it [the law] in full and are not required by the judaisers to do so" (352).

20. So, besides Burton, BAGD s.v. περιτέμνω 1; Thayer s.v.; Moule 107.

21. So, e.g., Lightfoot 222; Ridderbos 223, n. 5; Cole 181; Schlier 281.

22. Bruce 270; cf. Jewett, "Agitators," 202.

law") is only of confirmatory, not evidential, value to his thesis. Burton considers the absence of an expressed subject of "want" (*thelousin*, v. 13b, see AV) of little weight against his view, which is that v. 13a refers to the converts, not the Judaizers, since he argues that "the mind easily supplies as the subject of *thelousin* after *alla*[23] the judaisers who have been the principal subject of the discourse from the beginning of v. 12." But since *alla* introduces a contrast "which is directly contrary"[24] it is surely more natural to understand the unexpressed subject of "want" to be the same as that expressed in the preceding clause, namely, "those who do receive circumcision." In this case the close parallelism (which Burton himself observes) between vv. 12a and 13b ("want to make a fair outward and bodily show," "want you to be circumcised") shows that "those who do receive circumcision" of v. 13a are the same people as those "who are trying to force circumcision upon you" of v. 12a.[25] In other words, in both v. 12 and v. 13 Paul has only the Judaizers, not also their converts, in view.

Paul uncovers three motives for their efforts to compel the Galatians to be circumcised. *First,* they "want to make a good showing in the flesh" (v. 12a, RSV).[26] Here "in the flesh" is used in its general sense of "outwardly, before men" (cf. NIV), though probably Paul already has an eye to what he will say in v. 13b (hence NEB ". . . bodily show").[27] There a *second* motive is mentioned: "that they may boast in your flesh" (NASB) that is, in order that in your circumcised flesh (NEB "your having submitted to that outward rite") they may have a ground for boasting. Such "ecclesiastical statistics" would furnish evidence of the success of their proselytiz-

---

23. AV, RV, RSV, NASB "but"; NIV "yet."
24. BDF §447.1.
25. Cf. Bruce 269f. The logic here may be formulated thus:

The subject of 'want' (v. 13b)	(A) = (B)	'those who do receive circumcision' (v. 13a)
	(A) = (C)	'those who want to make a fair . . . show' (v. 12a)
Hence,	(B) = (C)	
	(C) = (D)	'[those] who are trying to force circumcision upon you' (v. 12a)
Therefore,	(B) = (D)	

26. Εὐπροσωπῆσαι (a NT hapax) is rendered "to have a good appearance," "to stand well with" by E. Lohse, *TDNT* VI: 779.

27. Cf. Lightfoot 222; E. Lohse, loc. cit.; E. Schweizer, *TDNT* VII: 130. Schmithals's understanding of v. 12 in terms of the Gnostic contempt of the flesh (*Paul and the Gnostics*, 55) is dismissed by Wilson as "surely a perversity of exegesis" ("Gnostics," 363).

ing mission[28] as well as evidence of their zeal for the law.[29] More important still, this would provide ground for boasting before God, since God would (supposedly) be pleased with their success in winning so many converts to Judaism.[30]

The *third* motive (second in order of mention by Paul) appears in v. 12b: "to escape persecution for the cross of Christ."[31] In view of the other two motives, the expression "their sole object" or "the only reason" (NIV) clearly cannot be taken literally; it is probably a rhetorical device for emphasis.[32] Here, as in 5:11, the cross stands for "the whole doctrine of salvation through the crucified Jesus as against that of justification by works of law,"[33] and is presented as the cause of persecution coming presumably from non-Christian Jews.[34] This persecution the Judaizers want to avoid by "striving for a compromise between the non-Christian Jewish position of orthodox Judaism and the non-Jewish Christian position of Paul."[35] The three motives are closely related: a good showing in the flesh provides not

28. Cf. Cole 181 (whence the phrase quoted); Schoeps, *Paul*, 77; R. Bultmann, *TDNT* III: 649; H.-C. Hahn, *NIDNTT* I: 228; H. Seebass, *NIDNTT* I: 675. Borgen, "Paul Preaches," 43 sees the two halves of v. 13 as forming "an antithetical parallelism" and the verse as "a word about wrong intentions in connection with the conversion of proselytes."

29. Schlier 281; cf. Bruce 270.

30. Duncan 190. With reference to these two motives, R. Bultmann suggests that they represent not the Judaizers' "conscious intention but their secret motive" (*Theology*, 1: 424); the suggestion is made in support of an earlier statement that "will" need not penetrate into the field of consciousness but may designate the self's hidden tendency (1: 223). See also the next note below.

31. Gk. τῷ σταυρῷ is thus dative of cause; cf., e.g., BDF §196; Moule 45; MHT 3: 242; Zerwick §58. With reference to this (v. 12b) and the second motive (v. 13b) Barrett 86 says that "we may and must distinguish between consciously held motives and the theological analysis of unconsciously held motives"; Paul may be "analysing submerged, unconscious motives" and seeing "more clearly into what the Judaizers were doing than they saw themselves" (85). Cf. the previous note above.

32. Cf. Betz 315: "the restrictive μόνον . . . is argumentative and not simply informative."

33. Burton 350; cf. Dupont, "Conversion," 190.

34. Cf. Harvey, "Opposition," 326. Others think of Jewish Christians stimulated by Zealot pressure (Bruce 269, in agreement with Jewett, "Agitators," 205), or the temptation to include the Christian Church in Judaism as a *religio licita*—a religion officially tolerated by the Roman imperial government (Manson, *Studies*, 164f., n. 1; cf. W. Gutbrod, *TDNT* IV: 1068, n. 202).

35. Guthrie 149. Cf. Machen 127. Barclay, "Mirror-Reading," 80f. warns against the danger of *mishandling polemics* here by concluding that "the opponents, who taught the law and circumcision, must have *played down* the message of the cross. . . . They may have been entirely happy to talk about the cross, even emphasize its saving significance, only failing, *in Paul's view*, to see its message as excluding obedience to the law."

merely an escape from persecution (by humans) but also a ground of boasting (before both humans and God). Of these three, it is the last—that of boasting—which appears to be the basic motive.[36]

3. THE MEANING OF THE CROSS (6:14-15)

14 *But God forbid that I should boast of anything but the cross of our Lord Jesus Christ, through which the world is crucified to me and I to the world!* 15 *Circumcision is nothing; uncircumcision is nothing; the only thing that counts is new creation!*

14 Over against the Judaizers who want to boast in the flesh (specifically in the flesh of those whom they are compelling to get circumcised), Paul disavows for himself[37] any ground of boasting except "the cross of our Lord Jesus Christ." To his contemporaries the cross bespoke unspeakable shame and its mention, even the very thought of it, provoked utter horror and sheer disgust;[38] but Paul exalts the cross of Christ as the sole ground and object of his boasting, thereby showing conclusively the absolute centrality of the cross in his thinking (cf. 1 Cor. 1:18, where he calls his message "the doctrine of the cross"). This means (cf. Rom. 3:27f.) that "all self-glorying is done away."[39] As C. H. Dodd put it, "pride in the Law has been displaced by pride in the Cross; pride in 'righteousness' as an achievement, by pride in that which empties him of pride."[40] "Cross" in this verse echoes the use of the same word in v. 12 and has the same significance as it does there, representing the atoning death of Christ as that which opens the way of justification by faith apart from the works of the law.

As Paul continues, the cross seems to gain a wider significance, as will presently appear. For in v. 14b he gives the reason[41] for the cross being his sole object of boasting: through the cross the world has been crucified to him and he to the world.[42] Here he refers to "the world" in its character as

36. Schlier 280. Cf. A. C. Thiselton, *NIDNTT* I: 680.
37. For μὴ γένοιτο ("God forbid") cf. 2:17; 3:21, where the phrase is used absolutely. Ἐμοί (literally "to me") is emphatic by virtue of its initial position. Ridderbos 224, n. 7 says that the entire construction "stands about half-way between a prayer and a curse."
38. On this see Bruce 271.
39. J. Schneider, *TDNT* VII: 576; cf. H.-C. Hahn, *NIDNTT* I: 228.
40. *NT Studies*, 78. Barrett 88 says of v. 14a: "The whole of Paul's criticism of the Judaizing, circumcising movement crystallizes here; and it is the ground of self-criticism that the Church has to apply in every generation."
41. The relative clause "through which . . ." has the effect of substantiating the preceding statement; cf. Schlier 281.
42. Since the cross is the instrument of crucifixion, "through which" correctly

"the epitome of unredeemed creation," that is, "of everything outside of Christ in which man seeks his glory and puts his trust."[43] For Paul himself this means primarily his former way of life as a Pharisee, his old world of inherited advantages and achieved successes (cf. Phil. 3:5f.).[44] The connection between him and that former world of his has been completely severed through the crucifixion of Christ; if it is right to see here a side-glance at an alternative meaning of the verb translated "crucify"—namely, "fence off"—Paul is saying also that the cross now forms a permanent barrier between the world and him and between him and the world.[45] How exactly the cross effected this break may be explained in terms of 2:19f. and 3:13f.: through participation in Christ's death, Paul has been set free from the law as the means of justification and from the old life of which the law was the principle.

It would appear, however, that Paul is here thinking of the cross not merely subjectively in its significance for himself, but primarily in its objective and eschatological character as the decisive event in salvation history which effected a radical separation between two worlds, so that between them there can no longer be any communication whatever. This understanding is supported by two considerations.[46] *First*, Paul speaks of the world being crucified to him as well as of himself being crucified to the world, and he speaks of them in that order; the thought thus clearly goes beyond that of his subjective experience to that of two objectively existent worlds, from one of which he has been transplanted into the other.[47] But since his transplantation from one sphere of existence to the other occurred by virtue of his participation in the historical crucifixion of Christ, then his transplantation first took place in Christ, whose cross made it possible. The underlying thought then is that the cross—standing for the Christ-event as a whole—marks the end of the old world and ushers in the new (cf. on 1:4).

15 *Second*, there is in this verse a significant difference from the otherwise closely similar statement of 5:6.[48] There the opposite of "circum-

---

understands δι' οὗ of the cross and not of the Lord (as in AV: "by whom"; Ellicott 136); "even if this phrase should refer to Christ, it is apparent here that it is Christ on the cross through whom Paul was crucified" (Tannehill, *Dying*, 63f. Cf. Betz 318). On the use of κόσμος ("world") without the article cf. MHT 3: 174f.

43. H. Sasse, *TDNT* III: 893 and Ridderbos 224 (cf. *Paul*, 92, 210) respectively.

44. Burton 354; cf. Hendriksen 245.

45. Cf. Bruce 271; *Romans*, 138; "Galatians Problems. 5," 267.

46. Cf. Vos, *Eschatology*, 48f. Tannehill, *Dying*, 64f. similarly judges that the present passage brings the cosmic-eschatological aspect to the forefront.

47. Cf. Ladd, *Theology*, 485; Ridderbos, *Paul*, 304; E. Brandenburger, *NIDNTT* I: 401.

48. It is probably due to the influence of 5:6 that some manuscripts have "in Christ Jesus" at the beginning of 6:15 (Metzger 599).

cision or uncircumcision" is "faith active in love," so that the verse refers unmistakably to the believer's subjective experience. But here the opposite of "circumcision or uncircumcision" is "a new creation."[49] "Creation" *(ktisis)* here is not the act of creation as in Rom. 1:20, but the result of the creative act (= *ktisma*) as in Rom. 8:20-22.[50] In the expression "a new creation," then, in contradistinction to the "faith active in love" of 5:6, the thought is objectively turned and the fundamental idea seems to be that of "incorporation into a new system of reality," the reality of God's kingdom, which is ushered in by "God's saving act in the cross of Christ."[51]

Paul is saying in these two verses (vv. 14f.) that Christ, by virtue of his coming and his atoning death on the cross, has inaugurated and brought about a new creation: his cross marks an absolute break between the new and the old world. Therefore, what matters now is no longer circumcision or uncircumcision, since that distinction belongs to the old world, but participation in the new order of existence.[52] This new order is characterized by a new relation to God which is bound to Christ and accepted by faith.[53] The

49. For this rendering of καινὴ κτίσις cf. also Betz 29, 31, 33, 319. For the distinction frequently made between the two words for "new" (καινός, νέος) cf., e.g., M. Dods, *EGT* IV: 373; Plummer, *Second Corinthians,* 85. It is better, however, not to press the distinction, since there are pairs of NT passages where the two words are used in similar contexts without any appreciable difference of meaning (cf., e.g., Bruce, *Hebrews,* 379 on Heb. 9:14; 12:24; *Colossians, Philemon, and Ephesians,* 147, n. 83, 358, n. 126 on Col. 3:10; Eph. 4:24; MM s.v. καινός). J. Behm, while stating that "the antithesis καινός/παλαιός ["new"/"old"] is wholly one of kind," thinks that nevertheless here "the aspect of time is also present" (*TDNT* III: 448f.). The divergence of the present verse "from the parallel G[a]l. 5:6; 1 C[or]. 7:19 in spite of the agreement in content" forms the basis of A. Oepke's judgment that it did not originate in a Moses-apocryphon, but "is original in Paul" (*TDNT* III: 989f.).
50. Schlier 282.
51. Vos, *Eschatology,* 49 (quoted); Ridderbos 226; H. Haarbeck, H.-G. Link, C. Brown, *NIDNTT* II: 671 (quoted). Similarly, Barrett, although he regards v. 14 as representing only "the subjective, existential view of salvation" (88), considers that in v. 15 we have moved away from that view "to an objective, metaphysical view": "Crucifixion and resurrection, and all that flows from them, are comparable only with the creation of the world. This is an act independent of man's existential response to it, but the indispensable condition of this response" (88f.).
52. This idea is emphasized by, e.g., Bring 268; Tannehill, *Dying,* 65; cf. H.-H. Esser, *NIDNTT* I: 385.
53. Cf. W. Foerster, *TDNT* III: 1034. This new relation issues in the new life and its expression; from this perspective, to belong to the new creation and to have faith operating through love (5:6) express basically the same reality (Ridderbos, *Paul,* 293). Chilton, "Galatians 6:15," 312 suggests that καινὴ κτίσις reflects "a theologoumenon current in contemporary Judaism" and should be translated "new creature" (AV, RV) or "new humanity"; Paul is asserting that "God has set aside the polarity of Jew and Gentile (*cf.* 3:28) in favour of an altogether 'new humanity.'" On this understanding, too, the fact of a new order of existence is implied.

cross symbolizes this break, both in its objective significance and in its subjective meaning for Paul, and so has become Paul's sole object of boasting. Here, too, we may discern an underlying connection between justification by faith and salvation history: the cross, which marks the line of demarcation between the old world and the new creation, also marks the line of demarcation between circumcision and the law on the one hand and justification by faith on the other, in that it rendered the former inoperative as a means of justification and brought the principle of faith into effect.[54]

4. THE RULE OF BLESSEDNESS (6:16)

16 *Whoever they are who take this principle for their guide, peace and mercy be upon them, and upon the whole Israel of God!*

16 The thesis of v. 15 is of such supreme importance to Paul that he makes it the rule of blessedness: the benediction of peace (on which see on 1:3) and mercy is pronounced upon all "who take this principle for their guide" as well as upon the "Israel of God." "Take . . . for their guide" is literally "will walk" (NASB); the verb has the same meaning as in 5:25.[55] The word rendered "principle" means primarily a ruler or straight edge for measuring and metaphorically a rule or standard.[56] "Mercy" is basically the grace of God,[57] although the word used has particular regard to the needy condition of the recipient, whereas the emphasis in "grace" is on the undeserved character of God's goodness. The order "peace and mercy" is the reverse of that found in other NT passages (1 Tim. 1:2; 2 Tim. 1:2; 2 Jn. 3; Jude 2; cf. the order "grace and peace") and puts the effect before the cause. "Peace be upon Israel" seems to be an echo of Ps. 125 (LXX 124):5. For these reasons "and mercy" has been considered an afterthought, added possibly to distinguish from the peace spoken of in the psalm the peace which is the possession of those who rely on God's mercy.[58] Whether this is

---

54. Thus, materially "the world" here is equivalent to "this age" and the "new creation" to "the age to come" (cf. Eph. 1:21), in full accord with the division of history which we have seen, e.g., in 3:23-25. This Pauline equation of the present aeon and this (old) world comes to linguistic expression most clearly in his use of σοφία τοῦ κόσμου ("wisdom of the world"), σοφία τοῦ αἰῶνος τούτου ("wisdom of this age"), and σοφία τοῦ κόσμου τούτου ("wisdom of this world") as equivalent expressions (1 Cor. 1:20; 2:6; 3:19, RSV); cf. H. Sasse, *TDNT* I: 203.

55. Gk. στοιχήσουσιν. Cf. H.-H. Esser, *NIDNTT* II: 452 ("keep to"); *pace* G. Delling, *TDNT* VII: 668 ("agree")—unless in the sense of NEB.

56. Gk. κανών, only here and in 2 Cor. 10:13-16 in the NT.

57. R. Bultmann, *TDNT* II: 484; cf. Ridderbos 227.

58. Cf. Guthrie 151; Burton 357f., who considers "and upon the whole Israel of God" a second afterthought.

so or not, the reference to the Israel of God need not be an afterthought. For the additional (nineteenth) benediction to the Eighteen Benedictions contains a prayer which asks God for "peace . . . and mercy on us and on all Israel thy people"; if Paul knew this prayer, the words "and upon the . . . Israel of God" would have come readily from his tongue.[59]

Paul's statement, particularly its last phrase, has been variously interpreted. (a) E. D. Burton would punctuate and translate it as "peace be upon them, and mercy upon the Israel of God," thus separating peace and mercy as being invoked, respectively, upon those who walk by the principle of v. 15 on the one hand and upon the true Israel of God, elect though as yet unenlightened, on the other.[60] This requires taking the second "and" *(kai)* "as slightly ascensive," which is not very satisfactory. Also, even if the words "and mercy" are an afterthought, this does not require that they be linked with what follows; the RV punctuation ("peace be upon them, and mercy, and upon the Israel of God") seems entirely acceptable. (b) If the second *kai* is taken as epexegetic (= "namely"; cf. NIV "even," RSV), the phrase may refer to the spiritual Israel as comprising the whole body of believers whether Jewish or Gentile.[61] But it has been objected that "it is doubtful whether *kai* is ever used by St. Paul in so *marked* an explicative force as must be here assigned."[62] (c) It is certainly more natural to take the *kai* as simply copulative (= "and" as in AV, RV, NASB, NEB), but the question still remains as to what "Israel" refers to.

The specifying phrase "of God" makes it unlikely that the reference is to Israel as such (or even the eschatological Israel in the sense of Rom. 11:26),[63] and Paul "can hardly have meant to bless the whole of Israel . . . , irrespective of whether or not they held to the canon of the cross of Christ."[64] The view that v. 16 refers to, respectively, "the Gentiles who believe the gospel and the Jewish Christians who recognize the unimportance of circumcision"[65] faces the objection that "whoever" *(hosoi)* would naturally include Jewish as well as Gentile Christians; moreover, particularly in the light of v. 15, it is improbable that Paul, with his concern for the unity of the church (cf. on 2:2), would here single out Jewish Christians as a

59. Bruce 274f.; cf. Schürer, *History,* II: 458. G. Stählin suggests that Paul's wish of peace for the Israel of God might be regarded as taking the place of the brotherly kiss (*TDNT* IX: 139, n. 234).

60. Burton 357f. Cf. Duncan 192f., though, unlike Burton, he does translate the second καί ("and").

61. E.g., Lightfoot 224f.; Zerwick §455ζ; W. Gutbrod, *TDNT* III: 387f.

62. Ellicott 139.

63. The view of F. Mussner, *Der Galaterbrief* (third edition, Freiburg, 1977), 417, n. 59, cited with approval by Bruce 275.

64. O'Neill 71. Cf. Hendriksen 246f.

65. Pinnock 89. Cf. Betz 323.

separate group within his churches.[66] Perhaps the least unsatisfactory view is to suppose that in the two parts of his benediction Paul is thinking first of those of his readers who qualify under the *hosoi* and passes from there on to the new Israel, the new people of God—both Jews and Gentiles being included in each instance.[67]

Since the benediction is invoked on both groups, the wider group may be by implication described, like the narrower group, as those who walk by the principle of v. 15, which in a certain sense sums up the content of the epistle and of the Pauline kerygma, at least as it unfolded itself in debate with Jews and Judaizing Christians.[68] In other words, Paul limits the blessing to those who follow the "norm of true Christianity,"[69] which recognizes that participation in the new creation is the only thing that matters. In this new creation circumcision or uncircumcision is irrelevant; that which is vital is a new relation with God which is accepted by faith—in other words, justification by faith.[70]

66. Cf. Bruce 274.

67. Schlier 283; Ridderbos 227; cf. K. H. Rengstorf, *TDNT* I: 734 ("the Israel of God" = "the new covenant people"); Bligh, "Church," 154 (= "the Body of Christ"). To some it has seemed doubtful that Christians generally could be called "the Israel of God" (Ellicott 139; Burton 358; cf. Richardson, *Israel*, 74-84). But not only Rom. 9:6; 1 Cor. 10:18; Phil. 3:3 but also Gal. 3:29; 4:23, 29 imply the idea that Christians are the true Israel. It may be that in the present instance Paul is led by the polemical context (cf. especially vv. 14, 17) to give this concept definite expression by actually calling Christians "the Israel of God," but that elsewhere he does not do so because, "as we may see from R[om]. 9-11, he neither could nor would separate the term [Israel] from those who belong to Israel by descent" (W. Gutbrod, *TDNT* III: 388). If this is accepted, there is no need to think that "the phrase 'Israel of God' is a tell-tale sign" that the last phrase of v. 16 is a post-Pauline gloss (O'Neill 71f.).

68. Schlier 283 (my translation); cf. H. W. Beyer, *TDNT* III: 598.

69. H. W. Beyer, *TDNT* III: 600; cf. J. Guhrt, H.-G. Link, *NIDNTT* III: 400.

70. Betz 25 claims that since it has a conditional curse at the beginning (1:8f.) and a conditional blessing at the end (6:16), Galatians is a "magical letter" (a category "well known from ancient epistolography"); that in addition to the "'art of persuasion' and its system of rational argumentation" Paul "also introduces the dimension of magic, that is, the curse and the blessing, as inescapable instruments of the Spirit, in order to confront the Galatians with the choice between salvation and condemnation."

This interesting theory is rendered suspect by the placement of magic arts (φαρ-μακεία, 5:20) and the Spirit on opposite sides of the Spirit-flesh antithesis and by the derogatory and condemning references in the Book of Revelation to the "magic arts" (Rev. 9:21, NIV; Gk. φάρμακα; cf. 18:23) and their practitioners (φάρμακοι: 21:8; 22:15).

Meeks, Review, 306 makes another valid criticism: "As a magical letter has 'automatic results,' so Paul also expects blessings to follow 'automatically' if the Galatians heed his admonitions, but curses, if they refuse. Yes, but this rather vague analogy conceals fundamental differences. Will the mere reading of the letter 'automatically produce the "judgment"'" [quoting Betz 25]? If so, what is the sense of the elaborate appeal to the will and emotion of the recipients which is precisely the purpose of those rhetorical devices that Betz has so ably described?"

Although this section (6:11-16) is separated from 5:2-12 by a long parenetic section (5:13–6:10), it has much in common with the earlier passage: running through both passages is the basic antithesis between faith and works, between righteousness by faith and righteousness by circumcision and the law. In 5:2-6, the antithesis is expressed as that between seeking to be justified by circumcision and law and being justified by faith, and Paul uses arresting language to point out that to go the former way is to cut oneself off from Christ. By implication, the way of justification is said to be by faith and is inseparably bound to the new life of love. In 5:7-12, the opposition is presented in terms of circumcision and the cross. The cross is a stumbling-block because it does away with circumcision as a means of justification, so that what is at issue is still the opposition between justification by faith and justification by works. In 6:12-16, the contrast is couched in terms of circumcision as a false ground of glorying and the cross as the true basis of boasting. Behind these contrasted objects of boasting again lies the fundamental issue of what matters (v. 15), and the answer categorically denies any value to circumcision and gives exclusive recognition to the new creation which involves justification at its very basis and center.

As already noted (see on v. 11), this section of the epistle is written by Paul with his own hand and in large letters and has the nature of a resumptive, summarizing, and conclusive statement. This serves to underline the importance of what Paul has to say here, and this in turn underscores the importance of the doctrine of justification by faith in his thought, since it is inseparably bound up with the cross and the new creation, both of which (themselves inseparably bound together) are seen to be of central significance to Paul.

B. CONCLUSION (6:17-18)

1. A FINAL APPEAL (6:17)

17 *In future let no one make trouble for me, for I bear the marks of Jesus branded on my body.*

17 This verse is best regarded as a separate paragraph unrelated to v. 18, which is the concluding benediction to the whole letter as v. 16 is to vv. 11-15.[1] "In future" is strictly "within the time that remains,"[2] but it,

---

1. Burton 359f.
2. Τοῦ λοιποῦ is an instance of the classical "genitive of time within which" (MHT 3: 235). More frequently Paul uses the accusative τὸ λοιπόν, meaning "from now

like "henceforth" (RSV; cf. NASB "from now on"), sufficiently expresses the sense.[3] The construction of the rest of the clause[4] shows that Paul is appealing for a stop to the trouble that was being caused him.[5] This appeal is addressed not to the agitators (for Paul could hardly appeal to them) but to the Galatians: they had not stood firm in the truth of the gospel but rather, succumbing to the persuasion of the agitators, had turned to another "gospel" (1:6f.; 5:7f.); moreover, in a volte-face of affection, they thought Paul was harboring hostile intentions towards them (4:15f.), thus causing him to be utterly perplexed (4:20). Now he tells them that they must stop causing him further trouble, the implication being: "you have caused me enough trouble already."

The reason Paul should be troubled no more is that he, unlike the agitators,[6] bears on his body "the marks of Jesus."[7] The "marks" branded on Paul's body were probably not tattoos, such as of the form of a cross or the name of Jesus, either in full or in a shortened form, despite the widespread use of religious tattooing in the Hellenistic world, since this was prohibited both by the Mosaic law (Lev. 19:28) and in Pharisaic teaching.[8] The "marks" are most widely and most reasonably interpreted as the wounds and scars left in Paul's body as a result of his sufferings for the gospel.[9] If the early dating and the South Galatian destination of the epistle preferred by this commentary are accepted, the specific reference may be to the marks left by his stoning at Lystra (Acts 14:19; cf. 2 Cor. 11:25), an incident which might be readily recalled by at least some of his readers.[10]

The background of Paul's usage has been seen as the branding of temple slaves and domestic slaves to denote ownership or the angelic branding in Ezek. 9:4 of the sighing faithful as a protective sign.[11] Whatever the

on" (1 Cor. 7:29, RSV) or used to indicate a transition to a new topic (Phil. 3:1; 4:8; 2 Thess. 3:1, NEB "and now" in the last two references).

3. Ridderbos 228 and Moule 39, 161 respectively.

4. Μή with present imperative; cf. Burton 360; *Syntax*, §165.

5. On κόπους παρέχειν (a phrase found only here in Paul) as "to trouble" cf. F. Hauck, *TDNT* III: 829.

6. This seems to be the force of the emphatic personal pronoun ἐγώ ("I").

7. O'Neill 82 interprets present tense "bear" as indicating that "Paul is about to be martyred; he is about to bear the marks of Jesus on his body." But this is unfounded: βαστάζω ("bear") here evidently means the same as ἔχω "to have on oneself" (F. Büchsel, *TDNT* I: 596). Σῶμα ("body") need not be regarded as having here the specialized meaning of "person" (S. Wibbing, *NIDNTT* I: 234f.); it denotes simply the physical, corporeal body (E. Schweizer, *TDNT* VII: 1063; Ridderbos, *Paul*, 115).

8. So, rightly, O. Betz, *TDNT* VII: 663.

9. E.g., O. Betz, loc. cit.; S. Wibbing, *NIDNTT* I: 235; MM s.v. στίγμα; Bultmann, *Theology*, 1: 193; Burton 360; Betz 324.

10. Cf. Bruce 276.

11. E.g., Lightfoot 225; Burton 361; and O. Betz, *TDNT* VII: 663, n. 46 respectively.

specific background, we may take these "brand-marks of Jesus" (NASB) as indicating "the personal relation of Paul to his Master with all the security which that brought with it."[12] They are called the marks "of Jesus" not only as a sign of ownership, nor merely because they were incurred on account of Jesus' name,[13] but probably also because they gave palpable proof that Paul was suffering with his Lord (cf. Rom. 8:17; 2 Cor. 1:5; Phil. 3:10), that he was continuously bearing in his body the dying of Jesus (cf. 2 Cor. 4:10), and that with his sufferings he was completing "what is lacking in Christ's afflictions" (Col. 1:24, RSV).[14]

The "brand-marks of Jesus" in Paul's body stand in antithesis to the mark of circumcision in the flesh of the Judaizers' converts: if the Judaizers boast in circumcision as the sign of God's covenant with Israel (cf. Rom. 2:25-29) and in the circumcised flesh of their converts (Gal. 6:13), Paul appeals to the marks of Jesus as the new eschatological sign marking the Church as the true circumcision (Phil. 3:3) and the new Israel (cf. on v. 16).[15]

2. FINAL BENEDICTION (6:18)

18 *The grace of our Lord Jesus Christ be with your spirit, my brothers. Amen.*

18 With the exception of Romans which concludes with a doxology (16:27; but cf. v. 20; 15:33), Paul's letters uniformly end with a benediction which replaces the conventional "farewell" (e.g., Acts 15:29). The various forms which the benediction takes are an indication that it had not yet become a fixed formula. "The Lord" is the subject in 2 Tim. 4:22a (cf. 2 Thess. 3:16); but more commonly the subject is "grace," and under this heading the benediction takes three forms. The simplest is "Grace be with you (all)" (Col. 4:18; Eph. 6:24; 1 Tim. 6:21; 2 Tim. 4:22b; Tit. 3:15); Gal. 6:18 is an example of the longer form: "The grace of our/the Lord Jesus

---

12. MM s.v. στίγμα.
13. So Ellicott 140 and Guthrie 152 respectively.
14. Cf. O. Betz, *TDNT* VII: 663; Ridderbos 228; Hendriksen 248; Bruce 248 (who notes that the last thought is not prominent in this passage).
15. Cf. O. Betz, loc. cit.; R. P. Martin, *NIDNTT* II: 573; C. Brown, *NIDNTT* I: 235. "What, then, is the significance and function of such a remark at this point?" asks Brinsmead 47. He answers: "Rhetorical texts and literary examples reveal that one of the most effective final appeals, in a forensic case, was to present one's wounds received in action, at the same time belittling the claims of the opposition. Paul here evidently makes a last appeal for a favorable decision." If this is correct, we may compare Paul's effective use of the voluntary oath in 1:20.

(Christ) be with you (all)/your spirit" (Rom. 16:20; 1 Cor. 16:23; Phil. 4:23; 1 Thess. 5:28; 2 Thess. 3:18; Phm. 25); while the most elaborate, trinitarian form is found only in 2 Cor. 13:13.

It has been suggested that the mention of the readers' "spirit" here is due to the emphasis on life in the Spirit in the preceding context.[16] But in other epistles where there is no such emphasis the expression "your spirit" similarly occurs in the final benediction (Phil. 4:23; 2 Tim. 4:22a; Phm. 25). Probably in these concluding benedictions "your spirit" and "you" are synonymous,[17] and the most that can be said is that Paul sometimes refers to the readers' "spirit" probably because—the spirit being the "God-conscious" aspect, as the "soul" is the "self-conscious" aspect, of the inner life[18]—"it is in the spirit of man that the operations of grace make themselves felt."[19] Gift and Giver are inseparable: the fact that "the Lord be with you" and "the grace of the Lord be with you" are interchangeable means that "God Himself is present in His gift; in His gift He gives Himself."[20] Paul's desire for his readers then is that they may have the gracious indwelling presence of the Lord Jesus Christ.[21]

Here only in Paul's letters does the word "brothers" occur in such a special position—at the end of the sentence. Paul wishes to emphasize that in spite of his converts' altered attitude towards him (4:15f.) his love for them remains unchanged; for all the severity of language he has had to use (4:20), he assures them once more in closing that he still regards them as "brothers." His sincerity is emphasized by the final formula of confirmation, "Amen" (cf. Rom. 16:27).

SUMMARY OF THEOLOGICAL CONCLUSIONS: THE STATUS OF "JUSTIFICATION BY FAITH" IN PAUL'S THOUGHT AS SEEN IN GALATIANS

There is a modern tendency to question the traditional understanding that "justification by faith" is at the center of Paul's theology and to relegate it

---

16. Rendall 191f.; Guthrie 152.

17. Ridderbos, *Paul*, 121; E. Schweizer, *TDNT* VI: 435; cf. H. Stratham, *TDNT* IV: 509 (here "spirit" is used for "soul").

18. F. F. Bruce, *EBC* 1160b.

19. Ellicott 140.

20. W. Grundmann, *TDNT* VII: 778.

21. Burton 362. Μετά with genitive ("with") is used here, as throughout Paul's final benedictions, and denotes close association or attendant circumstances (as in 1 Thess. 3:13), whereas σύν with dative, also translated "with," is used to express intimate personal union (e.g., Col. 3:4; cf. 1 Thess. 4:17; M. J. Harris, *NIDNTT* III: 1206f.).

instead to the periphery of his thought. We have elsewhere offered a brief survey of the modern debate on this issue;[1] our purpose here is to summarize the exegetical findings from our study of Galatians which bear on this topic, and in the light of these findings to reach a conclusion regarding the significance of "justification by faith" for Paul's understanding of the gospel.[2]

(1) *Its antithetical statement.* The relation of justification to faith is positively stated in three formulas: (a) "through faith in Christ Jesus" (*dia pisteōs Christou Iēsou,* 2:16a)—faith in Christ is the means of justification;[3] (b) "through this faith [in Christ]" (*ek pisteōs Christou,* 2:16c); cf. "through faith" (*ek pisteōs,* 3:8, 11, 24)—the change from *dia* to *ek* being merely stylistic;[4] (c) "in Christ" (*en Christọ,* 2:17a)—justification takes place in Christ, by virtue of the believer's incorporation into him.[5] Righteousness, which is the status of being right with God, is bestowed in justification (2:21; 3:6),[6] and is attainable only by and as the grace of God (2:21; 5:4),[7] hence by faith alone (cf. 5:5).[8] It is derived from the death of Christ, the very purpose of which was to provide an objective ground for the obtaining of righteousness/justification through faith (2:21; 3:13f.).[9] All this may be summed up by the statement that justification is *by grace, through faith, in Christ* (Christ being both the object of the believer's faith-union and the objective ground of justification).

Negatively put, justification is not by works of the law (*[ouk] ex ergōn nomou,* three times in 2:16).[10] Law, as a principle of justification, is diametrically opposed to the way of faith and can bring only a curse (3:10-12);[11] it is unable to provide righteousness (vv. 21f.);[12] to seek to be justified by law is not only entirely futile but definitely hurtful for believers (5:2-4).[13] To rehabilitate the law as the means of justification and as the authority in the believer's life is tantamount to making the believer a transgressor of the law (2:18).[14]

The absolute antithesis between justification by faith and justification by legal works runs through the major part of the epistle (2:11–6:18): it

1. Fung, "Status of Justification."
2. The following references are all to earlier pages of the present volume.
3. Cf. pp. 114f.
4. Cf. pp. 116 (a), 139f.
5. Cf. p. 119.
6. Cf. pp. 125f. (b) and (c), 135.
7. Cf. pp. 126 (c), 223f.
8. Cf. p. 227.
9. Cf. pp. 126 (c), 147–151.
10. Cf. pp. 113f., 117 (c).
11. Cf. pp. 141–146.
12. Cf. pp. 162f.
13. Cf. pp. 221–224.
14. Cf. p. 122 (d).

is explicitly stated in 2:16; 3:2, 5, 11f.;[15] it all but lies on the surface in 3:21f., 24; 5:2-6;[16] and it underlies the contrasts between slavery and freedom in the Hagar-Sarah analogy (4:21-31)[17] and between the cross and circumcision in 5:11 and 6:12-16.[18] It also extends to the form of expressions like "by faith in Christ" *(ek pisteōs Christou)* versus "by works of the law" *(ex ergōn nomou)* (2:16, RSV),[19] "by hearing with faith" *(ex akoēs pisteōs)* versus "by works of the law" (3:2, 5, RSV), and "in Christ" *(en Christǭ,* 2:17) versus "in terms of law/by way of law" *(en nomǭ,* 3:11; 5:4).[20]

(2) *Its polemical orientation.* As we have seen, the doctrine of righteousness/justification by faith is polemically directed against the Judaizers, in particular their demand for circumcision and observance of the law as necessary conditions for salvation. This polemical orientation is reflected in (a) the emphatic repetition of the doctrine throughout the major part of the epistle (2:11–6:18); (b) the antithesis between justification by faith and justification by legal works (cf. [1] above); (c) the prominent role played in the epistle's argument by the concept of sonship to Abraham, in terms of which justification by faith is presented (3:7-14),[21] and which is itself shown to be materially identical with sonship to God (3:26-29);[22] and (d) the exegetical use made of the Genesis story of Hagar and Sarah (4:21-31).[23] The evidence thus suggests that the formulation of the doctrine, and especially the argumentation employed, may in part have been conditioned by the position Paul was combating.

(3) *Its evangelic significance.* The Antioch incident clearly establishes that Paul conceived of justification by faith as the very truth of the gospel which could brook no compromise (2:14).[24] This was his own position: this understanding of the gospel was what he preached to the Galatians and what they held to for a time (5:7);[25] he considered that to be seduced away from this truth would be to succumb to an evil influence (5:8);[26] and he believed that if the Galatians were to submit to cultic observances as a matter of religious obligation, thus causing the principle of justification by faith to be set aside, his own apostolic labors over them would be in vain (4:11).[27] It

15. Cf. pp. 115, 130–133, 143–146.
16. Cf. pp. 162–165; 168–170; 221–224, 312.
17. Cf. pp. 206–212, 219 (d).
18. Cf. pp. 240f. (c), 312; 302–311.
19. Cf. p. 116.
20. Cf. p. 119.
21. Cf. pp. 138–140, 152f. (b).
22. Cf. pp. 170–176, 177 (2).
23. Cf. pp. 219f.
24. Cf. pp. 126f.
25. Cf. pp. 235f.
26. Cf. p. 236.
27. Cf. pp. 193f..

is thus evident that for Paul, the doctrine of justification by faith is an integral part of the apostolic gospel; it is, indeed, a fundamental statement of the gospel itself.

(4) *Its experiential importance.* Paul describes or at least interprets his own conversion experience in terms of justification by faith (2:16), thus showing that the essence of the doctrine is to be traced to a time as early as his conversion itself.[28] The same experience is attributed to the other Jewish Christians, including Peter, who were with Paul in Antioch and who shared with him the common knowledge of the way of justification by faith (vv. 15f.).[29] Justification by faith was involved at the very start of the Galatians' Christian experience (3:1-5) and this is fully in accord with the fact that it was also the foundational experience of Abraham's relation to God (v. 6).[30] Thus, as demonstrated in Abraham, the Jewish Christians at Antioch (Peter, Paul, and the others), and the Gentile believers of Galatia, justification by faith is an experience which stands at the very inception of Christian existence. Certainly for Paul, his religion was deeply rooted in the knowledge of his justification.

(5) *Its soteriological connections.* Justification by faith stands in intimate connection with adoption to sonship and reception of the Spirit. It is involved in reception of the Spirit (3:1-6),[31] and the promised blessing of the Gentiles' justification finds fulfillment in the bestowal of the Spirit on those who have faith (3:8, 14; 4:28f.).[32] The promise also finds fulfillment in sonship to Abraham, which is equivalent to sonship to God (3:26-29).[33] Thus justification, adoption, and reception of the Spirit appear as different expressions for the fulfillment of the same promise, and may be regarded as interwoven if distinct aspects of the single experience of faith-union with Christ.[34] This is their logical relationship: justification by faith provides the basis for adoption to sonship, which in turn is evidenced by reception of the Spirit (3:23f.; 4:1-7).[35]

Justification by faith is also intimately connected to the new life of union with Christ (2:20), which is a life of faith working through love, for the faith which justifies also receives the Spirit of Christ who produces the life of love within the believer (5:6).[36] Because of this intimate connection between justification and the new life, the ethical imperatives are a natural

28. Cf. pp. 118, 127.
29. Cf. pp. 113, 117 (c).
30. Cf. p. 136.
31. Cf. p. 136.
32. Cf. pp. 153 (c), 213f.
33. Cf. pp. 170–176.
34. Cf. p. 177.
35. Cf. pp. 187, 194.
36. Cf. pp. 230–232.

outcome of the theological indicatives of the gospel.[37] Further, justification by faith stands in close association with baptism, inasmuch as baptism is the visible sign and expression of faith (3:26f.).[38]

(6) *Its salvation-historical setting.* Paul supports his teaching that justification is by faith and not by works of the law by appealing to Scripture. For the negative part of this thesis, that justification is not by works of the law, Paul argues that the Psalmist already taught that justification could not be by means of law (2:16),[39] and that Deuteronomy teaches that all who hold to legal works are under the law's curse (3:10).[40]

For the positive statement that justification is by faith alone, Paul appeals to Hab. 2:4 (in 3:11)[41] and, supremely, to the example of Abraham and to his relation to Moses and to Christ. God's promise to Abraham concerning the Gentiles was in effect a promise of the blessing of justification by faith and as such was a preannouncement of the gospel (3:8); justification by faith is therefore what God intended from the time of Abraham as his abiding principle of dealing with mankind.[42] This original covenant of promise with Abraham and his seed could not be set aside by the law, which came in as a later dispensation (3:15-18)[43] designed for the very purpose of subserving the promise (vv. 19-22).[44]

Rather than being set aside by the law, the covenant found fulfillment in Christ, whose death delivered believers from the curse of the law and opened the door of justification by faith to the Gentiles (vv. 13f.).[45] Thus it became possible for believers to become God's full-grown sons and receive the Holy Spirit (4:4-7).[46] For the coming of Christ marked the cessation of the dispensation of law (3:23-25)[47] and ushered in the new dispensation of faith, through which believers become sons of God and the true offspring of Abraham (3:26-29).[48] To put it in a different way, the coming of Christ marked an absolute break between the old aeon, with its principle of legal observance as the ground of boasting, and the new, with its principle of boasting in the cross of Christ (6:14f.).[49] Salvation history is thus linked with the apocalyptic doctrine of the two aeons, with the coming of Christ—

37. Cf. pp. 232, 278–283.
38. Cf. pp. 173f.
39. Cf. pp. 117f.
40. Cf. pp. 141f.
41. Cf. pp. 143–145.
42. Cf. pp. 138–140, 152.
43. Cf. pp. 153–158.
44. Cf. pp. 158–166.
45. Cf. pp. 147–152.
46. Cf. pp. 182–187.
47. Cf. pp. 167–170.
48. Cf. pp. 170–176.
49. Cf. pp. 308f.

which put into effect the principle of justification by faith—as the line of demarcation, the turning point, in both. Thus justification by faith is firmly set in salvation history as the fulfillment of God's original covenant of promise with Abraham and as the very purpose for which God sent his Son into the world.

Conclusion. In the light of these findings, it may reasonably be concluded that, far from being a "subsidiary crater" in Paul's doctrine of redemption (as A. Schweitzer and others would have us believe), the doctrine of justification by faith is, despite its polemical orientation, of central importance in Paul's understanding and presentation of the gospel. More precisely, the centrality of justification by faith in Paul's thought may be defined as follows: On the one hand, it does not exhaust the content of the Pauline gospel; like adoption to sonship, reception of the Spirit, and the beginning of the new life, and coincident with them, it is one aspect of that redemption which God has effected in Christ. On the other hand, it is not just one aspect like any other; rather (as the last four considerations above, [3-6], clearly show) it stands out as the most fundamental and prominent aspect of God's one redemption in Christ and of the unitary event of the believer's incorporation into and union with Christ.[50]

---

50. With these conclusions cf. the summary and conclusion of our study on the teaching of justification by faith as expressed in the Corinthian letters: Fung, "Corinthians," 257f.

INDEX OF SUBJECTS

Paul (cont.)
196-98; on impartiality of God, 95-96; on intemperance, 259-60; and "I-Thou" relationship to Jesus Christ, 122-24; and James, 74-76, 89; and Jerusalem Council, 9, 14, 17, 21, 27, 28, 87-104; lack of interest in historical Jesus, 76-77; misrepresentation of the law, 141-43; missionary activities in Syria and Cilicia, 79-84; and motives of circumcision party, 108, 302-6; on motives of the Galatian agitators, 200-2, 237-38; not subordinate to the Jerusalem church, 16-17, 75-76, 81, 84, 87-89, 101, 104; oath of truthfulness in Epistle to the Galatians, 79; personal appeal to the Galatians, 195-204; and Peter, 73-74, 78; on Peter's hypocrisy toward Gentile Christians, 109-11, 121; Pharisaic training under Gamaliel, 71-72; pre-conversion devotion to Pharisaic traditions, 57-58, 62, 71-72; pre-conversion persecution of the Church, 55-56, 58-62, 82-83; recognized as apostle to the Gentiles, 97-101; response to Christ's revelation, 68-71; second visit to Galatia, 9; second visit to Jerusalem, 85-90; on spiritual pride, 289-91; on support of the ministry, 292-93, 295; Titus converted by, 86; on unimportance of circumcision, 307-8, 311; and unity of the Church, 90, 111, 126-27; use of rabbinical allegory, 156; on vices of the flesh, 253-61; visits to Jerusalem, 9-14, 16-17, 18, 20-22, 27-28, 69-70; visit to Damascus, 26-27; welcomed by the Galatians, 198-99; and wickedness of the world, 40-41. See also Jerusalem Council.
Peter: accused of hypocrisy toward Gentile Christians, 107-11, 126-27; as apostle to the Jews, 97-98; and Gospel of Mark, 74; and justification by faith, 113; Paul and, 73-74, 78; Paul on his hypocrisy toward Gentile Christians, 109-11, 121; Paul's confrontation with at Antioch, 104-11, 126-27
Pharisaic traditions: Paul's pre-conversion devotion to, 57-58, 62, 71-72

Righteousness: and faith, 134-36, 138, 225-28, 241, 281, 317; and grace, 125-26, 281; not obtainable through the law, 162, 165-66, 168, 170; Paul's definition of, 142, 145; and salvation, 225-27
Romans, Epistle to the: compared to Epistle to the Galatians, 24

Salvation: crucifixion of Christ as basis of, 128-30, 132-33, 177-78, 305, 306-9, 319; righteousness and, 225-27; through Christ and justification by faith, 278-83, 316-17, 319-20
Samaritan: parable of and love of neighbor, 246
Sarah: as analogy to new covenant of faith, 204-11, 217-20, 317; equated with the Church, 210-11
Scripture: justification by faith supported by, 117-18, 134-36, 137-40, 143-46, 152-53, 154-58, 166, 212
Sermon on the Mount: and love of neighbor, 246
Sinai: Hagar equated with, 207-9
Slavery: denial of the gospel as return to, 188-94
Spirit. See Holy Spirit.
Spiritual pride, 289-91
Stephen: accusations against, 60-61; martyrdom of, 81
Syria and Cilicia: Paul's missionary activities in, 79-84

Thessalonians, Epistles to the: compared to Epistle to the Galatians, 23-24
Timothy: circumcision of, 240
Titus: and circumcision, 13; converted by Paul, 86; subordinate position of, 12-13; as uncircumcised Gentile, 90-93, 96, 99

Vices of the flesh: Paul on, 253-61

Women: as Christians, 175-76

Zealots: as Galatian agitators, 5-7

INDEX OF AUTHORS

INDEX OF SCRIPTURE
REFERENCES